ST. JOSEPH CHURCH CARPINTERIA

Parish history

Dear Friends:

St. Joseph's parish is a vibrant presence to the entire community of Carpinteria. With approximately 1,700 registered families, this faith community has a rich tradition and history.

Its faith journey is traced back to the Franciscan friars accompanying the expedition of Captain Gaspar de Portola in 1769. Originally called Misposno, according to popular tale the native Chumash Indians were fashioning a canoe of pinewood; hence the soldiers called the place Carpinteria (a carpenter shop) even though Fray Crespi named it San Roque.

In the 1800's the people gather faithfully for Mass at the home of Gabriel Hernandez and Don Carlos Rodriguez in Santa Monica Rd.

This faith community continued to grow in number and strength eventually in 1933 was officially established as a parish, and in June 1934 it welcomed its first resident priest.

In 2008, our parish will be commemorating its 75th Anniversary, which will be observed through several religious, and multi-cultural events highlighting the wonderful mosaic, which composes the varied aspects of our parish life, it's Church building, grounds, parish reach-out programs, ministries, and all other ways through which our faith life is expressed and nurtured as it continues to be a Catholic presence fulfilling its evangelizing mission.

This historical book is a wonderful witness of the "seamless garment" of the faith, which has been handed down to us, and a tribute to the love, and dedication of those before us.

Sincerely in Christ,

Rev. Adalberto Blanco

Pastor

The Archdiocese of Los Angeles

A History of
THE ARCHDIOCESE OF
Los Angeles

and its precursor jurisdictions
in Southern California
1840-2007

MSGR. FRANCIS J. WEBER

—————

with appendices of
Parochial Foundations
by
Hermine Lees
and
Elementary Schools
by
Sister Joanne Wittenburg, S.N.D.

Archbishopric of
Roger Cardinal Mahony
(b. 1936)

R	Reformed curial administration at Los Angeles		1986
O	Ordained to the priesthood for Diocese of Fresno		1962
G	Graduate Study at Catholic University of America		1963
E	Estelle Doheny Collection auctioned		1986~1987
R	Removed chancery offices to Wilshire Boulevard		1997
	✦ ✦ ✦ ✦ ✦		
M.	Metropolitan Archbishop of Los Angeles		1985
	✦ ✦ ✦ ✦ ✦		
M	Minor seminary ~ Los Angeles College		1950
A	Appointed Cardinal priest		1991
H	Hosted Pope John Paul II in Los Angeles		1987
O	Our Lady of Angels Cathedral erected		1997~2001
N	Named auxiliary bishop of Tamascani		1975
Y	"Young Man of the Year" (Fresno)		1967

Msgr.
Francis J. Weber
old country priest

OFFICE OF THE CARDINAL

A Shepherd's Prologue

History never stays written very long as is demonstrated by this voluminous book which renders obsolete an earlier treatise by the same author issued just sixteen years ago.

This tome commemorates the seventieth anniversary of the establishment of the Archdiocese of Los Angeles by Pope Pius XI. That much has happened to God's people in the intervening years is obvious by just a glance at the chapter headings.

Los Angeles is now the epicenter of the Catholic Church in the United States. Long the nation's largest archdiocese, the one-time Pueblo de *Nuestra Señora de Los Angeles* has also emerged as the trend setter for the post Vatican II Church in the modern world. That three cardinals of the universal Church are native Angelinos comes as no surprise.

Since the publication of the earlier book, the cathedral of Our Lady of the Angels has taken its place as the largest Catholic cathedral in the United States. And while size itself is not the ultimate distinction, the *Wall Street Journal* describes our cathedral as being "the most impressive large interior space ever built in Los Angeles."

I am particularly grateful to Monsignor Francis J. Weber for his extraordinary skills and talents as the premier "Historian of California" in preparing this unique and comprehensive volume. He has the endearing gratitude of me and countless numbers who will read this insightful history with delight.

Finally and fittingly, this book itself is the most extensive, comprehensive and elegant of any of its kind yet published in our nation's annals. Where else but Los Angeles!

As impressive as statistics may be, I am here to testify that the Catholic people in this archdiocese surpass the ability of words to describe. May the Lord bless us all as we continue our trek along California's *El Camino Real.*

Roger Cardinal Mahony

PREFACE

By its very definition, a "preface" traditionally alerts the reader to the subject matter of the book, the extent and/or limitation of its coverage, the rationale of its presentation and how the contents of the overall narrative interface one with the other.

While those ingredients are already spelled out in the Table of Contents, we also need to point out that spatial limitation dictates the exclusion of topics which are no longer recognizable in their original form. Hence entries for such items as "Mary's Hour," "Youth Education Fund, Los Angeles Orphanage" and others which helped significantly to shape the modern archdiocese, are longer a part of the local landscape, and, therefore, are not included in this book. While this narrative may be the most extensive of any ever written on an ecclesial jurisdiction in the United States, it makes no pretention of being an encyclopedic in breadth.

We are told by the ancients that a good author is known by what is omitted. My late father put it a little differently when he suggested that we "leave something for the next person to do." Three areas purposely go untreated; in this area; We made only a minor nod to ecclesial finances about which the writer knows little and understands less; we have omitted any serious reflection about the pedophilia scourge which will reverberate for several decades yet to come and, finally we made no attempt to address the so-called "vocational crisis" in the archdiocese which some would consider more a lack of effectual discernment than a dearth of potential candidates. There is some repetition of statistics, in areas where the narrative is necessarily overlapping.

In May of 1907, Msgr. Robert Hugh Benson, in a paper read before the Society of Saint Thomas of Canterbury, said that "It has been very well observed that there is no such thing as an impartial historian. Every man who sets out to trace the development of life, whether in politics, religion, or art, is bound to do so with some theory in his mind. The historian, or the theologian, who is most nearly impartial is not he who has no view, but he who is aware of other views, and can give them due consideration."

The legendary Professor of American Ecclesial History at the Catholic University of America, Msgr. John Tracy Ellis, once said that Church historians are "modern day evangelists" insofar as they continue telling and updating the story of God's relationship with His people.

This book is the latest attempt to chronicle the noble saga of the Catholic Church in what has become the largest community of God's people in the United States of America. The first of these accounts, written and compiled by Dr. Charles C. Conroy, in 1941, was entitled *The Centennial*. It was issued to commemorate the hundredth anniversary of the establishment of the hierarchy. A man unique in his generation, he had served as editor of *The Tidings* for thirteen years. While he also oversaw the curial archives, his organizational talents were not as effective as his historical insights.

Century of Fulfillment, appearing in 1990, purported to tell the story of "The Roman Catholic Church" in the Archdiocese at Los Angeles, 1840-1947. With all its shortcomings, Archbishop Roger Mahony graciously referred to it "a fascinating historical saga." The narrative crammed into 536 pages was arranged around the seven bishops and archbishops who governed the Church during that pioneering century. Several years later the coverage was expanded to include the archbishoprics of James Francis Cardinal McIntyre and Timothy Cardinal Manning.

Now, the story has been totally rewritten updated and expanded to include representative laity, clergy and religious, the ethnic composition of the area, its vast school system, charitable outreach, health care and cemetery facilities. Catholic Action and allied institutions are also included as well as a generous sprinkling of relevant sidebars.

Despite a number of requests, thirty-six elementary schools did not provide photographs for this book. And, in a relative few cases, the publisher authorized changes in the text which were not substantiated by the author.

It is a pleasure to acknowledge the assistance of many people in the preparation of this book, namely Hermine Lees, editor of the annual directory for *The Tidings*, who wrote the parochial entries; Sister Mary Joanne Wittenburg, S.N.D., who compiled the section on elementary schools; Mr. Kevin Feeney, A.C.A., who digitized the manuscript for publication, Ana Carrera who typed the original manuscript and Bill Loughlin who served many years on the editorial staff at *The Tidings*.

Msgr. Francis J. Weber

FIRST MASS IN CALIFORNIA
FOURTH CENTENARY
1602-2002

Archdiocese of Los Angeles

Table of Contents

OVERVIEW

CALIFORNIA THE PLACE

California is a remarkable place, by almost any measuring rod. With only 10 to 15% of its 158,693 square miles regarded as comfortably habitable, the state has been the most populous in the Union for over a decade. With 3/4th of its surface consisting of rolling hills or mountains, the Golden State still accounts for more inhabitants than 111 nations!

For whatever value they serve, statistics indicate that California deserves "empire" status. With an economy ranking sixth among the world powers, its gross product is exceeded only by the United States, the Soviet Union, West Germany, the United Kingdom and France. Californians are more prosperous, longer-lived and more mobile than their counterparts in other states. Per capita income exceeds that of any country, including the United States. Presently California is edging out Japan for fifth place in Free World Manufacturing. Its overall export-import trade outranks a hundred nations.

California wineries produce four of every five bottles consumed in the United States and over 200 farm products are grown on the 8,000,000 acres of land in 400 varieties of soil composition. Residents of California have more telephones than any country, except the United States. At last count, the vehicular registration placed the state fourth in the community of nations. Variety is the spice of life too. California has the driest and wettest climatic zones in the nation. It snows more in the mountains of California than it does at the North Pole!

These are but a few of the reasons why California, as late as 1848 the most distant place on earth from major population centers, affords such fascination to onlookers. Religiously and historically, it is doubtful whether any section of the American continent offers a more absorbing montage of projects, events and personages. In his welcoming address to Bishop Joseph Sadoc Alemany, John A. McGlynn stated that "no portion of this great continent" presented a more interesting field for the missionary than California. Every bay and river, every mountain and valley, throughout the length and breadth of this beautiful land is,

in the name it bears, a silent but unimpeachable witness of the efforts ... in extending the Kingdom of Christ.

Another pioneer struck a similar vein, pointing out that the saga of California's discovery and development, is the story of its religion. "The sweetly suggestive Catholic nomenclature of the mountains and valleys, coast-line and interior plains of our State, are the legacy of the Apostles of the land." Nowhere in the world has the calendar of saints and the sacred objects of Catholic devotion been drawn upon as in California to designate even the most insignificant places.

As it did a half century ago, the Golden State shines with renewed luster to the world as the home and haunt of beauty - "a region where abides the creative spirit of art, and where there remains for the American world to cherish and make use of one of the most precious possessions any people may have, namely, visible symbols and links of tradition, joining the recent with the past and supplying a glorious perspective for the future. And these symbols are the missions." The late Michael Williams said that "every crumb of adobe in their walls is precious. Every scrap of history or legend concerning them is more valuable than fine gold from the Californian hills. Their inspiration for the millions of people who have gazed upon them, or who will so gaze, the influence they exert upon thought and so upon life itself, and the gracious history of the period from which they spring, these things are what put California in a place by herself - and make her a state *sui generis.*"

LAND OF PROMISE

California has experienced everything in recent years - riots, floods, droughts, fires, earthquakes and now killer bees. Yet, the Golden State is still the garden spot of old planet earth. One often recalls and affirms what Fray Junípero Serra said: "In California is my life and there, God willing. I hope to die."

California is truly a state of superlatives. Twelve percent of the nation's residents live in California, an area that boasts of 64,500 millionaires, 57% of them women! Well over 56% of the state's population own their own homes, and 90% have at least one car.

Despite the rape, mayhem, robbery and murder, California is still El Dorado to refugees from boredom, poverty, stagnation and despotism. A favored statistic, quoted for the benefit of easterners, is that Blue Canyon, California, is the snowiest town in the country with a mean average of 243.2 inches.

However decadent it may appear to outsiders - weakened by unemployment and inflation, demoralized by crime, deluded by cultists, corrupted by pornographers, debased by junk bond dealers, decimated by psychopaths and pillaged by rioters - California remains a never-never land of riches, fame and freedom to millions around the world. Despite pockets of poverty, Californians are fabulously wealthy in other ways.

In a booster pamphlet issued in 1886 by the Illinois Association, one reads that "in this grand country, we have the tallest mountains, the biggest trees, the crookedest railroads, the dryest rivers, the loveliest flowers, the smoothest ocean, the finest fruits, the mildest lives, the softest breezes, the brightest skies and the most genial sunshine to be found anywhere else in North America". The pamphlet goes on to say that "we welcome those sojourning in a 'City of Angels' where their hearts will be irrigated by living waters from the perennial fountains of health, happiness and longevity."

Angelenos are used to being misunderstood. The November 22, 1943 issue of *Life* carried a feature story about California's southland which stated that "Los Angeles is the damnedest place in all the world," a comment typical of eastern cynics.

Realistically, Los Angeles is the most interesting metropolis in all the world. In altitude, it ranges from 5,049 feet in Tujunga (which is higher than all but a few mountains east of the Mississippi) to below sea level at Terminal Island. Los Angeles is divided by both a river and a mountain range. It is the only major city in the country large enough to have forest fires within its limits! It boasts of snow-clad mountains and sunshine beaches at the same time, with a 40 degree difference in temperature in a single day. Los Angeles completely surrounds full-fledged municipalities and unincorporated county areas.

There has always been a strange loyalty to the rhythmic flow of life in Southern California. Perhaps that was best expressed by a youngster who, when asked where she came from, answered, "I was born in Los Angeles at the age of six."

PUEBLO DE NUESTRA SEÑORA DE LOS ANGELES

The *Pueblo de Nuestra Señora de los Angeles* was established on September 14, 1781, within the parochial confines of San Gabriel Mission, with a contingency of eleven families, or forty-four people. Four square leagues of land, good for planting all kinds of grains and seeds, about three-fourths of a mile west of the river, on a ledge rising above the present Alameda Street, were set aside for the furthest extension in the presidial district of San Diego de Alcala.

Fray Junípero Serra first visited the *pueblo* on March 18, 1782, seven months after its foundation, en route to San Gabriel. He referred to the town endearingly as *La Porciuncula*, though he did not describe it. His biographer relates how the inhabitants of those days worked in the fields, ate tortillas, beans and tamales and, for recreation, played cards.

Though Serra and his confreres harbored serious reservations about the expediency of establishing the *Pueblo de Nuestra Señora de los Angeles*, the foundation, like its sister metropolis to the north, San Francisco, bears that distinctively Seraphic imprint that can only be predicated of the earliest penetrators into this far-away Province of California.

Franciscan influence in Los Angeles reflects, at the local level, what the friars accomplished along the whole expanse of the Pacific Slope. Even Governor Pedro Fages, whose relationship with Serra was anything but cordial, admitted, in 1789, "that the rapid, pleasing, and interesting progress both in spiritual and temporal matters ... are the glorious effect of the apostolic zeal, activity and indefatigable labors of these missionaries."

That viewpoint has been generally sustained, even by the most hostile of observers. The openly antagonistic Frances Fuller Victor, for example, once remarked that "the spectacle of a small number of men, some of whom certainly were men of ability and scholarship, exiling themselves from their kind, to spend their lives in contact with a race whom it was impossible in a lifetime to bring anywhere near their level, excites our sympathy and commendation." The early Franciscan heritage has perdured into the 21st century. Indeed, Fray Junípero Serra's biographer stated that "nowhere else does Serra have so conspicuous a location today" as he does in contemporary Los Angeles.

The handsomely sculptured bronze statue of the *Presidente*, now prominently enshrined in the Old Plaza area of the city, embodies one of the nation's most meaningful tributes to a religious founder. Fray Junípero is also remembered in the names of numerous streets, schools, plaques, buildings and institutions.

The Franciscan influence has been manifested rather consistently since the earliest days. One creditable author acknowledges that up to 1854, the only organization in Los Angeles upholding any standard of morality "whatever was the Roman Catholic church. It erected houses of worship, hospitals and schools; it was the pioneer in all good works." Little wonder that there is a renewed interest in the work that Serra and his band of Franciscan collaborators accomplished in California the more so when one recalls that Los Angeles today is second only to Mexico City in the number of inhabitants who carry the blood and speak the beautiful tongue of the old vice-royalty of New Spain.

LOS ANGELES - SOME REFLECTIONS

Historical commentators are quick to observe that almost everything in Southern California has been imported — plants, flowers, shrubs, trees, water and even religion!

More than three decades ago, the late Carey McWilliams pointed to the unprecedented influx of peoples — a factor that today accounts for the multi-ethnic nature of the onetime *Pueblo de Nuestra Señora de Los Angeles.*

The Indians were the first to inhabit the area. And though they are mostly gone now, they left an indelible mark behind in such names as Cahuenga, Malibu, Mugu and Pacoima.

Then came the Catholic *pobladores* from Sonora who laid out the original plaza on a bluff above the river named by Fray Juan Crespi to honor Our Lady of the Angels.

For a while after the war with Mexico and the discovery of gold, Los Angeles remained a small and insignificant town. But that was soon to change.

Statehood came, in 1850, and then, following the Civil War, the railroads reached out to touch Los Angeles, bringing newcomers from the south and midwest, many of them lured westward by the well-publicized sunshine.

The roots of the Bible were solidly transplanted by the great midwestern migration. Los Angeles remains predominantly Protestant, though the importance of the Catholic faith was first attested, when the Archbishop of Los Angeles became the first cardinal in the western United States.

Though the city is famous for its revivalists and cultists, they have probably drawn attention out of all proportion to their numbers. Studies indicate that the great majority of churchgoers belong to the traditional faiths.

The Chinese and Japanese arrived; French, Poles and German Jews also came and many of the beach areas became popular resort meccas for English tourists.

Early in the last century, the Mexican population began rising again, this time forming the bulk of the migratory work force. The Blacks, who presently constitute 12.5% of the population, began their treks in 1900.

And the waves of immigration roll on. In the last decade, Vietnamese and Koreans, with their distinctive contributions, have flooded into Los Angeles to join dozens of other Asiatic groups, like the Samoans, more of whom live in Los Angeles than reside on the Island of American Samoa itself.

The people thronging to the area have generally been an adventurous and inventive lot. In Hollywood, for example, creative minds have entertained and informed the whole world, reflecting both America's manifold problems and its unique promise.

A major port city, the aircraft and electronics industries expanded to meet the challenges of World War II and then spun around to handle contemporary transportation and communication needs.

As it welcomed the Vicar of Christ, this largest of the world's cities dedicated to Our Lady provided a haven for its perpetual transplants. It amazes, amuses and eventually absorbs. New arrivals are confronted with culture shock — the climate, the freeways, the lifestyles and the ethnic mix.

But one can rest assured that new blood will keep Los Angeles alive, vigorous and growing as it begins inching towards its tricentennial.

LOS POBLADORES

Romanticists are wont to think that the *Pueblo de Nuestra Señora de los Angeles* was settled by Spanish grandees and *caballeros,* sophisticated descendants of the *conquistadores.* A close look at the record reveals, however, that the original founders or *pobladores* were a motley lot, there was not a full-blooded white family among them, but they were pioneer stock, and, with three exceptions, they stayed and built the town we know today as Los Angeles.

When plans were completed for the envisioned *pueblo,* Fernando de Rivera y Moncada journeyed to Mexico to recruit settlers for the town. There after a whole year of persuading, he succeeded in interesting only twelve families, or forty-six people and, of that number, only eleven families, or forty-four people, actually made the trek.

The outfitting of the settlers took place at Alamos, a small town on the Mexican mainland not far from the Gulf of California. Seven of the families enlisted at Rosario, three at Sinaloa, and one at Alamos. The small group, accompanied by an army contingent, set out for their new home on February 2, 1781. Though it is not widely known or emphasized, the overwhelming majority of the founders of the *Pueblo de Nuestra Señora de Los Angeles* were Catholics of Negro racial strain.

Of those forty-four *pobladores* ultimately arriving at the projected site, the only people of unmixed Caucasian race in the whole community were two Spanish men. The settlers, who represented a mixture of Indian and Negro with here and there, a trace of Spanish, can be broken down into four racial strains:

3 Indian families	8 people
2 Indian-Caucasian families	8 people
4 Negro families	15 people
2 Negro-Caucasian families	13 people

Intermarriage among the Latin American natives and Europeans produced a multitude of castes. Children of an Indian mother (in an Indian-Caucasian union) are considered mestizos; whereas those of a Negro mother (in a Negro-Indian union) are classified as mulattos. By this enumeration, the forty- four founders of Los Angeles were:

Caucasian	2
Indian	16
Negro	26

Using the hyphenated system for the children of all mixed marriages, the classification would be:

Caucasian	2
Indian	12
Indian-Caucasian	4
Negro	17
Negro-Indian	9

If these statistics prove nothing else, at least they dispel the notion that there were any blue-blooded Spanish Dons among the Catholics who pioneered the City of Our Lady of the Angels. Quite the contrary is the case for there were more Blacks among the founders of Los Angeles than any other racial group, and a realization of this factor, useful for the social historian confirms that, these noble *pobladores* "sprang from hardy stock and the blood of true pioneers coursed through their veins."

EXTENDED ECCLESIAL FAMILY

During the Holy Father's visit to Los Angeles, Pope John Paul II reached out to greet the entirety of God's people in Southern California. Gathering to welcome him at the Los Angeles Memorial Coliseum were representatives from the other historical centers of Catholicity in this portion of the Lord's vineyard.

Among the Christian communities of this great nation, few if any have a greater claim to antiquity than the city and people bearing the hallowed and revered patronage of Saint Didacus. Discovered by Rodríquez Cabrillo in 1542, named by Sebastían Vizcaíno in 1602 and inaugurated by Fray Junípero Serra in 1769, San Diego bears the added distinction of being the seat of the first bishopric for the Californias.

San Diego is a precious place in California for that is where it all began for Christ along the Pacific Slope. Here, on America's western shores, was reared the first

CALIFORNIA 1769 1969

United States 6 cents

cross, built the first church and established the first modern city. Here too sprang the first cultivated field, the first palm, the first vine and the first olive tree to blossom into fruitage. And most important of all, here the blood of the first martyr was poured out upon the ground as the seedling for Christianity. From this missionary outpost, at the very edge of the known world, the gray-robed sons of Saint Francis pushed the Spanish frontier north to Sonoma, carving out of the wilderness that path later popularized in literature as the King's Highway.

Along that *Camino Real* went emissaries of the Spanish realm to claim and possess the land, to develop and harness its natural resources and to acquaint its inhabitants with the duties and privileges of citizenship. Down that same roadway traveled the missionaries of Christ to proclaim and extend the Kingdom of Heaven, to evangelize and civilize its diverse peoples and to win a whole new race to the Christian way-of-life.

In this newest of the world's empires, Christ was King and the friars were His soldiers. They claimed this golden land in His name and possessed it for His glory — by living and practicing those Christ-like virtues of poverty, chastity and obedience. Through the ministry of Fray Junípero Serra and his confreres, the Mission of San Diego de Alcalá became the first tabernacle of God in Alta California. From this far Western cradle of Christianity, the Gospel message was brought first to the Indians and then to their multiracial successors as God's People.

Plans for a separate ecclesiastical jurisdiction for that district of the old Diocese of Monterey-Los Angeles comprising Central California had been considered at various times since 1866. In a letter to a friend, Bishop Thaddeus Amat predicted that "within a few years another bishop will certainly be established and form a new Diocese." No official action was taken at that time but early in 1889 Giovanni Cardinal Simeoni told Bishop Francis Mora that Roman officials found it difficult "to see how one person, however industrious, can effectively provide for the demands and necessities of the Church" in so extensive an area.

The matter was given serious attention and in September of that year Archbishop Patrick W. Riordan of San Francisco suggested to officials of the Sacred Congregation of Propaganda Fide the feasibility of a separate diocese at Monterey encompassing the six counties of San Luis Obispo, Monterey, San Benito, Tulare, Fresno, Inyo and those parts of Merced, Santa Cruz and Santa Clara not already attached to the Archdiocese of San Francisco.

Bishop Mora exhibited little enthusiasm for the proposal believing as he did that smaller units would not be financially viable. On February 24, 1890, the Archbishop of San Francisco reported that those he had consulted in the matter "were of the opinion that the line should be drawn north of Santa Barbara County and south of Kern County and south from San Bernardino."

Several additional reports were submitted to Rome later that year and circulated among the members of the congregation. In 1894, the cardinals endorsed Bishop Mora's views and voted to put aside the question of dividing the diocese in favor of appointing a coadjutor for California's southland.

Rumors of a division were revived after Bishop Thomas J. Conaty's death in 1915, by the long delay that ensued before the appointment of a successor. The territorial integrity of the Diocese of Monterey-Los Angeles remained intact, however, until 1922, when Bishop John J. Cantwell, acting on the advice of Gaetano Cardinal De Lai, petitioned Pope Pius XI to divide the unwieldy jurisdiction into more manageable units. A favorable response to the request came in June of 1922, with the announcement that the Holy Father had approved plans for removing the twelve northernmost counties from the Diocese of Monterey-Los Angeles and forming them into the separate ecclesiastical jurisdiction of Monterey-Fresno.

The most recent adjustment of ecclesiastical boundaries affecting Central California's twelve counties resulted in separate episcopal seats being established at Fresno and Monterey.

The origins of the Diocese of Orange, the tenth ecclesial district formed for the State of California, can be traced to March 11, 1889, when the presently-designated county was established from the loosely-knit cluster of *ranchos* then comprising the southeastern part of Los Angeles County.

Probably no other of the nation's 3,049 counties can match the temperate climate, geographical attractions and scope of religious, educational and recreational facilities adorning the 782 square mile area known as Orange County. It is bounded geographically by the counties of Los Angeles, San Bernardino, Riverside, San Diego and forty-two miles of Pacific coastline.

Orange County has been one of the nation's most spectacular growth areas. During the 1960s, its advance in population exceeded that recorded in forty-one of the United States.

Orange has evolved from an abundantly-rich agricultural region into a progressive, industrially-oriented metropolitan area. Inasmuch as three-fourths of the county's acreage is subject to urbanization, there is every reason to believe that Orange is destined to be an even more dominant force in the industrial and financial life of California. Indeed, its average rainfall (15 inches), rate of sunshine (from 60 to 80% of the year) and mean temperature (from 48 to 76 degrees) all portend a future of unlimited proportions, to say nothing of the recreational facilities and potentials.

Catholic penetration, on a permanent basis, can be traced to All Saints Day, in the year of American Independence, when Fray Junípero Serra founded the seventh of California's missions at San Juan Capistrano.

The creation of an ecclesial district encompassing the two counties of San Bernardino and Riverside was announced by Archbishop Jean Jadot from the Apostolic Delegation on July 18, 1978. Appointed chief shepherd of the new Diocese of San Bernardino was Father Philip Straling, Pastor of Holy Rosary Church (now the Cathedral), a native of the area.

Carved from the massive 36,000 square mile parent jurisdiction of San Diego, the new diocese was the eleventh established within the State of California. One of the last authorized by Pope Paul VI, the new diocese comprises a geographical area of 27,047 square miles.

Borders of the Golden State's newest jurisdiction extend from the 11,000 foot high Telescope Peak to the floor of Death Valley, some 2,280 feet below sea level in San Bernardino County and from the 10,830

foot high San Jacinto Peak to the Salton Sea, 230 feet below sea level in Riverside County.

The physical boundaries of the two counties are larger than four New England states. The area abounds in such geographic and geological features as twisted rocks and fossil beds, all of which indicate that the Pacific Ocean once extended into what is now desert land.

POPES AND CALIFORNIA

The influence of Peter's successors in California has been evident in many ways over the years since Christianity was first proclaimed in this area. The first of the popes to make his mark in California was Clement XIV (1769-1774). It was he who issued a special indult, on July 10, 1774, whereby Fray Junípero Serra was authorized to confer the Sacrament of Confirmation in the missionary foundations along *El Camino Real*.

The documentary evidence concerning episcopal jurisdiction in Alta California can be traced to Pope Pius VI (1775-1779) who created the Diocese of Sonora on May 7, 1779. Although the popes who governed the Church between 1800 and 1830 (Pius VII, Leo XII and Pius VIII) are not known to have personally dealt with the inhabitants of California, there is recorded evidence that their presence in Peter's Chair was known and acknowledged.

Pope Gregory XVI (1831-1846) created the Diocese of Both Californias on April 27, 1840 and appointed Fray Francisco Garcia Diego y Moreno to be the area's new bishop. On July 29, 1853, Pope Pius IX (1846-1878) created a Metropolitan Province for California, advancing the Right Reverend Joseph Sadoc Alemany to the Archbishopric of San Francisco and the Reverend Thaddeus Amat to the Bishopric of Monterey. Three years later, he named Saint Vibiana patroness for the Church in Southern California.

Pope Leo XIII (1878-1903) further provided for God's people along the Pacific Slope by creating the Vicariate Apostolic of Marysville (1860), Diocese of Grass Valley (1868), Diocese of Sacramento (1886) and the Diocese of Salt Lake City (1891).

It was during the pontificate of Pius X (1903-1914) that Patrick Harnett, Rector of Saint Vibiana's Cathedral and Vicar General for the Diocese of Monterey-Los Angeles was created California's first monsignor. The first pontiff to send a special message to the inhabitants of California was Pope Benedict XV (1914-1922), who conveyed his greetings through Archbishop Edward J. Hanna.

Lay people were honored by Pope Pius XI (1922-1939) who bestowed the *Pro Ecclesia* medal on Mary Julia Workman and a papal knighthood on J. Wiseman Macdonald in 1924. He created the Diocese of Reno in 1931 and the Metropolitan Province of Los Angeles in 1936.

Eugenio Cardinal Pacelli, who became Pope Pius XII (1939-1958) was the first pontiff to have visited California. He blessed the San Francisco-Oakland Bay Bridge on October 28, 1936. In 1939, he conferred the first title of papal nobility in the area upon Carrie Estelle Doheny and, in 1952, he named the Archbishop of Los Angeles to the Sacred College of Cardinals.

The papal consistory at which Pope John XXIII (1958-1963) was elected to the Chair of Peter was the first in which a Californian, James Francis Cardinal McIntyre, participated. In 1962, the Holy Father created dioceses at Oakland, Santa Rosa and Stockton. Pope Paul VI (1963-1978) also provided for growth development in the Golden State by creating dioceses at Fresno, Monterey and San Bernardino-Riverside.

DIOCESE OF BOTH CALIFORNIAS

The historical framework surrounding the formation of curial government for the Church in the Californias can be traced to 1681, when spiritual jurisdiction over the Peninsula was in dispute between Juan Garabito, Bishop of Guadalajara, and Fray Bartolomew de Escanuela, Bishop of Durango. The latter, contending that Baja California belonged to Nueva Vizcaya, customarily delegated faculties to California-bound missionaries, until he was gently told not to meddle in peninsular affairs.

The feasibility of advancing the internal provinces of northwestern New Spain to diocesan status was formally suggested as early as 1760. Renewed impetus for the plan came eight years later with the proposal to form Sonora, Sinaloa and Lower California into a separate ecclesiastical jurisdiction.

In 1775 Bishop Antonio Marcarulla informed Fray Junípero Serra that his Diocese of Durango exercised authority over future Spanish settlements in California in virtue of the canonical prerogative assigning all undesignated territories to the nearest established jurisdiction. That claim was flatly rejected by Fray Junípero Serra, as was the less convincing assertion of the Bishop of Guadalajara who argued that Alta California belonged to his diocese as "a logical extension of the peninsula over which he did have legitimate authority."

On May 7, 1779, acting upon a recommendation from Spanish officials at Madrid, Pope Pius VI created the Diocese of Sonora, comprising the provinces of Sonora, Sinaloa and Both Californias. For the first time, Alta California, hitherto a totally independent field of missionary endeavors, fell within defined canonical boundaries. The newly created Diocese of Sonora, entrusted to Fray Antonio de Los Reyes, was almost entirely a missionary territory. Communications between Sonora and the Californias by land was impossible and the Franciscan prelate, finding himself isolated from the furthest confines of his diocese, satisfied his episcopal obligations by delegating the Franciscan *Presidentes* as Vicars Forane for Sonora.

At least one prominent historian feels that "Spain should have asked for a bishop for the Californias, considering the huge territory, even though churches were few and the income nothing." Indeed, the thought of a mitre for Fray Junípero Serra possibly did cross the minds of Spanish officialdom. The *Presidente's* biographer recalls that after the establishment of Mission San Carlos. "His Reverence learned that a courier at Madrid had written to the Reverend Father Guardian of our college... that a great honor was waiting the Reverend Father Junípero." As soon as news of the "great honor" reached Monterey, Serra decided against any distinction that would forestall his work as an apostolic missionary among the infidels. He even took the extreme precaution of writing an influential acquaintance at the royal court, asking that he veto any further consideration of regal favors, should such ever come up for discussion.

The faculty of administering the Sacrament of Confirmation, bestowed by succeeding Popes on the *Presidentes* in California, was not renewed in 1803. That factor greatly disturbed Father Narciso Durán. In a letter to the Mexican chief of state, written on September 22, 1830, Durán was the first to suggest that it was time to petition for the erection of a diocese and the appointment of a bishop. The frightful chaos that befell the Church in the post-secularization period strengthened Durán's views that a canonically established curial government would be an effective and practical alternative to the existing status.

At a meeting in Santa Barbara, on May 27, 1835, Fray Narciso Durán and Francisco Garcia Diego drafted a formal memorial to the government suggesting that creation of a bishopric was the only means of providing adequately for the ecclesial needs of Alta California. That proposal was widely discussed and carefully studied by both Church and civil authorities at the Mexicali capital and on September 12, 1836, a formal request to that effect was approved and submitted to the Holy See. On April 27, 1840, Pope Gregory XVI approved the petition and issued the customary papal bulls inaugurating a diocesan system of government for the Californias.

The modern era of the Church had begun.

ARCHDIOCESE OF LOS ANGELES

Though already launched toward its tricentennial, there is still something fresh and exciting about the one-time *Pueblo de Nuestra Señora de Los Angeles*. The story of its progress, from Hispanic colonial foundation to international center for learning, art and commerce is as much a work of imagination as it is of history.

Historians and others maintain that more than any other major city, Los Angeles has achieved its unique place in human annals because a handful of pioneers - from the Kings of Spain to the barons of land, rail and industry - dreamt and decreed that it would be so, and because thousands of others, working people from Sonora and Indiana, Shanghai and Odessa, bought and built accordingly.

Los Angeles is not perched aside the confluence of major waterways or along a vital commercial route; it is not blessed with a great natural harbor or outstanding physical location; neither was it built atop some ancient center of human habitation or upon a pre-existing religious cult. About all the city ever had and continues to have is an unequalled place in human imagination. But, that's what really counts when all the chips are down.

If New York is identified on bumper stickers as the "Big Apple," and Chicago as "gangsters gulch," then Los Angeles must surely be the city of the giant dream, the grand illusion and the hard reality.

Unimpressed by its own past and certainly not intimidated by that of its sister cities, *El Pueblo de Nuestra Señora de los Angeles* is a place where everyone is entitled to a second, even a third chance.

Angelenos have never measured the cost nor considered the contradictions of their accomplishments. Their quest for water, to cite an outstanding example, is a monumental feat of human ingenuity and skill.

Or, again, when pressing demands of new immigrants and the financial interests of aggressive developers converged in postwar Los Angeles, the San Fernando and San Gabriel valleys blossomed forth with suburban housing tracts that defied demographers around the globe.

Probably no community in all of recorded history managed to house so many of its working-class and middle-income people so well, while continuing to provide them with amenities usually associated only with the wealthy. For the thousands who continue to pour into the area annually, Los Angeles is the community that invented itself. It remains the city of exceptions and exceptional "dreamers."

And why not? After all, was it not the "Dreamers of God" who began it all for *El Pueblo de Nuestra Señora de los Angeles?*

THE PICZEK TABLEAUS

One of the most interesting (and surely the most artistic) features of the Archival Center at San Fernando Mission is the series of six mosaic tableaus adorning the eastern wall of the building. Designed by the talented Isabel and Edith Piczek from a theme suggested by Timothy Cardinal Manning, the 48" by 32" panels portray the geographical history of the Church of Los Angeles since its inception, in 1840, as the Diocese of *Ambas Californias.*

The making of these mosaics followed a complicated procedure which dates back to pre-Roman times. The initial sketches were made, revised several times and then a final color plan was drawn to scale. Finally, the six scenes were rendered to full size in a black and white cartoon. The Piczek Sisters then dispatched the cartoon to the Italian fabricator, where a reverse photocopy was made.

The mosaics were fashioned in one of the many studios at Pietra Santa. This ancient, sister-city of Carrara, has been the world's mosaic center for uncounted centuries. There are over a hundred different colors and shades of Byzantine tile in the completed mosaic renditions. The only non-ceramic pieces are the gold ones which are glass over laid with 14 carat gold leaf.

The mosaicists glued the thousands of tiny pieces of tile into place on the photocopy. When completed, match marks were drawn on the reverse of the paper in blue crayon. The completed mosaics were then sealed into zinc containers (to protect them from dampness), crated and shipped to San Pedro aboard the *Zim Genova.* They arrived early in March, 1982.

Installation is a crucial part of the overall project and requires the careful craftsmanship of a master tilemason. Ralph McIntosh, who is the recipient of numerous national awards, was chosen for the task. The methodology for installing mosaics is as old as the art form itself, little changed from Roman times. After anchoring galvanized metal lath firmly to the structure, the installer mixed a non-organic solution of lime, sand and cement as the base into which the mosaic tiles were imbedded. Each tiny piece was fitted blindly into place, following carefully the numerical masterplan drawn up by the fabricator. Using a water solution, the paper was peeled off. The entire surface was then grouted and cleaned with a mild chemical solution.

The erection of these stunning mosaic tableaus is not alone a feat of artistic excellence, but an historical panorama of California's Catholic heritage. How fitting its use for the Archival Center.

Growth Patterns — Archdiocese of Los Angeles

AMBAS CALIFORNIAS

FRANCISCO GARCIA DIEGO

MONTEREY

JOSEPH SADOC ALEMANY

MONTEREY-LOS ANGELES

THADDEUS AMAT

FRANCIS MORA

THOMAS CONATY

GEORGE MONTGOMERY

JOHN CANTWELL

LOS ANGELES SAN DIEGO

JOHN CANTWELL

LOS ANGELES

TIMOTHY MANNING

J. FRANCIS A. McINTYRE

JOHN CANTWELL

LOS ANGELES

TIMOTHY MANNING

NOMENCLATURE

William Hazlitt, the English critic and essayist, once likened "a name fast anchored in the deep abyss of time" to "a star twinkling in the firmament, cold, silent, distant, but eternal and sublime." The preservation of the place-names from the days of early Spanish occupation has always been a matter of state pride to Californians.

The joy of the tourists "in the stately names which distinguish California from the Smithville States" was a human and laudable reaction, according to Charles F. Lummis, and one that should be shielded against the simple carelessness of those unaware of what those appellations signify. That the Golden State's rich and diversified nomenclature perdures is no accident of history. As early as 1905, the legislature directed that "as far as possible, the old Spanish names, where given to cities, towns and villages in this state, should be preserved in their original forms." Around many of the early California names hovers "an atmosphere of consecration, the aroma of ancient and romantic associations, the poetry of a pastoral age such as no other state in the union and no other country of the world ever had."

That nomenclature is especially cherished by Catholics diffusing as it does "a delightful aroma of piety" over the vast expanses of the noble California commonwealth. A journalist once suggested that the constant recurrence of this sacerdotal terminology "gives California an air of belonging to the patrimony of St. Peter." He further observes that "Holy Mother Church stands well in this notable land of gold and the vine. It was Catholics—the noble and ingenious Franciscan monks-who taught Californians what was in their soil, and created the conditions which render life so delicious here today. It is a land worth striving for to a verity."

Even with the passage of two centuries, dictionaries abound in the richly significant place-names which the missionaries scattered with a zealous prodigality over the area. One authority boldly asserts that there are "more saint names - more 'Sans' and 'Santas' - on the map of California than on the map of any similar-sized area of the world." Those names, harkening back to the beginnings of a unique movement in history, allow something of the charm, challenge and sacrifice of the pastoral age to linger in the smog-cluttered atmosphere of modern times.

The reverence which an area should bear for its place-names was spelled out by Robert Louis Stevenson:

None can care for literature in itself who does not take a special pleasure in the sound of names; and there is no part of the world where nomenclature is so rich, poetical, humorous and picturesque
as the United States of America. There are few poems with a nobler music for the ear, a songful, tuneful land; and if the new Homer shall arise from the Western continent, his verse will be enriched, his pages sung spontaneously, with the names of states and cities that would strike the fancy in the business circular.

A METROPOLITAN DISTRICT

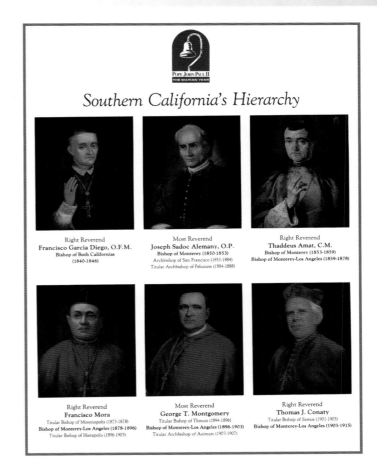

Southern California's Hierarchy

Right Reverend
Francisco Garcia Diego, O.F.M.
Bishop of Both Californias
(1840-1846)

Most Reverend
Joseph Sadoc Alemany, O.P.
Bishop of Monterey (1850-1853)
Archbishop of San Francisco (1853-1884)
Titular Archbishop of Pelusium (1884-1888)

Right Reverend
Thaddeus Amat, C.M.
Bishop of Monterey (1853-1859)
Bishop of Monterey-Los Angeles (1859-1878)

Right Reverend
Francisco Mora
Titular Bishop of Mosynopolis (1873-1878)
Bishop of Monterey-Los Angeles (1878-1896)
Titular Bishop of Hierapolis (1896-1905)

Most Reverend
George T. Montgomery
Titular Bishop of Thmuis (1894-1896)
Bishop of Monterey-Los Angeles (1896-1903)
Titular Archbishop of Axitum (1903-1907)

Right Reverend
Thomas J. Conaty
Titular Bishop of Samos (1901-1903)
Bishop of Monterey-Los Angeles (1903-1915)

The geographical derivation of the 8,762 square miles presently comprising the Archdiocese of Los Angeles can be traced to April 27, 1840, when Pope Gregory XVI created the parent jurisdiction from the already-established See of Sonora.

Boundaries for the gigantic Diocese of Both Californias were the Colorado River in the east, the 42nd degree of north latitude (Oregon line), the Pacific Ocean in the west and all of Baja California. The title was officially changed to Monterey in 1849.

The subsequent transfer of sovereignty in California made a further delineation of boundaries imperative. On April 17, 1853, Bishop Joseph Sadoc Alemany received word that the Sacred Congregation of Propaganda Fide had removed Peninsular California from its attachment to the Diocese of Monterey.

Several months later, on July 29, Pope Pius IX created a Metropolitan District at San Francisco. The southern parallel of the parish at San Jose was fixed as the demarcation between the new Archdiocese of San Francisco and the larger but suffragan Diocese of Monterey.

The Monterey jurisdiction, which encompassed all of Southern California, remained territorially intact for the next seven decades. On July 8, 1859, Bishop Thaddeus Amat was authorized to move his episcopal seat to Los Angeles. At that time he was also permitted to add that city's name to the diocesan title.

During the subsequent years, there were a number of proposals for dividing the large and unwieldy Diocese of Monterey-Los Angeles. As early as 1866, Bishop Amat confided to a friend that he expected, "within a few years," to see another bishopric formed in the southland.

While no official action was taken by Amat, his successor, Bishop Francis Mora, petitioned the Holy See several times for a reduction of his jurisdiction. The proposal was shelved temporarily, in 1894, when Mora was given a coadjutor.

Rumors of a division were revived after Bishop Thomas J. Conaty's death, in 1915, and were sustained by the long inter-regnum that ensued before the appointment of John J. Cantwell.

Early in 1922, Bishop Cantwell asked that the 90,000 square mile Diocese of Monterey-Los Angeles be dismembered, with twelve counties formed into a separate jurisdiction. Pope Pius XI acquiesced and, in June, created the new Diocese of Monterey-Fresno. The larger area, known as the Diocese of Los Angeles-San Diego, embraced the remaining southland counties stretching to the Mexican border.

The final major alteration in the southland occurred on July 11, 1936, with the erection of a second Metropolitan District in California, at Los Angeles. Simultaneously, the four southern-most counties were fashioned into the Diocese of San Diego. Included in the newly-formed Province of Los Angeles were the suffragan Sees of Monterey-Fresno, San Diego and Tucson.

In January of 1948, the Apostolic Delegate informed officials at Los Angeles that in order to avoid confusion with the older Archdiocese of Puebla de Los Angeles, in Mexico, the southland's jurisdiction would henceforth be known officially as the Archdiocese of Los Angeles in California.

The archdiocese retained its geographical integrity from 1936 until June 18, 1976, when Pope Paul VI created a new diocese for Orange County. Remaining in the parent See were the counties of Los Angeles, Ventura and Santa Barbara.

The assertion made in 1903, that California's glory "lies not in the fact that her wilderness was conquered, nor that her priceless treasures were unearthed, but in the propagation and marvelous growth of religious faith" has lost none of its force, even with the passage of eight decades.

The Archdiocese of Los Angeles, largest of the state's twelve ecclesial divisions, encompasses an area of 8,762 square miles, or the totality of Los Angeles, Ventura and Santa Barbara counties. Ranking first among the nation's 183 juridic units, in

January 2005 the archdiocese provides for the spiritual needs of 2,561,602 Catholics with 1,313 priests serving 281 parishes.

In order to facilitate its apostolic mandate of spreading the Gospel message, the Church's educational system in the southland enrolls 72,186 youngsters in 231 elementary schools, 35,682 teenagers in fifty-eight secondary schools and 8,850 students in five colleges and universities.

The latest statistics indicate an annual enrollment of 236,000 public school youngsters in the various programs operated by the Office of Religious Education. Students ranging from kindergarten to twelfth grade are engaged in pedagogical pursuits in after-school, Saturday and Sunday sessions. Teacher-training courses are available throughout the archdiocese.

The extensive involvement of the Church in the active apostolate is exemplified by its network of seventeen general hospitals, which accommodated 959,780 patients in 1984. An additional six special hospitals or sanitaria looked after the physical needs of numerous other persons.

These and other statistics have been described as the "dry bones" of history, yet one can easily perceive that ecclesial accomplishments in the Archdiocese of Los Angeles indicate a vibrant and healthy Catholic populace, firmly dedicated to the furthering of Christian ideals.

LARGEST ECCLESIAL JURISDICTION IN THE U.S.A.

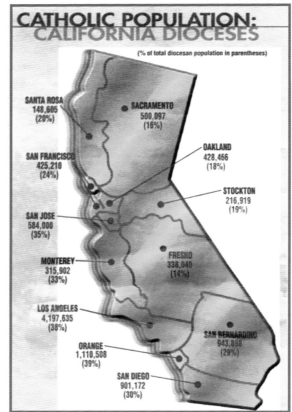

CATHOLIC POPULATION: CALIFORNIA DIOCESES

(% of total diocesan population in parentheses)

SANTA ROSA 148,605 (20%)

SACRAMENTO 500,097 (16%)

SAN FRANCISCO 425,210 (24%)

OAKLAND 428,466 (18%)

STOCKTON 216,919 (19%)

SAN JOSE 584,000 (35%)

MONTEREY 315,902 (33%)

FRESNO 338,040 (14%)

LOS ANGELES 4,197,635 (38%)

SAN BERNARDINO 943,698 (29%)

ORANGE 1,110,508 (39%)

SAN DIEGO 901,172 (30%)

Since 1983, the Archdiocese of Los Angeles has been the largest ecclesial district in the United States. Interestingly enough, the runner-up to Los Angeles in California is the Diocese of Orange, which was only severed from its parent jurisdiction in 1976. The figures are based on those reported by the nation's thirty-five Latin and Eastern Rite archdioceses and 150 Latin and Eastern Rite dioceses as enumerated in the Official Catholic Directory.

Naturally, the Church's growth reflects the civil structure. The metropolitan area of Los Angeles continues to grow at a phenomenal rate. Its 34,000 square miles encompass an area larger in population (13.4 million) than all the states except California, New York and Texas.

It has the largest Hispanic market, with predominate population of Hispanic heritage or origin, as well as the largest Asian Pacific islander market, with 8.2% of the population of Asian heritage or origin.

There are 157 separate incorporated cities in the district, ranging in size from

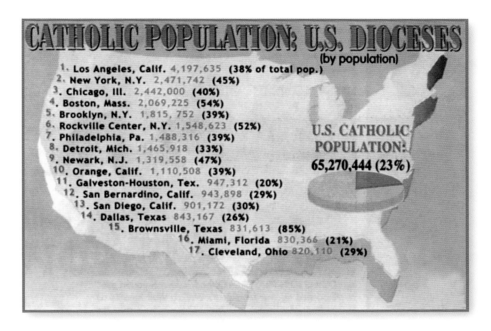

CATHOLIC POPULATION: U.S. DIOCESES (by population)

1. Los Angeles, Calif. 4,197,635 (38% of total pop.)
2. New York, N.Y. 2,471,742 (45%)
3. Chicago, Ill. 2,442,000 (40%)
4. Boston, Mass. 2,069,225 (54%)
5. Brooklyn, N.Y. 1,815,752 (39%)
6. Rockville Center, N.Y. 1,548,623 (52%)
7. Philadelphia, Pa. 1,488,316 (39%)
8. Detroit, Mich. 1,465,918 (33%)
9. Newark, N.J. 1,319,558 (47%)
10. Orange, Calif. 1,110,508 (39%)
11. Galveston-Houston, Tex. 947,312 (20%)
12. San Bernardino, Calif. 943,898 (29%)
13. San Diego, Calif. 901,172 (30%)
14. Dallas, Texas 843,167 (26%)
15. Brownsville, Texas 831,613 (85%)
16. Miami, Florida 830,366 (21%)
17. Cleveland, Ohio 820,110 (29%)

U.S. CATHOLIC POPULATION: 65,270,444 (23%)

Los Angeles (3.3 million) to Vernon (ninety) people. It is first in manufacturing shipments, with 75.7 billion in 1986 as compared with 71.5 billion for second-place Chicago. (The Archdiocese of Chicago was formerly the largest in the nation.) Upwards of 77 million tourists come every year, many of them to shop in an area which is fourth in production of apparel after New York, California and Pennsylvania.

Ranking third in the manufacture of furniture, to cite another example, Los Angeles and its metropolitan area is a major market for imported cars. And the area is not all highway either, but ranks just behind Washington and Oklahoma in the quantity of land devoted to agriculture.

Financially, the area has a firm base. It is the savings and loan capital of the United States, having eleven of the fifty largest such institutions headquartered here. Savings deposits total $104.4 billion, nearly twice that of second-ranked Chicago. For those who distrust American banks, there are 120 foreign banks located here.

In terms of gross national product, the metropolitan area of Los Angeles ranks tenth among the nations of the world. In 1986, the GNP was $275 billion, putting it ahead of Brazil, India, Mexico, Australia, Spain, the Netherlands and Switzerland.

In 1968, James Francis Cardinal McIntyre said that "Los Angeles would become a world center with an orientation to the Pacific." His Eminence may not have been a prophet in the scriptural sense, but he was exceedingly shrewd at reading the signs of the times. His successor was no less astute. Timothy Cardinal Manning likened Los Angeles to Ellis Island (in New York), a multi-cultural archdiocese, destined to take its rightful place as the flagship of the American Church.

When Pope John Paul II came to the archdiocese, in September of 1987, he found the Church experiencing what Archbishop Roger Mahony described as "a New Pentecost, a vigorous growth in faith and in diversity of peoples, a renewal of spirit and joy in our Lord Jesus Christ and in the tradition of Fray Junípero Serra".

ARCHDIOCESE AT HALF CENTURY

Just half a century ago, California became the only state in the Union to have two ecclesial provinces. In retrospect, the creation of a Metropolitan District at Los Angeles was an act of genius for in just a few decades the onetime Pueblo de Nuestra Señora de los Angeles would become the largest archdiocese in the United States.

As early as 1922, Bishop John J. Cantwell foresaw that "the time will come when there will be a diocese of San Diego and at that time the Bishop of Los Angeles will be made an archbishop." Fourteen years later, the tremendous growth of the Los Angeles-San Diego jurisdiction compelled Cantwell to petition the Holy See for a new diocese in the area of San Diego.

In his request, Cantwell suggested that if formation of a second metropolitan province in California was not advisable after the removal of San Diego, it would be legally preferable for the remaining jurisdiction to bear the title Los Angeles-Santa Barbara, to distinguish it from the already-existing Episcopal Diocese of Los Angeles.

Cantwell's attachment to the dual title was based on the added contention that "the Catholic bishop has enjoyed a seniority over all others in civil affairs. This seniority came not only from the right of priority of the Catholic Church in California, but also because of the wide jurisdiction of the Bishop, which always embraced more than the City of Los Angeles."

The statistical breakdown submitted with the proposal was impressive:

County	Residents	Catholics
San Diego	209,477	46,000
Imperial	60,894	11,320
Riverside	82,266	12,823
San Bernardino	133,878	96,443
Totals	486,515	166,586

7 Academies	244 Religious Women
9 Schools	44 Religious Men
2 Hospitals	73 Secular priests
1 Orphanage	53 Parishes

Remembering the unhappy financial aftermath associated with the formation of the Diocese of Monterey-Fresno, Bishop Cantwell carefully anticipated the complexities connected with his latest proposal, noting that, "I am very solicitous that there should be no controversy after the diocese is divided to intensify by any bitterness the discontent that many priests feel when they are cut off from the Mother Church."

Bishop Cantwell made it clear to the apostolic delegate that he would "prefer very much to have no division until such a time as the Holy See is satisfied that an equitable division has been made".

On September 9,1936, Archbishop Amleto Giovanni Cicognani notified Cantwell that "the new ecclesiastical province has been established and Your Excellency has been named archbishop." The papal bulls, dated July 11, were made public after their appearance in

L'Osservatore Romano. In part, the decreee addressed to the newly created archbishop read:

> Today with the counsel of Our venerable Brethren, the Cardinals of the Holy Roman Catholic Church of the Sacred Congregation in charge of Consistorial Affairs, We have by Our Letter "Nimas Amplas" raised your Cathedral to the rank and dignity of a Metropolitan Church under the name of Los Angeles and have granted to it and to its Archbishop all the rights, privileges, honors and prerogatives which other Metropolitan Churches and their Archbishops throughout the world possess and enjoy.

> By this same Letter, We make known your elevation to the clergy and people of your Archdiocese. We command in the Lord our venerable Brothers, the Bishops of Monterey-Fresno, Tucson and San Diego, to acknowledge you as their Metropolitan.

The Southland welcomed the papal action enthusiastically as is obvious in the various editorials of the time. One quoted an observation of Bishop Cantwell to the effect that "The high honor that has come to me is a tribute that comes from the most venerable, conservative and at the same time the most progressive power on earth as a distinguished recognition of the importance and stability of the city of Los Angeles." When the canonical erection of the new province took place on December 3, 1936, the previously existing boundaries for the Provinces of San Francisco and Santa Fe were readjusted permitting the Dioceses of Monterey-Fresno, San Diego and Tucson to be incorporated into the new metropolitan Province of Los Angeles.

A brief issued by the Apostolic Delegate noted that the new Diocese of San Diego, with its episcopal seat at St Joseph's Church, would incorporate the counties of San Diego, Imperial, Riverside and San Bernardino.

The ceremonies of formal erection, held at St. Vibiana's Cathedral, were broadcast by radio throughout the southland. The sermon for the occasion was delivered by Cantwell's long-time episcopal confrere and friend, Archbishop John T. McNicholas, O.P.

The Inaugural ceremonies were presided over by Archbishop Amleto Giovanni Cicognani, the Apostolic Delegate. Forty-one members of the hierarchy attended the event as well as the public reception held the following Sunday in the Shrine Auditorium.

The address on behalf of the laity, delivered by J. Wiseman Macdonald, a prominent local attorney, was one of historical importance inasmuch as it outlined Cantwell's major accomplishments since his arrival in the southland nineteen years previously.

REACHING FOR TRICENTENNIAL

Even those outside her fold must accord the Catholic Church a special "historical pre-eminence" in discussions about the earliest days of Los Angeles.

The "Catholic presence" in the area now comprising the City of Los Angeles actually pre-dates the city by a dozen years. The very name derives from the diary of Fray Juan Crespi, who introduced the Feast of the *Portiuncula* into California's vocabulary.

And it was a group of Catholics, most of them predominantly

Negro in racial strain, who effected the actual foundation of *El Pueblo de Nuestra Señora de Los Angeles*, in the fall of 1781.

Fray Junípero Serra, the *Presidente* of the California Missions, first walked the dusty pathways of the *pueblo* the following year. Interestingly enough, he and his Franciscan companions initially objected to the establishment, feeling that premature Spanish towns would infringe upon the Indian and mission prerogatives. And they did!

In any event, despite the reservations of the friars, the *pueblo* has borne, from the very outset, the unmistakable seraphic imprint of those dedicated pioneers who came to share their religion and civilization with an aboriginal people.

Los Angeles continued for some years to be a "Catholic" enclave, with most of its inhabitants worshipping, at least sporadically, at the Old Plaza Church. Oh, that's not to say that the *pueblo* was, by any means, a virtuous city. Unfortunately, the Catholic Church has always been blessed (or cursed) with more than its share of renegades.

On January 17, 1837, just a year and a half after Los Angeles had been raised to the status of a city, the *ayuntamiento* or council passed, without a dissenting voice, a resolution declaring that "the Roman Catholic apostolic religion shall prevail throughout this jurisdiction."

While there is no evidence that this expressed but never enforced "establishment of religion" benefitted Catholics, it did provide adherents with a unique distinction in Western Americana's historical annals.

Plans were unveiled to open a Catholic school in the city in 1849 and two years later the institution opened its doors with twenty-six "scholars." Bishop Joseph Sadoc Alemany entrusted the administration of the school to the Picpus Fathers.

As late as 1853, Harris Newmark said that "nearly all the population was Catholic." Another creditable authority noted that "up to 1854, the only organization in Los Angeles upholding any standard of morality whatever was the Roman Catholic Church. It erected houses of worship, hospitals and schools, it was the pioneer of all good works".

And while it all changed following the onrush of the gold seekers, Los Angeles continued through the decades to be a unique haven for religious-minded peoples of all creeds.

In a survey of local history published in 1967, Christopher Rand observed that "there are probably more religions in Los Angeles than in the whole previous history of mankind." And it all started with the Catholic Church, in 1781.

DECADE OF GROWTH

Catholicism in the State of California during the past decade shows one of the most phenomenal growth patterns of the Church in modern times and the following figures reflect, if only confusedly, the major results of this development.

Based on the latest national figures, there are 11,222,889 Catholics in the state's twelve ecclesiastical jurisdictions. A cardinal, an archbishop and thirty four bishops direct the activities of 2,073 diocesan and 1,545 religious priests caring for 1,069 parishes and 184 missions.

A total of 4,618 sisters and 471 brothers staff 117 diocesan and private high schools and 568 elementary schools. Enrollment is fixed at 70,833 in Catholic high schools and 180,083 in parochial grammar schools. Thirteen colleges and universities serve 41,197 students. There are three diocesan seminaries with 231 aspirants coupled with nine religious seminaries or scholasticates serving 561 seminarians.

Under the release-time program on the secondary level 84,850 public school students receive Catholic instruction each week while 435,430 youngsters participate in the program on the elementary level.

A large percentage of California's clergy teach in the Church's educational system: 73 are exclusively engaged in this work with another 118 brothers and 545 sisters devoting the major part of their time to the classroom; 15,254 lay teachers augment the program on a full-time bases.

Forty-two general hospitals serve California's Catholic population. This past year 4,814,356 people were treated in those institutions. The Church operates fifteen orphanages with 849 resident children and last year supervised the placing of 1,488 youngsters in foster homes.

There were 194,777 infant Baptisms recorded in parochial registers, while 9,149 adult converts were received into the Faith. 28,789 couples were united in holy matrimony, and 38,581 were listed in the burial records.

Within the state, Catholicity has grown at a proportionately slower rate than it has in the nation at large. In California, Catholics make up 32% of the population as contrasted with 20.9% a decade ago.

CALIFORNIA CATHOLIC CONFERENCE

The Decree on the *Bishops' Pastoral Office* in the Church considered it "supremely opportune everywhere" that bishops belonging to the same nation or region form an association which meets together at fixed times. Such had long been the practice in the United States. In the years immediately following Vatican Council II, the nation's bishops re-organized the existing National Catholic Welfare Conference into the United States Catholic Conference.

Incorporated on January 1, 1967, under the laws for the District of Columbia, the Conference assists the American bishops by uniting the People of God where voluntary collective action on a broad interdiocesan range is needed. The USCC provides an organizational structure and the resources needed to insure coordination, cooperation and assistance in the public,

educational and social concerns of the Church at the national or interdiocesan level.

California is one of the twenty-eight states which has adapted many parts of the USCC structure to the local Church. There are variances, of course, but the California Catholic Conference has generally the same objectives and goals as the larger organization, except that it deals exclusively with the fifty-eight counties of California.

The California Catholic Conference was formally established by the Golden State's hierarchy in February, 1971. It was an outgrowth of the California Conference of Catholic Health Facilities and the Catholic Schools of California, organized two years earlier. The functions of the Conference fall into three general categories: (a) providing liaison with state departments and with the legislature, (b) disseminating infor-

mation to Catholic associations and organizations, to other state conferences and to the USCC and (c) coordinating interdiocesan activities in the areas of education, welfare and related items.

An informational newsletter is published monthly and a large amount of correspondence is maintained with the archbishops and bishops attached to the twelve ecclesial jurisdictions of California. Organized as a direct result of Vatican Council II and the 1971 Synod of Bishops, the California Catholic Conference is actively involved in a myriad of public affairs integral to the preaching of the Gospel and the betterment of justice, peace and general welfare.

The California bishops are a policy making body. An executive director coordinates the day-to-day activities of the Conference, assisted by office personnel who serve as staff to the bishops. Associated with the CCC are the diocesan directors of welfare and social service agencies, the superintendents of schools and coordinators of religious education, campus ministries and Catholic cemeteries.

Among the arms of the California Catholic Conference are Divisions of Education, Hispanic Affairs and Social Welfare. Another satellite group closely affiliated with the California Catholic Conference is the California Association of Catholic Hospitals.

The existence of the CCC confirms the conciliar belief and ideal that "when the insights of prudence and experience have been shared and views exchanged, there will emerge a holy union of energies in the service of the common good of the churches."

HIERARCHY

ORDINARIES

FRANCISCO GARCIA DIEGO Y MORENO
(1840 – 1846)

Francisco Garcia Diego y Moreno was born on September 17, 1785, at Lagos de Moreno, Mexico, the son of Francisco and Ana Maria (Moreno) Garcia Diego. Invested with the religious habit of the Order of Friars Minor at the College of Nuestra Señora de Guadalupe on November 26, 1801, Francisco was ordained a priest on November 14, 1808 by Bishop Prime Feliciano Marin de Porras of Linares.

Upon completion of his service as Novice Master for the Franciscan community at Zacatecas, Fray Francisco Garcia Diego was elected *Comisario-Prefecto* of the missions attached to the Apostolic College. In 1832, he led a contingency of friars to peninsular California and then north to Alta California, arriving at Santa Clara Mission where he labored for several years.

On April 27, 1840, Pope Gregory XVI erected the Diocese of Both Californias naming Fray Francisco Garcia Diego as the proto bishop of the new jurisdiction. The friar was ordained (consecrated) by the Right Reverend Antonio Maria de Jesus Campos on October 4, 1840 at the National Shrine of Our Lady of Guadalupe just outside Mexico's Distrito Federal.

Upon his return to Alta California, Bishop Garcia Diego took up residence at Santa Barbara Mission where he lived for the relatively few years of his episcopal tenure. Beyond opening a seminary at Santa Ines Mission, the prelate was frustrated in bringing his other objectives to completion because of the economic, political and religious challenges in the region.

The bishop succumbed on April 30, 1846, probably from tuberculosis. He is buried in a vault on the epistle side of the sanctuary at Santa Barbara Mission.

JOSEPH SADOC ALEMANY
(1850 – 1853)

Joseph Alemany was born July 13, 1814 at #9 Rambla del Paseo in the ancient town of Vich, Spain, the third youngest of Antonio Alamany and Micaela de los Santos Cunill. In 1830, Joseph Alemany (he preferred and always used the "e" rather than the "a") entered the Priory of Santo Domingo and, on September 23, 1831, took solemn vows as a member of the Order of Preachers (Dominicans) at which time he was given the name "Sadoc."

After philosophical studies at Tremp's Priory of San Jaime de Pillars and theological training at Gerona's Priory of Our Lady's Annunciation, Joseph completed his sacerdotal preparations at Viterbo's Priory of Santa Maria dei Gradi. He was ordained to the priesthood by Bishop Gaspar Bernardo Pianetti on March 11, 1837, at Viterbo's Cathedral of San Lorenzo.

Following reception of a lectorate in theology and extensive courses in English at the Urban College of Propaganda Fide, Father Alemany was sent to the United States. Arriving on April 2, 1840, he was assigned to Saint Joseph's Priory in Somerset, Ohio.

Naturalized as an American citizen on April 15, 1841, Father Alemany served at Zanesville, Nashville and Memphis. He was elected Master of Novices in 1847 and, the following year, he was named Major Superior for Saint Joseph's Province in which capacity he attended the Seventh provincial Council of Baltimore.

Appointed Bishop of Monterey on May 31, 1850 by Pope Pius IX, Alemany was consecrated on June 30 in Rome's Church of San Carlos al Corso by Giacomo Cardinal Franzoni, assisted by Archbishop Giovanni Stefanelli and Patriarch Guiseppe Valerga.

Disembarking at San Francisco on December 6, 1850, the newly appointed Bishop of Monterey immediately journeyed to Santa Barbara, where he presented himself to the Vicar Capitular of the vacant jurisdiction, Fray Jose Maria Gonzalez Rubio. He was formally installed on January 28th. While in Santa Barbara, Alemany issued his first pastoral letter in which he exhorted Catholics in California to a greater "purity of morals" in the practice of their faith.

By the end of the following year, Alemany had established himself at Monterey where he designated the *presidio* Chapel of San Carlos Borromeo as his cathedral. On December 21, 1851, at Alemany's request, the Diocese of Monterey was separated from its attachment to the Metropolitan District of Mexico City. Alemany also took steps to establish a vicariate for peninsular California. He invoked a diocesan synod which was held in San Francisco on March 19-23, 1852.

While attending the First Plenary Council of Baltimore, Bishop Alemany initiated proceedings for the recovery of the Pious Fund of the Californias, a legal action that remained prominent in American juridical annals until its ultimate solution in 1967. On July 17, 1853, Alemany laid the cornerstone of what would become Saint Mary's Cathedral in San Francisco.

On July 29, 1853, Pope Pius IX created the Metropolitan District of San Francisco with Alemany as its first archbishop, a distinction bestowed on only six other districts during the longest rein in history. On November 18, 1855, Alemany was invested with the sacred pallium by his suffragan, Bishop Thaddeus Amat, C.M., of Monterey.

Alemany oversaw erection of the Vicariate Apostolic of Marysville on September 27, 1860, and the selection of Eugene O'Connell as its first incumbent. Later, O'Connell became Bishop of Grass Valley (later Sacramento).

Alemany attended all the sessions of Vatican Council I, 1869-1870, where he actively supported the definition of papal infallibility. He spoke several times to the assemblage, always with distinction and poise. In thirty-five years, Alemany's sheepfold at San Francisco grew to an impressive 400,000 Catholics, served by 160 clergymen in 131 churches and twenty-five chapels at stations.

After prolonged negotiations with the Sacred Congregation of Propaganda Fide, Alemany secured the appointment of a coadjutor archbishop in the person of Patrick W. Riordan in 1883.

Upon acceptance of his resignation by Pope Leo XIII, on December 28, 1884, Joseph Sadoc Alemany was given the titular See of Pelusium. He returned to Spain, where he spent the final years of his life as a humble religious in the Order of Preachers.

Death claimed the prelate on April 14, 1888 in the city of Valencia, where he was endeavoring to re-establish his Order's ancient Province of Aragon. He was interred on the epistle side of the main altar in the chapel of Santo Domingo.

Alemany's remains were disinterred in January of 1965 and returned to San Francisco where, after services conducted in old Saint Mary's Cathedral, he was placed in a vault alongside his successors at Holy Cross Mausoleum in Colma.

THADDEUS AMAT Y BRUSI, C.M.
(1853 – 1878)

Thaddeus Amat, C.M., born December 31, 1811 at Barcelona, Spain, the son of Pedro and Martha (Brusi) Amat, was received into the Congregation of the Mission (Vincentians) on January 4, 1832. Ordained a priest on December 23, 1837 by Hyacinthe Louis de Quelen of Paris, Amat arrived in New Orleans on October 9, 1838. He served at posts in Perryville, Cape Girardeau and Saint Louis until 1847 when he

became rector of Saint Charles Seminary in Philadelphia. He attended the Seventh Provincial Council of Baltimore.

Consecrated (ordained) Bishop of Monterey on March 12, 1854 by Giacomo Cardinal Franzoni in the chapel of Propaganda Fide, Rome, Amat arrived in California with the relics of Saint Vibiana, under whose patronage he erected a cathedral in 1876. He was installed at Monterey on November 25, 1855.

Amat issued his first pastoral letter in 1854 and authored a catechism on matrimony (1864) which was used widely throughout the United States. He moved to Southern California and had the name of the diocese changed to Monterey-Los Angeles in 1859. Amat attended the sessions of Vatican Council I (1869-1870) and brought to an end the first phase of the settlement for the Pious Fund of the Californias (1875). Later, he engaged in a protracted canonical dispute with the Franciscans at Santa Barbara.

Bishop Amat died at Los Angeles on May 12, 1878 and was interred beneath the main altar in Saint Vibiana 's Cathedral. In 1962, his remains were moved to the episcopal vault at Calvary Mausoleum, and then re-interred in the new Cathedral of Our Lady of Angels in 2004.

BISHOP FRANCIS MORA
(1878 – 1896)

The fourth of the southland's bishops, Francis Mora, was born on November 25, 1827 in the 12,414 square mile Principality of Catalonia, in the north-eastern corner of the Iberian peninsula.

Christened on the very day of his birth at Gurb, Francisco was enrolled on the parochial roster of the 5th century church of San Andres. He entered the Conciliar Seminary of San Joachim as a student for the bishopric of Vich. After several years there he was accepted as a divinity student by Bishop Thaddeus Amat, the newly consecrated Bishop of Monterey-Los Angeles.

Raised to the priesthood on March 19, 1856, his initial assignment was to the *presidio* chapel of San Carlos Borromeo at Monterey. Later he served at San Juan Bautista Mission and then became pastor of the parish of the Immaculate Heart of Mary in Pajaro Valley, Watsonville. For a while he also functioned at San Luis Obispo Mission. Mora was called to Los Angeles and the pastorate of the old Plaza Church of Nuestra Señora de los Angeles in 1863, a position he held for the following fifteen years.

On July 25, 1866, Mora was named Vicar General for the Diocese of Monterey-Los Angeles and, when the health of Bishop Thadeus Amat began to decline, Mora was appointed Coadjutor bishop of the diocese. He was consecrated on August 3rd. He became the residential bishop of the 75,984 square mile Diocese of Monterey-Los Angeles on May 12, 1878.

During his episcopal tenure, Mora encouraged the formation of a Catholic newspaper, selected the sites of several cemeteries, combated the local activities of the American Protective Association and expanded diocesan services and out-reach programs. There was modest expansion of educational services, establishment of several teaching communities of women and convocation of a synod.

After sustaining injuries in a carriage accident, Bishop Mora asked for and was given a coadjutor in the person of George Montgomery. With Montgomery's elevation, Mora handed over his crozier and returned to Spain where he lived for the final years of his life.

The bishop died on the thirty-second anniversary of his episcopal consecration in 1905. He was interred in the local cemetery at Sarria until 1962, when his remains were returned to Los Angeles. He is now entombed in the Cathedral of Our Lady of the Angels.

BISHOP GEORGE MONTGOMERY
(1896 – 1903)

When Bishop George Montgomery succeeded Bishop Francis Mora on June 10, 1896, anti-Catholic bigotry in the guise of the American Protective Association was rampant. The need for vigorous leadership to defend the Church was fully met in this able prelate.

Chancellor of the Archdiocese of San Francisco, he was consecrated April 8, 1894, shortly after Bishop Mora's request for a Coadjutor had been approved. Immediately he assumed almost complete administration of the Diocese of Monterey and Los Angeles for the ailing Bishop Mora.

This was the year when the A.P.A. was showing alarming power in the Los Angeles city elections. Bishop Montgomery acted promptly and decisively, organizing a branch of the Catholic Truth Society and instituting a series of popular lectures on Catholic doctrine. By the end of the century the wave of bigotry had subsided.

When the precarious health of Bishop Mora compelled him to resign and he returned to his native Spain, Bishop Montgomery continued his vigorous program of establishing Catholic prestige in Southern California and at the same time providing for the spiritual needs of an expanding population.

He was the first native American bishop of the diocese. Born in Daviéss County, Kentucky, December 30, 1847, he was ordained to the priesthood by James Cardinal Gibbons, Archbishop of Baltimore on December 20, 1879.

On February 3, 1903, Bishop Montgomery left Los Angeles to become Coadjutor Archbishop of San Francisco. But his life was cut short by appendicitis, from which he died after a week's illness, January 10, 1907. He was mourned throughout the entire state, for he had proved himself not only a dynamic churchman, but also a great civic leader and an outstanding American.

During nearly nine years of residence in the southland, Bishop Montgomery achieved widespread respect through his numerous associations and activities not only for himself but for all Catholics. He was a fearless and convincing speaker.

An inscribed plaque to his memory was placed on the pulpit in the Cathedral of St. Vibiana. Bishop Montgomery High School in the South Bay area is named for him.

THOMAS J. CONATY
(1903 – 1915)

In his younger days, Thomas James Conaty, second Rector of the Catholic University of America, was described in terms as realistic as they were poetic: "We can easily imagine him a Peter waking up Europe to the crusades, but would find it hard to see in him the same Peter in a hermit's cell. God made him an active man, and in every agitation for the people's health he is the angel who, stronger than the rest, can best stir the waters".

Thomas James Conaty was born in Kilnaleck, County Cavan, Ireland, on August 1, 1847, the son of Patrick and Alice Lynch Conaty. Two years later the infant was brought to the United States by his parents who settled in Taunton, Massachusetts. The boy grew up in the Old Colony State and after attending the local public schools, he entered Montreal College on December 30, 1863, transferring four years later to Holy Cross in Worcester. Under the patronage of a cousin, Conaty returned to Montreal in 1869 and enrolled at the Grand Seminaire. He was ordained for the Diocese of Springfield on December 21, 1872, by the Most Reverend Ignatius Bourget.

The following spring Father Conaty was named curate at Saint John's Church in Worcester and in 1880, when the parochial boundaries were adjusted, Conaty was given charge of the newly erected parish of the Sacred Heart.

That the years of his pastorate were filled with activities is understandable in view of his reputation as an "agitator who loves the work of the multitude." A school, rectory, convent, gymnasium and finally a church were built and, within a few years, the parish had no less than sixteen societies to coordinate its many-phased apostolate.

Father Conaty organized the Diocesan Temperance Union in 1877 and for some years there after was active in that movement. His prominence on the national scene was enhanced by his presidency of the Catholic Summer School of America. It came as no surprise when Pope Leo XIII selected Conaty for the rectorship of the Catholic University of America.

With the completion of his term in Washington, Conaty was named Bishop of Monterey-Los Angeles in 1903. In California, Conaty became involved with a host of activities. He purchased a newspaper for the diocese, took an active interest in all manner of laity groups, was a pioneer in charitable and hospital works and educational expansion. He brought a number of Religious women to the diocese, worked closely with Saint Vincent College and even tried, unsuccessfully to build a new cathedral.

Conaty interacted well with ethnic groups and was a close collaborator with movements to better the conditions of native Americans. A noted preacher, he was involved in ecumenical activities. He died at the seaside town of Coronado on September 18, 1915.

ARCHBISHOP JOHN J. CANTWELL
(1917 – 1947)

The first Archbishop of Los Angeles was a man of vision. Seventy years ago reading well the signs of potential and real growth for Southern California, he boldly proposed to the Holy Father the need for establishing a Metropolitan District for Los Angeles.

Though the people of a new era probably associate him mostly with the high school bearing his name, John J. Cantwell left his mark, and a prominent one at that, in the Catholic annals of California's southland. In fact, he was a pioneer whose stature contrasts favorably with the Golden State's great missionary founders. The prelate's accomplishments were as spiritually profitable to the faithful of his day as they are statistically phenomenal to those of a succeeding generation.

The archbishop was a far-sighted man whose programs envisioned the time when, in fulfillment of the prediction made early in his tenure, Los Angeles would become the largest city in the United States. His instinctive qualities of leadership, augmented by efficient organization, careful planning and gentle persuasion were a rallying point for the creative talent in that elite corps of highly competent subordinates which he fashioned into his official family.

John Cantwell was one of seven California prelates from the Emerald Isle. Born in Limerick, he was baptized in Saint Michael's Church on December 7, 1874, the only one of Patrick and Ellen Cantwell's ten children not initiated into the Mystical Body at the ancestral city of Fethard. Sent at the age of six to the Patrician Monastery National School and later to the nearby Classical Academy, young Cantwell began early to prepare for the clerical life he was to share with three of his brothers in the archdiocese of San Francisco. From Fethard, John went to Sacred Heart College in Limerick near the home of his grandparents on George Street.

The future bishop entered Saint Patrick's College at Thurles, one of Ireland's renowned missionary seminaries in 1892, and spent the following seven years preparing for his ordination. He was raised to the priesthood on June 18, 1899, at the hands of Robert Browne, Bishop of Cloyne in the 19th Century Cathedral of the Assumption.

Soon after his ordination, Father Cantwell arrived in San Francisco and served for the next five years at Saint Joseph's Church in

Berkeley. An enthusiastic promoter of educational activities, he helped to organize the Newman Club at the University of California and taught classics at Saint Joseph's Presentation Convent. In 1905, he became secretary to Archbishop Patrick W. Riordan and nine years later was promoted to Vicar General under Archbishop Edward J. Hanna. He was named to the long vacant Diocese of Monterey-Los Angeles in 1917, after having refused an appointment to Salt Lake City some years earlier. The staggering problems facing the young bishop on his arrival in Los Angeles were manifold, but he took as his yardstick the sage advice of his longtime friend Father Peter C. Yorke:

Don't start by building a cathedral… get the little ones to love Christ… concentrate on Christian education of the youth and you will be a great success in the eyes of the Lord.

During an episcopate that stretched over three full decades, Cantwell saw his original diocese divided twice, first in 1922 when the Monterey-Fresno area was detached and again in 1936 when San Diego became a distinct ecclesiastical jurisdiction. In the latter year Los Angeles became a Metropolitan See thus making California the only state in the Union with two separate provinces.

By the time of his death on October 30,1947, Archbishop Cantwell had developed a bustling, sprawling diocese of a few churches and schools into one of the major provinces in the nation.

As noted in Cantwell's biography by his long-time friend and collaborator, the archbishop "was a worthy successor to the prelates who preceded him. He piloted the Church of Los Angeles from a frontier rim of the Christian world to the edge of greatness in the family of American jurisdictions."

JAMES FRANCIS CARDINAL McINTYRE
(1948 – 1970)

Fulton J. Sheen once credited the second Archbishop of Los Angeles with being the greatest spiritual inspiration of his life, "not because of what he told me about the priesthood, but because of the way he lived it."

James Francis Aloysius McIntyre was born on June 25, 1886 in mid-Manhattan, the son of James and Mary (Pelley) McIntyre. After the death of his mother in 1896, James Francis was reared by a cousin, Mrs. Robert F. Conley.

He spent several years in the employ of H. L. Horton and Company, an investment house on the New York Stock Exchange. Young McIntyre took night courses at New York City College and Columbia and, following the demise of his father in 1915, he entered the preparatory seminary for the Archdiocese of New York.

The next year he enrolled in Saint Joseph's Seminary at Dunwoodie where he spent five years until May 21, 1921, when he was raised to the priesthood by Patrick Cardinal Hayes.

Immediately after ordination, Father McIntyre was appointed assistant to the pastor of Saint Gabriel's Church where he remained until September 1923, when he was named Vice Chancellor and liaison officer between Cardinal Hayes and the curial staff.

He became Chancellor in 1934, and, on December 27th of that year was designated a Private Chamberlain by Pope Pius XI. Two years later, on November 12, 1936 he was promoted to the Domestic Prelacy.

After the arrival of Archbishop Francis J. Spellman in 1939, Msgr. McIntyre became a member of the Board of Consultors for the Archdiocese of New York.

On November 16, 1940, Pope Pius XII appointed him Auxiliary Bishop of New York. He was consecrated by Archbishop Spellman in Saint Patrick's Cathedral on January 8, 1941.

Bishop McIntyre was made Vicar General of the archdiocese on January 27, 1945 and, eighteen months later, on July 20, 1946, the Holy Father advanced the prelate to Coadjutor Archbishop of New York. On February 7, 1948, Archbishop McIntyre was transferred to Los Angeles as the eighth occupant of the jurisdiction originally established in 1840 under the title of Ambas Californias.

Shortly after his installation at Los Angeles, Archbishop McIntyre set about to reorganize the archdiocesan curia, to erect a new chancery, and to refurbish Saint Vibiana's Cathedral - all of which he deemed necessary to the efficient management of a jurisdiction encompassing an area of 9,508 square miles with a steadily increasing Catholic population.

Pope Pius XII elevated Archbishop J. Francis A. McIntyre to the cardinalate, presenting him with the scarlet galero in Saint Peter's Basilica on January 12,1953, as the twelfth American member of the Sacred College.

Undoubtedly Cardinal McIntyre's greatest contribution was his program for expanding Catholic educational facilities. In the first fifteen years of his tenure, Catholic schools were tripled from 141 to 347, an average of one a month.

In addition to serving a significant role in the Central Preparatory Commission for Vatican Council II, the cardinal attended all the sessions of the council and was active in its deliberations.

After his retirement, Cardinal McIntyre spent the final nine years of his life serving as a parish priest at Saint Basil's in mid-town Los Angeles. By the time of his demise, on July 16,1979, he was the acknowledged "Elder Statesman of the American Hierarchy".

TIMOTHY CARDINAL MANNING
(1970 – 1985)

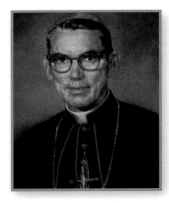

Trained in the noble tradition of the Cantwell years, seasoned in the expansionary complexities of the McIntyre archiepiscopate and steeped in the spirit of Vatican Council II, Timothy Cardinal Manning has left an impressive imprint on the pilgrim Church of Our Lady of the Angels.

One of the four children of Cornelius and Margaret (Cronin) Manning, Timothy was born Nov. 14, 1909, at Ballingeary, County Cork, Ireland. In 1915, he enrolled at the local National School and seven years later advanced to the educational facilities operated at nearby Cork by the Christian Brothers.

His preparation for the priesthood began in 1923, at Mungret College, a secondary school staffed by the Society of Jesus for the foreign missions.

The youthful clerical aspirant was attracted to California by an appeal on behalf of the Diocese of Los Angeles-San Diego. Leaving Ireland in October 1928, he traveled to Menlo Park where he joined the student body of St. Patrick's Seminary.

He was ordained to the priesthood by Bishop John J. Cantwell on June 16, 1934, in Saint Vibiana's Cathedral. His initial assignment was that of curate at Immaculate Conception Church in Los Angeles.

The following year, Father Manning was sent to Rome for post-graduate studies at the Pontifical Gregorian University, where he received the doctorate in Canon Law in 1938.

Upon his return to Southern California, Father Manning was named secretary to Archbishop Cantwell, a post he occupied for eight years. In 1943, he was made a papal chamberlain and, two years afterwards, was promoted by Pope Pius XII to the domestic prelacy.

On August 17, 1946, Msgr. Manning was appointed Titular Bishop of Lesvi and Auxiliary of Los Angeles. Episcopal orders were bestowed on October 15, by Bishop Joseph T. McGucken, then Apostolic Administrator for the Diocese of Monterey-Fresno. At the time and for a goodly while thereafter, Bishop Manning was the "Benjamin of the American Hierarchy."

With the appointment to Los Angeles in 1948 of Archbishop J. Francis A. McIntyre, Manning was named Chancellor. From 1953 to 1967 he also occupied the pastorate of Saint Gregory's, a parish on the western rim of downtown Los Angeles. On Nov. 29,1955 he became Vicar General of the archdiocese.

A popular speaker and writer, Bishop Manning published a chapter of his doctoral thesis dealing with Clerical Education in Major Seminaries, a fifty page treatise called *The Grey Ox* and the entry for the "Archdiocese of Los Angeles" in the *New Catholic Encyclopedia*.

A number of his sermons and addresses have appeared in various ecclesiastical journals in recent years. The bishop served the commonweal in several capacities during his tenure as Auxiliary of Los Angeles, including a fifteen year stint on the Los Angeles City Library Commission and a lengthy term as a director of El Pueblo de Los Angeles Commission.

Upon realignment of ecclesial boundaries in Central California. Bishop Manning was named to the newly-erected Diocese of Fresno on Oct. 24, 1967.

Bishop Manning's work in the eight counties of the San Joaquin Valley was described as "a servanthood of justice and reconciliation." In eighteen brief but intensely fruitful months, he created a diocesan housing commission, established four new parishes and five missions, approved formation of a priests' senate, authorized a task force to marshal resources for inner city and minority groups, shared the bitter anguish of the Delano labor dispute and visited each of the eighty parishes scattered through the 35,239 square mile jurisdiction.

Bishop Manning was recalled from Fresno to the scene of his earlier priestly labors on May 6, 1969 as Coadjutor to James Francis

Cardinal McIntyre. Assigned to the titular See of Capri, Archbishop Manning was re-named Vicar General and given the pastorate of Saint Brendan's Church.

Upon the retirement of Cardinal McIntyre on January 21,1970, Archbishop Manning became Chief Shepherd of the Church of Los Angeles, encompassing the 9,508 square miles of Los Angeles, Orange, Ventura and Santa Barbara counties. He received the pallium, symbolic of the metropolitan office, on June 17,1970.

In addition to pursuing administrative and expansionary policies, Archbishop Manning established a priests' senate, an inter-parochial council and a clerical personnel board. He energetically supported a host of ecumenical involvements and warmly endorsed the Cursillo movement. He personally chaired the Commission for Liturgy, established a spirituality house and erected an Archival Center, to mention but a few of his many activities

He made a solemn pilgrimage to Mexico City's National Shrine of Our Lady of Guadalupe, where it all began for California, there to thank the Mexican people for their role in bedrocking the faith along the Pacific Slope. It was also in 1971 that the archbishop was elected proto-president of the newly-created California Catholic Conference.

In his concern for and identification with the archdiocesan founded and sponsored Lay Mission Helpers, Manning visited missionaries in South Africa, Rhodesia, Ghana, Kenya, Malawi and Uganda. It was while en-route to another segment of that far-flung apostolate early in 1973 that he received word that Pope Paul VI once again had honored the People of God at Los Angeles, by naming him to the College of Cardinals.

Though the Catholics of Orange county were given their own diocese in 1976, Los Angeles continued to expand and was acknowledged as the largest ecclesial jurisdiction in the United States.

ROGER CARDINAL MAHONY
(1985 Onwards)

Catholics in California's southland rejoiced when word reached them that one of their own was returning to be the fourth Archbishop of Los Angeles. Their new prelate was the fourth native of Los Angeles and the twenty-third Californian called to the episcopate.

Roger Michael Mahony's ecclesial pedigree is deeply imbedded in the area's heritage. His relationship to Cardinal Timothy Manning, for example, goes back almost forty years. It was in the pages of *The Tidings* for October 18, 1946, that their kinship began. That issue, describing Manning's consecration as Auxiliary Bishop of Los Angeles, carries a picture of a ten-year-old Roger and his twin brother, Louis.

Thirteen years later, Bishop Manning conferred the minor orders of Lector and Porter on Mr. Mahony and, the following year, those of Acolyte and Exorcist. In 1967, when Bishop Manning was named to the Diocese of Fresno, Mahony served as chief liaison between the new Ordinary and retiring Bishop Aloysius J.Willinger.

Roger Mahony was born to Victor James and Loretta Marie (Baron) Mahony on February 27, 1936. His entire elementary training was acquired at St. Charles School in North Hollywood, where he fell under the pastoral tutelage of the late Msgr. Harry Meade.

Photo credit: VICTOR ALEMAN / 2MUN-DOS.COM

In 1950, Roger entered Los Angeles College, the preparatory seminary for the Archdiocese of Los Angeles. He was among the initial enrollees at Mission Hill's Queen of Angels Seminary, in1954.

Upon completing his collegiate courses at St. John's Seminary, Camarillo, Roger asked for and received incardination as a clerical aspirant for the Diocese of Monterey-Fresno.

Roger received priestly ordination at the hands of the Most Reverend Aloysius Willinger on May 1, 1962. A few days later, he was assigned to a curacy at Saint John's Cathedral, Fresno. In the following fall, Bishop Willinger asked Father Mahony to take further studies at the National Catholic School of Social Service in Washington, D.C..

Soon after returning to Central California in 1964, Father Mahony was named diocesan Director for Catholic Charities and Social Service, an assignment he held for six years. In September, 1964, he became Administrator (and later Pastor) of Saint Genevieve's Parish, Fresno.

Among other positions occupied by the tireless priest during the late 1960s were executive director for both the Catholic Welfare Bureau and the Infant of Prague Adoption Service, as well as chaplain of the diocesan Saint Vincent de Paul Society. He also found time to teach during those years at Fresno State University and Coalinga College.

Long interested in the apostolate to Hispanic peoples, Father Roger Mahony served a term on the board of directors for the West Coast Office of the Bishops' Committee for the Spanish Speaking. He has also been active as Secretary for the United States Catholic Bishops Ad Hoc Committee on Farm Labor.

There was time for civic responsibilities too. Father Mahony has been affiliated with the Fresno County Economic Opportunities Commission, the Alcoholic Rehabilitation Committee, the United Crusade, the Community Worship, the Urban Coalition and the Fresno Redevelopment Agency.

It was recognition of those manifold duties that prompted the Junior Chamber of Commerce to proclaim Father Mahony "Young Man of the Year for 1967." It was also in that year that he was named Honorary Chaplain to His Holiness, Pope Paul VI.

In 1970, shortly after the transferral of the Most Reverend Hugh A. Donohoe to Fresno, Msgr. Mahony was appointed diocesan chancellor, a position he continued to hold after his episcopal consecration on March 19,1975, as titular Bishop of Tamascani. He became Pastor of Saint John's Cathedral in 1973.

Bishop Mahony was transferred to Stockton as residential ordinary in 1980, and presided over the pastoral needs of that 10,023 square mile, six county diocese

---

Shortly after he was seated in the historic *sedes* of Los Angeles, Archbishop Mahony began preparations to completely reorganize the jurisdiction in preparation for its entry into the 21st century. The three county archdiocese was divided into episcopal vicariates and regional deaneries in an attempt to more effectively meet the needs of those inhabiting the nation's largest archiepiscopal see. Catholics were asked to express their priorities for discussion at a convocation scheduled in anticipation of an archdiocesan synod.

Those who have known the fourth Archbishop of Los Angeles since seminary days can testify that he personifies those traits outlined in the Directory on the Pastoral Ministry of Bishops as necessary for episcopal candidates: "unfailing kindliness and courtesy, a good and upright disposition, a steady and sincere character, a mind that in every way is both open and provident."

AUXILIARY BISHOPS

Very little research has been done over the years about the history and role of "auxiliary" bishops. According to the new Code of Canon Law, an "auxiliary" is appointed without the right of succession to a residential bishop. His rights, duties and privileges are delineated in the bull issued by the Holy See at the time of appointment.

Though they participate fully in the plenitude of priesthood, "auxiliary" bishops lack what Canon Law calls "Jurisdiction." They may exercise their office only in conjunction with and at the direction of the residential bishop. It is understood, however, that what an "auxiliary" bishop is able and willing to do should not be delegated to someone else.

At the time of his appointment, an "auxiliary" bishop is assigned to a titular diocese, generally in a place in the Near or Middle East where the Church flourished in earlier centuries. Interestingly, the appointee may not visit that area without authorization from Rome.

Since Vatican Council II, "auxiliary" bishops have a deliberative vote in ecumenical gatherings. Their role in regional episcopal conferences is determined by local legislation. In the United States, they have a vote in all matters except those touching on finances.

AUXILIARY BISHOPS OF LOS ANGELES		
PRELATE	**YEARS**	**TITULAR SEE**
1. Joseph T. McGucken	1941-1955	Sanavus
2. Timothy Manning	1946-1967	Lesvi
3. Alden J. Bell	1956-1962	Rhodopolis
4. John J. Ward	1963-1996	Bria
5. Joseph P. Dougherty	1969-1970	Altino
6. William R. Johnson	1971-1976	Biera
7. Juan A. Arzube	1971-1993	Civitate
8. Thaddeus Shubsda	1977-1982	Trau
9. Manuel D. Moreno	1977-1982	Tamagrista
10. Donald W. Montrose	1983-1985	Vescovio
11. William J. Levada	1983-1986	Capri
12. Carl A. Fisher	1987-1993	Tlos
13. Armando X. Ochoa	1987-1996	Sitifi
14. G. Patrick Ziemann	1987-1991	Obba
15. Sylvester D. Ryan	1990-1992	Remesiana
16. Stephen E. Blaire	1990-1999	Lamzella
17. Joseph M. Sartoris	1994-2002	Oliva
18. Thomas J. Curry	1994	Ceanannus Mor
19. Gabino Zavala	1994	Tamascani
20. Gerald Wilkerson	1998	Vincennes
21. Edward W. Clark	2001	Garder
22. Oscar A. Solis	2004	Urci
23. Alexander Salazar	2004	Nesqually

Prior to Vatican Council II, the function of an "auxiliary" ceased with the death or transfer of the residential bishop to whom he was assigned. Presently, "auxiliary" bishops are named to the see itself and retain their office during vacancies.

The appointment of "auxiliary" bishops is not of ancient origin, though some of the early commentators point out that Linus and Cletus were referred to in the annals as "vicars" or "auxiliaries" to Peter at Rome.

From the 14th to the 19th centuries, "auxiliary" bishops were fairly common in Spain, Poland, Germany and pre-Reformation England. The first "auxiliary" named for the United States was Sylvester Horton Rosecrans who received Episcopal ordination as titular of Pompey and auxiliary of Cincinnati on March 25, 1862. It was almost thirty years later when John Brady was named "auxiliary" of Boston.

California's proto "auxiliary" was Bishop Denis J. O'Connell who was assigned to San Francisco in 1908. He served there until 1912, when he was transferred to the residential bishopric of Richmond.

The practice of naming "auxiliary" bishops in the Archdiocese of Los Angeles dates from 1941 and the appointment of Joseph T. McGucken to the titular see of Sanavus. Since then, there have been a total of twenty-three "auxiliaries" assigned to the southland jurisdiction.

As of this date, there are more than ninety "auxiliary" bishops in the United States. The country with the next largest number is Poland (58), followed by Germany (41). Italy has twenty-eight, with Brazil and Spain with twenty-four each. There are 553 "auxiliary" bishops world-wide, with six countries mentioned accounting for 48 percent of the total number.

In what Gregory Baum described as a "truly parliamentary speech," Auxiliary Bishop Gerald McDevitt of Philadelphia addressed the conciliar fathers of Vatican Council II on November 13, 1963, scolding them for using the term "merely" when referring to titular bishops, especially those serving as "auxiliaries." He convinced his listeners that it was an important issue which touched the very nature of the episcopacy.

According to current practice, an "auxiliary" may be requested when the diocesan or residential bishop cannot adequately fulfill all his episcopal duties as the good of souls demands. The two most common reasons given are the "vast extent" and / or the "great number" of Catholics in the particular jurisdiction.

In the Archdiocese of Los Angeles, the largest ecclesial district in the United States, Roger Cardinal Mahony wanted each of the five pastoral regions to be presided over by an "auxiliary" bishop.

CALIFORNIA'S TITULAR SEES

Among the many uses of the term "ancient" by ecclesial historians is one associated with those centers of Christendom that were once thriving centers of Catholicity, but have since become only monuments to an earlier age. Such areas, known as "titular" sees, are mostly cities of Northern Africa, the Middle East or Spain that had to be abandoned because of schism or Islamic rule. *The Annuario Pontificio* devotes 233 pages to enumerating titular sees.

Because of the proliferation of retired and auxiliary bishops in the last quarter century, the Holy See has had to increase the number of

RT. REV. THOMAS GRACE, D.D.
MOST REV. PATRICK W. RIORDAN, D.D.
RT. REV. DENNIS J. O'CONNELL, D.D.
RT. REV. THOMAS J. CONATY, D.D.
HIERARCHY OF CALIFORNIA.

titular sees. In July of 1995, the Vatican announced the establishment of twelve new titular sees named for former jurisdictions in the United States. Until that time, only Bardstown, Kentucky enjoyed that status. Most of the ones in the United States are areas which ceased to be active see cities simply because of a decision to merge dioceses or transfer diocesan headquarters to another city.

Histories of diocesan and titular sees are often complex. The See of Monterey in California, for example, established on November 20, 1849, became the Diocese of Monterey-Los Angeles in 1859 and Monterey-Fresno in 1922. On December 15,1967, the original title was restored when the Diocese of Monterey-Fresno was divided. "In California" was added to distinguish the diocese from that of Monterey in Mexico.

Among the dozen new titular sees is Grass Valley, California, erected in 1868 and transferred to Sacramento in May of 1886. The history of the state's first titular see is both interesting and amusing.

When, on March 3, 1868, the Vicariate Apostolic of Marysville was elevated by Rome to the status of a diocese, the Roman decree directed that the title and episcopal seat was to be in Grass Valley. Bishop Eugene O'Connell (1815-1891) was obviously not consulted about the change and his letters to Roman authorities over the next few years reveal why he opposed and resented the change.

He told the Prefect of the Sacred Congregation of Propaganda Fide that "Marysville much more deserves the dignity (of having its named used) than the town called Grass Valley. Truly the transfer from the city of Marysville to Grass Valley is going from the greater to the lesser in every sense."

In another letter, written on July 31, 1870, O'Connell had the temerity to sign himself "Bishop of Marysville" and it was yet three more years before he could bring himself to acknowledging his status as Bishop of Grass Valley. O'Connell was so irritated by the new title that he adamantly refused to take possession of the newly-designated Saint Peter's Cathedral in Grass Valley. He wrote to a friend in Ireland that his installation had not yet occurred and he intended to wait until "the final translation of my remains" takes place, at which time "the change will no longer be a fiction of law."

O'Connell's metropolitan, Archbishop Joseph Sadoc Alemany of San Francisco, wisely took no action and allowed O'Connell to remain in Marysville. He was probably more amused than upset at his suffragan's intransigence. Like most ecclesial squabbles, the matter eventually resolved itself, though not before O'Connell indignantly complained to Rome that the Apostolic Bull erecting Grass Valley had been erroneously directed to "Daniel" rather than "Eugene" O'Connell.

Shepherds of the Flock
Southern California

E P I S C O P A T E		
	Francisco Garcia Diego, O.F.M. Bishop of Both Californias	1840~1846
	Joseph Sadoc Alemany, O.P. Bishop of Monterey	1850~1853
	Thaddeus Amat, C.M. Bishop of Monterey	1853~1859
	Bishop of Monterey~Los Angeles	1859~1878
	Francis Mora Bishop of Monterey~Los Angeles	1878~1896
	George T. Montgomery Bishop of Monterey~Los Angeles	1896~1903
	Thomas J. Conaty Bishop of Monterey~Los Angeles	1903~1915
	John J. Cantwell Bishop of Monterey~Los Angeles	1917~1922
	Bishop of Los Angeles~San Diego	1922~1936
	Archbishop of Los Angeles	1936~1947
	James Francis Cardinal McIntyre Archbishop of Los Angeles	1948~1970
	Timothy Cardinal Manning Archbishop of Los Angeles	1970~1985
	Roger Cardinal Mahony Archbishop of Los Angeles	1985

Msgr. Francis J. Weber old country priest

Chronology of Bp. Francisco Garcia Diego
(1785~1846)

F R A N C I S C O G A R C I A D I E G O		
	Father Theodore Arentz sketches prelate's life	1912
	Republic's president writes to Gregory XVI	1839
	Assistant Guardian at Zacatecas	1832
	Novice Master at Zacatecas	1816
	Came to Alta California	1836
	Ignacio del Rio invests friar with habit	1801
	Seminary established at Santa Ines	1844
	Comisario-Prefecto of Zacatecas	1828
	Ordained priest at Saltillo	1808
	✦ ✦ ✦ ✦ ✦	
	Governor Figueroa dies at Monterey	1835
	Authored Novena de Divina Pastora	1832
	Refuge of Sinners named patroness	1843
	Consecrated at Mexico's National Shrine	1840
	Initial Pastoral Letter to nascent diocese	1835
	Appeals for bishopric at Mexico City	1835
	✦ ✦ ✦ ✦ ✦	
	Died at Santa Barbara Mission	1846
	Interior Minister pledges Pious Fund	1840
	Episcopate moved to Santa Barbara	1842
	Garcia Diego born at Lagos de Moreno	———
	Obispo de Ambas Californias	1840

Msgr. Francis J. Weber old country priest

Chronological Chart for
Joseph Sadoc Alemany, O.P.
(1814~1888)

J O S E P H S A D O C A L E M A N Y		
	Journeyed to Mexico	1852
	Ordained Priest	1837
	Sent to United States	1842
	Erected Saint Mary's Cathedral	1854
	Provincial of American Dominicans	1848
	Hague arbitration ~ Pious Fund	1856
	✦ ✦ ✦ ✦ ✦	
	Summoned first diocesan synod	1852
	Arrived on planet Earth	1814
	Died in Valencia, Spain	1888
	Opened Catholic school in Los Angeles	1851
	Consecrated Bishop of Monterey in Rome	1850
	✦ ✦ ✦ ✦ ✦	
	Audience with Blessed Pius IX	1852
	Left for retirement in Spain	1885
	Entered Dominican novitiate	1830
	Metropolitan Archbishop of San Francisco	1853
	Assisted at Vatican Council I	1869~1870
	Named titular Archbishop of Pelusium	1885
	Year restos returned to California	1965

Msgr. Francis J. Weber old country priest

Chronology of
Bishop Thaddeus Amat, C.M.
(1811~1878)

T H A D D E U S A M A T		
	Transferred to Monterey ~ Los Angeles	1859
	Hague Arbitration ~ Pious Fund	1856
	Appointed Bishop of Monterey	1853
	Departed for the United States	1838
	Died at Los Angeles	1878
	Entered Congregation of the Mission	1832
	United States citizen	1841
	Saint Vibiana's Cathedral consecrated	1876
	✦ ✦ ✦ ✦ ✦	
	Arrived in California	1855
	Missionary in Middle United States	1838~1853
	Assisted in establishing St. Vincent's College	1865
	Traveled to Vatican Council I	1869

Msgr. Francis J. Weber old country priest

Chronology of
Rt. Rev. Francis Mora
Bishop of Monterey~Los Angeles
(1827~1905)

F R A N C I S M O R A		
	Founder of the Cause Newspaper	1890
	Returned his soul to the Lord	1905
	Advanced to the bishopric	1873
	Named pastor of Watsonville	1860
	Catalan-born at Gurb	1827
	Immigrated to the United States	1854
	Succeeded Bishop Thaddeus Amat	1878
	✦ ✦ ✦ ✦ ✦	
	Made Vicar General of Monterey-Los Angeles	1866
	Ordained to the Priesthood	1856
	Retired to Sarria, Spain	1896
	Accompanied IHM Sisters from Olot	1871

Msgr. Francis J. Weber old country priest

Chronology of the Most Reverend
George T. Montgomery
(1847~1907)

G E O R G E T. M O N T G O M E R Y		
	Greeted planet Earth	1847
	Enrolled at St. Charles College, Catonville	1870
	Ordained to priesthood	1879
	Returned his soul to the Lord	1907
	Graduated from St. Mary's Seminary, Baltimore	1879
	El Hogar Feliz begun for youngsters	1877
	✦ ✦ ✦ ✦ ✦	
	Tidings established in California's southland	1895
	✦ ✦ ✦ ✦ ✦	
	Made chancellor-Archdiocese of San Francisco	1879
	Organized Knights of Columbus ~ Los Angeles	1898
	Named Coadjutor Bishop, Monterey~Los Angeles	1894
	Transferred to Archdiocese of San Francisco	1903
	Given key to City of Los Angeles	1900
	Opened Catholic Truth Society in southland	1897
	Montgomery Family: Zachariah and John	1825-1900 1858-1911
	Earthquake and Fire devastation	1906
	Rumored for Archbishopric of Manila	1903
	Yorke preached at installation, Los Angeles	1896

Msgr. Francis J. Weber old country priest

Chronology of Right Reverend
Thomas J. Conaty
(1847~1915)

THOMAS J. CONATY

Total diocesan students ~ 10,545	1915
Home for the Aged	1904
Ordained to the priesthood	1872
Montreal College	1863
Appointed to episcopal titular See of Samos	1901
Sacred Heart parish, Worcester	1880~1897
✦ ✦ ✦ ✦ ✦	
Japanese apostolate in Los Angeles	1912
✦ ✦ ✦ ✦ ✦	
Catholic University of America, rector	1897~1903
Organized Diocesan Temperance Union	1877
New Testament Studies	1898
Apostolate for Indians	1905
Transferred to Monterey~Los Angeles	1903
Young Men's Institute	1896

Msgr.
Francis J. Weber
old country priest

Archbishopric of
John Joseph Cantwell
(1874~1947)

JOHN J. CANTWELL

Joined staff of Archbishop Patrick W. Riordan	1904
Opened two seminaries in Los Angeles	1927 & 1939
Helped Hispanic refugees in Southland	1929~1947
Named Bishop of Monterey~Los Angeles	1917
✦ ✦ ✦ ✦ ✦	
Jurisdictional boundaries adjusted	1922 & 1936
✦ ✦ ✦ ✦ ✦	
Celebrated centennial of California hierarchy	1940
Archbishop (metropolitan) of Los Angeles	1936
Newman Club chaplain ~ Berkeley	1899
Three brother priests: James, William and Arthur	
Welcomed the N.A.A.C.P. to Los Angeles	1921
Emigrated to the United States	1899
Limerick, Ireland, birthplace	1874
Legion of Decency founder	1934

Msgr.
Francis J. Weber
old country priest

Archbishopric of
James Francis Cardinal McIntyre
(1948~1970)

J. FRANCIS A. McINTYRE

Jubilee celebrated at Saint Basils	1971
✦ ✦ ✦ ✦ ✦	
Founded Lay Mission Helpers	1955
"Runner" on Wall Street	1899
Archbishop's Fund for Charity	1951
Named to Titular See of Cyrene	1940
Coadjutor Archbishop of New York	1946
Instructional Television Department	1967
Succumbed at Saint Vincent's Hospital	1979
✦ ✦ ✦ ✦ ✦	
Attended Vatican Council II	1962~1965
✦ ✦ ✦ ✦ ✦	
Masterminded school tax relief	1951 & 1958
Invested with the pallium	1948
Named Cardinal Priest	1953
Transferred to Los Angeles	1948
Youth Education Fund	1949
Relocated minor seminary	1954
Enrolled at Dunwoodie	1915

Msgr.
Francis J. Weber
old country priest

Archbishopric of
Timothy Cardinal Manning
(1909~1989)

TIMOTHY MANNING

Titular Bishop of Lesvi	1946
Installed in Diocese of Fresno	1967
Metropolitan Archbishop of Los Angeles	1970
Ordained priest	1934
Team Ministry program begun	1973
Hibernia's only Prince of the Church	1973~1989
Youngest bishop in the world	1946
✦ ✦ ✦ ✦ ✦	
Mary's Hour farewell	1989
Attended Vatican Council II	1962~1965
Natal day in Ireland	1909
Named pastor of St. Gregory's Parish	1953
Inaugurated Priests' Senate	1970
Nominated Cardinal priest	1973
Golden sacerdotal jubilee	1984

Msgr.
Francis J. Weber
old country priest

Archbishopric of
Roger Cardinal Mahony
(b. 1936)

ROGER M. MAHONY

Reformed curial administration at Los Angeles	1986
Ordained to the priesthood for Diocese of Fresno	1962
Graduate Study at Catholic University of America	1963
Estelle Doheny Collection auctioned	1986~1987
Removed chancery offices to Wilshire Boulevard	1997
✦ ✦ ✦ ✦ ✦	
Metropolitan Archbishop of Los Angeles	1985
✦ ✦ ✦ ✦ ✦	
Minor seminary ~ Los Angeles College	1950
Appointed Cardinal priest	1991
Hosted Pope John Paul II in Los Angeles	1987
Our Lady of Angels Cathedral erected	1997~2001
Named auxiliary bishop of Tamascani	1975
"Young Man of the Year" (Fresno)	1967

Msgr.
Francis J. Weber
old country priest

Three priest of the Archdiocese of Los Angeles are now members of the College of Cardinals, viz., Roger Mahony, William Levada and Justin Rigali.

CLERGY, RELIGIOUS AND LAITY

THE PERMANENT DIACONATE

When Pope Paul VI restored the order of deacon as a permanent ministry in the Latin Church, on June 18, 1967, James Francis Cardinal McIntyre was heard to say that "we will leave the implementation of that directive in Los Angeles to my worthy successor." That the cardinal was enthusiastic about the potentialities of that ministry is obvious from the positive vote he cast when, on April 23, 1968, the American bishops petitioned the Holy Father for its use in the United States "both to complete the hierarchy of sacred orders and to enrich and strengthen the various ministries of work in the United States with the sacramental grace of the diaconate."

The following October, the Holy See granted the request of the NCCB "to establish in the United States the permanent diaconate for married and unmarried men of mature years in those areas where they are needed." Bishop Fulton J. Sheen ordained the first permanent deacon, former Anglican priest Michael Cole, in June of 1969. On September 22,1971, the Bishops Committee on the Permanent Diaconate issued a series of guidelines for the formation of that ministry in the United States.

As was the case with many of his episcopal contemporaries, Archbishop Manning was not initially enamored about establishing the permanent diaconate in Los Angeles. He felt that the chief relevance of restoring that ministry would be in missionary areas of the world where it would sacramentally enhance the office of catechist. He wondered whether it was really needed in the United States, noting that, with the

exception of witnessing marriages and conferring baptism, most diaconal functions could be performed by any delegated lay person. In any event, the archbishop remained open-minded on the notion and asked the newly established Priests' Senate to look into the matter and report back to him with suggestions.

In May of 1971, a subcommittee of the senate commissioned Fathers Joseph George and Mario Antoci to study how best to organize and administer the permanent diaconate in the Archdiocese of Los Angeles. Seeking the advice of prominent local clergymen and lay people, they proceeded to draft a series of proposals. At that juncture, then Archbishop Timothy Manning signalled his unequivocal endorsement by appointing Father Peter Healy to be director of the diaconate ministry in Los Angeles. It was one of the wisest and most important appointments of his archiepiscopate.

Timothy Cardinal Manning and the proto permanent deacon class.

Working with George, Antoci and their collaborators, Healy drew up a "position paper" in March of 1972 which defined the program's academic, spiritual and outreach objectives. The draft was reviewed by the archbishop and his staff and, finally, in April, a thirty-five page booklet on *The Permanent Diaconate* was completed and distributed. That booklet was further fine-tuned and, on December 14, Manning wrote to the *pro tem* President of the Priests' Senate complimenting members for the "immense zeal of energy" which they had expended in the "superb master plan." The archbishop accepted the draft as a "working document, recognizing the validity of the suggestions and recommendations contained therein." He appointed a committee of priests to assist Healy, comprising Fathers John Danagher, Michael Lenihan, Armando Ochoa, James Nash and Anthony Leuer.

The archbishop envisioned selecting twelve candidates for the initial program, which would stretch over two and a half years. There would be an additional year to "evaluate the effectiveness of their position" and, with that done, "we would then be in a position to consider the next class of candidates and the successive classes thereafter on a regular basis." He designated the parochial hall at Immaculate Conception Church as the headquarters for the training sessions.

The archbishop was later to note that "one of the beauties of the Church since the Second Vatican Council is the visible and in-depth meaning given to the hierarchy which Jesus established for the service of His people in the Church. It was always true in the ranks of bishops and priests, but lacked the completion of the permanent order of the diaconate. This is now established and the Church is thereby enriched."

Manning further observed that "in the Church of Los Angeles we have inaugurated and pursue a program of training that is discreet, profoundly spiritual and coordinated to serve the needs of the local Church. This demands a measure of sanctity and sacrifice from each ordained deacon." Manning wanted the Catholic people in the archdiocese to understand that Vatican Council II had not simply restored the diaconate but, drawing on the roots of the early Church, it re-created a precious channel for better and more fully serving the needs of the Church in the modern world.

The process for choosing candidates entailed the following objectives: (1) to select candidates who exhibit qualities of faith, moral integrity and adequate intellectual ability; (2) to replace in some way the ethnic, cultural and social fabric of the Church community of Los Angeles and (3) to provide men capable of ministering to the needs of the Church at Los Angeles.

A breakdown of the original class indicated how well Father Healy and his advisers had done their work. It was truly a "catholic" group of twenty-five people.

Ordination for the proto class of deacons was scheduled for October 7, 1975 at Saint Charles Borromeo Church in North Hollywood. One newspaper told how "in recent centuries the diaconate was reserved for men preparing for the priesthood, but the permanent diaconate, open to married men, was restored by Pope Paul VI in 1967." It was clear in Manning's homily that his initial skepticism for the diaconate had turned to enthusiasm.

The assignment of the new deacons was anything but haphazard. Lengthy interviews with the candidates and prospective pastors and/or agency directors were held and every effort was made to maximize the special talents of the newly ordained. A review process was also introduced, whereby questionnaires were filled out annually by every one involved in the appointment

ANTHONY BROUWERS
(1912-1964)

Monsignor Anthony Brouwers (1912-1964) was recognized internationally as an "Apostle of the Missions." His memory is very much alive today, even a quarter century after his premature demise. Born in Los Angeles, young "Tony" Brouwers attended Sacred Heart Parochial School, Cathedral High and Los Angeles College. He was ordained a priest in Rome on December 8, 1938. A few years later, he was appointed to the archdiocesan matrimonial curia. In 1947, he became secretary to the then Bishop Timothy Manning and the following year, he was named director for the Propagation of the Faith.

Always a popular speaker, the energetic young priest was a favorite of young and old alike. In 1950, he established the Saint Vibiana's Guild to encourage and train aspiring artists. Five years later the far-sighted priest "began one of the most advanced and visionary developments in the Church" with his establishment of the Lay Mission Helpers, a group of people who volunteered to serve a minimum of three years in the missionary outreach of the Church.

The next year, he founded the Mission Doctors for the same purpose. Since the first departure ceremony on July 4, 1956, over 800 people have been sent to the missions, all because a dynamic priest had the courage to pursue a dream. Shortly thereafter, Father Brouwers began establishing a network of Mission Circles whose function it was and is to offer their prayers and financial support for the missionary program. Over 200 of the circles were ultimately erected.

Carpenters, teachers, nurses, pilots, administrators, doctors and journalists were only a few of the professional and non-professional people recruited for the missions. Before long they were running hospitals, operating schools and editing newspapers throughout Africa, Latin America, New Guinea and parts of the American southwest.

Brouwers was honored by two pontiffs when he was made a papal chamberlain by Pope Pius XII in 1950 and a domestic prelate by Pope John XXIII in 1959. The Papal Volunteer program inaugurated by the Holy See was modeled in great part on the program developed in Los Angeles. The monsignor was active in a host of other projects too. And somehow he found time to administer the busy, inner-city parish of Saint Paul between 1959 and 1964.

Monsignor Brouwers made four extended tours of the African continent to determine the needs of the missions there and to visit the Lay Mission Helpers already at work in that huge area. He authored a weekly column, "Mission Chats" for *The Tidings* wherein he kept alive the spiritual and physical challenges of the missions.

His final missionary labor was on the frontier of suffering. Though stricken with spinal cancer in his last years, he never slackened his pace or lessened his enthusiasm. As mentioned in an editorial by Alphonse Antczak in *The Tidings*, "it should not be forgotten that there was a holy man here named Anthony Brouwers. *Que en paz descanse.*"

VALENTINE CLOSA
(1841-1916)

Among the clerical pioneers of the Diocese of Monterey-Los Angeles, none surpasses in virtue or accomplishments those of Father Valentine Closa (1841-1916), a native of Vich, Spain. Born to humble parents, Valentine was educated at the local diocesan seminary. Adopted for service in California by Bishop Thaddeus Amat, he was ordained to the priesthood on June 19,1872.

After a few months of service at the Plaza Church of *Nuestra Señora de los Angeles*, Father Closa was assigned to San Juan Bautista Mission as associate to the legendary Father Cyprian Rubio. He eventually succeeded Rubio and spent the rest of his earthly sojourn among the small community attached to the Old Mission.

Like most priests then and now, there was nothing dramatic in Closa's life. He was content with performing his ministry away from the limelights of center stage. One commentator wrote that "Closa never allowed the boredom of daily routine to distract him from his primary goal of administering the sacraments and looking after the needy. He was one of that legion of clergymen who serve out their lives in happy anonymity. But he was no less a hero to his people."

A rare glimpse into Closa's life occurred in 1874, when a young man wrote about his visit to San Juan Bautista Mission for the *San Jose Herald*. He noted that after dining, he "walked out to the old Catholic Mission and wondered at its ancient tumbledown adobe walls, and from its peculiar surroundings became anxious to know something of its history." The door was locked so he "knocked at the door of the Father's study, and upon his answering the bell, made acquaintance with the object of our visit. He is a gentlemanly, modest, unassuming, mild-mannered man, and without inquiring, we saw upon the door, 'Rev. V. Closa.'"

"He took us to the entrance and unlocked the swinging gates and we walked into the ancient cathedral that has stood there for nearly one hundred years. There is something supernatural about this place of worship; everything was as still as death, nothing being heard but our footfall on the bare thick floor."

The writer said that Closa told him that the paintings hanging in the church "were painted many years ago, in Mexico." He described the baptismal font at which seven thousand people were baptized. As they passed through the church, Closa "reverently pointed to a slab near the altar, saying that directly under it, Father Estevan Tapis was buried" seventy years earlier. Closa showed his visitor some clothing that belonged to Tapis. He had seen the remains of Tapis and told how "the hair and beard of the priest looked as natural as ever."

The Old Mission was severely damaged in the earthquake of April, 1906. Father Closa asked Fremont Older, editor of the San Francisco *Bulletin*, to help inaugurate a movement for restoration. Older organized a fiesta which raised enough funds to stabilize the building and keep it from collapsing.

Closa suffered most of his life from chronic bronchitis and, on March 8,1916, he died quietly in his quarters at San Juan Bautista. In its issue of March 13, *The Tidings* told its readers that "the Angel of Death last Thursday morning called to his eternal home one of the oldest priests of the diocese." The account said that Father Closa "had been ill for some years, and almost blind, having suffered several strokes of paralysis."

The funeral was described in great detail. We are told that "all San Juan Bautista and the surrounding country mourned when, on Monday last, the remains of the beloved priest were laid away at the foot of the Cross in the cemetery overlooking the mission and the beautiful San Juan Valley."

JUAN COMAPLA
(1824-1878)

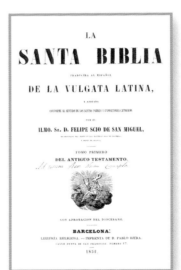

The provenance of the six volume set of *La Santa Biblia* given to the Archival Center by Miss Rosario Curletti of Santa Barbara is most interesting. Written onto the title page of each book is the simple phrase: "*Ad usum* Rev. Juan Comapla."

Juan Comapla, the son of Juan and Francisco (Senna) Comapla, was born at Batet, Spain, on May 10, 1824. He entered the seminary as a clerical candidate for the Diocese of Gerona, in 1845. Shortly before completing his theological training, John affiliated himself with Bishop Joseph Sadoc Alemany and was incardinated into the Diocese of Monterey. He came to the United States in 1853.

If one were to accept the evidence available in the annals, John was ordained to the priesthood no less than three times! Records in the San Francisco Chancery Archives indicate that he was advanced to holy orders on January 10, 1853, while the Catholic Directory for 1878, gives the date as January 1, 1854. A third authority suggests March 13, 1854.

In any event, Father Comapla was appointed to Santa Ines on April 25, 1854. While in that position, he also served as Vice Rector and later Rector of the diocesan seminary. The Catalan priest subsequently ministered at San Luis Obispo.

In 1861, Comapla was appointed Pastor of San Buenaventura Mission. A local historian wrote that the priest eventually became "the best loved, and in some ways perhaps the most remarkable of the long line of priests" at the Old Mission. Sol N. Sheridan goes on to state that Comapla's rule, gentle, benign, always seeking for the best of his people, lasted until 1876. No man in all the sleepy old village of San Buenaventura was more highly regarded than this good priest. The parish at that time embraced everything between Rincon Creek and San Fernando and never did Comapla "hesitate to go upon a call, however long nor however he might be fatigued by his labors."

The priest "drove an old surrey, and might be seen at any time, night or day, on the rough roads of that time going about his parochial duties. " Benjamin Cummings Truman, a pioneer California journalist, visited San Buenaventura in the late 1860s and he referred to Father Comapla as "a very pious, but an altogether delightful man and a person of brilliant attainments."

According to Truman, "Father Comapla had a very good library... and he pointed with marked respect to three engravings which adorned the walls of his study: George Washington, Stonewall Jackson and Robert E. Lee whom he looked upon, so he informed me, as great soldiers and good men."

The initial steps toward restoring the old church at San Buenaventura occurred during Father Comapla's pastorate. In addition to covering over the exposed roof beams with a false ceiling, he had a wooden encasement placed atop the disintegrating floor tiles.

The popular and energetic pastor died unexpectedly at Los Angeles, on January 11, 1878. His name remains enshrined at San Buenaventura and it was he for whom Padre Juan Canyon, eight miles up the beach toward Rincon, was named.

The books in question were likely used by Comapla in his seminary studies. Published by *Libreria Religiosa* and printed by Pablo Riera at his shop in Barcelona's *Nueva Calle de San Francisco*, the scholarly tomes are translated from the Latin Vulgate and edited for publication by Felipe Scio de San Miguel. It was probably after the priest's demise that his books were either sold or given to friends. Miss Curletti recalled that the books had belonged to her mother as long as she could remember.

JOHN DUNNE
(1903-1995)

For eleven years *The Tidings*, official newspaper for the Diocese of Los Angeles-San Diego and later the Archdiocese of Los Angeles, was guided by a remarkable man, Father John Dunne. Things were a lot different in 1931 when young Father Dunne, fresh from a three year course in Moral Theology at The Catholic University of America, walked into the cramped offices of *The Tidings* for the first time. The paper was then located on the second floor of a building at 130 East Second Street.

There were only 21/2 people on the editorial staff-Patrick Henry, George Andre and Charles Conroy. Old "Doc" Conroy, himself a former editor, "only counted for half because he was also a professor at Loyola College in Westchester."

There was no ticker tape machine in those days. International and national news was delivered from NCWC by post, except for those non-infrequent days when the mailman "fell in" with friends at the local pub. There were two ancient typewriters in the office and they could be heard clanking away from early morning until late evening. Occasionally a friend from *The Times* would drop by to share a juicy ecclesial morsel for local Catholic consumption.

Dunne saved his pennies and was eventually able to purchase a linotype machine along with the other equipment needed for printing the newspaper. From there on the weekly was produced at its own plant, a factor which saved money and improved efficiency.

Things were vastly different for the Church in those days. The old Diocese of Los Angeles-San Diego stretched from Santa Maria to the Mexican border. There were 284 parishes serving a Catholic population of 292,000.

Interestingly enough, though there are now eleven times as many Catholics in about a fourth of the area, the circulation of *The Tidings* was not greatly larger in the 1980s than it was seventy-five years earlier. And that doesn't speak very well for the reading habits of earlier people.

Though the curial offices were just a block away, Bishop John J. Cantwell rarely came to *The Tidings* office, and even less frequently did he use the telephone. "He left us alone," said Dunne, "except when he sent Barney (Msgr. Dolan) over with some official notices."

Dunne recalls only once being called on the episcopal carpet. He had hinted editorially that President Hoover favored certain actions of the Ku Klux Klan. "His Grace was displeased, to say the least." It was a brief scolding which began in this fashion: "Father Dunne, a gentlemanly priest would not have accused the President of the United States of being anti-Catholic. Your little Irish mother would not approve."

Then, just as curtly, the bishop stood up and said: "You may go, Father." As he passed through the office, he heard one of the secretaries whisper: "Go, and sin no more Father!"

When asked whether he "liked" Bishop Cantwell, Dunne replied: "We came from the same part of Ireland. The Cantwells had been prominent churchmen for generations. It ran in their blood. Though he lacked the commoner's touch, he was the right man for this rinky-dink diocese at the time."

The Tidings was more magazine than newspaper in the 1930s. There were upwards of a dozen regular columnists and weekly features that came by mail or messenger each week. "First we put the ads in place, then the regular fare and, finally, the news." And "when there was space left, we flipped a coin as to who would write the fillers."

There were concerned Catholics around the diocese in the 1930s who acted as unpaid stringers, mailing or bringing in local items. Photographs were mostly amateurish but quite usable. There was no sports section, but there was a great enthusiasm for such literary items as book reviews. Father John Devlin, for example, attended the Philharmonic every week and would often mail in the program along with his observations on a performance.

Pastors and others were good about keeping *The Tidings* informed about activities at the parochial level. Mary Sinclair and Ethel Bosert cranked out whatever official items there were. "We were much more a family in those days," said the monsignor.

While there may have been less journalistic sophistication during the Dunne years, the paper was attractively printed and highly informative. There was no television and little radio, so Catholics appreciated the role of *The Tidings* as the official newspaper for the sprawling diocese.

The energetic Father Dunne served as diocesan spokesman for eleven years until October of 1942, when he received his "Dear John" letter thanking him for his years of editorship. Then it was on to the pastorate at Saint Teresa's.

One stands in utter amazement at the marvelous things people like Msgr. Dunne were able to accomplish in those years. What fun it was to talk with this living testament of an earlier age. People in the twenty-first century need to know what the pioneers of earlier times did to make the Church in Los Angeles what it is today.

THOMAS F. FOGARTY
(1902-1966)

For the longtime pastor of Saint Brendan's Church, the "whole world was, as it ever should be for the pastor, his parish and people." This alone accounts for the spontaneous expression of grief manifested by the overflow crowds of faithful parishioners flocking to the four public obsequies for their departed shepherd.

Though born in Brooklyn, on August 27, 1902, Thomas Francis Fogarty, was raised and educated in Ireland. He studied for the priesthood at Saint Patrick's Seminary and was ordained in the Thurles' Cathedral for service in the Diocese of Los Angeles-San Diego on June 12, 1927. During his first thirteen years in the southland, Father Fogarty served as curate at Saint Monica's Church (Santa Monica), Saint John's and Sacred Heart Churches (Los Angeles), Holy Rosary (San Bernardino) and Saint Anthony's Church (Long Beach). In 1938, he was named pastor of Saint Frances of Rome Parish in Azusa. Two years later, following a brief period as administrator at Saint Kevin's, Father Fogarty was entrusted with the pastorate of Saint Brendan's.

In the physical order he found indebtedness when he came to his flock and the early years there were occupied in retiring that obligation. For the Sisters, he renovated and later rebuilt completely the convent. The school was first modernized and then replaced altogether. He brought to completion the shell of the parish's landmark Gothic church and subsequently saw it consecrated. For his fellow priests there was the dream of a new home and that too eventually became a reality.

Possessed of a keen Irish wit, a scholarly mind and a deep human sympathy, Father Fogarty became a part of each family in his square-mile parish, ever acknowledging the dignity of the laity and their prominence in the overall mission of the Church. It has been remarked that "with jealousy for his flock's welfare, he sought always the best, the perfect-and even when it was man's best, he felt the lack of Divine perfection and went on and on, still searching .

Thomas Francis Fogarty entered personally into every activity affecting the spiritual and material welfare of his parishioners, thus anticipating by several decades the role of the contemporary priest as outlined by Vatican Council II. Long ago this zealous shepherd realized that the clergy "cannot be of service to men if they remain strangers to the life and conditions of men."

To the pastor of Saint Brendan's as to the prelates of the recent ecumenical council, the priestly office was not confined to the care of the faithful as individuals, but also properly to the formation of a genuine Christian community. This concept of public service explains why Father Fogarty was no less accessible to his people after being elevated to the domestic prelacy in 1957.

Ever a man in a hurry, the last of the monsignor's many projects was finished only weeks before his death. At last he could and did repeat those lovely words of the evangelist: "I have brought you honor upon earth, I have completed the task which you gave me to do."

Rarely has such genuine grief been recorded at the loss of a pastor as when news of Monsignor Thomas F. Fogarty's sudden and unexpected demise spread among his people. But this good shepherd left something more enduring than mere human sadness. Those who knew him best would have no hesitation in re-echoing those sentiments formulated into eulogistic terms by a former curate:

We rejoice that a good soul, afflicted with the restlessness of Augustine here on earth, has crossed through the portals of death to find the eternal rest that awaits the just… and, while, in the words of the Canticle "he is now standing on the other side of this very wall-gazing through the windows, peering through the lattices" of his memorable' works among us, each, in our turn, will call to him for help as we continue on the same road going home.

FLORIAN HAHN
(1850-1916)

Gerrman-born Father B. Florian Hahn (1850-1916) was once described by the head of the Bureau of Catholic Indian Missions as "a good, pious, zealous and prudent priest who got the good will and confidence of all who knew him." Young Hahn came early in life to the United States, where he spent some years as a printer before entering the Congregation of the Precious Blood. He was ordained at Castagena, Ohio, on June 8, 1882.

After serving at a number of parishes in the midwest, Father Hahn was appointed pastor of Assumption Church in Reed, Ohio. There he reorganized the parish and became a local celebrity. He was later transferred to the Indian school at Rennselaer, Indiana, and it was while ministering at that institution that he decided to devote the remainder of his life to caring for the spiritual needs of native Americans.

Bishop Francis Mora heard about Father Hahn's work with the Indians and, in 1890, invited him to take charge of Saint Boniface Industrial School at Banning, in the Diocese of Monterey-Los Angeles. For almost a quarter century, Father Hahn rode on horseback, by wagon and in automobile across the desert areas of the diocese preaching to the (mostly Indian) inhabitants from San Gorgonio Pass to the Mexican border and as far east as Indio.

By the time of his death, Hahn left a legacy of eleven mission churches and two parishes, one in Banning and the other in Beaumont. It was indeed an impressive record and one for which Hahn was given the papal title, "missionary apostolic."

During his years at Banning, Father Hahn utilized his skill at printing by writing and publishing *The Mission Indian*, a monthly periodical which assisted substantially to support the Indian school. He also published several books during those years, including Archbishop J.B. Salpointe's *Soldiers of the Cross*, a collection of notes on the ecclesial history of New Mexico, Arizona and Colorado.

Father Hahn's twenty piece band became famous throughout the diocese. The talented priest, an expert on Gregorian chant, reportedly could himself play every instrument in the band. Though his native language was German, Father Hahn developed a fluency in English surpassed by few priests on the west coast. Bishop Thomas J. Conaty, a gifted orator in his own right, once said that he "preferred Father Hahn over all the preachers he had ever heard."

Despite the fact that he was plagued by ill health in his final years, Father Hahn never slackened in his pace. He was a perpetual motion machine for Christ. He died at Oxnard, on August 3, 1916. Father Hahn was among the most admired priests in California. In the homily preached at Hahn's funeral obsequies, Msgr. Thomas J. Fitzgerald attributed Hahn's intellectual and missionary success "to a unique and observable spiritual depth."

"Those who have heard him at the altar recite the Holy Sacrifice of the Mass could not but be struck with the intelligent, natural devotion that seemed to have possession of the man in the articulation of every syllable; in parts he seemed to go outside of himself and be, as it were, carried off in ecstasy."

JOSE MUT
(c. 1835-1889)

Jose Mut (c. 1835-1889) was among the clerical candidates recruited for the Diocese of Monterey-Los Angeles during one of Bishop Thaddeus Amat's visits to his native Catalonia. After completing his theological studies with the Vincentian Fathers at Cape Girardeau, Missouri, Mut came to Southern California where he was ordained on December 12, 1862. His first assignment was at the Plaza Church of Our Lady of the Angels.

In 1866, Father Mut was appointed pastor of San Juan Mission. In that position, he was also entrusted with the care of Catholics at San Luis Rey Mission and the Asistencia of San Antonio de Pala.

At Capistrano, Mut took up residence in a "mere hole in the mission building" and for the next two decades the dedicated cleric tended his scattered flock. A visitor to the Old Mission in the 1880s described Mut's living quarters, noting that "by no possibility could any chamber be more gloomy, unfurnished, generally dilapidated and desolate."

"A battered old pine table stood in the middle of the floor and, beside it, a mended chair. Another, with a rawhide bottom, stood beside the door. There was no glass in the one window. An old and worn black priest's coat hung against the wall and the cheapest variety of cotton umbrella leaned beside it. The only sign of creature comfort, the one human weakness of the place, was a little bag of cheap tobacco and a wooden pipe that lay beside the spectacles."

Zephryin Engelhardt told how "on one of his trips to the various Indian mission stations, Father Mut had occasion to bless the grave of a man whose name figured somewhat prominently in the early days." The man was Jose Antonio Pico, the elder brother of the notorious Pio Pico.

Benjamin Cummings Truman visited San Juan Capistrano and published his views about Father Mut. One fascinating story revolved around an old record kept by Fray Gregorio Amurrio dated May 7, 1778, in which were recorded these words: "We prayed fervently last evening for the success of the colonists under one George Washington, because we believe their cause is just and that the Great Redeemer is on their side."

Early in May of 1888, Father Mut was transferred to the north and made pastor of San Miguel Mission. It is recorded that "to his energy it is due that the row of buildings comprising the ancient convento was preserved. Many of the rafters were decayed and others broken, so that the roof with

its heavy tiles threatened to collapse at any time…" With $3,000 collected from local inhabitants, "the energetic priest replaced the rotten timbers and broken tiles with new material and, thus rendered the rooms habitable and safe."

Charles F. Wilcox attended Mass at San Miguel 1889 and, in a subsequent essay for *Ave Maria* magazine, he noted that "the Spanish priest, Father Mut, was the celebrant, and preached, in a quaint but pleasant manner, a practical sermon on the gospel of the day. The English tongue, spoken by a Spaniard, takes on a certain dignity and softness, decidedly foreign but delightful to the ear." Wilcox was much impressed by Mut who, he said, was "cheerfully giving his life to the obscure and arduous care of this post and three or four more outlying chapels of this parish."

Worn out by his missionary labors along California's *El Camino Real*, Father Joseph Mut died on October 15, 1889. His remains were interred in the cemetery at San Miguel, where a modest stone marker recalls the memory of the Catalan priest.

and who engraves their virtues on the tablets of love and memory."

Those who read Roche's *El Rodeo* columns between 1957 and 1973 were as impressed by his style as they were by their content. To the very last, the monsignor was a master of phraseology.

The record needs to show that Roche departed significantly from his predecessors insofar as he was exceedingly conservative, almost reactionary in many of his views. During his editorship, *The Tidings* lost much of its credibility among those imbued with the so-called "spirit" of Vatican Council II.

Yet, when he retired, he was praised by Timothy Cardinal Manning for his "sensitive and capable management of the paper. *The Tidings* has reflected a true image of the Church and the archdiocese under your loyal priestly mind and heart."

His Eminence went on to express the hope that "we can all call upon your experience regularly for the continued guidance of the official newspaper of the archdiocese." And that he did for the following decade.

PATRICK ROCHE
(1912-1982)

In 1957, the pastor of Holy Name parish in central Los Angeles, Msgr. Patrick Roche (1912-1982) was named editor of *The Tidings*, the sixth priest to occupy that position since 1895. Born in Lynn, Massachusetts, Patrick graduated from Holy Cross College before entering Saint Mary's Seminary in Baltimore as a clerical candidate for the old Diocese of Los Angeles-San Diego. He was ordained in 1938.

During the earliest years of his ministry, Father Roche worked mostly in educational assignments, both as assistant principal and associate superintendent for Catholic Schools. Like his two sacerdotal predecessors, Roche held a doctorate from The Catholic University of America and that training served him well for the sixteen years he shepherded the grand old lady of the Catholic press. Admittedly succeeding to the editorship of *The Tidings* was a tremendous challenge. There was still a steady flow of local news stories about the continued growth of parishes and schools, development of the seminary system, expansion of the Confraternity of Christian Doctrine and the activities of such organizations as the Lay Mission-Helpers who were sending people from Los Angeles to missionary areas around the world.

Roche consistently encouraged his staff members. He told one writer, just a few days before he died, that "Catholics walk taller when they learn about their roots. The honest writing of history is an apostolate that influences the mainspring of the commonwealth." He frequently quoted and endorsed John Steven McGroarty's definition of a friend which states that "a friend is one who writes the faults of his brothers and sisters in the sand for the winds to obscure and obliterate

CAJETAN SORRENTINI
(1815-1893)

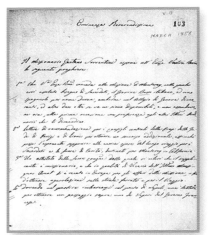

Though Father Cajetan Sorrentini was undeniably one of the most controversial of California's post-mission clerics, his fifty-four years in the ministry constitute an intriguing chapter in ecclesial annals. Born in Italy on August 7, 1815, the son of Giuseppe and Anna Maria Sorrentini, Cajetan studied at the Eternal City's prestigious *Colegio Romano*. He was ordained on September 19, 1839.

An "Apostolic Missionary" attached to the Sacred Congregation of Propaganda Fide, Father Sorrentini was assigned to the Chair of Theology at the diocesan seminary in Amalfi, Naples, a post he occupied for several years. Early in the 1840s, Sorrentini was sent to Jerusalem as a special "visitor." His delicate assignment was that of investigating charges of Franciscan affiliation with the Masons. During his three years in the Holy Land, Sorrentini was also influential in building Saint John's Hospital. He was eventually recalled to Rome because of ill health.

Sorrentini was present in the private oratory of the Urban College of Propaganda Fide for the episcopal ordination of the Right Reverend Thaddeus Amat. In November, 1854, Sorrentini arrived in California with Bishop Amat and shortly thereafter was entrusted with the pastorate at Monterey.

A few years later, Father Sorrentini was transferred to Santa Barbara as Pastor of Our Lady of Sorrows. He figured prominently in the dispute that Bishop Amat had with the Franciscans. In 1857, he was sent to Rome with a detailed account of the controversy. Unfortunately for all concerned, Sorrentini had previously run afoul of Father

Bernardino de Montefranco, the Franciscan Master General, in the Holy Land. Sorrentini was not one who could easily disguise his hostile attitude to the friars.

Upon his return from Europe, Sorrentini was released from the jurisdiction of Bishop Amat for service in what is now the Diocese of Alexandria, Louisiana. In 1861, he was made Pastor of Saint Mary Magdalen dei Pizzi, in Philadelphia. Between 1864 and 1871, Sorrentini occupied a similar position in New Castle. After four years at Pottstown, Pennsylvania, Father Sorrentini was appointed Pastor of Saint James, in Wilmington, Delaware. He also served as chaplain for the Italian work crews brought into that area for railroad construction.

Sorrentini then got into a dispute with the local bishop, an encounter which motivated his return west. Back in California, the priest was assigned to Sacred Heart Parish, Salinas. There he remained for sixteen years, building a new church, parochial residence, schoolhouse and cemetery. Father Sorrentini observed the golden jubilee of his priestly ordination in 1889, an event attended by hundreds of his friends from all over the country. He lived on until June 30, 1893.

A profound scholar, accomplished linguist and talented musician, Father Sorrentini was a colorful priest whose contributions are still evident in the landscape of California's Catholic heritage.

CYRIL VAN DER DONCKT
(1865-1939)

Father Cyril Van der Donckt was a native of Quaremont, Belgium. He was ordained in Louvain on June 24, 1887 for service in the Vicariate Apostolic of Idaho. Within three months, the youthful cleric had arrived and was busy at work in that far-flung post.

According to his own testimony, Father Van der Donckt was the first priest ordained for the vicariate. During his earliest years in Idaho, he attended to the spiritual needs of native Americans scattered around the fourteen counties comprising the vicariate. He served as pastor of a parish in Pocatello in the late 1890s.

For reasons of health, Father Van der Donckt came to the Diocese of Monterey-Los Angeles in 1921 and for the next decade was chaplain at the Los Angeles County Hospital. A letter in his file indicates that "he acquitted himself well and was devoted to his work."

Father Van der Donckt wrote several books over the years, including *Eucharistic Miracles, Christian Science and Spiritism Tested* and *Christian Motherhood and Education*. A writer in *Ave Maria* characterized the latter book as being "full of good advice for parents and educators."

The priest was a prolific versifier. He kept a quasi-diary into which he recorded his reflections in verse form. Father David McAstocker, a prominent Jesuit writer, encouraged Van der Donckt to have a selection

of his verses published. In 1934, Father Van der Donckt issued a limited edition of *Metrical Memories*, a 382 page book bearing the *imprimatur* of Bishop Edward J. Kelly of Boise. Three years later, a second, expanded edition appeared, along with an index to the larger text. Reviewers liked the book. R.H. Thompson said it was a "fine contribution to poetic literature."

Though Van der Donckt doesn't appear to have been one of John J. Cantwell's favorites, the priest dedicated his collection of *Metrical Memories* to the Bishop of Los Angeles-San Diego.

Included among his verses are two tributes to Cantwell, both composed to honor the prelate's silver anniversary of priestly ordination in 1914.

J oy gratitude and pride
O 'erflow your followers' heart today,
H igh Priest dear, long with us abide!
N e'er poured God powers in nobler clay.
C hampion of the Spirit's sword and spear,
A ngels high envy your career:
N o monuments, reared by human hands
T ow'r higher than those your toil has raised,
W hile loos'ning sins' and sorrows' bands
E ternally God hence be praised!
L ook down on you the Queen of priests,
L ure she us all to heaven's feasts!

J oin , priests, nuns, women, maidens, boys
O n this day, to acclaim our grand
H igh priest: his thanks to share and joys
N one's more revered throughout the land;
J ust, true, his words and deeds e'er urge
C harity to all: hence efforts surge
A ll men to teach, for Christ to win.
N eath his enlightened, prudent lead,
T o war 'gainst error, vice and sin;
W hilst giving host the Apostles' creed,
E nlarging bounds of higher freedom.
L oud sing we hence: "Through Christendom
L oved, praised be Christ *"in aeternum"*!

RELIGIOUS

WILLIAM P. BARR, C.M.
(1881-1964)

The late Father William P. Barr was eulogized by Archbishop Timothy Manning as "the greatest master of the spiritual life we have known." Indeed, the Vincentian educator combined, in his priestly role, the offices of father, advisor, legislator and disciplinarian without diminishing or compromising the paternal atmosphere within which he trained two generations of clerical aspirants.

Born in New Orleans, on January 7, 1881, William Patrick Barr's pre-seminary education was acquired from the Christian Brothers. He entered the Apostolic College of the Vincentian Fathers, at Perryville,

Missouri, in 1893, and pronounced his vows as a member of the Congregation of the Mission, on January 8, 1899. Subsequently sent to Rome's Apollinaris Seminary for completion of studies in philosophy and theology, both of which disciplines awarded him doctorates, he was ordained on December 19, 1903, by Archbishop Joseph Ceppetelli, the Patriarch of Constantinople.

Father Barr returned to the United States, in 1905, to become director of students and novices at Saint Mary's of the Barrens, in Perryville. For the following decade he also taught dogmatic theology at the Vincentian motherhouse. In 1923, Father Barr was appointed rector at Perryville, a position he occupied until 1924, when he was sent to Denver to manage the erection of that city's new theological seminary. In 1926, he was named Provincial of the Western Province and it was during his tenure that the Vincentian Fathers assumed direction of the newly constructed preparatory seminary at Los Angeles.

Upon completion of two terms as provincial, Father Barr became rector of Kenrick Seminary, Webster Groves, Missouri. In that more relaxed atmosphere, he became a well-known figure as speaker and educator in the Saint Louis area and a popular retreat master for clerical groups throughout the nation.

Father Barr began another term as provincial in 1938, but was forced to resign a year later because of ill health. With the opening, at Camarillo, of Saint John's Seminary, Father Barr heeded Archbishop John J. Cantwell's plea to assume the rectorship "on a temporary basis" until the institution was firmly established. During his ten years there a host of the southland's future levites were inflamed with the desire to emulate Father Barr's sublime ideal of priestly perfection, of which his life was so striking an example. In the years after 1949, Father Barr served as rector of Saint Mary's Seminary, in the Galveston-Houston Diocese. It was there that the renowned educator quietly observed the golden jubilee of his priestly ordination.

That his "communicability" with young people never faltered explains how Father Barr could return to the teenage level, during the latter part of his life, as a popular professor of religion at Queen of Angels Seminary, Mission Hills. His active apostolate was terminated by a paralytic stroke which forced him to spend his remaining years confined to Saint Vincent's Hospital, in Los Angeles, where he died on June 20, 1964.

Throughout his sixty-one years in the priesthood, Father William P. Barr exhibited all the desirable traits and none of the negative qualities associated with leadership. To his loyalty for the Church, love for learning, impatience with mediocrity and insistence on theological precision he added a very understanding attitude towards the frailties of human nature. He was among the last of a long line of outstanding Vincentian seminary professors whose very presence commanded respect and emulation.

ALBERT BIBBY, O.F.M. CAP.
(1878-1925)

In a reference to Father Albert Bibby, O.F.M. Cap., the Catholic *Bulletin* for April, 1925, declared: "To pass through life without meeting one who conveys the impression that he is cast in the mold of the Redeemer is to miss meeting an influence for the permanent uplifting of the soul. Those who had the joy of Father Albert's friendship can well look forward to meeting him in Heaven."

Thomas Francis Bibby was born at Muinebheag (Bagenalstown), County Carlow, on October 20, 1878. The youngster grew up in Kilkenny, within the shadow of the Capuchin Abbey, and, on July 7, 1894, joined the Franciscans at Rochestown. Fray "Albert" was ordained on February 23, 1902. Always a brilliant student, the young cleric took graduate courses at the Royal University. After completing his studies there, he was appointed Professor of Philosophy and Theology at Saint Kieran's College.

Father Albert spent many years at Church Street, where he served as provincial secretary from 1913 to 1919. It was while working in that capacity that he became one of the pioneers of the Gaelic League. During his years in Dublin, Father Albert was known for his marked piety. His saintly selflessness endeared him to all walks of life. His confessional was one of the most sought-after in all of Ireland. Always a frail and delicate man, Father Albert was buoyant in spirit. His cheerfulness in adversity was possibly the most attractive aspect of his many-faceted personality.

In the uprising of 1916, Father Albert served the spiritual needs of the Volunteers in the North Dublin Union area. From that time on, he was prominently identified with the movement for national independence. Father Albert's views eventually incurred the displeasure of British authorities and he was exiled from the country in mid-1924.

The Irish friars were entrusted with the old mission at Santa Ines in that year and on November 20th, Father Albert was named pastor of the historic California missionary foundation. Although his enforced exile was a mighty burden, Father Albert welcomed the opportunity of serving under the patronage of Saint Agnes, for whom he had long been a devotee.

The famous Irish patriot-cleric died on February 14, 1925, far from the land he loved so dearly and the people he served so faithfully. The first of the Irish friars to succumb in Western America, Father Albert was buried at Santa Ines. In 1958, his remains were returned to Ireland, where they were interred at the friars' cemetery at Rochestown, County Cork. At the time of his death, the Catholic press in Eire proclaimed that "the Catholic Church has lost a gifted scholar and a saintly priest; Ireland a loyal and devoted patriot."

NEWMAN EBERHARDT, C.M.
(1912-1995)

Newman Charles Eberhardt (1912-1995) spent almost his entire priesthood, well over half a century, walking along California's *El Camino Real*. He endowed the priestly image with all the virtues the world associates or should associate with priesthood.

Born in Chicago on July 10. 1912, Newman Eberhardt attended local Catholic schools before his affiliation with the Congregation of the Mission. Professed in 1932, he was ordained to the priesthood in 1939, just prior to World War II. The youthful Vincentian was then sent to Rome where he acquired a licentiate's degree in Sacred Theology at the *Athenaeum Angelicum*. Some years later, he received his advanced degree in history from Saint Louis University.

Assigned to Saint John's Seminary at Camarillo in 1941, Father Eberhardt spent his early professional years teaching philosophy, patrology and history. During the summers, he taught at De Paul University in Chicago. Eberhardt's reputation was firmly established on the national level with his publication, in 1961-1962, of *A Summary of Catholic History*. That two volume compendium was described by one reviewer as "an accurate, readable and comprehensive" treatise.

Another scholar writing for the *Catholic Historical Review* was "impressed by the generous bulk of material succinctly compressed into its 900 pages; by the prevailing tone of objectivity; by the refusal to slur over awkward facts; by the adroit summaries of major issues, and by the great attention given to the secular background."

The name "Eberhardt" thereafter became a recognized tradition in seminaries throughout the nation. One prominent authority explained that phenomenon by observing that "Father Eberhardt's style is simple, uncomplicated, historical rather than apologetic, with an occasional touch of humor."

In 1964, Eberhardt's supplementary study, *A Survey of American Church History*, appeared on the bookstalls. It too was greeted with wide acclaim. The late Hugh H. Nolan described the 308-page book as "a truly valuable work for seminaries, novices, college students, and the general Catholic reader." It is a sound, attractively written and carefully documented study.

In 1972, without slowing his pace at Camarillo, Father Eberhardt embarked on a third career, a teaching aposlolate for the Permanent Deacon Program in the Archdiocese of Los Angeles. Two nights a week, after a full schedule with the seminarians, he drove fifty-five miles to Los Angeles, where he functioned as academic coordinator and teacher in the training classes. Eberhardt's national reputation was confirmed in 1981, when fellow members of the American Catholic Historical Association elected him second vice-president.

In his lectures and books. Father Eberhardt always treated the Church with deference, respect and love. Perhaps more than others, he knew the Church's human imperfections and shortcomings, but he always chose to dwell on what was good and uplifting.

Vicariously, as spiritual director and academic professor, Father Eberhardt touched the lives of hundreds of thousands of Catholics in the Metropolitan Province of Los Angeles. He epitomized what is best in the evolving traditions of the Church probably because he always abided by his own dictum; "An historian ought to give testimony, not prophecy."

Eberhardt died suddenly in his room after returning from his customary morning walk on May 26,1995. He had turned in his grades for the semester and was working on a homily for the Feast of the Ascension. Placed next to his casket at Saint Vincent's Church in Los Angeles was the *Pro Ecclesia et Pontifice* medal which he had been awarded by Pope John Paul II in 1989. Roger Cardinal Mahony, seven bishops and over 300 priests concelebrated the Mass of the Resurrection.

Eulogizing Newman Eberhardt would be redundant. Everyone has his or her memories of "Ebbie" as they knew him. He was one who performed well all the priestly tasks: He recited his breviary, he read Holy Scripture, he made his meditation, he said the rosary, he did his spiritual reading and he practiced the virtues. Truly Ebbie did all things well. And he did them in an unobtrusive, almost hidden way. In a busy world, he found time for the Lord, for students and for everyone who knocked on his door. Seeing his light on was a sign that all was right with God and man. And that light was like a vigil lamp in the sanctuary, it never seemed to go out.

ZEPHYRIN ENGELHARDT, O.F.M.
(1851-1934)

Although libraries abound with books on the California missions, there are few that add substantially to the studies of Father Zephyrin Engelhardt, O.F.M., the first Catholic historian to wade through the maze of source materials scattered around the state.

Born at Bilshausen, Hanover, Germany, on November 13, 1851, young Charles Anthony Engelhardt was brought to America in 1852, where he spent the remainder of his eighty-two years. He was ordained in 1878, and shortly thereafter was sent to do missionary work among the Menominee Indians of Wisconsin. Serving in various capacities during the next decade, he was well-prepared for the appointment to the Indian Boarding School at Harbor Springs in 1894. There he installed a printing press and published a monograph on the saintly Indian maiden, Katherine Tekakwitha, in the Indian language of the Ottawans.

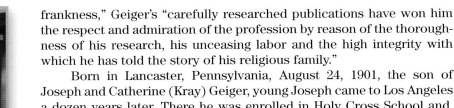

In 1900 Father Zephyrin came to Banning's Indian School and remained there until his transfer to Mission Santa Barbara. Already the author of several small volumes, he directed his whole attention to the now famous historical collection known as the Santa Barbara Mission Archives. His notes from the United States General Land Grants Office in San Francisco include many of the 2,000 original letters, reports and orders written by missionaries, governors, and viceroys which were subsequently destroyed by fire.

Among the first works published by Engelhardt at Harbor Springs was his *Franciscans in California* which appeared in 1897. This slender volume served in later years as the ground-plan for his series on *The Missions and Missionaries of California*. The four books were issued between 1908 and 1915, and rated from one reviewer the comment that "from many points of view... Father Engelhardt is the most indispensable of all the historians of California."

In the years after 1920, the well-known German friar began issuing small monographs on the local history of individual missions. Sixteen volumes ultimately appeared in the highly useful series and, in most cases, these books remain the principal sources on their subjects. The "Dean of California Historians" did not restrict his endeavors to books alone. He was a frequent contributor to periodical journals, both under his own name and under his two pen-names, *"Der Bergman"* and *"Esperanza."*

Ever the crusader, Engelhardt was anything but a retiring, colorless compiler of records. He wrote with a view to historical accuracy of fact rather than to attractiveness of style and method. His works represent an exhaustive study of the work of the Franciscans on the mission frontier. Charles Chapman observed that it was as "a great chronological sourcebook of mission history, as a kind of Franciscan Bancroft that Father Engelhardt's work is primarily important."

The passage of time, discovery of new sources and development of a more scientific approach suggests that Engelhardt's tomes should be revised and updated. But until that is done, it can be said that his writings are the principal thesaurus of historical lore regarding a glorious chapter in this nation's ecclesiastical annals.

MAYNARD J. GEIGER, O.F.M.
(1901-1977)

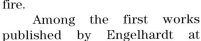

On May 23, 1972, Father Maynard J. Geiger, long-time archivist and historian at Mission Santa Barbara, quietly observed his golden jubilee in the Order of Friars Minor. Characterized by the late W. W. Robinson as one who "writes as he talks, with clarity, ease and frankness," Geiger's "carefully researched publications have won him the respect and admiration of the profession by reason of the thoroughness of his research, his unceasing labor and the high integrity with which he has told the story of his religious family."

Born in Lancaster, Pennsylvania, August 24, 1901, the son of Joseph and Catherine (Kray) Geiger, young Joseph came to Los Angeles a dozen years later. There he was enrolled in Holy Cross School and, later, Loyola High School. In 1919, he entered Saint Anthony's Preparatory Seminary, in Santa Barbara, as a clerical candidate for the Order of Friars Minor. At the time of his investiture with the Franciscan habit, July 15, 1923, young Geiger was given the name "Maynard," which has since become a familiar entry in the library card catalogues around the literary world.

Upon completion of his philosophical studies at Saint Elizabeth's, in Oakland, he was ordained to the priesthood by Bishop John J. Cantwell, on June 9, 1929, at Mission Santa Barbara. Between 1933 and 1937, Geiger took advanced courses in history at The Catholic University of America and it was during those years in the nation's capital that his proto-publications appeared, dealing not with California, but Florida. The friar's doctoral thesis, published in 1937, prompted the observation that "the work of Dr. Maynard Geiger on the *Franciscan Conquest of Florida* probably represents the best single specialized volume on Spanish Florida."

After finishing his graduate work in Washington, Father Geiger's interest turned westward. His imprint, however, remained indelibly impressed on Florida's annals and authorities in that field conceded that the meticulous Franciscan had "accomplished an undertaking of great importance for historical scholars interested in Spanish Florida." His work was formally recognized, ten years later, with bestowal of the Cervantes Medal Award by the Hispanic Institute.

Soon after returning to Santa Barbara, Father Geiger was appointed mission archivist, in which position he organized and augmented the vast quantities of original manuscripts and documents that Father Zephyrin Engelhardt and others had accumulated over the decades. The first tangible result was a *Calendar of Documents in the Santa Barbara Mission Archives*, which historians and other scholars greeted as "an outstanding contribution to the study of California mission history."

After 1947, Father Geiger's energetic efforts to update the archival relevancy tripled its quantity of holdings. The initial collection was enriched with an additional 8,000 pages of transcripts relating to the Serra Cause alone.

Inasmuch as a well-written life is almost as rare as a well-spent one, special attention must be given to Geiger's monumental biography of Fray Junípero Serra. Between 1941 and 1958, he traveled 100,000 miles through Europe and the United States locating, photostating and collecting materials in 150 public and private libraries and archives for the beatification process. His personal involvement in the subject never compromised the friar's impartiality and he unswervingly treated Serra with less sentiment and more objectivity.

In Geiger's opinion, the role of chronicler was one of utmost importance for it is he who makes available the basic sources. "There is no substitute for documents: no documents, no history, and I might add, no chroniclers, no documents." The works of Maynard J. Geiger are now and will long remain among the truly significant contributions to the field of American ecclesiastical history. The subtitle of his Serra biography, "The Man Who Never Turned Back," also characterizes the energetic friar who spent long hours seven days a week, for almost forty years, in a bare-walled Santa Barbara cell, slowly but ever so accurately grinding out the story of the Franciscan spiritual conquest along the New World's Pacific Slope.

Like the Master whom he served so faithfully in this life, Father Maynard Geiger was a prophet in his own land: yet generations after the peace marchers, draft protestors and social dissidents are relegated to the annals, the scholarly works of this humble friar will be re-membered and utilized as achievements of lasting merit.

MARY SCHOLASTICA LOGSDON, D.C.
(1814-1902)

Celebrating
125 Years
of Progress
1856-1981

In the words of Henry T. Hazard, Mayor of Los Angeles, Sister Mary Scholastica Logsdon (1814-1902) was a "kindhearted, generous, true and devoted" member of the Daughters of Charity. The following address was given by the City Treasurer, William H. Workman, at Caledonia Hall on October 7, 1902, just a month after the eighty-eight year old nun passed to her eternal reward.

The life of Sister Scholastica was a retired one; but her days and nights were filled with a noble devotion to the cause of humanity. Her name did not appear in public periodicals, her deeds were unrecorded, she cared not for worldly fame, but the good work she accomplished so quietly and unostentatiously, is manifest today in the lives of countless women of Southern California, and radiating from their lives to the lives of their children and their children's children. It is but just and meet that some one that knew her should speak of her now that she has gone from our midst, for the lives of noble men and women have a mighty influence on the lives of all. In our age of selfishness, it is refreshing to dwell on the life of one who labored always for others; who, without material re-compense, or even a desire for such remuneration, gave freely and lovingly of her best efforts for the cause of the orphan and the helpless, and for the education of the young.

Sr. Scholastica was born in Maryland in March of 1814. In her girlhood she was associated with the family of our late honored pioneer, J. De Barth Shorb. In August of 1839, she became a member of the well-known Order of Sisters of Charity, that, in every part of the civilized and uncivilized world carry on the work of devotedness in behalf of the helpless—this being the peculiar characteristic of their Company.

Nobly did Sr. Scholastica exemplify in her life the true spirit of her Order. She labored first in Mississippi, was called thence to important offices of trust in the Motherhouse of the Sisters of Charity at Emmitsburg, Maryland, and in 1855 was named leader of a band of six Sisters appointed to exercise their gentle ministry in the far distant and newly-inhabited region of California.

It required a brave and faithful spirit to undertake this work, and Sr. Scholastica and her associates were well chosen. Every pioneer knows how far away California seemed in those days when no railway stretched its connecting band of steel across the American continent; when vague and strange reports were circulated regarding the primitive life of the Far West; when prairie schooners led travelers through the terrors of Indian attack. Across the plains, or a long voyage by steamer, via the Isthmus of Panama was a tiresome journey. It required indeed a staunch heart to venture into this unknown world; and above all, it demanded courage inspired by such faith as Sr. Scholastica possessed for women to undertake this journey that they might minister to those in need. All honor to the noble pioneers of California!

Sister Scholastica and her companions reached San Francisco on the steamer Sea Bird, *in January, 1856. By the sixth of the same month they had arrived at San Pedro. General Banning's celebrated stage conveyed them to Los Angeles, the scene of their future life work. Ignacio del Valle, with characteristic hospitality, gave the Sisters shelter until a home was secured for them at the corner of Alameda and Macy Streets. Here the Sisters lived for many years; the property, on which was a small frame house, was purchased from Mr. B.D. Wilson. The house, familiar to all, had been brought in sections from New York, via Cape Horn. The sections were marked to facilitate reconstruction.*

Ere long the Sisters gathered around them the orphans, who have always been their special care. In connection with their Asylum they had a school for children and young ladies, and in this school many of the prominent and worthy mothers and grandmothers of Southern California received their education. The people of Los Angeles regardless of religious differences, gladly welcomed the Sisters and gave them generous assistance. To need their help was the only ticket of admission to their sympathy; color, race, or creed, did not enter into the consi-deration.

In the year 1889, on the fiftieth anniversary of the life of Sr. Scholastica as a Sister of Charity, her friends gave her a substantial proof of their love and esteem in the gift of a purse of $3,000 which the good Sister at once devoted to the building fund for the erection of a new and more commodious home for the rapidly increasing number of orphans. On February 9,1890, the corner-stone of the magnificent Orphanage now overlooking the city was laid.

When the home was completed, the Sisters took possession of it and here, surrounded by a family of nearly four hundred orphans, Sr. Scholastica whose life was all gentleness and peace, even in the midst of trials, folded her willing hands in the last long sleep.

LEO (FRANCIS MEEHAN), F. S. C.
(1881-1966)

In the 1920s, Brother Leo (Dr. Francis Meehan), the distinguished Professor of Literature at Saint Mary's College, Oakland and Moraga, was acknowledged to be "the shining star among the new constellation of Christian Brother intellectuals." Born on October 8, 1881, the son of James Meehan and Mary Ellen Gallagher, Leo graduated from Saint Peter's School in San Francisco and, in 1897, entered De La Salle Institute at Martinez. A mostly self-educated man, Brother Leo served as instructor in English at Sacred Heart College between 1903 and 1908.

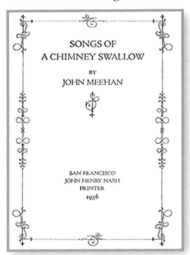

He then went to Saint Mary's College, where he became a full professor. In the following decade, he was sent to The Catholic University of America and there earned a doctorate in humane letters. During subsequent years, Brother Leo became the most famous Christian Brother in the United States. He lectured to more than two thousand different audiences in the 1920s and 1930s, often in the opera house at San Francisco.

He participated in lecture series which featured such figures as Winston Churchill and Sherman Anderson. It was an exciting time for Brother Leo who also offered courses at the College of the Pacific (Stockton) the University of California (Berkeley) and U.C.L.A. Speaking on education and literary topics Brother Leo was also a regular commentator over the then massive radio network of the National Broadcasting Company.

In 1930, Brother Leo was named Chancellor at Saint Mary's College, a position in which he functioned as college president and academic dean. In that role he determined to enhance the intellectual atmosphere at the college by making Moraga a cultural center for the whole bay area. He launched a rather ambitious extra-curricular program of public academies, faculty lectures, dramatic productions, symphonic recitals, operatic presentations, civic awards and learned publications.

Throughout his academic career, Brother Leo represented the viewpoint that exalted humanistic and literary studies at the expense of vocational and technical education. Within a relatively short time, Saint Mary's became a center for liturgical music in the western United States. And during that time, Brother Leo was also instrumental in launching The *Moraga Quarterly*, a journal that became a leading literary publication. Though he claimed that his resignation, in 1932, was prompted by a desire to devote more time for outside academic interests, it was widely known that Brother Leo was opposed to Saint Mary's becoming a "football factory."

Critics conclude that Brother Leo's publications were neither profound nor distinguished, but he had few peers in the country. Often writing under such pen names as "Will Scarlet" and "Leslie Stanton," he authored hundreds of articles, four plays, a few novels and several literary critiques. His college textbook on English literature was used throughout the nation.

In August of 1941, after forty-two years in religious life, Brother Leo received a dispensation from his vows and returned to lay life. Writing his famous *Living Upstairs* a year later, Leo said that "I feel that I have done my work, such as it is, it is now time to retire." He married DeNaze Brown, a convert to the Catholic Church, in 1946 and lived out the final years of his life at Casa Delia Madonna in Southern California's Lake Sherwood area.

When he died, in 1966 at the age of eighty-five, he was still referred to, even in obituaries, as "Brother Leo."

EUGENE SUGRANES, C.M.F.
(1878-1942)

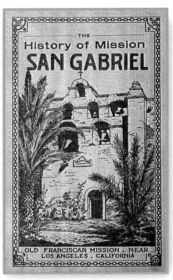

The story of San Gabriel Mission could not be told without reference to Father Eugene Sugranes who came to the "pride" of the California missions early in the 20th century. Born at Castellvell, Spain, the youthful Sugranes entered the seminary at Tarragone where he was known by his classmates for a "spirit of piety and love of books."

Entering the Missionary Sons of the Immaculate Heart of Mary (Claretians) in 1902, he completed his theological training at Santo Domingo de la Calzada. Ordained priest on July 5, 1903, he left shortly thereafter for Mexico. He came to the United States and, in 1905, was assigned to San Marcos, Texas.

At the invitation of Bishop Thomas J. Conaty, the Claretians took charge of San Gabriel Mission in 1908. Father Sugranes was among the first members of his community to serve in California, working at Yuma and the Old Plaza church of Nuestra Señora de los Angeles.

Sugranes became acquainted with the legendary Father Zephyrin Engelhardt and through him developed an interest in the history of the missions. He wrote numerous articles for the *Southern Messenger*, *The Tidings* and *Our Sunday Visitor*. Though he spoke English with a pronounced accent, he was able to write the language with an impeccable accuracy.

He published a life of Anthony Claret, as well as a manual of prayers, the *Florilegium*, which was for many years the official manual in Claretian houses throughout the United States. In 1927, he wrote a history of the Claretians in California.

In 1909, Sugranes published *The Old San Gabriel Mission* which he based on "historical notes taken from old manuscripts and records." The book was basically a compilation of articles written earlier for *The Tidings*.

John Steven McGroarty issued a "commendation" for the volume which he characterized as constituting "the most elaborate and complete history of the Mission San Gabriel that has yet appeared in print." He emphasized that the book had been compiled "from the mission records handed down by the Franciscans who built it and held possession of it until secularization and after." In McGroarty's view, Father Sugranes was "eminently fitted by education, training and experience to be the historian of San Gabriel. Moreover, his whole nature and his sacred profession of the missionary priesthood and his nationality makes him a sure interpreter of mission history and tradition."

In an ad which Charles Fletcher Lummis wrote for the *Out West Magazine*, in August of 1910, the book was described as "a critical study of art, antiquity and architecture of this best-preserved landmark by one who has for years been in touch with mission customs and traditions."

That the book was well-received is attested by a revised version which appeared in 1917 under the title *Glory of San Gabriel*. Four years later, another edition was issued to commemorate the 150th anniversary of the mission's foundation.

After his service in California, Father Sugranes established a house of studies for the Claretians in Washington, D.C. During his final years, he served in Chicago and it was there that he died on April 15, 1942.

Father Sugranes left behind an enviable reputation for learning and piety. Especially he is remembered in the bibliographical annals of California for his writings about San Gabriel Mission where even today his indelible imprint is plainly visible.

XAVIER SHAUER, D.C.
(1838-1912)

Archbishop Fulton J. Sheen tells how Almighty God, after He had created Adam, looked around and said to Himself: "I can do better than that! Then He created woman."

Sister Xavier Shauer was born in Munich, in 1838. She was brought to the United States ten years later, where she subsequently entered the Daughters of Charity, at Emmitsburg. She made her religious vows in 1857.

Shortly after her profession, Sister Shauer was among a group of six nuns who volunteered to serve the People of God along California's *El Camino Real*. Her tiny band sailed from New York, on November 22, 1855, arriving at San Pedro early the following January. The final miles of their journey to Los Angeles were traversed on a stage provided by Phineas Banning.

On May 29, 1858, the Sisters opened the first medical dispensary, in the house of Cristobal Aguilar, a small adobe building at Earth and Alameda Streets, near the Plaza. Sister Xavier was among the historic pioneers who moved on to larger quarters, in a two-story edifice, on Chavez Lane in the early 1860s. Though the new infirmary was bigger, it had no water and all the linen had to be carried to the river for washing.

Gifted with a rich, sweet voice, Sister Xavier organized the choir and led the youthful chanters in singing the praises of God. She taught herself Spanish and was soon able to communicate with her students in their native tongue. In 1859, Sister Xavier was transferred to San Juan Bautista. Although privations there were many, her "light heart and sunny disposition cheered all and the Sisters recalled with pleasure the happy days she spent" with them. She went from San Juan to Virginia City as one of the pioneers for a foundation to assist orphans and after a few years of faithful work there, was recalled to Los Angeles.

The German-born nun proved to be a heroine during the smallpox epidemics that ravaged California's southland. For three months in 1877, she courageously fought the dreaded scourge at the isolated "pest house" in Chavez Ravine. She was also on hand to assist victims of the virulent disease when it re-occurred in 1885. In whatever duties she was employed, Sister Xavier always displayed tact and devotedness. During her long religious life "only the good Master knows how many souls, blinded by error or passion, were by her brought back to the service and love of God." In her final years, frequent attacks of illness gradually weakened her robust constitution. She died at Los Angeles, on November 26, 1912.

The accomplishments of women such as Sister Xavier Shauer recall Pope Pius XII's statement that "Christianity pure and simple, grasping the essential values in womanhood, has discovered and cultivated in woman missions and offices which are the true foundation of her dignity and the reason for a more genuine exaltation of her sex." This brief glance at the life of Sister Xavier gives a deeper understanding of a hymn used in the Roman Breviary for the Feast of Holy Women:

> *High let us all our voices raise*
> *In that heroic woman's praise*
> *Whose name, with saintly glory bright,*
> *Shines in the starry realms of light.*

EMERGENCE OF THE CATHOLIC LAITY

Visitors to the west often express dismay about the impersonal cordiality existing in the Golden State between clergy and laity. Indeed, the laity have long since "emerged" in California to take their place as a vital part of the apostolic endeavor. The role of the laity was the subject of a sermon preached by Bishop Thomas J. Conaty at Saint Vibiana's Cathedral on February 10, 1907, to representatives of the American Federation of Catholic Societies.

The Southern California prelate reminded his listeners that throughout history, "the union of the clergy and the laity had been the upbuilding of Christianity and the spreading of the Gospel of Christ." At the same time, he took cognizance of the perils inherent in an indifferent laity such as England had in the Tudor days and France in the pre-Revolution era. While he was no apologist for the crusades, Conaty observed that those who engaged in these campaigns manifested an admirable zeal and love "in answering the appeals of Peter the Hermit and Saint Bernard…"

An intelligent knowledge of religion, an earnest devotion to truth, a love for the Church and its doctrine, and a willingness on all occasions to teach the truth, is demanded from all our people. I feel the need for a renewal of the spirit of the ages of Faith, the feeling of a divine calling to be not only members of the Church but also partners and cooperators in every work of the Church.

Conaty spoke of charity and education, of reformation and relief work, and observed that the Catholic layman is called to those activities of religious endeavor just as much as he is to more ordinary Church duties. "The Catholic layman should be found practicing and defending the domestic virtues, an unflinching enemy to divorce, living his life so that all men would find him without fear or reproach; he should be intelligently informed upon principle of government, loyal to the State, incapable of dishonesty and untruthfulness and filled with devotion to civic responsibility." Dwelling upon the obligations of Catholics as loyal citizens, he noted that Catholics should always be model members of society, expressing in their public life the character and goodness of their holy Faith.

Professional men, in Conaty's opinion, should always realize the force of the eternal precepts and the spirit of eternal justice "and should be models of faith, intelligence and probity." Referring to the work done on the national level, the bishop commended the generosity whereby the Church had developed its magnificent cathedrals, churches, schools and institutions to answer the demands of mercy and charity.

In a strong plea supporting the Federation of Catholic Societies, the Bishop of Monterey-Los Angeles stressed its effort "to inspire zeal in the work of religion." He urged his congregation to centralize and unify the efforts of the organizations into one well-defined desire to serve the Church, to be its faithful ally in all the works of religion and charity, to unite with the good men of all creeds against the evils threatening its very foundations.

Concluding his observations, the prelate said that "the battle cry is for God and country, for home and for the individual, against evil in every form, for Christ and His Church, for faith and virtue. The inspiring motive guiding our life work should be to conquer the world for Christ."

MARTIN AGUIRRE
(1858-1929)

Martin Aguirre was one of the last of the old-time California sheriffs. Playing a significant part in the days when Los Angeles was a sleepy little adobe town, he lived on to occupy center stage when the same city became known for its skyscrapers, automobiles and entertainment industry.

In an essay for the *Quarterly of the Historical Society of Southern California*, Margaret Romer said that "the story of Martin Aguirre's life is a Western thriller that sounds, in spots, like fiction, but is actually true."

Born in San Diego, the son of Jose Antonio and Rosario (Eustudillo) Aguirre, Martin grew up within a family who had extensive land holdings between Santa Ana and San Diego, as well as in the San Jacinto area. After his mother's death, Martin moved to the *Pueblo de Nuestra Señora de Los Angeles,* where he lived with his cousins, the Wolfskills. He subsequently graduated from Saint Vincent's College when that institution was the only one of its kind in the southland.

Martin's earliest employment was as foreman in the Wolfskill Orange Packing Company. There, he did everything from picking and crating oranges to selling them at the public market. According to a description in the Los Angeles *Herald* for February 26, 1929, Martin "was not a very large man, but had a fine physique, muscles like iron. He was always very neatly dressed and conducted himself with the manners of a born gentlemen, a credit to his Catholic faith."

In 1885, Martin Aguirre was elected sheriff of Los Angeles County, a position in which he was entrusted with preserving order. Harry Carr recalled that "he had the fighting courage of a bull terrier, the tender sympathies of a lady and a soul unblemished by dishonor." Governor Henry T. Gage named Aguirre warden of San Quentin Penitentiary in 1899. There, under the most unfavorable circumstances, he straightened out the discipline by being strict, but unwaveringly fair.

Returning to Los Angeles a few years later, Martin again affiliated himself with the sheriff's department as Chief Criminal Deputy. He took up permanent residence in a suite of the old Baker Hotel on Main Street. During the flood of the Los Angeles River, in 1886, Aguirre became a local hero by personally riding along Center Street warning inhabitants to abandon their homes. Time and time again, he rode into the roaring flood waters, bringing out survivors. He was credited with saving nineteen lives.

Martin never married. He loved people, enjoyed visiting with them and was a frequent and welcome guest in the homes of his many friends and relatives. He was honorary "uncle" to more youngsters than any of his contemporaries.

In the shadow of the office where he worked for so many years, the one-time constable sheriff and warden died on February 25, 1929. In its story about "the last old sheriff," one local paper spoke extensively of how "deeds of valor" marked the "life of this veteran officer who had served the city since adobe days".

The funeral for one of California's most colorful peace officers was held at the Plaza Church of Our Lady of the Angels which Martin had attended most of his life. His body was interred at Calvary Cemetery.

ANTONIA
(1807-1828)

The conciliar Fathers of Vatican Council II, in the first ever document setting forth official teaching on the lay apostolate, noted that "by performing their ordinary work according to God's will," the laity most assuredly "make progress in the holiness" characteristic of God's people. Though only hinted at in conciliar decrees prior to the 1960s, the notion of the "lay apostolate" has existed in the Church since the days of our Lord in Jerusalem. It is reflected in many of the early patristic writings.

Fray Junípero Serra and the pioneer missionaries who labored along *El Camino Real* were keenly aware of the sanctity inherent in their neophytes. In many of the entries made by the friars in the register books, there is mention of outstanding virtue. An example is that of a neophyte who was born, reared and died at Santa Cruz Mission. She became a role model for her contemporaries and she retains that distinction today. According to entry #1364, Antonia, the two day old daughter of Proyecto and Fabiana was baptized by Fray Andres Quintana on April 4, 1807.

Her whole life was spent within a few miles of the Old Mission and it was there, on April 26,1821, that she married Severo Usculti de la Ra de Churissaca. Fray Luis Gil, who witnessed the exchange of vows, noted that "the ceremony was performed at a Mass attended by all the Indian populace." There were two children born to the couple: one in May of 1824 (Maria Magdalena) and the other in April of 1827 (Angela del Ssmo Sacramento).

It was also in 1827 that Santa Cruz became a port-of-entry by order of the President and Congress of the Mexican Republic, an action that permitted foreign vessels to stop there for trading purposes. During the ensuing months, the area's Indians were ravaged by several European diseases, including a virulent strain of measles which devastated the local population.

Antonia responded to the call for volunteers to look after the infirm and eventually she too contracted the dread disease. *The Libro de Difuntos* indicates that she "died of an acute measles with severe chills." When the youthful Antonia was interred in the cemetery at Santa Cruz on April 26, 1828, Fray Luis Gil noted that "as a single person as well as in her married state, she gave splendid testimony of her faith not with extraordinary actions, but fulfilling with exactitude her duties as a virgin and later as a married woman".

"Always modest and quiet, she did not like crowds and mundane diversions but constantly and promptly performed the works assigned to her. She was a young woman who fulfilled the obligations of her state with perfection doing the ordinary and common tasks as best she could for the love of God. She became too good for this world and so she passed to a better life. Such Christians do not die, they are reborn. She received with fervor the sacraments of Penance, Holy Eucharist and Extreme Unction during the three days of her illness and fever."

According to Harry Kelsey, Mead Fellow at the Huntington Library, Antonia, "certainly seems to have lived a saintly life, if the testimony of the *padre* is any guide."

FRANK M. BALFOUR
(1856-1915)

A glance at the relatively short life of Frank W. Balfour (1856-1915) reveals a man who arose, in a period of only fifteen years, from practical obscurity to widespread esteem as one of Southern California's foremost public figures. Originating in London and educated at Saint Edmund's College, Balfour completed his studies at La Belle, France. Following a short apprenticeship in Hanover Square's Electrical Institute, the young Englishman journeyed to Canada, where he embroiled himself in the perilous speculations of cattle raising.

Local annals record Balfour's name among the thousands of immigrants wandering westward, in the 1880s. Soon after his arrival in Southern California, "it became the good fortune of the then young city of Pomona to claim and thereafter hold his allegiance as a citizen." Balfour's loyal, energetic and patriotic qualities soon acclimatized themselves to new surroundings and numerous positions of public and private trust were bestowed upon him.

While employed for the firm of James Taylor and Company, Balfour helped to survey much of present-day Pomona, as well as several neighboring towns. His personality forged a vital relationship with the municipal affairs of Pomona and it was his honor, along with fourteen others, to draft that city's charter. Balfour subsequently chaired Pomona's Board of Health and directed its Chamber of Commerce. For several years, before his association with the Southern California Edison Company, Balfour functioned as the city's postmaster.

Apparently it was a rare day that did not see him engaged in some piece of committee work for the betterment of industrial, fraternal, social or political conditions of his fellowmen. Balfour was active in the Knights of Columbus, the Elks, the Fraternal Brotherhood and the Catholic Foresters.

One contemporary observer noted that "the memory of his life, fragrant with nobility of character and rich in achievement, is a solace and an inspiration to all who knew him." Bishop Thomas J. Conaty felt that "the beauty of Frank Balfour's character... sprang from his faith in God, his conscience was enlightened by the teachings of his Church and his heart was strengthened by the grace of its sacraments."

In a moving tribute before the Newman Club of Los Angeles, J. Vincent Hannon described Balfour as a most conspicuous figure in his community, as a loving, dutiful husband and father. But first and foremost, Frank W. Balfour was "a practical Catholic. He realized that the Divine Founder of the Church left in the sacraments the means of grace and strength to enable mortal man to live the life of rectitude that would lead him safely to his destined land."

KATHERINE BELL
(1844-1926)

Katherine Bell, the daughter of Nicholas A. Den, was fond of recalling that she arrived on the scene when California was in the pastoral phase of its development. Shortly after her birth, the Mexican flag was lowered over the Pacific Slope and in its place was hoisted the banner of the stars and stripes.

Born in one of Santa Barbara's old adobes, on July 22, 1844, Katherine grew into womanhood in the Channel City. There she married and raised her family and there she died on June 9, 1926, within the sound of the very bells that rang out the day of her birth.

She was part of the life known only to the pioneers. Her education came not alone from books, but also from her association with those who directed the forces of the state and who, in a short half century, brought California from a wilderness into a prominent position among the galaxy of states.

According to the Santa Barbara *Daily News*, Katherine "was recognized as an authority on the history of Santa Barbara County and its early-day families." That same account went on to say that "probably no other person knew the history of the county and of its early families as did Mrs. Bell, who was reared in an atmosphere created by its traditions and, as a child, absorbed its history and romance."

Katherine played a unique role in the gradual development of the area. "Her active mind and her unusual literary genius made her a most interesting writer and companion." The eminent California historian, Zoeth S. Eldredge, was known to consult frequently with Mrs. Bell about the events and dates associated with the early days of Santa Barbara.

Katherine's husband, John, was a prominent landowner in the area. He was a native of Tahiti, where his father operated a large sugar plantation. While Herman Melville was writing *Moby Dick*, he met the Bells and later devoted a chapter to Katherine in which he recalled that once, "taking a pensive afternoon stroll along one of the many bridle-paths which wind among the shady groves in the neighborhood of Taloo, I was startled by a sunny apparition. It was that of a beautiful young Englishwoman, charmingly dressed, and mounted upon a spirited little white pony: she was the wife of Mr. Bell (happy dog!), the proprietor of the sugar plantation." He concluded by characterizing Katherine as "the most beautiful white woman I ever saw in Polynesia."

During her busy lifetime, Katherine wrote often for the Santa Barbara *Morning Press* and *The Grizzly Bear*, the official organ for the Native Sons and Native Daughters of the Golden West. In those essays she described the events of her time in a charming style that endeared her to all of California.

In 1931, the Bell family published Katherine's "Reminiscences of Old Santa Barbara" under the title *Swinging the Censer*. This they did "not only as an affectionate tribute to her memory, but also as a contribution to the historical archives of California." Her chapter on "A Miraculous Saint's Adventure" is a classical portrayal of Francis of Assisi.

Katherine Bell belonged to the generation that inspired Mark Twain, Francis Bret Harte and other writers who brought renown to California. As Charles S. Storke observed, Kate never made a profession of literature "but her recollections attracted attention among those who appreciated good writing."

JOHN J. BODKIN
(1841-1918)

John J. Bodkin, the eleventh of fifteen children, was born at Tuam, County Galway, Ireland, on November 25,1841. He came to the United States in 1867, and took a teaching position at Saint Genevieve, Missouri. In 1869, he moved to Texas where he taught in "the first Catholic school in the City of Dallas, the school being conducted in the pastoral residence, a small four room cottage." Shortly thereafter he married Marian O'Brennan in the Cathedral at Saint Louis. It was during his years in Texas that Bodkin edited the *Dallas Free Press*.

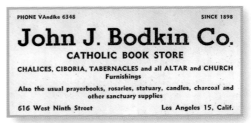

Bodkin came to the Golden State in July of 1875, and the next year was followed by his wife and two children, Elizabeth and Thomas. The family first took up residence in San Gabriel. In subsequent years Bodkin lived and taught in public schools in that city and various parts of Los Angeles County. The next five Bodkin children were born in California. During his early years on the west coast, Bodkin traveled in the interest of securing subscriptions and advertising for the *California Catholic*. When financial conditions forced the newspaper into bankruptcy, Bodkin resumed his teaching career in the Los Angeles County Public School system.

Early in 1898, the Right Reverend George T. Montgomery, Bishop of Monterey-Los Angeles, asked Bodkin to become associated with *The Tidings*, offering to personally underwrite his investment in that struggling journal. Bodkin complied and by the end of the year had purchased full control of the paper from its founder, Patrick W. Croake. Before the passage of many months, the new editor had enlarged the paper and the number of its readers was "greater and its influence wider than any other weekly paper published in this section." There was nothing pretentious about the journal in those years. It was "put to bed" and printed in a small press room in the basement of the Y.M.C.A. at Second and Broadway.

Bodkin was keenly aware that "the support which a newspaper receives determines its quality" and he took considerable care to emphasize that *The Tidings* was not a political sheet nor a partisan organ, for "while the editor has his own political convictions, and pronounced ones at that, he does not consider the columns of *The Tidings* the place to ventilate them." It was Bodkin's opinion that "the chief value of a Catholic paper lies in its treatment of local topics," and he resisted several suggestions about enlarging the journal, feeling that "its small size is one of the chief recommendations of *The Tidings*."

Late in 1904, Bishop Thomas J. Conaty purchased the paper as the official Catholic Publication of the Diocese of Monterey-Los Angeles. As his final issue drew near, Bodkin remarked with justifiable pride that "there is not a city in the country where Catholics and their religion are more respected or where the entire secular press is more favorably disposed towards our people." After his retirement from journalism, Bodkin devoted full attention to the religious goods store which he had opened in December of 1899. When death finally claimed the pioneering editor, on January 25, 1918, one of his contemporaries noted:

"There have been wiser and abler men in the world than our old-time confrere, John Bodkin, but there have been few more sincere, when embarked on a worthy cause!"

ETHEL BOSSERT
(d. 1992)

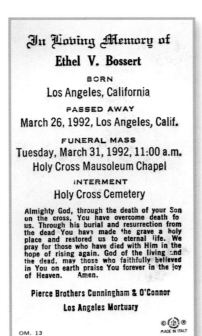

The Feast of Our Lady of the Angels in the year of the Lord, 1986, richly deserves to be remembered by the Catholics of Southern California. For on that day, Ethel Bossert closed out a sixty year career of uninterrupted service to the Church of Los Angeles, a record unparalleled in the Golden State's religious annals.

A private person to the very last of her days in the Chancery Office, Ethel confided very little for the public record. This much we know— that she was born in Los Angeles, at the old Clara Barton Hospital. She and her brother attended elementary school in Ocean Park.

Her first contact with the Catholic Church came during her teen years as a student at Saint Mary's Commercial School in Boyle Heights. Shortly after her conversion, Ethel became a member of the first class at Conaty (Catholic Girls) High School. In 1926, after completing her education at Venice High, Ethel took a "temporary" position with Steve Sullivan, who was spearheading the drive to raise funds for Los Angeles College,

the preparatory seminary for the Diocese of Los Angeles-San Diego.

She was assigned a desk in the chancery, which was then located in the Higgins Building, at 108 West Second Street, across from Saint Vibiana's Cathedral. When the drive was finished, Bishop John J. Cantwell invited Ethel to join Mary Sinclair and Pat Powers on the permanent curial staff. Though she worked at numerous tasks in the next six decades, Ethel was associated mostly with the chancellors of the diocese, including such outstanding churchmen as Bernard J. Dolan, Joseph T. McGucken, Alden J. Bell and Benjamin G. Hawkes.

In the spring of 1932, when the diocesan offices were relocated, Ethel took up her work on the seventh floor of the then new Petroleum Securities Building, on West Olympic Boulevard at Figueroa. She recalls the ever-gracious Carrie Estelle Doheny insisting that she and Mary Sinclair take their meals with the staff of the Doheny Oil Company on another floor of the building.

The chancery was relocated in August of 1951, this time to 1531 West Ninth Street and there Ethel rounded out her service to the Archdiocese of Los Angeles. She alone has the distinction of having worked for all four of the southland's archbishops!

While researching an article for the golden jubilee of the archdiocese, we noticed that the earliest letters relating to that epochal event bear the initial "b," an indication that they were typed by Ethel Bossert who, in 1936, had already logged ten years of service to God's people!

Though her mark remains on tens of thousands of letters, reports, memoranda and journals, Ethel always preferred to work behind the scenes. Only once did she emerge from the shadows, and that time by obedience. It was January, 1929, and she appeared with Bishop Cantwell in a photograph published in the *Los Angeles Times*. The late Monsignor John J. Devlin, for whom Ethel worked in her earliest days at the chancery, once remarked that she was "the most professional, qualified and loyal person" he had known in all his long and distinguished ministry.

That testimony, made a quarter century earlier, was echoed by Timothy Cardinal Manning who said that "for half a century and a decade more, Ethel Bossert served the Church in Los Angeles in a manner unique among its hand-maidens. She was intimate to all the doings that were transacted at the headquarters of the Church. In that capacity she preserved a confidentiality that made her a treasured person. No one's light will ever shine brighter."

MARY BOYLE
(1885-1964)

Mary Boyle deserves a place among those whose total lives were devoted to the service of the Church in California. Because her life was so hidden, this will probably be the only memorial she will ever have.

Born to James and Mary (Hurley) Boyle at Saint Louis, Missouri, Mary was baptized at Saint Malachy's Church by Father C. Ziegler on September 27, 1885. In November of 1917, shortly after coming to the west coast and just a month before the arrival of the newly-appointed Bishop of Monterey-Los Angeles, Mary became the housekeeper at the old episcopal residence at 717 South Burlington Avenue.

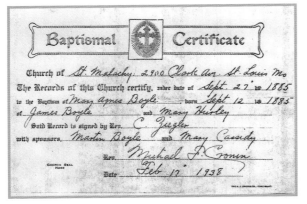

She continued in that position when the residence was moved to the King Gillette Mansion at #100 Fremont Place in 1927. For almost a half century, forty-seven years to be exact, Mary Boyle looked after the episcopal residence and those who lived there. Whether it was a banquet for thirty-five visitors or a simple breakfast for the archbishop, Mary was always the gracious and efficient host who made guests and residents alike feel at home.

Mary catered especially to seminarians and her oatmeal cookies were a favorite with several generations of seminarians who came to serve Holy Mass each day in the archbishop's chapel. There was always a modest gift for the servers at Christmas-time and more often than not it was something she had been given by the archbishop. She was fond of "recycling," to the extent that there was nothing left of her earthly possessions when her life was over.

To Archbishop John J. Cantwell, Mary Boyle was as important to the operations of the archdiocese as the Vicar General. He once wrote on her birthday card: "To Mary, one of the brightest treasures of the local Church. I thank the Lord every day for your selfless service and dedication." On those rare days when there was no liturgy offered in the chapel at Fremont Place, Mary would take the Wilshire bus to La Brea and then walk south three blocks to Cathedral Chapel for the 6:30 a.m. Mass.

When I visited her in 1964 at Santa Teresita Hospital in Duarte, shortly after her leg had been amputated, she showed me an envelope which contained her "most valued possession." It was a note on mono-grammed stationery which read: "Thank you, Mary, for your gracious care of this humble pilgrim." It was signed "Eugenio Cardinal Pacelli." The future Pope Pius XII had been a house guest at Fremont Place in October, 1936.

Miss Boyle was proud of her calling. She had business cards printed with her name and the words "Archbishop's Housekeeper" embossed in bold letters. To her, housekeeping was a ministry and she performed it well.

In his reflections, Timothy Cardinal Manning said that "God is not so concerned about what a person does for a living, but how well she or he does it." By that yardstick, Mary Boyle was an outstanding, even heroic practitioner of virtue. She did everything well because, to her, "housekeeping was a vocation of service for the Lord."

James Francis Cardinal McIntyre was with Mary when she died at Santa Teresita Hospital on October 24, 1964. Her funeral was conducted at Cathedral Chapel. In his homily, Msgr. Benjamin G. Hawkes said that "Mary resembled her namesake in Holy Scripture always busy about the needs of others, little concerned for her own comfort."

GEORGE HENRY CARSON
(1829-1901)

George Henry Carson, short and sturdy in appearance, was a shrewd business man who left an indelible mark on Southern California. His name still adorns the city founded on part of his extensive ranch holdings. Born in New Jordan, New York, on March 23, 1829, George, the eldest son of John C. and Sophia Cady Carson, was destined to be a considerable influence on the California skyline.

In 1841, the Carson family began moving west, settling for awhile on a farm in Illinois. George enlisted as a drummer boy in Company F, Seventh Regiment of the Illinois Volunteers. Later he became a bugler and regular soldier in active service, positions he held throughout the War with Mexico. Following his discharge, young Carson joined Chapman's Rangers and served in the campaign to suppress a Navajo uprising.

George spent several years as a merchandiser in Texas and New Mexico, a trade in which he managed to accumulate a considerable amount of money. In 1852, he went to Mexico and there engaged in the cattle trade. Early the following year, he drove a herd of sheep to Southern California. Later he spent time working as a carpenter.

George Carson become active in local politics and was elected to the Los Angeles City Council. Subsequently he served as Public Administrator and, in that capacity, he got to know Manuel Dominguez. While serving as Public Administrator, George also involved himself in construction work and is credited with having erected the first brick building in Los Angeles in what was known as the Childs Block.

After marrying Maria Victoria Dominguez on July 30, 1857, George worked in the hardware business for a few years before moving his family to *Rancho San Pedro*, where he became chief assistant to the elder Dominguez. George brought his considerable managerial acumen to the rancho and, during his tenure, the Dominguez holdings grew and stabilized. Grain and dairy farming were added to the *rancho* and George devised a method for shipping grain and wool to eastern markets.

Following the death of Manuel Dominguez, George Carson supervised the management of the lands inherited by his wife. His was the principal guiding hand in protecting the interests of the other Dominguez daughters.

George, a firm disciplinarian, controlled his own family of fifteen children in every respect. After the allotment of tracts to his offspring in 1885, George and Victoria built a large two story house for their family on a slight incline just north of the original Dominguez homesite.

In later years, George Carson also took a special interest in improving the strains of dairy cattle and sheep. He also raised thoroughbred horses and developed some of the best trotting and carriage stock in Los Angeles county.

George Henry Carson died at his home on November 20, 1901, at the age of seventy-two. His passing was given full coverage by the local press. The funeral was an elaborate ceremony with a long procession to Saint Vibiana's Cathedral and then on to Calvary cemetery.

For George Henry Carson, the Catholic faith was a "given." His whole life was anchored to the Church. He once confided to Bishop Francis Mora that he "never made a decision without first praying for divine guidance."

BARTHOLOMEW DOWLING
(c. 1820-1863)

The name of Bartholomew Dowling is not outstanding in the anthologies of literature pertaining to the American occupation in California; yet this Irish poet deserves to have his name remembered for he may yet emerge as a "bright light" in an otherwise darkened period of literary development.

Dowling was born in Listowel, County Kerry, Ireland, in the early 1820s. He is known to have arrived in California about 1852 among that horde of men seeking their fortunes along the Gold Dust Trails. Not finding his riches in mining, Dowling retired to the seclusion of Crucita Valley in the Contra Costa Hills, where he built a small home and settled down to farming. During his years on the ranch and later in San Francisco, Dowling was employed as a staff writer for *The Monitor*, and in 1856, P. J. Thomas induced him to join the paper as a full-time editor.

Undoubtedly the chief reason for his obscurity was the practice he followed of not signing his work. Even his commercial poems usually appeared anonymously or under the *nom de plume* of "Hard Knocks" or "Southern." Favorite of Dowling's signature was "Masque." *The California Pioneer* carried many of his writings. "Reminiscences of the Mines" depicts the California of Gold Rush Days in dramatically graphic fashion. Of all his poems appearing in the *Ballad Poetry of Ireland* only one bears his true name.

Until the publication of *Forgotten Pioneers* by Thomas F. Prendergast in 1942, the only sketch of Dowling's life was that in a volume entitled *Irish Poets and Novelists*. Therein is printed a brief biography "by a gentleman who for more than twenty years enjoyed the personal friendship of the deceased poet." Dowling's heroic ballad "The Brigade of Fontenoy" came out in 1889, in the little volume *A Chaplet of Verse* by California Catholic Writers. The *Irish Monthly* picked it up and ranked its author among the "brilliant galaxy of gifted young Irishmen who threw themselves and their fortunes into an inspiring national movement".

Very little is known about the poet's education, although it was said that "he was versed in the Latin and several of the modern languages," a fact made obvious by his writings. Dowling's translation of Beranger's poems was published at San Francisco and his facility with the German language made the English version of the poems an instant success. Like many poets, Dowling was something of a romanticist. He avoided, as much as possible, the public life of San Francisco, preferring instead to read his books and jot down personal observations for later editorials. Although his personal opinions were sometimes expressed in *The Monitor* and in other publications, Dowling had no special attraction to politics and kept out of the public eye whenever possible.

Dowling's death was brought about by an accident late in 1863. His remains were laid to rest at Calvary Cemetery where a handsome monument, erected by his brother, "marks his grave and perpetuates his name." Perhaps the simple Irish Faith that inspired Dowling's life is nowhere more evident than in his translation of Theodor Korner's "Prayer During Battle."

> *Father, I call to Thee!*
> *Roaring around me the cannons storm;*
> *Like a shroud their lightnings enwrap my form.*
> *Guide of the battles, I call to Thee:*
> *Father! Today be a guide to me.*

JOHN FILMORE FRANCIS
(1850-1903)

"A career which elevates one's own self and at the same time reaches out and helps to raise those with whom one comes in contact has an influence so widespread as to be immeasurable. To the City of Los Angeles has been given such a character in the late John F. Francis."

Very little is known about the early life of John Filmore Francis (1850-1903) beyond the fact that his earliest years were spent mostly in Europe. A native of Clinton, Iowa, Francis was fascinated by military life, and, at the age of sixteen he enlisted in the Kansas Volunteer Cavalry where he had many thrilling experiences in the Indian campaign on the Western Kansas frontier in 1867. Afterwards "he spent several years adventuring over the plains and mountains of Wyoming, Colorado and California, obtaining a rich fund of information, so that by the time he came of age he was in possession of valuable ideas regarding this great country."

Shortly after coming to the west coast, Mr. Francis married the socially prominent Maria de los Reyes, the last of the direct descendants of the Dominguez family. Contemporary accounts speak of Francis as one whose personal qualities endeared him to every level of society. An able conversationalist with keen powers of observation, the jurist was acknowledged as discreet, adroit and considerate of the feelings of his fellowmen. Harrison Gray Otis portrayed Francis as "essentially a good citizen and never a self-seeker." The publisher of the *Los Angeles Times* remarked that Francis "repeatedly declined to stand for public office, but as a private citizen in the civic ranks, never was there a better soldier." In 1897, he was president of *La Fiesta de Los Angeles* and as such was largely instrumental in securing the success of that function, which formed so important a part of the social life of the city.

John Francis was converted to the Catholic Faith in 1891, largely through the influence of Father Joachim Adam, Vicar General of the Diocese of Monterey-Los Angeles. Even before adopting Catholicism, however, Francis was a man of deep religious feeling. On May 25, 1899, John Francis and several other outstanding Catholic laymen of the southland established the Newman Club whose avowed purpose was (and is) "the advancement of religious toleration in accordance with the Constitution of the United States; the expression of members' sentiments on matters of interest to Catholics and promotion of social intercourse among its members."

At the time of his death in Los Angeles on July 4, 1903, Francis was eulogized by *The Tidings* as "a good husband, a kind neighbor, an upright citizen, but above all, he was a good Catholic." It is recorded in the annals that Saint Vibiana's Cathedral could not hold the people who gathered to pay to the noble life of John F. Francis their last tribute of respect. Bishop Thomas J. Conaty characterized him as a man whose "life was a constant sermon of the value of the Catholic Faith," and one whose "greatness was his goodness."

MARIE WALSH HARRINGTON
(1907-1986)

The person of Marie Walsh Harrington, the matriarch of the San Fernando Valley, is a woman whose name is indelibly inscribed on the walls of the Old Mission, as well as on the bibliographical rolls of Western America. A native of Santa Monica, Marie was by profession a journalist. Her first book, *The Mission of the Passes*, occasioned a personal commendation from Eugenio Cardinal Pacelli who became Pope Pius XII in 1939.

To this day, her subsequent book on *The Mission Bells of California* remains the standard authority on a subject that continues to fascinate readers all over the world. During years that stretched from the depression to the space age, Marie's byline appeared above a veritable litany of essays in magazines, journals and newspapers throughout the west. She was the official biographer for the Hearst newspapers in Los Angeles.

Her last and probably best book was about the man she married, a personal account of the life and career of Mark Raymond Harrington, published in 1985 by the Great Basin Press. Marie knew Mark for many years before they were married. She once said that the first time she met him, she knew that they would one day marry! She quickly added: "Oh, I didn't tell him then, I just got in line." She became the fourth Mrs. Harrington in 1949.

There were many facets of Marie's life that were absolutely fascinating. One relates to her close relationship with Archbishop Francisco Orozco y Jimenez, the famed and fugitive Archbishop of Guadalajara, who spent several years of his exile during the Mexican persecutions hidden away in her home. Marie's assistance to the archbishop and her concern for the plight of Mexican Catholics persecuted by a hostile government was officially acknowledged by Pope Pius XI who awarded her the *Pro Pontifice et Ecclesia* medal in 1933.

In the early 1980s, shortly after the Archival Center for the Archdiocese of Los Angeles was opened at San Fernando Mission, Marie founded *Las Damas Archivistas*, a group of docents who conduct tours of the Historical Museum and perform other duties of vital importance. It was at Marie's insistence that *California's Catholic Treasury* was written as a guide to the Historical Museum of the Archival Center. The members of *Las Damas Archivistas* use that text as a handbook for learning about the artifacts on display.

For many decades, San Fernando Mission was the focal point of Marie's life. In mid 1981, she presented the Old Mission with twenty-one Indian baskets that had belonged to her late husband. They are on permanent exhibit in one of the rooms of the mission, just across the way from her longtime home.

Those who worked with Marie will always recall her as a determined, forceful (one might even say stubborn) person, one who outlived many of her doctors and defied the rest. When she was told that she had only a few months to live, she simply shrugged her shoulders and said: "We'll see about that." She lived another four years.

Marie Harrington epitomized in her person all that was best in mission history and lore. Were her own biography ever written, it would read like the chapters from one of her many books and articles pages of the past, alive in the present, as a guide for the future.

RYOZO FUSO KADO
(1890-1982)

Ryozo Fuso Kado has been designated as "the greatest builder of Catholic shrines in the West and perhaps in the whole country." Most of his ninety-one years were spent "gathering up boulders overlooked by others and squeezing and stretching them to fit like jigsaw-puzzle pieces to create dells, grottoes, shrines and artificial waterfalls that look like nature's work."

R. F. Kado was born at the base of Mount Fuji in Japan to a devout Buddhist family of tea growers. He later became a Methodist and, after coming to the United States in 1911, entered the Catholic Church.

Kado's wife and two children subsequently followed him into the "one true religion whose truth is eternal." Shortly after his arrival in America, Kado apprenticed himself to Chotaro Nishimura, an internationally recognized stone craftsman. "Mr. Nishi," as he was known, had designed part of the Imperial Garden in Tokyo and the Presidential Gardens in Mexico City.

In later years, Kado earned his own reputation as an architectural gardener, winning plaudits also for developing and propagating the Epiphyllum, or flowering cactus, a highly popular parasitic shade plant. Mr. Kado lived an exciting and often troubled life. His thriving nursery business was closed at the outbreak of World War II, when he and his family were forcibly sent with other Southern California Japanese-Americans to the Manzanar Relocation Center, a mile-square internment camp in the desert east of the Sierra Nevada.

Following a short interval in New York after the war, Kado and his family returned to California, in 1946, penniless, but anxious to begin anew. "After all," he stated, "where else in the whole world would we have the chance to start again?"

The eighty shrines and grottoes erected at sixty-five Catholic churches, cemeteries, schools, hospitals and homes during his lifetime earned for Mr. Kado the reputation of being "the country's busiest rock-garden builder." Most ambitious of his undertakings, according to an article in the *Saturday Evening Post*, was one he started, in 1946, on a barren hill overlooking Holy Cross Cemetery in the southern section of Los Angeles. Completed in 1969, it is an eye-filling spread of gardens surrounded by a massive 400-foot rock wall out of which arises a thirty foot high grotto. Within the wall, the three shrines of Our Lady of Lourdes, Saint Ann and Saint Joseph, blend together 700 tons of ornamental rocks so ingeniously that they resemble a giant outcropping of natural serpentine. "This is Kado's art with rocks, making them look as though they had always been there."

Over twenty replicas of the Lourdes grotto, the first built for the cloistered Carmelites in Alhambra, convinced Mr. Kado that rocks have character and are loaded with life and rhythm. R. F. Kado was a happy man, working at his chosen vocation. He expressed in stone and flowers the Faith he found so many years ago. He dedicated himself to the task of building shrines "so that people who pass by and stop to say a prayer, may reach up their hearts to God in a much-troubled world, and thereby gain solace and consolation."

J. WISEMAN MACDONALD
(1866-1942)

J. Wiseman Macdonald, "a man of broad sympathies, of fine intellect and high ideals," was born at Mazomanie, Wisconsin, on January 17, 1866, the son of Allan and Eleanor (Wiseman) Macdonald. Descended from the Macdonald's of Clanranald, in the Western Highlands of Scotland, James received his education in the land of his ancestors and at the Grant School, in Lancastershire. By the time of his return to the United States, the young man was steeped in the best traditions of a family that had been solidly Catholic for over a thousand years.

Admitted to the bar before the California Supreme Court, in 1892, J. Wiseman Macdonald was a lawyer by instinct as well as training. Early in his long legal career, he "gained wide recognition as a lawyer of fine natural ability, supplemented by an education in the law, extensive and comprehensive." In addition to his busy legal practice Macdonald lectured on corporation law for many years at the University of Southern California. He served two terms as trustee for the Los Angeles Bar Association. Throughout his life he had "an active and energetic interest in all civic affairs," serving, at various times as Director of the Bank of Italy and the Hibernian Savings Bank of Los Angeles as well as President of the Dimond Estate Company of San Francisco.

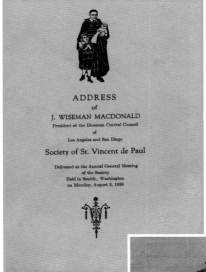

During the twenty-two years Macdonald occupied the presidency of the Saint Vincent de Paul Society, he won an abiding place in the hearts of the poor and downtrodden in California's southland. It was Macdonald's long and tireless dedication to charitable activities which brought him the papal knighthood from Pius XI, in February, 1924. That recognition, the first such ever accorded in California, was bestowed as a reward for faithful and devoted service to the Church and religion.

His charitable involvements were accelerated after the premature death of his wife, Jane (Boland) Macdonald, in 1919. From his suite of offices in the Higgins Building, Macdonald employed his manifold talents to further Catholic activities with utmost fidelity and rare ability. Macdonald's "very manner, his expression, his countenance, his reasonings, the tact with which he approached difficult situations, the keen light that he threw on abstruse subjects, his eloquent familiarity with the Spanish tongue, were the qualities that made success in his profession, and he had them at his command. His appearance in courts of the land was always such as to command respect."

Possibly the most outstanding ecclesiastical honor given to the well-known jurist was his selection as keynote speaker for the public reception held, on December 6,1936, at the elevation of Los Angeles to the status of metropolitan archiepiscopate. The death of J. Wiseman Macdonald, on November 21, 1942, deprived the People of God in Southern California of a distinguished and eminent lawyer, a sympathetic friend of the poor and a high-toned Catholic gentleman.

JOHN STEVEN MCGROARTY
(1862-1944)

Of John Steven McGroarty, it was said that no man has caught the spirit of California from the beginning of the coming of the Spanish padres down to the present time and gathered it together into one continuous golden thread such as this great man has done. "His sense of the religious basis of the original settlement of our state not only illumined his writings about that portion of her history, but ran down through his appreciation of modern-day California."

Named Poet Laureate of the Golden State on May 15, 1933, McGroarty later represented his adopted commonwealth in the United States Congress as a representative from the eleventh congressional district. His column in the *Los Angeles Times*, appearing under the title "From the Green Verdugo Hills," was published for over forty years and won for McGroarty a place in almost every home in the southland. A man of endless talents, the Pennsylvania-born author and poet spent his early years in teaching, journalism and politics. Although licensed to practice law in Pennsylvania and Montana, McGroarty spent his life in California and it was there he won his fame.

Though he wrote a number of books, both prose and poetry, the name of John Steven McGroarty will best be remembered for his famous Mission Play, a production seen by almost 2,000,000 spectators, most of them non-Catholics, including President Calvin Coolidge and William Butler Yeats, the famous English poet.

The idea of the play came from Frank Miller, founder of the Mission Inn in Riverside. Miller, himself a Quaker, wanted McGroarty to write a Nativity Play which could be shown each Christmas season at Riverside. The completed production told the story of the bringing and founding of Christian civilization to the Western shores of America. After Vice President Thomas R. Marshall saw the play, he remarked to McGroarty, "Some men may write a history, dry as dust; some may produce a drama, full of fire but wholly false; but it has been given to you to blend historic accuracy with dramatic power, and thus both to please and instruct mankind."

In addition to his books on California lore, McGroarty served as editor for some years of *The West Coast Magazine* and his contributions to that journal are a valuable part of California's Catholic heritage. This great pioneer, born just a month after Lincoln's Emancipation Proclamation, went home to God on the eve of his 82nd birthday, August 7, 1944. The night before he died, the gentle poet answered a query about his health in the lines of his last poem:

When I have had my little day
My chance at toil, my fling at play,
And in the starry silence fall
With broken staff against the wall,
May someone pass, God grant, that way,
And, as he bends above me say:

Goodnight, dear comrade, sleep you well,
Deep are the daisies where you fell,
I fold your empty hand that shared
Their little all with them that feared
Beside you in the rain and sun
Goodnight, your little day is done.

DANIEL MURPHY
(1855-1939)

The man for whom Daniel Murphy High School is named was "an eminent citizen, a man who in the days of his strength was a leader in public affairs, whose advice in critical circumstances was eagerly sought and always respected." Born in the farming community of Hazelton, Pennsylvania, on September 20, 1855, the son of Thomas Murphy and Anne Rafter spent his early years as a developer of oil interests throughout the expanses of Oklahoma. In the late 1870s, after becoming interested in railroading, young Murphy came to California as an employee of the Southern Pacific.

Murphy belonged to a generation of men whose rugged individualism contributed mightily to the growth of American civilization. Gifted with physical strength, rare intelligence and common sense, he faced and surmounted the problems that confront every pioneer. Descended as he was from a people acquainted with poverty and self denial, Daniel launched his business career with a courageous heart and mighty vision. At Needles, which he helped to develop as a townsite, Murphy established a mercantile house, opened a bank, provided domestic and commercial utilities and inaugurated a chain of refrigerating plants for the Santa Fe Railroad.

Shortly after the turn of the century, Murphy expanded his business interests to Los Angeles, where he engaged in petroleum and cement production, and participated in organizing the Brea Canyon Oil company. He was also among the founders of El Segundo's Standard Oil refinery in 1911. During World War I, Murphy lent his talents to the inauguration of the Los Angeles Shipbuilding and Dry Dock Company.

A notice in the diocesan newspaper, for May 18, 1906, records that "Mr. Dan Murphy has lately returned from a visit to Needles and the theatre of his old and new mining interests. If there is anything in which the Irish-American shows superior quality it is in procuring gold and silver out of the earth, and Dan is no mean hand at that."

Daniel Murphy never allowed temporal success to diminish his reliance on Almighty God. Tried as he was in the furnace of affliction, the poor, the widow and the orphan never appealed to him in vain. He served as a trustee for the diocesan seminary and a board member for the Catholic Welfare Bureau as well as the Convent of the Good Shepherd. His heart was as big as his noble frame, and social organizations like the Red Cross, Travelers' Aid and Community Chest rarely looked his way without results. Bishop John J. Cantwell noted that Daniel Murphy "made the recipient of his bounty doubly happy because he always gave with pleasure and not with reluctance."

The stage of his life was darkened before the curtain fell, inasmuch as Murphy's final years were heavily burdened by the ailments of advancing age. On September 14, 1939, just a year and a half after the death of his wife, Antoinette, the eighty-three year old pioneer passed away quietly at his stately home, 2076 West Adams Boulevard. "A mighty oak had fallen by the wayside and Los Angeles mourned an eminent citizen."

AGUSTIN OLVERA
(d. 1877)

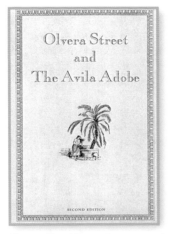

Agustin Olvera, for whom the famed Olvera Street in the Plaza area of Los Angeles was named, was a youngster from Mexico City who came to Alta California in 1834 with the Hijar and Padres Expedition. Very little is known about Olvera's early life, though his subsequent accomplishments indicate that he had a rather extensive education. An uncle, Ignacio Coronel, had been a well-known teacher in Mexico.

The youthful Olvera lived with his uncle on the Corralitos Ranch, in Santa Cruz County, until 1839, when he decided to take up his permanent residence in Southern California. In 1842, Governor Juan B. Alvarado named Olvera commissioner for the lands then comprising San Juan Capistrano Mission and, the following year, he was advanced to the position of Justice of the Peace.

On May 23, 1842, Agustin married Concepcion Zefferina Arguello and that union was blessed by five children. Unhappily, Concepcion died just a decade later. Agustin subsequently married Refugio Ortega, the widow of Edward Stokes.

In 1847, Olvera represented Governor Pio Pico at the signing of the Treaty of Cahuenga, an agreement that ended the fighting in California during the Mexican War. The treaty was confirmed at Guadalupe-Hidalgo on February 2, 1848. Following ratification of the latter treaty, Olvera was asked by the governor to supervise transferral of California to American officials, a diplomatic task that he performed with characteristic dignity.

Two *ranchos* were granted to Olvera in 1845 and the titles to both were subsequently confirmed by the United States Land Commission. Olvera later acquired the large Tujunga Rancho. Olvera was among the first to accept American citizenship. He was admitted to the bar and became a prominent local lawyer. In 1846, Governor Bennet Riley appointed him justice of the Peace for Los Angeles, a position he had held earlier during the Mexican regime.

On April 1, 1850, Olvera was named first Judge for Los Angeles County. That was an important position insofar as Olvera was called upon to decide cases and set precedents in a host of private matters and appeal cases. Olvera was also director of the Court of Sessions. When the State Legislature created the original counties, it placed their control and management under the Court of Sessions. Hence Olvera was also the proto chief executive officer for Los Angeles county.

A prominent Catholic layman, Olvera was active in many ecclesial affairs. An article in the *Weekly Star* for June 5, 1858, tells how his residence was decorated for the festival of Corpus Christi, an annual event in which many of the local citizenry participated. Agustin Olvera lived in California fourteen years as a Mexican citizen and twenty-nine years as an American. He was widely recognized as a man whose public trust was beyond question.

He died in 1877 and the name of his home, which originally faced the *Plaza de Nuestra Señora de los Angeles*, later was given to the street leading north from the plaza.

LEO POLITI
(1908-1996)

Leo Politi was not only among the nation's premier author illustrators, he was a folk-hero to generations of youngsters who grew up with his books and were nurtured with his gentle but persuasive love for the simple joys of life. For half a century, Leo deftly blended the old and the new into a colorful pageantry, depicting early California history and describing the great wealth of tradition brought to these shores by Spanish, Mexican, Italian and Chinese peoples who adopted California as their home of choice in the New World.

Born at Fresno, in 1908, Leo returned with his family to their native village of Broni, in Northern Italy. There he first developed an interest in artistically portraying the warmth of familial relationships.

At fifteen, Leo won a national scholarship to the University of Art and Decoration in the Royal Palace of Monza, near Milan. It was during the ensuing years that his sketches were recognized and extolled. His first illustrated book, one which he had never seen and which doesn't even bear his name, was an Italian text for deaf-mute children.

Upon graduation as a *Maestro d'Arte*, Leo taught art and augmented his income by textile and tapestry designing. In 1930, he returned to the United States and shortly thereafter took up permanent residence in Los Angeles. Eight years later he married Helen Fontes.

Leo Politi's literary career began with *Little Poncho*, a children's story he wrote and illustrated for Viking Press in 1938. That volume was the first in a long series of volumes he either composed himself or illustrated for others.

Over the years, Leo won practically every award and prize offered in his discipline. In 1949, *Song of the Swallows* earned the prestigious Caldecott Medal from the American Library Association for the nation's most distinguished picture book. *Moy Moy*, a book about Chinese-Americans in Los Angeles, won Politi further acclaim, this time for a truly "significant contribution to the field of illustration." Others of his prizes included the Regina Medal from the Catholic Library Association which was bestowed for Politi's "continued distinguished contributions to childrens books."

Besides excelling in painting, sculpture and design, Leo studied architecture and utilized its principles in his work. His books about Los Angeles became classics and elicited from such authorities as Carl Dentzel the comment that Politi "has done the most to call attention to the need to preserve the grace and heritage" of our city.

Foremost among Leo's broadsides is that portraying the youthful Fray Junípero Serra which he did for the Serra Bicentennial Commission in 1984. With the touch of a master artisan, he captured the spirit of optimism and love that characterized the life of California's religious pioneer.

Leo was stooped, his face craggy and weathered, his eyes large and luminous behind thick lenses. But he was full of wonder, like the little children in his pictures. He radiated great warmth and quiet humor. He was an indigenous part of California's landscape who will never die or be diminished in the hearts and souls of his public One of Politi's oldest friends and most ardent admirer, Timothy Cardinal Manning, contended that "the artistic genius of Leo Politi is his gift of being able to penetrate the heart of a child and to reproduce in his works the innocence and loveliness of those who reflect the Kingdom of God."

JOSE DE LA ROSA
(1790-1891)

Though the claim that Jose de la Rosa was California's first printer is disputed, it is known that his was the first printing of English in the area, a distinction he achieved while working for Thomas Oliver Larkin, the United States Consul at Monterey.

Born at Puebla de los Angeles, to Jose Florencio and Maria Antonia de la Rosa, the youngster was raised in a family long respected for its skills in the printing trade. Jose served in the War for Mexican Independence and during that time held a prominent position in the government's printing office at Mexico City.

In 1833, General Antonio Lopez de Santa Ana dispatched de la Rosa to Monterey with a printing press. There are nine extant publications bearing de la Rosa's imprint, all of them dating from 1844-1845. Jose moved to Sonoma in the early 1840s, where he became a protege of General Mariano Guadalupe Vallejo, the military comandante for San Francisco Bay.

After the Bear Flag Revolt, de la Rosa remained a close personal friend of Vallejo, whose family referred to him as "Don Pepe." He was named *alcalde* of Sonoma, in 1845, and became the grantee of the nearby Ulpinos Rancho. About 1880, Jose moved to San Buenaventura, where he took up residence with Harold L. Kamp and his family. He worked in a host of trades. He was a skilled tailor, expert watchmaker and talented musician.

During his last dozen years, the never-married de la Rosa became a familiar character in the community of San Buenaventura. He was known by his contemporaries as a cheerful man, a "quiet, polite and intelligent gentleman."

A statewide celebration was held in San Buenaventura's Union Hall to mark his 100th birthday. Jose spoke on that occasion and then played his guitar for the guests. One news account remarked that "his accuracy of touch and the agility of the movements of his hands and fingers was wonderful."

Mary M. Bowman noted that shortly before Jose's death, "time had dealt gently with him. His hair was quite abundant and not entirely gray. The upper teeth were firm and even, the eyesight dim, but his hearing good and memory clear." Jose de la Rosa died at 101 years of age on December 28, 1891. His funeral was held at the Old Mission, where he was eulogized as a fine Christian gentleman of high moral standards and strict religious observance. The local newspaper editorialized that "it was a fitting send-off for one who had been such a respected formulator of the area's objectives."

J. F. REGIS TOOMEY
(1898-1991)

While out-of-town a few years ago, I read in a local newspaper about the death of J. F. Regis Toomey, one of Hollywood's most durable and widely-known actors. According to the wire reports, Toomey's most notable and memorable accomplishment was "taking part in what was billed as the longest on-screen kiss in Hollywood history."

Perhaps that 158 second encounter with Jane Wyman, in "You're in the Army Now," is reason enough for a headline. But I have more authentic memories of Toomey than that. I knew him forty years ago when I was a youthful curate at Saint Victor's Parish in West Hollywood. To me, he was all the things one could associate with a Catholic layman, an actor who epitomized the very best in the Motion Picture Industry.

I once introduced Regis to the members of the Altar and Rosary Society as "an actor who is a Catholic." He didn't like that description and pointed out that he preferred being a "Catholic who is an actor." Being Catholic came first in Toomey's priorities. And his wasn't just a nominal affiliation with the Church. He attended daily Mass and took an active part in all our parochial functions.

He lived with his wife in a modest little home at 1257 Sunset Plaza Drive. Jobs were hard to find in the industry–even for a man of his stature. We always knew when Regis was working because he tithed on

every pay-check he ever received.

Regis was a native of Pittsburgh. Born on August 13, 1898, he did graduate work in drama at the Carnegie Institute of Technology. Initially he wanted to be a lawyer and he looked the part of a jurist in his always neatly-tailored suits. But he signed on temporarily with a vaudeville act and later decided to make the stage his career.

He toured England in George M. Cohan's "Little Nelly Kelly" and, in 1928, he appeared with Chester Morris in "Alibi," the first all-talking melodrama. Three years later he played opposite Clara Bow in "Kick In." Once he let me page through his scrapbook, where there were playbills of his starring roles in "Spellbound," "The Bishop's Wife," "Show Boat" and "Voyage to the Bottom of the Sea."

In television, Regis often played a priest or a policeman. He appeared in several series, including "Dante's Inferno," "Hey, Mulligan" and "Petticoat Junction." He often played the victim of screen violence. "I die well," he once said. He was "killed" so often that he wondered if he qualified as the "mortician's 'Man of the Year'."

Cecil B. De Mille once asked Regis to play a part in "Union Pacific" where he would be terminated by Anthony Quinn. He said it wasn't all that bad because he died in Barbara Stanwyck's arms. "If you gotta go, that's as good a way as any."

Regis had reached the grand age of ninety-three when he died peacefully at the Motion Picture Hospital in Woodland Hills. He played his screen and stage roles well, but he really excelled in his private life. For what you saw was what he was—a role model for contemporary Catholics.

ROGER WAGNER
(1914-1992)

Martin Bernheimer, music critic for the *Los Angeles Times*, said that Roger Wagner was something of a genius on the podium, and a splendidly feisty old walrus off it. He knew how to blend vocal sounds with uncanny flexibility, sensuality, color and point. He was a showman *par excellence* and, luckily, his generous ego was matched by his talent.

Born at Le Puy, France, Wagner orginally wanted to be a priest. At the age of seventeen, however, he decided to pursue a career in music. He spent five years studying organ and researching Gregorian chant. Coming to Los Angeles, Wagner sang in the MGM Studio chorus in the mid-1930s, where he worked with Jeanette MacDonald and Nelson Eddy in the film "Naughty Marietta."

Later he served as organist and music director for Saint Joseph's Church, a post he occupied for over thirty years. Annual choral concerts attracted music lovers to downtown Los Angeles and led to Wagner's selection as supervisor of youth choruses for the Los Angeles Bureau of Music.

He established the Los Angeles Youth Concert which evolved into the Roger Wagner Chorale in 1948. The chorale toured Europe and Latin America, sang for movies and even performed at rock concerts. Wagner served as guest conductor with choruses around the world and was often accompanied by his wife Janice and their three children.

An authority on medieval and Renaissance music, Wagner wrote scholarly essays and engaged in teaching for several decades on the UCLA faculty. He was noted for identifying such talented opera stars as Marilyn Horne and Marni Nixon.

Praised by critics as a conductor who drew rich sounds from his singers, Wagner possessed the flair and energy of a showman. He was passionate about music and demanding of those who worked with him. Possessed with a quick, frequently wicked wit, Wagner's considerable charm was easily matched by his acerbic tongue. More often than not, his sarcasm was benign, such as when he greeted a sing-along audience with this admonition "I hope you're in better voice than you were last year."

After a 1957 appearance at New York's Town Hall, music critic Howard Taubman called Wagner's group "a highly disciplined ensemble which can cope with anything." Leopold Stokowski observed that "there are supremely great choruses in England and Italy, but yours is second to none in the world."

In 1964, Wagner co-founded the Master Chorale, an aggregation of more than a hundred professional and amateur singers. That group functioned as a Los Angeles-based group, while the separate Roger Wagner Chorale, with fewer singers, concentrated on touring.

Upon his retirement in 1986, Roger Wagner was given the title "music director laureate." In later years, Wagner continued working as his health permitted. By the time he died in Dijon, France, on September 17, 1992, Wagner had become a nationally acclaimed music figure whose career spanned nearly five decades.

Referred to by one writer as a "mercurial conductor," Roger Wagner was a dominant figure in American choral music. There was a

"priestly" ingredient in his work which gave the talented musician a unique status in the world's entertainment capital.

CONSULTATIVE BODIES

REGIONAL AND PAROCHIAL COUNCILS

By 1974, a fair number of parishes in the Archdiocese of Los Angeles had already established parochial councils. "Shared responsibility is the reality of a new age in the Church" was the theme of a message by Timothy Cardinal Manning endorsing the movement. He said that such sharing "allows for the involvement of all the faithful" and was typical of the early Church. "No superficial attempt to capture this spirit will suffice" he said. "The parish council is an excellent forum for the development and expression of these gifts by which all things are re-stored in Christ."

Today each of the five regions in the Archdiocese of Los Angeles has a regional pastoral council which addresses the common goals, concerns, challenges and the sharing of resources. Their goals are:

* greater participation of all members of the Church through consultation and collaborative ministry;

* collaboration between clergy, religious and laity in setting direction and vision for the local Church;

* the development and support of effective Parish Pastoral Councils;

* the development and support of the Archdiocesan and Regional Pastoral Councils;

* the development and support of Parish Finance Councils.

ARCHDIOCESAN AND PAROCHIAL FINANCE COUNCIL

The notion of an archdiocesan financial advisory board dates back to the McIntyre era when the cardinal singled out and utilized the talents of a host of people prominent in the local business community. In one of his earliest decisions on June 11, 1970, then Archbishop Timothy Manning asked six people to serve as a small Advisory Committee "from whom we might seek counsel on financial matters." That group met several times annually throughout his tenure and their imprint is plainly evident on a variety of programs affecting the four counties comprising the Archdiocese of Los Angeles.

A formal Archdiocesan Finance Council was inaugurated in March of 1986, as the key financial advisors to the Archbishop of Los Angeles. The council was mandated to meet once a month. Members were given five year terms which were renewable.

Each year the Finance Council prepares a budget of income and expenditure over the coming year for the governance of the archdiocese. The payments and objectives of the Council were to advise in developing and implementing.

a). The ideals and principles upon which the Catholic Church was founded and for which it stands;

b). The effective administration and general welfare of the archdiocese, its clergy, and its personnel;

c). The advancement and reputation of the archdiocese within the sphere of influence of the individual members of the Council;

d.) The means necessary to provide adequate financial support for the archdiocese;

e). Such other and additional purposes and objectives as consistent with the foregoing.

The Church recognizes the extent of the responsibility that goes with fiscal management of the various operations that constitute the typical parish. This was provided for by Canon 537 which requires every parish to maintain a Finance Council to assist the pastor in his duties of administering the temporal goods of the parish.

In May of 1998, the 150 member archdiocesan Pastoral Council voted unanimously to endorse formation of parish financial councils in the 207 parish Archdiocese of Los Angeles.

CLERGY MISCONDUCT OVERSIGHT BOARD

In 1994, the cardinal formed a Sexual Abuse Advisory Board. Its purpose was to provide advice to the Vicar for Clergy in dealing with complaints of abuse and in refining policies and practices. The Board consisted of pastors as well as priests, psychologists, social workers, attorneys and victims or parents of victims. The Vicar for Clergy presented the factual situations to the Board using pseudonyms for the accused priests and victims. The Board discussed each case and offered its wisdom, usually by consensus, but did not make a formal recommendation. Instead, the advice of the various members of the Board was conveyed by the vicar to the archbishop. The question of a return to ministry remained a judgment of the archbishop based on the recommendations of therapists and the Board and on the ability of the archdiocese to monitor the priest's activities.

Eight years later, Cardinal Mahony established a Clergy Misconduct Oversight Board headed by retired Presiding Superior Court Judge Richard Byrne. Expanding the functions of the earlier advisory panel, the new board, composed of thirteen members representing a broad spectrum of the community, was given new authority to review and strengthen all existing programs to end sexual abuse.

The Board is now an entity directly answerable to the archbishop with formal written recommendations. All cases of sexual misconduct by clergy are presented to the Board. The Board's meetings and records, including its recommendations, are strictly confidential.

When an allegation is received, the accuser is directed to the archdiocese's Coordinator for Victim Assistance. Civil authorities are notified, and the accused is informed of the allegation. The case is brought before the Board, which receives a report of each allegation lodged against a priest or deacon. The Board reviews all the relevant information and may request additional information as necessary.

Among other things, the Board makes written recommendations to the archbishop concerning:

* Compliance with California's child sexual abuse reporting laws;

* Whether the needs of the victim or victims are being addressed and pastoral outreach has been extended to every victim and his or her family;

* The type of notice to be given to the parish staff and community.

As of February 1, 2004, the Board had twenty-eight meetings. It had reviewed thirty-seven cases of reported abuse of minors, the vast majority of which happened before 1987. The Board's recommendations have been instrumental in the decision-making of the cardinal and other archdiocesan officials.

Policies on sexual abuse remain under regular review, with an eye to considering "best practices" around the country that could enhance practices in the archdiocese. Recently three former FBI special agents were hired to assist the archdiocese with investigations.

"SAFEGUARDING THE CHILDREN PROGRAM"

As a response to what future historians will surely classify as the "worst scandal ever in the American Catholic Church," the Archdiocese of Los Angeles adopted a "Safeguarding the Children Program" in 2002 whereby victims harmed by sexual abuse at the hands of priests, religious, deacons or other ministers of the Church could obtain therapy and spiritual direction.

Though the scandal touched most areas of the Catholic Church in the United States, it affected the Archdiocese of Los Angeles more severely than many other places because of the sheer numbers of people comprising the largest ecclesial jurisdiction in the country.

In the morgues of news media, is a mountain of materials tracing the evolvement of the scandal from its outset as it unfolded in the newspapers, magazines, journals, radio reports and television commentaries. With the passage of time, a future sociologist-historian will be able to prepare a study of what transpired and how it played out in the nation as a whole and the archdiocese in particular. Even at this early stage, norms adopted and implemented by the National Conference of Catholic Bishops have taken hold whereby the Church is dealing aggressively with this problem.

While a single case of this malady is reprehensible, it needs to be said that the problem is not as rampant as newspaper and television reports would indicate. Statistics are few, but one survey of 2,400 priests in the Archdiocese of Chicago over a forty-year period puts the percentage rate for all kinds of sexual misbehavior at 1.8%, which is considerably beneath the incidence in the general population. Priests are human beings and, as such, they reflect all the traits, good and bad, that enhance or taint human nature.

Gary Schoener, a nationally recognized expert on sexual abuse, expressed a widely-accepted opinion that "true pedophilia is very rare among all clergy, and now there is no evidence that it is more common among clergy than laypersons."

And it should be observed that sexual abuse of young people is not just a Catholic problem. The *Christian Science Monitor* reported on April 5, 2002, that most American Churches being hit with the child sexual abuse allegations are Protestant, and most of the alleged abusers are not members of the clergy or staff, but Church volunteers.

Though comparative data is not readily available, there are indications that this is not a problem just in the Church. For example, the Gallup Organization reported that 1.3 million children were assaulted in 1995. Most instances of abuse take place in families, where it remains a hidden but very real problem. According to Dr. Garth A. Rattray, "about 85 percent of the offenders [of child sexual abuse] are family members, babysitters, neighbors, family friends or relatives."

A second and troublesome aspect of this scandal have been attempts made over the years by bishops and others of "covering up" the whole matter. To some extent, that is true. In their defense, up until fairly recent times, most psychologists have believed that pedophilia was treatable. Now we are told there is no cure.

In earlier times, acting on what was the best available medical and psychological advice, a number of pedophiliacs were sent to treatment and then some few were put back into active service. Belatedly, the bishops are better informed and have adopted a zero tolerance for these cases. We can be assured, however, that critics will keep recalling the well-intentioned mistakes of the past.

Roger Cardinal Mahony and other members of the hierarchy have openly acknowledged "the failure of bishops and other Church leaders to deal wisely with this misconduct." The president of the Catholic League has noted that "there is much blame to go around". Among the culprits are some priests, many therapists, some lawyers, some alleged victims and some in the media.

Unfortunately, down through the ages, there have been scandals, indiscretions and outright crimes perpetrated by the clergy in almost every century. Today's scandals, bad as they are, are simply the latest manifestations of the power of evil in the world.

The French king once took Cardinal Richelieu to task for not complying with one of his directives. He yelled at Richelieu "Your Eminence, I will destroy the Church if it doesn't comply with my wishes." The cardinal smiled and said: "Your Majesty, our priests have been trying to do that since apostolic times and have been unsuccessful."

Christians are reminded that from arid deserts will come streams of running water and out of the deepest darkness will come the light of God's peace and good news. Darkness gives place to sunlight in the early hours of every day.

This horrible scandal will pass, but it will probably take a long time for its wounds to heal because communications today are immediate and universal. The Lord has promised to be with His poor, mud-splattered Church until the end of time. Forgive your priests, pray for them and encourage vocations. For some inexplicable plan of Divine Providence, priests are designated ministers of the sacraments, which are the normal means for communicating God's graces to His people. God has chosen to publicize the sins of His chosen people from the time of David, the King. Even among Christ's innermost apostolic family, one of the twelve denied Him, another doubted Him and a third betrayed Him. But the early Church was strengthened by the scar tissue of those unpleasantries.

Tomorrow will be a better day!

SYNODS

Since pre-Christian times, the term "Synod" has referred to a meeting or assembly. Tertullian introduced the term into the West as a means of describing Christian gatherings at which ecclesial matters were discussed.

Since the 17th century, the term Synod has been exclusively reserved for diocesan meetings, and that's how "Synod" was used in the 1917 Code of Canon Law. Canonically, a "Synod" is defined as a legitimate assembly of clergymen convoked by a bishop for the purpose of discussing and adopting (or legislating) measures necessary and useful for the welfare of a diocese.

Our purpose here is not to explain how a Synod functions, why or whether there should be one or what can be expected at its conclusion. Rather, here the concentration is on how the previous eight Synods influenced the Church as we know it today in Southern California.

Prior to 1840, the Church in the Californias was a missionary enterprise presided over by a small cadre of Franciscan friars under the leadership of a *presidente* who derived his authority and legitimacy from an "apostolic college" whose purpose and operation was minutely spelled out by the *Laws of the Indies*. Despite stupendous challenges, 142 friars established twenty-one frontier outposts along California's *El Camino Real* in what was then the Rim of Christendom. Those beleaguered and homesick missionaries baptized nearly one hundred thousand Native Americans in a period of seventy-one years.

With the premature secularization of the missions and the gradual entry into California of Europeans, Americans and others, the Church needed a wholly new operational format. As early as 1836, the few remaining friars asked the Mexican Government to petition the Holy See for diocesan status. Pope Gregory XVI responded on April 30, 1840, by establishing the Diocese of Both Californias and placing the governance of the huge geographical area in the hands of Francisco Garcia Diego y Moreno, a Mexican friar from the Apostolic College of *Nuestra Señora de Guadalupe in Zacatecas*. The annals testify that the early years of diocesan administration were difficult indeed, with few priests, practically no resources and a handful of missions rapidly falling into decay.

After a dozen years, with a new bishop installed at Monterey, it became obvious that the young diocese, with its long distances and poor communications, desperately needed some basic operational guidelines to insure its very survival. Bishop Joseph Sadoc Alemany, educated in Europe and experienced in the pastoral ministry of mid-America, wisely decided to adopt practices utilized effectively in the eastern part of the United States.

The first of California's ecclesiastical Synods was summoned on February 10, 1852. Bishop Joseph Sadoc Alemany wanted that assemblage to serve jointly as a spiritual exercise and an occasion for discussing necessary diocesan business. The Synod met on Friday, March 19, and remained in session until the 23rd. Meetings were held at Saint Francis Church, on Vallejo Street, in San Francisco. In attendance at this important legislative gathering were Friars Jose Maria Gonzalez Rubio, Jose Jimeno, Francisco Sanchez and eighteen other priests of the California jurisdiction. The decrees that emerged from state's initial Synod were concerned principally with such matters as tithes and clandestine marriages between Catholics and non-Catholics.

The clergymen in attendance also advised the bishop to urge the Mexican government to comply with its stated commitments to the California Church. Among other actions was that touching upon mission property. Alemany noted "all the priests of the diocese, assembled in the diocesan Synod, concur with me in urging the United States Land Commission to confirm to me the Mission properties." Subsequent testimony given by Fray Jose Jimeno, on April 20, 1854, indicates the lengths to which the Synodal participants concerned themselves on this important topic:

> I was present at a conference of the Catholic clergy of California in 1852, which assembled on March 19ᵗʰ at San Francisco. A resolution was adopted requesting and empowering the bishop to apply to the Government for the Church lands through the State.

Similar testimony, from Fray Francisco Sanchez, further corroborates the feeling of the local clergy:

> The Conference of the Catholic clergy of this diocese in 1852 adopted a resolution to claim from the United States Government the churches, sacristies, adjoining buildings, cemeteries, gardens, orchards and vineyards as property of the Church, and one section of land at each mission for the Church, and one league of land at each mission for the care of the Indians.

Though approved in 1854 at the initial Synod for the Archdiocese of San Francisco, the following regulations were actually drafted at Monterey two years earlier:

HOLY DAYS OF OBLIGATION.

January 1	Feast of the Circumcision of Our Blessed Lord;
January 6	Feast of the Epiphany;
February 2	The Purification of the Blessed Virgin Mary;
March 19	Feast of Saint Joseph;
March 25	The Annunciation,
	The Ascension of Our Lord and Savior:
	Corpus Christi,
June 24	Feast of Saint John the Baptist;
June 29	Feast of Saints Peter and Paul;
August 15	Assumption of the Blessed Mother;
September 8	Nativity of Our Lady;
November 1	Feast of All Saints;
December 8	The Immaculate Conception;
December 25	Nativity of Our Lord and Savior.

FEASTS OF DEVOTION.

July 4	Feast of Our Lady, Refuge of Sinners;
August 9	Feast of Saint Emigdius;
December 12	Our Lady of Guadalupe.

DAYS OF FAST.

The Quattuor (i.e. seasonal fast days);
Lent: Vigils of Pentecost, Saint John the Baptist, Saint Peter, All Saints;
Christmas; Fridays and Saturdays of Advent.

FORMS OF MARRIAGE.

Since the decrees of the Council of Trent are promulgated here, the marriage of two Catholics before a civil judge or other witnesses is invalid if there is a priest in the parish: moreover they fall under excommunication reserved to the Bishop or Vicar General. But if one of the parties be a heretic and validly baptized and there be no other canonical impediment the marriage is valid by concession of Pius IX who extended to this diocese the concession which Benedict XIV made for Holland.

THE CONFESSOR.

The Confessor must examine the penitent in Christian doctrine before First Communion, marriage and Easter duty Communion.

Synodal activity occupied much of Bishop Thaddeus Amat's time during his episcopate. A circular letter was sent to all the priests on February 28, 1862, announcing a diocesan Synod for the second Sunday after Easter. The notification directed that the prayer *Ad Postulandum Gratiam Spiritus Sancti* was to be recited at Mass daily immediately before that already being said for the pope until the conclusion of the Synod. It had been exactly a decade since the first Synod and many new problems faced the Church that only a meeting of this nature could resolve. Fifteen priests were present for the solemn opening on May 4 at the first such gathering of its kind in Los Angeles. Of primary concern were the transitional problems resulting from the diocese's transfer from Mexican to American jurisdiction, together with a more precise definition of disciplinary laws not in accordance with legislation of the provincial councils held at Baltimore. Much consideration was also given to matrimonial cases occasioned by the large influx of non-Catholics into the southern part of the diocese. Secret societies likewise received attention, as did the question of abstinence from meat on certain days. In regard to the last item, it might be pointed out that abstinence had been a troublesome problem for many years, indults having been sought and obtained at various times allowing the use of lard and other commodities in the preparation of foods consumed on Fridays. However, it was not until the 1880s that a final and satisfactory solution of that thorny problem was reached. In fact, parts of the Diocese of Tucson continued to partake of meat on days of abstinence until the middle 1950s, claiming for their justification an old papal indult given to Spain at the expulsion of the Moors. Wakes were no longer to include drinking and dancing, and processions to the church and cemetery were to be more dignified, which meant a prohibition of the customary firing of guns and the lighting of firecrackers. There were to be no further burials within the church itself, despite the long tradition that had accorded this honor to prominent citizens and infants. All liturgical ceremonies were to conform to the rubrics of the *Rituale Romanum*.

Other matters faced the participants of the second Synod. Up to that time, thirteen parishes had been erected; two new ones were in the process of formation with several others in the planning stage. Still, the need for priests remained a paramount problem. On one occasion the bishop noted that:

> From every part of this immense diocese, the people ask for priests to attend to their wants, but all in vain. There are no priests

to be sent to them, there being only sixteen in all the diocese, a number quite insufficient to administer to the spiritual wants of the numerous Catholics.

One of the reasons for Amat's convoking of the Synod was his desire to consult the priests about the forthcoming provincial council at San Francisco, which had been formally announced on September 6. Thus when that meeting opened on October 19, Amat was fully prepared to present the needs of the Church in Southern California to this initial provincial gathering. Amat's typically judicious use of time was exemplified by his itinerary on the way to San Francisco. He traveled through the gold mining town of Aurora and then to Carson City making visitations and administering confirmation. Shortly after his arrival in the Bay City, he issued a circular letter announcing the erection of an association authorized by Rome whose object, he said, was "the protection of the rights of the Holy See, attacked in these times by evil and impious men in order to obtain from heaven, through prayers and alms-giving, the assistance that the Vicar of Christ needs to govern the Church with freedom and independence." Amat urged his people to avail themselves of the indulgences and other privileges available to those promising to pray for the Holy Father during this time of trial. With the publication of his circular letter, Amat's attention was concentrated on the business of the provincial meeting, which lasted for several days. It was the first such meeting and the bishops expressed the hope that it would set a precedent for future gatherings where the problems of the Church in California could be discussed.

One of Amat's methods of informing his people about meetings such as that held at San Francisco was the circulation of pastoral letters. On May 7, 1865, for example, he issued a letter calling attention to the approaching golden jubilee of Pope Pius IX's ordination and repeating his earlier request for prayers to sustain the Holy Father. Amat attributed the persecution of the pope to his strenuous position as the champion of truth and justice, which had been the characteristic quality of his pontificate. In another pastoral, published early in 1869, the bishop noted the appropriateness of directing "a few admonitions, regarding some of the principal points that may affect Christian obligation." His presentation of doctrine emphasized that the Church, as the guardian and depository of the faith must go forth not to a single point in the globe, but to the whole world, always preaching not to individuals but to everyone.

In a tone reminiscent of our own day, Amat stated that the Church teaches what Christ teaches; her rules are His rules; her ways are Christ's ways. He went on to speak of the sad plight of the pope but pointed out that suffering seemed to be a characteristic of the rulers of Christendom. "There can be no true liberty, progress and civilization," he concluded, "without the fear of God and submission both to Him and to them by whom He governs the world in temporal and spiritual concerns."

The bishop used his pastorals to promulgate several of the earlier Synodal decrees, noting the duties, not only of the laity but also of the clergy. "Your duties to them (pastors) are their rights, and their duties to you are also your rights." In the matter of the laity's generosity, he said he could not refrain from expressing gratitude and praise for the zeal that some had shown in contributing to the poor and promoting the glory of God. And yet, he observed, poverty was still widespread and therefore, they had "only to look to the actual state of your churches throughout the diocese and to the several localities which actually need a place of worship to see the needs that still face them."

In 1869, Bishop Amat had summoned the third Synod, which met at the Plaza Church of *Nuestra Señora de Los Angeles* in Los Angeles. Among other matters discussed was the drafting of a diocesan catechism for the instruction of children. Many of the pastors were still using the old *doctrina* which had been so successful in earlier times, but it had been prepared for strictly missionary areas and Southern California was gradually developing in a way that set it apart from the earlier times. It was also decided at the Synod that an annual collection would be taken up for the maintenance of diocesan orphanages, which were experiencing anxiety because of inadequate funding.

Amat asked for suggestions regarding the approaching Vatican Council, telling the priests that he would be their spokesman at the conclave later that year. One of the questions settled was that of stole fees, which up to that time had not been regulated in the diocese. Amat set the general formula, which he later had printed for distribution, and originated the laudable custom of having all such fees accrue to the parishes and not the individual priests as was done in the eastern United States. Finally, a prohibition against intermarriage with Protestants was emphasized. The scarcity of marriageable women had led many Anglo-American Protestants to seek out the daughters of Hispanic Catholic families. Catholics were advised to avoid participating in lay associations, secret societies and social outings. The Odd Fellows and the Sons of Temperance were mentioned specifically. Priests were advised to discourage their people from attending social events sponsored by non-Catholics. It would be another century before the concept of ecumenism was approved and then encouraged by the Church.

The fourth Synod, convened in 1876 in the Church of Our Lady of the Angels, issued fewer decrees. It lasted until May 7, when the bishop imparted the apostolic blessing and adjourned the meeting. In addition to reaffirming the earlier decrees, the bishop officially acknowledged and approved regulations adopted at the provincial council held at San Francisco. Several liturgical admonitions were contained in the statutes, most of which had previously gone unenforced because of the missionary status of the diocese. Nonetheless, Amat insisted that these observations were only becoming in a jurisdiction, which had now risen to some degree of stability within the framework of the American Church. The fourth Synod was the last in which prohibitions were emphasized. Thereafter, the bishops concentrated on positive measures.

Nor was Bishop Amat's knowledge of councilor matters confined to California. On March 19, 1866, Archbishop Martin Spalding asked him to submit a schema for the forthcoming plenary council, which was scheduled to open at Baltimore on the first Sunday in October. As apostolic delegate to the council, Spalding was anxious to have opinions from the nation's bishops especially those versed in legal matters. In July, Amat sent a circular to all the priests of the diocese informing them of the coming council in Baltimore. The bishop announced his own plans to attend the council and requested that each parish begin a triduum of prayers for the fruitful deliberations of its participants. The *Sacramento* sailed from San Francisco on August 18 with Archbishop Alemany, Bishop Amat and Bishop Eugene O'Connell and three other priests. The voyage took them to Panama where they traveled overland and then up the Atlantic seaboard to New York.

The council at Baltimore formally opened on October 7. Several items on the agenda pertained especially to the Far West, including the recommendation of Alemany that the Vicariate of Marysville be elevated to diocesan status. Of more immediate concern to Catholics in Southern California was the suggestion that a seminary be set up in Barcelona for the education of priests destined to labor in Spanish-speaking areas of the United States. It was a favorite project of Amat's and one on which he had been working several years. He read a letter from Alessandro Cardinal Barnabo endorsing the plan. Nothing came of this idea at the time but the matter came up a year later in Amat's correspondence with Spalding. He then said:

> If you thought proper, Most Reverend Archbishop, to devise some means by which this could come to the knowledge of the prelates of these States as several of them labor under great difficulties for want of missionaries; and according to all appearances, in Spain we could get a good supply, and without great expense. They could likewise be trained in a manner suitable for our missions; I doubt not, that some might be willing to join in the undertaking ...

No definite action was taken by the bishops, however, and the question remained in abeyance throughout Amat's life. The fourth and last public session of the council was held in Baltimore's historic Cathedral of the Assumption on Sunday, October 21. A solemn Mass was celebrated by Archbishop John Odin, C.M., of New Orleans attended by President Andrew Johnson and several of his cabinet members.

Small though the diocesan educational system was, by 1889 the program was capable of accommodating all youngsters interested in obtaining a Catholic education. For that reason, in the fifth Synod for the Diocese of Monterey-Los Angeles, held in July of that year, Bishop Francis Mora directed that "all Catholic parents must send their children to parochial schools, unless at home or in other Catholic schools (e.g., academies), they are sufficiently informed or, if for a cause judged worthy by the bishop, and with remedial compensations observed, they are allowed to send them elsewhere."

The question of another diocesan Synod surfaced during a meeting of the diocesan consultors on April 25, 1912. But it was decided, by virtue of the about-to-be published *Code of Canon Law*, that it would be better to wait so as to avoid duplicating or rendering inapplicable any part of the Church's broader legislation. During the years after inauguration of a new bishop in 1917, remote plans were afoot to convene a Synod. In October of 1925, Bishop John J. Cantwell informed his advisors that work should begin.

As he approached the end of his first decade as chief shepherd for the Church in California's southland, Bishop Cantwell announced the convocation of yet another Synod, the sixth to be held in the area and the first in forty years.

The Synod provided a superb opportunity for appraising the development of ecclesial growth in the Diocese of Los Angeles-San Diego. Cantwell declared the purpose of the Synod was "to build on what went before." An essay in *The Tidings* noted "it would be unjust to discount the splendid work of the energetic and self-sacrificing pioneers, whose labors were nothing less than heroic."

While acknowledging that the "foundations of the missionary *padres* are well known" and that "their fame has traveled the world over," *The Tidings* went on to say that "we must not forget the tremendous effort and untiring zeal of those who came after them. During what might be called the Spanish regime, when bishops and priests left their distant homes across the seas to come to California, the trying work was carried on amid the destruction wrought by the devastating hand of mission secularization." But then there dawned a brighter era. As the Spanish-speaking clergy gradually gave way to their English-speaking counterparts "Spain gave fewer of her sons to the California Church and Ireland, that great mother of priests, became a never failing source of clerical recruits for the far western mission."

In his opening remarks to those attending the 1927 Synod, Bishop Cantwell could not say enough in praise of the area's "glorious pioneers," pointing out that it was upon the foundations they laid, in the midst of trials and difficulties, that the mighty superstructure of the strong ecclesial establishment we know today was built. After enumerating the deeds and virtues of "a score of priests, many of whom were with us until recently and all of whom are still fresh in our memories," Cantwell said that "to these worthy pioneers and to all their collaborators, our hearts turn with deep feelings of gratitude for the unceasing labors of themselves and their faithful people which prepared the way for the glories of today."

One era builds upon another. The growth of the Church in the southland after 1889 had been nothing short of phenomenal. A local newspaper reported that the increase of population brought "with it activity and expansion without parallel in Catholic annals. Increased material facilities, coupled with intense spiritual vigor has been achieved under the direction

of a young and energetic shepherd whose capacity for leadership and untiring zeal are a source of wonderment to all."

In *The Tidings* for December 16, 1927, the statistics of ecclesial growth between 1889 and 1927 were carefully catalogued, along with the interesting observation that only one priest who attended the earlier convocation was still alive, the jovial Father Patrick Grogan, patriarchal pastor of San Buenaventura Mission. It is doubtful if Grogan or any of the others who processed into Saint Vibiana's Cathedral for the 1889 Synod "dreamed in moments of wildest reverie what marvels the future held." The remarkable growth of the Church in Southern California had only just begun.

When the Synod of 1889 was held, diocesan government in California was barely forty-seven years old. Yet, within less than a half century, the Church in that area had "come of age," ready to take its place within the family of American religious communities. In 1889, there were only thirty-two priests, secular and religious, laboring in sixteen parishes and looking after twenty-two mission stations scattered around the vast diocese. When Cantwell came to the Diocese of Monterey-Los Angeles in 1917, there were 234 priests. The number of parishes had grown to ninety-three, with 109 mission stations. The next decade saw a further increase, with 405 priests (272 secular and 133 religious) working in 195 parishes. The most striking increase had occurred within the area covered by the City of Los Angeles. The three parishes in 1887 had become twenty-five in 1917 and seventy by 1927.

By 1927, there were seventy-two parish schools with 16,483 pupils in attendance and eleven diocesan high schools, with 1,717 students. Colleges, academies, orphanages, etc. numbered twenty-three, with 3,672 youngsters on the rolls. Statistics recorded the overall number of youngsters receiving Catholic instruction at 21,872.

Those who researched the figures used for an article appearing in *The Tidings* for December 16, 1927, were conservative about their prognostications for the future. Yet, experience had taught them "to accept willingly the predictions which in other places would be laughed to scorn." Hence, they confidently predicted "we of the present generation expect even greater marvels of expansion to follow."

The 240 statutes in the 1927 Synod, written in classical Latin, were arranged in an order analogous to the *Codex Juris Canonicis*, with eight chapters dealing with clerics, religious, laity, sacraments, holy places, Divine Worship, magisterial teaching and temporalities. The fifty-three page book containing the statutes was carefully compiled and indexed by Rome-trained Father Henry Gross.

A commentary on the 1927 Synod concluded with these words: "Who can measure the glories of the future or weigh the amount of material construction and spiritual vigor that will follow, when the solid foundations that are being laid today will have been built upon by the generations to come." Those statements proved modest indeed in the years that followed.

Among the suggestions made by Roman officials when Los Angeles was elevated to archiepiscopal status in 1936 was that a Synod be convened. It being wartime, preparations were kept to a minimum. The seventh of the Synods for the Church in Southern California was held during the annual clergy conference at Saint John's Seminary in Camarillo in July of 1942. Among the nine amplifications of the earlier decrees was legislation regulating clergymen attendance at horse races, ownership of automobiles, mixed marriages and technical advice for the Motion Picture Industry. Archdiocesan taxes were also adjusted to reflect the economical needs of the times.

By the late 1950s, the Archdiocese of Los Angeles was well on its way to becoming the largest ecclesial jurisdiction in the United States. Clearly it was time to update and expand the Synodal legislation of previous years. Imitating the example of Pope John XXIII, who had called a Synod for the Diocese of Rome prior to the opening of Vatican Council II, James Francis Cardinal McIntyre announced plans for a Synod in the Archdiocese of Los Angeles in June of 1959. During the ensuing months, a host of committees met and discussed a wide range of potential legislation. Several hundred priests and religious, together with dozens of consultants, were involved in the process. The draft statutes were read to the clergy in three different parts of the four county Archdiocese.

The complete statutes of earlier Synods were reviewed by the committees to which particular parts were assigned, and ample opportunity was afforded for the presentation of new material, as well as the omission of obsolete considerations.

On December 12, 1960, the feast of Our Lady of Guadalupe, more than 700 priests gathered at Saint Vibiana's Cathedral where the completed statutes were presented to and then formally approved by the cardinal. The new statutes specified the rules and recommendations that would thereafter govern the conduct of the clergy, the religious and the laity within the archdiocese in the light of contemporary conditions. Relationships between the priest and his people were defined and guidance was offered for enriching the spiritual life of the priests and the souls entrusted to their ministry.

Precise provisions were made for the pastoral care of Catholics from the cradle to the grave, with regulations touching every phase of life from the rebirth of Baptism to the solemnity of Christian burial. Among the synodal statutes were specific rules governing marriage preparations, pastoral care of the sick and infirm, the conduct of parish schools, catechetical instructions and the dissemination of Catholic literature.

Fresh encouragement was given to such wholesome customs as the blessing of mothers after childbirth, the practice of daily Mass, reception of Holy Communion and the recitation of the Rosary for the dead in the parish church. New impetus was given to the growth of parochial societies such as the Holy Name, the Legion of Mary, St. Vincent de Paul, and the Sodality of Our Lady, and to those organizations that aid the Propagation of the Faith.

The 181 statutes adopted were made available in a forty-three-page booklet sent to the clergy early in 1961. Though there was little new in the legislation, it evoked some clerical grumbling that the 1927 prohibition against priests' attendance at horse racing was re-stated, along with the penalty of suspension for violations.

On several occasions during the archiepiscopate of Timothy Cardinal Manning, suggestions surfaced about a Synod. Though he was a canon lawyer, Manning exhibited little interest in such a convocation, arguing that "first we need to get over and assimilate the (directives of) Vatican Council II and all the regulations following in its wake."

While the Synod as presently structured is deeply rooted in canonical history, the 1983 Code of Canon Law extended participation at the Synod to specified "members of the Christ's Faithful." Earlier, only priests were allowed to participate, at least in the final stages, and that made good sense since priests were the ones most closely affected.

American bishops especially have embraced the consultation process in a way that gives new meaning to the whole notion of collegiality Yet it needs to be pointed out, in the final analysis, that the local bishop is the sole legislator. The duty of all others is to provide him with an abundance of evidence and facts that he can use in drafting the final text which will then be forwarded to the Holy See.

THE SYNOD OF 2003

The 2003 Synod had its origins in the Apostolic Letter of Pope John Paul II, released on the Feast of the Epiphany, 2001, wherein the Holy Father issued the invitation to proclaim in word and deed the mission of Christ and the Spirit.

As expressed in *The Tidings*, Los Angeles is the largest and fastest growing archdiocese in the United States of America, with an estimated five million Catholics within its borders. Parishes in the archdiocese report serving two and a quarter million Catholics directly, roughly half of that population. Moreover, parish reports indicate that the average number of Catholics served was almost eight thousand.

However, estimates based on ethnicity as reported by the U.S. Census indicate that the average number of Catholics per parish is close to nineteen thousand. Parishes are making enormous efforts, and many are quite successful, but the challenge remains ever greater. Eighty-seven parishes report serving more than ten thousand people. However, the above census estimates show that one hundred and ten

parishes have a population of more than twenty thousand Catholics. Non-participating/inactive Catholics constitute the largest "religious" body in the United States.

Like the Church in many countries, there are many baptized persons in the archdiocese who, for a variety of reasons, are not active in the life of their parishes or the local Church.

Roger Cardinal Mahony said that what is called for is a major reorientation in our thinking about ministry as well as in our ministerial practice. At the conclusion of a Pastoral Letter, the cardinal convoked a Synod for the Archdiocese. The Synod was an invitation for the People of God to engage in a process of prayer, dialogue, discernment and decision to meet the needs of the people in the archdiocese at this time.

The Cardinal went on TV say that Catholics in California's southland are living amidst the third great wave of immigration in this country. The first and second waves brought immigrants primarily to the shores of the Eastern seaboard in the first two centuries of this nation. The third wave, growing in strength and numbers since 1970, has brought peoples from Mexico, Central America, South America and the Far East to the California shores.

We count this as an enormous gift, rich in vitality and diversity. But the gift also brings with it huge challenges, not least of which is that of language, as well as that of reaching out to serve diverse cultures, respecting the other, and deeply appreciating, not merely tolerating, difference and uniqueness. With these changes there has also been the pain involved in the changing composition of existing parishes.

While recognizing that "lay ministries" are flourishing in unprecedented numbers, the lessening presence of priests required drastic steps to the contemporary challenges of ecclesial life.

During the synodal process, those involved at the parochial and regional level spoke out and their voices have been heard. What have they said? Above all they stressed the need for evangelization:

To announce in word and deed the Good News of the Lord,
The time of God's favor,
The transformation of the world,
And the coming of the Reign of God when truth, holiness, justice, love and peace will prevail.

Through prayer, dialogue, discernment and decision is at the heart of the synod, six pastoral initiatives emerged above all others. These will give shape to the Archdiocese Los Angeles as we seek to live in the communion of the Spirit, able to respond to the changing needs of the people in the archdiocese, the mission is:

to those who are not evangelized and to those Catholics who are inactive or alienated from the Church;
to the vast numbers of people who have come to our shores;
to the vast number of those Catholics who no longer claim Church affiliation;
to youth and young adults;
to ourselves, who are still in need of conversion to the Gospel;
and to the generations that will succeed us.

With the acceptance of the synodal directives, a permanent office of the Synod was established and it will continue over the years ahead to implement the wishes and conclusions of those who participated in the process.

ETHNIC
COMPOSITION

POLYGLOT ARCHDIOCESE

The Archdiocese of Los Angeles probably has the most diverse Catholic population of any jurisdiction in North America and perhaps in the whole world. One writer has suggested that this diversity explains why the area is "so precious in the sight of the Lord."

According to the latest figures, there are ninety-nine ethnic groups represented in the Archdiocese of Los Angeles. Holy Mass is offered regularly in thirty-seven languages and occasionally in twelve additional languages.

Surely the situation has changed appreciably since 1924, when the relatively small Los Angeles boasted of sixteen foreign language newspapers reaching approximately 250,000 persons.

The diversity of peoples in this area of the Lord's vineyard is hardly a recent development. On April 27, 1927, Bishop John J. Cantwell wrote to the Apostolic Delegate in Mexico telling him that "we have here a large number of refugees, lay and cleric, and I think that this diocese in the past few years has become the largest Mexican diocese outside of Mexico."

Fourteen years later, Cantwell, by then the Archbishop of Los Angeles, addressed a letter to the clergy in which he observed that "California, and our own City of Los Angeles, have been joined by many bonds to the great country of Mexico." He went on to say that "the large number of Mexicans who have come to California, and indeed to the Southwest," have brought "the finest traditions of their own land in music, in art, in sculpture and in painting."

Cantwell, preparing for a trip to Mexico's Shrine of Our Lady of Guadalupe, invited those interested in accompanying him to participate in this tribute to the "Empress of the Americas." He said that "a visit by our people to the City of Mexico would be a gracious compliment to the hierarchy and Catholics of a country that has sent so many of its children to California."

During the mid years of his tenure, James Francis Cardinal McIntyre was confronted with the beginnings of sizable ethnic immigration by peoples who brought with them many of the same problems and challenges that earlier faced Catholic leadership on the eastern

Nation

"The New Ellis Island"

Immigrants from all over change the beat, bop and character of Los Angeles

By 10:30 a.m., the Northwest Orient jumbo jet was in its berth at Los Angeles International Airport, simmering down after the 13-hour flight from Manila. It had disgorged its captain, crew and 284 passengers, including the unbearably excited young Santiagos.

The five siblings, ages 24 to 33, were about to join their parents, whom they had last seen in 1979. They stepped through the passport stamper's booth and up to the desk of the Immigration and Naturalization Service official, a sympathetic woman, for fingerprinting and more stamps. They carried their things (a portable tape player, a jar of noodles soaked in vinegar, bath slippers) past the Department of Agriculture inspector and out. The young Santiagos had never been

to Los Angeles, let alone the U.S. And yet, as of last Thursday afternoon, they were here to stay.

Los Angeles is being invaded. Two hours after the Santiagos arrived a Pan American jet landed with 76 Vietnamese refugees on board. And all those immigrants standing in anxious L.A. airport queues, mainly Asians, are only the western flank. At the INS checkpoints to the south in San Diego, nearly 2,500 Mexicans, Salvadorans and Guatemalans are waved through each month. Many more, perhaps 50 times the legal arrivals, slip quietly over the border.

Each immigrant, whether he crossed the Pacific on a 747 or the Rio Grande on a compatriot's shoulders, is bristling with old-fashioned ambitions. Each harbors a plan, or at least the rough vision of a better life. More and more head for the new ethnic metropolis. "Los Angeles," says Rand Corporation Demographer Kevin McCarthy, "has become the natural embarkation point to the U.S. There's no question that it is the new Ellis Island." L.A. has no central processing facility like Ellis Island, or any Pacific Coast Statue of Liberty, no romantic symbol for every country's immigrants. But during 1982, according to Rand estimates, more than 90,000 foreign immigrants settled there, and since 1970, more than 2 million. The exotic multitudes are altering the collective beat and bop of L.A., the city's smells and colors. And a deeper transformation is under way.

Immigrants have landed there before, of course, though never in such numbers. "We find ourselves suddenly threatened," said the last Mexican Governor of California, in 1846, "by hordes of Yankee emigrants . . . whose progress we cannot arrest." Southern California in particular has always been full of transplants becoming Americans.

TIME, JUNE 13, 1983

seaboard. In addition, immigration from the Orient began in the 1970s. In every case, McIntyre endeavored to obtain lingually and culturally sensitive and qualified priests to look after their spiritual needs, all the while insisting that, eventually the new immigrants should take their place alongside those whose parents or grandparents had come to the United States and/or California in earlier times. While a whole treatise could be written about this fascinating phase of McIntyre's archi-episcopate, there is only room in these pages to cursorily mention the larger groupings.

The chancellor of the Diocese of Monterey-Los Angeles pointed out, in 1921, that "it is the wish of the Holy Father that national churches, as far as possible, be dispensed with in the United States." That being the case, there was little encouragement given to establish-ment of such parochial units in the Southern California jurisdiction.

Like most of his predecessors in the California episcopate, McIntyre did not like, encourage or allow the formation of "national" parishes in Los Angeles. His experience in New York convinced him that such groupings caused far more problems than they solved. He often pointed to downtown Chicago, where earlier generations had built three or four Catholic national churches within blocks of one another. Invariably, as youngsters grew up speaking English, the need and usefulness of such parishes and churches disappeared and neighborhoods were left with empty houses-of-worship. While he encouraged retention of the best old world traditions and lingual diversities, the cardinal felt that the more readily immigrants became Americanized, the sooner they would start moving up the economic ladder.

From 1970 to 1980 Los Angeles County experienced a change of landslide scale in its ethnic composition. For the county as a whole, there was only a six percent increase in population, from 7.04 million to 7.48 million persons. But the population of Spanish (or, inter-changeably, Hispanic) origin increased by 97 percent, from 1.05 million to 2.07 million, while the number of non-Hispanic whites declined 21 percent, from 5.02 million to 3.99 million. Simultaneously the non-Hispanic black population grew by 24 percent reaching 0.93 million, and the non-Hispanic population of all other races (mainly Asians) skyrocketed from 0.23 million to 0.50 million, an increase of 123 per-cent (Southern California Association of Governments, 1984).

Even in the early 1970s the Archdiocese of Los Angeles was fast becoming the most diverse Catholic population of any jurisdiction in the United States, maybe in the whole world. Timothy Cardinal Manning was attuned to these developments, as perhaps few others were. One of his favorite quotations and one which he used often when speaking to newcomers was first uttered by Bishop John J. Cantwell when he addressed the National Association for the Advancement of Colored People in 1921: "Neither your fathers nor yourselves, nor the people whom I represent, have been strangers to intolerance. You and I know full well, to our sorrow be it said, what comes from an intolerant bigotry."

Manning established the practice of having an annual Migrant's Day Mass at Saint Vibiana's Cathedral and he rarely missed being there himself. In 1979, he exhorted those present to "pass on to your children your faith and the fine things of your culture." Addressing them as "My fellow immigrants," he said that "the church was home and haven for all peoples and generations." Noting that there were eighty languages then being spoken in the archdiocese, he pointed out that "all cultures

have different traits and talents and each enriches the nation that receives it. Jesus willed to experience every part of the human story," the cardinal said. "He had no shelter at birth. He moved with his parents to a land whose customs and language they did not know and lived there in a ghetto. Jesus is sanctifying the whole experience of exile and migration." In this nation, materialistic and overly-scientific, the cardinal called on immigrants to show the joy of faith, a dimension of life that money cannot buy.

On another occasion, Manning declared that no one is an illegal alien in the Church. He told a congregation of a thousand people, comprised of sixteen nationalities that "from every point of the compass we come together to create one family. Each one of us has equal rights." He related how recently he had been with the Holy Father in Vancouver, British Columbia:

We had a small private dinner together. He was asking about Los Angeles. I told him that we have eighty-three different languages spoken here and also that there are a large number of undocumented people here. In a beautiful gesture he raised his finger and said: "Undocumented in the state, yes, but not in the Church." There is no such thing as an undocumented person. There is no illegal alien in the Church. Here, we are together. We have a common father, successor to Peter. We go to him and he tells us what in this time and place we must do to give witness to the fact that we are the family of God. With great joy we can tell the large community of Los Angeles that even though we come from every nation under the sun, here in this house we are one family, under one common father, and our mother is the Church.

In 1978, Manning created a vicariate for the Multilingual Apostolate and appointed Father Felix S. Diomartich Episcopal vicar for that ministry. Over the ensuing months, directories were issued containing location of Masses celebrated in different languages, along with a list of priests conversant in various lingual strains for the Sacrament of Reconciliation. Diomartich assured those who felt that this ministry was divisive that "all immigration is destined to be absorbed into the American mainstream."

By the time of his retirement, Manning could point to multilingual churches or centers serving the Chinese, Croatian, Czech, Filipino,

German, Hungarian, Italian, Japanese, Korean, Lithuanian, Polish, Portuguese, and Vietnamese peoples, along with seven Eastern Rites, Nativity of the Blessed Virgin (Ukrainian-Byzantine), Our Lady of Mount Lebanon (Maronite), Our Lady Queen of Martyrs (Armenian), Saint Andrew (Russian-Byzantine), Saint Anne (Melkite-Byzantine) and the Cathedral of Saint Mary (Byzantine-Ruthenian).

By 1987 California had become a haven for immigrants, a new home for the refugees and migrants, a place where people from every continent have come together to fashion a society of the most varied ethnic diversity… "As a result, the Church is truly Catholic in the fullest sense, embracing people and cultures of the widest and richest variety."

The statistics show that by 1995, the Latino population in California was 7.6 million - up by nearly 70% in one decade, to account for about 37.4% of California's population. By 1995, the Asian population increased to 3.8 million or 20% of California's population - up by 140%; and non Hispanic white represented 31%. Meanwhile the Blacks comprise about 3.8%.

In his *Quinquennial Report* for 2004, Roger Cardinal Mahony reported that Los Angeles had become an ethnically diverse city. "In such cultural diversity, where no one is the majority, more than one hundred languages are spoken daily." The pluri-culturalism consists of: 44% Hispanic (Mexican, Salvadoran, Guatemalan and other Latin American countries); 31% Euro-American (European, Canadian and others who identify themselves as "White, non-Latinos"); 15% Asian (Japanese, Chinese, Filipino, Korean, Vietnamese and 47 other nationalities); 10% African-American; 0.4% Native Americans (Indians).

Ethnic groups are served in California's southland by fifty-five priests who have come from all over the world to serve peoples of their nations of origin. Clergy gatherings resemble the General Assembly of the United Nations.

The largest number of foreign-born priests hail from Ireland (105), while twenty-seven come from the Philippines. The next largest groups are from Spain (14), Vietnam (14), Korea (8), India (6) and Italy (6).

During 2004, in an effort to further streamline and update the Church's outreach to non-Anglo Catholics residing in the Archdiocese of Los Angeles, Roger Cardinal Mahony gathered those diverse ethnic ministries under a single coordinator in the person of newly ordained Auxiliary Bishop Oscar A. Solis.

AFRO-AMERICANS

When Pope Paul VI visited the martyrs shrine in Uganda, he reflected on the theme of how Black peoples had enriched "the Church with their unique and treasured gifts of negritude." Indeed that gift was present in the New World from almost the beginning of European penetration. The first Blacks came with the Spanish Explorers like Cabeza de Vaca and there was reportedly a priest with Coronado's expedition in the 1500s.

When the City of *Nuestra Señora de Los Angeles* was established in 1781, its founders were Hispanic peoples of mostly Black and Indian ancestry. One of the area's earliest landowners was Maria Rita Valdez de Villa, a Mexican lady whose grandparents were Blacks.

Shortly after the turn of the last century, Black Catholics were recorded in parochial register books throughout the southland, many of them having migrated from Louisiana. One writer observed in 1918 that "Negros are to be found in almost all the Christian denominations in Los Angeles. There are a large number of Roman Catholics, most of whom are members of the cathedral parish and their numbers are constantly increasing."

One of the more prominent civic figures in those years was Noah Thompson, a Black writer, journalist and politician. His wife, Eloise Bibb Thompson, a devout Catholic, was a poet and writer who often had her work published in *The Tidings*.

Bishop Thomas J. Conaty was highly esteemed by the area's Black Catholics. When he died in 1915, *The California Eagle* noted that "The (Black) race indeed loses one of its staunch friends." In an earlier issue, the editor said that "Bishop Conaty in line with Archbishop John Ireland, James Cardinal Gibbons and others of this great Church have been in the last decade a mighty force in scales of justice for the Negro."

Bishop Carl Fisher working the crowds at a first Communion service.

Conaty's successor was also an outspoken champion. On November 28, 1921, Bishop John J. Cantwell delivered a benchmark address to the N.A.A.C.P. in which he put on record his strong feelings toward the race issue as it affected the local scene. At the same time, Cantwell foresaw new opportunities for missionary work among the Blacks in the United States. His goal was to give those living in Los Angeles "one of the best organized social centers in the country."

When Saint Victor's Center was launched in 1922, Cantwell noted that there would be further openings for Black Catholics as they became aware "of their hopes and aspirations and a fuller development of the fine qualities that characterize their race, a deep religious instinct, love of family life and a devotion to their Church."

In 1927, a large church and a two-story rectory were inaugurated at 53rd Street and Hooper Avenue under the patronage of Saint Odilia.

It was not a center for Blacks alone, as indicated by the census rolls which abounded in Irish and Italian names.

It was also in 1927 that a chapter of the Knights of Saint Peter Claver, a Catholic fraternal society, was established in Saint Patrick's Parish. The first chapter established in the west coast, it became a vibrant organization for Catholic activities in the southland. Though he had provided a fraternal organization for the Blacks, Cantwell was never pleased about their being excluded from other groups. He wrote to Joseph Scott, a prominent Catholic layman, complaining that "there should be a place in the Knights of Columbus for our Negro Catholics." He eventually won his point.

The manifold contributions made by Black Catholics to California is nowhere more evident than in the Hollywood film industry, together with television, night clubs and theaters, all of which attracted Catholic actors and actresses, performers, musicians and other entertainers from other parts of the nation and the world.

As early as 1917, jazz pianist Jelly Roll Morton arrived on the southland scene. Others came in-later years, notably film actor-comedian Steppin Fetchitt (converted to the Catholic Church in the 1930s) actress-singer Ethel Waters, actress Fredi Washington and singer-actress Lena Horne.

Jazz singer Billie Holiday came to Los Angeles in the early 1940s and took an active part in the establishment of the Capitol Records Company in Hollywood. Later she was a popular performer on the night club circuit. Another group who contributed mightily to the arts were the Rene Brothers. Initially, Otis worked as a bricklayer and Leon as a pharmacist. They later started an orchestra and wrote numerous hit songs, including "When the Swallows Come Back to Capistrano."

Other Black Catholics native to Los Angeles were band-singer Ivie Anderson, writer-musician Elizabeth Laura Adams, dancer Carmen de la Vallada and prima ballerina (with the Metropolitan Opera) Janet Collins. Another singer-actress who identified herself with the Catholic Church throughout her life was singer-actress Dorothy Dandridge.

In the mid 1940s, the Catholic Interracial Council was established "to oppose all forms of discrimination directed at minority groups of all races and colors and to make known the Catholic point of view on both legal and extralegal practices of segregation on account of race or color."

Chairman Daniel Marshall spoke to a gathering of the council in February of 1945, assuring his listeners that the superintendent of Catholic Schools for the Archdiocese of Los Angeles "would not permit discrimination in the parochial schools on account of race and color." In 1948, the Catholic Interracial Council was involved in what became a major civil rights victory. Father Joseph della Torre, a priest attached to Saint Patrick's parish in Los Angeles, appealed to the council for assistance in having the state's anti-miscegenation law nullified. A legal case was instituted and tried in the courts. On October 2nd, the California State Supreme Court ruled the law unconstitutional, thus allowing Sylvester Davis, a black, and Andrea Perez, a white, the legal right to marry in a Catholic ceremony.

When President Ronald Reagan and the members of the United States Congress formally approved the designation of Martin Luther King's birthday, January 12, as a national holiday in 1984, Timothy Cardinal Manning used that occasion to issue a pastoral letter on racism in which he called on "all of our two million plus Roman Catholics to reflect on the need for racial harmony." He invited each of the parochial communities in the archdiocese "to pray for the courage to live the principle of human dignity, for we are many people living as one people of faith." Noting that Southern California had been "enriched with a variety of ethnic groups that are like blood transfusions into our culture," he noted with pleasure that "our schools, institutions and parishes have become more aware of and responsive to the needs of what is now a world community. Yet there remains a grave responsibility which rests on us to be advocates of racial harmony. We must uproot and isolate all negative feelings and banish from us all fears of change, all paternalism, all stereotypes and scapegoating. Racial harmony is an imperative. The racial question in all its ramifications, is ultimately a moral/ethical one. The fullness of Christian life cannot exist where racial hatred resides."

Manning had a special place in his list of priorities for the Knights and Ladies of Saint Peter Claver. He once told members attending a national convention that they should be "stand-ins for Christ." Stars in Hollywood have stand-ins who resemble them and stand in their stead while lights and cameras are adjusted. When St. Paul writes of "putting on Christ," he means that we should be stand-ins for Christ "so that our bearing, our language, our actions will show that Christ is walking again among us."

By 1986, California had become one of the states with the largest number of Black Catholics (102,895). On December 29th of that year, Pope John Paul II announced the appointment of a black auxiliary bishop for the Archdiocese of Los Angeles. Father Carl A. Fisher, a Josephite priest, was consecrated auxiliary bishop.

Though their numbers are relatively small in relationship to California's overall population, Black Catholics have made their presence felt in the artistic, social, civic and political sphere of influence. Researchers like John LeFlore are gradually unearthing historical evidence and statistics that confirm the tremendous contributions made by Black Catholics to the Golden State.

The African-American Catholic Center for Evangelization serves approximately 25,000 American Catholics within the Archdiocese of Los Angeles, in collaboration with local parishes and organizations such as the Knights of Peter Claver and the Ladies Auxiliary, to develop and support programs of evangelization and education.

ARMENIANS

The second World War, which resulted in the devastation and displacement of countless millions of people who were uprooted and forced into labor camps and factories all over the countries occupied by Germany, saw thousands of Armenians homeless or destitute in the most primitive living conditions.

A large number of Armenians eventually settled in the East Los Angeles/Montebello area, and they were fraternally received and helped by their fellow Armenians who had been established here for many years.

On December 11, 1951, Father Michael Akian came to Los Angeles and established an Armenian Catholic Community. That same year, upon the invitation of James Francis Cardinal McIntyre, Gregory Cardinal Agaganian, Patriarch of the Armenian Catholics visited and celebrated the Armenian liturgy in the cathedrals of Los Angeles, Fresno, and San Francisco. It was James Francis Cardinal McIntyre who entrusted to them Our Lady Queen of Martyrs, the first Armenian Catholic church in California.

A memorandum in the archives indicates that in 1975 there were 7,000 Armenians in Los Angeles belonging to the eight Orthodox churches. Members of the two major groups were more closely affiliated with the Catholic Armenian rite than they were with each other.

Two years later, a large influx of Armenians mostly from Beirut, came to Los Angeles because of the civil war in their homeland. Estimates put the number at 20,000.

Timothy Cardinal Manning presided at a Mass offered at Our Lady Queen of Martyrs parish in Boyle Heights early in 1985 when the Apostolic Exarch of Armenian Catholics made a visitation to his people in Los Angeles. Manning expressed his "profound respect and reverence for the primacy and beauty of this rite which adorns the Catholic Church. I would beg you who are inheritors of this rite to preserve it, to assist at it, to live it, and to assure that your children do not lose what you have inherited."

In a visitation report with the pastor of Our Lady Queen of Martyrs Armenian Catholic church in 1990, it was related that the Los Angeles parish was one of eight in the Armenian Eparchy of the United States and Canada. That parish encompassed the western United States and accounted for 2,000 families of about 10,000 people. An Armenian school was in operation in La Crescenta.

ASSYRIAN CHALDEAN

Most of the Chaldean Catholics in the United States are natives of Iraq, with many coming from other areas of the Middle East.

Father Ibrahim Ibrahim who belonged to the Apostolic Exarchate for the Chaldeans in the United States, came to Los Angeles in 1979 where he served as proto pastor of Saint Paul Chaldean Church in Montrose.

In 1982, Ibrahim was named first exarch of Saint Thomas Chaldean Church in the United States with residence in Southfield, Michigan. Later the parish of Saint Paul was moved to North Hollywood where Bishop Ibrahim dedicated the new church on September 12, 1987.

ORTHODOX CHURCHES
and
EASTERN RITE CATHOLIC CHURCHES
of the
LOS ANGELES AREAS

ST. ANDREW'S RUSSIAN-BYZANTINE RITE
CATHOLIC CHURCH
538 Concord Street, El Segundo 90245
322-1892

1976

POPULATIONS OF CATHOLIC CHURCHES	
1. Albanian Church	under 1.000
2. Armenian Church	363.000
3. Bulgarian Church	15.000
4. Byelorussian Church	105.000
5. Chaldean Church	304.000
6. Coptic Church	197.000
7. Croatian - Church of Krizevci	49.000
8. Ethiopian Church	203.000
9. Georgian Church	under 5.000
10. Greek Church	2.345
11. Hungarian Church	282.000
12. Italo-Albanian Church	64.000
13. Maronite Church	3.222.000
14. Melkite-Greek Church	1.252.000
15. Roman (Latin) Church	1.000.000.000
16. Romanian Church	1.119.000
17. Russian Church	3.500
18. Ruthenian Church	533.000
19. Slovakian Church	222.000
20. Syrian Church	138.000
21. Syro-Malabar Church	3.886.000
22. Syro-Malankar Church	327.000
23. Ukranian Church	5.160.000

Chaldeans are descendants of the ancient Babylonians and Assyrians. According to tradition they received the Christian Faith from the Apostle Thomas. The liturgical language is Aramaic, the language spoken by Jesus.

North Hollywood has the unusual distinctions of being home to three Eastern Rite Catholic Churches; Saint Paul (Assyrian Chaldean), Saint Anne (Melkite Greek) and Jesus Sacred Heart (Antiochene Syrian.)

BRACEROS

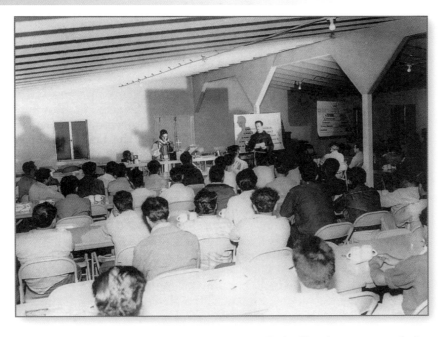

One area in which Los Angeles excelled all other areas of the southwest was its outreach to migrant workers, generally referred to as *braceros*. James Francis Cardinal McIntyre never favored the law that allowed them to work in the United States because he felt that it attracted persons into an unknown and often unfriendly land. In the late 1950s, when labor camps were set up in Orange and Ventura counties, the cardinal endeavored to provide chaplains to visit the camps and look after their spiritual needs. In Orange county, there were camps at Fullerton, Anaheim, Irvine, Villa Park and Tustin employing about 3,000 citrus workers. Father Raphael Toner, M.SSs.T., administrator at La Purisima Mission at El Modena coordinated Masses, confessions and other sacraments for those contract workers. He also distributed rosaries, pamphlets and other religious articles, along with the Catholic weekly newspaper *La Frontera* from Tijuana. Toner and the other priests assisting in the program were paid directly from the Chancery Office. In 1960, the annual report on the spiritual care of *braceros* in Orange county indicated that upwards of 5,000 men were active in the program. Television programs in Spanish were shown as were visual aids in Catholic doctrine. As the years progressed and the number of *braceros* escalated, the ministrations of local clergy kept pace.

In mid-1955, provisions were made to care for the approximately 4,000 *braceros* in Ventura county who were located in fifteen different camps. The largest concentrations were at camps in Oxnard, Saticoy and Camarillo. A priest was acquired from Mexico and, with the assistance of seminarians from Saint John's Seminary, he made periodic visits to the various camps on a weekly basis. McIntyre wrote to Rome for faculties to allow priests to offer evening Mass more than once a day, a provision then given rarely. Missions were preached and a series of radio messages was beamed out to the county weekly over stations KASA and KVEN. In later years, additional *bracero* camps were opened in Santa Barbara and Los Angeles counties. It was an ambitious apostolate and one which has received little or no recognition in the annals.

A feature story in *The Tidings* told about spiritual ministrations at the Somis Labor Camp, home for "250 *braceros*, Mexican nationals, brought into the U.S. for field work under terms of an agreement between the two nations." Noting that their contract carried no provisions for "spiritual care," the article explained how a priest journeyed to the camp twice weekly for Mass and other sacraments. The camp manager had acquired a former barracks building which the workers had renovated for a chapel dedicated to Our Lady of Guadalupe. After the celebration of Mass, seminarians would recite the rosary, teach catechism and write letters to families back in Mexico. Located in a picturesque eucalyptus grove, the chapel was looked after by Legion of Mary members from nearby Camarillo. "To the men, the chapel makes this corner of a strange land less alien."

Among the reports contained in a publication for the Bishops' Committee for Spanish Speaking was one in 1958 in which a priest told about his ministry in Ventura County. He said that "only this last year I gave 1,018 lectures by radio. I preached daily at Mass and on Sunday I celebrated three Masses. I celebrated Mass daily at night among the

twenty-five camps. We also had fifty-two Sunday Holy Hour devotions. It was difficult to hear their confessions because of the large numbers. As I was sick three months I could only preach twelve missions in twelve camps, but I expect to do more in 1959. This last year they had the largest bracero camp in the United States. An enormous salon was turned into a chapel where Mass was said each Sunday. There was a special playground which was kept orderly and clean. One day we had a solemn High Mass in the open at this camp for more than 3,000 *braceros* who all sang together and then marched in a solemn procession in groups of four carrying candles. I ministered to some 6,000 *braceros* in Ventura County."

In mid-1955, the Apostolic Delegate to the Church in the United States, wrote to McIntyre asking about the conditions of Mexican workers who had crossed the border "secretly" and were obliged to live hidden lives. He wondered what was being done for them spiritually. McIntyre replied that the subject had "been the occasion of much concern in the Southwest." He explained the migratory worker program and how they were provided for in various labor camps. But he noted that the so-called "wet-back" situation was a totally different problem. Such "enter illegally and of course without family. They mix with their Mexican confreres. In many instances, they continue without difficulty until by some means or other, they come in contact with the law. Meanwhile they live with Mexican families and do not constitute a particular group to be served. In fact anonymity is an advantage. Besides, many of them wish to return as soon as their purpose is served and rejoin their families. Our Catholic Welfare Agency tries to help them whenever difficulties arise."

CAMBODIANS

Archimandrite Alexei Smith is Director of Ecumenical and Interreligious Affairs for the Archdiocese of Los Angeles.

Between 1975 and 1979, an estimated 1.6 million inhabitants of Cambodia were tortured or killed by the Khmer Rouge in their native homeland. Most Cambodian immigration to the United States occurred in the 1980s when nearly 70,000 immigrants arrived in California, 27,000 of whom settled in Los Angeles county, 17,400 choosing to live in Long Beach where Our Lady of Mount Carmel Church became the only Catholic church in the United States specifically catering to Catholic Cambodians.

A report in *The Tidings* stated that in 1990 there were about 40,000 people of Cambodian descent living in the archdiocese. Those few who were Catholic, mostly converts, were looked after by a French-speaking missionary who spoke and celebrated the Liturgy in their native language.

Three years later, the director of the Cambodian Catholic Center estimated that there were about 200 Cambodian Catholics in the

Archdiocese of Los Angeles. Auxiliary Bishop Carl. Fisher said that the future of their local community looked bright, noting that the purpose of the Catholic Center was "to help these people to coalesce as a community."

CHINESE

There was a strong affinity for the Chinese among Western missionaries who lived and worked in China for generations and were forced to leave after the outbreak of war with Japan. While the Chinese had their roots deep in California history their numbers in the southland did not grow rapidly until after the turn of the century and what few there were did not profess the Christian faith. However, by the time of World War II, there were enough in Los Angeles to launch what became Saint Bridget's Catholic Chinese Church.

The Catholic Chinese Center at Saint Bridget's has functioned since 1939.

As noted by Immaculate Heart Sister Noemi Crews, the center was launched with several unique challenges: First, the central part of Los Angeles already included three other major ethnic Catholic churches, as well as two established Catholic schools. Secondly, the center's location, between Cathedral High School and the Pasadena Freeway, precluded any appreciable growth and, finally the garb and culture of Anglo priests and religious provided a major obstacle to the initial reception of the Church in the residential and commercial sections of Old Chinatown.

It was in 1939 that Father John Cowhig, a missionary from China who had returned to the United States for health reasons, first began to organize a Catholic presence among the southland's Chinese community. Archbishop John J. Cantwell was highly sensitive to the need expressed so eloquently by Cowhig and other members of the Columban Fathers. Cowhig took up residence temporarily at Cathedral High School as he began reaching out to the local Chinese community.

After making a thorough demographic study of the area, Father Cowhig chose the present site at the north end of Chinatown, for his foundation. The edifice on Cottage Home Street opened on Christmas day in 1940.

When the Chinese Catholic Social Center was dedicated under the patronage of Saint Bridget, on June 7, 1942, Archbishop Cantwell said that "the kindly Mother Church, knowing no racial barriers or political compromises, stretches out her arms to enclose in her embrace the Chinese people of this community."

A language school was also begun at Cathedral High School and that endeavor proved to be enormously successful. Young people were anxious to learn more about their roots and, soon thereafter, a club was organized for sporting activities. The Sisters of the Immaculate Heart of Mary were asked to assist in the project and formal classes were offered at Queen of Angels High School, a program that lasted until 1951. The Catholic Chinese Academy that flourished in Chinatown was highly esteemed by all the local inhabitants, most of whom had relatives or friends evangelized by Catholic missionaries in their homeland.

The archbishop was an avid supporter of the center as evidenced by a letter to a benefactor in New York: "You will be happy to hear that our Chinese Mission is filled to capacity and overflowing." The donor had paid for the original building and it was he who asked that it be called "Saint Bridget's Catholic Chinese Center". He also stipulated that Holy Mass be offered there weekly.

Bishop Ignatius Wang

Except for the nursery and kindergarten, the center's school was closed in 1951, at which time the youngsters were sent to a Catholic school a few blocks away. In the mid-1960s, new waves of Chinese immigrants called for enlarging and modernizing the center. Expanded facilities were also made for liturgical activities. Today, Saint Bridget's Catholic Chinese Center is recognized as a permanent and cherished part of the Los Angeles Chinatown community.

A festive archdiocesan celebration occurred in January of 2004 when San Francisco Auxiliary Bishop Ignatius Wang, the first Chinese to serve in the American hierarchy, came to the Cathedral of Our Lady of the Angels to celebrate the Year of the Monkey for the Asian Catholic community. Roger Cardinal Mahony joined the festivities to rejoice with the Chinese People in "their culture and way of life."

COPTIC EGYPTIANS

The Coptic rite, one of the most ancient in Christendom, traces its roots to Saint Mark, the Apostle. Today, Egypt boasts the largest Christian presence in the Arab World with nearly 400,000 members of the Eastern rite Coptic Catholics.

In 1986, a Coptic Catholic community was established in Los Angeles and five years later Saint Mary Coptic Catholic Church was dedicated by His Beatitude, Patriarch Stephanos II Ghattas. It was the only Coptic Catholic church west of the Mississippi River. The following December, it was announced that Father Hanna Badir, the pastor, had been named Bishop of the Diocese of Ismalia in Egypt.

CREOLE AND CAJUN

Of all the peoples who reside under California's umbrella of color, none is more historic and interesting than the Creoles and Cajuns known for their Catholic faith, French language and large families.

The Cajuns living in Los Angeles emigrated to the west from Louisiana. They were immortalized by Henry Wadsworth Longfellow in an epic poem telling about their expulsion from New Brunswick and Nova Scotia (Acadia) by British troops in 1755, when they refused allegiance to the British crown. By 1790, about 4,000 of those Acadians had settled in the fertile bayou swamps along the Gulf of Mexico.

Linguists reckon that the name "Cajun" is a corruption of "Acadians." Their speech patterns combine bits of ancient French with words taken from English, Spanish, German, native American languages and Afro Americans. Their distinctive music, played by fiddles, distonic accordions and triangles, often has a haunting quality of sadness.

Creoles have a different background. They are a people who originated in one of the New World's possessions of France, Spain or Portugal. "Creole" is a French word which came from the Spanish "criollo" which, in turn, was adapted from the Portuguese "crioulo." According to Webster's dictionary, it means "a slave born in the master's household."

The Creoles came to New Orleans prior to migrating north through rural Louisiana where some remained. Their dialect is a soft, idiom-rich jargon grounded in French.

Zydeco, the Creole counterpart of Cajun music, incorporates blues and jazz. Its unique Afro-Caribbean sound comes from a percussion instrument known as the frottoir, a corrugated metal vest which the instrumentalist plays with spoons.

Louis H. Metoyer, editor of *Bayou Talk*, a monthly newspaper circulated to Creoles in twenty-five states, says that most of the 20,000 families in Los Angeles came from Louisiana in two major

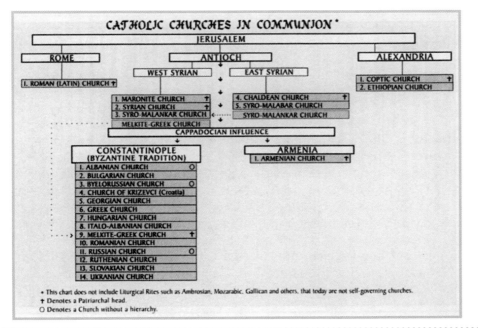

CATHOLIC CHURCHES IN COMMUNION *

JERUSALEM

ROME	ANTIOCH	ALEXANDRIA
	WEST SYRIAN / EAST SYRIAN	1. COPTIC CHURCH †
I. ROMAN (LATIN) CHURCH †		2. ETHIOPIAN CHURCH

1. MARONITE CHURCH †	4. CHALDEAN CHURCH †
2. SYRIAN CHURCH †	5. SYRO-MALABAR CHURCH
3. SYRO-MALANKAR CHURCH	SYRO-MALANKAR CHURCH
MELKITE-GREEK CHURCH	

CAPPADOCIAN INFLUENCE

CONSTANTINOPLE (BYZANTINE TRADITION)	ARMENIA
1. ALBANIAN CHURCH ○	I. ARMENIAN CHURCH †
2. BULGARIAN CHURCH	
3. BYELORUSSIAN CHURCH ○	
4. CHURCH OF KRIZEVCI (Croatia)	
5. GEORGIAN CHURCH	
6. GREEK CHURCH	
7. HUNGARIAN CHURCH	
8. ITALO-ALBANIAN CHURCH	
9. MELKITE-GREEK CHURCH †	
10. ROMANIAN CHURCH	
11. RUSSIAN CHURCH ○	
12. RUTHENIAN CHURCH	
13. SLOVAKIAN CHURCH	
14. UKRANIAN CHURCH	

* This chart does not include Liturgical Rites such as Ambrosian, Mozarabic, Gallican and others, that today are not self-governing churches.
† Denotes a Patriarchal head.
○ Denotes a Church without a hierarchy.

migrations. The first occurred after World War II when they journeyed west to find employment and good schools for their youngsters. They settled in what is now known as South Central Los Angeles.

Metoyer points out that "When we left Louisiana, we didn't leave our values there. We packed them and brought them with us. And they are interwoven within the Catholic faith." He goes on to note that "one of the distinct things about the Creoles, as well as the Cajuns, is that they have large families. Extended family is just as important as immediate family."

The second migration took place in the 1960s and it was then that Metoyer and others came to the Pacific rim. The archdiocesan Creole Cultural Heritage Liturgy was inaugurated at that time. In Los Angeles, the Cajuns and Creoles have preserved what is best in their traditions. Over 5,000 gathered in June of 1993 at Long Beach for the seventh annual Southern California Cajun and Zydeco Festival. There, actor John Delafise and the Eunice Playboys exhorted the people to reach out and touch a hand.

One Anglo observer at that event wrote that "the music is part of the pie. The rest of it is these wonderful people who are very family oriented. They're real Catholics, and I feel at home here. They get together, and they celebrate life and community. And that's their gift to the Church."

CROATIANS

1962   1962

ALOYSIUS CARDINAL STEPINAC·BORN MAY 8, 1898·DIED FEBRUARY 10, 1960

Help Croatian Bishops and Clergy

The presence of Croatians in Southern California stretches back a century. Towards the end of the 19th century, small groups of Croatians from the shores of the Adriatic sea began settling in the area where they found a climate much like that in their native Dalmatia. In the early 1900s, other groups from Herzegovina came to the west coast and became involved in the heavy construction industry. Croatia was baptized, civilized and inspired by the Catholic Church. The zenith of the glorious history of Croatia coincides with the religious progress of its people.

Croatians were welcomed to the Diocese of Monterey-Los Angeles by Bishop Thomas J. Conaty who encouraged the

formation of a church dedicated to Saint Anthony. Early on, many parishes offered their facilities for services and gatherings.

In the December 9th, 1910 issue of *The Tidings* was a report that "Saint Anthony Croatian Church, of which Reverend Anthony Zuvish is the pastor, will be solemnly dedicated next Sunday morning at 10 o'clock." It was noted that "the pretty little church" had a seating capacity of 350 people. Bishop Conaty gave a sermon which set the tone of the event:

"My dear children of the Croatian people, I know you and your pastor are happy today in your own church. I am happy with you because today you have proved that you are children of that gigantic people whom Holy Father Leo XIII called a Vanguard of Christianity."

Over the ensuing years, a number of Croatian organizations were established, all of which helped solidify the community and foster frequent social activities. In 1933 the cornerstone of a new hall was blessed by Bishop John J. Cantwell. Erection of that building necessitated moving the rectory from Alpine Street to Grand Avenue.

Tragedy befell their mother country in the late 1940s when communism forced many Croatians to flee to California. In 1953, James Francis Cardinal McIntyre reported to the Apostolic Delegate that the "parish (of Saint Anthony) draws the Croatian people from all over Los Angeles." He also noted that there was a large group of Croatians living in San Pedro where they found employment in the fishing trade. He noted that most of the latter came from Dalmatia and Herzegovina.

The cardinal also spoke out against the forced imprisonment of Aloysius Cardinal Stepinac, Archbishop of Zagreb, who had been horribly mistreated by the Tito government of Yugoslavia. In one of his many statements on that issue, McIntyre stated that in "their long history of 1300 years, the Croatians have often been compelled to put aside plow and pen, and to fight with sword, ever alert to defend their freedom, their religion and the frontier of Western Christian civilization."

Among the many Croatian cultural accomplishments was the release of "Croatian Melodies" in the 1970 by the Tamburitza Club. That stereo record was a major contribution to the ethnic music of those days.

In 1988 Franjo Cardinal Kuharic, Archbishop of Zagreb, visited Los Angeles where he told people that "the east offers the cross with Christ, the west offers Christ without the cross. That's the problem! "

CUBANS

The work of James Francis Cardinal McIntyre with the Cuban refugees is among the most memorable and significant of any parallel program anywhere in the world. In 1962, he organized the Cuban Refugee Resettlement Committee and, within two years, that organization had relocated the second largest number of refugees outside the New York area. John F. Thomas, an official in the United States Department of Health, Education and Welfare, issued a statement commending the program, saying that "we would like to express the deep appreciation of the Federal government for the work accomplished by the Cuban Resettlement Committee of the Archdiocese of Los Angeles."

The cardinal took an active part in the various outreach activities of the committee. On one occasion, after a group of children gave him a statue of Our Lady of Charity of Cobre, the patroness of Cuba, he took the occasion to encourage youngsters to learn English. He told them about having traveled to Cuba in the days when he was stationed in New York and he spoke about the large Cuban colony that he knew in Manhattan. McIntyre received many signs of affection from the Cuban refugees, including a plaque which assured him they would "be forever grateful for the fatherly spirit with which he has taken care of all our needs during our stay in the archdiocese."

Even as late as 1967, an average of 200 Cubans a month were still coming to Los Angeles. In 1968, the 10,000th Cuban refugee arrived, just five days after being airlifted from his homeland. It was estimated that about half the total number of Cuban refugees coming to California had been located under Catholic auspices.

On several occasions, Timothy Cardinal Manning offered endorsement and encouragement for the Federation of Cuban Catholic Youth, or the *Comunidades Cristianas Federadas* which, he said, was "a source of great joy." He was "edified by their dedication to the lay apostolate" and described the members as "authentic apostles while you remain close to the priests who share your ideals." The cardinal also encouraged support of those acting as sponsors for Cuban refugees which were coming to the archdiocese in great numbers.

CZECHOSLOVAKIANS

In 1950, estimates placed the number of Czechs and Slovaks living in Los Angeles at 2,498 and double that number of offspring living in the archdiocese. By 1964, the number exceeded 10,000 due partly to the fact that a large number of their families moved to California from the

On June 22, 1969, James Francis Cardinal McIntyre visited the Czechlovakian parish in Los Angeles.

east for health reasons and also because of the country's favorable immigration policies.

A report to James Francis Cardinal McIntyre indicated that there were twelve organizations comprised of about 1,500 members who met at the Sokol Hall on North Western Avenue. They attended Mass at Blessed Sacrament church in Hollywood where they were cared for by Father Adolph Pelikan, S.J.

McIntyre followed their progress closely. At a Mass celebrated for the 1100th anniversary of the death of Saint Cyril, the cardinal referred to exiled Czechoslovakians as "living martyrs of the Church of Silence." At that time, Bohumil Smutnik, secretary of the Czech Mission, was awarded the Benemerenti Medal personally by McIntyre.

The cardinal said he was "proud to have so many Czechoslovakians living in this archdiocese" and he welcomed them, observing they had "demonstrated love of the faith and love of the Church. They have

Jaime Cardinal Sin visits a Filipino community in Los Angeles.

suffered and it has made them stronger." Thinking back to his New York days, McIntyre said he had "lived a long time, long enough to see much history made. When I was Chancellor in New York I had to provide priests for many groups of immigrants driven from their lands or who came here to make a new life. I know how they feel, and I know how they have enriched these United States with their arts and crafts and hard work."

Timothy Cardinal Manning enjoyed getting out of his "Ivory Tower" as often as he could. In October of 1970, he received bread and salt, symbols of Slavonic hospitality at Loyola High School from a group of Czechs celebrating the Feast of Saint Wenceslaus. He praised them as "good people who have come to the United States, not to clamor for rights, but to seek a chance to live in freedom." He compared them to the Irish, who, he said, also came to the United States "to breathe free air."

The Irish know what it is to be hanged for the wearing of the green and the love of the faith, and I can sympathize with the Czechoslovakian people who also have come here to start new lives. We have not come empty-handed. We have enriched this culture, weaving a bright and resplendent garment. I belong here with you, sharing the same faith and same sacrifices.

FILIPINOS

At the turn of the twentieth century companies along the west coast began recruiting Filipino laborers to replace Chinese and Japanese workers, mostly in agricultural pursuits. Between 1922 and 1929, 5,513 entered the Port of Los Angeles. Though like earlier Asian immigrants, Filipinos faced a strong nativist presence in California. By 1930, there were 30,470 of them living in California.

During those years Catholic Filipino Clubs began springing up in California. Besides providing protection from Protestant proselytism, those clubs served to assist immigrants in adjusting to life in the American Catholic Church.

America's bishops, especially the ones in the west, were long opposed to erecting national parishes and the Filipinos gradually adjusted to survive in territorial parishes dominated by Anglos.

Population of Los Angeles County by Ethnic Group, April 1, 1980 and July 1, 1986			
Ethnic Group	**1980**	**1986**	**% Change**
Total	7,477,566	8,331,200	11.4
Non-Hispanic white	3,999,481	4,037,916	1.0
Born in the U.S.	3,504,440	3,540,608	1.0
Born outside the U.S.	495,041	497,308	0.5
Hispanic	2,018,594	2,486,364	23.2
Mexican	1,610,982	1,780,754	10.5
Born in the U.S.	664,843	697,984	5.0
Born outside the U.S.	946,139	1,082,770	14.4
Other Spanish	407,612	705,610	73.1
Born in the U.S.	117,119	142,512	21.7
Born outside the U.S.	290,493	563,098	93.8
Black	947,345	1,029,544	8.7
Born in California	278,842	381,978	37.0
Born in Other U.S.	631,576	600,870	−4.9
Born outside the U.S.	36,927	46,696	26.5
American Indian, Eskimo and Aleut	54,489	64,876	19.1
Asian/Pacific Islander	457,656	712,499	55.7
Chinese	94,450	154,686	63.8
Born in the U.S.	16,868	20,836	23.5
Born outside the U.S.	77,582	133,850	72.5
Japanese	117,551	111,079	−5.5
Born in the U.S.	77,184	71,654	−7.2
Born outside the U.S.	40,367	39,425	−2.3
Filipino	100,121	180,811	80.6
Born in the U.S.	12,385	17,833	44.0
Born outside the U.S.	87,736	162,978	85.8
Korean	64,455	128,064	98.7
Born in the U.S.	2,456	2,848	16.0
Born outside the U.S.	61,999	125,216	102.0
Vietnamese	25,930	43,523	67.8
Other Asian/Pacific Islander	55,149	94,336	71.1

With the second wave of Filipino immigration, from 1940 to 1960, a ministry was established for them in Los Angeles, where they were given their own church, Saint Columban at 1035 Defora Street. It was blessed by Archbishop John J. Cantwell on January 12, 1945. Two years later it was relocated in the city's oldest fire department, Chemical Company No. 2.

The archbishop had a special fondness for the Filipinos, partly because his longtime chauffeur, Alex Navarro (1890-1968), was with him from the 1920s. When Alex wanted to purchase a house, he found that there was a restrictive covenant against Orientals. Cantwell's secretary, Father Joseph T. McGucken, later Archbishop of San Francisco, signed the necessary papers to validate the purchase. Two of Alex's daughters, Marie Alexis and Lenore, became college professors and members of the Immaculate Heart Community.

There were approximately 40,000 Filipinos in California in 1942, nine thousand of whom resided in the Archdiocese of Los Angeles. The predominantly male population, most of whom hoped one day to return to their homeland, found seasonal work or were employed as domestics.

The Filipino Naturalization Act of 1946 permitted Filipinos to become American citizens and many sought and acquired better paying employment and educational opportunities in their adopted country.

In mid-1956, Bishop Alejandro Olalia of Lipa, in the Phillipines, apparently complained to the Apostolic Delegate in the United States that the Filipino people in Los Angeles and other areas were not receiving adequate religious attention. The charge irritated McIntyre who said he had received no complaints. While acknowledging that it wasn't always possible to obtain Filipino priests, "the fact is that all services are available to the Filipino people throughout the archdiocese in both English and Spanish." He told the delegate that the 35,000 Filipinos in the greater Los Angeles area were widely scattered and did not live in clusters, as was the case with other nationalities. He noted that there was a Filipino parish conducted by the Columban Fathers which serves its people effectively. That church also served as a "social center and a national gathering point for the Filipino people. Inasmuch as most spoke English and/or Spanish, there was no reason why they also couldn't attend other parishes in the archdiocese. McIntyre felt that "they are better Americans and better Catholics by attending the parish church of the area in which they live," noting that they "are received everywhere with equality."

One of the many outreach activities of the Filipinos was the Rosary Group Apostolate which was begun in 1970. Within a few years that movement spread all over the Greater Los Angeles, as well as Orange and San Diego counties. There were eighteen major groups under the umbrella of the Federation Rosary Groups.

In 1980, Manning praised the Filipino community for its "sustaining love for the Blessed Mother" which he felt was " a source of great hope to the Church in Los Angeles." He rejoiced that they had "not allowed such a great tradition of prayer to diminish in these days." In another letter, Manning "observed with gratitude the growth of the number of Filipino people coming to our shores. They are faithful, loyal members of the Body of Christ. In their love for the Church they speak the Gospel message with eloquence."

Timothy Cardinal Manning

The Filipino community in Los Angeles came of age on February 2, 1990 when Roger Cardinal Mahony inaugurated the Filipino Pastoral Ministry, appointing Rev. Loreto Gonzales, its first director. By the beginning of the next decade, there were approximately a half million Filipinos in the Archdiocese of Los Angeles, 85% of whom were Roman Catholics. Given their talent and numbers, Filipinos became a tremendous force for good in the larger community. They now constitute the largest Asian American population in California and second largest ethnic group in Los Angeles, second only to Hispanics.

In July of 1989, in St. Bernard Church, Los Angeles, the chancellor for the Archdiocese Msgr. Stephen Blaire said before a large gathering of priests and parish leaders that the "Filipino people bring a unique contribution. You bring your own culture and you want to meet your needs as a people in Los Angeles, but also you want to contribute to the whole life of the community, to the Archdiocese of Los Angeles, to Southern California."

The Filipino Pastoral Ministry has three primary goals:
1. To integrate Filipinos and make them more active in the parishes. Filipinos are potentially a tremendous resource to the parish.
2. To encourage Filipinos to share their rich cultural and religious heritage with the larger ecclesial community, through events like the Simbang Gabi, Marian devotions, Filipino Holy Week and San Lorenzo Ruiz celebrations.
3. To provide pastoral care and services to Filipinos, through ministries that cater to the Filipino-American youth, families and the elderly, especially those experiencing difficulty with cultural adaptations.

The Filipino community has grown significantly over the last ten years. According to the Bureau of Census 2000, the Filipino is the largest Asian American population in California with 918,678. In the Archdiocese of Los Angeles, the Filipino population is 281,045.

On February 10, 2004, Father Oscar Solis was ordained as Auxiliary Bishop of Los Angeles, the initial American Filipino bishop in the United States. His ordination was the first of its kind in the new Cathedral of Our Lady of the Angels.

FRENCH

The French played a prominent role in the interesting drama of California's heritage. Handicapped though they were by internal revolutions and faltering governments, the French were just as eager as others for a place in the Pacific sun. Not being powerful enough for unilateral action to acquire the area outright, France played a discreet role, striving to cultivate the good will of the Californians. Her agents were enthusiastically received and her subjects were treated as natives rather than foreigners.

The first effective contact dates from 1786, and the arrival at Monterey Bay, of the first foreign contingency to visit California after Spanish occupation. Jean Francois de Galaup, Comte de La Pérouse, had been commissioned by King Louis XVI to expand geographical knowledge by searching out such areas as the Northwest Passage. The Comte de La Pérouse was equally intent on appraising the commercial and political potentialities of the whole Pacific Slope.

That seaman's attractive and colorful personality is reflected in his personal observations about the California missions, where "the monks, by their answers to our questions, left us in ignorance of nothing concerning the regime of this kind of religious community."

Wright Howes maintains that "of all modern exploring voyages to the Pacific those of Cook, La Pérouse and Vancouver were the most important."

In 1817, Camille de Roquefeuil dropped anchor in San Francisco Bay. His ship was the first one flying the French flag to enter that port. A lieutenant in the merchant navy, Roquefeuil's objective was to demonstrate the possibility of trade with China which was then almost at a standstill.

A decade later, Auguste Bernard Duhaut-Cilly sailed along the Pacific Slope and became the initial "outlander" to be intimately acquainted with Hispanic California. That French navigator's published observations constitute the most extensive contemporary account of California's missions and settlements for the period.

Abel Aubert Du Petit-Thouars came in 1837. A keen observer and a man of considerable intelligence, he kept a careful diary of his voyage which he envisioned as helpful for French foreign commerce, especially the whaling industry.

The colorful flag of Orleanist France was brought to California in 1839 by Cyrille Pierre Theodore Laplace, who was concerned about the possibility for French colonial establishments in the Pacific.

Eugene Duflot de Mofras, a young attaché at the French embassy in Mexico City, ploughed the California waters in 1841, examining and reporting on the area's institutions, resources, history and prospects. An advance scout of King Louis Philippe, Duflot de Mofras industriously sent back his findings and later published a two volume illustrated account of his trek.

An observer of later generations, Frank Monoghan, wrote that "it was enthusiasm rather than bitterness that prejudiced the minds of French travelers to America during the eighteenth century." On the California scene, "the English and French travelers were the most prominent, and their results were the most far-reaching; but of those visiting and writing of Mexico and California, the French easily surpass the English."

Even this most cursory glance at early French influence in and concern for the west coast indicates that before the admission of California to the Union, there were many who hoped to acquire the area for France.

GERMANS

In the 1880s, Bishop Francis Mora was anxious to provide for the German speaking people who had moved into the Diocese of Monterey-Los Angeles from the east and middle west. Most of them were concentrated in the area around 12th and Los Angeles streets, in Los Angeles. He was able to acquire a priest fluent in German from Milwaukee and, in 1888, when Father Joseph Florian Bartsch arrived, Saint Joseph's parish was established as only the fifth parochial entity in Los Angeles.

Then Auxiliary Bishop Timothy Manning at a meeting of the German Catholic Federation in 1956.

Father Bartsch organized the parish on what were the outskirts of the city in the midst of a pear orchard. The priest received tremendous cooperation and within a year Saint Joseph Parish had its first church on Santee Street between 12th and Pico Boulevard.

On January 1, 1889, Father Bartsch celebrated the first Mass in the new church. An essay for the *California Chronicle*, records that "the neat church edifice is 70 feet long and 32 feet wide, with the sacristy and priests housed in the rear."

In 1893, Bishop Mora confided the parish to the Franciscans who had earlier accepted German-speaking parishes in Northern California. About a decade later, when the permanent German Gothic church was built, Bishop George T. Montgomery answered criticism in these words: "Some have questioned the economic wisdom of building such a large and magnificent structure. But let me assure you no mistake has been made. It is better by far to go into debt and build something that will answer the needs of a growing city like Los Angeles, than to expend less money on a church that a few years hence would be far too small to accommodate its membership."

For many years, Sr. Joseph's was a parish of small businesses and families. Santee and Maple streets were noted for beautiful homes, many of them owned by families of German descent who had long been active in the parish. As young couples married, they founded homes in the parish and took their place in parish life. With the boom days of the 1920s came a series of changes which had an important bearing on the future of the parish.

The predominantly Italian community on Wilson and Hunter Sts. to the east was suppressed when the Union Pacific Railroad moved into the area. Part of this territory was annexed to St. Joseph's. Since the families in this district lived so far from the church, the chapel of the Mother Cabrini Day Home on Mateo and Enterprise Streets was opened to them for Sunday Mass, and looked after by one of the priests from St. Joseph's. The Day Home became a catechetical center, and the Sisters of the Sacred Heart worked very zealously for many years in the area.

By the time of World War I, the number of Germans living in the area had diminished considerably and those who remained found it prudent to downplay their attachment to the motherland.

Nonetheless, in 1929, when the German Catholic State Federation Convention was held in Los Angeles, a goodly number of locals attended. The meeting was presided over by Joseph Geiger, whose son would become the great Franciscan scholar of the mission era. Even at that late date, there were clusters of Germans still residing in Saint Joseph Parish.

GUAMANIANS

Roughly 50% of Guam's population is Catholic and among those who have immigrated to Los Angeles the percentage is upwards of 90%. Most are fluent in English and have integrated well into already established parishes. Today they are concentrated mostly in Carson, Long Beach and Wilmington.

HISPANIC

Hispanics in the United States rightly point out that their ancestors were here long before the Pilgrims. The image of the nation as a land settled exclusively by immigrants from northern Europe is a pious myth which, historically, has anti-Catholic roots.

Especially is that true in California where the Spanish-speaking population has grown enormously in recent years. Los Angeles has become one of the world's largest Hispanic metropolises and the growth pattern gives no indication of diminishing. Recent demographical studies indicate that Hispanics in Los Angeles comprise well over a third of the population, thus forming the largest single ethnic market in the United States.

While such Catholic prelates as Archbishops John J. Cantwell and J. Francis A. McIntyre foresaw the trends, even they would have been astounded that nearly one-fifth of the entire Hispanic population in the United States and 54% of the state's Hispanics now reside in Los Angeles.

Figures such as these explain what motivated Pope John Paul II, during his 1987 pastoral visit, to say that "This land is a crossroads… experiencing both the enrichment and the complications which arise from this phenomenon." He noted that this massive influx is "a symbol and a kind of laboratory, testing America's commitment to her founding moral principles and human values."

Of the millions of persons of Hispanic background in the United States today, an estimated 85% identify themselves to census takers as Catholics. Yet there is precious little room for complacency because the loss of Spanish-speaking Catholics to Protestant proselytism is disturbingly high.

In an address to the National Conference of Catholic Bishops, the papal Pro-Nuncio observed that "much of the challenge to the Church… lies precisely in stemming this outflow of our brothers and sisters from our faith. And this will happen by providing them the same supportive ecclesial environment that nurtured the faith of earlier generations of Catholics of other ethnic and cultural origins-Irish, German, Italian, Polish, and the rest."

The Church in California has even closer ties to its Mexican-origin Hispanics than other areas in the southwest. Its proto bishop, a native of Lagos de Moreno, was consecrated for the newly-created Diocese of Both Californias in Mexico's National Shrine of Our Lady of Guadalupe. The inaugural of a Spanish language weekly Catholic newspaper in Los Angeles, *Vida Nueva*, is the most recent recognition by the Church of the importance attached to Hispanic culture and its survival along the Pacific Slope.

A few years ago, voters in California joined sixteen other states in approving a controversial measure designating English as the state's "official language." Those Catholics who favored that initiative were probably unaware that the state's earliest missionaries couldn't speak English, that its first bishop was Mexican-born, that three of his successors were Hispanics, and that the area's first pastoral letters, homilies and catechetics were written and communicated in Spanish.

Soon after his canonical installation at Saint Vibiana's Cathedral, Archbishop J. Francis A. McIntyre set out to develop a comprehensive program for dealing with what others called the Mexican-American "problem," but what he referred to as the Hispanic "challenge."

Members of the Hispanic Encuentro,
Mount Saint Mary's College, 1985.

Enlisting the assistance of Father Augustine O'Dea, the archbishop felt that by defining the scope of the "challenge," he could thereby come up with the best methodology for dealing spiritually with what was even then the largest foreign language group in Southern California.

At that time, Hispanics were the fastest growing group in the area, with a birth rate of forty-two per one thousand, a factor complicated by an ongoing emigration from Mexico. McIntyre estimated that 40% of the Catholics in the archdiocese were Mexican-American by birth or origin and fully half of the baptisms were accounted for by Mexican babies.

While 80% of the Mexican-Americans claimed to be Roman Catholic, only 30% practiced their faith, with the women more committed than their spouses. The largest concentration of them had come from Chihuahua, Sonora, Sinaloa and Baja California where they had little if any educational opportunities or association with the Church. For that reason, the archbishop felt that religious instruction programs for the children were imperative. Most observers felt that there was very little discrimination against them such as is found in other regions of the Southwest. Those living in and around Los Angeles were "better off here not only socially and economically," but also had better opportunities for religious worship and religious instruction than they had experienced in the parts of Mexico from which they came.

McIntyre was puzzled and upset by Protestant proselytization among the Mexican-Americans. Available figures indicated that most Protestant denominations admitted that their largest proportional increases came from converts from among the Latin American people. At the same time, when the Church had been able to give them adequate religious instruction, as well as Church facilities, Protestants inroads were minimal. Most of the Protestant successes were occurring in colonies where there was no Catholic church or religious educational center.

Assessing the goals of the Church among these people, McIntyre saw "the greatest need" as being the erection of more parochial schools. Next was the need for more Religious men and women and catechists to work among public school children. Also necessary were more Settlement Houses in Mexican-American districts and boarding homes to accommodate court wards. He noted that juvenile delinquency among the Mexicans was high and he thought that a trade school for boys would greatly alleviate that problem. He viewed the average Mexican-American colony as being "entirely disorganized." There was very little responsible leadership and he felt that the Church should take measures to develop that quality by offering, where possible, "greater opportunities for higher education." He advocated scholarships in Catholic colleges, as well as training courses preparatory for civil service jobs.

Already the archdiocese was at work. In particular McIntyre told about his envisioned drive for funds with which to build two high schools on the east side of Los Angeles as well as five grammar schools, two of which had already been inaugurated. He mentioned the work being done by the Catholic Youth Organization as providing "a healthy outlet for their energies in those districts where there is a second generation." Young people were often confused by the old fashioned culture of their parents and the manners of the United States which were frequently "presented to them under the worst possible auspices.

We need to give archdiocesan support to the associations of Mexican youths - for boys and girls - encouraging pastors to develop such organization in their parishes." Of particular benefit was the renewed emphasis on teaching Spanish in the archdiocesan seminaries.

Perfunctory courses had given way to new and more effective programs. Courses in Hispanic culture, history of proselytism and pastoral methods were being offered. Seminarians were encouraged to speak Spanish at meals, during their recreation periods and on walks. More gifted students were given the opportunity of a visit to Mexico City. McIntyre concluded by calling for greater cooperation with the Bishop's Committee for the Spanish speaking, suggesting that Archbishop Robert E. Lucey's "tendency to overemphasize the social side at the expense of the religious" might need to be re-examined. He noted that "some of the older bishops of the southwest, who had long lived with the Mexican-Americans had suggested privately that the committee would be on more solid foundation if in time it were headed by a prelate more universally acceptable."

In the recent past it had been fashionable, if not historically correct, to criticize members of the Catholic hierarchy in the United States for not doing enough for Mexican Americans. One writer, in an essay entitled "Chicano and Catholic," declared that "simple honesty demands that high tribute" be paid to people like James Francis Cardinal McIntyre for the pioneering work he did "in training and assigning priests specifically to this work" within his jurisdiction. Speaking only for Los Angeles, the Church was indeed very active in looking after Mexican-Americans in many ways. The first obvious example would be that of supporting and partially financing the apostolate of the Bishops' Committee for the Spanish Speaking which had its headquarters in San Antonio, Texas. At a time when priests were at a high premium number-wise, McIntyre released two of them to act as directors of the Committee, Fathers John J. Birch and Matthew Kelly. The publication for that Committee, published quarterly and entitled *Our Catholic Southwest* together with the minutes of the meetings of the Committee, indicate widespread concern and action on behalf of Mexican-Americans in the Archdiocese of Los Angeles.

Timothy Cardinal Manning's love and affection for Mexican-Americans stretched back to his earliest days in California. When asked about that, he replied that "when I came to Menlo Park, I was so busy explaining my own heritage that I never even thought about poking fun at others who were also alien to American culture." In a feature story by a local newspaper, shortly after Manning became Archbishop of Los Angeles, a writer said that Manning had "turned his attention to the problems of the poor, particularly Mexican-Americans who account for more than one-half of the archdiocese's 1.7 million parishioners." He established an inter-parochial council composed of twenty parishes in the east side *barrio* of Los Angeles and its first project was a voter registration drive. "The Church has also established a center to deal with Chicano immigration problems, and expanded its bilingual adult education courses."

Speaking at the *First Encuentro Hispano de Pastoral* in 1973, the cardinal said that the time was ripe "for opening the door, the beginning of a great enrichment," Speaking to some 350 delegates, Manning said:

We in this country have reached a state of spiritual impoverishment, for the things in which we had put our trust have deceived us. We are coming to realize that it is religious faith alone that we can trust and rely on. And that faith has been mysteriously and magnificently preserved in the people of Hispanic culture. This event, this *encuentro*, cannot be evaluated solely in terms of the conclusions that may come from it. This event is the releasing of a potency of faith inherent in that culture.

Manning's Spanish was probably better than many of his priests. He never hesitated to offer Mass and even preach in Spanish, though he preferred to have someone more fluent than he deliver the homilies at Masses. He made it a point to learn the background of every group to which he ministered. Often he knew more about the Mexican-American heritage than did his listeners. He once told John Dart of the *Los Angeles Times* that "All Latinos, because of their Roman Catholic heritage, belong to the (Catholic) Church," even if they no longer go to their parish for baptism.

By mid 1972, Los Angeles had the largest population of Mexicans of any city in the world, save Mexico City and Guadalajara. And, of those people, 90% were at least nominal Catholics.

Wanting to upgrade and strengthen the Church's ministry, Cardinal Manning inaugurated a Vicariate for the Spanish speaking in late 1973. Throughout his archiepiscopate and that of his successor Hispanics and others of Latin heritage were served well in the Archdiocese of Los Angeles.

In the 2004 *Quinquennial Report* for the Archdiocese of Los Angeles, Roger Cardinal Mahony reported that "the Hispanic population is, according to most estimates, about 75 percent of the Catholic population of the archdiocese. The diversity within the Latino population is also quite complex. Latinos come from all parts of Latin America, with most arriving from Mexico and Central America. About 75 percent of the Latinos are Mexicans or of Mexican descent, followed by approximately 14 percent Salvadorian, 6 percent Guatemalans, and the remaining are from other countries in Central America, the Caribbean and South America." There was a high mixture of races, with more than 40 percent of the African-American and Asian women giving birth in the Los Angeles County General Hospital to children of Hispanic fathers. In Los Angeles, more than 50 percent of all births are of Hispanic children. In the City of Los Angeles, 42 percent of the residents speak Spanish, compared to the 41 percent who speak English only.

HUNGARIANS

Bishop John J. Cantwell visited Hungary in 1938 while enroute to the Eucharistic Congress. His letter from Budapest said that "The weather is warm, but not warmer than the reception I received from your countrymen."

In his missive Cantwell further recalled:

No race has overcome successfully more difficulties in this country than the Hungarian people. The Hungarian language is so different from all other languages that the early immigrants found it hard to get their place in the community. It is now a long time since Count Beldy and his three companions, Boloni, Wesselenyi and Balogh arrived in this country. They were pioneers,

*Father Mathias Lani assists fellow Hungarians
in packing supplies for the needy.*

mittee, established by James Francis Cardinal McIntyre under the watchful eye of Father Mathias Lani, were Hungarians. A report for 1951 indicates that upwards of 3,000 persons were processed, located and employed through this agency. Lani reported to McIntyre that "most of the new arrivals are fine, religious and church-going people." Volunteers were organized to teach the new immigrants language skills, along with the other amenities needed by candidates for American citizenship.

Stories were run in *The Tidings* about the immigrants at least monthly. In June of 1956, for example, an essay appeared about an ethnic German family who spent more than three years in a miserable and overcrowded refugee camp in Linz, Austria. Most of the Hungarian refugees were initially affiliated with Saint Stephen's parish where Lani was pastor, until they could be relocated.

In one of his *El Rodeo* columns in *The Tidings* Alphonse Antczak recalled how "displaced persons from refugee camps in Europe were arriving here regularly in long trains. They were met, always at dawn, at the Union Station by Father Mathias Lani, pastor of St. Stephen's, 37th and Woodlawn, and volunteers of Catholic Resettlement. St. Stephen's was a gateway to America and a new life for thousands of European refugees. Fr. Lani was one of the great priests of the Church of Los Angeles. By sheer energy and force of personality he resettled thousands - got them homes, got them jobs."

Many prominent lay and civic leaders visited the parish, including Josef Cardinal Mindszenty in 1974. His words on that occasion were

personifying in themselves the noble traditions of the Hungarian race. The great patriot, Louis Kossuth, whose name is honored wherever liberty is loved, came to this country as far back as 1851. It was not until the decade between 1899 and 1909 that immigration from Hungary developed and reached its highest peak. Hungary has now given to the United States honorable citizens of over three-quarters of a million. The Hungarians gave, as did other immigrants of this country, labor and toil and sweat in the great Eastern and Middlewest cities, in factories, in iron works and in mines. The names of many an Hungarian child of American birth is found on the honor-roll of those who fought under the Stars and Stripes in the World War.

The Saint Stephen Society had been founded in 1927 to prepare the way for the foundation of a Hungarian parish. In February of the following year, Bishop Cantwell asked Father Mathias Lani "to take care of my Hungarian people." Mass was offered for the first time under the protection of Saint Stephen, King of Hungary on April 22, 1928. A church was dedicated on April 6, 1930. On that occasion the bishop said that "we of Los Angeles rejoice when the Hungarian people come together to do as their forefathers often did, to dedicate a church to the glory of God that will perpetuate among us the noblest traditions of a noble and historic race. We are confident that this new church will grow in numbers and they who come in and out of its portals will be models of Christian virtue and practice, and exemplars of the highest type of American patriotism."

In August of 1944, the American-Hungarian Relief Organization was founded "uniting churches of many different denominations as well as labor and civic groups" to benefit the impoverished Hungarian homeland. Later the rectory of Saint Stephen Church became the Office of the Archdiocesan Catholic Resettlement Committee. Over successive years, Msgr. Edward Wade, Father Arnold Biedermann and other local priests looked after spiritual needs of the parish.

The primary beneficiaries of the Catholic Resettlement Com-

*The American Hungarian Relief Organization
was among the recipients of charitable activity*

classic: "If you have no faith, you have nothing." The relief work was monumental in scope. Saint Stephen's Church became the "Ellis Island" of Los Angeles.

Timothy Cardinal Manning wrote in 1978 that his years in the curial offices of the archdiocese "spans forty years; hence I am aware with first hand evidence of the shepherding of God's people that has been accomplished in Saint Stephen's this half century. It is essential that the religious and cultural traditions of a people should be preserved in a new land. The Church is enriched by this variety of gifts."

INDONESIANS

The first Catholic Indonesian families came to the Archdiocese of Los Angeles in the mid 1960s. They were among the 300,000 who found it necessary to leave their then homeland, the former Netherlands East Indies.

Finding the weather in the eastern part of the United States unpleasant, many decided to settle along the west coast. About a third of the repatriates, among them the Marees, are Catholic. Many settled in Saint Pius X parish in Santa Fe Springs.

The Indonesian Catholic population in the Archdiocese of Los Angeles number upwards of 500 families.

IRISH

Save for the Spaniards themselves, the only ones appearing in the record of achievement to extend the frontiers of New Spain into the wilderness of *Las Californias* were Irish. Certainly it was altogether fitting, that those two great nations, Ireland and Spain, which had shared the Faith since penal days, should have cooperated so harmoniously in Christianizing California.

That the Golden State is a beneficiary of the Irish spirit hardly needs emphasis. Here, the sons of Erin have added much to the composite American, made up as it is from various European, Asiatic

Josef Cardinal Mindszenty visited the Chancery Archives on June 21, 1974.

and African stocks. The spiritual disciples of Saint Patrick, co-patron of the Archdiocese of Los Angeles, have softened California wit, added to its tenderness, increased the spirit of good fellowship, augmented its social graces and increased our poetical imagination.

The Irish priesthood has a long and noble heritage in Southern California, though, in all fairness, it should be noted that even before her ministers came, the Faith carried over from Ireland was securely locked away in the hearts of a people who never forgot their religion, despite being deprived for many years of its priestly services.

One historian of California, speaking of the Irish missionaries who followed Bishop Eugene O'Connell to the Southland described the stream of the Emerald Isle's clergy who have so faithfully served this far-western apostolate:

From the Apostolic colleges of Ireland, they came; from St. Kieran's in Kilkenny, from St. Patrick's in Carlow, from St. John's in Waterford, from St. Patrick's in Tipperary and from All Hallows in Dublin. Nor were these messengers of peace all silver-haired divines who had borne the heat and burden of the day, but bright young clerics, just fresh from the anointing at the hands of the bishop, fortified with the continence of the Virgin, the burning zeal of the Apostle, and the spirit and welfare of their fellowmen till death would meet them at the end of the trail.

Joseph Scott, Patriarch of the Irish in Western America.

That long list of Irish missioners perdures to the present day. In Southern California alone, 42 percent of the deceased secular priests and 39 percent of those presently serving in the Archdiocese of Los Angeles proudly claim the Emerald Isle as their place of birth. Los Angeles takes justifiable pride in the accomplishments of those who have been with her through the years since her infancy, those who have helped to make her name glorious in the eyes of the world.

The area is grateful to those trail-blazers who assisted in pushing back the forces of ignorance and barbarism. She is mindful of those who, in the not-so-easy pioneering days, struggled, sometimes at the sacrifice of their own lives, to see that justice prevailed within her borders; of those who freely gave of their time, talent and resource that a stable government might be universally established. California is thankful for those children who have brought her honor.

The Golden State, if she is highly respected today as a benevolent and godly commonwealth, a peaceful and desirable place to live, recognizes her great Irish builders as humble men of God, who by teaching and good example, added their share of knowledge, culture, courage and faith to the state's development.

Pope Pius XI once said of the Irish: They are "everywhere, like the grace of God." Truly, the monuments of Ireland are erected "everywhere," not monuments of cold marble or chilled stone but monuments of living nations whose Faith she had founded, fostered or revived and whose manners she has purified, refined and gilded with superb Christian wisdom.

It would indeed be difficult to define the limits of the spiritual service of the Irish race in this or any other area, and that, perhaps, is why the Holy Father said they are "everywhere, like the grace of God. Everywhere, they are found the champions of morals, the apostles of liberty and the emancipators of people, and races, Everywhere, like God's sunshine giving warmth and glow to a cold and neo-pagan civilization. Truly the Irish pioneers of California were great men and the reward of great men is that, long after they have died, one is not quite sure they are dead!"

ITALIANS

In very few regions of the United States have Italian activities been so important and successful as on the west coast. From the very earliest explorations up to the present time, Italians as individuals and as a group have consistently shared in the work and sacrifices which made possible the constant growth of the Pacific Coast.

The first Italian to anchor in California waters was probably Captain Allesandro Malaspina, who in the years 1786-1788, made a controversial scientific voyage around the world in the service of Spain. A valiant navigator of Florentine origin, Malaspina (1754-1809) is given recognition for having explored the Pacific Coast in great detail. Juan Bonifacio was the first Italian colonist. He landed at Monterey in 1822, where he secured work as a hide and tallow stevedore. Bonifacio became a naturalized Mexican citizen and raised a large family.

The earliest full description of California and its inhabitants written by an Italian, was that of Paolo Emilio Botta, a physician aboard a French vessel commanded by Auguste Duhaut-Cilly. Another early Italian description of California and Oregon was the vivid account of the missionary, Louis Rossi, entitled *Six ans en Amérique Californie*

James Francis Cardinal McIntyre receives invitation to Italian Catholic Convention in Long Beaxh in 1964.

Luigi Providenza was the co-founder of the Italian Catholic Federation.

et Oregon, published at Paris, in 1863. Leonardo Barbieri was a highly-talented artist who painted portraits of members attending the state constitutional convention, in 1849. Barbieri's paintings hang in the Monterey Customs House.

King Victor Emmanuel II appointed Leonetto Cipriani the first Sardinian Consul, at San Francisco, in 1850. He it was, in later years, who supposedly offered President Abraham Lincoln a plan to kidnap Confederate General Pierre Beauregard. In 1859, Cipriani's successor, Federico Biesta, inaugurated *L'Eco della Patria*, the first Italian newspaper west of the Mississippi.

Biesta estimated that there were 6,000 Italians in California by 1850. He remarked that "the Italian population is one of the best, most active and hard-working in California. Strong, industrious, and accustomed to suffering and toil, our nationals tend to their own affairs without taking part in those regrettable disorders that the heterogeneous people of the state give vent to from time to time." He went on to say that "generally, whether in San Francisco or in the interior, the Italians thrive and prosper in their businesses, and there is probably not a village in all California in which Italian business is not well represented, just as there is not a mining district where companies of Italian miners are noted for their good conduct, their fraternal harmony, and for the energy which they bring to their work."

One of the most successful of the Gold Rush arrivals was Domenico Ghirardelli, who traveled through the Mother Lode towns selling chocolate and hard candy. His heirs long continued to operate the Ghirardelli Chocolate Company. Southland residents especially would endorse the words of President Calvin Coolidge that "Italians have immensely contributed and are still contributing with their skill, with their love for liberty, with their genius for science, arts and humanitarian deeds, to make this country what she is today."

Italian settlers have been involved with Southern California's *El Pueblo de Nuestra Señora de los Angeles* since 1823, when Giovanni Leandri opened a general store on the plaza. Father Blas Raho (1806-1862), a native of Naples was assigned to the Plaza church of Nuestra Señora de los Angeles in 1856. Described "as a genial, broadminded Italian," he was noted for his gardening ability, his beautiful chrysanthemums and for his improvement of the church grounds and efforts to raise funds to repair the church following the heavy rains of 1860.

In subsequent years, scores of Italians, attracted by the mild climate, came to the area where they cultivated the lands and operated small businesses. Among those early pioneers was Segundo Guasti who became a prominent wine merchant. By the early 1920s, Italians accounted for nearly 11% of the city's population, and by the 1980s there was 107,000 Italian Americans or 4% of the total population.

The parish of Saint Peter in downtown Los Angeles has always been an umbrella for the Italian community of the archdiocese, since 1915 embodying the religious and cultural roots cherished by every Italian.

The annals substantiate Bishop John Cantwell's remarks to the Apostolic Delegate, in 1933, when he told him that "the Italian people have never been neglected in the Diocese of Los Angeles - San Diego." A non-territorial parish had been set up for the Italians during Thomas J. Conaty's episcopate. A temporary frame church served the area in the years after 1904, and on July 4, 1915, the stone memorial chapel of Andrew Briswalter in old Calvary Cemetery was placed at the disposal of the people. Boundaries were given to Saint Peter's in 1922, when it was detached from Sacred Heart Parish and entrusted to the Salesian Fathers. A population shift brought about establishment of Our Lady Help of Christians Church in late 1924, and the older Saint Peter's then reverted to its earlier status as a mission station cared for by the Claretians from the Old Plaza Church.

Later years witnessed the revitalization of Saint Peter's and, by 1944, a new church was necessary to accommodate the increased numbers. The historic red sandstone chapel was destroyed by fire on June 13, 1944, while being taken down to make room for a larger church. The tragedy brought on a renewed effort to complete the new edifice which was dedicated on July 21, 1946.

While Cantwell acknowledged that "the Holy See in many countries is not anxious to encourage national churches," he went on to point out that Rome "has no objection to a large number of people who are collected together, perpetuating the best traditions of their race. It was to further that objective that he gave his approval, in 1936, to Luigi Providenza's proposal for the formation of the Italian Catholic Federation. The ideological persecution of the Church in Italy had left its mark on many emigrant Italians and it was thought that this excellent organization, embracing as it did both spiritual and social activities, would help to offset the unfavorable conditions of many resettled Italians.

California is the story of an Italian Catholic Federation heritage fulfilled, resources developed and beauty cultivated. Catholicism in the Golden State is likewise the narrative of saint-named cities and mission-marked heroism brought to the twentieth century with vitality and promise.

In the early 1920s, a survey indicated that a vast majority of the Italians and Italo-Americans in Southern California had become alienated from the traditions of their Catholic religion. Mainly responsible for that sad condition were such factors as anti-clericalism, lack of Italian-speaking priests, poor education and, above all, the mentality that economic and social betterment would be accelerated by breaking all ties with their background, foremost of which was the Catholic faith.

In an attempt to reverse that trend, Father Albert Bandini and Mr. Luigi Providenza decided to establish an organization whose primary and ultimate aim would be the reactivation of the spiritual seed which was dormant in so many Italian hearts and souls. The first meeting of the Italian Catholic Federation took place on June 15, 1924 in San Francisco's Church of the Immaculate Conception. Archbishop Edward J. Hanna approved the structure and statutes and, on December 7, the initial branch of the I.C.F. was inaugurated with 300 members.

It was the founders' intention that the I.C.F. should be the instrument for anchoring the Italian descendants to a family apostolate, uniting husband, wife, children and relatives in sacred enthusiasm. That ideal was further implemented through establishment of the *Bolletino*, which has been published monthly since 1925.

From the very outset, the Italian Catholic Federation sponsored missions, retreats and radio programs by Jesuits, Salesians, Josephites, Franciscans and Dominicans to awaken "a more intense Christian life among the Italian population of California." The I.C.F. was introduced to California's southland in 1931, with foundation of the San Roque branch at Santa Barbara, on November 22. Presently, the Archdiocese of Los Angeles is the largest field of work for the I.C.F., with fifty-eight branches in the three county area.

Though envisioned as primarily a parochial society upon which the local pastor could rely for his work the I.C.F. was destined by God's grace to encompass a spirit and vitality that has grown to several hundred active branches. The Italian Catholic Federation observed the golden jubilee of its establishment in 1974, with publication of a 112 page book on *The First Fifty Years*. Therein, the "reason" for the I.C.F. was nobly stated by Msgr. Robert Brennan: "to bring back people to the Body of Christ." The long-time archdiocesan director of the I.C.F. for Los Angeles went on to describe the organization as "an idealogical, beautiful expression of Catholic Action."

JAPANESE

*Japanese celebrate seventy-five years
at Saint Francis Xavier, 1988.*

The origin of the Japanese mission on the west coast was related by *The Monitor* of San Francisco in 1913. A certain Leo Hatakeyama of Los Angeles wanted a priest to hear his confession. Speaking no English, he wrote to his native land offering "to send his confession in a registered letter" and asking that a priest "return the penance and absolution by mail."

Apparently the case was referred to the Bishop of Monterey-Los Angeles, the Right Reverend Thomas J. Conaty. The prelate immediately contacted the Maryknoll Fathers in Massachusetts who, in turn, forwarded the request to the Paris Foreign Mission Society. One of their priests, Father Albert Breton, was sent to Los Angeles and told to organize facilities for the Japanese Catholics in the Golden State. Father Breton arrived in Los Angeles on October 12, 1912 where he found a Japanese colony of 10,000. Although a relatively small number was Catholic, those who did profess the Faith were found immensely anxious to have their needs cared for by a fellow countryman.

It was noted in one journal that "the work of locating the Japanese Catholics in California is being done by Fr. A. Breton, a member of the Society of Foreign Missions in Paris. Long residence in Japan had given Father Breton the advantage of a thorough knowledge of the language and literature of the country. His present residence is Los Angeles." There were about fifty Japanese members of this first Catholic Mission dedicated to the Japanese in America, originally located at 707 West Second Street.

Education of the children was the first perplexing problem. Of the 60,000 Japanese in California, 8,000 were going without a Catholic education. At Father Breton's request, four Catechist-Lovers of the Cross (later known as the Japanese Sisters of the Visitation) from Nagasaki came to Los Angeles to open Saint Francis Xavier Mission School. With the aid of the Franciscans, Daughters of Charity and the Helpers of the Holy Souls, the education and evangelization of the emigrated Japanese advanced rapidly and was greatly encouraged. Many works sprang up... Kindergartens, orphanages, sanatoriums, grammar schools, language schools, music schools, night schools and Sunday Schools.

Breton's influence was felt throughout the state. In San Francisco Archbishop Patrick W. Riordan set up a home and club room at 2158 Pine Street, for classes on "religious and secular instruction." The priests of Saint Mary's Cathedral looked after the foundation during Father Breton's absences in the southland. One contemporary journal told its Catholic readers that "it is needless to speak of the merits of the work, or to suggest the propriety of cooperation. The success of Saint Francis Xavier's mission, and the zeal and self sacrifice of his converts shows us what grace can do among these wonderful people; and the labors of the modern Catholic missionaries in Japan should inspire us to supplement their work on the Pacific Coast."

After World War I, Father Breton was recalled to Japan where, ten years later, he became the Bishop of Fukuoka. In San Francisco the Jesuits took over the work and the Society continued its activities among the Japanese until 1925, when the Divine Word missionaries assumed the charge. Sacramento's apostolate was assumed by the Franciscan Sisters of Niagara, while in Los Angeles and Seattle the Fathers and Sisters of Maryknoll took up the task.

The Japanese apostolate came to a thundering halt on Pearl Harbor day, and overnight the streets of the Japanese communities were abandoned. When the hostilities ended, the people returned to their homes "taller in stature, with the pride of men and women who had proven their faith and loyalty to the land of their adoption by the sacrifice of their sons in that nation's defense."

After World War II, a number of the Japanese interned during the hostilities returned to Los Angeles. Only a small number of them were Catholic. A report sent to the clergy of the archdiocese in 1954 said that "out of a total Japanese population of almost 40,000 in Los Angeles County, Catholics number scarcely 1,200. Father Everett Briggs, a Maryknoller, looked after the Japanese Catholics. With the endorsement and encouragement of James Francis Cardinal McIntyre, Father Briggs served as editor, publisher and treasurer of three Japanese Catholic newspapers, all of which were printed and distributed mostly in Japan. All three tabloids were devoted to giving the Catholic answers to social problems of the day, an important task in Japan where communist propaganda was then prevalent. Saint Francis Xavier Chapel, which was operated under the auspices of Maryknoll, also sponsored a fifteen minute program each Sunday on KBLA. Those programs, in both English and Japanese, were widely circulated. Archbishop John J. Cantwell was quite sympathetic with the plight of California's Japanese during the dark days of World War II. He remarked to a friend that they are "very good people... excellent Catholics," contrasting them to other Orientals "who readily come into the Church but do not always stay put." Cardinal McIntyre personally participated as often as he could in all the outreach activities for the Japanese people.

LITHUANIANS

Though the Lithuanian enclave in Los Angeles, composed mostly of refugees, has never been a "national" parish, it has pretty much functioned in that capacity. Established in 1941, the parish was placed under the patronage of Saint Casimir, the only canonized saint in Lithuania's 600 years history of Christianity.

It was on June 1, 1941 that Archbishop, John J. Cantwell formally granted permission for the Lithuanians to establish a parish in a home at 2411 Third Avenue, between Washington and Adams Boulevards.

In 1948 the original church was sold and another site acquired.

Lithuanian Catholics have been active in the archdiocese since 1941.

Educational facilities were launched and, on November 4, 1951, Archbishop J. Francis A. McIntyre dedicated the new church. A report submitted the following year states that there were approximately 700 registered members of the parish, along with a Sunday school with forty-two students.

Bishop John J. Ward receives offertory gift at Mass for Lithuanians.

Meanwhile in October of 1952, the *Lithuanian News* was begun with a circulation of 1,100 families. Two years later "to promote community spirit and Lithuanian heritage, the so-called Lithuanian Day" was sponsored which drew hundreds of persons from all parts of Southern California.

In 1959 the issue of attaching a "national" status to the parish was discussed with chancery officials. James Francis Cardinal McIntyre concluded the deliberations by noting that there was no precedent for national parishes in the Archdiocese of Los Angeles.

In 1957 a school was established and two years later the parish was given territorial boundaries. The new school was dedicated on March 20, 1960.

There was a great love and affection for the Lithuanian colony in Los Angeles and each year Cardinal McIntyre or one of his delegates would attend a Mass in August for the liberation of Lithuania and the other suppressed nations. In 1957, McIntyre himself presiding at the ceremonies, said "it was our hope and prayer that your noble contributions to American life will ever be sustained." He joined "in expressing sympathy to your brothers and sisters in the homeland as we ask God's bountiful blessings upon them."

When asked by the Lithuanian R.C. Priests' League of America in February of 1960 to allow "a salaried Lithuanian priest" to come to Los Angeles and to engage in work among the Lithuanians exclusively, the cardinal politely demurred, noting that the parish where most of them worshipped was already presided over by a Lithuanian pastor. He felt the archdiocese would "not welcome the injection of a greater and perhaps predominate national spirit" in their lives in Los Angeles.

When a new church was in preparation, in 1961, the archdiocesan newspaper observed that Saint Casimir's parish had "more displaced persons than any other parish in the archdiocese." It also noted that the parish had become "an orientation center to help former Lithuanians in their adjustment to American life."

Archbishop Timothy Manning was always anxious to endorse appeals for the Lithuanian people. In January of 1971, he signed a petition and issued a formal statement protesting Soviet treatment of Lithuanians, one of whom had been forcibly removed from a U.S. Coast Guard Cutter. In a public statement, Archbishop Manning lamented "the forced abduction of a Lithuanian seaman from the protection of our own Coast Guard, with whom he had sought asylum, and the cruel and inhuman sentences passed by the Soviet Union upon a young Lithuanian and his wife who dared to strive for freedom." The archbishop said that "these incidents point up in dark colors one of the great tragedies of our times, namely, the enslavement and repression of a proud nation who had lived peacefully on the shores of the Baltic from time immemorial."

The tragic loss of freedom in Lithuania was always on the minds of that nation's refugees in Los Angeles. An editorial in *The Tidings* for March, 1968 noted that the annual observance independence "has been somber, sorrowful, underlined with the grim accent of defeat and tragedy." It went on to say that:

> The Lithuanians are a proud people who have lived peacefully on the shores of the Baltic from time immemorial. Their language is the oldest in Europe today. They were united into a state in the year 1251, and by the 15th century their nation extended from the Baltic to the Black Sea and almost to the gates of Moscow. Their fortunes gradually declined and the nation was completely taken over by Russia in 1795.

The next century was a period of struggle and national revival, and Lithuania won back her independence in 1918. Her sovereignty and independence were recognized by the Soviet Union in a peace treaty signed in 1920, and confirmed by other treaties in 1926 and 1939. But in 1939 the Soviet Union signed secret agreements with Germany and gave Hitler the release he needed to begin World War II. In violation of its solemn treaties, the Soviet Union forcibly occupied Lithuania in 1940.

During the Mass deportations between 1941 and 1950, more than 300,000 Lithuanians were swallowed up in Siberian slave labor camps. About 75,000 others were able to escape to the West, and about 30,000 Lithuanian freedom fighters were killed in guerilla warfare resisting the Soviet occupation. Thereafter, the history of Lithuania follows a familiar pattern of repression and tyranny.

Over the years, the three Los Angeles cardinals actively supported efforts to free Lithuania. In 1991, for example, Roger Cardinal Mahony said that "it is my prayer that Saint Casimir Catholic community will continue to live out its charge... with clarity, fidelity and commitment."

The eventual freedom, independence and reestablishment of Lithuania was greeted with great joy and celebration among those attached to Saint Casimir's parish.

KOREANS

Though the first Koreans moved to Los Angeles in 1905, there were only a handful living in the area prior to the late 1960s. When the *Korea Weekly* was established in 1969, James Francis Cardinal McIntyre sent a letter to the editor saying that he was "happy to learn that the Korean community in Los Angeles is establishing a medium of expression." He predicted that the reception of the newspaper would "be warm and gracious." A short article in *The Tidings*, the following year, noted that the Korean Catholic Association had grown "from thirty to more than 400 members in two years." McIntyre gave every encouragement to the Koreans, asking Father Lawrence J. Lee, a Korean priest, to offer Masses for them at Saint Vincent's Church each week. Perhaps even McIntyre did not foresee that by the early 1990s, the City of Los Angeles would boast of the largest Korean Catholic population outside the Orient.

The strongest element in Korean society is the Church and it is there that the major portion of their social interaction takes place. About 75% of Koreans attend weekly Mass, a remarkably high number in these days.

When a Korean airliner was shot down by a Soviet fighter plane in September of 1983, Manning sent telegrams to the Korean consul and to the Korean community in seven parishes of the archdiocese:

> On behalf of the Catholic community of Los Angeles which is enriched by so many Korean members, we wish to extend our sympathies to the nation and its people so sadly afflicted with tragedy. May the merciful Father of all give us consolation, forgiveness and peace. The Archdiocese of Los Angeles shares in the sorrow of the Korean community in the recent tragedy. Our prayers are promised for the consolation and peace of this worthy people and for God's mercy on us all.

In his greeting on an earlier anniversary, Roger Cardinal Mahony acknowledged "the vitality of the Korean Catholic communities within the Archdiocese of Los Angeles" as "a marvelous blessing and we thank God for the energy and strength of your Catholic commitment." "Today," he said, "in the Church at Los Angeles, Christ is Anglo and Hispanic, Christ is Chinese and Black, Christ is Vietnamese and Irish, Christ is Korean and Italian, Christ is Japanese and Filipino, Christ is Native American, Croatian, Samoan and many other ethnic groups."

The faith came to Korea in a most unusual way, through diplomatic envoys who journeyed to China each year to pay taxes at the Imperial Court in Beijing. There, they encountered Jesuit priests who gave them Catholic books and religious articles. And so, with the help of neither true missionaries nor priests, a group of Korean scholars began to study Catholic doctrine. They are recognized among the founders of the Church in Korea.

The Catholic community in Korea was formally established by Yi Sung Hun. The nascent grouping, calling one another "believing friends," abolished class distinctions, stopped offering sacrifices to their ancestors and spread the faith through books written in the Korean alphabet.

In 1785, the first in a long series of persecutions broke out. The growth of the Korean Catholic Church, up to 1883, was one of tremendous sacrifice. In 1869, alone, some 10,000 Catholics were sent to their death.

Father Andrew Kim (b.1821) began his ministry in 1843. He was arrested and beheaded just a year later. A number of French priests made other incursions, most of them members of the Paris Foreign Mission Society. In 1886, the Korean-French Treaty ended the persecutions and, thereafter, native seminarians were trained in Seoul.

Pope John Paul II traveled to Korea in 1984 and there canonized 103 of the Korean martyrs, including ninety-four lay people from nearly every walk of life. Also canonized was Saint Andrew Kim in the first such ceremony performed outside of Rome since the 13th century.

The most significant celebration during the 25th anniversary of the Korean Catholic Apostolate in North America was the blessing of the Shrine of Saint Andrew Kim Tae-gon at Holy Cross Cemetery, Los Angeles, on November 7, 1993.

Saint Andrew Kim, the first Korean priest, spear-headed efforts that brought the Catholic faith into his native land two hundred years ago. Only twenty-three years old when he died, Kim's martyrdom symbolized the peace and harmony that the Catholic message offers to a local society.

When the final pages of the history of the Catholic Church in Southern California are written, the chapter on Korean Catholics will figure prominently. The city of Los Angeles presently boasts of having the largest Korean Catholic community outside of Seoul with about 150,000 people.

MARONITES

The Maronites hold a unique position in the history of Eastern Christianity insofar as they were the only Church to have had a monastic origin; secondly they took a theological position which cut them off for centuries from the Holy See and, finally, in the 12th century, they alone effected a lasting reunion with the Latin Church.

Maronite priest, Father Peter Sfeir,
at Our Lady of Mount Lebanon church in 1947.

A parish was provided for the Maronites in Los Angeles in 1923 under the patronage of Our Lady of Lebanon. The Gold Medal was subsequently conferred upon Archbishop John J. Cantwell by the President of the Republic of Lebanon in appreciation of his kindness to the Maronites in Southern California.

The people of Lebanon were also recipients of Timothy Cardinal Manning's concern. He joined his prayers to those of Pope John Paul II, saying that "we are constant in our deep desire for a resolution that will be respectful and just for all religious persuasions in this country beset by violence. We cherish those among us whose origin and inheritance is Lebanese. The great traditions of the United States in humanitarian and peace keeping missions urge us to support and encourage our own government in its best efforts to accommodate that peace and justice for which we all hope and pray."

In mid 1966, James Francis Cardinal McIntyre entrusted to the Maronites the former parish and church of Saint Peter which is now Our Lady of Lebanon - Saint Peter Cathedral. The territory formerly belonging to Saint Peter was then assigned to the neighboring parishes of Saint Victor, Saint Ambrose and Saint Mary Magdalen. At that time there appears to have been about 500 families who transformed their allegiance to the parish bordering West Hollywood.

In 1980, Father John G. Chedid was named Auxiliary Bishop of St. Maron of Brooklyn, with residence in Los Angeles. He was advanced to the newly created Eparchy of Our Lady of Lebanon in Los Angeles in 1991, a jurisdiction encompassing Maronites living in thiry-three states.

MELKITES

Father Michael Bardaouil performs the liturgy in the Melkite Rite.

A Melkite presence in California's southland dates from 1909 when Father Geracimos Sawaya, a Basilian Chouerite priest, arrived in Los Angeles. Bishop Thomas J. Conaty asked if he would serve the spiritual needs of the Melkite and Maronite community. A church was begun in the 1920s and the parish of Saint Anne was organized with less than 250 persons.

On Christmas eve, 1964, a new church was opened and dedicated the following July 25th in North Hollywood. In 1973, His Beatitude, Maximos I (Hakim), Patriarch of Antioch, made a parochial visitation at the site on Moorpark Street. Since that time the liturgy in the Arabic tongue has been offered weekly at several locations in the archdiocese.

NATIVE AMERICANS

The apostolate to Native Americans is the oldest of the Catholic Church's spiritual outreaches in Southern California. Between 1769 and 1840, missionaries from Spain and Mexico provided the sacraments to Indians in missions at San Diego, San Luis Rey, San Juan Capistrano, San Gabriel, San Fernando, San Buenaventura, La Purisima, Santa Ines and Santa Barbara. During the subsequent decades, the bishops, priests and religious continued the apostolate to native Americans scattered throughout the area.

The Indians of California had been pretty much ground to pieces between the Spanish Conquest from the south up the coast, and the Anglos from the east and north across the mountains and over the desert. The pitiful condition of these people has been described as the result of fierce attack in which "never before in history has a people been swept away with such terrible swiftness." The normally peaceful attitude of the California native made him an easy prey to the greed of unscrupulous exploiters, a fact which accounts for their almost total lack of resistance to the seizure of their property and possessions.

That depravity had ruined even the lives of the state's 15,000 Christian Indians was noted in an account penned by a priest from Los Angeles shortly after the entry of California into the union:

Poor Indians of California, how abandoned they are and how deplorable is their lot.

Two Native Americans at Saint Thomas Indian School in Yuma, 1883.

This is a memorial to the Native Americans buried at San Fernando Rey de Espana Mission in Mission Hills

specialized work, Amat offered the project to the friars at Santa Barbara for their consideration. His proposal was declined though and it was some time before he could fill the need of the southern part of his diocese. Those natives living in and around San Luis Rey had, at least, nominal homes something which could not be said of the other areas of the state. In one report it was pointed out that,

To the missions they can never go again, with hope of finding a home. The successors of the friars are there, for a priest is stationed at all except two, I believe. Any Sunday a few Indians may still be seen near the altar, summoned by the chimes that once pealed over a smiling multitude gathered for worship or the harmless diversions wherein their happy hours passed away. The rest linger there in their straggling huts of brush or tile, trying to get a meager subsistence out of the small patches not yet taken up by whites-ill clothed, in filth and wretchedness, without food half the year, save what is stolen.

Commenting on the natives of Los Angeles, John Bartlett said he observed more Indians "about this place than any part of California" he had visited. "They were chiefly Mission Indians, that is those who had been connected with the missions, and derived their support from them until the suppression of those establishments." Some thought, however, that regression to the earlier program was not the answer. And even one writer later noted that "there are many well-meaning men, I know, who favor the idea of restoring them (the Indians) to the Missions: the measure is impracticable."

Contact with civilization daily ruins their race more and more, particularly because of that great agent of destruction which is called whiskey. There are whites who kill Indians just to try their pistols. Almost every week our little village witnesses from eight to ten murders; but it is during the night between Saturday and Sunday when the most abominable crimes are committed. Many times I have had to hear the confessions of some of these mortally wounded victims.

From the outset, Bishop Thaddeus Amat was deeply concerned about the natives, their poor living conditions, their maltreatment and most of all their spiritual direction which, he acknowledged, had often been overlooked. He told one of his correspondents that:

I have already taken steps toward obtaining the establishment of a religious community, either in San Luis Rey or in some other point more central to the Indians, whose object would be to attend to the civilization of the same; and another of the Sisters of Charity to perform the same duty toward the Indian females; the only means by which, in my estimation, we can effect a real and lasting good, especially if we can obtain assistance from the Superintendent [of Indian Affairs] for I must confess, that I feel myself unable to perfect this...

Bishop Amat meanwhile had been asked by an agent of the United States Government for several priests to take charge of the 3,000 natives living around the San Luis Rey area. Knowing something of the history of California and the successes of the Franciscans in that highly

Nonetheless, an act of Congress on March 3, 1853, authorized the gathering of Indians into reservations and the United States Government found it imperative for saving the very lives of the surviving Indians to adopt the methods of the Franciscan friars, the very mission system which Fray Junipero Serra and his bretheren wisely introduced in 1769 for saving the souls of the natives. Of course there were differences in the two systems; under mission rule, the natives were treated as children which was never the case on the Federal Reservations where the Indians were regarded as mere orphans and treated accordingly.

Establishment of reservations did not solve all or even a majority of the Indians' problems. That they were frequently ill-cared for by government officials can hardly be denied. Father Anthony Ubach at San Diego reported in 1873 that

> I have been seven years in this place and therefore amongst them as they form a large part of my congregation and during all this period of time, no Indian Agent or Commissioner has even come down among them to see how they get along.

Ubach's plea for honest and capable agents was based on the practical contention that "many thousands of dollars would be saved by the National Government if good honorable men would be appointed as its Indian Agents."

When the question of governmental assistance came up for reappraisal in 1875, a long report was addressed by a special commissioner to the Department of the Interior urging governmental action to avert utter starvation from the neglected charges. Credit in the report was given to what little Catholic missionary activity had been possible, and the commissioner freely stated that "it is an undeniable fact that to this day the Roman Catholic priests have a strong influence over the Mission Indians, which

influence might be exerted for their benefit if the Government would do its duty by the Indians." Obviously then, the Church was still a vital part of the native culture even though it was not often able to provide as much material assistance as might have been desired.

And certainly if the Church found itself unable to lighten the blows of secular indifference toward the California natives, the cause cannot be placed at the feet of the Bishop of Monterey-Los Angeles. Lack of personnel, paucity of funds and generalized apathy on the part of the state's white population combined to make this aspect of Amat's episcopate something less than a total success. Another generation would carry on this noble work in the mid-1870s when the Bureau of Catholic Indian Missions was set up in Washington to coordinate Catholic endeavors in this field on a national level.

One graphic example of Bishop Thomas J. Conaty's pastoral zeal was his deep concern for the spiritual and material plight of the few remaining California Indians. At the time of his arrival in the southland, the only places in the vast diocese where Indian children were receiving a Catholic education were the two schools operated by the Sisters of Saint Joseph, one at Banning, the other in San Diego. Only three priests were ministering exclusively to the natives, Father B. Florian Hahn at Banning, and Fathers Anthony Ubach and A.W. Schneider at Yuma. The bishop augmented their number by assigning two additional priests to the task. Almost immediately work was inaugurated at Sherman Institute near Riverside on a chapel. The pastor at St. Rose of Lima Church in Hanford, Father Patrick Brady, was assigned to care for the Tache Indians and Father George Freund at Kern was instructed to look after the Tejons attached to Our Lady of Guadalupe.

The outlying houses of worship for the mission stations of Pala were rebuilt in order to better accommodate the religious needs of the 850 Indians still there; the chapel at Cahuilla was renovated; two additional *capillas* were erected on the desert floor near Banning and another at Tache, near Hanford. Additional edifices at Santa Ines, San Jacinto and El Cajon were "expected to give preference of time and interest to the Indians." Two serviceable chapels located at La Jolla and Rincon were constructed entirely by Indian labor, with workmanship that would have reflected credit on any white carpenter.

An editorial in one journal observed, "The crowning work in this line has been accomplished at Saboba, California, through the munificence of Bishop Conaty and the hard labor of Father William Hughes and his Indians who have built, in the old mission style, a monument, in the shape of a chapel of concrete, that will probably endure as long as the Saboba Indians themselves." The repair of existing facilities was a concern too. When the central building at Saint Boniface Indian School was destroyed by fire in 1911, it was immediately replaced by Bishop Conaty and the generous people of the Diocese of Monterey-Los Angeles.

Conaty was not at all provincial in his outlook on this or any other matter. Though desperately short of clerical personnel qualified for the arduous missionary work among the Indians, the bishop did not hesitate to release one of his most valuable priests, Father Hughes, in 1910, for the more encompassing task of helping to direct the nation-wide activities of the Bureau of Catholic Indian Missions. Conaty's interest in the general welfare of the Indians was such that "while he made it a point to urge upon his diocese an annual collection as possible for the Colored and Indian Missions, he never made application for an allocation and never received one cent from the Lenten collection. He was willing that the proceeds should go to other dioceses less fortunately situated than his, and the only help he received from the Catholic Indian Bureau was for the meager support of St. Boniface's Industrial School at Banning."

A measure of the bishop's personal involvement in promoting the welfare of the California Indians is reflected in a written memorandum which President Theodore Roosevelt asked the prelate to submit following a visit by the Bishop of Monterey-Los Angeles to the White House in May of 1904. Conaty singled out three areas he thought the Chief Executive should examine regarding the 4,000 Catholic Indians in his jurisdiction. The first was marriage. Invalid and illegal unions were common, and the bishop felt that "it would be wise to urge upon the agents the advisability of recommending that all Indians belonging to any Church have their marriage performed by the clergymen in charge of their Church or Chapel, as many of them, especially the Catholics, realize the conscience obligation as to the sacramental character of the contract."

Another source of Conaty's anxiety was the liquor policy which, at that time, was very ineffective inasmuch as the Indian policeman was apt to be afraid of his fellows in the stringent enforcement of any required regulation. Conaty thought that the wholesale fear of jail would act as a repressing influence upon the Indian and the fear of the penitentiary would hinder the Mexicans and the Whites from invading the reservations with their wagons of liquor.

A third and most vexing difficulty arose from the undefined condition of land tenure among the Indians. When California was ceded to the United States, treaty provisions recognized inhabitants of the area, including Indians, as citizens of the Republic of Mexico with the privilege of emigrating there within a two-year period. Those wishing to remain in California would enter the United States under the same status as they enjoyed under Mexican rule; hence the California Indians were *ipso facto* citizens of the United States, though in most cases they were totally unaware of their legal standing. Their lack of knowledge often resulted in loss of holdings to unscrupulous white men. To remedy the evil and to save at least some of the land for the Indians, Congress set aside 85,000 acres in Southern California for the natives, empowering the President to have surveys made prior to erection of reservations. Though the total area eventually amounted to three or four hundred thousand acres, eighty percent of it was mountainous or desert.

The land remained subject to Congressional litigation, since it exceeded the original allocation. This last factor resulted in an almost constant molestation of the Indians by government officials. In addition, the small amount of arable land made it difficult for some of the reservations to give sufficient returns to the Indians for their industry in cultivation.

Bishop Conaty impressed upon the President the necessity of appointing honest agents to remedy this situation. He urged Roosevelt to consider naming the agents from a section as remote as possible from the reservations, so they would be free from the influence of white people in the vicinity. The prelate also suggested that the government send a good, reliable, unprejudiced inspector to make a thorough investigation of the area. Such a man should be instructed to consult, not only with the agent, but with the Indians, priests and ministers, as well as with those of us who have general charge of the spiritual affairs of the Indians.

President Roosevelt thanked the bishop for his memorandum and promised to take up the matter in detail with the Department of the Interior. Secretary E.A. Hitchcock later acknowledged the observations which Bishop Conaty "so clearly and intelligently set forth on the conditions of the Indians in Southern California" and asked the Indian Bureau for a full report on the situation.

In the opinion of California's poet laureate, John Steven McGroarty, Bishop Conaty might well have worn a Franciscan habit himself for "dear to him are the glories of his ancient diocese, dear to him are its ruins and dearer still the welfare in his care of those who are baptized by the early *padres.*"

The number of Catholic Indians descended from mission times residing within the Diocese of Los Angeles-San Diego, in the early 1930s, could not be exactly determined, though the figure was approximated at 4,800. Twenty-one station churches and chapels served their needs at such places as Campo, Capitan Grande, Pala, Pauma, Warner Springs, Arlington, Banning, Palm Springs, Saboba, Fort Yuma and Cahuilla. Two special schools were in operation, one at Arlington, the other at Banning, with an enrollment of about 300 youngsters. Four priests were engaged exclusively in caring for the Indians and four others worked with them on a part-time basis.

The esteem for James Francis Cardinal McIntyre among Native Americans was amply demonstrated by a feature story that ran across the wires of the NCWC News Service in April, 1958. It proclaimed that "the Apaches of Arizona have a new chief. His name is Red Robe Friend. In his own territory, he is better known as His Eminence James Francis Cardinal McIntyre. The investiture took place at the Statler Hilton hotel, before 1,000 members of the 144 Lay Mission Circles. The Apaches had come from Saint John's Mission, Komatke Village, to express their appreciation for the cardinal's aid to Indian missions. They said it in actions by their spirited dancing and in words by making Cardinal McIntyre a chief of their tribe."

By 1969, the archdiocesan newspaper estimated that there were about 45,000 Indians in the jurisdiction, about ten percent of whom were Catholic. Widely scattered, they were affiliated with fifteen tribes. The article noted that the native Americans no longer fought off the white man's gun fire with bow and arrow. "Instead, he fights the white man's indifference with calmness, patience and a courtesy that ought to be the envy of older Christian civilizations. He is not angry with the white man's rush to affluence. To curse the darkness is the one luxury the American Indian knows he cannot afford. He is too busy trying to reach the American dream."

Today the Archdiocese of Los Angeles is blessed with the largest urban population of people with some degree of Indian blood in North America. It is comprised of upwards of 100,000 Indians representing over 130 tribes in Southern California, of which roughly two-thirds are Roman Catholic.

The ministry to the Native Americans was formally established in November of 1989. Presently the major outreach is through the Kateri Circle, a community of Catholic Indians under the patronage of Blessed Tekawitha.

POLISH

The initial Polish imprint on Southern California can be traced to May 1, 1805, when Captain William Shaler's 175 ton Lelia Byrd put into a bay on Santa Catalina Island for repairs. Because the bay which served the weary seamen as an hospitable haven had not yet been designated with a name, Shaler, the proto navigator to visit and survey the area "took the liberty of naming it after my much respected friend, M. de Roussillon." The conferral of his Polish companion's name was the first such appellation applied in California by an American. Although Port Roussillon does not survive in the Golden State's geo-

Then Karol Cardinal Wojtyla visits a Polish church in Los Angeles on August 29, 1976.

graphic nomenclature, present-day Avalon remains the scene of the first link in what has become a formidable Polish presence in California.

The first Mass for Poles in Los Angeles was celebrated in Saint Vibiana's Cathedral in 1908. There were at the time sixty-five people in Los Angeles whose country of origin was Poland (Russia), along with another fifty-five from the "other" Poland.

The initial Polish church was built at 5134 Towne Avenue in the 1920s when the official United States census listed 2,516 Poles in Los Angeles. That number grew to 12,872 with the passage of another decade.

A church was dedicated on November 28, 1926 and, by 1940, there was also a school in operation. A new location was acquired on West Adams Boulevard where the first Mass was offered in a temporary structure on March 3, 1944. At that time the title and patronage of Our Lady of the Bright Mount was approved by Archbishop John J. Cantwell.

The "only Polish church is California" was dedicated by Auxiliary Bishop Timothy Manning on December 9, 1955. On August 29, 1976. Cardinal Carol Wojtyla (subsequently Pope John Paul II) offered Mass at Our Lady of the Bright Mount to begin celebration of the parish's golden jubilee.

Among the many Polish organizations founded in subsequent years was the Saint Stanislaus Club, begun in 1946 with the purpose of providing Catholic activity, social and spiritual; the Polish Fraternal Association in 1949, the Polish Center in 1967, the Polish American Credit Union in 1970 and the Polish Retirement Foundation in 1977. Described by one writer as "one of the brightest monuments of the Polish American heritage in Southern California, is the parish of Our Lady of the Bright Mount in Los Angeles."

Though their numbers have never been large, the Poles have left a noble record in western American annals. One writer says that "here in the sunny land they found freedom and new homes, they found friends and a measure of prosperity. They repaid the young commonwealth with the best that was in them." This they surely did and today their numbers even include a member of the California hierarchy, the Most Reverend Thaddeus Shubsda, who served as Bishop of Monterey.

The Polish Pope visits Saint Vibiana's Cathedral.

Bishop John J. Ward at a meeting for the Polish millenium in 1965.

*Father John Ryder
celebrates Russian Liturgy.*

PORTUGUESE

The Portuguese have a long and noble history in California. Juan Rodriguese Cabrillo, the European discoverer of California, was Portuguese, though he sailed in Spanish vessels. Many of the early Portuguese in Southern California came from the Azores and introduced such native crops from their homeland as sweet potatoes.

In the late 1870s, a Portuguese man named Fayal settled at what is now the corner of Sixth and Front streets in San Pedro. Later the Portuguese began gathering in and around the city of Artesia which was named for the artesian wells in the area. Their spiritual needs were served by a small church on the corner of Corley and 187th street dedicated to the Holy Family.

In 1947, the pastor purchased property on Clarkdale Avenue for a parochial school. As a tribute to the efforts of his Portuguese parishioners, the priest dedicated the school to Our Lady of Fatima. As the dairy farms gave way to the city of Cerritos and to other tract housing developments, the ethnic make-up of both the school and parish changed. Today, Our Lady of Fatima parish is composed primarily of Filipino, Chinese, Korean and Latins.

RUSSIAN GREEK

Russians in the southern part of their homeland, known as Molokans, came to Los Angeles as early as 1906. Before and after the 1917 revolution, there were sizable emigrations to the United States.

Archbishop John J. Cantwell welcomed them to Los Angeles where they functioned in Boyle Heights overlooking Hollenbeck Park. An article in *America* magazine described the "strange and lovely little chapel as one to arouse the interest of all American Catholics." The essay went on to say that it was "the first place of worship in the United States which belongs to the new Russian Catholics rite."

By 1937, there were reportedly 20,000 non-Catholic Russians living in and around Los Angeles, a fertile field for the peoples attached to Saint Andrew Byzantine parish. One writer said that "God is worshipped amidst sacred ikons, the opening and closing of doors, the majesty of eastern ceremony, and the sound of an ancient tongue. It is a Mass that reaches for its origins through Cyril and Methodius back to the more ancient Antioch of Peter and Paul." Father John Ryder, a Jesuit, was attached to the parish for many years. And he did much to popularize the Russian liturgy in parishes of the Latin Rite.

When the freeway took their property, the community moved to El Segundo where many of the Slovaks were working in the Standard Oil refineries. By 1986, most of the congregation was made up of non-Russian Byzantine Catholics. Their numbers had decreased to about forty persons. The pastor of St. Andrew Russian Church, Archimandrite Alexei Smith, also serves as archdiocesan Director for Ecumenical and Inter-religious Affairs.

RUTHENIANS-BYZANTINE

The Catholic Church has unity of faith in all things divinely revealed, but it does not have uniformity in worship, in matters of spiritual life and ecclesiastical discipline. Of the five Eastern Rites - Alexandrine, Antiochene, Armenian, Byzantine and Chaldean, by far the largest is the Byzantine Rite, while the Armenians are the smallest.

Statistics reveal that in 1985 in the United States, about 73% of Eastern Rite Catholics were members of the Byzantine Rite which is composed of four major ethnic traditions: Ruthenian, Ukranian, Melchite and Romanian. Byzantine Catholics began coming to the United States in significant numbers at the end of the 19th century.

The first Byzantine or Ruthenian Rite parish on the west coast, part of what was then known as the Eparchy of Passaic, New Jersey, can be traced to late 1956 when Father Eugene Chromoga arrived in Los Angeles. With the endorsement of James Francis Cardinal McIntyre, Father Chromoga established the parish of Saint Mary which functioned temporarily from the tiny church of Our Lady of Zapopan in North Hollywood. Weekly liturgy was celebrated in the Old Slavonic language and in English. Property was later acquired at 5324 Sepulveda Boulevard for a permanent church which was solemnly dedicated by Cardinal McIntyre on February 21, 1961.

In 1981, the Holy See established the Diocese of Van Nuys with Saint Mary's church as cathedral. The new diocese included thirteen western states with fifteen parishes. With a Byzantine population of 16,000, the diocese of Van Nuys was a suffragan to the Byzantine-Ruthenian Metropolitan Providence of Pittsburgh.

During the ceremonies of erection, Timothy Cardinal Manning sketched the background of the area named after a New Yorker of Dutch descent. He noted that "the area had been part of the San Fernando Mission lands and consisted in wheat fields" which he regarded as "comprising spiritual wheat fields."

Father Eugene Chromoga established Saint Mary parish for the Ruthenians or Byzantines in Los Angeles.

A copy of the Lord's Prayer in Syriac or Aramaic, the language spoken by Jesus.

A chancery and bishop's residence were erected for the area which was entrusted to the care of Bishop Thomas V. Dolinay. Due to the destruction caused by the Northridge earthquake, the diocesan headquarters were moved to Phoenix, Arizona, in 1994.

SALVADORIANS

Timothy Cardinal Manning was particularly vociferous in favor of the Salvadorians and attempts to deport them. He asked Secretary of State George Shultz to grant the refugees extended voluntary departure status, thus allowing them to remain until conditions subsided in their homeland. In part, his letter said:

"In recent times because of strife in their countries, extended voluntary departure status has been granted to, among others, Ugandas, Ethiopians, Poles, and Lebanese. Objective evidence exists of the high level of indiscriminate political terror and violence in El Salvador and of the particular liability of repatriated persons to persecution and death. These facts have been recognized by the United States High Commission on Refugee Affairs. It has designated all Salvadorans outside their country as political refugees."

"The Catholic Bishops of the United States have also taken cognizance of the facts of the situation. Motivated by a Christian concern for the human rights and welfare of the Salvadoran refugees, the bishops have, since 1981, asked that Salvadoran refugees be granted extended voluntary departure status. It is true that a nation must safeguard its borders. It is also true that these refugees are present among us in numbers greater than in any other American city. To recognize and ameliorate their plight is but to assert traditional American concern for God-given human rights, foremost of which is the right to life.

"Therefore, I ask that Salvadoran refugees in the United States be granted extended voluntary departure status, so they may have a safe haven until the end of the civil war in El Salvador enables them to return to safe and peaceful conditions."

According to the 2004 *Quinquennial Report* for the Archdiocese of Los Angeles, "immigrants from El Salvador arrive in the United States best equipped to assume leadership roles in the Church."

SAMOANS

The majority of Samoan Catholics in the Archdiocese of Los Angeles live in Long Beach and its environs. They constitute the largest Pacific island group in the southland. Samoans are mainly Polynesian, closely related to the native peoples of Hawaii, Tahiti, Tonga and New Zealand. American Samoans are United States nationals.

Most of the Samoans in the archdiocese live in or around Long Beach.

SYRIAN CATHOLIC OF ANTIOCH

The Syrians, in the ecclesiastical sense, are the descendants of the Aramaic Christians of ancient Syria, who have retained the early Christian Syrian rite of Antioch, and who live today chiefly in Iraq. There are Christians of the Syrian rite also in Syria, Lebanon, Egypt, and the United States.

Syrians came to Los Angeles in the 1990s and three years later purchased a former Mormon church and complex on Collins Street in North Hollywood.

Today Jesus Sacred Heart parish has upwards of 180 families from Orange County to Palmdale and Victorville to Santa Barbara. The parish belongs canonically to the Eparchy of Our Lady of Deliverance in Union City, New Jersey.

Liturgy is offered for the mostly Iraqui congregation in Aramaic, the language spoken by Jesus.

UKRANIAN BYZANTINE

The year 1984 marked the first centenary of the founding of the initial Ukranian Catholic parish in the United States. Immigrants to the west were mostly victims of persecution in the Soviet Union.

The Church of the Nativity of the Blessed Virgin Mary, at 2511 Third Avenue in Los Angeles, was founded in 1947 mainly by transplants and displaced persons who migrated to Southern California because of the mild climate.

They purchased the old Lithuanian church which was re-blessed on March 7, 1948. Five years later the parish site was moved to De Longpre Avenue in Hollywood. The parish still has allegiance to Saint Nicholas Eparchy in Chicago.

In 1968 the parish was visited by Patriarch Josef Slipyi, then on a worldwide tour of Ukranian communities. The air-borne apostle, like his counterparts of earlier ages, told his scattered peoples in several places that "they needed to keep their faith strong and without compromising their responsibility as American citizens. If you do not watch your children, they can disappear like drops of water in the ocean"

VIETNAMESE

Following the fall of Saigon in 1975, the first wave of immigrants from that country came to Southern California. They were composed mostly of government officials, army officers, doctors, lawyers, businessmen and other professional people. The next surge came in the late 1970s bringing in a different breed of Vietnamese: peasants and fisher folk fleeing poverty, young men evading conscription in the mother country's wars against China or those expelled by the communists as suspected surrogates of China. Escaping by the sea, often aboard rickety, overcrowded crafts, these boat people were lashed by savage storms or ran out of food and water. Many were robbed, raped and even murdered by pirates.

By 1983, there were clusters of Vietnamese in Burbank, San Gabriel, Altadena, East Los Angeles, El Monte, West Covina, Pomona, Whittier, Norwalk, Long Beach, Torrance, Culver City, Van Nuys and West Los Angeles.

In 1989 Archbishop Roger Mahony visited Vietnam. He reported that the Church there was "alive and vigorous" and "living out the Gospel in a difficult and complex situation with remarkable persistence and strength."

A number of parishes sponsored Vietnamese families, including San Buenaventura Mission in Ventura. Families were provided housing, employment and other necessities of daily life. In every case, those who participated were assimilated into parochial life.

In 1991, a series of by-laws were adopted by the Catholic Vietnamese community in the archdiocese. The five goals enumerated were:

* To preserve religious heritage of Vietnamese Martyrs and Saints-our ancestors and heroes and to promote the excellent aspects of our Vietnamese culture;
* To build up a Christian community of love and assist each other in the life of Faith;

* To make a commitment to the works of evangelization;
* To actively participate in and contribute to the activities of local parishes and those of the Archdiocese of Los Angeles in enriching themselves with Christian spirit and values and to carry out charitable works in the fourteen parishes with Vietnamese liturgies where social, and cultural activities are needed.

Timothy Cardinal Manning
with Vietnamese refugees at Camp Pendleton, 1985.

Bishop John J. Ward with Vietnamese Sisters of Mary
Immaculate who escaped from Hue, 1975.

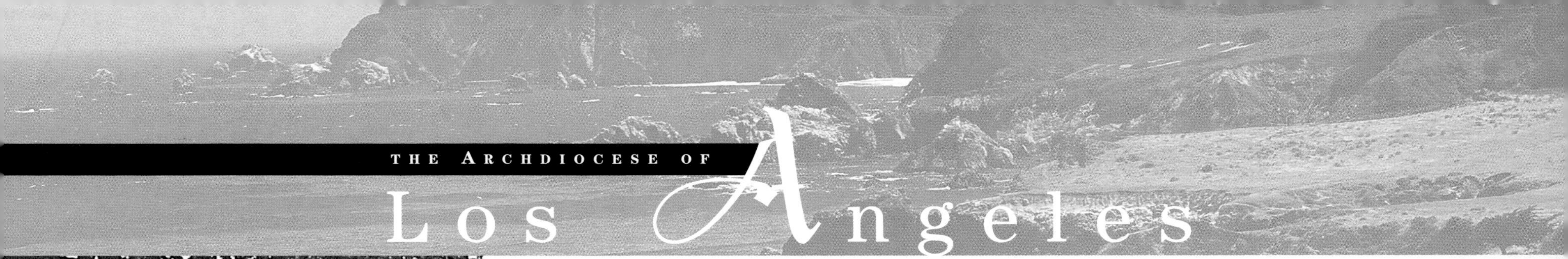

PARISHES

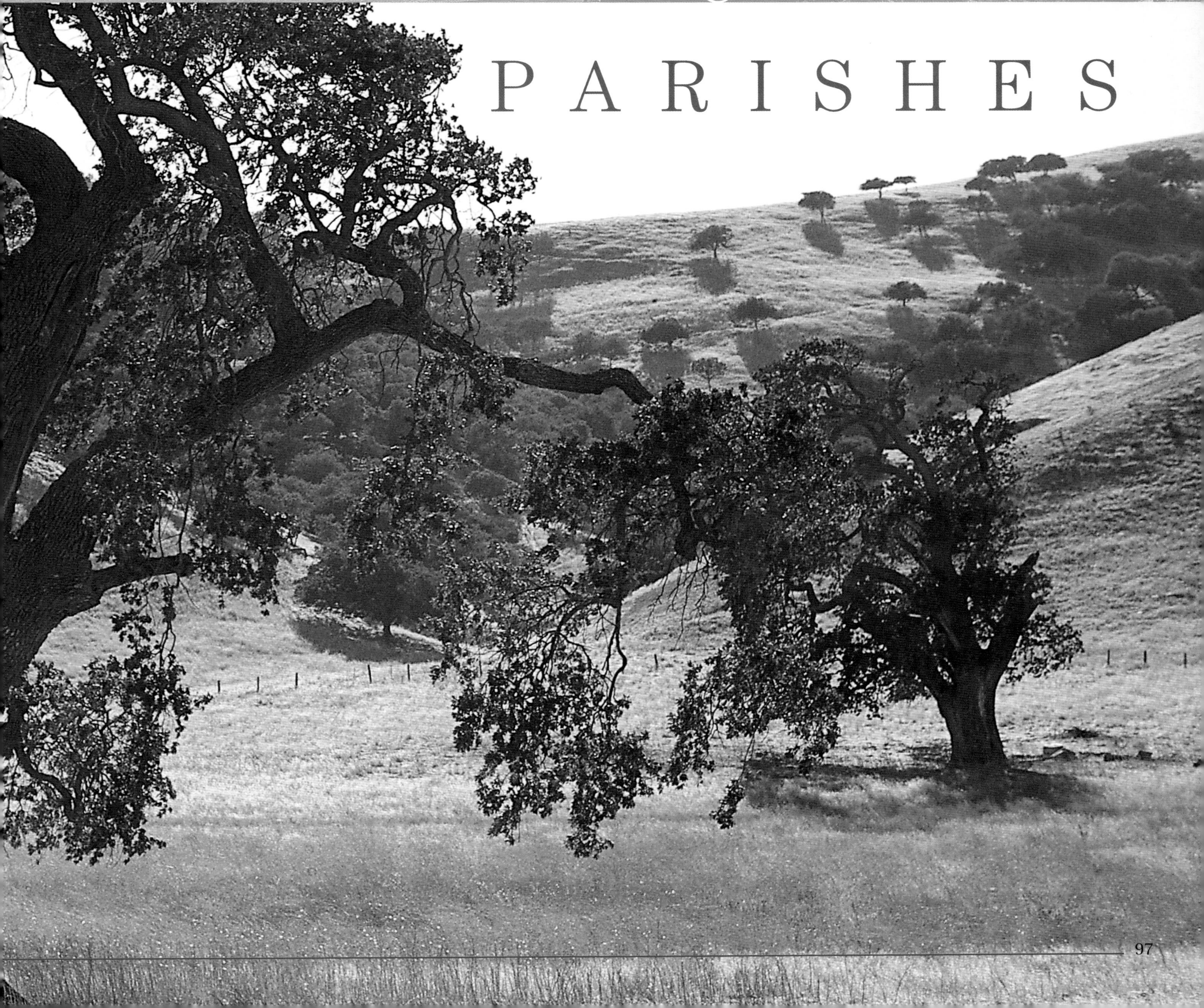

Cathedral of Our Lady of the Angels

2002

Cardinal Roger Mahony dedicated this second cathedral for the archdiocese September 2, 2002. The Spanish architect, Rafael Moneo, designed the church that seats 3,000 and has become a landmark in the downtown area, located on Temple Street and Grand Avenue. Saint Vibiana was the original cathedral for the city, opened in 1876, and named in honor of the third century virgin and martyr. For almost 120 years the church functioned as the center for the rapidly growing city, but renovations were insufficient to withstand several earthquakes that severely damaged the building, and it was closed in 1995. The new cathedral contains striking tapestries of 135 saints, immense bronze doors designed by Robert Graham and a chapel in the mausoleum area containing 6,000 crypts. Millions of visitors tour the imposing site each year.

Cathedral of Our Lady of Angels dominates freeway

All Saints

1926

This parish began as a mission in 1921 in the El Sereno area of Los Angeles. Father Paul Dillon was the resident pastor in 1926 followed by diocesan priests for the next forty-two years. One of the early pastors, Monsignor Patrick Shear, shepherded All Saints for eighteen years, built the school and convent, and enlarged the church. He was the first Archdiocesan director of the Propagation of the Faith. The Dominican Sisters from Wisconsin became the teachers. In 1968 the Minim Fathers took charge of the parish. Saint Francis of Paula founded the Order in Italy in the 15th century. Father Gino Vanzillotta, a native of Italy, became pastor and oversaw many changes in his twenty-two years of ministry. The present pastor is Father Jose Vega. The parish is located on Portola Avenue near Huntington Drive.

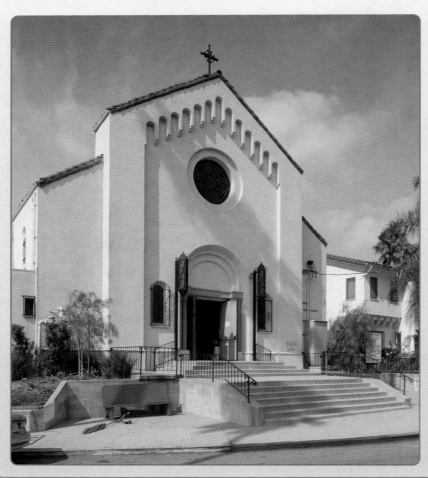

Ascension

1923

Father Patrick Dunne celebrated Mass for Ascension parish February 11, 1923. In the same year the new Diocese of Los Angeles-San Diego created eighteen parishes – part of the post-World War I building boom in Southern California. Bishop John J. Cantwell named the parish for the feast day of Christ's Ascension. The Aircraft Hall on Broadway served as the site for the first Mass where early residents were largely French-Canadian. After using a temporary chapel on Figueroa, a church was completed in 1925 by Father Louis Genest and the Sisters of Saint Joseph of Carondelet taught in the new school. Monsignor George Scott, son of the famous attorney, Joseph Scott, headed the parish from 1939 to 1946. The church is located on 112th Street and Figueroa. Present Pastor is Fr. Humberto Bernabe 2800 Saints.

Assumption

1927

This parish was one of seven early places of worship erected on the East Side of Los Angeles for Spanish-speaking Catholics, most of whom were fleeing persecution in Mexico. The first building was a small mission chapel until the church near Evergreen and Winter Streets was finished in 1961. For thirty-three years Father John Fosselman, a native of Iowa, headed the Boyle Heights parish and oversaw the church construction. Father Joseph McArdle, a former pastor, conceived the plans and made the purchase of the present site. The old church on Fresno Street, about eight blocks away, is still used for several Masses on weekends and twice during the week.

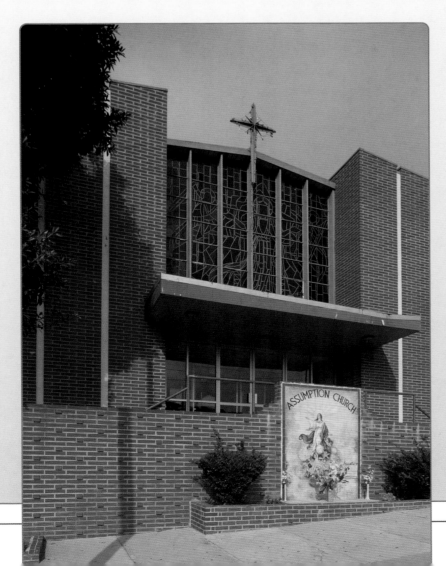

Blessed Sacrament

1904

The Catholic Church in famous Hollywood traces its history to the Indian village of Cahuenga where Masses were celebrated. By 1900 priests from the Cathedral of Saint Vibiana and the Plaza traveled to the former Indian village to serve Catholics in the area. In 1904 Father Daniel Murphy was appointed pastor. Five years later the motion picture industry arrived and an unusual partnership grew between the parish and fledgling movie-makers. Jesuit Fathers were appointed administrators in 1914 with Father William Deeney as pastor. A new church, frequented by many renowned stars, was built in 1928 on Sunset Boulevard. By the golden jubilee in 1954, the compete renovation of the church made it the "finest thing in Hollywood." Jesuit Father

Cornelius McCoy was pastor for twenty-five years. The area has changed dramatically in subsequent years.
1998 to present, pastor is Fr. Michael J. Mandala, S.J.

Cathedral Chapel

1927

Monsignor John Cawley became the pastor of what was originally envisioned as the "pro-Cathedral" for the Southland. The previous year the chapel of Saint John Vianney on Detroit Street was built for the students attending the junior seminary of Los Angeles College. Plans to build the initial church into a cathedral never materialized. Instead, the church located on La Brea Avenue near Olympic Bld was enlarged, remodeled and adorned by succeeding pastors – Monsignors Bernard Dolan and James Dolan. The parish school opened in 1930, staffed by Immaculate Heart Sisters. At the golden jubilee in 1977, Pastor Earl Walker estimated that at least thirty men from the parish had been ordained priests. The school on Cochran Avenue is now staffed entirely by the laity. Since 1998 Father Charles L. Schwehr is the current Pastor.

Christ The King

1926

This south Hollywood Church on Rossmore Avenue was established in October, a year after Pope Pius XI proclaimed the feast of Christ the King. Monsignor Peter Corcoran continued his pastorate for thirty-eight years in the parish that originally served much of the growing movie industry. In recent times its congregation had been predominantly Asian and Hispanic. The church is constructed in an Italian Byzantine style, modeled after Saint Sophia Basilica in Constantinople and Saint Mark's in Venice. By 1950 a series of stained glass windows by Joseph Tierney and murals by Belgian artist Marrissaael were added. The twelve-foot Carrara marble statue of Christ the King in front of the church was erected in 1957. The parish school opened in 1958 on Arden Boulevard and is still active. The faithful celebrate Mass in English and Spanish.

Cristo Rey

1939

Augustinian Recollect Father Jesus Domench started this parish in a small rented house that served as a temporary chapel, providing for the religious needs of the Spanish-speaking residents of the Atwater section of the city. His arduous efforts and the sacrifices of parishioners built a church in 1943, and by 1955 the mission church at Perlita Avenue and Chevy Chase Drive near Griffith Park received canonical status as a parish. For fifteen years Father Gabriel Salinas, former American superior of the Recollect Augustinians, headed the parish that was dedicated to the memory of the Mexican martyrs and their rallying cry of "Viva Cristo Rey." He died in 1972 at age eighty from injuries sustained in an automobile accident. The Augustinian Recollect Fathers still administer the parish.

Divine Saviour

1907

The parish of Divine Saviour had its beginnings in 1907 [when the Diocese was Monterey-Los Angeles]. Father J. W. Organisiak received permission from Bishop Thomas Conaty to open a mission for Polish-speaking Catholics. By 1914 the mission became largely English speaking and was formally erected as a parish. A frame church was built in 1924 and forty years later was replaced by an edifice on Cypress Avenue. With seating for 800 persons it has a distinctive hyperbolic parabola roof on steel girders. The altars are of Mexican onyx and Italian Carrara marble. Both the stations and statuary are Italian woodcarvings, all reflecting the various backgrounds of the parishioners. Although the parish borders the Southern Pacific freight yards, it also serves an area of homes in the Mount Washington area.

Dolores Mission

1945

In 1925 a small group of Catholics built a little wooden church on Eagle Street, near the Los Angeles River. Spanish-speaking priests from Saint Mary's came to minister to the small group until a new highway changed the area. Archdiocesan officials then purchased four lots in the area called "the Flats" at Third and Gless Streets and Our Lady of Talpa parish donated their old church for the corner lot. By 1945 the building was enlarged, renovated and named Nuestra Señora de los Dolores. The Missionaries of the Immaculate Heart of Mary staffed the parish of mainly Mexican immigrants located near the housing projects, and in 1950 opened a school. Father Herman Louwagie, C.I.C.M., was named pastor in 1970 and worked closely with the population of some 7,000 persons. The Jesuits took charge of the parish in 1980 with Father Francis Gallagher as pastor.

Holy Cross

1906

On November 4, 1906 Father Thomas Fahey, the founding pastor, celebrated Mass in a small, rustic cottage on South Main Street that later became the school. By 1913 the parishioners had erected a red brick Gothic building, considered at the time one of the most beautiful in the city, at a cost of $50,000. The Sisters of Saint Joseph of Carondelet staffed the school. In 1910, the first Holy Name Society in the city was established. The Long Beach earthquake of 1933 damaged both the church and school, but both were subsequently rebuilt and remodeled. In 1970, the Comboni Missionaries (Verona Fathers) were named to administer the parish. Another quake caused considerable damage in 1987. The following year the church re-opened despite extensive repair costs, primarily due to the restoration of the sanctuary. Since August 2004, the current pastor is Reverend Father Tesfalset-Asghedom MCCJ.

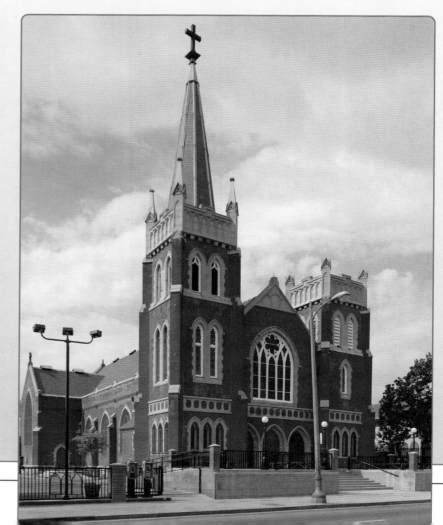

Holy Name of Jesus

1921

The roots of this parish extend to 1903 when it was part of Saint Agnes Church. An old wooden chapel served the neighborhood on Jefferson Boulevard until 1921 when Bishop John J. Cantwell established a canonical parish. Father Matthew Marron became pastor and erected a larger brick and stucco building in 1924. The Sisters of Loretto opened the school the same year. In 1953 a red brick church replaced the second building with a seating capacity of 700 and an eighty-foot-high tower. The first edifice was converted to an American Legion salvage store. Construction for a new school started in 1960 and two years later, on completion, an auditorium was added. In 1999 Jesuit Father Gregory Chisholm was named administrator for Holy Name of Jesus parish, which now serves primarily African American, Hispanic and Belizian parishioners. Current pastor is Rev. Paul Spellman.

Holy Spirit

1926

Both the church and the rectory for Holy Spirit parish, situated on the corner of Pico Boulevard and Dunsmuir Avenue, were completed in one year and then dedicated by Bishop John J. Cantwell on Thanksgiving Day, 1927. Father Patrick Concannon was the pastor of the church that exemplified Spanish revival architecture. Ten years later the school and convent were built and the Immaculate Heart Sisters staffed the school for thirty years. Father Michael Mullins from Ireland, a former chaplain in World War I, served as pastor for thirty years, retiring in 1968. The next pastor was Monsignor Patrick Dignan, former superintendent of archdiocesan schools. The parish community has changed through the years from those of European descent to primarily Hispanic, African-American, Filipino and Vietnamese. The current pastor Rev. Paul A. Susthyta arrived in February of 2000. He is responsible for the church's exterior and interior restoration displaying its original beauty.

Holy Trinity

1925

When this parish was established, the area of the city was known as Atwater Park. The church is located on Boyce Avenue near Glendale Boulevard and was formally dedicated in 1936. In 1965 James Francis Cardinal McIntyre dedicated the two-story brick parish school of eight classrooms, library and offices. That was during the pastorate of Father Daniel Gallagher who also built a rectory. He had been pastor for thirteen years when he died at age fifty-eight in 1964. The area, now known as Atwater Village, has a population of 75% Filipino with many Korean and Hispanic families in the parish. The congregation attends Mass in Spanish and Korean. At a Korean Center, located on San Fernando Road, liturgies are celebrated in English and Korean. Two of the former pastors are in residence – Fathers John J. Daly and Thomas Peacha.

Immaculate Conception

1909

This church was originally intended to be the site for a new cathedral, and in 1909 a chapel dedicated to Our Lady of Guadalupe was built on Ninth Street with priests initially attending from Saint Vibiana. Monsignor Francis Conaty became rector in 1914, and pastor in 1918, the year the school was built. In 1926 the name of the parish was changed to Immaculate Conception and a large basilica style church was planned. It was consecrated in 1954, during the pastorate of Monsignor Joseph Truxaw, who served from 1935 to 1972. During that time the Lourdes Grotto, the Rosary Chapel and the stained glass windows were installed. Immaculate Heart Sisters taught at the school for sixty-five years. Pope John Paul II visited the downtown church in 1987, and in 1989, the Operarios del Reino de Cristo priests from Mexico began their service.

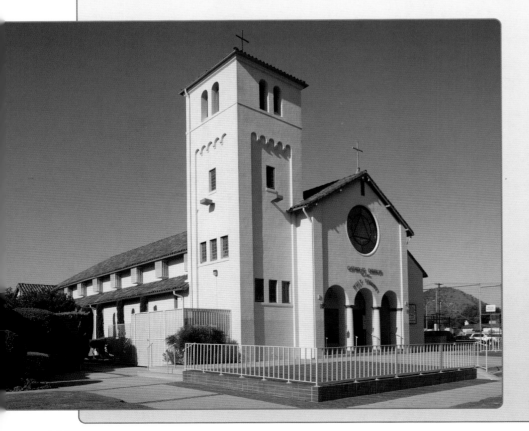

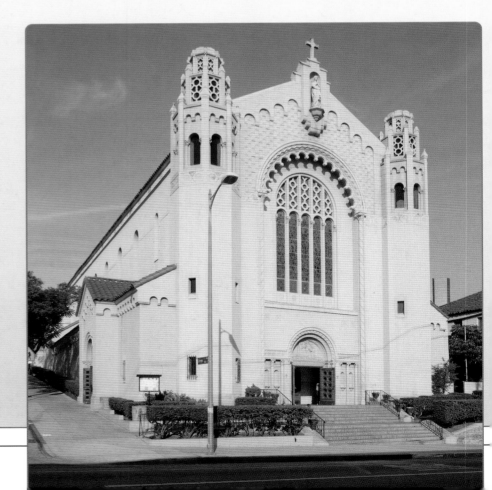

Immaculate Heart of Mary

1910

Father D. W. Murphy built a parish hall, rectory and school at Immaculate Heart of Mary in 1910, and two years later Bishop Thomas Conaty named Father Stephen Cain as pastor. The church building was finished the same year. A modified Gothic structure was erected in 1941 on Santa Monica Boulevard followed by a rebuilt school in 1955 staffed by Immaculate Heart Sisters. Monsignor John O'Donnell directed the construction of both the church and school during his thirty-one years as pastor. Steel spires were built in 1957 that added thirty-six feet to the height. Monsignor Carl Bell was pastor for eleven years at the parish where he had as a youth attended the elementary school. Religious Sisters of Charity now administer the school and Masses are celebrated in English, Spanish and Tagalog.

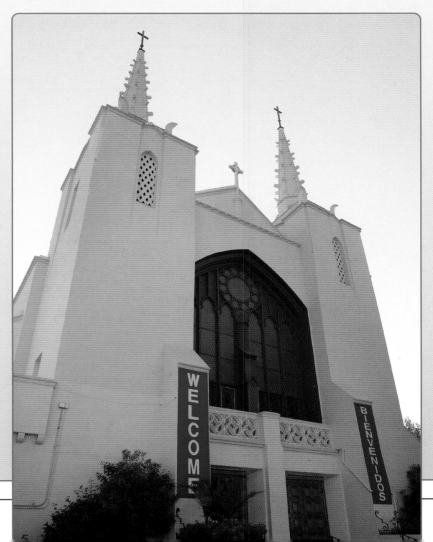

Mother of Sorrows

1923

Bishop John J. Cantwell established this parish at Main Street and 87th Place in 1923. Father Joseph Loughran was the pastor. It was dedicated in 1926. Monsignor William O'Donnell was pastor for thirty-one years and was responsible for starting the school that opened in 1948, staffed by Sisters of Notre Dame de Namur. Through the years the school has faced severe economic times in the low-income area of South Central Los Angeles. Various grants have assisted with tuition costs and other expenses. Father Perry Leiker supervised a liturgical renovation during his twelve-year pastorate as the church celebrated its 75th anniversary. The parish is predominantly Latino and African-American. Father Dario Miranda, born in Mexico City, was named administrator in 1999 and pastor in 2001.

Nativity

1920

In 1920, Father Edward J. Riordan celebrated Mass in the Dougherty residence on East 53rd Street, a year before the church was built. By 1925 a parochial school had been opened during the pastorate of Father John Clifford. The 1933 earthquake damaged the school and much of the church statuary. Father Henry Gross renovated the entire exterior of the church in 1936. Additional classrooms were added during the years to accommodate the increased influx of families in the South Central area. In 1950 Father Thomas Moran obtained ground for a convent. Father David Herrera was pastor from 1985 to 1996 during the time of the Los Angeles riots and the Northridge earthquake and started Spanish language liturgies at the parish. In 1997 Monsignor Timothy Dyer was named pastor, and the parish was clustered with Saint Columbkille in Team Ministry. Repairs to the church and remodeling was completed in march 2002.

Nativity of Blessed Virgin Mary

1948

(Ukrainian-Byzantine of Saint Nicholas Eparchy)

On March 7, 1948 Father Roman Lobodyeh dedicated the first Ukrainian Rite Church in Los Angeles. He came as a refugee from Poland the previous September to organize this parish and resided with the Vincentian and Franciscan Fathers before opening the church on Third Avenue. He had escaped to Cracow from the Soviets and served as a chaplain in forced labor and refugee camps. In 1957 Monsignor Michael Koltusky was named pastor and the church moved to 5154 De Longpre Avenue. He headed the parish for twenty-five years. Monsignor Peter Leskiw was appointed pastor in 1982 and oversaw extensive renovation of the church, parish hall and rectory. A golden dome and icons of two guardian angels facing the Madonna with Child and Christ the Teacher dominate the white stucco church. The parish center contains an exhibit on Ukrainian history.

Our Lady of the Bright Mount

1 9 2 6

The idea of a Polish church in Los Angeles originated in 1911 from a Polish Alliance group headed by Father Stanislaus Marciniak. A small church was built in 1926 at 52nd Street and Avalon Boulevard, by Father Bronislaw Krzeminski. He planned a church with property on Adams Boulevard purchased in 1944. Father Stanislaw Jureko completed a church in 1956 that featured a mosaic of the "Black Madonna" of Czestochowa. Father Jureko was pastor for nineteen years. During the pastorate of Father Zbigniew Olbrys, a member of the Society of Christ, the future John Paul II, Karol Cardinal Wojtyla, visited the Polish parish and preached at the Sunday Masses. From 1991 to 1995 Father Andrzej Maslejak administered the parish and is now Provincial of the Society of Christ. The pastor of the Polish parish is now Father Edward Mroczynski. In 2004 the administrator is Father Bogdan Molenda.

Our Lady of Guadalupe

(HAMMEL STREET)

1 9 2 3

This East Los Angeles parish, one of ten named for Our Lady of Guadalupe, was founded in 1922 when Bishop John J. Cantwell appointed Father Jose Grajales to minister to the Mexican immigrants in the area. Mass was celebrated in garages until a small church was built on Fisher Street. Through the early years many of those escaping persecution in Mexico found a refuge in this community. From 1957 to 1991 Monsignor William Atwill headed the parish and in 1967 built the church on Hammel Street, blessed by James Francis Cardinal McIntyre on July 16th. He was named Pastor Emeritus in 1991 and died in 2005. Parish outreach now includes the mission of San Felipe de Jesus Evangelization Center on Geraghty Avenue, where Mass is celebrated weekly, and Guadalupe House on East Dozier Street, a residence for seminarians preparing for the priesthood.

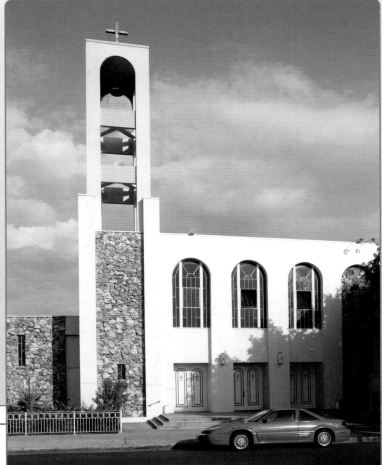

Our Lady of Guadalupe (ROSEHILL)

1928

As a Confraternity Center, this mission of Sacred Heart parish opened in 1924 and Father Antonio Arias celebrated Sunday Mass in a small hall on Mercury Avenue. The first resident priest was Father Alberto Lopez who came in 1928. A rectory moved from Sacred Heart was used until 1934. In 1945 Father Ramon Soriano became administrator at the small church. By 1953 the city decided to build a playground where the church stood, and through many donations and fundraisers, lots were purchased across the street where the church is now located. By 1954 the mission was named a parish and Monsignor Soriano served there for almost thirty-one years and was noted for his generosity and care of all parishioners. A school was blessed in 1961. Father Juan Enriquez served from 1989 to 1994 and the current pastor is Father Moises Apolinar.

Our Lady of Guadalupe Sanctuary

1929

A small hall on top of a hill in what was the Belvedere district served as the initial church that is now located on Second Street near Mariana Avenue. The site overlooks the city of Los Angeles and in the early 1930's became a center for many of the refugees from the persecution in Mexico. Monsignor Vincente Guzman was the founding pastor. His dream was to create a sanctuary similar to the Basilica of Guadalupe in Tepeyac, Mexico. A modest version was accomplished when the cornerstone was placed in 1941 and the church was completed that year with a seating capacity of 250. One of the main features of the church is the 48-foot mosaic and marble shrine of Guadalupe situated on Second Street. Father Leslie Delgado was named pastor in 1986 and completely renovated the interior of the church where each Sunday ten Masses are celebrated in Spanish.

Our Lady Help of Christians

1923

The Salesian Fathers staffed this parish erected for Italian residents of Lincoln Heights, northeast of downtown Los Angeles. Father Paschal Beccaria, the pastor, built a wooden church in 1924 and in 1930 constructed a new building. Father Nunzio Picarelli administered the parish from 1935 to 1941 and included the Spanish-speaking in his ministry. Monsignor Vincent Lloyd-Russell built the school and revived Mexican devotion and liturgical customs. In 1951 the Pious School Fathers, or Piarists, were named administrators and Father Enrique Pobla became pastor. In his ten-year pastorate, he built a school and a shrine to Saint Joseph Calasanctius, the European saint who established the first public free school and founded the Pious School Fathers who still guide the eastside parish.

Our Lady of Loretto

1905

Bishop Thomas Conaty established this parish for the northwestern part of the city in 1905. The pastor was Monsignor George Donahoe who in 1906 celebrated Mass in the Temple Street car barn before the church was built. In 1959 a modern concrete and brick church replaced that original red brick Gothic structure on North Union Avenue. A 90-foot bell tower adjoined the church and a seven-foot statue of Our Lady of Loretto was placed above the main entrance. Monsignor James Nash, pastor at the time, served there for ten years. He was followed by Monsignor John Languille, who was the director of the Catholic Welfare Bureau, and headed the parish for eighteen years. In 1988 the parish was placed under the care of the Divine Word Missionaries and Father Eamonn Donnelly from Ireland was the first of his order to serve there.

Our Lady of Lourdes

1910

Through the efforts of Benedictine Fathers who had already established Saint Benedict church in Montebello, the parish of Our Lady of Lourdes in the area of Belvedere started in 1910. Father Gratian Ardans said Mass in a dance hall on First and Indiana Streets for eighty people. A small frame church was built shortly after and by 1912 a rectory and hall were completed. A parish school opened in 1915 and in 1930 a church, recognized as an outstanding modern architecture example, was constructed by the second pastor, Father Edmund Basel. In 1958 a 54-square-foot mosaic of Our Lady of Lourdes' apparitions was added during the pastorate of Father Lawrence Spencer. Benedictine priests served the parish for seventy-eight years. Now Divine Word Missionaries serve the parish. Present pastor is Father Eamonn Donnelly SND.

Our Lady of Mount Lebanon
St. Peter Cathedral (MARONITE)

OUR LADY OF MT. LEBANON **1923**

SAINT PETER **1935**

MT. LEBANON-SAINT PETER **1966**

The original center for forty-five Maronite Rite families began in 1923 after a visit from Monsignor Joseph Daher from Lebanon. A house was purchased at Warren and Brooklyn Avenues and Father Paul Meouchi became the resident pastor. A church was built in 1933 on the same site. Pope Paul VI later appointed Father Meouchi Cardinal Archbishop of Tyre, Lebanon. The Maronites are named after Saint Maron, Apostle of Lebanon. Monsignor John Chedid became pastor in 1956, and ten years later the parish was moved to San Vicente Boulevard in West Los Angeles. In 1980 he was named a bishop of the Maronite church and then in 1994 the Eparch of Our Lady of Lebanon. Father Abdallah Zaidan is now rector of a parish that has over 1,500 families. Some liturgies are celebrated in Aramaic.

Our Lady Queen of Angels

1784

The Church of Our Lady Queen of the Angels is known as the Plaza or La Placita and was the only one named for the Blessed Mother in one of the largest cities of the world. With the earliest settlers to the area in 1781 came a priest who celebrated Mass and planted a cross on the site. Construction started in 1784 and ended in 1790 as an outreach of San Gabriel Mission. In 1826 it became a separate entity under the administration of the Franciscan friars. The Missionary Sons of the Immaculate Heart of Mary, the Claretian Missionaries, succeeded them. Over the years several restorations and expansions have occurred, and after the 1965 earthquake damaged the 1913 addition, a church was built back-to-back of the original. The Claretian Missionaries still serve the parish of mainly Mexican parishioners.

Our Lady Queen of Martyrs (ARMENIAN)

1952

The old San Antonio de Padua Church on Pleasant Avenue in Boyle Heights underwent complete refurbishing to accommodate the Armenian Rite established there by Father Michael Akian, C.M.Vd. The parish plant included the former Bronson House and the CYO settlement house that adjoined the church. The ancient Kingdom of Armenia in the third century became the first Christian nation, and Our Lady Queen of Martyrs is the first Armenian Catholic Church in the west. In 1985 the Apostolic Exarch of Armenian Catholics visited Los Angeles and Timothy Cardinal Manning presided at a Mass at the church, praising those who are "inheritors of this rite." In a visitation report of 1990 it was related that the parish was one of eight in the Eparchy of the U.S. and accounted for some 2,000 families.

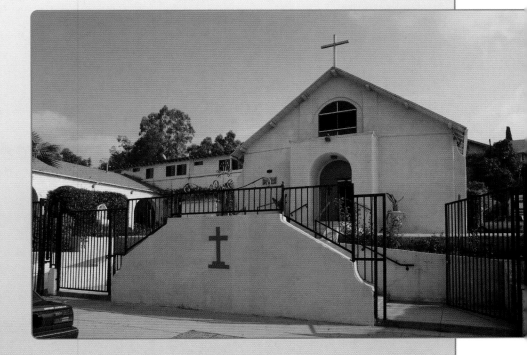

Our Lady of the Rosary of Talpa

1928

Priests from Saint Mary's parish in East Los Angeles first attended this small chapel where many of the Mexicans fleeing persecution in Mexico lived. In 1938 Spanish Vincentian Fathers were placed in charge of the church on Fourth Street. During World War II a former Japanese meeting hall was moved to the parish site and remodeled. A white stucco building was completed in 1943. Vincentian Father Joseph Cervera built the church, school, convent and rectory during his twenty-four years as pastor. La Purisima Chapel in 1960 was named a mission of the parish. The present church was built in 1974. Entering the church to the right is the statue of the Virgin of Talpa and to the left that of Our Lady of San Juan de los Lagos. Vincentian Fathers from Mexico now administer the parish. The current pastor is Rev. Silviano Calderon, C. M.

Our Lady of Solitude (LA SOLEDAD)

1925

Monsignor Michael Sheahan, a native of County Cork, Ireland, was the founding pastor of this East Side parish established for the Mexican community in the Belvedere area on Brooklyn Avenue. He organized the parish and built the church and school accommodating 140 children. In 1930 the Claretian Fathers were placed in charge and in 1946 added a grammar school. Local artist Rodolfo Vargas carved the famous wood statue, blessed in 1940, of Our Sorrowful Mother, clothed in black velvet and holding symbols of Christ's suffering. Father Louis Olivares was pastor from 1975 to 1981 and was a leading social activist in the Latino community. The Claretians administered the parish for sixty-nine years until 2000 when the parish was transferred to the Missionary Servants of the Word from Mexico. Current pastor is Reverend Father Julio Cesa Ibarra since 2003.

Our Lady of Victory

1966

Our Lady of Victory Mission was part of Resurrection parish in East Los Angeles until the parish was established in 1966 with Father Armando Salazar as administrator. It started with a small church, rectory and catechetical youth center on Herbert Avenue. The center had its roots in a garage and service station that served as a site for instruction for fifty years. In 1967 the parish was placed in the care of the religious congregation of the Missionary Servants of the Most Holy Trinity with Father Athanasius Goode, S.T., pastor. The Missionary Servants or Trinitarians were founded in Alabama in 1929 and work in many foreign countries. Timothy Cardinal Manning blessed the 500-seat concrete masonry church in 1976. The title of Our Lady of Victory has its origin in the 16th century, when Pope Saint Pius V established the feast.

Our Mother of Good Counsel

1925

The Augustinian Fathers have headed the Vermont Avenue parish since its founding. Bishop John J. Cantwell invited them to come from Pennsylvania to establish this parish. Father John O'Farrell was the pastor. In 1933 the school opened in two small cottages staffed by Immaculate Heart Sisters who continued teaching there for thirty-five years. A school building was erected in 1949. After World War II the parish also served the Rodger Young Village housing development nearby. In 1959 a concrete church was completed with a bell tower 138 feet high, and a larger-than-life-size crucifix above the main altar. Local liturgical artists Edith and Isabel Piczek designed and installed fifty-one stained glass windows. James Francis Cardinal McIntyre blessed the church in 1962. Augustinian Fathers still staff the parish.

Our Saviour

1957

A group of students formed the first Newman Club in 1923, and in 1944 Father Thomas Connelly, C.M. served as chaplain. In 1957 Bishop Timothy Manning blessed a permanent Newman Center at University Avenue and 32nd Street which replaced the old Newman clubhouse nearby. The building included a chapel for 300, choir balcony, auditorium, large library, chaplain offices and quarters for resident priests. Father Joseph Weyer became pastor, scheduled Catholic information classes and was also on the University of Southern California faculty. In 1967 the Servite Fathers were named to administer the campus parish, and during the 1984 Olympics Our Saviour Church served the spiritual needs of the athletes. In 1993 Father William Messenger, a native Angeleno and archdiocesan priest, became pastor. A parish center is planned in the near future. In 2005 Father Lawrence Seyer became administrator.

Precious Blood

1923

Monsignor Michael O'Halloran became pastor for the church on Hoover Street and Occidental Boulevard in 1923. In the early years Mass was celebrated in the home of Charles Murray and in a small temporary church. The first liturgy in the renowned Italian Romanesque church was offered on October 31, 1926 and Bishop John J. Cantwell dedicated the reinforced concrete building November 25. The Irish born pastor shepherded Precious Blood parish for almost forty-seven years. A parish school opened in 1950 and a parish auditorium was completed in 1951. Two years later the pastor finished ornamentation of the church interior. Originally the area comprised mostly elderly people residing in large homes, but now it is mainly an apartment house district. Since 2003 the Missionaries of Jesus serve the largely Filipino and Latino congregation.

Presentation of Mary

1925

Presentation parish in southwest Los Angeles was established in 1925 and the church was built the following year. The pastor, Father Francis Benson, was noted for encouraging several vocations to the priesthood and religious life. The church was dedicated to Our Lady under the title of her Presentation. Because the 1933 earthquake damaged the building, it was completely renovated in 1950. During the pastorate of Father John Rengers, a striking crucifix of hand-carved walnut was installed above the altar. Monsignor John Deady became pastor in 1964 and served for twenty-one years. During World War II he served with the Marines in the invasion of Iwo Jima. Father Gregorio Raymundo, from the Philippines and a university professor for twenty-five years, served as pastor for eight years. From 1997 Monsignor Benigno A. Rodriguez is the pastor of the church.

Resurrection

1923

Resurrection was one of seven parishes established December 12, 1923 by Bishop John Cantwell. Father William O'Regan was pastor for the East Side church and a rented home served as his rectory and chapel until a church could be built in 1924. Another church was built in 1965 during the pastorate of Monsignor Ramon Garcia, who headed the parish for nineteen years. Following him in 1973 was Father Donald Montrose, later named an auxiliary bishop of Los Angeles in 1983. Since 1984, Monsignor John Moretta, a native Angeleno, has served as pastor at the East Opal Street parish and has been actively involved in Right to Life issues. He founded El Centro Sagrada Familia and was chairman of the task force established by the Family Life Bureau to oppose school pregnancy clinics.

Sacred Heart

1887

This was only the fourth parish founded in the city of Los Angeles. A small committee raised enough funds to buy two lots on Sichel Street and Baldwin Avenue. Father Patrick Harnett was pastor. In 1890 the Dominican Sisters of Mission San Jose opened the school. The church was completely decorated by 1904 with massive tower, spire and stained glass windows. During World War II Father Timothy Galvin served followed by Father John Curran who was pastor until his retirement in 1973. The church faced enormous repair costs in 1989 resulting from years of earthquake damage. Many vocations were fostered from the parish including Bishop Alden Bell of Sacramento, Monsignor Anthony Brouwers (founder of the Lay Mission Helpers), Archbishop Robert Lucey, Bishop Joseph Sartoris and Fathers Tobias, Gilbert and Juan Romero. From July 2004 Fr. Mario Torros is the current pastor.

St. Agatha

1923

A temporary chapel was built at the corner of West Adams Boulevard and Mansfield Avenue when the parish was erected on December 12th, 1923 with Father Edward Bradley as pastor. There was one baptism in 1924 and by 1926 twenty-two children were instructed for First Communion. A rectory was constructed shortly after and in 1936 the Roman Basilica type church was completed. The year 1969 radically changed the parish boundaries with consequent change in demographics. Liturgies in English and Spanish include Gospel Music, and various ethnic cultures are honored in parish celebrations. In 1996 Father Kenneth Deasy became pastor and through town hall meetings has invigorated the church community, uniting the African-American and Latino groups and bringing about dynamic participation.

St. Agnes

1903

Saint Agnes was one of three parishes opened by Bishop Thomas Conaty in 1903 and was placed under the direction of Father Clement Molony. A temporary chapel was erected at West Adams Boulevard and Vermont Avenue and the church building was completed in 1907. The Gothic structure with twin towers became a landmark in the city. Original windows were later replaced with stained glass ones from Munich, Germany. Saint Agnes School opened in 1914. Father Molony directed all the buildings for the parish and served there for forty-six years until his death in 1949. Monsignor Patrick Dignan was pastor from 1949 to 1953. A Mediterranean-style church replaced the original building in 1961, and in 1967 the parish was placed under the direction of the Society of the Precious Blood priests with Father Bernard Schmitt as pastor.

St. Aloysius Gonzaga

1908

Bishop Thomas Conaty established this parish in November 1908. Father P. J. McGrath celebrated Masses in a bungalow on Crocket Boulevard and the church was built shortly thereafter, and then remodeled in 1922. The school opened in 1921 staffed by the Sisters of Mercy, who taught there for over fifty years. During the pastorate of Father William O'Regan, a nine-classroom school and auditorium were built with the auditorium used as a temporary church. In 1951 the parish center was completed, combining the church, school and meeting facilities when Father John Stapleton was pastor. Saint Aloysius was called an "island" parish, surrounded on three sides by the city of Los Angeles and Huntington Park on the other. Recent pastors, Fathers Robert Pizzorno and George Bellavista served as associates and administrators.

St. Alphonsus

IGLESIA DE SAN ALFONSO

1922

This parish was originally a mission chapel of Our Lady of Lourdes in East Los Angeles, administered by the Benedictine Fathers, and was named Saint Joan of Arc. Diocesan clergy were placed in charge in 1924 and the mission was made a parish with Father James Buckley as pastor. During the pastorate of Father Patrick O'Dowd, the parish name was changed to Saint Alphonsus. He headed the parish for twenty-seven years until his death in 1963 and was responsible for purchasing the present site on Hastings Street near Atlantic Boulevard. The church was consecrated in 1961 and a parish school and auditorium built in 1945. Relics of Saint Alphonsus Liguori were sealed in the altar stone. Two auxiliary bishops of the Archdiocese have served as pastors – Joseph Dougherty and Juan Arzube. The parish is mainly Hispanic, and the school remains an active center.

St. Anastasia

1953

A temporary church was built in 1953 that converted an old reservoir into a chapel for parishioners of the Westchester-Playa del Rey area. The parish was named for James Francis Cardinal McIntyre's titular church in Rome shortly after he was named to the Sacred College of Cardinals. Saint Anastasia was a fourth century martyr in Rome. Father James P. Diamond was the pastor and during his twenty-five years heading the church, the parish, school, convent and rectory were built. Several hundred men renovated the old reservoir into a chapel and again in 1955 helped to construct the school and outside equipment. In 1990 Monsignor Royale Vadakin was named pastor of the expanding parish. He served until 2003 when he was appointed Vicar General and Moderator of the Curia for the Archdiocese of Los Angeles.

St. Ann

A temporary church at the corner of Dorris and Blake Streets was obtained under the administration of Father William Schulte. In 1948 the cornerstone for a new building was blessed when Father Patrick Scott was pastor. Monsignor Kenneth O'Brien, pastor from 1955 to 1962, had also served in the Chancery Office for thirty-six years. He was a doctor of Canon Law and a Chor-Bishop in the Maronite Rite. Following him was Irish born Monsignor John Brosnan, pastor for twenty-three years of the parish that lies between the Los Angeles River and the eastern bluffs of Elysian Park on Blake and Riverdale Avenues. In 1986 another Irish priest was named pastor, Father Hugh Crowe, from County Galway, who had served in the Archdiocese as a parish associate and hospital chaplain since 1958.

St. Anselm

B ishop John J. Cantwell established this "Westside" parish in 1924, and a year later Father James Morris was named pastor and celebrated Mass in the rectory. During the early years, baptisms and marriages took place in the neighboring parish of Saint Brigid. The next pastor, Father Patrick Concannon, built a Tudor Gothic style church in 1926. The school opened in 1937 during the pastorate of Father Martin McNicholas. In 1943 Monsignor John K. Clarke was named pastor. He headed the Confraternity of Christian Doctrine for thirty-three years and founded the Borromeo Guild Book Store. He was pastor for thirty-eight years. In 1956 the original church was razed and a Spanish Mission style building was completed in 1958. The present pastor, Father Lawrence Shelton, was appointed in 1981 for the parish on 70th Street.

St. Anthony

CROATIAN

1910

This downtown parish on North Alpine and Grand Avenue was built originally by Croatian immigrants who came here in 1905 and attended Saint Peter's Church. In 1910 Father Anthony Zuvich arrived and the church was dedicated that year. Through the years most of the pastors have been Croatian, but two were Irish and one was Polish. Many ethnic organizations have contributed to the growth and maintenance of the parish which includes a Croatian language school for children. In 1996 a parish and cultural center opened, encompassing a 48,000-square-foot complex next to the church. Saint Anthony parishioners raised most of the funds and provided more than $400,000 for refugees and war victims in Europe. In 1950 Monsignor Felix Diomartich, a native of Croatia, was named pastor and served for thirty-six years followed by Father John Segaric.

St. Basil

1920

Father William Hughes, the pastor, secured property at Seventh and Catalina Streets and had a church erected in seventy-five days. In 1922 the next pastor, Monsignor Edward Kirk, had the original church moved to Wilshire Boulevard and Harvard to better serve parishioners. He inaugurated the devotions to Our Sorrowful Mother that became so popular that five separate services were offered each Friday. But in 1943, a fire consumed part of the wooden structure, and a store site became a church until repairs were completed. Monsignor Henry Gross served the parish until it was evident that a new structure was necessary. Under the supervision of the fourth pastor, Monsignor Benjamin Hawkes, a church was built on Wilshire Boulevard at Kingsley Drive, a spacious, modern building that seats over a thousand.

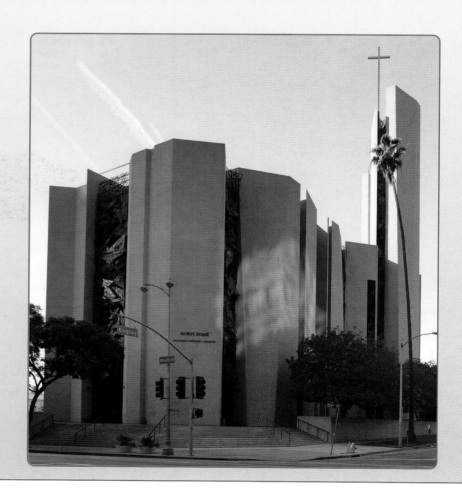

St. Bernadette

1947

This Baldwin Hills parish opened with a temporary church that was formerly the Sunset Fields Clubhouse with Father William J. Duggan as pastor. He had been the director of the Society for the Propagation of the Faith. For twenty-one years he served the material and spiritual needs of the parish, converting the clubhouse and two ancient adobes into the church, hall, rectory and school. The school was completed in 1955, staffed by the Sisters of Saint Joseph of Carondelet who still administer the school in the complex near the Crenshaw shopping center. Father Aidan J. Day was pastor from 1973 to 1982 when he died of smoke inhalation in a rectory fire. For the next seventeen years Father Patrick J. Gorman, a native of Ireland, headed the parish followed by Father Thomas King for four years. The present pastor is Father Allan Roberts.

St. Bernard

1924

Mass for this parish in the Glassell Park Area of Los Angeles was celebrated in the homes of parishioners until a church was built in 1925. Monsignor Harry Meade was pastor from 1932 to 1936 when he was appointed pastor of Saint Charles, a parish he served for over thirty-six years. The convent was built in 1941 during the pastorate of Monsignor Thomas Moran. Father Thomas Barry was pastor from 1949 to 1964 and supervised the remodeling of the church. Father Dennis Murphy, the first priest from the parish, administered Saint Bernard from 1960 to 1973 and helped build another church. Father Patrick McNulty, pastor for twenty years, retired in 1993 and lives at the parish as Pastor Emeritus. Father Gerald McSorley from Ireland was named pastor in 1993. In 1999 Saint Bernard's 4,000 families celebrated its 75th anniversary.

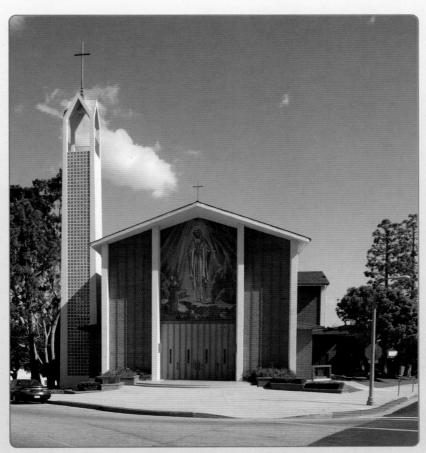

St. Brendan

1915

A temporary school auditorium served as the church for one of the "square mile parishes." Father William Forde was pastor and built the medieval Gothic style church in 1927. Bishop Timothy Manning consecrated the church in 1957 after altars were installed and the sanctuary remodeled. The pastor then was the well-known Irish priest, Monsignor Thomas Fogarty, who also built the school, hall and rectory. He remained at the parish for over twenty-five years and was responsible for a multitude of religious vocations. The famous Mitchell Boys Choir was also active during his pastorate. For twelve years Monsignor Patrick Roche headed the parish and also served as editor of The Tidings. Monsignor Jeremiah Murphy, former superintendent of high schools and colleges, was named pastor in 1988, a post he also held for twelve years. Present pastor is Msgr. Terrance Fleming.

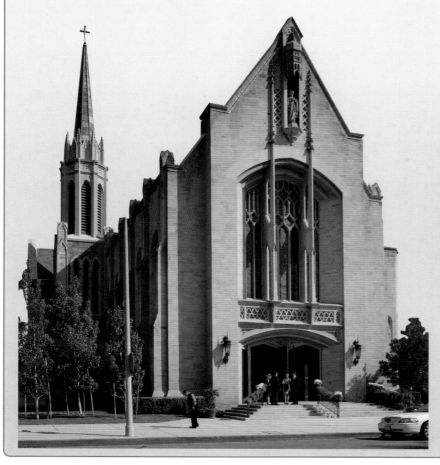

St. Bridget

Chinese Center

1940

In 1939 through the efforts of a missionary from China who had returned to the southland for health reason, an outreach to the Chinese community was inaugurated. Father John Cowhig took up residence at Cathedral High School and made a thorough demographic study of the area. He chose a site at the north end of Chinatown and a church was opened on Christmas Day in 1940. Archbishop John J. Cantwell dedicated the Chinese Catholic Center under the patronage of Saint Bridget on June 7, 1942. A language school was started at the high school and Immaculate Heart Sisters offered classes until 1951. By the mid-1960s as a wave of Chinese immigrants arrived, the center was enlarged and modernized. Salesian Father Joseph Cheng became administrator in 1994. Mass is celebrated in English and Cantonese Chinese.

St. Brigid

1920

Mass for this parish named for a sixth century Irish nun was celebrated on December 8, 1920 in a small house rented by the pastor, Father John Egan. By the first Sunday in Lent, 1921, a small frame church was dedicated, while the whole surrounding area remained mainly a gigantic corn field. During his long forty-four-year pastorate, he saw a prize-winning church built in 1954 under the supervision of Father James Nash. Monsignor Matthew Marron was responsible for the new school, and by 1979 the parish was assigned to the Josephite Fathers and Brothers whose primary work is ministry to the Black community. Father William Norvel thus became the first African-American pastor. He was a pioneer of Gospel music and vitally revived a parish spirit that resulted in some forty ministries. The current pastor is very Reverend Robert M. Kehrns, SSJ.

St. Camillus Center for Pastoral Care

1954

This center was originally founded to provide chaplains for local hospitals. Father Edmund Bradley founded the parish that served County General Hospital and the surrounding community of Lincoln Heights. It was named Saint Camillus de Lellis to honor the 17th century Italian saint who founded an order that cares for the sick and dying. From 1966 to 1976 the Missionaries of the Holy Family provided chaplains for the hospital and Juvenile Hall. In 1976 Father Walter Riendeau of the Congregation of the Blessed Sacrament became pastor. By 1987 when Father Don Kribs was named pastor, the transition was made from Saint Camillus to a Center for Pastoral Care, responsible for all the surrounding medical centers. Father Christopher Ponnet was named pastor in 1995.

Los Angeles

St. Casimir

LITHUANIAN

1941

This church was built by and for Lithuanians, most of them refugees from their native country. Monsignor Julius Macejauskas founded the parish then located on Third Avenue. Father John Kucinskas purchased the property at Griffith Park Boulevard and Saint George Street in 1948. He built a new church in 1951 and opened the school in 1957. For thirty-seven years he headed the parish that was home to scores of immigrants. He too had been a displaced person when he arrived in 1946. He organized a school for refugee children, edited the Lithuanian News and also published a book on the martyrs of Telsiai. The church remains a religious and cultural center for Lithuanian peoples. In 1984 Monsignor Algirdas Olsauskas was named pastor and in 2002 Father Stanislovas Anuzis was appointed.

St. Cecilia

1910

Although established in 1909, the dedication of the church in 1910 is more often used as a founding date. A school was erected and blessed in 1916 with the Sisters of Saint Joseph of Carondelet in charge. In 1920 Father Edward Brady, who headed the parish for thirty-four years, succeeded Father Paul Dillon. During his pastorate another church was built, a remarkable example of Lombard Romanesque style. The church was consecrated in 1943. Monsignor Laurence Clark was named administrator in 1973 beginning the system of team ministry clustered with the parish of Holy Cross. He continued this ministry until 1989. Father Thomas Peacha served as pastor from 1989 to 1997. The Comboni Missionaries were placed in charge in 1997 and continue in team ministry with Holy Cross parish.

St. Columban

FILIPINO

1945

The Columban Fathers, a foreign mission society, were entrusted with the care and leadership of the first Filipino parish in the Archdiocese. Father Francis Hoza, with the help of the Filipino community, converted an old 1892 firehouse into a suitable church that was used for twenty years. When Father Patrick Dermody was pastor, a formal church was planned in 1966, a simple two-story structure with hall and rectory on the lower level. The historic bell from the Philippines' national shrine was used in the tower. The old firehouse was razed. In 1987 Father Patrick Lavin was named administrator, and since 1996 Columban Father Colm Rafferty has administered the Filipino parish. Each year the parish celebrates the Sinulog festival to honor the Child Jesus.

St. Columbkille

1921

This parish was formerly a mission from Holy Cross church and originally extended to almost the southern extremity of the city. There was a building at the corner of 64th and Main Streets, but a complete parish plant was finished in 1923 with a school, convent and rectory. In 1936 the church and rectory were re-modeled and then re-dedicated. Father Thomas N. O'Toole was the pastor. Monsignor Timothy Galvin was pastor for twenty-six years, from 1946 to 1972. He was one of five brothers who were priests. Monsignor Michael Lenihan, an associate in 1964, was named pastor in 1972, followed in 1981 by Father Jules Mayer. The parish, built originally for Irish and German immigrants evolved into an African-American community and in the 1980's became largely Latino. It is clustered with Nativity church. The church was remodeled in 1999. Thanks to efforts of parishioners and generous donors. Current pastor is Monsignor Timothy Dyer named in January 1997.

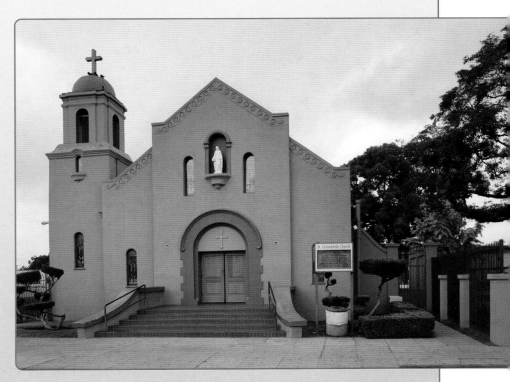

St. Dominic

1921

First established as a mission in 1920, Mass was celebrated in a private home, later in a store and finally in a tent. Priests from Saint Ignatius parish served the community, and in 1921 Dominican Fathers took charge. Father Francis Driscoll helped to build the school. A wooden chapel was erected, known later as "the Old Hall" and "DePorres Hall" and soon after, the Dominican Sisters of San Raphael were invited to staff the school. Through the 1930's and 1940's, the whole complex expanded and many societies were formed. Archbishop John J. Cantwell dedicated the structure of frame and stucco in 1940. For the 75th parish anniversary, Dominican pastor Father Paul Scanlon expanded and enlarged the facilities, acquiring a 10,000 square-foot Masonic Lodge as an activity center and home for the parish's Adeste program.

St. Eugene

1942

Father Patrick Casey, from Ireland, was the founding pastor of this parish named in honor of Pope Pius XII and Saint Eugene, a seventh century pope. For twenty years he headed the parish and during that time built a church, school, convent and rectory. He had to wait for over a year to obtain a permit to erect a bigger church because residents opposed the building, but the city planning commission finally granted permission. The church was built in 1955, in a style described as a contemporary California adaptation of Italian-Florentine. Monsignor Melvin Young was pastor from 1969 to 1972 followed by Father Anthony Duval. For more than twenty years, Father Patrick Walsh served the parish, both as associate and pastor. Father Sabas Mallya of the Apostolic Community of Priests became pastor in 2002.

St. Frances Xavier Cabrini

1946

Saint Frances Xavier Cabrini is not only the first American citizen-saint but she also lived and worked in Los Angeles and celebrated the silver jubilee of the order she founded, the Missionary Sisters of the Sacred Heart, in Saint Vibiana's Cathedral in 1905. The church built in her honor started with Mass in the home of Mary Knauff, who as a child knew the saint. Father Paul Konoske was pastor when there were fewer than 200 parishioners and served the parish for twenty years. A second church was built in 1955 and the temporary structure was converted to extra classrooms for the school. Monsignor John Rohde served from 1981 to 1988 when the concept of team ministry was introduced. Father David O'Connell headed the parish during its golden jubilee in 1996. From 1997 to 2006 Father Anthony Gonzalez was the administrator. In July 2006, Father Cesar Raffo will be the next pastor.

St. Francis of Assisi

1920

The original frame structure for the parish named for Saint Francis was in use for thirty-eight years until another church was completed in 1960. The pastor was Father Michael Conneally who built a rectory, school and convent. Two Paulist priests followed him, and in 1929 the Capuchin Fathers were appointed to head the parish. Capuchin Franciscan Father Celestine Quinlan was an associate for five years, then named pastor in 1962. The new building completed in 1960 faces Golden Gate Avenue, near Sunset Boulevard, and has a sixty-foot bell tower. Father Lawrence Caruso headed the parish from 1978 to 1985, followed by Capuchin Father Michael Mahoney. In 1991 the Canons Regular of the Immaculate Conception administered the parish until the Orders of Friars Minor came in 1999.

St. Francis Xavier Chapel

1912

Originally, the parish began as a station, under the direction of a French missionary priest, Father Albert Breton, who opened a meeting place for Japanese speaking residents. By 1920 the new Maryknoll Missionary Society took over. The school was opened in 1921 in the charge of the Foreign Missionary Sisters of Saint Dominic. Maryknoll Father Hugh Lavery built the church that contains outstanding examples of oriental art. During World War II when Japanese Americans were sent to relocation camps, he helped in obtaining fair prices for their property and stored their belongings. He served in the archdiocese for almost thirty years. Father Michael McKillop headed the parish for ten years and was honored by Japan for his work. Father James Habenicht served the parish from 1969, becoming pastor in 1986. In recent years the Atonement Fathers have administered the parish.

St. Gerard Majella

1952

Masses were celebrated in a skating rink, then for almost a year in a circus tent until a church was built in 1953 at Inglewood and Culver Boulevards. Father John Brennan celebrated the dedication Mass in honor of the Redemptorist lay brother and patron saint of mothers, Gerard Majella. Religion classes were held on Saturday in the large circus tent until Father Brennan built the brick school in 1954 and extended it to sixteen classrooms by 1958. Sisters of the Holy Names of Jesus and Mary staffed the school. Father John Doherty was pastor from 1965 to 1973, and during the pastorate of Father John McHugh, the parish celebrated its 25th anniversary in 1977. Father William Connor served from 1985 to 2001 when Father Martin Slaughter became administrator and then pastor in 2003.

St. Gregory Nazianzen

1923

Father Victor Follen celebrated Mass in a house on South Norton in 1923 and by the following year a small frame church was erected. By 1931 a brick school opened and in 1938 the church was completed. It is a spacious example of Italo-Gothic design of steel frame and concrete construction. For thirty years Monsignor Follen headed the parish and as a member of the building commission for the archdiocese contributed to the design and construction of more than a hundred churches and schools. Bishop Timothy Manning was pastor from 1953 to 1968 when he was named bishop of Fresno. As cardinal he revisited the parish in 1973. Monsignor Robert Brennan, pastor from 1968 to 1973, was also well known as the director of music for the Archdiocese. Father James O'Grady was pastor for ten years, followed by Monsignor Edward J. Johnson. Current pastor Alex H. Chung began serving as administrator in 2005.

St. Ignatius of Loyola

1911

The Jesuit Fathers purchased a half-block at Avenue 52 and Monte Vista in 1911 that included three small cottages so that a church and college could be established. One was the beginning of Saint Vincent College and the other Saint Ignatius church. Mass was celebrated in one of the cottages until a frame structure was completed. Father Richard A. Gleeson, S.J., opened the church and school. In 1914 the Jesuits turned over the care of the parish to the diocese and Father Thomas O'Regan was named pastor. He built a church and rectory. Father Jeremiah Burke completed the school and Father Patrick O'Donoghue, pastor from 1927 to 1944, built the convent. Monsignor Francis O'Carroll (1944-1970) built a church, rectory and school. Monsignor Alfred Hernandez served from 1978 to 1996. Father Arturo Velasco became the pastor at the end of 1996.

St. Jerome

1949

Mass was originally celebrated at the La Tijera Theatre. The church built for the Westchester area was eventually used for the school auditorium. Monsignor Thomas F. McNicholas, the pastor, was associated with the Holy Name Union for twenty-five years and was also principal of Bishop Conaty High School for ten years. He died tragically in 1966 just before the church was nearing completion. The structure is a 16-sided church that draws the assembly closer to the altar. Father Michael Walsh was the second pastor, followed by Father Edmund Maechler who served as pastor for fourteen years. Father James Kavanagh, from Ireland, served from 1988 to 2002 and during that time the church experienced the earthquake of 1994 that closed the building for six months. The diverse community includes African-Americans, Anglo, Latino, Nigerian and Asian peoples. The current pastor is Reverend Norman Priebe.

St. Joan of Arc

1943

Monsignor Eugene MacSweeney from Ireland was pastor of the parish in west Los Angeles that started in a small store building on Pico Boulevard. For a time a remodeled walnut packinghouse was used until 1954 when the modern church was completed, in Romanesque style with a bell tower rising seventy-five feet. The entire church was built of reinforced concrete and the roof has a covering of variegated colors. Above the main entrance is the text: "My house is the house of prayer." Monsignor MacSweeney headed the parish for thirty-two years, opening the school in 1947. He died in 1975. Following him was another Irishman, Monsignor Robert Condon who was pastor until 1983. Also from Ireland was Father John Cunningham, pastor from 1984 to 1995. In 1996 Father James Barnes, born Long Beach was named pastor.

St. John the Evangelist

1909

The area surrounding this parish was first called Hyde Park and was part of Saint Michael's where Father Emil Gerardi was pastor. He was transferred from there to start Saint John's and celebrated Mass in a wooden church in 1910. Sisters of Saint Joseph of Carondelet opened the school in temporary classrooms in 1925, and new buildings were completed in 1950 with an additional main building in 1964. During the pastorate of Monsignor Martin McNicholas, a church was dedicated in 1947. He was pastor for twenty-four years and died in 1967. Following him was Father Michael Haran from Ireland. In 1973 the parish was assigned to the care of the Divine Word Fathers and Father William Caffrey from New York was named pastor. Divine Word Father Charles Burns was pastor from 1982 to 1993. Then pastor was Father Melvin James. From 2005 present pastor is Fr. Damian Kabot, SVD.

St. Joseph

1888

Saint Joseph's was established for German speaking Catholics under the guidance of Father Florian Bartsch. In 1893 Bishop Francis Mora assigned it to the Franciscan Fathers and a church was dedicated in 1903, a striking Gothic edifice designed by Franciscan Brothers Adrian Wewer and Leonard Darscheid during the pastorate of Father Victor Aertker. The parish was only the fourth one in the city. Franciscan Sisters assumed educational duties in 1907 and continued until the building was razed in 1964. By 1922 many ethnic families lived in the area, and confessions were heard in English, German, Spanish, French and Dutch. On Labor Day, 1983, fire swept through the Gothic structure and completely destroyed the old church. A simple replacement opened in 1987 and Archdiocesan priests were assigned in 2001.

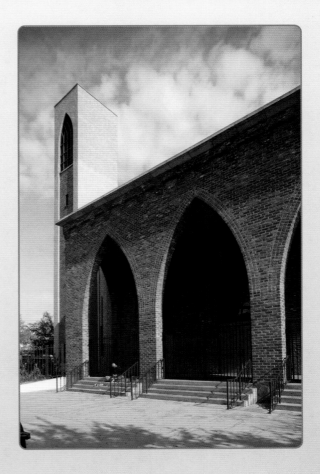

St. Kevin

1923

Irish, German and Italian families made up the parish in the early days when Father Joseph Loughran was pastor. Father Robert Lucey was the next pastor (later Archbishop of San Antonio, Texas). In 1948 Father Thomas Noonan was named pastor. He built the rectory and undertook construction of the church but died suddenly in 1954. Father James Deenihan followed and for eleven years headed the parish. He celebrated the dedication of the new church completed in 1956. Monsignor Patrick Collins, also from Ireland, was pastor until 1973. For fifteen years Father George Gunst was pastor of the parish named for an Irish saint of the sixth century. A cast-stone statue of Saint Kevin is above the main entrance. Father Leo Steinbock was named pastor in 1995 and retired in 2004.

St. Lawrence of Brindisi

CAPUCHINS CAME IN 1921

1908

Franciscan Capuchins have served at this parish on Compton Avenue in the Watts area since it was established in 1908. The parish was named for the 17th century Capuchin saint born in Lisbon who was noted for his scholarly works, great preaching and miracles. A school and convent were added in 1924, staffed by the Sisters of Notre Dame. In 1962 a two-story brick building replaced the old school that had withstood two earthquakes. Father Thomas Dowling was pastor from 1937 to 1951. He did much for the parish, liquidating the debt on both church and school and planning for a building dedicated in 1949. Father Valerian O'Leary served from 1961 to 1968 and was also the founding principal of Saint Francis High School. Capuchin Fathers Michael Walsh and Edward O'Keefe headed the parish from 1985 to 1998. 1998 to present Father Peter Banks is pastor.

St. Lucy

1981

The history of Saint Lucy's begins around 1940 when Father Antonio Bouquet said Mass in an empty store in City Terrace. A small chapel was completed in 1947, but it was a mission of Santa Teresita parish. The Burgos Foreign Mission Fathers were assigned in 1969 with Father George Duran as administrator. Plans for a church began in 1970 and Archbishop Timothy Manning blessed the two-story combination center and church in 1971. The Piarists Fathers were assigned to direct the mission in 1973 with Father Joseph Sole as administrator. Saint Joseph Calasanz founded the Order of the Pious Schools in the 17th century and started the first elementary school open to all children. Father Francis Boronat was administrator at Saint Lucy's. Father Vicente Casaus, from Spain, became pastor in 1996.

St. Malachy

1926

In November, 1926, Father Thomas Butler founded the parish and by 1927 Father Francis Woodcutter had built a church. Bishop John J. Cantwell dedicated the church in 1928. During the pastorate of Father Paul Early, the church and hall were renovated, a school and convent built and a rectory added all by 1949. In 1968 the parish was assigned to the Divine Word Missionaries with Father William Adams pastor. He headed the parish located near Central and 82nd Street for twelve years. The ethnic composition of the area changed through the years from mainly Spanish to African American when Father Fisher Robinson was pastor from 1980 to 1989. Father William Bonner was named pastor in 1989. In 1997 the parish received the annual Cardinal's Award.

St. Marcellinus

1957

Monsignor Thomas G. Hayes was the pastor of this parish near the Long Beach and Santa Ana freeways. He celebrated Mass in the upstairs dining room of Kelly's Restaurant. Next, a former Protestant church was used until 1959 when a church was completed and named in honor of the fourth century Roman martyr. In 1971 Father Peter Bullum, a native of Croatia, was named pastor and served until 1984. Father Jules Mayer, former pastor of Saint Columbkille and a native of Los Angeles, was named pastor in 1985 and is the only priest at the parish, with four Masses on the weekend. With over 200 students in religious education classes he relies mainly on volunteers. The original church, seating about 300 is still in use, but most of the parishioners are elderly.

St. Martin of Tours

1946

A native of Austria, Father Augustine C. Murray was the founding pastor of the parish named in honor of the fourth century bishop of Tours who had been a Roman soldier. Father Murray was also president of the Kolping Society, a post he held for fifty years. During his pastorate of twenty-eight years he built the church, school, rectory and convent for the Brentwood parish. The California mission-style church that opened in 1947 was two years later partially destroyed by fire. The school of eight classrooms opened in 1955. Father Murray retired in 1974 and died in 1989. Monsignor Lawrence O'Leary was named pastor in 1979. He had served as director of the Los Angeles Lay Mission Helpers and the Society for the Propagation of the Faith. For twenty-six years he headed the parish on Sunset Boulevard.

St. Mary

1896

The first church built in Boyle Heights was a small, red brick structure measuring only fifty by eighty-four feet. The pastor was Father Joseph Doyle. The Sisters of the Holy Names staffed the school, opened in 1907 when Father Joseph Barron was pastor. Bishop John J. Cantwell dedicated a larger church in 1926, an elegant Italian Byzantine-style building under the guidance of pastor Father Thomas O'Reagan. During the depression of 1929, the parish community underwent great economic problems, and only after World War II was the parish debt paid. A fourteen-classroom school was built in 1951. The Salesian Fathers were assigned to the parish in 1965 with Father Albert Negri as pastor. In the 1987 earthquake, the historic building suffered extensive damage. The Salesian priests are still in charge.

St. Mary

COPTIC

1991

In 1986 a small Catholic Coptic community was established for the traditions and celebration of this ancient liturgy. By 1991 Saint Mary became the first Coptic Catholic Church west of the Mississippi. Father Hanna Badir was pastor but soon after was named Bishop of the Diocese of Ismailia, Egypt. In accordance with custom he took the name of Jaoannes Zakaria. The Coptic rite, one of the most ancient in Christendom, traces its roots to Saint Mark the Apostle. The Patriarch of Alexandria, His Beatitude Stefanos II Ghattas, dedicated the wood-beamed, white stucco church in 1992. Today Saint Mary is one of only three Catholic Coptic churches in the United States. In 2001 Father Indrawes Bisada Kilada was named pastor of a parish where the liturgy is celebrated in both Arabic and English.

St. Mary Magdalen

1930

A temporary church and rectory were placed in charge of Father Francis C. Ott and in 1931 Bishop Thomas Gorman of Reno dedicated the building. A shrine with a life-size figure of Saint Mary Magdalen kneeling at the foot of the cross was constructed at the same time. Father John Conlon became pastor in 1932 and in 1946 built a new elementary school and convent. He headed the parish for twenty-three years and died in 1960. Father Christopher Kennedy, from Ireland, was pastor from 1968 to 1977 following the pastorate of Monsignor Thomas B. Morris. From 1979 to 2003 Father Patrick H. Sullivan headed a parish that sustained two serious church fires, both attributed to arsonists. Father Paul Sustayta was named pastor in 2004. Under his leadership an outdoor plaza wa&s created between the church and the rectory. In honor of the parishes 75th anniversary. In october of 2005 the exterior of the church was painted and new church doors built to entrance the church's architecture beauty.

St. Michael

1908

Dedicated to the Archangel Michael, the first of three church buildings opened in 1908 with Father Emil Gerardi pastor. Father Joseph Kaiser was pastor for eight years followed by Father Raphael Fuhr who headed the parish for seventeen years. The church was enlarged in 1921 and a new grammar school dedicated in 1926. In 1935 Monsignor Michael O'Gorman was named pastor, and in 1937 a church was built that incorporated rich symbolism. Archbishop John J. Cantwell dedicated the church that was consecrated in 1961. For fourteen years Monsignor Michael A. Lee, of Ireland, headed Saint Michael's and renovated the church, enlarged the elementary school and built a high school. Father William S. Vita was named pastor in 1961 and died three years later. Monsignor Lawrence Donnelly served the parish from 1967 to 1994 and was also spiritual director for the Legion of Mary.

St. Odilia

1 9 2 6

The parish of Saint Odilia was established as a "Negro national church" and most of the early parishioners came from Louisiana. Bishop John J. Cantwell dedicated the mission style church in 1927 in honor of the eighth century French saint who miraculously had her sight returned and was known as "the mother of the poor." Priests of the Society of African Mission headed the parish for sixty-six years. Father Edmund Schlecht from Belgium was the pastor and served for sixteen years. Father James Perrone was pastor for a dozen years. Other missionary priests who pastored the parish were Fathers Patrick Shine, Edward Galvin and Thomas O'Flaherty. In 1950 Saint John Bosco Mission chapel was opened on Duarte Street. By the early 1990's, the Missionary Society was succeeded by the Franciscan Friars of the Atonement, with Father Daniel Callahan pastor. The present pastor is Fr. Francis Eldridge, S.A.

St. Patrick

1 9 0 3

Father Peter O'Reilly was the pastor of this parish, one of three churches established in 1903. A school opened in 1904 and in 1907 Bishop Thomas Conaty dedicated a Gothic church of red pressed brick. Salesian priests were assigned to the parish in 1930 with Father De Matei pastor. The 1933 earthquake destroyed two of the three steeples of the church. A modern brick school was blessed in 1951 by a former parishioner, Bishop Joseph McGucken. The Gaelic heritage of the parish was modified through the years by Italians, Hispanics and eventually African Americans. The original frame schoolhouse was razed in 1959 when Father Alphonsus Straub was pastor. In 1971 another temblor destroyed the church. In 2003, ground breaking for another church took place.

St. Paul

1917

In the convent chapel of the Sisters of Mercy, Father John Lucey celebrated Mass for a new parish on Washington Boulevard. By December of 1917 he built a small brick church. In 1918 Father Thomas Blackwell was named pastor. He built a Romanesque style church in 1938 wherein the life of Saint Paul is painted on the nave walls. Impressive church bells were installed in 1956. For forty-one years Monsignor headed the parish and died at age seventy-five He was followed by Monsignor Anthony Brouwers, founder of the Lay Mission Helpers. He was pastor from 1959 until his death in 1964 and during that time replaced the school with a modern, fireproof building. Monsignor Harold Laubacher, who also directed the Lay Mission Helpers, followed in 1967, and then Bishop Thaddeus Shubsda. Monsignor Royale Vadakin came in 1980. In 1996, Guadalupe Missionaries arrived.

St. Paul the Apostle

1928

Bishop John J. Cantwell invited the Paulist Fathers to establish a parish in west Los Angeles in October 1928 near the University of California at Los Angeles. Father Henry J. Stark was the pastor. The church was dedicated in 1932, a school and convent in 1938. The Paulists are an American religious community founded in 1858 in New York, dedicated to convert work. At the parish they also direct the UCLA Newman Center and are chaplains at the Medical center. In 1958 a church was built during the pastorate of Father John Fitzgerald. The main architectural focus of the structure is the white travertine altar, faced with a Byzantine mosaic panel. Father John Mitchell followed as pastor in 1964, Father Joseph Flynn in 1970, Father John Carr in 1974 and Father William Edens in 1994.

St. Peter

ITALIAN

1904

A temporary frame structure on North Spring Street served the Italian community, with Father Tito Piacentini as pastor. By 1915 the chapel from old Calvary cemetery was moved to Broadway to serve the "little Italy" families in the area under the patronage of Saint Peter. In 1923 Salesian priests were assigned to the parish and in 1932 Claretian Fathers came and served for twenty-two years. A permanent church was built in 1947. The Scalabrini Fathers, Missionaries of Saint Charles, were placed in charge in 1961. Father Luigi Donanzan, pastor from 1962 to 1979, started a weekly radio program and rebuilt Casa Italiana, a cultural and social center for Italian-Americans. The annual Saint Joseph Table remains a highlight for the parish. San Conrado Mission, established in 1966, is served from Saint Peter's.

St. Raphael

1925

A year after the parish was established a church was built on Seventy-first Street. Father William Mullane was pastor and celebrated Mass in a storefront on Vermont Avenue. He was succeeded by Father Noel Dillon. In 1934 the Carmelite Fathers were assigned to the parish. In 1947 Father William Patrick Russell opened an elementary school under the direction of the Adrian Dominican Sisters. Father Matthias Ewing served as associate in 1966 and pastor from 1971 to 1979. The church built in 1926 is still in use and the congregation includes Hispanic, African American and Anglo cultures. Father Tracy O'Sullivan, a native of Chicago, was named pastor in 1994, his first pastorate in the archdiocese.

St. Sebastian

1924

The area was known as Sawtelle when this parish was founded, primarily to serve the residents of the "Old Soldiers' Home". Since 1886 priests from Santa Monica have ministered to the veterans in Holy Trinity Chapel. The founding pastor, Father Anthony Jacobs, rented a small house and walked to the Soldiers Home. By the end of 1924, a rectory and hall were completed, and four years later Father William O'Donnell became pastor. In 1945 Father Timothy O'Shea succeeded him and continued until his death in 1971. During that time a school was opened in 1950, staffed by the Daughters of Mary and Joseph. A church was constructed in 1972 and dedicated to the third century soldier-saint. In 2000 the Paulist Fathers were assigned with Father Gil Martinez as pastor until 2003. Currently, the parish is twinned with St. Joan of Arc, with Father James Barnes as administrator.

St. Stephen

1930

Sister of Social Service Fredericka Horvath gathered a group of Hungarians to form the Saint Stephen Society in 1927. Soon after, Bishop John J. Cantwell asked Father Mathias Lani from Hungary to care for the community. Through many sacrifices, three lots were purchased and a church completed by 1930. The congregation was mainly Hungarian, German, and Hispanic, and Mass was celebrated in all those languages. Father Lani established many parish groups as well as headed the archdiocesan resettlement program for persons displaced during World War II. He died in 1954, a pastor for twenty-four years, and his funeral featured one of the largest processions in the city's history. By 1967 the multi-language parish was assigned to the Norbertine Fathers with Father Benedict Horvath as pastor for twenty-three years. In 1st July 2006 the parish will be under the care of diocesan clergy. Father Bonnor will be the pastor.

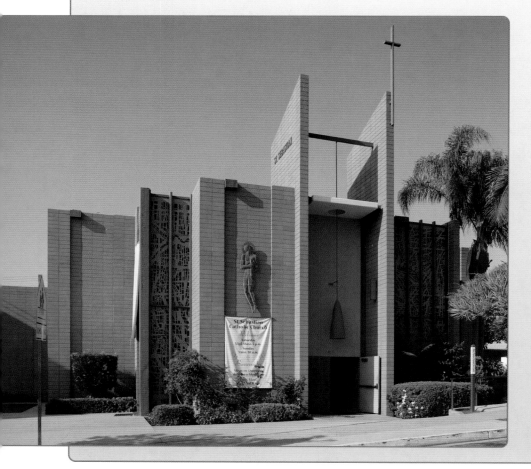

St. Teresa of Avila

1921

A temporary church and rectory were built in 1921 and replaced in 1929 by a mission style building at the corner of Fargo Street and Glendale Boulevard. The pastor was Father Patrick O'Donoghue, followed by Father Ernest J. LeGuyder, who served during the construction of the church. The school opened in 1949 during the pastorate of Father P. J. Beary. The original temporary church was converted into a parish hall. Father Anthony J. Reidy was pastor from 1952 to 1969 and continued in residence until his death in 1973. Father Thomas McLaughlin spent thirty years in the Silverlake district parish, twenty of them as pastor. During the pastorate of Father Kenneth Sullivan the school was expanded from six to nine classrooms. Father Alexander Salazar was named pastor in 1995. In 2004 he was ordained an auxiliary bishop for Los Angeles.

St. Thomas the Apostle

1903

This parish was named for the patron saint of the newly appointed Bishop Thomas Conaty. The pastor was Father John J. Clifford, who offered Mass in the convent chapel of the Immaculate Heart Sisters. By 1904 a church was ready on Pico Boulevard. Two years later he added a school. Numerous repairs and alterations were made over the years. In 1919 Monsignor John J. Gallagher was appointed pastor and in 1924 enlarged the church. He died in 1960, a pastor for 40 years. Monsignor Thomas J. O'Dwyer, who directed health, welfare and charity programs for the Archdiocese for forty years was pastor for six years. For ten years Father Paul Peterson headed the parish. Father (later Bishop) Dennis O'Neil was pastor from 1984 to 1998. In 1999 the church was seriously damaged by fire and re-opened in 2002. Current pastor since 1998 is Father Jarlath Cunnane.

St. Timothy

1943

Father William T. O'Shea was the pastor of the parish on Pico Boulevard and in his twenty years built the entire plant – church, school, rectory and auditorium. The original church was converted to an auditorium when the classical Spanish edifice was completed in 1949. It contains a 300 year-old Spanish altar and several other antique pieces. Cast-stone work adorns the 101-foot bell tower. Archbishop J. Francis A. McIntyre dedicated the church in 1950. The new school opened in 1958. Father O'Shea died three years later and Bishop John Ward was assigned pastor, the same year he became an auxiliary bishop for the Archdiocese. For thirty-three years he headed Saint Timothy's and in 1986 was appointed Episcopal Vicar for Our Lady of the Angels Pastoral Region. Bishop Ward retired in 1996. Reverend Father William Brelsford became the pastor since this time.

St. Vincent

1886

Saint Vincent parish was the third church established in Los Angeles. Services were held in the chapel of Saint Vincent's College. The Vincentian Fathers have always administered the parish located at Adams and Figueroa. The pastor was Father A.J. Meyer. Plans to build a church were delayed during World War I, but by 1925 through a gift from Mr. and Mrs. Edward Doheny, a magnificent church was built that resembles the church of Saint Prisca in Tasco, Mexico. The style is Spanish Renaissance with the exterior of the dome and bell tower done in Mexican tile. Decorations in the interior and exterior of the church represent images of Christ, Mary and saints, in particular a full color painting of Saint Vincent surrounded by orphan children. Three of the Vincentian pastors since 1970 were Fathers Joseph Dyra, Philip Van Linden and Bernard Quinn.

San Antonio de Padua

1926

Prior to a parish or a church building was a Catechism Center in charge of Monsignor Jesús Ramirez. Later Bishop John J. Cantwell built a church and Father Peter O'Dowd was appointed pastor. In 1928 Father Benito J. Dorca was named to the parish in Boyle Heights. Father Leroy S. Callahan built a rectory during his pastorate in 1934. Father (later Monsignor) Fidencio Esparza, who had fled persecution in Mexico, was named pastor in 1938. For thirty-eight years the Mexican born priest ministered to the Hispanic community, and each year conducted a pilgrimage to the shrine of Our Lady of Guadalupe in Mexico City. He also built the school on Bridge Street near Brooklyn Avenue. He died in 1988 at age eighty-nine. Father Alfred Hernandez followed as pastor and then Father Pedro M. Ciordia, from Spain, in 1979. From 1984 to 1995, Father Genaro Coronado was pastor. Since that time to the present, the pastor has been Msgr. Joseph Herres.

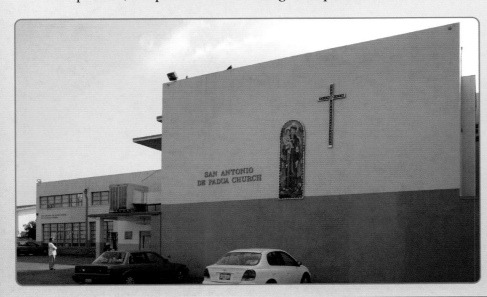

San Francisco

1982

In the early 1960s the Archdiocese purchased a former Four Square Gospel church for use as a social and catechetical center. Priests of the Burgos Foreign Mission Society celebrated Sunday Masses. Father Diosdado Martin, a native of Cuba, was the resident administrator of San Francisco Chapel from 1976. In 1982 the church was given regular parochial status with territorial boundaries, and Father Martin was named pastor. In 1988 Father Saul Rodriguez, a native of El Salvador, was assigned as pastor, and in 1991 Father Juan Romero was named administrator. Three years later he became pastor and created a gymnasium as an outreach for the youth in the area. In 1997 Father Severiano Castaneda, from Mexico, was named pastor of the parish on Olympic Boulevard.

San Miguel

1927

Bishop John J. Cantwell dedicated the Church of the Apparition of Saint Michael on February 12, 1928 in the heart of the Mexican district in Watts. The church was made possible by the parishioners of Holy Cross parish. The following year the Recollect Augustinian Fathers from Spain were assigned and Father Nicholas Zabalza was named pastor. In 1962 Father Joseph M. Santiago initiated plans for a hall that would also serve for catechism classes. By 1966 Sisters of the Love of God were operating a school. In 1966 Father Maximus Bortiri, from Spain, became pastor. Father Alphonse Gallegos was named pastor in 1977 and was later named Auxiliary Bishop of Sacramento. In 1998 diocesan priests were assigned to the Watts parish.

Santa Isabel

St. Elizabeth

1915

In 1914 three Claretian priests from the Our Lady Queen of Angels (La Placita) blessed a chapel near the corner of Boyle Avenue and Opal Street dedicated to Saint Elizabeth on her feastday. That became the first local parish established to care for the Spanish-speaking refugees from Mexico. A larger church was built later, called Santa Isabel. Father John Rossi was pastor from 1931 to 1939. Father Michael Sheahan, from Ireland, was named pastor and headed the parish for thirty-three years. The old church was demolished to make room for a freeway and Monsignor Sheahan built a new church and school. In 1973 the parish was entrusted to the Vincentian priests. The pastor was Father Pedro Villarroya of Spain, who was also a leader in the Hispanic community. The Vincentians served until 1989 when archdiocesan priests began to serve the parish.

Santa Teresita

1923

The original building was a confraternity center and Mass was celebrated in an old hall. One of the confraternity workers purchased a site for the church, hall and rectory. The church was built in 1926, attended by priests from Saint Vibiana Cathedral. The parish is a few blocks from the Los Angeles County / USC Medical Center. The pastors were Fathers Augustine O'Dea, William McGinley, Benito Dorca and J. F. Gambe. Father A.M. Boquet remodeled the church and built a hall in 1942. The school opened in 1950, staffed by Dominican Sisters of Mission San José. Father Joseph Lluent, from Spain, was pastor from 1965 to 1973 and continued building improvements. In 1973 the Piarist Fathers were assigned. Father Manuel Sanahuja was pastor from 1981 to 1983 and from 1990 to 1999.

Transfiguration

1923

Bishop John J. Cantwell established this parish in August of 1923 and named Father John Cotter pastor. He obtained a three-story building at Browning Boulevard and Western Avenue that served as a center for Mass, social hall and rectory. In 1924 he built a church at Van Ness and Santa Barbara Avenues. In 1930 Father James P. Buckley was named pastor and directed the parish for thirty-five years. Although the Depression delayed construction for several years, a new church in a modern Italian design was built in 1937 on property at Santa Barbara and Roxton Avenues. The older building was moved behind the church and served as a hall. Monsignor Buckely died in 1965 at age seventy. American artist, Velda Buys Gateley, did the mural painting above the main altar of the Transfiguration in 1947. Father John J. Hanly, from Ireland, was pastor for fifteen years. His successor, Father Jarlath Dolan launched the successful "A right of Hope" capital campaign in 1991. Monsignor Robert Howard led the church into the new millennium with Father Richard Martini continuing the legacy of Black Catholic Spirituality of Transfiguration.

Los Angeles

Visitation

1943

Father Thomas O'Sullivan, from Ireland, bought four acres near Sepulveda and Manchester Boulevards in the middle of an empty field in 1943 and celebrated Mass in a garage until a frame building could be erected. In just four years he completed the school, convent and rectory. In 1950 a church was erected in a modern adaptation of Italian Renaissance architecture, and a solemn Mass was celebrated on Christmas morning. Monsignor O'Sullivan directed the parish for forty-five of the sixty-nine years of his priesthood and fifteen years as pastor emeritus. He died in 1997 at age ninety-two. From Visitation parish were formed the parishes of Saint Jerome and Saint Anatasia. From 1980 to 1999 Father James O'Grady, also from Ireland, served as pastor of the church on 88th Street and retired as pastor emeritus in 1999 when Monsignor Timothy O'Connell became pastor.

Alhambra

All Souls

1913

A small brown wood building represented the first Catholic church in Alhambra where mostly German and Irish families lived. Father Philip Williams, Benedictine, was the pastor, followed by Monsignor Edward Kirk, Fathers Henry Gross and Matthew Maron. In 1921 the school was built and placed under the care of the Sisters of the Holy Names. In 1934 Monsignor Peter Hanrahan, from Ireland, was named pastor and continued his administration for thirty-eight years. By 1938 he completed the concrete church, and the school plant in 1949. Monsignor Hanrahan was also active in civic affairs and was the proto-archivist for the archdiocese. He died in 1981 at age eighty-five. Father Harold Ford headed the parish for sixteen years. Ethnic diversity of the parish changed during the years and now includes many Hispanics, Japanese, Vietnamese and Filipinos.

Saint Therese

1924

This Alhambra parish was the first in the U.S. to be placed under the protection of the Little Flower, a year before she was canonized. A combination church and school building were erected and the parish was assigned to the Carmelite (Discalced) Fathers who came from Ireland. In 1951, Archbishop J. Francis A. McIntyre blessed the new church, which has the character of a shrine dedicated to Saint Therese of the Child Jesus. The edifice was built in a modern Mediterranean style with a 120-foot-high bell tower. A statue of the saint is in a cascaded niche behind the main altar. Carmelite Father William Fenton served as pastor for two terms, a total of twelve years. In 1963 a modern reinforced concrete and brick school was built with a hall added soon after. The school celebrated its 75th anniversary in 2001.

Saint Thomas More

1948

An early temporary building was the former church and hall from All Souls, moved in sections to Fremont Avenue. Monsignor Patrick Coleman, the founding pastor, celebrated Mass in the chapel of Ramona Convent. By 1968 a building dedicated to the English philosopher and statesman Saint Thomas More was completed. Above and behind the main altar is a large stained-glass window depicting the marriage feast at Cana. The school opened in 1952 and was enlarged ten years later. Monsignor Coleman, an Irish native, retired after serving as pastor for thirty-two years. During his pastorate he was also responsible in helping resettle Vietnamese refugees. He died in 1988 at age eighty-four. The next pastor was Father Jeremiah O'Neill, also from Ireland, who headed the parish for almost twenty years. His successor was Father Paul Menke, a native Angeleno.

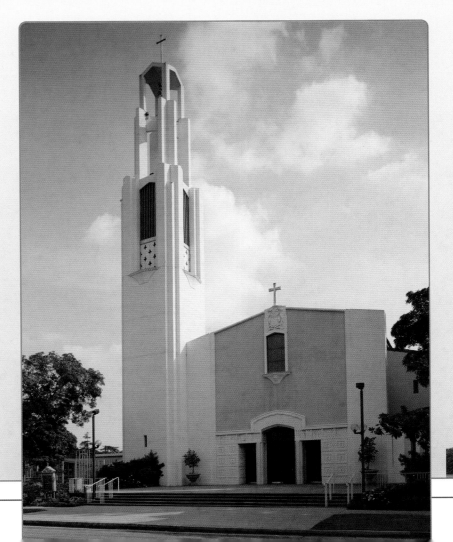

Sacred Heart

1935

Four years before the parish was established, the chapel of the Sacred Heart of Jesus served as a mission and center for Mexican immigrants. Monsignor George M. Scott was the pastor and first celebrated Mass on December 15, 1935. He was responsible for purchasing the site for a church and initiating the building program. In 1955 James Francis Cardinal McIntyre dedicated the California Mission style church during the pastorate of Monsignor Timothy O'Keeffe, pastor from 1940 to 1972. He it was who opened the school in 1948. Father Eugene Duffy, also from Ireland, shepherded the parish from 1972 to 1988 and initiated the parish council in 1973. Another Irishman, Father Jarlath Cunnane, was administrator, then pastor of the Altadena parish from 1988 to 1995.

Saint Elizabeth

1918

This Altadena parish was the first one established by Bishop John J. Cantwell as Bishop of Monterey-Los Angeles. Father Victor Follen offered Mass in a temporary chapel on February 10, 1918. He purchased property at Woodbury Road and Lake Avenue where groundbreaking took place in June. By October the church dedicated to Saint Elizabeth of Hungary was ready. The school opened in 1919. Monsignor William E. Corr was pastor for sixteen years and the church was completed in 1926. Eugenio Cardinal Pacelli (later Pope Pius XII) visited the parish in 1936. The outside shrine to Our Lady of Lourdes was planned by Monsignor Corr and dedicated in 1939. Father William Mullane headed the parish for twenty-three years. Monsignor Robert E. Brennan was pastor from 1962 to 1968. Msgr. Martin Slaught was pastor to 1992. Fr. Edwin Duyshart became pastor in 1998.

Annunciation

1949

Father Dominic Dale celebrated Mass on May 29, 1949 in the garage of the Mountain View Dairy in Monrovia, and that remained the church for eighteen months. Cows were milked across the driveway. This event gave rise to an early reference to parishioners as "the fallen angels who had holy cows." A church was soon built at Longden Avenue and Peck Road. A school opened in 1952 under the direction of the Franciscan Sisters of Penance and Christian Charity. From 1952 to 1971 Father Hugh O'Donnell, from Ireland, expanded the school and built a parish hall. Monsignor Roland Zimmerman headed the parish from 1973 to 1997. A native of Los Angeles, he also taught at Queen of Angels Seminary and several archdiocesan high schools. Father Eugene Herbert, a native Angeleno, was named pastor in 1999.

Holy Angels

1935

Father John Sheehy originally used a loading platform by the railroad tracks as a platform on which to celebrate Mass for the local Mexican workers in the early days of this parish. Employment and ranch life eventually changed sufficiently to warrant the establishment of the parish in 1935, headed by Father Gerald M. O'Keeffe who changed the original name from Our Lady of Peace to that of Holy Angels. A permanent church was completed in 1940 on Holly Street. The school was built in 1946 followed by a convent in 1949. For thirty-eight years the Irish priest served the parish and died in 1975 at age seventy-four. Another Irish priest, Monsignor Robert Walsh, guided Holy Angels for sixteen years and initiated many renovations. Father Patrick J. Daly, also from Ireland, was pastor for two years followed by Monsignor Norman Francis Priebe, a native of Nebraska, who was pastor for twelve years. A special ministry of the parish is an outreach program to the workers at the nearby racetrack.

151

Artesia

Holy Family

1931

Before the parish was established, Father Manuel Vicente, a native of Portugal, celebrated Mass for three years in the old Scott and Frampton building until a small church was built on South Corby Avenue. Bishop John J. Cantwell dedicated that church and Father Vicente served until his death in 1938. Monsignor Thomas English followed as pastor for two years followed by Monsignor John Hurley, another Irish priest. From 1943 to 1958 Father Patrick O'Connor, also from Ireland, headed the parish and opened a school in 1948 staffed by the Immaculate Heart Sisters. Father William Kelly, another Irishman, built on Clarkdale Avenue in 1961 a church with a shrine to Our Lady of Fatima. Succeeding pastors were Father Mario Matic, from Croatia; Father George Kass, from Iowa; Father John Twomey, from Ireland and for twelve years Monsignor Loreto Gonzales, of the Philippines.

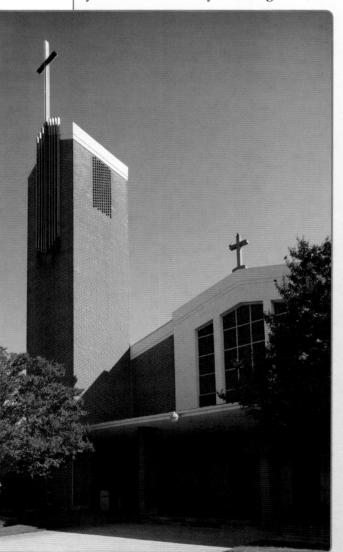

Avalon

Saint Catherine of Alexandria

1902

The first church on Santa Catalina Island was built in 1900 by Father Robert Byrne and the parish was established in 1902. The second church, built in 1912, and the rectory were destroyed by fire eight months later during the pastorate of Father Philip Williams, O.S.B. A third church was dedicated in 1913 by Father E. H. Fitzgerald. In 1950 a church was constructed near the beach and downtown Avalon when Father John J. Brennan was pastor. It was built in the style of California mission architecture with a statue of Saint Catherine of Alexandria in the tower. Further pastors and administrators were Father Cyril Navin, Father John Quinn, Father Brad Dusak and Father Robert O. Luck. In 1989 Monsignor Vincent McCabe, from Ireland, was named pastor and in 1993 Father Paul A. Siebenand, from Minnesota, was appointed.

Azusa

Saint Frances of Rome

1904

Prior to the turn of the century, priests from the San Gabriel Mission provided spiritual guidance to the residents of Azusa. Bishop George Montgomery celebrated Mass in the area in 1895. The resident pastor was Father Michael H. Geary in 1908, although the church, erected in 1904 and attended as a mission from Monrovia. In 1925 Father Peter J. Quinn rebuilt the original church and constructed a rectory. Father Albert J. Duggan was named pastor in 1950 and a school opened in 1952. He purchased property for a church building that was completed in 1959. James Francis Cardinal McIntyre blessed it in 1960. Monsignor Robert J. Stein headed the parish for fifteen years and founded the Saint Frances Food Bank. Father Edward Landreau was pastor from 1990 to 1998 before becoming pastor emeritus.

Baldwin Park

Saint John the Baptist

1946

An early chapel, built entirely by men of the area, served as a church during the pastorate of Father Hugh Regan. It was later enlarged and converted to a parish hall. A school opened in 1952 staffed by Benedictine Sisters. A new church was completed in 1957. The Spanish modern church had a seventy-one-foot tower. Monsignor John Flack, from San Bernardino, was named pastor in 1951 and during his thirty years at the parish also constructed the school, auditorium and catechetical center. Monsignor Peter Nugent, from Canada, was named pastor in 1981 and headed one of the largest parishes in the Archdiocese for nine years. During that time he helped establish the East Valley's Organization and initiated Mass in Filipino and Spanish. Father James Forsen served as pastor from 1990 to 2002. The current pastor is Father John G. Montejano, serving since 2002.

Bellflower

Saint Bernard

1923

When first erected in 1923 the parish was called Assumption and had a combination church and rectory on the corner of Center Street and Pacific Avenue. Early pastors were Fathers J. E. Fitzgerald, E. Villenure, Maurice Dee, Patrick O'Dwyer, Leo Lambrick and Roger O'Shea. Father Cornelius Sullivan, from Canada, served from 1940 to 1950 and built a school, a temporary church-auditorium, convent and rectory. Monsignor Michael Healy, from Ireland, headed the parish for twenty-five years, 1950 to 1975, and constructed the new church, a modernized Romanesque design that was a local landmark with a cross-topped, 72-foot-high tower. Father Philip McGrath, also from Ireland, headed the parish from 1976 to 1998. Father Thomas Feltz, from Ohio, served from 1998 to 2004.

Saint Dominic Savio

1954

The church named in honor of the youngest non-martyred saint, Dominic Savio, is part of the Salesian complex in Bellflower that includes an elementary and high school, all staffed by Salesians. The pastor, Father George Salbeck, a native of Germany, completed the temporary church and school. The next pastor, Father David Zunino added to the school and in 1970 Father Anthony DiFalco, of San Francisco, was named pastor. From 1980 to 1997 four other Salesians were named for the parish: Fathers Salvatore Giacomini, Harry Rasmussen, Christian Woerz and Harold Danielson. In 1997 Father Gael Sullivan, of Boston, was named pastor and by 2002 completed the present church on Bellflower Boulevard. Parishioners had waited since 1954 for the new church that Roger Cardinal Mahony dedicated in November 2002.

Saint Gertrude

1938

Father Patrick Casey was appointed to organize a parish that previously had been a mission attended from Downey. Within a year a church and rectory were built with much of the labor done by parishioners. In 1949 the church was moved to a site at Garfield Avenue and Florence Boulevard and completely remodeled. A school was built and staffed by Immaculate Heart Sisters during the pastorate of Father Thomas O'Malley. In 1953 Father Michael Galvin, from Ireland, was named pastor until his death in 1967 at age sixty. In 1976 Monsignor Henry Gomez, a native Angeleno and graduate of Cathedral High School, was named pastor. He had previously served as administrator at the parish. Dedicated in 1995, the present church was based on a simple design, but enhanced by motifs from early Christian churches.

Good Shepherd

1923

Much of the area around Santa Monica Boulevard and Bedford Drive was still open fields when Bishop John J. Cantwell established Good Shepherd parish in 1923. At the time, Father Michael J. Mullins counted only thirty Catholic families in the parish. He served there for fifteen years and built the original Mission style church. Monsignor Patrick J. Concannon, from Ireland, was pastor for twenty years. He died in the sanctuary after Mass at age sixty-three in 1958. During the thirty-two-year pastorate of Monsignor Daniel F. Sullivan, the church was completely renovated and its altars consecrated. Monsignor Sullivan died in 1993 at age ninety-three. Through the years the church became known as the "church of the stars" because many Hollywood movie stars were parishioners. In 1990 Father Colm O'Ryan, from Ireland, was named pastor and completed a second renovation.

Saint Finbar

1938

This parish is named for the seventh century Irish saint. Father John O'Brien, also from Ireland, celebrated Masses in an American Legion hall. A temporary church was built in 1940. Classes for children were held in tents and a school was completed in 1945. Seven years later, the permanent church was built with a 100-foot-high landmark campanile. Monsignor O'Brien retired in 1974 and died in 1982 at age eighty-three. Monsignor Kieran Marum, also from Ireland, was the next pastor. He introduced Masses in Spanish and helped to resettle Vietnamese immigrants.

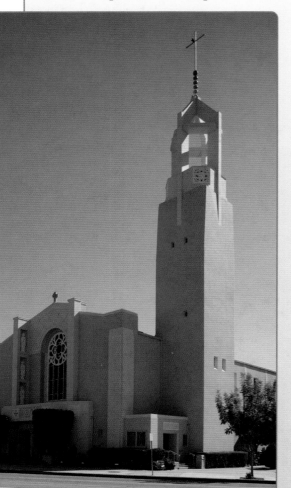

He was pastor for ten years and died in 1996 at age seventy-nine. The third pastor was Monsignor Robert Howard, a native of Indiana, who headed the parish for twelve years and continued the "sister parish" system with Saint Thomas the Apostle Church. Father Jose Holguin, a native Angeleno, was pastor for six years. Father Albert Bahhuth was appointed pastor in 2002.

Saint Francis Xavier

1954

This was the first parish in the Archdiocese to be staffed by Holy Cross priests. Father John P. Lynch, C.S.C., from New York and a former lawyer, celebrated Masses in Villa Cabrini Academy Chapel before a church was constructed. Near the site was the chapel erected by Saint Frances Xavier Cabrini, which overlooked the entire valley. The Cabrini Sisters made the parish site available from property Mother Cabrini had selected. A church and school were built in 1956. Father Lynch was pastor for eight years. Father William C. O'Connor, C.S.C., of Milwaukee, was the next pastor and served for fourteen years, followed by Father Van Wolvlear. The last two Holy Cross pastors were Fathers William Neidhart and Michael Couhig. Archdiocesan priest Father Richard Albarano was appointed pastor in 2000.

Saint Robert Bellarmine

1907

The parish was established under the name of Holy Trinity, and Father Edward Wright was pastor. Several pastors served the growing parish. In 1930 Monsignor Martin Cody Keating, of Connecticut, was appointed and obtained permission to change the name of the parish to Saint Robert Bellarmine. The church was completed in 1939 in the style of Colonial architecture to symbolize the "American Way." All the parish buildings were completed during his pastorate of thirty-eight years and reflected his commitment to the religious and political principles of the country. Monsignor Keating died in 1971 at age eighty-eight, a priest for sixty-two years. Monsignor Paul Seday, a native of Kansas, was pastor from 1969 to 1986. Monsignor Patrick O'Reilly, from Ireland, pastor for sixteen years, remodeled and renovated the buildings in 1990.

Blessed Junipero Serra

1988

The founding pastor for this parish was Monsignor Liam Kidney, a native of County Cork, Ireland and former high school principal. The parish was named in honor of Fray Junípero Serra, founder of the California Missions. Some 800 families were enrolled through volunteer census takers. Mass was temporarily celebrated in the chapel of Saint John's Seminary College. In 1995 Roger Cardinal Mahony dedicated the church, on Blessed Serra's feast day, July 1st. By then the parish had 1,800 families. The land whereon the parish is located, was part of the original Camarillo family ranch that Juan Camarillo donated for Saint John's Seminary. In 1999 Father Jarlath Dolan, also from Ireland, was named administrator and started a campaign to expand the original site to include a parish center and conference space. He was named pastor in 2000.

Saint Mary Magdalen

1940

Thirty years before the parish was established, the chapel of Saint Mary Magdalen was built by the Camarillo family and subsequently willed to the archdiocese for use as a parish church in 1940. Father Hugh Crowe, from County Galway, Ireland, was the pastor and served the parish until his death in 1951. Monsignor John Moclair, also from County Galway, constructed the parish school in 1954. For the next ten years Monsignor Denis J. Falvey of County Kerry, Ireland, headed the parish. From 1971 to 1999 Monsignor John C. Hughes, a native Angeleno, was pastor. During that time a church was built at Las Posas Road and Crestview Avenue, two miles from the original church, which then reverted to its original status as a chapel. Timothy Cardinal Manning dedicated the modern mission style church in 1976.

Our Lady of the Valley

1921

A recently retired Air Corps chaplain, Father Arthur Hutchinson, celebrated Mass in a restaurant on Sherman Way that eventually became a chapel. Bishop John J. Cantwell approved of the facility and thus the "Mother Church" of the valley was established in 1921. The next year a wooden building was completed and by 1931 the town called "Owensmouth" was renamed Canoga Park. Three pastors were appointed before 1943, Fathers John Cunningham, Hugh Crowe and Thomas English. Then Father John Hurley, from Ireland, was named pastor and for thirty-three years guided the parish through enormous changes. Father Hurley relocated the wooden church twice and in 1969 built a new structure and a school. Monsignor Hurley died in 1995 at age 91. Father John Murray renovated the church in 1995 after the Northridge earthquake.

Saint Joseph the Worker

1956

This parish was established on May 1st, the day on which the feast of Saint Joseph the Worker was celebrated for the first time. Father Austin J. Greene said Mass in the John Sutter Junior High School auditorium. A church was completed in 1957 and designed for future use as a parish auditorium. In 1966 the parish broke ground for a permanent church and in 1969 James Francis Cardinal McIntyre dedicated the brick and concrete building. Behind the main altar is a large marble panel with the mosaic figure of the risen Christ, designed by Isabel and Edith Piczek. Monsignor Greene, a native of Massachusetts, was pastor until 1981. He died that year at age seventy-four. The next pastor was Monsignor James Loughnane, from County Galway, Ireland, who served until 1993. Monsignor James Gehl, a native of Chicago, was pastor from 1993 to 2004. Father Kevin Rettig was named pastor of St. Joseph the Worker Church in 2004.

Saint Joseph

1933

The first pastor for the new church built in 1957 was also one of the five priests in the first ordination class of St. John's Seminary in 1940 - Father Francis W. Roughan, (named a Monsignor in 1981). The original church, built about two miles from the present site, is maintained as a chapel in the business district. Monsignor Roughan, a native Angeleno, served as pastor for seventeen years witnessing the blessing of the school in 1961 and the dedication of the new church by Bishop Timothy Manning in 1967. Parishioners volunteered in constructing the school as they had for the early church. Monsignor Joseph Kearney, a native of Spokane and a professional musician with the Crosby brothers, headed the parish for twelve years. For seven years Father Michael Jennett, of Burbank, served at St. Joseph followed by Father David Herrera whose short term of three years ended in 2000 when he died of cancer. The present pastor is Father Adalberto Blanco, a native of Mexico.

Saint Philomena

1956

Father Frederick Callahan headed the parish for twenty-one years and directed the building of the church, school, rectory and convent. He was a native of Worcester, Mass, and died in 1977 in the rectory at age sixty-seven. Monsignor William O'Toole, from Ireland, was named administrator in 1976 and then pastor in 1978. By then the Carson parish was comprised of twenty percent Polynesians, the biggest Samoan colony outside of the islands. For fifteen years Monsignor O'Toole shepherded the ethnically diverse parish. He was succeeded by Father Rizalino Carranza from the Philippines, pastor until 1999. Father Demetrio Bugayong, also from the Philippines, was named administrator in 1999 and pastor in 2000. An new church was completed in 2002 to serve Filipinos, Samoans, African-Americans, Latinos, Vietnamese, Koreans and Caucasians.

Saint John Eudes

1963

Parochial Masses were celebrated in Rancho San Antonio auditorium. The pastor, Monsignor Philip Grill, a native of Utah, served the parish for twenty-six years. During his pastorate he supervised the building of the entire parish plant and witnessed its growth from 800 to more than 2,500 families. The parish was one of six established in 1963, all named for founders of religious congregations. Father Robert McNamara, a native of Limerick, Ireland, was named pastor in 1988. Six years later the Northridge earthquake severely damaged the church and liturgies were held in the parish hall. By 1996 the church had been rebuilt and renovated with the addition of a sixty-five-foot tower and 15,000-square-foot parish hall that included meeting rooms and kitchen. Monsignor Peter Nugent, from Canada, was named the third pastor in 2001.

Our Lady of the Assumption

1947

Before this parish was established in 1947, Sacred Heart Chapel in Claremont was built in 1938 and served the Spanish-speaking people of the area. The pastor for Assumption was Father John Rengers, from Holland. He died in 1961 at age fifty-eight. The next pastor was Father Donald P. Strange, a native Angeleno, appointed in 1949, who headed the parish for fourteen years. He built the church, school and parish auditorium. Monsignor died in 1994 at age eighty-seven. Monsignor William J. Barry, a native of Akron, Ohio, was named pastor in 1963 of the only Catholic parish in the college town of Claremont. For thirty years he headed the parish and also administered several archdiocesan posts. Father Thomas Welbers, from Glendale, was appointed pastor in 1994.

Our Lady of Victory

1911

This parish was a mission of Saints Peter and Paul Church in Wilmington before 1911. Father Jeremiah Burke started with some fifty families in the area. The Dominguez family donated the property for the parish building. In 1929 Father Laurence O'Connor was named pastor and built a rectory to replace the one that had burned. Father Vincent Flynn, of County Tipperary, Ireland, began a pastorate of thirty-two years in 1937. He opened the school, built a church and convent. Father Flynn died in 1969 at age sixty-seven. That same year the parish was assigned to the Missionary Servants of the Most Holy Trinity, with Father Justin Furman as pastor. By 1998 the parish had a pastoral team headed by Fathers Stanley Bosch, Kent Weidie and Roberto Mena. The team is clustered with the parish of Sagrado Corazon, also in Compton.

Sagrado Corazon

1956

Father Francis Reilly, from Ireland, was pastor of Sacred Heart parish in Compton. He was also the spiritual director of the Ozanam School of Charity, a society for Catholic laypersons interested in extensive charity work. He died in 2001 at age seventy-nine. From 1971 to 1985 Father John Gubbins, a native Angeleno, headed the parish. Prior to his appointment as pastor, he taught Latin at the junior seminary. He died in 1999 at age seventy-two. Following him was Father Francisco Vitela, from Mexico City, who served from 1986 to 1998. He was ordained in Mexico and incardinated in 1976. In 1998 the pastoral team of the Missionary Servants of the Most Holy Trinity was assigned to the parish. The leadership team is the same that serves the parish of Our Lady of Victory in Compton. The Trinity Missionaries were founded in North America in 1929.

Saint Albert the Great

1949

Mass for the parish was celebrated in an auditorium on South Avalon Boulevard. By 1952 the church was completed, incorporating the work of several California artists and reflecting the style of Bavaria, homeland of Saint Albert the Great. Monsignor Patrick Redahan, from Ireland, guided the parish for five years. He died in 1998 at age eighty-nine. Monsignor James Dessert, from Missouri, also served for five years and died in 2001 at age ninety-six. From 1961 to 1969 Father Martin McGovern, from County Mayo, Ireland, headed the parish. He died in 1998 at age eighty-three. The Missionaries of the Holy Family were placed in charge in 1969 and Father Edward Zaborowski, a native of New Jersey, was named pastor. Comboni Missionary Father Bartholomew Battirossi, from Italy, was pastor from 1983 to 1997. Archdiocesan priests were assigned in 1997.

Sacred Heart

1927

First erected as a mission in 1911, the church was attended from Saint Frances of Rome Church in Azusa, but was established as a separate parish in 1927 with Monsignor Denis J. Falvey, from County Kerry, Ireland, as pastor. He built the rectory and served the parish for two years. Monsignor Patrick Carey served from 1936 to 1941. Father Hubert Vandenbergh, from Holland, was pastor from 1942 to 1948. He died in 1975 at age seventy-three. During the 1950-1979 pastorate of Monsignor Bernard Collins, a native of County Cavan, Ireland, a second church and school were built. He died shortly after his retirement in 1979 at age seventy-five. New parishes were formed from Sacred Heart due to the area's growth. Monsignor Patrick Reilly, from Ireland, served from 1979 to 1986 followed by Father Louis Stallkamp, a native Angeleno, who was pastor until 1994 when he died at age sixty-four.

Saint Louise de Marillac

1963

This Covina parish was named for the 17th century wife and mother who founded the Sisters of Charity with Saint Vincent de Paul. Monsignor James Walsh, of County Sligo, Ireland, was the pastor and used the Echo Sales Warehouse on Arrow Highway to celebrate Mass. For twenty-one years he shepherded the parish, building a church and school that was staffed by the Sisters of Notre Dame de Namur. Timothy Cardinal Manning consecrated a church in 1973 that received national recognition for its distinctive architecture and became a model for many other churches. Monsignor Walsh died in 1984 and Monsignor Robert Pierce, from Pasadena, was named pastor. A Confraternity of Christian Doctrine building and parish hall were completed in 1989 as part of the parish development program. Monsignor Pierce retired in 2001.

Cudahy

Sagrado Corazon y Santa Maria de Guadalupe

1992

Before the establishment of the parish, it was called the "Roman Catholic Mission in Cudahy". Monsignor Henry Gomez from the neighboring church of Saint Gertrude in Bell Gardens presided at Masses at various locations on Florence Avenue or wherever a place could be found to accommodate the crowds who wanted to worship. In 1992 the Missionaries of the Sacred Heart of Jesus began administering the parish when Bishop Carl Fisher found a nearby Methodist church that was selling property. A small church was built on Clara Street. But growing attendance made the small church inadequate, and parishioners built an additional open-air platform for more space. The parish soon had 500 baptisms a year and several fund raising efforts helped to build a larger church. The pastor is Father Antonio Garnica.

Culver City

Saint Augustine

1919

Father Patrick Hawe of Saint Monica's church had constructed a small frame building for the area mission that was served by priests from Redondo Beach and Saint Agnes. The first resident pastor was Father Thomas O'Toole, followed by Monsignor Michael O'Halloran, who enlarged the wooden church. From 1923 to 1938 Monsignor John O'Donnell headed the parish and invited the Daughters of Mary and Joseph to open a school. In 1936 a larger church was built that attracted nationwide attention for its network of steel rods welded into a single unit. Monsignor Leo Murphy (1937 to 1949) completed the expansion of the school and convent. Monsignor James McLaughlin, of County Leitrim, Ireland, served from 1949 to 1968 and built a Gothic style church in 1958. He died in 1968 at age seventy-five. Additional pastors were Father Regis Combs and Monsignor Ian Holland followed by Father Alfred Burnham, then today, Father Kevin Nolan.

Diamond Bar

Saint Denis

1971

Timothy Cardinal Manning chose the name for this parish, the patron saint of Paris. Father Donald W. Potthoff, of Los Angeles, served there for twenty-two years. The parish was originally a mission of Saint Angela Merici church in Brea and Masses were often said in local schools. Adjoining the Pomona Freeway, Diamond Bar was called the county's largest master-planned community. The original mission center included an auditorium for Mass, classrooms and kitchen. In 1989 a Spanish-style church building was completed that included a unique seating arrangement with pews in a semi-circle facing the altar. Monsignor James Loughnane, of County Galway, Ireland, was named pastor in 1993 and celebrated the 25th anniversary of the parish in 1996 that includes Anglo, Filipino, Korean, Chinese and Indonesian parishioners.

Downey

Our Lady of Perpetual Help

1909

Monsignor John McCarthy built the original church for this parish in the southwest part of Los Angeles County, but the first pastor was Father B. O'Rourke. Monsignor Thomas Blackwell, of Ireland, presided until 1918. Father John J. O'Brien, of Ireland, in 1930 erected a church of Romanesque architecture. In 1971 Monsignor Stephen Kiley of New York became pastor of the Downey parish. For thirty-one years Monsignor Patrick J. Carey of County Clare, Ireland, presided at the parish where he built the school, expanded the church and opened a parish hall. He retired in 1972 and died in 1978. Monsignor Michael Walsh of Ireland was pastor for twelve years. Monsignor John M. Young of Los Angeles was pastor from 1984 to 1991 during which time the quake-damaged church was rebuilt.

Downey

Saint Raymond

1956

Aschool and temporary church were combined in one building when this parish was established under the pastorate of Monsignor Patrick Cleary. The County Dublin priest headed the parish for twenty-five years. In the beginning, Mass was celebrated at Pius X High School. Bishop Timothy Manning blessed the new church built in 1958. The patron is the 13th century Spanish priest, Saint Raymond Nonnatus. Monsignor Robert Gipson of Los Angeles headed the parish from 1982 to 1998 when a parish hall was planned and renovation of the church was begun. In 2003 Father John W. Higgins from Indiana was named administrator. The parish also has a mission at Rancho Los Amigos National Rehabilitation Center and Mass is said at Los Padrinos Juvenile Hall in Downey on Sundays.

El Monte

Nativity

1923

Father Innocent Montanari celebrated Mass in a private home before constructing a church on Tyler Street. Father Michael Lalor, who succeeded him, built the rectory. In 1925 Father John Dignam completed the church building. Additional pastors were Fathers Jeremiah Lehane, Richard Hennessy, Albert Hurley and Anthony Kelly. In 1941 Father Denis Ginty of England was appointed and served the parish for thirty-two years. A church was completed in 1955 that replaced the original wooden frame building. It received the top award in the Catholic architectural competition. Father Ginty retired in 1973. Monsignor Robert Pierce headed the parish from 1973 to 1984, followed by Monsignor Peter O'Reilly of Ireland who served until 1992. Father Pedro J. Lopez of Ventura was pastor from 1992 to 2004.

Our Lady of Guadalupe

1973

The first Guadalupe Chapel was built in 1928 and Bishop Alfredo Galindo, a Missionary of the Holy Spirit priest served the mission in its early days, and in 1966 celebrated the ground breaking for a church. Father Juan Arzube (later Bishop) administered the parish before Father Marcos Nicolas was named administrator, then pastor. Father Nicolas, born in Spain, participated in the Spanish Civil War and volunteered for the Augustinian missions. In 1951 he came to the United States. Cardinal McIntyre accepted him as a diocesan priest. He died in 1997 at age eighty-six. Approved in 1972, the parish has had three churches in its half-century history. In 1986 Father Pedro Ciordia, a native of Navarra, Spain, was named pastor. He served the parish for twelve years. In 1998 Father Francisco Vitela, from Mexico City, became pastor.

Saint Andrew

RUSSIAN-GREEK CATHOLIC

1936

Archbishop John J. Cantwell established the original Saint Andrew Chapel in Boyle Heights on Fifth and Cummings Streets. The pastor was Father Michael Nedtotschin, a convert from the Russian Orthodox faith. Father John H. Ryder, an English Jesuit who adopted the Russian Rite, was pastor from 1939 to 1954. He was the first Jesuit to be ordained in the Russian Byzantine Rite. He established the Saint Andrew Russian choir. Father Fionan C. Brannigan, another English Jesuit, was named pastor in 1954 and within three years the parish moved to El Segundo. He died in 1972 at age sixty-eight. Jesuit Father Feodor Wilcock, from England, was named administrator in 1972. He died in 1985 at age eighty-four. Archimandrite Alexei R. Smith, followed as pastor. He is also the administrator of the Melkite Greek Mission, Saint Paul.

Saint Anthony

1925

Father Henry B. Tierney was the resident pastor, but Father Nicholas Conneally, pastor of Saint James, Redondo Beach had erected the building in 1915, when it was a mission of that parish and Saint Joseph, Hawthorne. The first years were very difficult and it was merged with the parish of American Martyrs in Manhattan Beach. In 1942 it was again an independent parish with Father Lawrence O'Connor as pastor. The property on Grand Avenue was purchased in 1955 and a school was built in 1956 during the pastorate of Father Luke Lynch. A church followed the next year. Monsignor Edward Maddox, of Los Angeles, was pastor from 1967 to 1974. Father Michael J. McNulty of Ireland was named to head the parish in 1974. Father James O'Grady, from County Mayo, Ireland, served from 1983 until 2001. Father James Anguiano, of Ventura, became pastor in2001.

Saint Paul

MELKITE GREEK MISSION

1987

The Eastern Rite church is under the jurisdiction of the Melkite Greek Catholic Eparchy of Newton, Massachusetts. No documents remain of the early history. It was founded as a mission of Saint Anne Melkite Greek Church in North Hollywood, with a plan to evolve into a parish on the west side of Los Angeles. When Rt. Rev. Alexei Smith was assigned to Saint Andrew Russian Greek Church, he was also entrusted with the Melkite rite. At first the liturgy was held in the rented Saint Paul Lutheran Church in West Los Angeles, but eventually the group moved to El Segundo. The two Greek Catholic communities share one building under the direction of Rt. Rev. Alexei Smith, a native Angeleno, who for many years has been in charge of the Office of Ecumenical and Inter-religious Affairs.

Our Lady of Grace

1945

The Discalced Carmelite Fathers established this parish in 1945 and dedicated it in honor of the Blessed Mother. Fathers Patrick Collins and Enda Somers, O.C.D. celebrated Mass in the Encino Women's Club. The school opened in 1947, followed by the convent. James Francis Cardinal McIntyre blessed the church building in 1962. The Carmelites returned to Ireland in 1958 and archdiocesan priests took over administration of the parish. Monsignor Francis Osborne, born in Pasadena, shepherded the parish for twenty-three years. He had served as a Navy chaplain in World War II and had moderated the Holy Name Society. He died in 2004 at age ninety-two. Father Gerald Wilkerson, of Iowa, (later bishop) administered the parish in 1982. He became pastor in 1985 and celebrated the parish golden jubilee in 1995. Father Austin C. Doran, of County Dublin, Ireland, became pastor in 1998.

Saint Cyril of Jerusalem

1949

Father Michael Lalor, of County Leix, Ireland, was the founding pastor and headed the San Fernando Valley parish for eighteen years. During that time he completed the parish plant and built a church in 1959. A school opened in 1950 staffed by Sisters of Saint Joseph of Carondelet. Father Lalor died in 1967 at age sixty-two, having just completed the building of a new church. The temporary church of 1950 was converted into a parish auditorium. The new structure combined traditional Gothic and contemporary design, with a stained glass window of Saint Cyril above the main entrance. Monsignor Christopher J. Bradley, of County Cavan, Ireland, was pastor from 1967 to 1971. Monsignor Cyril Navin, native of County Clare, Ireland, became pastor in 1971 and continued at the parish until 1996. Monsignor Carl Bell, of Los Angeles, was named pastor in 1996.

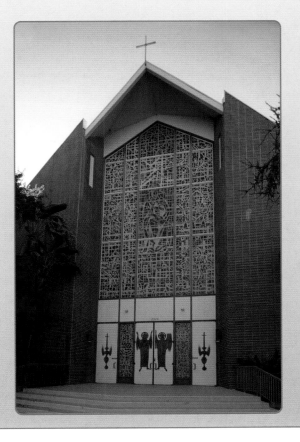

Fillmore

Saint Francis of Assisi

1926

Beginning in 1914, priests came from Santa Paula to offer Mass for those working in this agricultural region. By 1918 they also served the small town of Piru, where San Salvador Mission was later established as part of the parish. Father John J. Cox was pastor and later Monsignor Joseph Feehan. In the early 1940s, Monsignor Eugene MacSweeney, of County Cork, Ireland, was pastor. Father Joseph Alker administered the parish from 1955 to 1962. Monsignor Cornelius Ravlic, of Croatia, began his twenty-four years at the Fillmore parish in 1961. He built the church, hall and religious education center, and also the Piru Mission. He died in 2002 at age eighty-nine. Monsignor Sylvester O'Byrne, from County Dublin, Ireland, headed the parish for five years. He died in 2004 at age seventy-eight. Father Norman Supancheck was pastor from 1991 to 1996 during the Northridge earthquake. Father John Love was appointed pastor in 2005.

Gardena

Maria Regina

1956

The parish was named for the new feast of the Queenship of Mary, and Father Michael Casey, a native of County Limerick, Ireland, was the pastor. Mass was celebrated in the Junípero Serra High School auditorium. He directed all of the parish's development, including the sixteen-room school. James Francis Cardinal McIntyre blessed the church and school in 1958. Father Casey died in 1978 at age sixty-seven after directing the parish for a quarter century. Father Thomas Acton, from County Down, Ireland, was appointed pastor in 1978 and continued in that position for twenty-five years. During his pastorate, the immigrant Vietnamese community was welcomed and Mass was celebrated in Vietnamese and Spanish. He retired as pastor emeritus in 2003 and resides at the parish. The administrator of Maria Regina is Father Leo Alberg, from Montebello.

Saint Anthony of Padua

1910

The parish and a church both started in 1910 with Father William Powers as the pastor. Monsignor Raphael Fuhr, from Cologne, Germany, headed the parish from 1914 to 1918. He died in Rome, 1935 at age seventy-five. The parish was then made a mission of Saint Michael's, but in 1922 it again became a parish with Father Michael Lalor as pastor. A new church was dedicated in 1927. Father Lalor was pastor until the early 1940s. Father Augustine Murray, of Austria, was pastor for three years followed by Father Jerome O'Neill, of County Cork, Ireland, pastor for nine years. Father Joseph Hill, of Massachusetts, built a school, convent and rectory during his term of ten years. He died in 1965 at age 54. Father James Hansen was named pastor in 1966 and died in an auto accident in 1975. Father Peter McGee, of County Galway, Ireland, headed the parish from 1975 to 2000.

Holy Family

1907

Bishop Thomas Conaty told Father James Stephen O'Neill, a Boston native, to establish a parish in the new city of Glendale in 1907. He found a hall owned by the Grand Army of the Republic and celebrated Mass there. By 1921 he had built a church on East Lomita. The school opened in 1925 and was staffed by the Sisters of Charity of the Blessed Virgin Mary. They opened the high school in 1937. From 1923 to 1972 Monsignor Michael Galvin, from County Limerick, Ireland, headed the parish – his forty-nine-year term is one of the longest in the Archdiocese. The third pastor for two years was Monsignor Charles Cranham, of Minneapolis. For twenty-one years Monsignor Arthur Lirette, a native of Eureka, California, headed the parish until he retired in 1995. Father Joseph Shea of Van Nuys was appointed in 1996.

Incarnation

1927

The first two pastors of the Glendale parish were Fathers Emmett F. Panner and Thomas O'Sullivan who secured a building as a temporary church in 1928. Monsignor Michael Carvill, of County Down, Ireland, was named pastor in 1931 and headed the parish for forty-one years. During that time he built the church, school, auditorium, convent and rectory. The school opened in 1937 and its auditorium served as the church for fourteen years until the new church was built in 1952. Monsignor Carvill died in 1975 at age eighty-eight, a priest for fifty-two years. Monsignor Laurence O'Brien, of Winnipeg, Canada, was named pastor in 1972 and served until his retirement in 1986. From 1986 to 1999 Monsignor Eugene Frilot, a native Angeleno, headed the parish and retired as pastor emeritus. Father Paul Hruby, also a native Angeleno, was named pastor in 1999.

Saint Gregory

ARMENIAN

1998

In December of 1951 Father Michael Akian came to Los Angeles to establish an Armenian Catholic community. With the support of James Francis Cardinal McIntyre, in 1962 Our Lady Queen of Martyrs became the first Armenian Church in California, with Father Akian as pastor. He was succeeded by Father Clement Morian from 1964 to 1976 and Father Mesrob Topalian from 1987-1991. An increasing number of immigrants saw the need for a new church, and Father Raphael Minassian helped to establish Saint Gregory the Illuminator on east Moutain Street. He transformed the church into one reflecting in the Armenian architecture. In 2004 Father Andon Noradounguian was appointed to take the responsibility of the parish, and in 2005 Father Antoine Saroyan became the pastor.

Saint Dorothy

1958

Mass was celebrated at the Women's Club by a visiting priest from Azusa until James Francis Cardinal McIntyre appointed Father William Trower pastor. The parish was named for the fourth century martyr, the patroness of gardeners. The Missouri-born priest found an eager group of parishioners to start the parish. By 1960 the school had been built and in 1964 a church was completed. For twenty years Father Trower served the parish. He died in 1995 at age eighty-four. A native of County Galway, Ireland, Monsignor John Acton was the next pastor, and during his twenty-one years renovated the church, parish hall, youth center and school. He retired as pastor emeritus in 1999. In the same year Monsignor Michael Meyers, from Minneapolis, became pastor after serving nine years as director of the Propagation of the Faith in the Archdiocese.

Saint Mark University Parish

1966

The Paulist Fathers came to the University of Santa Barbara in 1966 to establish a traditional Catholic Newman Center for students. Father Robert Donoghue, from the missionary fields of Rhodesia, was assigned to set up a center and "store front" church. He celebrated Mass in Dos Pueblos Hall. A year later the church was built at Picasso Road. In 1969 the People Corps of the parish was formed to visit the elderly and neglected members of the community. Father Donoghue played an important role during the campus riots of 1970. The next pastor was Father Rudolph Vorisek who served from 1970 to 1976. Paulist Fathers who continued to serve as pastors were Philip Hart, 1978 to 1981, Kenneth McGuire, 1982 to 1990. Father William Edens, of Portland Oregon, was appointed in 1990 and Father Joseph Scott in 2002.

Goleta

Saint Raphael

1896

On land donated by Mrs. Rafaela Hill, Father Polydore Stockman, from Belgium, built the original church and was the first California priest to be named a monsignor. Jesuit Fathers administered the parish in 1908 and Father Octavius Villa organized the choir for what was still a mission of Our Lady of Sorrows. The earthquake of 1925 destroyed all the church records. In 1928 the Franciscans were appointed and Father Alfred Boedekker given full charge. Franciscans served until 1937 when Father Henry McHenry was appointed, followed by Father Thomas J. O'Sullivan who converted the hall into the church. During the pastorate of Monsignor William Harvey, a church was built. Monsignor Henry Van Son served from 1969 to 1978. Monsignor Stephen Downes, of County Dublin, Ireland, headed the parish for fifteen years, until 2002. Father Bruce Correio was appointed pastor in 2002.

Granada Hills

Saint Euphrasia

1963

The parish was named for Saint Mary Euphrasia Pelletier, foundress of the Good Shepherd congregation. Monsignor Laurence O'Brien, of Canada, celebrated Mass at Knollwood Country Club until the church was completed in 1966. James Francis Cardinal McIntyre dedicated the church in 1968. In 1964 the school opened in renovated buildings from Saint John Baptist de la Salle parish. Father Paul Kelly, from Iowa, served from 1972 to 1980 and during that time built the parish hall. Father Raymond Saplis, a native Angeleno, headed the parish from 1980 to 1998. The after-school program started in 1984, and a kindergarten began in 1988, followed by the religious education office and computer lab. Father Michael Wakefield, from Pasadena, was appointed pastor in 1998 and the church interior was updated.

Saint John Baptist de La Salle

1953

Father Edmund Bradley, from Arizona, celebrated Mass for the parish at San Fernando Mission until a temporary building was completed. The next year Monsignor Peter O'Sullivan, of County Tipperary, Ireland, started his pastorate of thirty-two years and oversaw the construction of the church, school, rectory and convent. He retired as pastor emeritus in 1986. For twelve years Father Michael Slattery, of Waterford, Ireland, headed the parish and faced unusual growth and calamity. The Northridge earthquake damaged the church, school and other buildings. He created a master-plan for the parish complex, rebuilt the school and installed a computer room. In 1998 Father Robert Milbauer, who grew up in Encino and attended Our Lady of Grace School, became pastor. The parish is named for the founder of the Christian Brothers, the eighteenth century French father of modern teaching methods.

Our Lady of Guadalupe

1867

The mission of Guadalupe was attended from Santa Ines Mission. A church was built around 1875 by Father Michael Lynch from Arroyo Grande. The town derives its name from the Guadalupe Rancho. In 1905, Guadalupe became one of the chapels of Saint Mary of the Assumption parish in Santa Maria. By 1913 the church had become an independent parish with Father M. Cordiero the pastor. Father John Early was pastor from 1940 to 1943. By 1958 a church had been built during the pastorate of Father Anthony M. Cambra from Spain, who headed the parish for twenty-two years. He died in 1977 at age sixty-seven. Father William Appling, of Nebraska, was pastor for seven years. He died in 1992 at age sixty-six. Father Julio Roman of Panama administered the parish from 1988 to 1994. Father Abel Suquilvide, from Argentina, was named pastor in 1995.

Hacienda Heights

Saint John Vianney

1965

Four years after this parish was established, a church and school of religion were completed. The parish patron is Saint John Vianney, the Curé of Ars, and a stained glass window above the main entrance bears his image. The founding pastor was Monsignor James A. O'Callaghan, a native Angeleno, whose pastorate lasted twenty-seven years. During the early 1980s the parish implemented the Renew plan, which included thematic homilies and handouts for twenty-seven consecutive Sundays, with small group discussions during the week. Monsignor O'Callaghan helped form the first Priest's Senate in the archdiocese and was highly esteemed by fellow priests and parishioners. He died in 2002 at age eighty-five. Monsignor John Kane was pastor from 1992 to 2001, when Mass was also celebrated in Chinese. Father Timothy Nichols, a native Angeleno, was named pastor in 2002.

Hawaiian Gardens

Saint Peter Chanel

1986

Archbishop Roger Mahony declared Saint Peter Chanel a parish in January of 1986. It had been a mission of Holy Family parish, Artesia, for seven years and is in the heart of the heavily Hispanic Hawaiian Gardens community. The pastor was Father Vincenzo Antolini, who had served seventeen yeas as a missionary in Brazil and was a member of the Oblates of the Blessed Virgin Mary. He had served the Catholic community in the area since 1980 and continued as pastor until 1991. Father Lawrence T. Darnell, O.M.V, of Memphis, Tennessee, was appointed in 1991. In 2000, Roger Cardinal Mahony dedicated the permanent church. Its main altar was one of the side altars of the former Saint Vibiana Cathedral that was donated to the church.

Saint Joseph

1920

The parish was originally a mission of Saint John Church in Los Angeles, in 1916. There was no church, but Father Jeremiah Burke celebrated Mass for the eleven Catholic families in the area who helped build the first church. The pastor in 1920 was Father Paul De Munck. In 1924 Father John Ford ministered to a hundred families and a second church was built. The school opened in 1928, staffed by the Sisters of Providence. Monsignor Patrick J. Redahan, of County Longford, Ireland, was pastor from 1955 to 1984. During that time a third church was completed in 1959, with a 98-foot carillon tower and forty-three stained glass windows. The 1928 church became an auditorium. He also expanded the school and parish library. In 1988 team ministry, with Fathers Joseph Moniz, of India, and Eugene Buhr, a native Angeleno, constituted the team. In 1999 Father Perry Leiker, of Los Angeles was named pastor.

Our Lady of Guadalupe

1958

A catechism school for Spanish speaking children started around 1920 and became a Hispanic center. By 1927 Father Jose Alba celebrated Mass for the growing community. Father Julio Torres, a refugee from persecution in Mexico, served the parish in 1934. Other Mexican priests continued there until 1942 when Monsignor Cyril Wood was named administrator. He improved the church, rectory and buildings used for catechism. By 1957 the Conventual Franciscans were appointed administrators and the following year James Francis Cardinal McIntyre established the mission as a parish. Father Edmund Krolicki, from Conneticut, was named pastor. A church was built in 1960, then the rectory, school and parish hall. Father Edwin Banach was pastor from 1970 to 1978 followed by Father Ralph Vala of Iowa. In 1997 Franciscan Father Gary Klauer was named pastor.

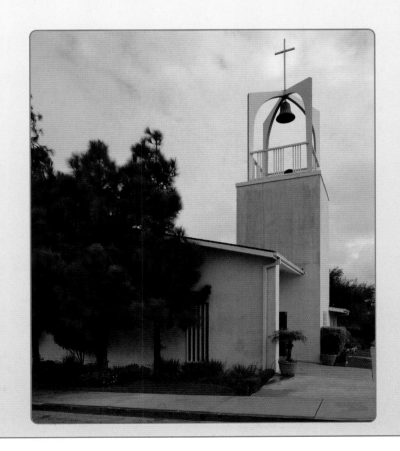

Saint Martha

1913

Father Mathias Ternes celebrated Mass in August of 1913 in the city of Vernon. The land for the church was donated by the Furlong family and named for Martha Furlong. The parish was formerly a mission of Saint Matthias parish. Monsignor Jesús Ramirez, from Mexico, was pastor from 1921 to 1944. The Missionaries of the Holy Spirit were named to the parish in 1952, and Father José Ibarrola named pastor, followed by Father Carlos Furber, from Mexico, who was pastor from 1956 to 1967 and from 1970 to 1976. He was also a noted columnist for The Tidings. During the pastorate of Father Salvador Carasa, the church was moved to the former site of Saint Matthias in Huntington Park. Father Enrique Ramirez, from Mexico, was pastor from 1985 to 1994. Father Roberto Saldivar was appointed pastor in 2005.

Saint Matthias

1913

The pastor was Father Mathias Ternes, from Wyoming, who named the parish for a disciple of Jesus. Later another 't' was added to the original spelling. A small frame building on Seville Avenue was the church. A school opened in 1924 during the pastorate of Monsignor Patrick Pierse, and in 1926 Monsignor Leo Murphy was appointed. He enlarged the church to accommodate the growing numbers of parishioners. Monsignor Thomas Morris was pastor for sixteen years and built a new church. In 1954 Monsignor Patrick Shear, a native of England, was named pastor, and during his twenty years at the parish he built schools, including a girls high school. From 1976 to 1999 Father Rody Gorman, from County Galway, Ireland, was pastor and then Father Abelardo Bailon, from Mexico, was appointed.

Saint John Chrysostom

1923

A chapel dedicated to Saint John Chrysostom was erected in 1911, and in 1923 Father Leo Garsse took charge of the parish. In 1928 a combination church and school was blessed by Bishop John J. Cantwell, during the pastorate of Monsignor James Buckley. Sisters of Saint Joseph of Carondelet staffed the school. In 1938 Father Anthony Reidy became pastor and moved the site. Monsignor Thomas Moran, of County Carlow, Ireland, built a modern Gothic church in 1961 and was pastor for twenty-two years. Monsignor Edward C. Maddox, a native of Los Angeles, was named pastor in 1974 and headed the parish until 1990. Monsignor Paul Montoya, of Wyoming, then served the parish for 15 years. Father Stephen S. Woodland, of Santa Monica, succeeded him in 2000. Today the administrator is Father Javier Altun, S.J.

Our Lady of Guadalupe

1964

The original stone church, built by the people of the area in ten months of hard work, was a mission attended mainly by priests from Saint Frances of Rome in Azusa. For Mass, people had to sit and kneel on the dirt floor. The mission was entrusted to the Verona Fathers, the Missionary Sons of the Sacred Heart in 1957. After that a small meeting hall, catechetical classrooms and rectory were added. In 1964 the mission became a parish, and Father Anthony Marigo, a Verona Father, built a church and catechetical center. In 1966 Father Aldo Cescatti, from Italy, was named pastor and served until 1976. Archdiocesan priest Father Patrick Hughes, a native Angeleno, was administrator in 1977 and then pastor from 1979 to 1999. Father Joseph Canna, a native of Italy, was named pastor in 1999.

La Cañada-Flintridge

Saint Bede the Venerable

1951

This parish was named for the English saint who was the most learned individual of his time. Father J. Paul Early, of County Roscommon, Ireland, celebrated Mass at Saint Francis High School. He opened the parish school. He died in 1962 at age fifty-nine. A permanent church was built in 1966 during the pastorate of Father Thomas Lahart, of County Tipperary, Ireland. He retired in 1972 and Father Joseph Eyraud was appointed. Monsignor Leland J. Boyer, of Sacramento, headed the parish from 1975 to 1994. He expanded the church property and added shrines to Saint Anthony and Our Lady of Guadalupe. Parishioners were noted for many outreach activities. Monsignor Francis Wallace headed the parish for ten years, and Monsignor James Gehl was appointed pastor in 2004.

La Crescenta

Saint James the Less

1955

Father Christopher Barry, from County Limerick, Ireland, celebrated Mass in a rented auditorium. The parish was named for one of the twelve apostles, who was the first bishop of Jerusalem. In 1958 James Francis Cardinal McIntyre blessed the church and school on a 10-acre site on Dunsmore Avenue. Monsignor Barry headed the parish for twenty-nine years and died in 1984. Monsignor Thomas Doyle, from County Waterford, Ireland, headed the parish from 1984 to 1998. During his pastorate he renovated the church, established a youth ministry and a senior citizen center. He also introduced the Renew program and created an award-winning garden area in front of the church. Monsignor Robert Gipson, a native Angeleno, was named pastor in 1998 and formed a parish council and liturgy committee. There are many Koreans in the parish.

Lake Hughes

Saint Elizabeth Mission

1959

This mission outpost was originally under the patronage of St. Mary parish in Palmdale with Father Martin Hiss as pastor, with one Mass celebrated on Sunday morning. By 1961 Father Charles Dachtler headed St. Mary's and also served St. Elizabeth's. In 1969 Father Dachtler was named pastor of Sacred Heart, Lancaster and the mission was then assigned to that parish and the Relgious Fathers of St. Joseph. When the new parish of Blessed Junipero Serra was established in 1987 at Lancaster, the mission became part of that growth with Father Mariano Biasio serving both churches. He was a native of Italy who served in the Antelope Valley as teacher, coach and priest for twenty-four years. In 1999, Congregation of Saint Joseph, Father Ernest Candelaria, from New Mexico, was appointed pastor of Father Serra parish, and also served the mission at Lake Hughes where Mass is still celebrated once on Sunday morning.

Lakewood

Saint Pancratius

1953

A native of Fitchburg, Massachusetts, Father Daniel Kielty, the proto pastor, had served with the Combat Engineers in World War II in Europe. Masses were held in the Lakewood Theatre and the first four school classrooms opened in 1955. The church was built in 1954. Father Kielty served for twenty-nine years and died in 1983. The parish patron is a fourth century Roman boy, martyred at fourteen. Monsignor Ronald Royer, of Santa Monica, an associate in 1976, was named pastor in 1983. His astronomy photos have appeared in several publications and he is known for his Royer Astrographic Camera. He was named one of the top ten astrophotographers in the world in 1988 and retired in 2002. Monsignor Joseph Greeley, of Long Beach, became pastor in 2002.

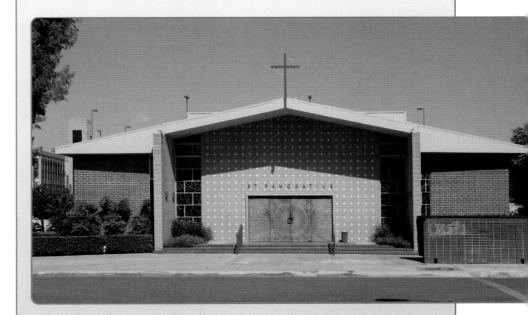

La Mirada

Beatitudes of Our Lord

1964

Father Matthew Marron, a native of County Sligo, Ireland, was pastor. Ground was broken for a temporary church and sixteen-classroom school in 1966. The church was designed as a future auditorium. Monsignor Marron headed the parish for twenty-seven years. Before his retirement in 1990, he witnessed another groundbreaking, this time for the church that would contain a hall, youth center, elementary school and religious education center. Father James Williams, from County Cork, Ireland, was named administrator in 1987 and pastor in 1990. Father Anthony Page is the third pastor, appointed in 1998. He is a native Angeleno and a former high school teacher at Bishop Conaty/Loretto and Daniel Murphy High Schools. The church was finished in 1991.

Saint Paul of the Cross

1956

The parish was named for the founder of the Passionist Fathers, in the then new city of La Mirada, which was formerly part of Norwalk. Monsignor Owen P. Jinks, a native Angeleno, served the La Mirada parish for twenty-seven years. When he began his pastorate, the area was known as the "largest olive grove in the world." He built the first temporary church, a sixteen-room school and convent. Monsignor Jinks died in 1983 at age seventy-two. Father Patrick J. Gannon, from County Roscommon, Ireland, was the next pastor and served the parish for twenty years. He retired as pastor emeritus in 2004. Father Roger Labonte, from Providence, Rhode Island, was appointed administrator in 2004.

Blessed Junipero Serra

1987

Congregation of Saint Joseph Father Mariano Biasio of Italy helped establish the parish, the second in Lancaster. It was named for the founder of the California Missions, Fray Junípero Serra, and is referred to as Father Serra parish. Father Basio was instrumental in designing the master plan that included a multi-purpose hall, church and other facilities. He died in 2002 at age seventy-seven. A memorial was installed in the vestibule of the church that was dedicated in December, 2002 by Roger Cardinal Mahony. Father Ernest Candelaria, C.S.J., from Albuquerque, New Mexico, became pastor in 1999. Father Candelaria also serves Saint Elizabeth Mission on Johnson Road in Lake Hughes. The mission was founded in 1959.

Sacred Heart

1890

There were very few Catholics in the Antelope Valley area when priests visited to offer Mass. In 1884 Father Patrick Bannon came monthly and in 1886 erected a church building. In 1910 Father Joseph Wanner rebuilt the church. A resident pastor was named in 1917. Monsignor Charles K. Kennedy, from Canada, came in 1928 and was pastor for nearly forty years. He built a church in 1956 and was chaplain at Civilian Conservation Corps camps and Muroc Army Base. The school opened in 1949. He died in 1968 at age seventy-four. Father Charles V. Dachtler, of Ohio, was pastor from 1968 to 1976 when he died at age sixty-six. Father John Alvarez, pastor for two years, was followed by Monsignor Jerome Elder of Ohio. He died in 2003 after thirteen years as pastor. Monsignor Timothy O'Connell, of County Cork, Ireland, was pastor for eight years, followed by Father John Vogel in 2000. Father Thomas Baker was appointed pastor in 2005.

La Puente

Saint Joseph

1 9 1 9

A chapel on Main Street named for Our Lady of Guadalupe served as the church in the area until Father Raymond Ferrer was named pastor. In 1922 Monsignor Bernard Dolan, from Ireland, was named pastor of Saint Joseph in 1919 and a church was completed. Father Felix Sheridan, from County Cavan, was pastor from 1933 to 1939. Monsignor Francis Coleman, from Ireland, was pastor for two years. The school opened in 1950 staffed by the Immaculate Heart Sisters. Father Edward Callahan, pastor from 1959 to 1971, built a church. He died at age sixty. Monsignor Edward Sexton, from Chicago, served from 1971 to 1983 when he died at age seventy. Monsignor Patrick Staunton, from County Mayo, Ireland, after serving as associate and administrator, was named pastor in 1983.

Saint Louis of France

1 9 5 5

This town in the San Gabriel Valley was named Bassett when the parish started with Monsignor James Mulcahy, of County Kerry, Ireland, as pastor. The parish grounds were originally a walnut grove and Sunday Masses were celebrated at Our Lady of Guadalupe Chapel in Puente before a temporary church was school were built in 1957. Monsignor Mulcahy headed the parish for thirty-two years, expanded the mission style church, built the school, convent, hall, rectory and center for religious education. He retired in 1987 as pastor emeritus. Monsignor David Sork, a native Angeleno, had worked for ten years in the formation of master catechists for the Archdiocese before serving as pastor from 1987 to 1999. Father Lorenzo, a native of Detroit, was appointed pastor in 1999.

Saint Margaret Mary Alacoque

1937

A temporary church was erected in January of 1937 and Father Timothy Lynch was the pastor. He was quickly succeeded by Father Louis A. Mulvihill. Monsignor Joseph Feehan from Illinois was pastor from 1937 to 1939, followed by Father Thomas Barry, pastor for six years. Father John V. Hegarty headed the parish for twenty-five years and saw the school, church, convent, rectory and parish hall completed. The old church was moved to Eshelman Avenue and used as a hall. From 1971 to 1978 Father Harold Cremins, of Los Angeles, headed the Lomita parish named for the seventeenth century French visionary saint. In 1978 Father Joseph Sartoris, a native Angeleno, was named pastor and remained for sixteen years. Later he was ordained an auxiliary bishop for the Archdiocese. Monsignor Patrick G. Thompson, another Angeleno, was appointed pastor in 1994.

La Purisima Concepcion

Established 1787
Parish 1910

Of the twenty-one California Missions, this is one or two that are state parks. Franciscan Fray Fermin Francisco de Lasuen founded the eleventh station in the mission chain and building began in 1788. A church was completed in 1802. After the severe 1812 earthquake, a new site was chosen. By 1845 the church lost control of the mission. The land was eventually donated to the park service. Restoration was completed by 1941. A nearby parish was erected in 1910 and Father John Reynolds was the pastor in 1910. Monsignor Thomas Morris, from Ireland, built a church and a number of pastors succeeded him. In 1955 Father Andrew McGrath, another Irish native, was pastor for thirty-one years and a church, rectory, school and convent were built. In 1987 Monsignor John Rawden from Ohio was named pastor, followed in 1994 by Father Richard Vega, a native Angeleno.

Queen of Angels

1972

Formerly a mission of La Purisima Church, it was established as a parish in March of 1972. Monsignor Michael J. Ryan, a native of County Galway, Ireland, was named pastor. The parish also traces its beginnings to La Purisima Annex School in Mission Hills that served as a center for Mass in 1964. Monsignor James A. O'Gorman, from County Leitram, Ireland, was pastor from 1977 to 1980 and had been a chaplain in two wars and decorated for valor. The next pastor was Father Paschal Hardy, from County Mayo, Ireland, who headed the parish for nine years and died in 1989 at age fifty-six. Monsignor John G. Fitzgerald, of County Kerry, Ireland, assumed the pastorate in 1989 after administering the parish in the area known as the "Valley of the Flowers." He previously served at La Purisima Concepcion in Lompoc.

Holy Innocents

1923

After the parish was established in December, 1923, Mass was celebrated at McFayden Funeral Parlor by Father Thomas Dowling, pastor pro tem, who was succeeded by Father Francis C. Ott. A parish hall was completed in 1925 and the church, situated on 20th Street, was dedicated in 1926. Father Albert Dontanville was named pastor in 1929. Father John J. O'Brien was pastor from 1941 to 1969 and in 1958 opened the parish school, staffed by Carmelite Sisters. Father Edward Sexton, of Chicago, was named pastor in 1969, followed by Long Beach native Father Robert P. Byrne, pastor for seventeen years. In 1989 Father Michael Gleeson, of County Tipperary, Ireland, headed the parish until 1995. Father Antonio P. Astudillo, from the Philippines, was appointed in 1995 to a parish that is now home to a growing Asian population. Present pastor is Father Peter Irving.

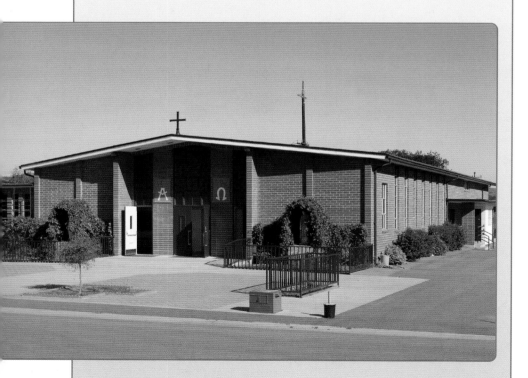

Our Lady of Refuge

1948

This parish was the first in the area established after World War II. In his twenty-one years as pastor, Father Hugh J. Vandenbergh, a native of Holland, directed the building of the church, school, auditorium, convent and rectory. He died in 1975 at age seventy-three. The school opened in 1953, staffed by the Sisters of Saint Louis, and a new church was completed in 1961, at the corner of Stearns Street and Los Coyotes Diagonal. Monsignor Dominic Daly, a native of County Limerick, Ireland, headed the parish for fourteen years. He died in 1986 at age eighty, having served the archdiocese for fifty-five years. He had been instrumental in establishing the Sorrowful Mother Novena at Saint Basil Church, a local popular devotion. Monsignor William O'Keeffe, a native of Ireland, was administrator in 1980 and named pastor in 1981.

Saint Anthony

1902

Father Raymond Ferrer started the first parish in Long Beach. A school was built in 1910 and a new church in 1914. Father James A. Reardon was named pastor in 1917, followed by Father John M. Hegarty and Father Robert E. Lucey, who later became Archbishop of San Antonio, Texas. A second school and a high school were later added, staffed by the Immaculate Heart Sisters. The 1933 earthquake damaged most of the buildings. The present church was dedicated in 1934. Monsignor Bernard J. Dolan, of County Roscommon, Ireland, who was named pastor in 1938, completely rebuilt the damaged church and installed Marian mosaic masterpieces. For thirty years he headed the parish, opened the high school and died in 1968 at age seventy-eight. Monsignor Ernest Gualderon, of Ohio, served the parish from 1968 to 1994.

Saint Athanasius

1933

The parish was a mission church from Holy Innocents for seven years while Father Maurice J. Ryan celebrated Mass in the first church building on Long Beach Boulevard. In 1933 Father Thomas O'Sullivan, of County Kerry, Ireland, was named founding pastor and continued until 1943. Father Joseph Feehan, from Illinois, headed the parish for thirty-four years. A church was built on Linden Avenue and blessed by Bishop Timothy Manning in 1951. The original church became the parish hall, but it was twenty-five years of growth and expansion that brought about the modern construction. Father John Gutting, a native of Saint Louis, headed the parish for twenty years, retiring in 1997. That same year Father William McLean, from Forest Hills, Massachusetts, became pastor of a mainly Latino community. Father Jose Luis Cuevas, a native from Mexico, came to our parish in 2005 and is presently the fifth pastor of the parish.

Saint Barnabas

1939

Services were held on the feast of Christ the King, October 29th, 1939, for 100 Catholic families in the area. Monsignor Thomas J. Foley, a native of County Tipperary, Ireland, was the pastor and headed the parish for twenty-nine years. During his term he built the entire parish plant. The church was dedicated in 1951 and a new rectory completed. The school opened in 1946. Monsignor Foley died in 1968 at age sixty-eight. The next pastor was Father Peter Conroy, from County Roscommon, Ireland, who served for nine years. Before his appointment, he had founded the Rosary Hour radio broadcast in 1949. He died in 1978 at age sixty-seven. Monsignor Christopher Kennedy, of County Roscommon, Ireland, was pastor from 1977 to 1992 followed by Monsignor John Twomey, of County Cork, Ireland who died in 2003 at age sixty-four. Monsignor Loreto Gonzales was subsequently named pastor.

Saint Bartholomew

1937

Monsignor Thomas F. Kennedy, from New York City, was the first pastor and continued to serve the parish for thirty-eight years. The church was dedicated in 1939 by Archbishop John J. Cantwell. The hall was completed in 1946. Bishop Timothy Manning dedicated the school, staffed by Immaculate Heart Sisters, and a convent in 1951. Monsignor Peter C. Caslin, of County Roscommon, Ireland, was pastor from 1975 to 1984. From 1984 to 1988, Monsignor Thomas McGovern, of County Cavan, Ireland, was pastor, and Monsignor Jerome Elder, of Ohio, took charge from 1991 to 2002. He died in 2003 at age seventy-two. In 2002 Monsignor Sean Flanagan, of County Dublin, Ireland, was appointed pastor, after serving at Saint Catherine in Reseda for two decades.

Saint Cornelius

1951

This parish was named for the Pope St. Cornelius, third century Pope, whose baptism marked the expansion of the Church to Gentiles. The founder was Father Michael J. O'Connor, a wartime chaplain born in County Kerry, Ireland, who celebrated Masses in the Lakewood Theater. In 1955 James Francis Cardinal McIntyre blessed additional rooms for a school that opened in 1953 when the temporary church was completed. The next pastor was Monsignor Francis Osborne of Pasadena, from 1955 to 1959, when Father Edmund Bradley of Arizona was appointed. For twelve years he headed the parish and directed the construction of a permanent church and rectory. He died in 1972 at age seventy-four. Monsignor John Folliard, from County Mayo, Ireland, was pastor for twenty-four years and retired as pastor emeritus in 1996, when Father Michael Reardon from Ireland became pastor.

Saint Cyprian

1944

When the parish was founded in June of 1944, the area was called Lakewood Village. Father Philip McKiernan, from County Cavan, built the church that was completed in 1946. For thirteen years he headed a parish that started with only 137 families. Father Patrick O'Connor, of County Kerry, Ireland, pastor for thirteen years, opened the parish school in 1948 and built the church in 1970. He died in 1971 at age sixty-seven. For four years Monsignor Joseph Pekarcik of Chicago was pastor, dying in 1990 at age sixty-seven. His pastorate was followed by that of Monsignor William Hollinger, a native Angeleno, who for thirteen years was also chaplain at Long Beach College. He died in 1988 at age sixty-eight. A native of Long Beach, Father Robert Byrne was pastor from 1989 to 1995, followed by Father Peter Foran, of County Mayo, Ireland.

Saint Joseph

1955

Iowa-born Father Walter A. Martin was the initial pastor of the parish in what was then Lakewood. During his twenty-three years he built the church, school, convent, rectory and gymnasium. The school opened in 1950, staffed by Sisters of Saint Louis. James Francis Cardinal McIntyre blessed the parish plant in September of 1957. Father Martin retired in 1978. In 1979 Monsignor John J. Reilly, a native of Long Beach, became pastor and headed the parish for a decade. He was an educator most of his priestly life and headed the High School Seminary in Mission Hills. He died in 1998 at age seventy-six. Father Douglas Saunders, of Milwaukee, Wisconsin, was also an educator, and directed the parish for eleven years that was then a mixture of Asian, African American and Latino families. In 2001, Father William Connor, from Connecticut, was named pastor. The parish celebrated its fiftieth anniversary June 26, 2005 with a Mass on the grass of the playing field.Cardinal Mahony presided and stayed for the banquet afterwards.

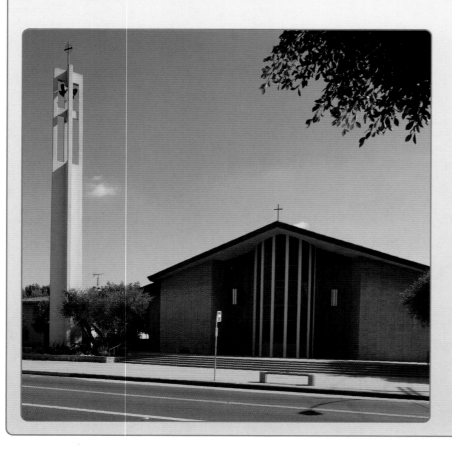

Saint Lucy

1944

Archbishop John J. Cantwell blessed Saint Lucy's Church, the eighth parish within the city of Long Beach, on Cota Avenue. Father Michael J. Lalor, of Leix, Ireland, celebrated the dedication Mass. He served there for five years. Father Hugh Regan, of County Galway, Ireland, was pastor from 1949 to 1972. In 1950 the school was completed and staffed by the Sisters of Mary Mother of God and later by the Sisters of Saint Francis of the Mission of the Immaculate Virgin. Father Regan retired in 1972 and died in 1984 at age eighty. Father John R. Keller, of Pasadena, was named pastor in 1972, and served for three years. Fathers Laurence Joy and Robert Pizzorno were team ministers for seven years. Father Richard Miskella, of County Wexford, Ireland, was pastor for ten years, and in 1996 Father Michael Roebert, of Detroit, was appointed.

Saint Maria Goretti

1955

Dedicated to a twelve-year-old Italian peasant girl who died in defense of her purity in 1902, the parish was established five years after the saint was canonized. During his fifteen years as pastor, Father Vincent Molloy, a native Angeleno, completed all the parish facilities, including a 16-classroom school. He died in 1970 at age fifty-six from a heart seizure. The next pastor was Father Thomas Ryan, of County Tipperary, Ireland, who headed the Long Beach parish for fifteen years. He died in 1988 at age seventy-three. Father John Kane of Nebraska served for seven years, followed by Father John B. Fitzgerald, a Long Beach native who headed the parish for eight years. In 2000 Monsignor Douglas Saunders, of Milwaukee, Wisconsin, was named pastor and redesigned the church interior.

Long Beach

Saint Matthew

1920

Bishop John J. Cantwell named Monsignor Thomas Morris, of County Longford, Ireland, the first pastor. He directed the building of the church, school and rectory. Mass was celebrated in the Brightman Home. By 1921 the school was completed and staffed by the Immaculate Heart Sisters, whose teaching tenure lasted until 1967. Monsignor Morris died in 1967 at age eighty-three. He was succeeded by Father Thomas O'Sullivan until 1932. For forty years Monsignor James Lynch, of County Cavan, Ireland, headed the parish. Just four months after his appointment, he had to cope with the 1933 earthquake that destroyed the church and other buildings. He retired in 1972 and died in 1986 at age eighty-eight. From 1972 to 1983 Fathers William Diamond and Lawrence Dunphy each served as pastor. In 1984 Father Gerald Meisel of Los Angeles became pastor.

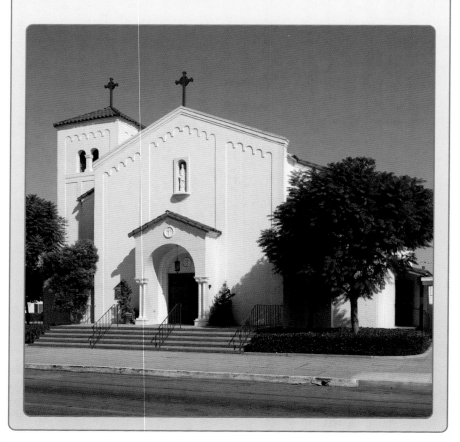

Los Nietos

Our Lady of Perpetual Help

1958

Originally built as a mission chapel in 1923 and then as a mission of Saint Pius X parish in Santa Fe Springs, this faith community became a parish in 1958. The area had its beginning in Rancho Los Nietos in 1784, and a church was built in 1893 in Whittier. Father Jose E. Lopez, from Mexico, was named administrator in 1956 and pastor in 1958. He completely remodeled and enlarged the former chapel. He died in 1966 at age seventy-seven. Monsignor Eugene A. Gilb, a native Angeleno, who served as both administrator and pastor until 1985 and built a church in 1973 on Norwalk Boulevard. Father Charles Ralston, from Hawaii, was pastor for three years and died of cancer in 1989 at age forty-three. Besides parish work, he was assistant super-intendent of elementary schools. Father Greg King, of Santa Monica, was pastor for four years followed by Father John Woolway of Los Angeles.

Saint Emydius

1925

The year the parish was established, Father J. T. Torsney built a church in honor of the fourth century bishop and martyr, who since 1863 has been the patron saint for protection against earthquakes in Southern California. In 1927 Father William O'Donnell became pastor, followed by Fathers Timothy Galvin, Stephen Kiley, John J. Sheehy, Michael Lalor and Richard Hennessy. In 1940 Father Charles J. O'Carroll, during his seventeen year tenure, completed the entire parish plant: an auditorium-church, a sixteen classroom school, a convent and rectory. He died in 1957 at age fifty-five. Monsignor Patrick J. McGuinness, of County Rosscommon, Ireland, was pastor for thirteen years and completed the church. He died in 1970 at age sixty-seven. Monsignor Michael McNulty, of County Mayo, Ireland, was pastor until 1974 and Father Donal O'Connor, of County Cork, Ireland, from 1974 to 1998. In 2000, Msgr. Herrera was appointed pastor. The inside and outside of the church was renovated and dedicated by His Eminence Cardinal Roger Mahoney on the Feast of Christ the King November 20, 2005.

Saint Philip Neri

1948

This parish was named for the apostle of Rome and founder of the Congregation of the Oratory. Father Bernard J. Butler, of County Roscommon, Ireland, directed the construction of the church and rectory. Mass was first celebrated in the new church in 1949. By 1954 the school opened, staffed by Sisters of the Holy Cross, during the pastorate of Monsignor John Birch. He was from Massachusetts and died in 1986 at age seventy-eight. From 1955 to 1968 Father Joseph Eyraud, a native Angeleno, headed the parish. He was a Navy chaplain in World War II and the first principal of Mater Dei High School. Father William Hollinger of Los Angeles was pastor for five years followed by Father Francis Seymour of New York, pastor for seven years. He died in 2004 at age seventy-three. Father Juan Enriquez of Mexico became pastor in 2003.

Malibu

Our Lady of Malibu

1947

Before the parish was established, Father Daniel Gallagher from Saint Jarlath's Church (later closed) said Mass for a small Malibu congregation. He helped erect the church until the appointment of Father Joseph Burbage, of County Longford, Ireland. In 1958 Father Burbage opened the school staffed by Sisters of Saint Louis. During the great Malibu fire of 1958, he remained with the fire fighters to save the church as flames came close. Father Burbage died in 1959 at age fifty-five. Monsignor James O'Callaghan, a native Angeleno, headed the parish from 1958 to 1961. Monsignor John Sheridan, of County Longford, Ireland, was pastor for twenty-five years. He was a national radio and television speaker, author, and writer for The Tidings as well as director of the Catholic Information Center. Father William Kerze, of Glendale, was named pastor in 1996.

Manhattan Beach

American Martyrs

1931

This is the first church erected in the United States under the title of American Martyrs. Father Leo J. Lambrick, of Toronto, Canada, built the church that had eight stained glass windows of the martyred Jesuit missionaries. In 1943 Monsignor Edmond O'Donnell, of Galbally, Ireland, was named pastor and during his twenty years built a complete parish plant, including a permanent church and sixteen-room school. He died in 1963 at age sixty-eight. Monsignor Patrick J. Dignan, of County Roscommon, Ireland, was pastor for four years and was superintendent of schools for twenty-two years. Father Robert Deegan, a native Angeleno, headed the parish for twelve years and was also director of Health and Hospitals for the archdiocese. In 1983 Monsignor John Barry, of County Cork, Ireland, was named pastor.

Maywood

Saint Rose of Lima

1922

A temporary church and rectory were built when the parish was established with Father William Power as pastor. The school opened in 1930 staffed by the Sisters of Notre Dame. A church was erected in 1937 when Father John Dignam was pastor. Archbishop John J. Cantwell dedicated the stucco and frame structure that was converted from the original building. In 1941 Monsignor Maurice J. Ryan, of County Tipperary, Ireland, was named pastor and built a church in 1954, rectory, convent and enlarged the school. He was pastor for thirty years and died in 1971 at age seventy-one. Monsignor John Cummings, from Scotland, headed the parish for the next four years. He died in 1979 at age seventy-six. For twenty-seven years Monsignor George Duran, from Spain, was pastor of the Maywood parish and in 2002 Father David Velazquez, of Mexico, was appointed.

Mission Hills

San Fernando Rey de España

Founded 1797

The seventeenth of the twenty-one California Missions was founded by Fray Fermin Francisco de Lasuen on September 8, 1797. Though never a canonical parish. It was an outpost between Los Angeles and Ventura and contained a compound of church, workshops, granaries and living quarters. A second church served the Indian community until 1806, but the period of 1811 to 1846 witnessed military intervention and corruption. By 1834 the mission lands were confiscated, but Franciscan Father Blas Ordaz remained from 1837 to 1847. In 1902 Father James E. Burns was named pastor of nearby Saint Ferdinand parish. Oblate Fathers administered the mission in 1922. That same year, Father Charles Siemes undertook the restoration. Father Charles Burns completed it in 1937. The fourth chapel was built in 1974. Monsignor Francis J. Weber oversaw the rebuilding of the convento after the 1984 Northridge earthquake.

Immaculate Conception

1904

Father John J. Sheehy gave Shamrock Avenue its name and built the original granite church, one of the most picturesque in the San Gabriel Valley. It was dedicated in 1906. Father John Power became pastor in 1919 and undertook construction of a school and convent. Father Matthew A. Marron continued development during his six years as pastor. For nineteen years, Monsignor John Moclair, of County Galway, Ireland, was the pastor. He died in 1961 at seventy-one. For twenty years Monsignor Maurice Dee, of Tipperary, Ireland, was pastor and built two additions to the school. He died in 1972 at age seventy-two. After the three-year pastorate of Father John McNulty, a team ministry of Fathers Eugene Buhr and John Foley administered the parish for thirteen years. Father Foley was pastor until 1992 and in 1997 Father Charles Ramirez was appointed.

Our Lady of the Miraculous Medal

1950

The parish church was the original building for Saint Alphonsus Church, which was moved to the Montebello site on Garfield in 1950. The founding pastor was Father Marshall Winnie of Sacramento who was the Western provincial of the Vincentian Community. He headed the parish for eight years and died in 1958 at age seventy-one. The school was built in 1954 and staffed by the Daughters of Charity. The church was enlarged in 1956 and Father John Donohoe built a church of "swept-wing" design in 1968. James Francis Cardinal McIntyre presided at the dedication. New York native Father Owen J. Quigley served twice as pastor for a total of nine years. He died in 1983 at age sixty-eight. For eleven years Father John Shine served as both associate and pastor. Father William Piletic was the last Vincentian pastor in 1995, when archdiocesan priest Father Juan Matas was appointed.

Saint Benedict

1906

Bishop Thomas J. Conaty invited the Benedictine monks to come to Montebello from Oklahoma to serve the Basque shepherds working in the nearby hills. Father Leo Gariador, O.S.B., built the first church that burned in 1910. Within the same year another church was opened, which stood through 1929, when Father Luke Eichenlaub completed a brick edifice. Father Albert Brousseau was pastor in 1929 and again in 1936 for a total of seventeen years. A new modern church was erected in 1959, and blessed by James Francis Cardinal McIntyre. Father Charles Massoth was pastor from 1971 to 1986, followed by Abbot Martin Lugo, a native Angeleno, who served for eight years. In 1998 when Father Louis Vanderley was pastor, the Benedictines relinquished the parish. The Augustinian Recollect Fathers were then appointed to administer the parish.

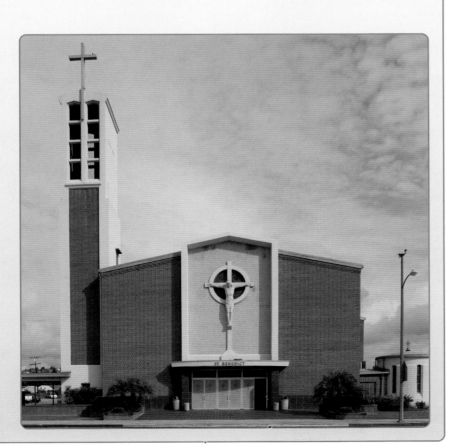

Saint Stephen

1921

From 1918 the parish was served as a mission of South Pasadena. In 1921 Father John J. Cox was named pastor. By 1928 a church and school were completed under the direction of Rev. Michael J. Conneally, of County Galway, Ireland. He died in 1940 and the requiem was held at Saint Stephen's with 200 priests attending. For thirty-two years Monsignor Charles O'Carroll, from Scotland, headed the parish and built the third church that was blessed in 1959. An outstanding feature of the 1959 design was the nearly life-size Stations of the Cross by artist John Henryk de Rosen. In 1965 sixteen classrooms were added to the school. Monsignor O'Carroll died in 1987 at age ninety. Father Carrol O'Sullivan, of London, served the parish from 1972 to 1991. A native of India, Father Eric Lewis, served for four years followed by Father Lawrence Estrada for seven years.

Saint Thomas Aquinas

1960

Father Maurice Evans, of County Kerry, Ireland, directed development of a complete parish plant during his pastorate of fifteen years. Mass was celebrated at Miraculous Medal parish before a former machine shop on Atlantic Boulevard was leased as a site. The parish church was completed in 1963. Father Brian Cavanagh, of County Kilkenny, Ireland, was named administrator in 1975 and pastor in 1979. For fifteen years he served during a time when more Asian families were moving into the area. Father Edward Dover, of Lompoc, was pastor from 1995 to 2001. Maryknoll Father Delos Humphrey helped administer the parish when an evangelization outreach to the Chinese community was formed. In 2003 Father Gabriel Lui of Taiwan was named pastor. In addition to English, Mass is also celebrated in Chinese, and Spanish.

Holy Redeemer

1925

A native of County Tipperary, Ireland, Father William J. Stewart, was commissioned to found a parish in the area that included not only Montrose, but also La Cañada, Flintridge, La Crescenta and Verdugo City. He selected the name for the church, and in two years the mission style building was completed. Monsignor Patrick Healy, of County Galway, Ireland, served the parish for forty-three years, enlarging the church and building a rectory, school and convent. Monsignor Healy died in 1969 at age eighty-nine, and at the time was the oldest priest in the Archdiocese. In 1970 Monsignor Paul Konoske, of Chicago, was pastor for five years, followed by Monsignor Fachtna P. Collins, of County Sligo, Ireland who headed the parish for seventeen years and completed the auditorium building. He died in 2003 at age seventy-eight. In 1992 Father John Foley of County Tipperary, Ireland, was named pastor.

Holy Cross

1982

Holy Cross began in 1925 as a mission to Saint Rose of Lima Church in nearby Simi Valley, but in 1982 it was established as its own parish. By 1984 Timothy Cardinal Manning was able to dedicate a building on the hilltop parish site of Peach Hill and Moorpark Roads. The founding pastor was Monsignor Joseph Cosgrove of County Galway, Ireland. The church and multi-purpose hall seated 850 persons, although the parish already had over 1,000 families. In 1993 Roger Cardinal Mahony dedicated the parish's new church, hall and administrative building. The rapid growth of the area necessitated the creation of facilities more in keeping with post-Vatican II liturgical practice. The 900-seat church was completed a year ahead of schedule and created a "year of celebration" for the parish, according to the pastor, Monsignor Joseph Cosgrove.

Saint Julie Billiart

1969

This parish was named for the foundress of the Sisters of Notre Dame de Namur who was canonized one week before the parish was established. During a four-year pastorate, Monsignor Robert Walsh, of County Sligo, Ireland, built a multi-purpose center, which combined a church, auditorium and Confraternity of Christian Doctrine under one roof. Father Patrick Meskill, of County Kerry, Ireland, headed the parish for twenty-three years and directed the building of a second church across from the original center. Archbishop Roger Mahony dedicated the Spanish style church in 1987, one of the first churches he dedicated after his appointment as archbishop. In 1996 Monsignor Michael Bunny, a native Angeleno, was named pastor. He remodeled the church for 1,600 registered families and built a full baptismal font for the building.

New Cuyama

Immaculate Conception

1969

As early as 1954, before there was a parish in this northern edge of the archdiocese, an Augustinian priest, Father Samuel D'Angelo, drove from Ojai to celebrate Mass in the home of Anne Connor who was the nurse for a local oil company. The community was part of Saint Mary's parish in Santa Maria, and Father Thomas Murphy made monthly trips to the oil town. By 1964 Augustinian, Father Richard K. Smith, celebrated Mass every weekend in the chapel that was a mission of Saint Thomas Aquinas parish in Ojai. (Father John F. Blethen had celebrated Mass only monthly prior to this.) A chapel was built in 1969 and Franciscan Father Leonard Kolodziej was appointed resident administrator. Father Michael Buckley served from 1980 to 1994. In 2000, Sister of Saint Joseph of Carondelet Mary Dorothea Quinn became the first woman religious named to direct a parish in the Archdiocese of Los Angeles.

North Hills

Our Lady of Peace

1944

In 1941 Archbishop John J. Cantwell dedicated a chapel administered by the Oblate Fathers. The first resident pastor, in 1946, was Father James Leheny, of County Sligo, Ireland. He built the school in 1951 and a church in 1954. He died in 1955 at age forty-nine. For five years Father John T. Conlon, of County Mayo, Ireland, headed the parish. He died in 1960 at age sixty. For almost twenty-six years Monsignor Joseph G. Schnieders, of Iowa, was pastor. During that time he built eight additional classrooms, a church hall and rectory. At the time, the school was the largest in the archdiocese. He also served thirty-three years in the Tribunal office. He died in 1986 at age seventy-one. Father James Ford, a native Angeleno, served from 1988 to 1994, when Father John Keese, of Wisconsin, was named pastor and renovated the church building in 2001.

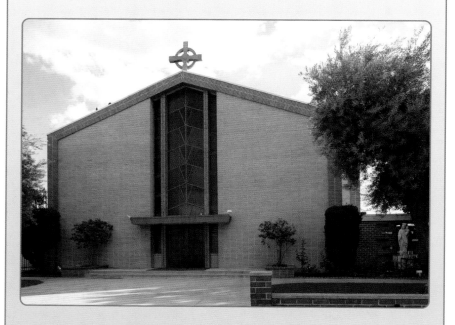

Jesus Sacred Heart

ANTIOCHENE SYRIAC

1992

Descendants of the ancient Aramaic Christians came from Iraq, Syria, Lebanon and Egypt to Los Angeles in the 1990s. By 1992 they purchased a former Mormon church complex on Collins Street in North Hollywood. The parish has some 450 families and belongs canonically to the Eparchy of Our Lady of Deliverance in Union City, New Jersey. The pastor is Father Yousif Habash. Parishioners come from Orange County, Palmdale, Victorville and Santa Barbara. There is one deacon and nine subdeacons. Divine Liturgy is said in Arabic, English and Aramaic, the language spoken by Jesus. The Sacrament of Penance is offered in English, Arabic, French and Assyrian.

Saint Anne

MELKITE-GREEK

1926

The first church that served the Melkite community was erected on North Hoover Street by Father Geracimos Sawaya and was completed by Monsignor Clement Salman, the pastor from 1929 to 1952, the time of his death. The next pastor was Father Michel Bardaouil, a native of Lebanon. For nineteen years he headed the Byzantine rite church and was responsible for the construction of the edifice on Rye Street in North Hollywood. Ancient Byzantine and Moorish architectural styles were used to create the distinctive, circular church. In 1962 Father Bardaouil was elevated to the rank of Archimandrite. Monsignor Maximos Mardelli, a native of Syria, was named to head the parish in 1971 followed in 1980 by Archimandrite Maxim Chalhoub, also a native of Syria, who served for five years. Father Albert Wehby was appointed in 2000.

North Hollywood

Saint Charles Borromeo

1920

Originally a mission of Holy Trinity (now St. Robert Bellarmine) Church in Burbank, Mass was celebrated in the Mulhall home by Father Ernest Leguyader. The parish was established in 1920 with Father Anselme Bois as pastor, followed soon after by Father Leo Murphy. During the pastorate of Father Emmet Panner, the church was named and the building enlarged. In 1927 Father Edward Riordan came for two years followed by Father Michael Lalor until 1936 when Father Harry C. Meade was appointed. He was a native of Michigan and served the parish for more than thirty-six years and built two churches, one in 1938, the other in 1959. The school opened in 1939. Father Meade died in 1978 at age eighty. Monsignor Kevin Keane, of County Sligo, Ireland, followed and was succeeded by Monsignor Thomas Kiefer, of Missouri, pastor for sixteen years. Monsignor Robert Gallagher, of Los Angeles became pastor in 2000.

Saint Jane Frances de Chantal

1948

Father Thomas Lahart of County Tipperary, Ireland, named the parish in honor of the saint who founded the Congregation of the Visitation in the seventeenth century. Before a church was constructed, Mass was celebrated in a barn, under a circus tent and in a public school. Father Lahart headed the parish for fifteen years and completed the church. In 1963 the Carmelite Fathers were entrusted with the parish, and Father Norbert G. Piper, of Chicago, was named pastor. From 1966 to 1973 Father Joseph Gilmore, of New York, headed the parish and died in 1989 at age eighty-one. Father Shane Tahney, of Chicago, was pastor until 1981 when Father Sebastian Meyer, of Detroit, became pastor. The next three pastors were Carmelite Fathers Roy Ontiveros, Chris Pieklo and Michael Higgins. Father Patrick Gavin, of Michigan, was named pastor in 2003. Father Ferdinand Lansang, O. Carm. was appointed pastor in 2005.

Saint Patrick

1948

An old farmhouse served as a temporary site for Mass when Father Joseph Bauer, a native of Wisconsin, served as the pastor for fifteen years. He directed the building of the church and school in the area that was once vineyards and a turkey ranch. He became a monsignor in 1962 and died in 1963 at age sixty. Father Michael Gormally, of County Galway, Ireland, was pastor for sixteen years. The school was opened in 1952, and Father Gormally added a four-room unit in 1964, bringing the complex to a total of sixteen permanent classrooms. The Religious of the Sacred Heart of Mary staffed the school. Father Gormally died in 1979 at age sixty-one. Father Henry Johnson, of Pasadena, was pastor for seven years, and in 1986 the Missionary of Africa priests formed a team ministry. In 1998 Father Gregory King, of Santa Monica, became pastor.

Saint Paul

ASSYRIAN CHALDEAN

1980

The founding pastor of the Chaldean Church was Father Ibrahim Ibrahim, a native of Iraq. For a time he used a former Methodist church for services. The Chaldeans are descendants of the ancient Babylonians and Assyrians who received the faith from the Apostle Thomas. The original congregation of eighty grew to over 240, composed mostly of immigrants from Iraq, Iran and Lebanon. Father Ibrahim was fluent in Arabic, Assyrian, Aramaic, French, Italian, English and German. In 1983 Father Mikhael Bazzi was appointed, and in 1987 Father Emanuel Hanna Shaleta became pastor until 2000. For one year Father Poulus Khozaran served as pastor, succeeded by Father Noel Gorgis in 2001.

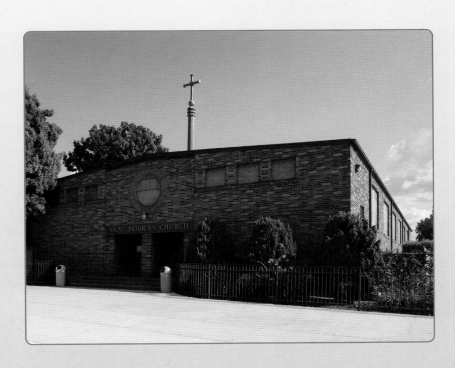

Our Lady of Lourdes

1958

Mass was celebrated at Rancho San Antonio before permanent facilities were completed in 1960. Monsignor Paul E. Stroup, of Fort Wayne, Indiana, directed a complete parish plant and developed an outstanding liturgical music program. The school opened in 1959, staffed by Immaculate Heart Sisters. Monsignor Stroup headed the parish for twenty-five years and was also a member of the Priests' Senate. He died in 1983 at age sixty-six. In 1986 Father George Brincat, a native of Malta, was named pastor. He had been an associate pastor since 1978. Monsignor Peter Moran, of County Galway, Ireland, was named pastor in 1983, almost ten years before the Northridge earthquake severely damaged the church. In 1995 Roger Cardinal Mahony rededicated the church after the earthquake renovations and a new baptistry were completed.

Saint John of God

1950

This Norwalk parish was named for the "beggar for the poor," and the title was given to Father Louis Buechner, the founding pastor from Michigan, in a letter from Archbishop J. Francis A. McIntyre. Early liturgies were celebrated in the Norwalk Theatre. During his twenty-two years as pastor Father Buechner built the church, school, convent and rectory. In 1968 a permanent church was erected on Pioneer Boulevard. Monsignor Thomas Doyle, of County Waterford, Ireland, was the next pastor and for ten years continued the growth and expansion of the parish. In 1984 Monsignor Bernard Leheny, of County Sligo, Ireland, was appointed and initiated programs that ministered to youth, young adults and seniors. Mass is celebrated in Spanish, and an active Filipino community is part of the parish life. A parish center opened in 1996.

Saint Linus

1961

The parish patron was the immediate successor of Saint Peter who died a martyr. Father Michael J. McNulty, of County Mayo, Ireland, celebrated early Masses at the Elks Hall on Rosecrans Avenue. In 1964, James Francis Cardinal McIntyre blessed the church and school on Shoemaker Avenue. The school was staffed by Sisters of the Holy Faith. Father McNulty headed the parish for nine years. Father Gerald J. Moschel, of Peoria, Ill., was pastor for seven years and also founding principal of Saint Paul High School. Monsignor Timothy O'Connell, of County Cork, Ireland, and head of the Family Life Bureau was pastor for nine years, followed by Father Joseph Brennan of Van Nuys. In 2004 Father Anthony Gomez of Covina was named administrator of the Norwalk parish.

Saint Thomas Aquinas

1919

A mission chapel attended by priests from Ventura and Santa Paula served this rural community from 1903 until 1919 when Father E. Ylla began to celebrate weekly Mass. Fathers John Killian, W. F. Verhalen and John Moclair followed. The Augustinian Fathers took charge of the parish in 1923, but the original church had been destroyed by fire. A school opened in 1955 when Father Philip Holland was pastor. During the six-year pastorate of Father John F. Blethen of San Diego, a new church was completed in 1963. From 1969 to 1975 Father Richard K. Smith of San Diego headed the parish. He died in 1987. In 1977 Father Thomas J. McLaughlin, of Ohio, served until 1987 when Father James Clifford, of Illinois, became pastor, followed in 1989 Father Patrick Keane, of San Diego. Father Michael J. McFadden was appointed pastor in 2006.

Mary Star of the Sea

1963

The original church was located in Port Hueneme at Santa Clara and San Pedro Streets, a location that later was purchased by the Harbor Redevelopment Commission. In 1942 the church was attended as a mission of Santa Clara parish and after 1959, Saint Anthony's. A temporary church was built on Pleasant Valley Road in 1965 when Father Russell Karl was pastor. For fourteen years the Missionhurst Fathers led the parish with Fathers Michael Cattaert and Joseph Dewaele as pastors. In 1983 the Augustinian Recollect Fathers were appointed with Father Francis De la Vega of Nebraska as pastor. Church construction started during the pastorate of Father Paul Goni, of Spain and in 1997 the building was completed and blessed by Roger Cardinal Mahony. Father Euben Capacillo served for three years and in 2003 Father Antonio Zabala, of the Philippines, became pastor.

Our Lady of Guadalupe

1958

Early history records that a church was brought from Mexico around 1911 by Father Jesus Ramirez and assembled in Oxnard. Our Lady of Guadalupe was then a mission of Santa Clara. In 1958 the parish was established as Christ the King with Missionary of the Holy Spirit Father Joseph J. Arredondo of Mexico as pastor. He served two other terms as pastor from 1964 to 1970 and 1976 to 1985. He died in 1999 at age eighty. The original mission of Our Lady of Guadalupe was destroyed by fire in 1958 and in 1970 Archbishop Timothy Manning blessed a new church. Formerly called Christ the King, the new edifice and parish was dedicated to Our Lady of Guadalupe. "Christ the King" became a mission outpost of the new parish church. Father Jose Madera of San Francisco was named pastor and in six years was followed by Father Arredondo. Missionaries of the Holy Spirit serve the parish and Christ the King mission. Since February 2005 Father Ricardo De Alba is the current pastor.

Saint Anthony

1959

St. Anthony's was the second parish established in Oxnard and covered more than twenty miles of coastline, including Oxnard Beach, Port Hueneme and Point Mugu. Father Michael Condon, of Dublin, Ireland, was the founding pastor. During his thirty-one years as pastor he built the church, rectory and the sixteen-classroom school. He first celebrated Mass in Santa Clara High School auditorium, and by 1964 a new church was built on C Street graduating class of 1941. He died in 2001 at age eighty-six. Father Robert Folbrecht, of New Jersey, administered the parish for two years when Monsignor Condon was named pastor emeritus. Monsignor Richard Loomis, of Texas, headed the parish for five years and in 1996 Father George Sullivan, of Santa Paula and a member of Saint John's Seminary class of 1976 was named pastor.

Santa Clara

1885

Early settlers in Ventura County had called the Oxnard region "New Jerusalem," the name still in use when Father Juan Comapla from San Buenaventura Mission celebrated the completion of a small church there with the first Mass in 1877. In 1885 Rev. John Pujol was named the first pastor of Santa Clara parish, which experienced such rapid growth that by the turn of the century it was clear that the now bustling town of Oxnard needed a larger and more centralized church. Father Pujol and his assistant, Father John Laubacher, broke ground for a new church in 1903. The first Mass was celebrated in the new Santa Clara Church on August 14, 1904, and the little church in New Jerusalem became Santa Clara Chapel, still serving the needs of the El Rio community today. When Father Pujol retired in 1910, Father John Laubacher served as pastor until his death in 1918. The Parish school, St. Joseph's Institute, founded by the Sisters of St. Joseph in 1901, became the present day Santa Clara Elementary School and Santa Clara High School. A cemetery and mausoleum were completed, and Santa Clara's pastor was instrumental in establishing St. John's Hospital in 1914. Pastors over the next fifteen years were Revs. John J. Clifford (1918-1922), James A. Reardon (1922-1923), James O'Neil (1923-1925), J. J. Sheehy (1926-1930), Fred Wekenman (1926-1930), and Michael G. Sheehan (1930-1934). In 1934, Monsignor Anthony J. Jacobs, originally of The Netherlands, was appointed pastor, a position he held until his death thirty years later. He was followed by Monsignor Joseph Sharpe (1964-1974), Father Michael O'Shea (1974-1977), and Monsignor Charles O'Gorman (1978-). Under the leadership of Msgr. Peter Nugent (1989-2001) and Father Jon F. Majarucon (2001-present), the church was retrofitted and renovated in preparation for the hundredth birthday of the beautiful neo-Gothic structure, celebrated on August 22, 2004.

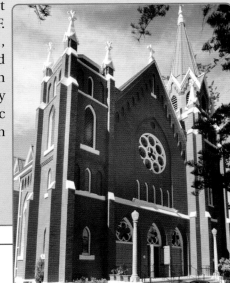

Pacific Palisades

Corpus Christi

1950

The only parish named for the feast of the Body of Christ was also unique in that a school was built before a church. The school opened in 1951, staffed by the Sisters of Saint Louis. The founding pastor, Monsignor Richard F. Cotter, of County Cork, Ireland, first celebrated Mass in the New Horizons Theater. For twenty-nine years he guided the parish and was responsible for the award-winning church built in 1964. He retired in 1979 and died at age eighty-four. From 1979 to 1987 Father Neville Rucker served as pastor. Father Juan Enriquez was in the parish from 1995 to 2003. For thirteen years Monsignor John Mihan, a native Angeleno, served the parish and also worked in the archdiocese as superintendent of elementary schools and other educational fields. In 2000, Monsignor Liam Kidney, of County Cork, Ireland, was named pastor. He had also served in education, as administrator of high schools and in radio and TV ministries.

Pacoima

Guardian Angel

1956

Bishop John J. Cantwell dedicated a church in 1929 as a mission of Saint Ferdinand that served then some 100 families. The first priest assigned was Oblate of Mary Father Alphonse Jalbert who helped the needy by raising farm animals and having a vegetable garden. Father Robert Koerner served the mission for fifteen years and opened a school and convent. In 1958 the mission was changed to a parish and Father Paul Stroup became pastor. He completed the school. The Spanish Vincentian Fathers were assigned to the parish in 1966 with Fathers Narciso Gonzalez, Celso Garcia and Pedro Villarroya succeeding as pastors. In 1973 Fathers John W. Rohde and George M. Miller were appointed in a team ministry. In 1990 Father Jose Holquin headed the parish, and Father Steven Guitron served as administrator beginning in 2003.

Mary Immaculate

1 9 5 4

Mass was celebrated at the Moose Club near Laurel Canyon Boulevard when the Oblates of Mary Immaculate began their ministry in an area that was formerly part of Saint Ferdinand's parish. The founding pastor was Father Harold Conley, from Massachusetts, a former missioner and wartime chaplain. By 1957 a church and sixteen-classroom school were completed and Bishop Timothy Manning blessed the complex when Father Joseph B. Billman was pastor. He headed the parish for twelve years and was followed by Father John J. Kelly of Chicago. In 1974 Father Joseph Scales, also of Chicago, was named pastor. Father Luis Valbuena, of Spain, was pastor for six years. During the pastorate of Father Thomas Rush, the Northridge earthquake severely damaged the church and school. It was rebuilt in 1998. Father James Fee of New York was appointed in 1999.

Saint Mary

1 8 9 0

In 1890 Saint Mary was a mission church of Sacred Heart in Lancaster, serving the small Catholic community in Palmdale. In the 1920s, on property donated by the Jack Stinson family, a church was built on Ninth Street East, and dedicated by Bishop John J. Cantwell in 1924. Father Lawrence O'Connor was assigned as resident pastor in 1943 when it reverted to being a mission of Sacred Heart Church. Father William Kelly was assigned in 1948, and by 1952 it was again a parish with Father Martin C. Hiss as pastor. Four years later a new church was built, and later a rectory and school. Father Charles V. Dachtler became pastor in 1960 and in 1968 Monsignor Michael J. Moran was pastor and remained for twenty-one years. Father Dorian Rowe, of Denver, was named pastor in 1987 and Monsignor Stephen Downes in 2002. Dedication of the new church December 8, 2005.

Panorama City

Saint Genevieve

1950

Monsignor Michael J. Ryan, of County Galway, Ireland, was the founding pastor of the church dedicated to the Patroness of Paris, and in his twenty-one years at the Panorama City parish opened both the elementary and high schools, directed the building of temporary and permanent churches. At first, Mass was celebrated in the Panorama Theatre before the temporary church was built and until the permanent structure was completed in 1966. Monsignor Arthur Thomas Kiefer, of Saint Louis, headed the parish for four years followed by native Angeleno Monsignor John Cosgrove. His pastorate, from 1975 to 1989, followed many years as an educator. He died of a sudden heart attack in 1989 at age fifty-nine. Father Charles Hill, of San Diego and also an archdiocesan educator, was pastor from 1989 to 1999.

Paramount

Our Lady of the Rosary

1934

Before the parish was established, the area was known as Clearwater and residents attended Mass across great distances in nearby churches. At one time Monsignor Thomas Blackwell commuted by horse and buggy from Downey to celebrate Mass. It is one of two parishes named under this title of Mary in the archdiocese. The first resident pastor was Father Vincent Flynn who served for three years, followed by Father Joseph Fehan, of Illinois, who died in 1990. From 1941 to 1961 Father Henry J. McHenry, of Dublin, was pastor and completed the entire parish plant – permanent church, school, auditorium, convent and rectory. He died in 1963 at age eighty-one. Monsignor Bernard O'Reilly, of County Longford, Ireland, headed the parish for twenty-five years. Father Edward Dober, a native Angeleno, was named pastor in 1994.

Assumption
of the Blessed Virgin Mary

1950

Monsignor Timothy Crean, from County Kerry, Ireland, was not only the founding pastor of the church in the northeast area of Pasadena, but also headed the parish for thirty-four years. He retired as pastor emeritus in 1984 and died in 1999 at age ninety. In its early years, 300 parishioners gathered for Mass in Saint John the Baptist Chapel on Foothill Boulevard, known locally as the "little green church". The first church and school, staffed by Sisters of the Holy Child Jesus, were dedicated in 1952, and by 1970 a permanent church seating 900 was completed. The parish was established at the same time that the dogma of the Assumption was proclaimed by Pope Pius XII and was one of the first to be named in honor of this Marian title. In 1984 Monsignor Augusto Moretti of Italy was named pastor and headed the parish for eighteen years. He retired as pastor emeritus in 2004.

Saint Andrew

1886

Although Father Patrick Harnett was the first priest to say Mass for the Catholics of Pasadena, it was Irish Father Andrew Cullen who was appointed the resident pastor in 1888. He asked that the parish be named for the apostle Andrew. In 1890 Irish Father Cornelius Scannell started his six-year pastorate and began the school staffed by Sisters of the Holy Names. Father Patrick Farrelly and Father William Quinlan, both Irish, were the next two pastors who continued to expand the educational ministry of the parish. Monsignor John McCarthy, of New York, headed the parish for twenty-six years, building a new high school and church. The structure was modeled after the Basilica of Saint Sabina in Rome. In 1944 Bishop Joseph McGucken was appointed pastor. Monsignor James Hourihan, of County Cork, Ireland, was pastor for twenty-seven years. He was succeeded by Monsignor Tobias P. English, from Templebraden, County Limerick, who served as pastor for seventeen years.

Saint Philip

1921

Father Daniel O'Connell, of County Cork, began his pastorate in 1921 by celebrating Mass at the East Side Hardware Company on Colorado Boulevard. Yet a church was ready by Advent. By 1927 the school opened. Father O'Connell died in 1937 at age fifty-two, and the next pastor was Irish-born Father Thomas O'Regan, who directed the parish for twenty years and acquired property on Hill Avenue for a permanent church completed in 1951. He died in 1957. Monsignor William North, of Chicago, was then named pastor, built the parish center and Newman Club and headed the parish for twenty-two years. He was also editor of The Tidings. The next two pastors had only short terms. Monsignor Carl Gerken died in 1982 and Monsignor Clifford Parker drowned in an accident in 1986. Monsignor Gary Bauler was pastor for eleven years, and in 1998 Father Joseph Moniz of India became pastor.

Saint Francis Xavier

1939

The Redemptorist Fathers administered this parish as a mission from Saint Mary's in Whittier when the area was simply called Pico. The first diocesan resident pastor was Father George Pausch, from 1946 to 1949, completed a church building in 1943. Monsignor Percy J. Bell followed him for one year. In 1963 the church needed to be enlarged and a multi-use conference room was added. A two-classroom hall was built for the 600 public school children who received religious education from Our Lady of Victory Missionary Sisters. Father Pascal Nocero, from New Jersey, was named pastor in 1971 and headed the parish for nineteen years. He retired as pastor emeritus. Father Jorge Peñaloza, a native of Peru ordained in Italy, was appointed in 1989 for the Pico Rivera parish. He had previously headed the Catholic Maritime Ministry.

Saint Hilary

1950

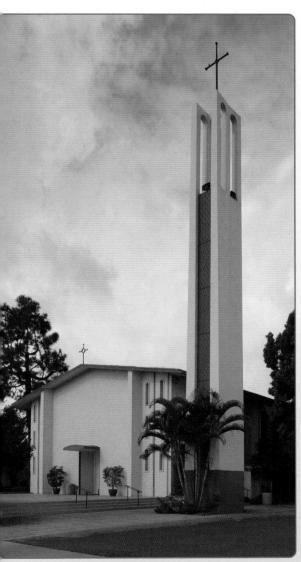

The founding pastor was Monsignor Percy J. Bell of Canada, brother of Bishop Alden J. Bell. He built a complete parish plant during his twenty-two-year pastorate at Saint Hilary, and in 1958 inaugurated the program of perpetual adoration of the Blessed Sacrament that has continued ever since. The church and school, staffed by the School Sisters of Notre Dame, were dedicated in 1952 when the parish had 1,700 children under the age of ten. Residents of the area of Pico and Rivera debated at one time to name the town Serra City. Father John Killeen of County Clare, Ireland, headed the parish for twelve years. He died in 1991 at age sixty six. Monsignor Christian Van Liefde of Belgium was pastor until 1999 when Father Peter Joshua Lee of England was appointed. He was ordained a Benedictine in 1989 and joined the Archdiocese of Los Angeles in 1996.

Saint Mariana de Paredes

1950

Father Herve M. Trebaol, a native Angeleno, was the founding pastor of the parish named for the young saint, Maria Ana, who died in 1644 at age twenty-six in Ecuador. He served the parish for twenty-one years, building the church and school. He died in 1971 at age sixty-nine. He was an Army chaplain during World War II. Monsignor Matthew Kelly, another native Angeleno, headed the parish for five years, followed by Father Gerald Maechler, also of Los Angeles. They both died in 2002. From 1981 to 1993 Father Gerald McSorley, of County Tyrone, Ireland, was pastor of the parish where he was first assigned after his ordination at All Hallows Seminary in 1964. Father Fernando Iglesias from Spain headed the parish for ten years and retired as pastor emeritus. Father David Gallardo, of Santa Monica, was named administrator in 2003 and pastor in 2004.

Sacred Heart

1967

The church built in 1935 as well as the school built in 1949, were mainly the work of donated parochial labor. The parish was originally a mission of Saint Joseph's and erected mainly for the Spanish-speaking people of the area. Father Angel Beta, of Spain, was the administrator until parochial status was approved in 1967 and he was named pastor. For thirty-five years he ministered at the Pomona parish, directing the construction of a new church in 1971 and building a convent for the Felician Sisters, who staffed the school. He retired in 1972 and died in 1989 at age eighty-three. Monsignor Joseph Kearney of Spokane, Washington, headed the parish for four years, and was for nineteen years spiritual director of the Catholic Labor Institute. He was followed by Monsignor Manuel Sanchez of Spain, pastor for ten years. Father Juan Silva, of Mexico, was appointed pastor in 2001.

Saint Joseph

1886

Before this parish was established, San Gabriel Mission friars occasionally celebrated Mass at different ranches. In 1886 Father Patrick J. Fisher was named pastor of a parish that reached from the San Gabriel River to San Bernardino. Father Fisher invited the Holy Names Sisters to start a school that eventually became Pomona Catholic High School. In 1905 Father Joseph Nunan replaced the original chapel with a Normandy style church that survived until 1956 when a Mission-Mediterranean building was completed. Monsignor Thomas P. English, of County Limerick, Ireland, headed the parish for thirty-one years, overseeing the division of the parish into four surrounding ones. He died in 1975 at age seventy-three. Father Bernard Flanagan, of Omaha, shepherded the parish for twelve years and died in 1987 at age fifty-six. Father Maurice O'Mahony of Dublin was pastor for ten years. Father Roberto Jaranilla Jr. of Philippines, was appointed pastor in 2005.

Saint Madeleine

1963

This parish is named for Saint Madeleine Sophie Louise Barat, a 19th century woman who founded the Religious of the Sacred Heart. The first pastor was Monsignor Robert Gara, of County Dublin, Ireland, who served there for seven years. He died in 2000. Father Vincent Barrett, of Iowa, headed the parish for four years and died of cancer in 1985. Native Angeleno Father Joseph Sartoris was also pastor for four years and later was named an auxiliary bishop for the archdiocese. Monsignor Andrew Tseu, born in China, succeeded Father Sartoris and guided the parish for twenty-three years. He had two priest brothers, one in China and one who served in Los Angeles, and the family traced its Catholicity to the 16th century in China. In 2001 Father Alejandro Aclan, from the Philippines, was appointed to his first pastorate at Saint Madeleine.

Saint John Fisher

1961

Originally the parish was named Saint Peter Alcantara in honor of a 16th century Spanish mystic, but the title was changed to prevent confusion with other parishes in the area also named for Saint Peter. Monsignor Thomas J. McCarthy, of Massachusetts, was the founding pastor and under his direction the church, school and parish buildings were completed. He was also the editor of The Tidings for seven years and pastor for thirteen years. Monsignor McCarthy died in 1978 at age sixty-seven. Father Vincent Barrett of Iowa was pastor for nine years and died in the last year of his pastorate, 1985. Monsignor Eugene Gilb, a native Angeleno, headed the parish for fourteen years and renovated the church which received a design award in 1995 when the building was dedicated. He retired as pastor emeritus in 1999 and Monsignor David Sork, also a native Angeleno, was appointed pastor.

Redondo Beach

Saint James

1 8 9 2

Before a resident pastor was appointed, local Catholics gathered in the home of Dr. Gregorio del Amo and attended Dominguez Memorial Chapel, which later became Saint James Church. Father Raphael Forthiar was the first rector and served the parish for fourteen years. A new red brick church was built during the term of Monsignor Nicholas Conneally in 1914. Father James Deenihan completed the school in 1918 and built the convent for the Sisters of Saint Joseph of Carondelet. Monsignor George Donahoe was pastor for seven years and built the hall. He died in 1943. For nine years Father William Forde headed the parish, renovated the school and hall and redecorated the church. Monsignor James O'Gorman, of Ireland, built the third church and served for twenty-one years. He died in 1986 at age eighty. Father Gerald Walker was pastor for thirteen years and Father Timothy Nichols for twelve.

Saint Lawrence Martyr

1 9 5 5

The founding pastor, Monsignor Daniel P. Collins, of County Limerick, Ireland, started construction on a temporary church, school and rectory one year after the parish was established. By 1964 the permanent Mediterranean style church was started. Monsignor Collins headed the parish for twenty-six years through continual growth and retired as pastor emeritus in 1981. Monsignor Michael Lenihan, of County Kerry, served from 1981 to 2002. Renovation of the church began in 2000 and Roger Cardinal Mahony blessed and formally dedicated all the changes, including painting and mosaics, in 2001. In 2002 Monsignor Paul Dotson, of Hollywood, was named pastor. He had served in several capacities at the Archdiocesan Catholic Center, the tribunal and cemeteries department and was pastor of Saint Bernardine of Siena for twelve years.

Saint Catherine of Siena

1949

The parish hall served as the church for the founding pastor, Monsignor John Hackett, of County Tipperary. By 1952 the first four-classroom unit and a convent were built, and by 1964 construction of a permanent church began. Because of enormous growth, three new parishes were established from the original parish – Saint Bridget of Sweden, Our Lady of Lourdes and Saint Joseph the Worker. In 1974 the parish noted its silver jubilee, listing more than 2,000 families from the original 400, most of them World War II veterans. Monsignor Hackett retired as pastor emeritus in 1981 after serving thirty-two years. He died in 1988 at age eighty-three. Monsignor Sean Flanagan, of County Dublin, Ireland, served the parish from 1981 to 2002 and oversaw ten months of renovations needed as a result of the Northridge earthquake. Father Paul Vigil, a native Angeleno, was named pastor in 2003.

Saint Elizabeth Ann Seton

1981

For nine years this rapidly growing parish in Rowland Heights used a temporary building for liturgical celebrations before the permanent church was completed in 1990. Monsignor Michael F. Killeen, of County Clare, Ireland, was named pastor in July, 1981, and for twenty-four years has served at the parish named for the first native-born U.S. saint, who was a mother, widow, religious and foundress of the American Sisters of Charity. Saint Elizabeth Ann Seton was canonized in 1975 and this parish is the only one named in her honor and the only Catholic church in Rowland Heights. In September, 1990, Archbishop Roger Mahony dedicated a new church that was designed by Armando Ruiz as a contemporary building with classical accents, featuring a separate Blessed Sacrament chapel. The previous building became the parish hall.

San Dimas

Holy Name of Mary

1922

The early history of San Dimas indicates that it was an unincorporated area, also known as La Verne. The early mission of Our Lady of Guadalupe in La Verne became a parish in 1939 with Father Juan Padilla as pastor. He designed and built the church. The Sacred Hearts Fathers were given charge of the La Verne and San Dimas churches in 1954. In 1957 the parish adopted the name Holy Name of Mary and the temporary church was completed. The new parish combined the two mission chapels of Our Lady of Mount Carmel, San Dimas, and Our Lady of Guadalupe, La Verne. It was blessed two weeks after the death of Father Thomas Lyons, who served for only two years. Sacred Hearts Fathers have continued to head the parish. In 2004 the new church was completed with Father Thomas Mullen, of Ireland, as pastor.

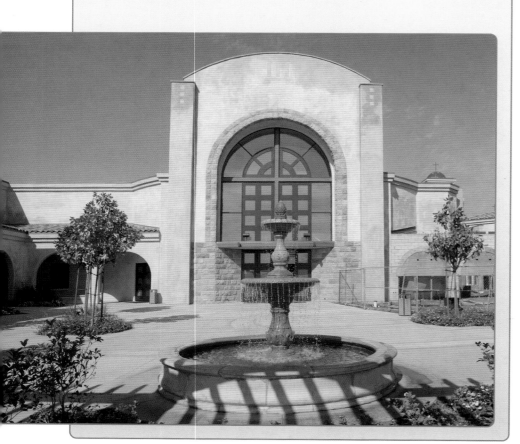

San Fernando

Saint Ferdinand

1902

St. Ferdinand is the oldest parish in the San Fernando Valley. Father James F. Burns was named pastor and Father A. LeBelleguy succeeded him in 1903 followed by Father James S. O'Neill. Later the Claretian Fathers were placed in charge. In 1912 the parish returned to diocesan clergy with the pastorate of Father Gerard Bergan. Father J. B. Roure served until 1923, when the Oblates of Mary Immaculate took charge under Father Charles Siemes. Father Charles Burns served from 1938 to 1944. With Father John J. O'Connell, groundbreaking took place in 1948 for a new church. Father Edward Lynch was pastor in 1956 and died in 1962. For three years Father Edward Collins was pastor followed by Father William McHugh from 1966 to 1972. Father Paul Maher, pastor from 1979 to 1985, was followed by Father Paul Waldie. Father Paul Nourie was appointed in 1998. Father Stephen Conserva was appointed pastor in 2006.

Santa Rosa

1927

This parish was a mission of Saint Ferdinand in 1924 when the Oblate Fathers built the first church. A resident priest was appointed in 1927. Father William Grant, O.M.I., built the church hall in 1949, and in 1955 Father Raymond R. Knopp, O.M.I, directed the construction of the school, staffed by the Franciscan Sisters of the Immaculate Conception. Bishop Timothy Manning blessed the new wood frame and stucco church of traditional Spanish mission design in 1962 when Father James Whelan, O.M.I. was pastor. It replaced the old church that was two blocks away. Father Luis Valbuena, O.M.I., of Spain, and pastor from 1966 to 1972, established the first bilingual adult school in the United States Additional Oblate pastors includeed Fathers Amador Lopez, David Ullrich, Pablo Wilhelm and Carlos Alarcon, appointed in 2002.

Saint Anthony

1945

In 1926 a small church was erected at the corner of Del Mar and Emerson Avenues in the Wilmar district. It was then a mission of Saint Stephen in Monterey Park. In 1932 the building was enlarged. Archbishop John J. Cantwell made it a separate parish in 1945 with Father James McGovern as pastor. That same year the church was moved to San Gabriel Boulevard and Marshall Street. The school opened in 1948 staffed by the Sisters of the Holy Names. In 1955 Monsignor James Glennon, of County Roscommon, Ireland, was named pastor and directed the parish for twenty-six years. The permanent church was completed in 1957 with an eighty-foot tower that was a landmark for the community. Monsignor Patrick Thompson, a native Angeleno, was pastor for thirteen years, and Father Michael Gleeson, of County Tipperary, Ireland, was appointed in 1995. In 2006 Father Huy Nguyen was appointed administrator pro tem.

San Gabriel

San Gabriel Mission

Established 1771
1908

Franciscan Padres Benito Cambon and Angel de la Somera erected this fourth of the twenty-one missions September 8, 1771 on the original site some four miles from the present church near the Rio Hondo River. It is the "Mother Church" of the archdiocese. Four years later it was moved to the Mission Drive location. Through the years, the "Pride of the Missions" has been damaged by earthquakes, ravaged from neglect and secular administration. The Franciscan Order ministered until 1834 when the government took over. It was reclaimed in 1843. After almost fifty years the Claretian Fathers took over in 1908 with Father Felix Zumarraga as pastor. In 1956 the Chapel of the Annunciation was built nearby to accommodate the growing number of parishioners. Claretian Father Ralph Berg, former provincial, is the current pastor.

San Marino

Saints Felicitas and Perpetua

1938

The old Miguel Blanco adobe dating back to the Mission days served as a chapel and parish house prior to completion of the Italian style church in 1948. Archbishop James Francis A. McIntyre dedicated the church in July of 1948. It was the first church of any denomination in the city of San Marino. Monsignor William Fox, of County Tipperary, Ireland, was named the first pastor and served for thirty-four years, directing construction in 1950 of both church and school, staffed by Sisters of the Holy Names. He died in 1975 at age seventy-five. Father Gerald Moschel, of Illinois, was named pastor in 1973, followed shortly after by Monsignor Lawrence Gibson, of Glendale, who headed the San Marino parish for almost thirty years and retired as pastor emeritus in 2003. Father Paul K. Fitzpatrick currently serves as administrator.

Holy Trinity

1924

Father James O'Mahoney was pastor of the parish that opened November 11, 1923 when Sunday Mass was celebrated in a motion picture theatre on Pacific Avenue. The following year Father John W. Meehan organized the parish and then built a church in 1927 on O'Farrell Street. In 1929 Father Patrick J. Beary, of County Limerick, Ireland, was named pastor and served four years. During the Depression years the parish returned to the care of Mary Star of the Sea. When it was reactivated in 1946 Monsignor George Gallagher was named pastor and served the parish for thirty-three years. In 1962 a new brick church was completed overlooking the Los Angeles Harbor. Monsignor Gallagher died in 1983. From 1979 to 2004 Father Thomas Glynn, of County Roscommon, headed the parish. Father Joseph Brennan became pastor in 2004.

Mary Star of the Sea

1889

Bishop Francis Mora, who headed the Diocese of Monterey-Los Angeles, blessed the new parish in 1889 when there was only a small wooden structure on West Ninth Street. The first regular pastor was Father Charles Tanquerey. In 1905 a larger church was built on Vinegar Hill with Father Michael Conneally as pastor. For seven years Father Patrick McGrath headed the parish and started a school staffed by Immaculate Heart Sisters. In 1919 Father Maxim Benso, of Italy, became pastor and secured more land to expand the parish. For twelve years Father James McLaughlin headed the parish and established the "Apostleship of the Sea." Monsignor George M. Scott was pastor for twenty-nine years and built the parish's third church, convent, school and rectory. He died in 1986. Monsignor Thomas Kiefer, pastor for nine years, was followed by Monsignor Patrick Gallagher in 1984.

Saint Peter

1965

The Los Angeles Harbor church was originally named Holy Trinity and dedicated in 1927 by Bishop John J. Cantwell. The San Pedro Chapel was then a mission of Holy Trinity until it became an independent parish in 1966 and was named Saint Peter. The Fathers of the Congregation of Saint Joseph, founded in Turin, Italy, have directed the parish since its founding. Saint Peter's parish was their first California foundation. Father Emil Martinelli, C.S.J., of Italy, was the first pastor and served until 1974. He died in 1976. Father Bruno de Santi, of Italy, headed the parish from 1974 to 1983. He had been the provincial of the order in Argentina and Chile. Father Claudio de Agostini, C.S.J., of Italy, was appointed in 1983. Confessions at the parish are heard in English, Spanish and Italian.

Holy Cross

1973

Holy Cross parish was originally a mission of Our Lady of Guadalupe church in Santa Barbara, which had been part of Our Lady of Sorrows. It is located in the Mesa district southwest of downtown at Cliff Drive. The church building was erected in 1959 with a temporary rectory on Ricardo Avenue. The former pastor of Our Lady of Guadalupe, Monsignor Thomas Hayes, became the founding pastor for Holy Cross. He was a native of New Orleans and alumnus of Cathedral High School. He headed the parish for eighteen years and directed the building of the parish Confraternity of Christian Doctrine center that opened in 1976 and was used for classrooms and meetings. Monsignor Hayes died in 2001 at age eighty-six. Monsignor John Young, a native Angeleno, was pastor for five years and in 1996 Josephite Father Ludovic DeClippel, of Belgium, was named to head the parish.

Mission Santa Barbara

Established **1786**
1915

The "Queen of the Missions" was the tenth of the twenty-one missions on the El Camino Real in California. It was founded by Fray Fermin Lasuen founded this mission on the feast of Saint Barbara, December 4, 1786. Since its founding, the mission has survived several earthquakes, reconstruction and renovation. In 1795 the quadrangle was completed, but the 1812 earthquake damaged many buildings. By 1820 a new structure was finished. The first bishop of both Californias, Francisco Garcia Diego y Moreno, is buried there. The 1925 earthquake required extensive repair. The mission is the only one administered by Franciscan Fathers from its beginnings. In 1915 Father Dominic Gallardo became pastor of the parish. United States presidents and British royalty have visited this widely photographed mission. Father Virgil Cordano was pastor for fifteen years.

Our Lady of Guadalupe

1928

The history of this parish can be traced to the chapel of the Royal presidio of Santa Barbara. From that congregation was formed the parish of Our Lady of Sorrows, and in 1913 this mission for the Mexican people was established, near the train station. In 1928 Bishop John J. Cantwell appointed Father Alexander J. Oyarzo pastor. Father Peter O'Dowd served for nine years and Monsignor John Curran for four. Father Manuel Canseco was pastor when the parish had its silver jubilee. Monsignor Matthew Kelly, a native Angeleno, served for fifteen years. He died in 2002 at age eighty-seven. Monsignor Thomas Hayes was pastor for two years. For twenty-three years Monsignor Fernando Valle, of Guatemala, headed the parish. He died in 2001. Father Guillermo Garcia was pastor for five years and Father Rafael Marín-León, of Spain, was appointed in 2003.

Our Lady of Mount Carmel

1856

On the feast day of Our Lady of Mount Carmel, July 16, 1856, a priest from Santa Barbara Mission celebrated Mass in a field and announced that a chapel would be built in the area. The parish is one of the oldest in the Archdiocese. Bishop Thaddeus Amat laid the cornerstone March 1, 1857. A frame structure built in 1898 replaced the chapel. Father William Lonergan was the first resident pastor and Father Anthony Serra, from Barcelona, was pastor for thirteen years. In 1929 Father John Cox struggled through the Depression years, but received a donor gift of a new church in 1936. Father John Meehan was pastor for thirteen years, and founded the parish school. Monsignor Ozias Cook served for sixteen years, and retired in 1978. Father Henry Van Son, of Holland, was pastor for twelve years, then Monsignor Sylvester O'Byrne and Father Maurice O'Mahony.

Our Lady of Sorrows

1856

The historic Presidio Chapel, erected in 1786 under the care of the Franciscan Fathers from Santa Barbara Mission, formed the beginning of this parish. The Franciscans served until 1856 when the parish was canonically declared. An early pastor was Father James Vila who headed the parish for almost forty years. In 1863 the church building was destroyed by fire, but the relics of Saint Vibiana were saved. Monsignor Polydore Stockman built the school. In 1908 the Jesuit Fathers administered the parish. The 1925 earthquake destroyed the church but a new Romanesque style edifice was built in 1929. Father Joseph R. Stack, S.J., was pastor for several years. Other Jesuit pastors were Fathers James Deasy, William J. Tobin, Edward J. Whelan, Martin Brewer, Francis Gallagher and Carroll Laubacher. Father Luis Quihuis, S.J. was named pastor in 2001.

San Roque

1953

San Roque school opened in 1936 as part of Santa Barbara Mission. One room was used as a chapel until a former Army chapel was moved onto the property and remodeled. The parish started in 1953 with Franciscan Fathers in charge. It was named for Saint Roque, a 14th century saint noted for curing victims of the plague. In 1958 Father Luke Powleson, O.F.M., of San Francisco, was named pastor and in his sixteen-year pastorate directed construction of the Italian-Spanish style church and school addition. The old building was converted into the parish hall. Father Powleson died in 1974 at age seventy-three. Monsignor Vincent McCabe, of County Leitrim, Ireland, headed the parish from 1974 to 1988. Monsignor John Rohde was the next pastor and Father James Ford, a native Angeleno, was appointed in 1994. The church was completely renovated in 2001.

Blessed Kateri Tekakwitha

1998

This parish was named for the Native American virgin of the Mohawk tribe who was beatified in 1980. In 1995 Roger Cardinal Mahony broke ground for the first parish in the archdiocese named for a Native American Indian. It was then a mission of Saint Clare Church in Canyon Country and Monsignor Edmond Renehan ministered at both. For several years Catholics in the Santa Clarita Valley celebrated liturgies at Arroyo Seco Junior High School because the area was one of the fastest-growing regions of Los Angeles County. In 1998 the parish was officially established. Father Michael Slattery, of County Waterford, Ireland, who headed Saint John Baptist de La Salle Church in Granada Hills was named founding pastor. A multipurpose facility was completed at Copper Hill Drive and Tamarack Lane with plans for a sanctuary and administration building.

BLESSED KATERI TEKAKWITHA CATHOLIC CHURCH
Armet Davis Newlove Architects

Rendering from Victor Newlove or Armet, Davis, Newlove AIA Architects.

225

Our Lady of Perpetual Help

1944

In the days when the area was Newhall, priests from the Plaza would travel by train to say Mass on Sunday in a dance hall for Catholics at the surrounding ranches. Eventually a church and school were built for the Mexican population in the area and Father Philip Garcia, O.F.M. became pastor. The first church was built in 1914 and was part of Saint Ferdinand parish until this parish was established in 1944. Monsignor Thomas O'Malley, of County Cork, Ireland, headed the parish until 1948. Father Josuah Kennedy was pastor from 1948 until 1954. Father Henry Banks came in 1954 and was there for 22 years until his death on October 4, 1976. Father Henry Banks, of County Leitrim, Ireland, was pastor for twenty-two years and built the church, school, hall, library and rectory. A Sunday Mass center was also established at Canyon High School. Father Banks died in 1976. Father Patrick Power, of County Waterford, Ireland, headed the parish for twenty-three years and died in 2003. Monsignor Paul Montoya became pastor in 2000.

Saint Clare

1978

Timothy Cardinal Manning established this parish in February 1978. Masses were celebrated in the Canyon High School gymnasium before a multi-purpose center was erected. Geographically it was one of the largest parishes in the archdiocese, and Monsignor Edmond M. Renehan, of County Kilkenny, Ireland, was named administrator. The parish was a mission of Our Lady of Perpetual Help church in Newhall but was dedicated in 1989 and Monsignor Renehan was named pastor. The hall was named for Father Henry J. Banks, pastor of Our Lady of Perpetual Help in Newhall. The parish is named for Saint Clare, the 13th century saint and collaborator of Saint Francis, who founded the Order of Poor Clares. Early explorers named the river Santa Clara and the towns of Newhall and Saugus became Santa Clarita.

Santa Fe Springs

Saint Pius X

1954

Established on October 10th, Saint Pius X was one of the first parishes named for the 20th century "pope of Christian Doctrine." Father James F. Burke, of Brooklyn, New York, was named pastor and the parish then covered the areas of Santa Fe Springs, Los Nietos and parts of Norwalk. Before the church was built, the Little Lake School auditorium was used for Sunday Mass. James Francis Cardinal McIntyre blessed the church and school in 1957. The sixty-foot high bell tower was an area landmark. Father Burke headed the parish for eighteen years. He died in 1979. Monsignor Glen A. Rademacher, of Bakersfield, headed the parish for six years. He had spent thirty-two years as a chaplain in the military service. He died in 1998 at age eighty-one. For sixteen years Father John McHugh, of County Leitrim, Ireland, was pastor. Father Pedro Lopez was appointed in 2004.

Santa Maria

Saint John Neumann

1986

The pastor of Saint Mary's Church in Santa Maria, Monsignor James Colberg, was the first to announce that a parish would soon be established nearby named for the one-time bishop of Philadelphia, John Neumann. He was the first American male saint. Father Emigdio Herrera, of Michoacan, Mexico, was named administrator in 1986 and the following year named pastor. In his sixteen years at the parish, Father Herrera developed numerous programs including the Guadalupanas, Cursillo, English and Spanish Marriage Encounter, a youth group and a weekly Spanish prayer scheduler. He was named a monsignor in 2000. Father Vaughn, a native of Riverside, was named pastor in 2002. The challenges of the parish include offering religious education for public school children and preparing for as many as forty baptisms several times a month.

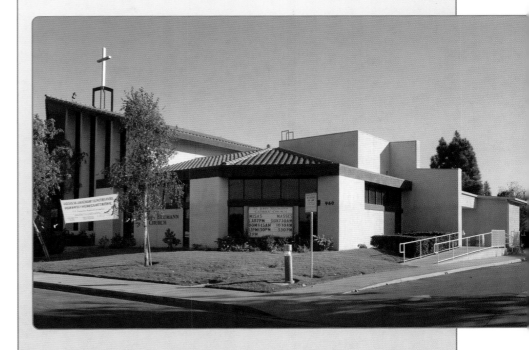

Saint Louis de Montfort

1963

Father Vincent McCabe, of County Leitrim, Ireland, was named administrator and then pastor of Saint Louis de Montfort, which was originally part of Saint Mary's in Santa Maria. Mass was celebrated in an old Army mess hall at the Santa Maria Airport. In 1964 land was acquired at Clark and Harp Streets in the unincorporated Orcutt area for a church where Mass was first celebrated on January 30, 1965. That year the church was dedicated and the majority of parishioners came from Vandenberg missile base. Monsignor McCabe headed the parish until 1975 when the Josephite Fathers were given charge. Father Anthony Runtz, C.J., was pastor for nine years and built the rectory and hall. Father Guilermo Garcia, C.J., pastor for five years, was followed by Father Mark Newman, C.J., of England, who was appointed in 1990. Father Charles Hofschulte, C.J. was appointed pastor in 2001.

Saint Mary of the Assumption

1905

Father Mathias Ternes celebrated Mass for the Catholic families in Santa Maria on August 20, 1905 in the opera house, and the following year a church was built. In 1912 Father John Coen was named pastor, followed by Fathers F. J. Dubbel, James O'Mahony, John Morgan and A. J. Hurley. For thirty-three years Monsignor Thomas Murphy, from County Tipperary, Ireland, headed the parish, opened the school and directed the new construction in 1959 that replaced the fifty-three-year-old church that was converted to the auditorium. Monsignor Murphy died in 1966 at age seventy-one. In 1964 Monsignor Kieran Marum, of County Kilkenny, Ireland, headed the parish for ten years. A new parochial center opened in 1973. Monsignor James Colberg, of Los Angeles, was pastor for twenty-five years, 1974 to 1999. Father Rizalino J. Carranza, from the Philippines, was appointed pastor in 1999.

Saint Anne

1908

The original church was a small frame chapel with most of the materials and labor donated by parishioners under the direction of Father Patrick Hawe, then pastor of Saint Monica's. Bishop Thomas Conaty dedicated the chapel on April 12, 1908. The Sisters of the Holy Names opened the school in 1908, and classes were held in the chapel until 1923 when the school was built. Saint Anne Shrine opened in 1916 with a statue erected on a stone pedestal. In 1935 an altar was constructed for services in the annual novena. By 1952 a more elaborate niche was built. The chapel, shrine and school remained part of Saint Monica's parish until 1951 when Monsignor Cyril Wood was appointed pastor. He was from Middlesex, England, and headed the parish for thirty-six years. He died in 1987 at age seventy-four. Father Michael Gutierrez, a native Angeleno, was appointed pastor in 1999.

Saint Clement

1904

This Ocean Park parish was originally part of Saint Monica's, but was put under the patronage of Saint Clement in 1904. The area was then one of Southern California's most popular summer resorts. Pastor Michael L. Hennessy completed work on the church, two blocks from the waterfront, opened the school and served the parish for twenty-three years. He died in 1926. Monsignor Patrick Pierse, of County Kerry, Ireland, was pastor from 1926 to 1951. He remodeled the church, the rectory, and built the convent. Father John Cummings was pastor for sixteen years. He died in 1979. Father William Williams, of Idaho, directed the parish for almost twenty years, until 1990. Father Edward Berumen, of Monrovia, was appointed in 1990 and Father Tomas A. Elis, of Panama, was named pastor of Saint Clement in 2002. In 2006 Father Anthony Gonzalez was appointed pastor.

Saint Monica

1886

The history of the parish began in 1886 when Father Patrick Hawe was assigned to the Bay District. A rectory and church were built in 1888 and Bishop John J. Cantwell dedicated a new church in 1925. A school building was added in 1930. Father Hawe died in 1923 and Monsignor Nicholas Conneally was appointed. He served for twenty-six years and erected the statue of Saint Monica in Palisades Park in 1935. In 1949 Monsignor Leo J. Murphy was pastor, followed by Monsignor Raymond J. O'Flaherty, of Kansas City, pastor for twenty-four years. He also served as secretary of the Catholic Welfare Bureau for sixteen years. He died in 1988. Monsignor Anthony Duval, of Canada, served for eight years. Monsignor Lloyd Torgerson was appointed in 1987, overseeing renovations after the 1994 earthquake.

Our Lady of Guadalupe

1942

Although this parish had mission status for many years, a resident priest was present for most of its early history. Father Anthony Cambra administered the church from 1943 to 1947. A combination catechetical center and social hall was built in 1950. Members of the Spanish Foreign Mission Society took charge in 1958 with Monsignor Jenaro Artazcoz as pastor. He served until 1963, followed by Father Jesus Gomez, I.E.M.E. In 1973 the Santa Paula parish was entrusted to the Franciscan Fathers and Father Duncan MacDonell, of Huntington Park, was pastor until 1980. Father Joseph Zermeno, O.F.M. served from 1980 to 1990 and Father Rene Juarez, O.F.M. was pastor for eight years. Father Nelson Trinidad was administrator. The Canons Regular of the Immaculate Conception was the next religious order to administer the parish and Father James Garceau, C.R.I.C. was appointed pastor, then Father Arturo S. Gomez, C.M.F. was named administrator. Finally Father Charles Lueras, C.R.I.C. was named administrator in 2006.

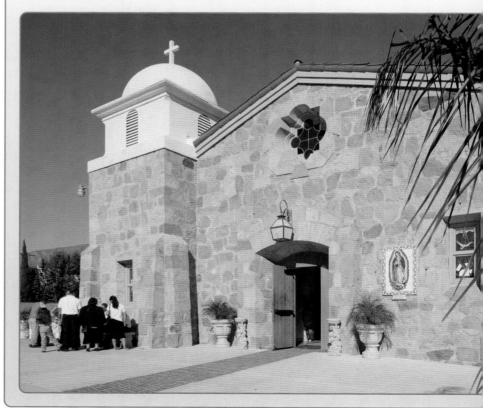

Saint Sebastian

1896

Father John Pujol first attended to this church as a mission from El Rio. In 1891 a church was built and in 1896 Father Patrick Grogan was named pastor. In 1902 the church was enlarged and dedicated and Father Pujol again took charge. Father P. Gerald Gay in 1904 built the rectory. Eight other pastors followed, one of them, Father John Joseph Cox, returned in 1924 and served until 1932. Father Maurice Ryan was pastor until 1937, followed by Father William McGinley. In 1938 Father Daniel Sweeney was named pastor. Several other priests served for short terms and in 1949 Father James Nevin built the school. Father Joshua Kennedy, of County Tipperary, Ireland, headed the parish for eighteen years and retired as pastor emeritus in 1972. Monsignor Matthew Kelly was pastor until 1987, followed by Father James Rothe, of Burbank, in 1987.

Cathedral of Saint Mary

BYZANTINE-RUTHENIAN

1956

St. Mary's is the first Byzantine Church in California. The Rite originated at Constantinople during the fourth and fifth centuries. By the 19th century, immigrants brought the Byzantine Rite to America. The Cathedral of Saint Mary was established in August of 1956 when Bishop Nicholas T. Elko granted permission for a priest to minister in Los Angeles. Father Eugene Chromoga, of Saint Louis, was named the first pastor and celebrated Divine Liturgy at Nazareth House and was granted the use of the facilities of Our Lady of Zapopan Mission. A church on Sepulveda Boulevard was dedicated in 1961. In 1969 Father Paul Fetch, of Pennsylvania, was appointed pastor, followed by Father Eugene Linowski. Father Michael Moran was named rector of the church when the new Eparchy of Van Nuys was established in 1982 and Father Melvin Rybarczyk in 2004.

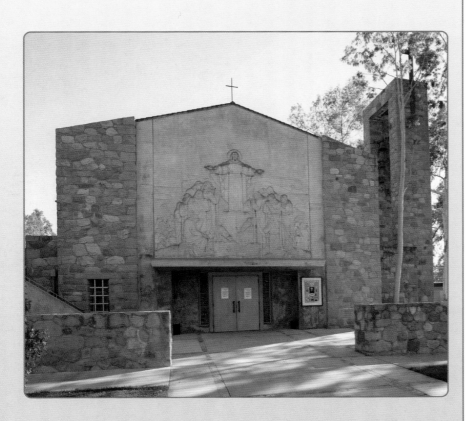

Saint Francis de Sales

1938

Father William McGinley was in charge when the parish was established on Fulton Street. Father James O'Mahony, of County Kerry, Ireland, served from 1945 to 1960 and built the church in 1959. The school opened in 1949 and was conducted by the Religious of the Sacred Heart of Mary. Father O'Mahony died in 1960. He had been a pastor of seven parishes in the archdiocese. Monsignor James Nevin, of County Waterford, Ireland, was pastor from 1949 to 1954 and built an eight-classroom building and the convent. He died in 1981, the same year Father Kevin Larkin, of County Cork, Ireland, was named pastor. The Northridge earthquake of 1994 severely damaged the church and destroyed the bell tower. Father Larkin oversaw the reconstruction, completed in 1995 with an Earthquake Memorial Garden dedicated as a memorial to the earthquake victims.

Saint Rita

1908

The original church was a small chapel named for Saint Teresa and built by a retired priest, Father M. W. Barth, in 1908. Five years later the church was moved nearer the center of town and in 1919 Father Francis Woodcutter was appointed pastor. He obtained permission to change the name of the parish to Saint Rita. For some years the Passionist Fathers had charge, and a new church was built in 1925 by Father A. Scannell, C.P. In 1951 archdiocesan priests were assigned. In 1970 under Monsignor Thomas O'Malley, of County Cork, Ireland, the third church was built at Baldwin and Grandview Avenues. Father Lawrence Coen was pastor for two years and Monsignor Robert Gara, of County Dublin, was pastor from 1974 to 1988. Monsignor Joseph Cokus, of Pittsburgh, was pastor for sixteen years, and in 2004 Father Richard Krekelberg was appointed.

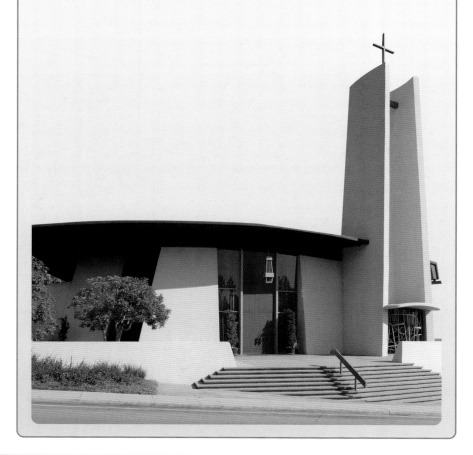

Saint Peter Claver

1972

The parish of Saint Peter Claver covered the southeastern corner of Ventura County, including the area formerly known as Santa Susana. Father James McKeon, of Detroit, was named administrator and continued as pastor for nineteen years. At first Father McKeon said daily Mass in his living room, a block from a public high school where Sunday Mass was celebrated for many years. The parish was named for the 17th century Spanish Jesuit priest who labored thirty-three years for African slaves in the New World. Father McKeon died in 1999 at age seventy-one. Father Dennis Mongrain was pastor for six years and blessed the ground for a permanent church in 1996. Monsignor Gary Bauler, a native Angeleno, became pastor in 1997, and in 1998 a permanent church was dedicated to replace the parish center that had been used for twenty-three years.

Saint Rose of Lima

1921

Originally a mission of Santa Clara in Oxnard, the parish was named for the 17th century saint of Peru. Bishop Thomas Conaty in 1913 blessed the church that had previously been a Presbyterian chapel. The pastor was Father L. Philip Genest. Before a new church was built almost fifty years later, pastors were Fathers Michael Healy, Francis Coleman, James Glennon, Dominic Daly and Peter O'Sullivan. During the pastorate of Father Patrick McDonagh, of County Sligo, Ireland, the school opened in 1964 and the new church was completed in 1968. He died in 1972. Monsignor Sylvester O'Byrne, of Dublin, Ireland, was pastor for thirteen years. Monsignor O'Byrne died in 2004. From 1985 to 1995 Monsignor Michael Bunny, a native Angeleno, was pastor. Father Michael Carcerano, of Torrance, was named pastor in 1996.

Solvang

Old Mission Santa Ines

Established 1804
Parish 1853

Fray Estevan Tapis, presidente of the California Missions, celebrated the first Mass in the Santa Ynez Valley on September 17, 1804. The Mission was built of adobe by Indian artisans and was the location of the first college and seminary in the state. The 1812 earthquake damaged most of the buildings, but the chapel was rebuilt in 1817. The Mission is named for Saint Agnes, a fourth century martyr. Franciscans were in charge until 1850 and for a time the Picpus Fathers directed the college and mission. In 1924 the Franciscan Capuchin Fathers were in charge and continual restoration took place, beginning with Father Alexander Buckler. He died in 1930. Recent appointments include Capuchin Fathers Camillus MacRory, Roger Anderson, Cyril Kelleher, James Cleary, Donal Burke, Robert Barbato and Michael Mahoney who was named pastor in 2001.

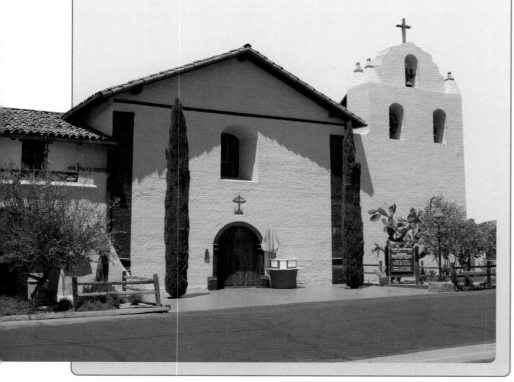

South El Monte

Epiphany

1956

Services for this El Monte parish were held at the auditorium of the Wilkerson School on Doreen Avenue when Father John J. Hill, of Massachusetts, was appointed pastor. The first Mass in the church was offered on Christmas Day, 1958. The parish school, directed by Bernardine Franciscan Sisters, opened in 1959. Monsignor Michael A. Hunt, of County Waterford, Ireland, headed the parish for twenty-six years, from 1958 to 1984 when he died at age sixty-nine. He directed construction of the church and school. In 1982 at the silver jubilee of the parish, 2,200 families were registered. Monsignor Joseph Greeley, of Long Beach, was pastor for ten years and Father Tomas Elis, of Panama, headed the parish from 1998 to 2001. Father Pedro Esteban, of Spain, was appointed pastor in 2002. The parish is the only one in the archdiocese named in honor of the Feast of the Epiphany.

Saint Helen

1931

Father Thomas Butler was the founding pastor of the church then located at Madison Avenue and Firestone Boulevard. Subsequent pastors until the new church was completed in 1950 were Fathers Terence O'Donnell, 1934-46, James McLaughlin, 1946-47 and Anthony Kelly, 1947-70. In 1950 during the pastorate of Father Kelly, the church on Firestone was constructed in Spanish colonial style and blessed by Archbishop James Francis A. McIntyre. The school opened in 1941 under the supervision of the Sisters of Notre Dame. In 1970 Father Samuel Hynes, of County Tipperary, Ireland, was named pastor and under his direction the parish hall was erected in 1974. He retired in 1976 as pastor emeritus and died in 1995. For twenty-two years Father Jerome Bouska, a native Angeleno, headed the parish. In 1999 Father John Provenza, of West Covina, was appointed pastor.

Holy Family

1910

Bishop Thomas Conaty established the parish in 1910 and appointed Father Richard J. Cotter as pastor. Mass was celebrated in a small cottage until 1928 when the Spanish Baroque church was dedicated. Succeeding pastors were Monsignor Michael O'Gorman, Monsignor Edward Kirk, Monsignor Michael J. Galvin and Father William J. Clancy. Father James Morris was named pastor in 1926 and served for twenty-eight years. Monsignor Leo Murphy, of Redlands, was pastor for seventeen years. He died in 1972 at age eighty-one. Monsignor Thomas McGovern, of County Cavan, Ireland, served from 1971 to 1984. Monsignor Clement J. Connolly, former secretary to Timothy Cardinal Manning and from County Limerick, Ireland, was named pastor in 1984. During his pastorate the entire parish plant has been renovated with a new hall and school, and additional property were acquired for future expansion.

235

Sun Valley

Our Lady of the Holy Rosary

1937

Originally the town of Sun Valley was called Roscoe when Father Michael O'Shea from Ireland celebrated Mass at a plumbing shop on San Fernando Road for eleven families. In 1939 Archbishop John J. Cantwell dedicated the new church. From 1939 to 1974 several archdiocesan priests served as pastors, including Father Thomas Noonan, Father Augustine Murray and Monsignor Stephen Kiley. For twelve years Monsignor Robert Brennan headed the parish. He died in 1986 at age seventy-eight. Father Louis Pick, of the Netherlands, built the new church with twice the capacity of the original. In 1974 the Sacred Heart Missionaries administered the parish and the pastors were Father Eugene O'Sullivan, Father Jerome O'Mahony and Father Thomas Jordan. In 1993 the Scalabrinian priests were appointed to serve the parish. Father Richard Zanotti was named pastor in 2002.

Sylmar

Saint Didacus

1957

Monsignor William Duggan, of County Leitrim, Ireland, was the pastor for the parish named for the 15th century Franciscan lay brother who labored in Spain, the Canary Islands and Rome. The area was formerly part of Saint Ferdinand's. The parish center was at Glenoaks Boulevard and Astoria Street. Masses were celebrated in the Sylmar Community Building. A church was completed in 1958 and the school opened, staffed by the Sisters of Saint Joseph of Newark. Bishop Timothy Manning blessed the church in November of 1960. Monsignor Duggan was pastor until 1971. Monsignor Peter Amy, a native Angeleno, was appointed pastor in 1981 and the parish silver jubilee occurred the following year during which Timothy Cardinal Manning celebrated Mass for all former and present parishioners.

Saint Luke

1946

On July 14, 1946, Father James Hourihan hosted some 150 people on a lawn in Temple City to inaugurate this parish in the San Gabriel Valley. In 1947, the priests lived in an old farmhouse on Cloverly Street and the Immaculate Heart Sisters taught in an old Army barracks. Bishop Timothy Manning celebrated Mass four years later in the new California mission-style church. Monsignor Hourihan was pastor until 1955. Monsignor John Birch, of Massachusetts, headed the parish for almost thirty years and led the parish through many changes. He died in 1986 at age seventy-eight. The Memorial Center at the parish was dedicated in his honor in 1993. Father Thomas King, of Venice, California, was pastor for twelve years and founded the first Parish Council in 1988. Father Donald Grasha, of Ohio, was named pastor in 1999.

Saint Paschal Baylon

1960

This parish is named for a 16th century Franciscan lay brother known for his kindness to the unfortunate and for many miracles, particularly in healing the sick. Father Thomas Greaney, of County Limerick, Ireland, started the new parish on a ten-acre site in 1960. During his twenty-three years as pastor he built the church, school, convent and parish buildings. When he started there were some 600 families and Mass was held in the old Acorn Theater. At his retirement there were 2,900 families. He died in 1988 at age seventy-two. Monsignor Joseph George, of Buffalo, New York, became pastor in 1983, after serving on Saint John's Seminary faculty for fifteen years. He saw the completion of an extensive renovation project that included moving the altar into the assembly and updating the sound and lighting systems. Father Dave Heney, who grew up in Saint Paschal Baylon, became pastor in 2002.

Torrance

Nativity

1924

Father Edward Riordan was pastor of a parish that for some years was a mission attended from Gardena. The rectory was built in 1926 and the Spanish style church was dedicated in 1939. Subsequent pastors were Fathers Emmet F. Panner, Thomas Kennedy, Daniel Hurley and Joseph V. Fitzgerald. Monsignor Joseph Bauer, was pastor from 1940 to 1944. The school opened in 1948 during the pastorate of Father Patrick McGuinness, staffed by the Sisters of Saint Joseph of Orange. In 1974 Timothy Cardinal Manning was the principal celebrant for the golden jubilee Mass when Father Patrick McHugh was pastor. Father McHugh was from County Sligo, Ireland, and headed the parish for twenty-five-years. Monsignor Paul Albee, of Pasadena, was pastor for two years and Father Alfred J. Hernandez, a native Angeleno, became pastor in 2000.

Saint Catherine Laboure

1947

This church was named for the French nun to whom the Blessed Virgin made known the Miraculous Medal. Father Patrick Masterson founded the parish in the area that was called Lawndale which included an old winery, a grape orchard and two old houses. Mass was celebrated in a rollerdome until the church was dedicated in 1948. The school opened in 1952 staffed by the Sisters of Saint Joseph of Cluny, and a new church was constructed in 1956. Father Raymond Tepe, of Illinois, was pastor for twenty years, overseeing all the new construction. He died in 1969 at age sixty-three. In 1969 Father John McNulty became pastor and in 1972 Father Joseph L. Zwissler, from Kansas, headed the parish for fifteen years. He died in 1987 at age sixty-three. Father John O'Byrne, of County Tipperary, Ireland, first an associate, became pastor in 1987.

Tujunga

Our Lady of Lourdes

1920

Father Joseph Tonello, an Italian priest and musician, celebrated the first public Mass at the home of Mrs. Catherine Forster. A church committee headed by the legendary poet laureate, lawyer and journalist, John Steven McGroarty, decided to build a church that was completed in 1921. Succeeding pastors were Fathers William J. Steward, Peter Corcoran and P. A. McCusker. From 1939 to 1949 Monsignor Denis J. Falvey headed the parish and directed the building of the second church in 1941. The church site was donated by John Steven McGroarty. During the pastorate of Monsignor Edward Wade, 1966 to 1979, a new contemporary church was dedicated. Father (later Bishop) Sylvester Ryan, of Catalina Island, was pastor for seven years and Father George Brincat, of Malta, for six. Father Mark Strader, of Torrance, became pastor in 2000. Father Freddie Chua from the Philippines has been named administrator in 2005.

Valinda

Saint Martha

1958

The temporary church of 1959 was designed as a future parish auditorium in the city that was then La Puente. Monsignor John McNamara, of Massachusetts, was the founding pastor and shepherded the parish for twenty-three years. The Sisters of the Love of God, a Spanish community, opened the school and when the parish celebrated its silver jubilee many improvements were added. Groups in the parish included Cursillo, Marriage Encounter and the Christian Family Movement. Father Juan Romero, of New Mexico, was pastor for three years. Monsignor William Leser, of Ohio, headed the parish from 1984 to 1994. Father William Easterling, of Whittier, became pastor in 1996 directing a parish composed of mainly Filipino, Latino and Anglo parishioners. The church was redesigned with the altar, ambo and baptismal font centralized in the main interior.

Saint Bridget of Sweden

1955

Although construction of the church and school was long delayed by zoning difficulties, Father Patrick McGoldrick started groundwork in 1956. He oversaw construction of the church and school that opened in 1957, staffed by Irish Sisters of Charity and lay teachers. A native Angeleno, he was the first graduate of Cathedral High School to be ordained. He died in 1972 at age sixty-two, having spent seventeen years at the parish named for the saint, a mother of eight, mystic, widow and foundress of the Order of Our Savior in the 14th century. Monsignor John Young, of Los Angeles, headed the parish from 1972 to 1983. Monsignor Laurence Clark, of Rhode Island, was pastor for six years and had been a Navy fighter pilot during World War II. He died in 2001. Father Raymond Morales, a native Angeleno, became pastor in 1997.

Saint Elizabeth

1920

Since 1912, Saint Elizabeth's was a mission of Holy Trinity Church in Burbank before it became a parish in 1920. Father Clarence. A. Kimmons was appointed pastor, followed by Father Edmund Keohan, of County Waterford, Ireland. During his term of twenty-three years, he built the two-story school that was put in charge of the Sisters of Providence of Saint Mary of the Woods. He died in 1947 at age sixty-six. From 1947 to 1971 Monsignor Patrick O'Dwyer, of County Tipperary, Ireland, headed the parish and directed the building of the new church, hall and school additions. He died in 1971 at age seventy-one. Monsignor William M. Duggan, of County Leitrim, Ireland, was pastor for eighteen years and instituted a host of organizations including the Service Center. He died in 1990 at age seventy-five. Father Paul Hruby was pastor for five years and Father John Bruno, R.C.J. became pastor in 2001.

Saint Mark

1923

Before a church was dedicated in 1924, Father Michael Lalor celebrated Mass in Angelo's barbershop for the few all-year parishioners of this largely resort area. The school opened in 1949 staffed by Sisters of the Holy Names. A new twelve-room facility was built in 1953. Another church was built in 1955 on Coeur d'Alene Avenue under the direction of Monsignor William North, who was both pastor and editor of The Tidings newspaper. The parish center opened in 1963. Monsignor North headed the parish for twenty-three years and died in 1989. Monsignor Michael Hoban, of County Kilkenny, Ireland, headed the parish from 1970 to 1989. He died in 1992 at age seventy-two. Father Roderic Guerrini, of Dublin, Ireland, became pastor in 1989. He had previously served as a Jesuit missionary in Zambia, Africa for fifteen years. Father Michael Rocha was appointed pastor in 2002.

Our Lady of the Assumption

1954

The parish was first a mission of San Buenaventura Mission when Monsignor Daniel Hurley was assigned as pastor to this church on Telegraph Road. A mural on the façade of the church, created by the artist Millard Sheets, depicts the first Mass celebrated in Ventura in 1769. He also created the Assumption mural in the sanctuary. A native of County Cork, Ireland, Monsignor Hurley shepherded the parish for eighteen years, directing construction of the church and school. He died in 1982 at age eighty-seven. Monsignor Donal Mulcahy, of Ireland, was the next pastor. In 1997 Father Michael Jennett, of Glendale, became pastor. The school opened in 1957 with a lay teaching staff and is now administered by Sisters of Notre Dame who left in 2004 and also bears the name first given to the area by the Portola expedition of 1769. Father Steve Davoren was appointed pastor in 2005.

Sacred Heart

1 9 6 6

The mission church of Sacred Heart in the town of Saticoy was raised to parochial status in May of 1966. Monsignor Arnold Biedermann, of Austria, was named pastor. The small church was moved in 1915 to the site at Telephone Road and Saticoy Avenue when Father Emilio Ylla ministered to the Catholics in the area. Monsignor Biedermann built a church for the new parish in 1968 and a rectory a year later. By 1980 a school opened with some seventy pupils. More classrooms were added in the following years that were used as a kindergarten, science room and library. Monsignor Biedermann headed the parish for twenty-six years and retired as pastor emeritus. Father Daniel O'Sullivan, of County Limerick, Ireland, became pastor in 1992 of the parish now listed in the city of Ventura.

San Buenaventura Mission

Established 1 7 8 2
Parochial 1 8 4 3

Fray Juníipero Serra founded the ninth of the California Missions on Easter in 1782. It was the last mission he personally founded. Painfully infirm, he died two years later after thirty-four years of missionary labor. The permanent building was completed in 1809, but the 1812 earthquake partially destroyed it. After 1840, the Franciscans left their administration and the mission became a parish church. Father Jose Maria Rosales became pastor. From 1878 to 1896 Father Cyprian Rubio was pastor. Father Patrick Grogan, a native of County Roscommon, Ireland, was revered as the last living link with the Spanish Friars. He headed the mission for forty-two years and died in 1939 at age seventy-nine. Father Aubrey O'Reilly was pastor for twenty years followed by Monsignor Francis J. Weber. Monsignor Patrick O'Brien, of County Clare, Ireland, became pastor in 1981 and died in 2005.

Holy Angels Church of the Deaf

1987

Archbishop Roger Mahony canonically erected this parish for the deaf on March 31, 1987. It is designated as a personal parish for the deaf and hearing impaired Catholic community of all three counties of the archdiocese. The parish uses the old Santa Marta Center that had been a Catholic Social Service Center in the industrial area of the city. Father Brian Doran, of Dublin, Ireland, was named pastor. The church, rectory and hall are used as a center for deaf ministry. There are seven other personal parishes for the deaf in the country and an estimated 2,600 families with a deaf member in the archdiocese. The 1987 earthquake delayed the opening, but liturgies were celebrated in 1989. Mass is celebrated in American Sign Language. Father Thomas Schweitzer, of Long Beach, became pastor in 1998.

Saint Lorenzo Ruiz

1991

In 1989 some 200 families joined for worship at Collegewood School at Saint Martha's Mission, an offshoot of the parish in neighboring Valinda. In 1990 Father Dennis Vellucci, of Rhode Island, was named administrator and larger quarters were secured in the Vogel Business Center. On September 8, 1991, Saint Lorenzo Ruiz was established as a parish with Father Vellucci as pastor. Mass was celebrated in warehouse space until 1995 when a new hillside multipurpose hall/church was built. Outside the church is a huge bronze statue of Saint Lorenzo Ruiz, the first Filipino saint, donated by eight parish families. Roger Cardinal Mahony blessed the new church in March of 1996. Father Vellucci died in 2002 at age fifty-six. Father Michael J. Carroll, of County Cork, Ireland, became pastor in 2000. Father Tony P. Astudillo was appointed pastor in 2005.

Saint Christopher

1954

Father Samuel Hynes, a native of Tipperary, started organizing this new parish in 1954 and celebrated Mass in the Covina Theatre as plans were made for a permanent church. The school opened in 1955 with the Benedictine Sisters. Father Hynes was pastor for two years. Monsignor William Keith Bramble, a native Angeleno, was named pastor in 1956. By 1963 the permanent church was completed and dedicated by James Francis Cardinal McIntyre. For thirty-three years Monsignor Bramble headed the parish, built the church, erected the school, rectory and convent. Parish growth changed the ethnic mix to Vietnamese, Korean and Filipino. Monsignor Bramble died in 1994 at age eighty-one. Monsignor Helmut Hefner, a native of Yugoslavia, was pastor from 1989 to 1995. Father Nestor Rebong, from Manila, became pastor in 2002.

Saint Ambrose

1922

The founding pastor of the parish started three new churches in the diocese, and Saint Ambrose was one of them. Father Thomas O'Toole, of County Wicklow, Ireland, built the church, convent, rectory and school during his more than twenty-five years as pastor. The old church was replaced in 1950 and a new rectory built. He was also an Army chaplain during World War I. Monsignor O'Toole died in 1960 at age eighty. Monsignor Maxim Benso, from Italy, headed the parish from 1960 to 1972 and opened an auditorium for parish activities. Father Edward Hempfling, of Oklahoma, was pastor for five years. For ten years Father Robert Bradley, of Pittsburgh, headed the parish and in 1987

Monsignor John Beattie, of County Armagh, Ireland, became pastor for three years. Father William Wolfe, a native Angeleno, became pastor in 1999.

Saint Victor

1929

Bishop Thomas Conaty accepted the offer of a small wooden church in what was then the village of Sherman as the site for Saint Victor church. Victor Ponet donated the property in 1906. The church was named for the first African Bishop of Rome who died a martyr. For many years the church was a mission administered by priests from Blessed Sacrament Church and Saint Ambrose. Father Daniel Murphy was the first of pastors until 1925 when Father Vincent Shepherd became the resident priest. In 1929, the legendary Monsignor John J. Devlin from Ireland became pastor for forty-five years. He opened the school, built the convent and a new rectory. He died in 1977 at age seventy-nine. By 1959 the old wooden church was replaced by a new building. Monsignor George Parnassus, from Pasadena, became pastor in 1977 and Monsignor Jeremiah Murphy was appointed in 2003.

Saint Jude

1970

St. Jude, the patron of difficult and desperate cases, was chosen as the saint for the parish that was established in June 1970. Father Thomas O'Connell, of County Tipperary, Ireland, was appointed pastor. By 1980 a church was completed that included a shrine of Saint Jude where a weekly novena was conducted. The parish site was on five acres at the corner of Foxfield Drive and Lindero Canyon Road. Father O'Connell retired as pastor emeritus in 1995 and died in 1999. Monsignor William Leser, of Ohio, became pastor in 1995. He had served for many years in the Marriage Tribunal. In 2002 the building underwent a complete renovation and structural repair. On Christmas Eve, the scaffolding was finally removed for the four p.m. liturgy. Prior to that Mass was celebrated in the parish hall.

245

Saint Maximilian Kolbe

1992

This parish was named for the priest who gave his life to spare that of a Jew in a Nazi concentration camp during World War II. In the beginning, the founding pastor, Monsignor Peter A. O'Reilly, celebrated Mass at Oak Hills Elementary School. By 1994 parishioners gathered in the Pavilions shopping center in Oak Park, using Suites A6 and A7 for liturgies and parish activities. The storefront site lasted for six years until the new worship space was completed on Kanan Road in Westlake Village. Roger Cardinal Mahony celebrated the three-hour dedication liturgy on March 19, 2000. The new parish home on a seven-acre site is designed to emulate a village, utilizing a series of arcades and courtyards to connect the building elements including a meditation area. Monsignor O'Reilly, of County Longford, Ireland, has headed the parish since 1992. Msgr. O'Reilly retired July, 2005 and was replaced by Fr. Patrick O'Dwyer.

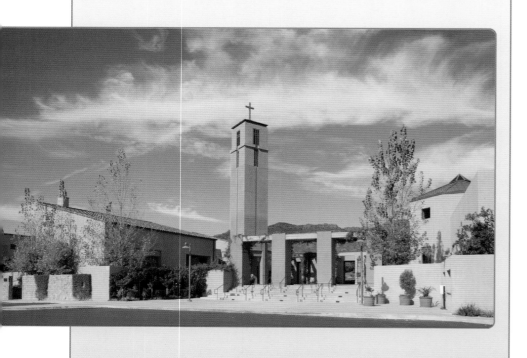

Saint Bruno

1955

The founding pastor was Father John McCormick, of Saint Paul, Minnesota. Mass was celebrated in a citrus warehouse and then in a circus tent. By 1956 the church was ready for use and the parish school opened conducted by the Sisters of Mercy. Father McCormick headed the Whittier parish for eighteen years and died in 1973 at age sixty-two. The parish is named for the 11th century German theologian and founder of the Carthusian Order. Father John Cooley, a native of New Mexico, became pastor in 1973 and retired as pastor emeritus in 1993. That year Father Patrick O'Dwyer, of County Tipperary, Ireland, was named pastor. In 1997 a new parish center was built, named in honor of Father Cooley who had served the parish for twenty-three years. The building was completed in 200 days and has meeting rooms, a library and music room.

Saint Gregory the Great

1951

This parish that opened in October of 1951, was named for the sixth century Benedictine Pope who was responsible for the conversion of much of Western Europe. Father Michael Galvin, from Ireland, was appointed pastor. By 1952 a church was built and Father Leo Mackey, from Ireland, was named pastor. Bishop Timothy Manning blessed the new church in 1953. The school opened in 1954, staffed by the Dominican Sisters of Houston, Texas. For twenty-four years Father Mackey headed the parish, built the church and auditorium and a new rectory in 1968. He died in 1976. Monsignor Donald J. Ruddy, of Iowa, was first an associate at the parish, then administrator and pastor from 1976 to 1998, serving some forty-two years at Saint Gregory's. He retired as pastor emeritus and died in 2000 at age seventy-one. Father John Schiavone became pastor in 1998.

Saint Mary of the Assumption

1893

Bishop Francis Mora established this parish under the patronage of Saint Mary in 1893 and named Father A. Montanarelli as its first pastor. Father P. J. Grogan succeeded him followed by Father Denis J. Hurley, C.M., Father James More, C.M. and Father E. A. Antill, C.M. who was pastor from 1910 to 1922. The church was destroyed by fire in 1912. The Redemptorist Fathers were placed in charge in 1922 with Father Marcellus Ryan, who built a new church, school and convent in 1923. Eight new parishes were formed from the original area serviced by this parish to accommodate the city's growth. Father Alexander Chapoton served from 1927 to 1933 and Father Edward Mattingly for nine years. Construction for the third church began in 1957. The 1987 Whittier earthquake, during the pastorate of Father Donald MacKinnon, damaged the church and demolished the school that was reopened in 1991.

Wilmington

Holy Family

1929

Father Luciano Gonzalez left his native home in Jalisco, Mexico, to escape religious persecution in 1928. He came to volunteer at Saints Peter and Paul Church and minister to the area's growing Mexican settlement. He celebrated Mass for the people under a ramada of burlap. He was named pastor when Bishop John J. Cantwell formally established the parish in 1929. His successor, Father Francisco Arias y Cortes built the first church in 1929-30. Father Manuel Canseco was named pastor in 1947. In 1950 the school opened staffed by Carmelite Sisters of the Sacred Heart. In 1951 the Oblates of Mary Immaculate were assigned to the parish. Father Charles Burns, O.M.I., headed the parish for six years. Father Jesus Alonso, O.M.I. was pastor for seven years. Archdiocesan priests were assigned with the arrival of Monsignor Joseph Greeley in 1996.

Saints Peter and Paul

1866

When Father Anthony Ubach erected a church in 1865 in the port city, it was the only Catholic house of worship south and west of the Los Angeles Plaza for twenty years. He celebrated the first Mass on November. 19, 1865, and visited the congregation regularly from the Plaza Church. Other priests continued the trip until 1886 when Franciscan Father Henry N. Morgan was appointed resident pastor. Succeeding pastors lived either in Wilmington or San Pedro. Bishop John J. Cantwell dedicated the new church in 1931 when Father B. J. Schiaparelli was pastor. The school opened in 1945 in remodeled Army barracks and the permanent school opened in 1951 with Monsignor John Dunne as pastor. Monsignor John Brennan was pastor for twenty years, Monsignor Clement Morian, from Rumania, for nine years and Father Peter Irving, of New York, became pastor in 1993.

Saint Bernardine of Siena

1962

This parish is named for the 15th century Franciscan saint who was called the Apostle of Italy and the greatest preacher of his time. James Francis Cardinal McIntyre appointed Monsignor Richard Murray, from Louisiana, as pastor in 1962. The area was formerly served from Our Lady of the Valley and Saint Mel's parishes. A temporary church and school conducted by the Sisters of the Immaculate Heart opened in 1965. Monsignor Murray retired as pastor emeritus in 1989. Monsignor Paul Dotson, a native of Hollywood, headed the parish for three years, building a new church that replaced the one that needed structural repair and liturgical renovation. During the construction period, the parishioners worshipped for a year in a large canvas tent. The new building enables the congregation to sit closer to the altar. Father Robert McNamara, of Limerick city, Ireland, became pastor in 2001.

Saint Mel

1955

The Woodland Hills parish is named for the fifth century Irish abbot and bishop. All three pastors who served the church since its founding in May of 1955 have been from Ireland. Monsignor Michael O'Connor, the founding pastor who died in 2005 was from County Kerry and headed the parish for almost thirty years. He retired in 1984 as pastor emeritus. The complete parish plant of church, school, hall, convent and rectory was blessed in May of 1958. The Immaculate Heart Sisters staffed the school that opened in 1957. Monsignor John Naughton, of County Mayo, headed the parish for five years and also retired as pastor emeritus. He had served twenty-eight years as a United States Air Force chaplain. A parish center opened in 1989. Monsignor Padraic Loftus, of County Mayo, became pastor in 1990 and had first served at the parish when he came to Los Angeles in 1974. After the Northridge earthquake in 1994, the church was completely renovated after serious damages, a new organ, one of the finest in Southern California, was donated by Mary D. Allen. A new activity center was built as well as a new preschool.

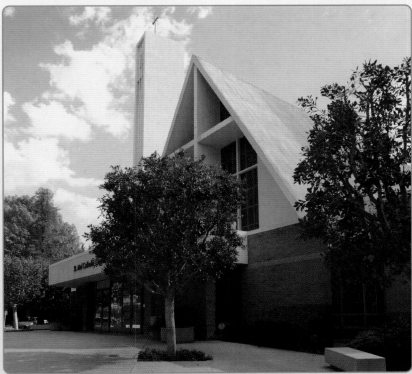

EDUCATIONAL OUTREACH

HISTORICAL OVERVIEW

ARCHDIOCESAN SEMINARIES

California is one of those singular areas of the Church universal where the notion of a seminary system predated by ten years the actual establishment of a diocesan government.

As early as the 1830s, The Presidente of the California missions, Fray Narciso Duran, suggested a seminary for the education of young men who felt inclined toward the ecclesiastical state. Six years later, the Franciscan Comisario Prefector, proposed establishing a college "to which all the youth of the Californias may flock, as well as many of the Indians of the various idioms, in order to receive the education and knowledge peculiar to their state." In his initial pastoral letter, Bishop Francisco Garcia Diego y Moreno announced to the faithful of the diocese of both Californias that, in compliance with the decrees of the Council of Trent, he would direct his attention to the erection of a seminary as the object of his first episcopal endeavors. Shortly after arriving in the newly created diocese, the Franciscan prelate opened California's first seminary at Mission Santa Barbara. Located in the rear apartments off the corridors facing the patio, the embryonic institution functioned for about two years until the number of students and lack of facilities necessitated more commodious quarters.

Early in 1844, for the purpose of expansion, the bishop petitioned Governor Manuel Micheltorena for a grant of land adjacent to Mission Santa Ines to be used for the building of a permanent seminary. Complying with this request, the governor authorized transfer to the Church of Rancho Canada de los Pinos, a parcel of land eventually amounting to 35,499 acres. On May 4th, Bishop Garcia Diego formally inaugurated the partially completed edifice, placing the state's first college under the patronage of Our Lady of Guadalupe. Although the school was moved in later years to San Isidro, it remained in operation until 1882.

The extreme poverty of the Church, the absence of an educational tradition and the political and social unrest then prevalent, account for the unspectacular accomplishments of the area's pioneer seminary. That the college functioned for as long as it did can be attributed to its acceptance of students other than those preparing for the priesthood. Despite its humble beginnings and the many hardships facing the seminary, those early years of growth and development were important ones for the history of the Church in California. Zephyrin Engelhardt, the Franciscan chronicler, regarded the college as representative of "a transition period between the glorious days of old when saintly and industrious friars reaped a harvest of souls and the modern far-flung province that has passed its Second Spring."

In the 1850's Archbishop Joseph Sadoc Alemany had those seminarians studying for San Francisco moved to Mission Dolores while clerical students from the southland were either sent abroad or to one of the educational institutions in the eastern part of the nation.

Bishop Thaddeus Amat built St. Vibiana Cathedral in the 1870s.

When Saint Vincent's College opened at Los Angeles in 1865, Bishop Thaddeus Amat reserved the right to educate seminarians for his diocese in the Vincentian-staffed institution, although there is no evidence that the college ever had a formal seminary program. Subsequent Southern California prelates used the facilities of San Francisco's seminary system as well as those provided by Saint Thomas (Denver), Saint John's (Collegeville), Mount Saint Mary's (Emmitsburg), Saint Mary's (Baltimore), The Catholic University of America (Washington D.C.) and numerous foreign seminaries.

In 1924, Bishop John J. Cantwell revealed plans for a minor seminary and urged the southland's faithful to make the realization of such a proposal the object of their annual pre-Pentecost novena. Pointing out that such a preparatory school was an absolute necessity in the diocese, the bishop noted that only the generosity of the Catholic people could bring this dream to fruition.

In January of 1926, Bishop Cantwell issued a pastoral letter concerning the envisioned seminary. He stated that "the soil is adapted to foster the growth of the old Faith, and although the harvest is plentiful, the children of the soil are not forthcoming to meet the demand for laborers." The prelate observed that the See of Los Angeles-San Diego was no longer an infant diocese dependent on external material assistance; and, since it was financially self-supporting, it should be also spiritually independent. Studies showed that the dearth of vocations was due, in large measure, to the absence of a local program for clerical recruiting and training, both of which could be alleviated considerably by erection of a minor seminary. On the national level, experience had indicated that aspirants to the priesthood could be encouraged efficiently only in those areas where preparatory schools flourished. In California, as elsewhere, the future efficacy of the Church depended upon establishment of a local institution to train priests.

In the same pastoral letter, the bishop observed: "The time has now arrived when, in obedience to the wishes of the Holy Father, and in duty to ourselves and posterity, it becomes necessary to raise funds for the immediate erection of a seminary." He went on to state that such an undertaking would admittedly require the laying aside for a time of certain parochial activities but that a concentration of energy on the broader field of diocesan advancement was a worthwhile sacrifice.

The Olympic Auditorium in Los Angeles was the focal point for a meeting of the lay and religious leaders of the diocese who gathered to inaugurate plans for a fund drive. Archbishop Edward J. Hanna came from San Francisco to address the largest meeting of Catholics ever held in the southland. Edward Laurence Doheny launched the campaign by a generous gift and, as General Chairman of the Junior Seminary Committee, directed letters and personal appeals to prominent Los Angeles civic leaders among whom, he stated, were many "ever ready to assist any cause which brings to our country and our fellow citizens a contribution for betterment."

During the intensive three-month drive, pastors exchanged pulpits and a speaker's bureau provided qualified laymen to address various groups throughout the diocese. The first door-to-door campaign ever conducted in the diocese was, by all standards, a tremendous success.

So enthusiastic was the bishop with the results that he acquired and remodeled temporary quarters on 21st Street, west of Grand Avenue, for students wishing to begin their seminary work in the fall of 1926. Seventy seminarians registered for the term beginning on September 7th, in the new institution staffed by the Fathers of the Congregation of the Mission.

Since the new building on Detroit Street was ready for occupancy early in the next year, March 27th was chosen for the formal dedication and inauguration of Los Angeles College. On the occasion, a prominent attorney remarked that, "the opening of the seminary commences a new era of instruction and religious advancement, the importance of which can scarcely be overestimated… To start a seminary in vision only, and in less than two years thereafter to produce a site, a great seminary building, furnished and equipped, an ample endowment fund, a school faculty, and sixty-five students, with everything in perfect functioning order, is a feat probably unparalleled in the history of such enterprises."

At the time of the dedication, Bishop Cantwell, stating that the building of a major seminary could not long be delayed, publicly acknowledged the gift made by Juan Camarillo to the diocese of a hundred acres of land near the town bearing his family name, to be used specifically for a theologate. It was the donor's intention that the new institution, to be known after his patron saint, would occupy the knoll formerly dividing the two historic Ranches of Calleguas and Las Posas.

Theoretical planning for the new institution, slowed by the economic stress of the depression years, stretched out over the next decade. On September 29,1936, the Right Reverend John J. Cawley reminded the pastors of the diocese that "one of the obligations of the archbishop is to provide a new senior seminary for the education of young men for the priesthood." Not long afterward, Archbishop Cantwell explained the reasons why such an institution was necessary and what plans had been formulated for its construction. Noting that the preparatory seminary had occasioned a radical increase in the number of native vocations, the archbishop looked forward to the day when Los Angeles would be "practically self-sustaining in a spiritual and religious way as it is already in things material." He called attention to the fact that the creation of a new ecclesiastical jurisdiction in Southern California was an "implied command" to erect those institutions found in the sister-provinces of the nation: "What better monument to record the creation of the Archbishopric of Los Angeles than the erection of a Major Seminary — a School of Philosophy and Theology that would bring to completion the work begun when the Junior Seminary was founded?" Archbishop Cantwell stated that he had proceeded along such lines only after long deliberation and prayer. His decision rested upon the solid principle that "the needs of the diocese as an organic unit cannot be ignored by those who have the spirit of the universal Christ within them." Later, in an address to the Knights of Columbus, the archbishop keynoted the campaign as the greatest work for the permanency of religious life yet attempted in California.

The drive, begun on February 11, 1938, has been regarded as the most significant work ever undertaken to consolidate the apostolic labors of more than a century and a half of work by the Church in California. Those who gave generously of their time and energy to make the drive successful overlooked no possible means of communication: one group scheduled a series of radio talks; another conducted oratorical contests; the thirty thousand school children in 160 parochial and high schools distributed circulars; a force of 800 workers canvassed the 185 parishes of the archdiocese. Working diligently to increase the number of native California clergy, these volunteers responded to the archbishop's appeal on behalf of the proposed educational institution. Considerable support was also evidenced by Archbishop Cantwell's friends in the non-Catholic community.

By the time the campaign had drawn to a close in March, seventy-five percent of the goal had been subscribed. On the following May 10th, Monsignor John J. Cawley officiated at ground breaking ceremonies at Camarillo and from that time onwards, weekly reports of the building progress were featured in the archdiocesan newspaper. When construction was practically finished in the early part of the following year, the archbishop issued an invitation to the people of the archdiocese to participate in cornerstone-laying ceremonies scheduled for the Feast of Saint Joseph.

The first scholastic term began on September 12, 1939, when sixty-seven students presented themselves at the practically completed seminary. The formal dedication took place on October 14, 1940, exactly a century after California's first bishop received the fullness of the priesthood in the Basilica of Our Lady of Guadalupe. Fifty members of the hierarchy attended the event presided over by the Most Reverend Amleto Giovanni Cicognani, Apostolic Delegate. The Archbishop of Mexico City, Luis Maria Martinez, celebrated the Pontifical Mass for the festive occasion.

No major additions were made to the physical plant at Saint John's Seminary during the first sixteen years of its existence. Early in 1955, plans were completed for enlarging the enrollment potential by erecting a third wing, together with an adjoining utility building at the eastern terminus of the then existing campus, a program made possible by the Archdiocesan Education Fund.

On September 19, 1956, thirty-nine students occupied *Aedes Sancti Thomae* for the first time. His Eminence, James Francis Cardinal McIntyre, dedicated the new structures on October 2nd. Principal speaker for that occasion was the Very Reverend William P. Barr, the seminary's first rector. With great eloquence he thanked the Catholic populace of Southern California for their "farsighted benevolence."

The new buildings, described by the Ventura County Building Commission as "the finest in the district," consisted of a two-story residence wing and a single story unit containing classrooms, a science laboratory, a radio station, a student canteen and recreational facilities.

In order to attain more fully the "highest standard of general education and learning" envisioned by Pope Pius XI and his successors, the Archdiocese of Los Angeles was among the first ecclesiastical jurisdictions in the United States to establish the three-unit system of seminary education. The purpose of the overall program was to bring clerical training more in line with the prevailing American pattern of high school, college, and post-graduate study.

Prior to 1961, Saint John's College, a fully accredited institution incorporated under the laws of the State of California, had been operated as two divisions, the lower branch attached to the preparatory seminary at San Fernando, the upper section to the theologate at Camarillo. In the latter year, plans were announced to amalgamate the two units into a seminary-college occupying a single physical plant on property contiguous with the already existing major seminary.

Offering courses in the liberal arts and empowered to grant academic degrees, Saint John's College began operation as a self-contained school in the fall of 1961. Francis Cardinal Spellman dedicated the new institution on June 25, 1966, as part of celebrations honoring the Archbishop of Los Angeles on his eightieth birthday. Assisting at the ceremonies were the Cardinal Archbishop of Guadalajara and numerous prelates from the western part of the nation.

While the first twenty-five years at Saint John's can be described as brick-and-mortar years, the second quarter century was devoted primarily to internal development. With the seminary's monumental structures firmly in place, the major thrust shifted towards maximizing the spiritual and academic programs that followed in the wake of Vatican Council II. That this ambitious endeavor was eminently successful is attested to by the commendatory report issued when a team of papal visitators minutely scrutinized the seminary's curriculum and interviewed its faculty and students in 1984.

In its first half-century of service to the Church of Southern California and elsewhere, Saint John's Seminary, with its religious, diocesan and lay-staffed faculty, has sent forth more than 700 well-trained and pastorally-orientated bishops and priests to jurisdictions all over the western United States.

CATHOLIC EDUCATION

The remarkable and unparalled accomplishments in the field of Catholic education in the area now comprising the Archdiocese of Los Angeles are unique in the annals of American Catholicism.

According to the command of Christ to His apostles, the office of teaching takes chronological precedence over even the sacramental and liturgical ministry. "Go, therefore, teach all nations..." The apostles, obeying that divine mandate, placed the work of teaching ahead of every other activity. Saint Paul himself affirmed: "Christ did not send me to baptize but to preach the Gospel."

That age old mandate, coupled with a long series of exhortations from the Baltimore Councils, explains why bishops in the United States over the last century have attached such importance to Catholic schools. The hierarchy in California has an especially long and enviable record in the educational apostolate.

Catholic schools as we know them today trace their beginnings to the early years of the 20th century and the episcopate of Thomas J. Conaty (1847-1915) who came to national prominence as Rector of The Catholic University of America.

He was ranked among the first and most zealous promoters of the Catholic school system long before his arrival in California as Bishop of Monterey-Los Angeles. Fortunately, the broadmindedness and civic activity, which characterized his earlier life, were continued with notable effect throughout his incumbency in the southland.

During the episcopate of Bishop George T. Montgomery (1847-1907), Conaty's predecessor, a fairly extensive system of parochial elementary schools in the 80,000 square-mile diocese had been inaugurated. Secondary education, however, had been generally confined to a handful of academies scattered over an area equal in size to the combined states of Pennsylvania, Maine and Massachusetts. First among Conaty's priorities was the encouragement of additional academies as well as central high schools patterned after those in Philadelphia.

Shortly after his installation, the bishop set up a Diocesan Board of Education to coordinate what had previously been a loosely organized program with considerable local autonomy. The aim of the board was to provide a continuous program of study from kindergarten through college under Catholic auspices. Periodical school visitations, standardized textbooks and improved teacher training were paramount goals. In addition to introducing the normal secondary curriculum of languages, mathematics, history, music and science, some of the academies also offered commercial and business branches.

By 1907 Conaty could report that there were thirty educational institutions functioning in the diocese with a total registration of upwards of 5,600 pupils in all the grades from primary to university. Material growth, in itself, was not paramount among the bishop's goals, and though expansion did come rapidly, he assured the people of Southern California that the Church intended to erect such buildings that would be a pride to the city and a credit to the diocese.

Through his earlier work with the Association of Catholic Colleges, Conaty recognized that the work of education depends on the training of teachers. It was this conviction that impelled him to inaugurate, in 1904, annual summer conferences at which educators of national prominence were invited to lecture. According to one newspaper account, the object of these institutes, the first of their kind held west of the Mississippi River, was to keep the teaching Sisters in touch with the latest advances in methods of teaching and the constantly developing pedagogic program.

Conaty believed that the sacrifices Catholics made for parochial schools could only be understood in the light of the obligation which they felt in conscience to train mind and heart together toward a union with God. While harboring no quarrel with public instruction, he pointed out that the drift of such education for may years had been toward complete neutrality in religious and moral matters, a factor which was causing thinking people to demand more religion in education.

In the bishop's mind, the basic principle of the whole Catholic educational movement was unalterably cemented to the same purpose for which the Church exists, namely, "to establish the Kingdom of God in the lives of men and women." Such a dedication it was that motivated a growth of educational facilities in the Diocese of Monterey-Los Angeles between 1903 and 1915 far out of proportion to the meager financial resources available to the bishop.

Soon after the appointment of John J. Cantwell (1874-1947) to the Diocese of Monterey-Los Angeles in 1917, the young Irish-born prelate received some sage advice from an old and respected friend, Father Peter C. Yorke of San Francisco. The legendary "priest of the working-man" advised Cantwell:

Don't start out by building a cathedral, Bishop ... get the little ones to love Christ... concentrate on Christian education of the youth and you will be a great success in the eyes of the Lord.

The admonition was well given and better received. In his initial pastoral letter, the new Bishop of Monterey-Los Angeles called on his clergy to assist in putting every Catholic child in a parochial school, noting that "the hope of a Christian future, the preservation of faith, the welfare of families, the prosperity of nations and the Christian character of our civilization depend upon the Christian education of our children."

In Cantwell's opinion, the Catholic school was an essential part of a parish. After the Church, it was the most important place because it was the conservator of faith and morals, and the training ground of future champions of religion and morality. So dedicated was the bishop to the ideal of a parochial school in every parish that it was later remarked that he favored the building of schools over permanent churches.

In his plans of placing "Catholic education within easy reach," Cantwell revamped the diocesan Board of Education in 1918. Over the subsequent fifteen-year period, the loosely connected network of academies, elementary and high schools of the far-flung jurisdiction were gradually molded into an integrated school system of considerable proportions.

The bishop used every means to improve the quality of diocesan education and even endorsed plans to organize a national standard system for private schools, feeling as he did that "there is nothing that would be of greater benefit to the cause of education than general supervision of education by Federal Authorities." The prelate pointed out that "just as inspection has improved the standard of our orphan asylums and clerical institutions, so would such inspection by civil authorities be a help to our schools."

Cantwell also encouraged teachers to work for Normal School Certificates, recalling that the accrediting of Catholic schools to the universities had given them prestige and a guarantee to the parents that the schools are all that was claimed for them. Along these lines, Cantwell anticipated by some years the Sister Formation Program by organizing, as early as 1924, a Diocesan Teachers Institute, an idea that had spread to the national level by 1937. In 1925, an elaborate series of summer sessions was made available to the religious of the diocese.

In 1922, Bishop Cantwell inaugurated a modified form of the central high school program used by Bishop Philip McDevitt a decade earlier for girls in Philadelphia. Patterned on this plan, Cantwell opened Bishop Conaty Memorial High School where young ladies were accepted from all over the city on a competitive basis. A few years later, a similar institution was provided for boys at the newly founded Cathedral High School. The bishop's policy was spelled out in an address he made at the latter institution's dedication:

... I want every high school boy in our diocese to feel that school is a place not for the rich, not for the poor nor for any other class in particular, rather it is a place for all boys to be educated, to be trained for true citizenship.

When J. Francis A. McIntyre (1886-1979) came to California in 1948, he found detailed plans and a healthy financial nest egg set aside for a new cathedral which his predecessor had long wanted to build on Wilshire Boulevard. Though recognizing the need even then for an adequate cathedral in the southland, the newly installed Archbishop of Los Angeles felt uneasy about the overall program, especially in view of what he considered more pressing priorities.

McIntyre met individually with his official consultors and, in each case, he prefaced his remarks with a single query: "Would it not be better to erect schools so that a future archbishop will have educated Catholics to worship in his new cathedral?"

After determining and shaping the consensus of his advisors, McIntyre composed a letter to the major donors whose contributions had already been received. He offered either to refund their offerings or to divert them to an expansion fund for Catholic schools. McIntyre later recalled that not a single one of the several thousand donors asked for the return of the money.

From his own experience, McIntyre knew that the greatest "leakage" from the Catholic Church occurred in the teenage years. For that reason, he directed the major portion of his concern towards

increasing the number of archdiocesan secondary schools. From the very outset, McIntyre proceeded along a threefold track-inviting Religious communities to open private secondary schools, encouraging pastors of larger parishes to expand existing facilities into the secondary level and, where neither plan was feasible, to establish a system of archdiocesan high schools. It was an ambitious endeavor, which could only have succeeded in Los Angeles.

McIntyre's vision of education was reflected in the many pastoral letters he wrote during his tenure as Archbishop of Los Angeles. In 1948, for example, he observed that "Catholic education is today in greater demand than at any time in our history..." On another occasion, he noted that it was of "primary importance that the youngsters be enrolled in our Catholic institutions."

At every opportunity, the cardinal reminded his people about "the advantages of higher education." At the head of McIntyre's priorities for Catholic schools was their transformation into institutions on a professional par with or even above their public counterparts. Many of the measures introduced in the 1950s were a direct outgrowth of his hands-on leadership in the educational apostolate.

A national survey in 1949 revealed that schools in the archdiocese were among the best equipped in the country. In an era before it became popular, archdiocesan officials adopted plans for a second language that was usually Spanish. And McIntyre was adamant that his schools be properly and adequately outfitted. Finally, there was the formation of a corps of archdiocesan supervisors whose duty it was to assist teachers and others in utilizing the best pedagogical methodology then available.

In 1949, after discovering that there were four applicants for every available seat in the existing high schools, McIntyre organized the first in a series of Youth Education Fund rallies, campaigns that proved to be the most extensive of their kind in the country. As to why the campaigns emphasized high schools, the cardinal said that the need there was the most acute. The average parish could not afford to have its own high school and such institutions serve regions rather than parishes. It was then that he announced new secondary schools were in preparation for San Fernando, East Los Angeles, Westchester, Whittier, Pasadena, Sierra Madre, Redondo Beach, Torrance, Covina, Azusa, San Pedro and Santa Barbara.

A national magazine observed in 1953 that McIntyre's "most notable achievement, among the lengthy list since assuming leadership of the Los Angeles archdiocese, has been in the educational field where he has taken the initiative as a builder of schools."

Late in 1958, the cardinal once again wrote to his clergy telling them that our "high schools program has developed beyond our expectations." But, because of high registration, he still needed to double the number of classrooms within a few years.

It is part of the official chronicle that no other area in the United States, or probably anywhere else, raised more money, erected more schools and expanded more energy on Catholic education than did the Archdiocese of Los Angeles or its archbishop who, himself, never had the benefit of attending a parochial school. And always, priority went to the poor and to those who had waited longest and needed help the most.

The last high school in what was then the Archdiocese of Los Angeles was opened in 1965; and there the story abruptly ends. Despite the fact that the Catholic population since then has increased by 136%, no secondary schools have been inaugurated over the past thirty-six years and there is none on the drawing board.

There are many valid reasons behind the shift in educational emphasis and concern from that of the earlier years. Among others, statisticians would cite:

a) The exorbitant and escalating costs of construction and staffing;

b) the dissolution of traditional religious life, with the consequent diminution in availability of brothers and sisters;

c) constant shifting of demographics in Southern California communities;

d) fluctuation and unpredictability of the birthrate due to the pill;

e) shifting of emphasis in archdiocesan priorities and funds in the wake of new and diversified post-Vatican II ministries;

f) prohibitive and necessary rise in tuition rates;

g) increased dissemination of alternate education and/or catechetical programs;

h) the upsurge in maintenance costs for existing buildings which are now half a century old;

i) increasing demands of accreditation agencies.

The detailed story of the remarkable educational achievement at the secondary level during the tenure of the southland's first two archbishops has been adequately portrayed in John Joseph Cantwell, His Excellency of Los Angeles and His Eminence of Los Angeles, James Francis Cardinal McIntyre.

One school never opened (Catherine McAuley, 1970); several changed their patronage (Saint John Vianney to Daniel Murphy, Regina Caeli to Queen of Angels Academy and Saint Joseph to Pomona Catholic); three schools operated under the same name (Marymount-Los Angeles, Santa Barbara and Palos Verdes); a couple merged (Conaty-Our Lady of Loretto and Cantwell-Sacred Heart); others were sold (Marymount in Santa Barbara and Corvallis in Studio City); one moved to another's campus (Saint Matthias to Pius X); and six became part of the Diocese of Orange (Cornelia Connelly, Marywood, Mater Dei, Rosary, Saint Michael and Servite).

Because co-instructional high schools were often listed in earlier archdiocesan directories as separate institutions, one for boys and the other for girls,* the overall number of secondary schools has varied over the years.

In a recent news article, the editors of *America* noted that "Catholic schools in Los Angeles give low-income and minority children a quality education at half the cost of public schools." A study, by the San Francisco-based Pacific Research Institute showed that Catholic high schools in the Los Angeles Archdiocese spend less than $5,000 per student annually and elementary schools about $2,200 per student, compared with $9,029 per student in the Los Angeles Unified School District. But despite the lower spending, said the study, Catholic schools have fewer dropouts and send a greater percentage of their students to college than do public schools in the same neighborhoods.

PAROCHIAL HIGH SCHOOLS

HOLY FAMILY HIGH SCHOOL

Founded in 1937, Holy Family High School is a parish secondary institution for girls. From the outset, it has been staffed by the Sisters of Charity of the Blessed Virgin Mary. One class was added each year until the four year college preparatory course was completed.

By 1946, there were 210 students at the Glendale school. It was early recognized as one of the seven "progressive" high schools in the archdiocese whose curriculum offered, in addition to a full college preparatory course, classes in homemaking, physiology, sociology, physics and chemistry. At that time, about half of the graduates went on for further education.

Our Lady's Sodality was very active at Holy Family. One of the distinctive features of the sodality was its Cooperative Library Association. The idea for such a library was conceived by the girls them-

selves. Money was raised in a variety of ways to purchase books and encourage students to read. The only criteria was that the books had to be Catholic in tone and theme.

In 1949, there was a dramatic rise in enrollment with an unprecedented ninety freshmen, thus bringing the total roster to 250 girls. Under an elective system, functional courses were offered to equip the students for entrance into the fields of business or for the important vocation of homemaking. Student initiative was further developed through activity in the Student Body Association.

When students returned in 1950, there was a new schoolhouse underway at Holy Family. The young ladies also found additional courses, including one in "Charm and Personality." Located on East Lomita Avenue near Elk, the two story structure allowed for doubling the student body. The building was a reinforced concrete and brick structure in a modified mission style.

In 1954, the high school was physically separated from the elementary grades. In the new facilities were a cafeteria, assembly hall, shower and locker rooms, laboratories, domestic science facilities and updated classrooms.

There were 350 students at Holy Family in the mid-1950s. The school was well into its eighteenth year and administrators looked forward to many more years of productive service to the local community.

By 1960, the curriculum was expanded to meet the needs of a busier age. The science department acquired new equipment for biological study. A micro-projector allowed an entire class to see an enlarged view of a slide. To cope with the increasing complexity of international affairs and their impact on the lives of local peoples, elective courses were offered in history.

Even conversational French was introduced for honor students. A fourth year of mathematics was added to allow accelerated students to engage in pre-college work. As was always the case, religion classes were the focal point in the curriculum with emphasis on developing the intellect and strengthening the will for adult Catholic citizenship.

In 1961, a student member of the Mariner Scouts presented a statue of Our Lady Queen of the Sea to the new nuclear submarine *Scamp*. The two-foot high wooden statue, designed by Mrs. Fred Chase, was presented in a formal ceremony on the ship itself.

For its silver jubilee, Holy Family High School's students engaged in the Summer School of Catholic Action in San Francisco. Local demonstrations by guild members were staged throughout the academic year.

Over the years, the young ladies consistently took an active part in raising money for the poor. They devised a social action club and personally engaged in visiting and looking after the indigent in the area.

MARY, STAR OF THE SEA HIGH SCHOOL

Groundbreaking ceremonies were held in San Pedro on February 12, 1950, for a new Catholic junior high school. Roy Better, representing the Board of Education, welcomed the 750 persons attending the event. He praised the fine spirit of cooperation between Catholic and public schools, citing the high educational standards of parochial schools. The legendary Joseph Scott, father of the pastor, discussed the role of Catholic schools as a positive response to communism.

The Immaculate Heart Sisters, who formed the original faculty, welcomed James Francis Cardinal McIntyre in 1953 for the official dedication. It was the tenth high school built through assets provided by the Youth Education Fund.

The two story brick building was the first unit of what was expected to become a large coeducational high school serving the harbor area. Until the additions could be made, students were accommodated in rooms of the neighboring grammar school.

Included in the new complex were a modern science laboratory, a library, study hall and health, faculty and homerooms. The sports facilities were scattered and included a nearby city park which was used for football practice. For baseball, the youngsters utilized the local Army-Navy gymnasium.

In 1963, seven more classrooms were added, along with a biology-art room, sewing units and basement multi-purpose rooms with seating capacity for 450 persons. Enrollment advanced from 314 to 500.

When, in 1959, Fermin Lasuen High School opened, Mary Star became a girls' high school. With the closure of Fermin Lasuen, in 1975, Mary Star reverted to being co-educational.

Over the years, the curriculum was a challenging college preparatory track. The school placed high in academic Decathlon and stressed responsibility and leadership. Roughly 70% of the graduating classes went on to four year or two year colleges. Many ethnic peoples lived in the San Pedro area, the largest of which were Asian, Slavic and Hispanic.

In 1996, Mary Star received a gift of twenty-seven acres from surplus Navy property for the purpose of relocating the high school which found itself operating in a cramped square block downtown neighborhood. A capital campaign was begun to raise an estimated $7.5 million, making it the second largest construction project in the history of the archdiocese.

Former Secretary of the Department of Education, Dr. William Bennett, participated in fund raising programs supporting the new Mary Star of the Sea High School in 1998. Praising the work of Catholic schools, Bennett stressed the notion of instilling morals and character in students, something that had been a feature in the San Pedro school from the earliest days.

Bennett applauded the Navy's decision to give the property to the school, saying that the new structures would be a literal interpretation of "beating swords into plowshares."

SAINT ANTHONY HIGH SCHOOL

It was in 1920 that the Sisters of the Immaculate Heart of Mary founded and staffed a co-educational high school under the patronage of Saint Anthony. Located in San Pedro, the school received its first accreditation from the University of California on July 12, 1922. The first graduation, consisting of two students, took place in 1923.

The actual dedication of new educational facilities took place on May 23, 1927. The edifice was beautiful in design, ultra-permanent in construction and expressive of the highest and most modern standards in utility. Bishop Cantwell was extremely pleased and proud of Saint Anthony's. He congratulated the throng present for the ceremony, stating that Catholic schools teach reverence for constituted authority and appreciation for its inviolability and endurance.

Unhappily, the school was destroyed in the 1933 earthquake and had to be rebuilt. Yet, within a year, a new building was in place and the school was again functioning as a full course high school with 200 students in attendance.

The athletic program, inaugurated in the 1930s, was active in the Catholic League. During the 1940s, both a gymnasium and a football stadium were built. Many of the "Saints" went on to various colleges and universities to become All American Greats.

In 1941, a new schoolhouse was erected at Seventh Street and Olive Avenue. It was placed under the tutelage of the Holy Cross Brothers from Notre Dame, Indiana. That building contained eight classrooms, a library, physics and chemistry laboratories and administration offices. It was fireproof and earthquake resistant.

Saint Anthony Athletic Field opened in 1947 at 4832 Clark Avenue. The following year, the school won the CIF 4-A football Championship. And, in 1953, the baseball team became league champions, as did the track team.

Two separate schools rather than one that was co-educational, Saint Anthony housed many organizations present in both divisions. One was the Sodality that oversaw all manner of outreach programs. Officers were chosen for the Sodality in a democratic way and members were involved in planning many activities.

The girls' school reached a record enrollment in 1948, with 517 names on the roster. Each year, the first week was given over to a special "Friendship Rally" whereby all new students were personally welcomed to the San Pedro campus. The Glee Club was also active, with 300 young ladies signed up to study both secular and religious music. In 1949, a new library was added to the school along with six new classrooms and an audio-visual room.

Four students were declared winners of the coveted Naval Reserve Officers Training Corps in 1950. They had successfully passed rigid mental and physical examinations with thousands of other Long Beach youths.

A school bus was acquired in 1952. Facilities at the school's Memorial Stadium were expanded, with shower, locker and equipment rooms. Landscaping of the field and addition of a baseball diamond adjacent to the football field made the school a most attractive campus.

Over the years, there were many vocations at Saint Anthony's. By 1958, twenty-one had been ordained to the priesthood. Three had entered the brotherhood and fourteen were in various novitiates.

The old cafeteria was converted into a "Home Living Suite" in 1961. Girls returning to school were able to utilize sewing rooms, kitchen facilities and modern cooking devices. Such conveniences as dishwashers, refrigerators, waste disposals and washers and dryers were ready for use.

In 1965, Jean Raders was named a Presidential Scholar, one of only 121 chosen for that honor nationwide. Students were occupied in all sorts of programs such as resettlement, pantry work for the poor and volunteer programs.

As the school observed its fiftieth anniversary, Saint Anthony's became co-educational in the normal sense of the term. Most of the organizations were merged in such a way that both boys or girls could take an active part.

On and on the school moved. Today, graduates brag that before the seaside city had the Queen Mary, the Spruce Goose, tidelands oil bonanza, the Grand Prix, modern marina and shopping malls, Saint Anthony High School was educating and morally shaping Catholic young people for important roles in society.

SAINT GENEVIEVE HIGH SCHOOL

In February of 1959, it was announced that a new co-educational Catholic high school would be opened that fall at Saint Genevieve's parish in Panorama City. Assisted by the Youth Education Fund, the new school would serve families of many surrounding parishes in the San Fernando Valley. The school would be conducted by the Sisters of Saint Joseph of Newark who also had staffed the parochial elementary school.

Plans called for modern building techniques to be utilized in the two-story structure. Steel and concrete would be combined with Roman brick piers. Aluminum and glass window-wall units would cover the interior. There were to be ten regular classrooms, a library-study hall, a science laboratory and a lecture room.

When the school actually got under way, a three-course curriculum was offered: three sections of general and one of business education. A Special Honors course was pitched to students achieving higher placements.

James Francis Cardinal McIntyre blessed Saint Genevieve's High School on October 16, 1960. By that time, there were 323 ninth and tenth graders. In his address for the occasion, the pastor noted that "Our people are extraordinarily cooperative. Through their sacrifices, they not only put up half the cost of the building, but they also contributed generously to the Youth Education Fund." At that time, local families were mostly in the middle income bracket, with a few professional people.

As the next two years progressed, the final levels of high school were added. Nineteen parishes were served with a total enrollment of 550 students. The school was known for its excellent sporting facilities.

In 1962, construction began on a ten classroom addition to the main building, a factor that allowed for the doubling of enrollment. Academically, the school offered complete college preparatory as well as general and business courses.

There were 108 graduates in 1963. The school reached its maximum enrollment of 850 that fall. A wholly new range of learning methods was inaugurated. Physics, mathematics, modern chemistry, aural-oral French and Spanish and the structural approach to Latin were among the offerings.

Students did well in other endeavors. In 1970, the Valiants vanquished Agoura before 6,000 fans at Birmingham High Stadium. Earlier, the Valiants had been monarchs by capturing the CIF's Small School title. And the band swept all sorts of competitions the following year, winning no fewer than fifteen first place awards in their first full parade competition.

In 1974, the Salesian Sisters arrived in Panorama City, instilling a whole new vitality to the high school. During subsequent years, the sisters added immeasurably to the academic stature of the institution.

In 1976, Saint Genevieve High School boasted of six finalists in the National Merit Scholarship competition. Winners had distinguished themselves among a highly select group of students representing less than one half of one percent of the nation's graduating seniors.

A journalist visited the school in 1975 and reported that "Friendly" was the word best describing the spirit of the youngsters. The 920 students hailed from twenty-five parishes. The writer also noted that the parents were generous with their time and energy.

A graduate from Saint Genevieve, Laura Slattery, finished her studies at West Point, the United States Military Academy, in 1988. She ranked 118th in a class of 980 cadets, 90% of whom were boys. Later she served for five years in the armed services.

SAINT MONICA HIGH SCHOOL

A new high school was dedicated on January 4, 1940, under the patronage of Saint Monica. At the ceremony, Archbishop John J. Cantwell congratulated the pastor, Msgr. Nicholas Conneally, for this latest fulfilling chapter about the educational outreach of the Archdiocese of Los Angeles.

The school was one of the first, if not the first, in the country with outstanding sound reproduction facilities. At the inauguration, John McCormack's motion picture "Song of my Heart" was shown to visitors. The school began with nine classrooms and a spacious playground.

Administration of secondary education in the Bay District was entrusted to the Sisters conducting the Academy of the Holy Names. On the roster in those beginning days were names of 229 enrollees.

According to local legend, Fray Junípero Serra offered Holy Mass in Santa Monica in 1770. He was also credited with naming the place. City fathers, mindful of that tradition, erected a statue of Saint Augustine's mother at the intersection of Wilshire Boulevard and Ocean Avenue. In 1948, the Irish Patrician Brothers took over the administration of the school.

In 1951, there were nine members of the Sullivan family enrolled in the various grades of education at Santa Monica. The father was a fireman and his wife worked full time as a housewife. The family resided just a few blocks from the school.

At that time there were three general courses offered, college preparatory, general and commercial. Extra curricular activities fulfilled the spiritual, mental, social and athletic needs of the students who were separated into girls' and boys' departments.

By 1954, there were 400 girls and 320 boys at the school. To provide for the growing student body, additional faculty members were added. Expansion in the boys' division allowed for courses in business law, economics and mechanical drawing. For the girls, there were modern business machines, which assisted them to be "office-ready" when they graduated.

Carpenters, painters and plumbers were active during the summer months of 1955 expanding facilities still further. Improvements included a new fiberglass stage curtain. A life-size painting of the Blessed Mother, executed by the artist Eric Sauer, greeted returning students.

A completely new wing, added the next year, was constructed of reinforced concrete type 1 construction. Included in that unit were twelve classrooms, study halls, multi-purpose quarters and several laboratories. By 1957, the school could accommodate 1,000 pupils.

Enrollment was not reserved to Saint Monica's parish. There were students from the San Fernando Valley and Redondo Beach, together with others from twenty-five neighboring parishes. A shop program was inaugurated along with classes in metal graphic arts, wood shop, radio and television.

In 1976, the U.S. Air Force Academy Catholic Cadet Choir visited Saint Monica's High School. The 125-member choir presented several programs for students and their parents and friends.

During the 50th graduation, in 1988, Timothy Cardinal Manning came to the school bringing a "telegram from God". His Eminence spoke to the 169 graduates about their valued place in the Catholic laity, telling them "to always be willing to walk the extra mile."

SAN GABRIEL MISSION HIGH SCHOOL

Plans were begun early in 1949 for a new high school attached to the parish of historic San Gabriel Mission. Boys and girls attended the school, but in separate classes. There were to be joint school activities and social functions.

In order to give students a well-balanced education for living in accordance with Catholic philosophy, a five-fold development program was planned embracing the spiritual, intellectual, aesthetic, social and physical. The school offered a full college preparatory curriculum with a commercial major for boys and a choice between a homemaking and a commercial major for girls.

The school opened in temporary quarters at All Soul's elementary in Alhambra. Only ninth grade students were accepted the first year. Groundbreaking for the high school was held on January 10, 1949, at Santa Anita Street and Broadway in San Gabriel. Plans called for a two-story school building to be of reinforced concrete with a tile roof in keeping with the architectural style of the Old Mission.

The school moved into its first full term in the fall of 1950. Approximately 300 freshmen and sophomores were on the roster with the Claretian Fathers and the Dominican Sisters of Mission San Jose on the faculty.

James Francis Cardinal McIntyre journeyed to San Gabriel for the official dedication on January 13, 1951. He was pleased to see the thirty-two rooms, which included a library, classrooms and laboratories. There was even a temporary cafeteria, showers and lockers located in the basement.

The archdiocesan superintendent of education observed that the mission bells first rung in the area 180 years earlier. "We cannot build a social conscience in a moral vacuum, but must go back to our heritage of inalienable rights and trust in God."

By 1955 there were 875 pupils in the school where "both the religious and lay faculty pledged themselves unstintingly to conformity with the Catholic educational axiom that Christian education is a training in correct evaluation."

There was an intensified schedule of intramural sports that featured post-game dances and other social get-togethers. Beside the regular courses of study, there were a host of elective subjects, including drama, speech, journalism, photography, driver education, first aid, band, mechanical drawing, typing, glee club and printing.

The 930 enrollees came from thirty parishes by 1956. Annual functions included a general retreat and a closed retreat for senior girls at the Monastery of the Angels in Hollywood. A marching band with new uniforms in the California pioneer style became known nation-wide.

In 1960, the school went public with its idea to develop each student spiritually, morally, intellectually, physically and socially, a goal actualized through a wide variety of subjects under the general heading of college preparatory and business programs. A wide variety of clubs provided an opportunity for everyone to advance his or her special talents, extend academic interest and earn the value of initiative.

A representative share in scholarships granted to graduates and a good record by its students in colleges and universities indicate the maintenance of high academic standards at San Gabriel Mission High School.

The school band performed at the Los Angeles Coliseum in September of 1962. An average of a hundred students each year were in one or another musical program in a discipline that developed, mellowed and matured.

The fiftieth anniversary class presented a mural to the school in 1963. Painted by Edith and Isabel Piczek, the artistic panel featured "Christ the Teacher" and overlooked the school playground.

In 1970, the boys' department at San Gabriel Mission High was closed and students were merged with those at La Salle in Pasadena. The move allowed the school to offer an expanded curriculum to the remaining girl students.

PRIVATE CATHOLIC HIGH SCHOOLS

ALVERNO HIGH SCHOOL

In 1960, plans were announced to open an archdiocesan girls' secondary school in Sierra Madre. The Franciscan Sisters of Christian Charity agreed to staff the new school which began the fall term with 150 freshmen.

Located on a thirteen-acre section of the former Barlow Estate, the academy was a concrete-block structure with a crushed tile roof. It was designed to match in color and texture buildings already on the campus. The buildings were designed on several levels, with thirteen homerooms, two large science laboratories, a workroom for individual science projects, a language laboratory and an audio-visual studio. Buildings already on the property were remodeled to provide library facilities, music instruction and an arts and crafts center.

Saint Francis of Assisi and Our Lady of Guadalupe were selected as co-patrons of the school, which was part of the ongoing Youth Education Fund established by James Francis Cardinal McIntyre. The name of the school derives from the Mount of Avernia in Tuscany where Saint Francis of Assisi went for solitude and meditation. Alverno was the only school within the city of Sierra Madre.

Faculty members told reporters that the campus was "the most beautiful in the archdiocese." The contemporary style of the buildings was bright and colorful, with wide expanses of glass and cement panels in pastel shades. The concrete masonry structure, mostly one story, surrounded three sides of a garden quadrangle. The educational focus

at the academy was college preparatory. There were also homemaking and business courses offered.

By 1962, there were 400 enrollees at Alverno. A special committee formed by the parents' association began a cultural program for students that allowed them to attend concerts and take special tours of museums and other educational centers in the area.

There was always an outreach program in evidence at the academy. In 1964, for example, eight tons of used clothing was collected for the needy in Mexico. The "wagon train of charity," the fifth in the school's history, included 120 students, thirty parents and several members of the faculty. The clothing was personally delivered to the hospital of the Sisters of the Sacred Heart, the Casa de Cuba orphanage and the Casa del Niño Pobre Orphanage. The recipients entertained their guests with songs and dances.

In 1968, Pamela Ann Anicichi, an alumna of Alverno, was named the Rose Parade Queen for the following year. She received nationwide coverage for the event and was interviewed on television and radio. And, in 1971, Pam Steel was awarded first place in the Foreign Language Speech Contest at Saint Mary's College, winning among contestants from twenty-seven high schools. Sara O'Gara was one of six students from Southern California selected for a trip to the National Capital as a winner of the Junior Science Symposium sponsored by the United States Army in 1984.

In 1978, the Franciscan Sisters turned the institution over to a board of the Immaculate Heart Community who responded to the search for a Catholic community to assume legal sponsorship of the school. Alverno continued its founding tradition as a Catholic, private, independent school for girls.

Alverno High School welcomed forty Japanese exchange students to the campus in 1989. In the United States, to augment their knowledge of English, the students were housed at homes of the school's parents.

CATHEDRAL HIGH SCHOOL

Cathedral High School, which guarded the approaches to Chavez Ravine long before the Dodgers moved to Los Angeles, began in 1925 in a building on the property of Sacred Heart parish. Two years later, a structure was completed on the site of Old Calvary Cemetery. The first diocesan boys' high school, it was staffed by the Christian Brothers who continue the time-tested Lasallian philosophy of assisting in the salvation and intellectual formation of the common person.

In 1931, a building was added to the original schoolhouse. The number of graduates grew to seventy-six in 1937. Three years later, the Arroyo Seco freeway was constructed at the west side of the campus. In 1941 a new gym was erected by Archbishop John J. Cantwell. That building was a modern one-story structure, with floor space for basketball, spectator bleachers and a built-in stage. There was even an alcove for a portable altar. In the front were offices, a reception area, cloakrooms and quarters for physical education that was an integral part of the institution's life. Already by that time the school's alumni were men eminent in their professions and in civic and religious life of the city of Los Angeles.

Sports have always been an outstanding spectre at Cathedral. In 1943, the track team gained top honors in the annual All Southern California Catholic High School Meet.

In 1949, the school opened its fall term with a new, completely equipped manual arts program housed in an up-to-date shop building. With existing academic and commercial departments, the school became the first of such institutions to introduce a manual arts curriculum. The new building fronted a 220 foot front along North Broadway and extended ninety-seven feet west in the shape of an L. It included an 80 x 40 foot woodshop, a drafting room, a lecture room, two classrooms and a complete visual aid library with projection equipment for use in shop instruction.

With the inauguration of the fall term in 1949, there were 700 boys enrolled at Cathedral High. The school's college prep courses included English history, geometry, Latin, Spanish, chemistry, physics, trigonometry and solid geometry. The commercial-academic courses consisted of sufficient academic requisites to enable students to enter college, together with such commercial subjects as bookkeeping, shorthand, typing, business math and English, commercial law and the like. Religion was a requisite in all classes.

Located at 1253 Bishops Road, the school offered a curriculum that, while fully accredited, allowed students to fill in multiple deficits. Cathedral has always been a typical boys' school providing unique opportunities for physical, social and spiritual training that developed and prepared for mature status.

Throughout its history, Cathedral High has also encouraged extra-curricular activities, among which were a band, a glee club, newspaper and yearbooks. A Marian Society and Y.C.S. Alumni gatherings included Communion Breakfast, twice each academic year.

Three additional buildings were begun in 1960. The new units, joined by covered walkways, formed a large C, opening southward toward the auditorium-gymnasium. These structures replaced the original 1925 building that no longer met the city code requirements. Auxiliary Bishop Timothy Manning blessed the new units on April 24, 1963.

The school's production of "Fiddler on the Roof" won many accolades in 1973, including the Mayor's Adult Committee Youth Award. Cathedral won the traveling trophy for the highest achievement in a single production. That same year the senior class won over $100,000 in college scholarships and other financial assistance.

Further building came in 1987 with erection of a multi-story educational center housing classrooms and a science laboratory. At the same time, plans were announced to provide additional scholarship assistance for needy boys.

Cathedral now functions as a private Catholic high school for young men. The school community takes pride in being a Christian community where students pursue an academic life in an atmosphere, which forms and develops their beliefs and commitment in a supportive educational environment.

CHAMINADE COLLEGE PREPARATORY

In 1952, the Marianists purchased the Cheviot Hills Military Academy and opened a school for boys named for the founder of their community, Father Chaminade. Eight years later, a new site was acquired in Canoga Park. With the closure of Saint John's Military School in Chatsworth, Chaminade expanded to a dual campus institution for students of the West San Fernando Valley. The school opened its doors to girls in 1972.

Chaminade collaborates with the families it serves to provide a challenging Catholic education in the Marianist tradition, which encompasses the whole person. A family spirit is used to provide a nurturing, caring environment attentive to the moral and religious development of students.

School officials have endeavored to recruit students with a diversity of cultural, religious and economic backgrounds and mould them together in an active and varied curricular and extracurricular program.

A Blue Ribbon School of Excellence, the mission at Chaminade is that of forming a morally aware and academically capable cadre of young people to be outstanding contributors to themselves and the future of their country.

CRESPI CARMELITE HIGH SCHOOL

Designed to serve the educational needs of the western San Fernando Valley, Crespi High School was located adjacent to the parochial plant of Our Lady of Grace in Encino. Named for Fray Juan Crespi, the life-long companion on Fray Junipero Serra, the school was erected as part of the Youth Education Fund.

The school's patron, one of California's greatest missionaries, explorers and chroniclers, came to the area in 1769 with Gaspar de Portola. In addition to serving as chaplain, Crespi was also the official diarist for the expedition. Much of California's nomenclature originated with the friar, such as Los Angeles and Encino.

The first unit was a modern, two-story unit of reinforced brick with an initial capacity for 600 boys. In the proto building were facilities for sixteen classrooms, a science laboratory, library, study hall and offices.

At the opening in 1959, there were 120 students. Administration of the school was entrusted to the Carmelite Fathers of the Chicago Province who had been working in the Los Angeles educational apostolate for a quarter century.

By the time the second class arrived at Encino, the library had been outfitted with seating capacity for ninety-two students. The Crespi Mothers Club started the library project by donating and cataloguing over 300 books. Another development was a cafeteria where students could get hot, nourishing meals. Specially designed typing desks were installed with new typewriters. The Fathers Club leveled the football field, installed automatic sprinkler systems and planted fresh turf.

Dedicated by James Francis Cardinal McIntyre on March 11, 1962, the school already had accommodations for 650 students. A locker-shower building had been provided adjacent to the athletic fields.

The physical development of a school is more easily catalogued and simpler to explain than its interior activity. At Crespi, it has always been a thrust to assist students in carrying out their mental prayer. Interior conversation with the Lord was fostered by having periods of silence following all school Masses. The reading program required book reports on the lives of the saints and doctrine of the Church as well as literary masterpieces.

A language lab was installed in the summer of 1963. It was a modernized version of equipment used by the armed services and adapted to high school needs. Besides honors programs in English and mathematics, a college credit Latin acceleration course was established at Crespi.

Scholarship and cooperative Catholic spirit have traditionally marked the atmosphere of Crespi High School. The college prep course was designed to interest as well as reward participants. And there were scholarships that allowed students to cover early college curriculum while still in high school.

In 1968, a new multi-purpose building was erected. It included a 10,000 square foot gymnasium with the first indoor Tartan floor in California, together with an oratory chapel, a kitchen with serving accommodations, shower and locker rooms and coaches' offices.

Christian service programs date from 1974. Teenagers found out how satisfying is work with handicapped children and hospitalized seniors. Services of some kind for approximately two hours a week became an accepted part of the Crespi schedule.

Students won accolades too. James Carrabino received an appointment to the U.S. Naval Academy at Annapolis; Michael Zepf got a similar appointment to the U.S. Air Force Academy and Christopher Hall was awarded a research internship at the United Nations European Headquarters in Geneva.

DON BOSCO TECHNICAL INSTITUTE

In its issue for April 14, 1955, the *Post Advocate*, a newspaper serving the San Gabriel Valley, announced that a "new $3,000,000 technical high school specializing in the instruction of trades and crafts" would be opened to boys in the following fall. Located at 1115 North San Gabriel Boulevard, the school was entrusted to the care of the Salesian Fathers.

Not truly a "trade" school, Don Bosco is a unique institution combining a complete academic program with the technical training for leadership in industry and college. It was planned as a pre-engineering, technical-academic high school whose overall purpose was that of developing students into creative individuals able to work with new machines, products, structures and processes.

The first school of its kind in the west, it was designed to include classrooms, a general science laboratory, a drafting room and an assembly room. When finished, it would be a T-shaped structure 160 feet long and sixty-four feet wide, with wings extending 130 feet at one end. The whole complex was planned to allow future expansion.

Initially, the school was equipped to offer shop programs in auto mechanics, photo offset printing and commercial binding. There was also a machine shop, a cabinet shop and quarters for practical metallurgy.

The idea for the school came from James Francis Cardinal McIntyre who always considered the institution the favorite of his many educational outreaches. He remained active as Chairman of its Board until his retirement. Blessing the school on May 16, 1956, the cardinal noted that it would have a place in the atomic cities of the future, eternally reflecting the influence of the Church. The twenty-acre complex was advertised as a "school that shows the shape of things to come."

There were ninety-four graduates in the first commencement class in 1959. The cardinal was there to note the historic event. Though admitting that he had projected his own imagination into the school, he thanked Almighty God noting, "it has not been human wisdom that has foreseen and developed this institution." He envisioned the school as "a new growth from virgin California soil."

A new gymnasium-recreation building was begun in 1961. Its hyperbolic paraboloid roof was the largest of its kind in Southern California. Covering 19,000 square feet, it accommodated two basketball courts, seating for a thousand persons and two training areas.

Over the years, other shops were added, including industrial drafting, which specialized in such technical areas as electrical, structural, architectural, and aerospace, all of which figured into the program of developing highly skilled young men for the new challenges of the industrial world.

The 143 graduates in 1964 represented thirty neighboring communities extending from Reseda to Long Beach. Sixteen of the southland's leading industrialists were actively associated with the school. That group, embracing many industrial and professional firms, attested to the value of the school.

In its first decade, Don Bosco chalked up a wide range of firsts. The school boasted of having all races and religious faiths represented. Its nineteen buildings served as an intramural athletic and recreation model for other schools. There were seven fields in the technology curricula: automotive, cabinetmaking, electronics, drafting, mechanical technology, metallurgy and photolithography. There were also twenty-five social clubs and societies in such areas as amateur radio, drama, debate, choral and instrumental music, language, science, rocketry, riflery and sports.

From the outset, religion played a prominent part at Don Bosco. A newspaper story in 1969 testified that eighty students were active in the Sodality of the Blessed Virgin's forty-year local tradition of helping young people in the city's southside and eastside. Twice weekly, students toured the neighborhoods tutoring small children on the catechism.

The school also adopted a five-year program leading to the Associate of Science degree in 1968. Under that plan, students in the 11th and 12th grades were assigned college semester credits toward a technical major. Over the years, numerous graduates were given appointments to the armed forces academies. In 1974, Daniel Dubois and Douglas Vermillion were appointed, one to the U.S. Merchant Marine Academy and the other to the U.S. Military Academy at West Point.

By the 1980s, Don Bosco was deeply involved in the field of computers. A computer lab allowed students to learn keyboarding, standard word processing and database, as well as spreadsheet programs. IBM donated much of the equipment. Today, the school features computer service, construction, design, electronics, graphic communications, manufacturing, materials science, power and transportation.

FLINTRIDGE SACRED HEART ACADEMY

For many years Flintridge Sacred Heart Academy has been equipping young women with the skills to meet life's challenges and the Christian attitudes to make the world a better place.

Founded in 1931 by the Dominican Sisters of Mission San Jose, the academy is situated on a picturesque elevation above the sea, overlooking the two beautiful cities of Pasadena and Altadena. The view over the broad San Gabriel Valley commands the admiration of visitors looking for a glimpse into California's rich historical heritage.

Before its purchase by the Dominican Sisters of Mission San Jose, the buildings and site of forty acres was the former Flintridge-Biltmore Hotel, erected in reinforced concrete by Senator Frank Flint. Built and equipped as one of the state's finest resort hotels, it became one of the best-appointed schools in the Archdiocese of Los Angeles.

A writer in *The Tidings* in 1947 said that the "classrooms, recreation parlors and chemistry laboratories offered unlimited material for speculation and many a geometrical theorem meets an untimely end as a distracted student tries to visualize what the former occupants of the school did back in the old days."

In 1950, construction began on a new U-shaped structure to enclose a patio on three sides. It was to house six academic classrooms, a combination study hall-assembly room and science, art, journalism, typing and sewing rooms. The reinforced concrete with tile roof followed the same Spanish colonial architecture of the earlier buildings.

Archbishop J. Francis A. McIntyre blessed the new building on October 14, 1951. The speakers were delighted that the leveled hilltop site was large enough for future additions. There were 115 high school and twenty-two elementary youngsters on the campus. Temporary classroom space was also provided for 136 pupils from nearby Saint Bede's parish.

The large and airy classrooms were conducive to good study habits, and the students took every opportunity of expanding their learning experience of the foothill communities.

In 1952, the Sodality program was enlarged to place renewed emphasis on the spiritual life of the youngsters. This in turn allowed for greatest participation to Catholic Action.

An auditorium was added in 1956 and two years later, Flintridge Sacred Heart enlarged its music program. The aim of the school was restated as "not only education of the intellect but primarily the formation of character, the development of native abilities and the fostering of sound religious principles."

By 1961, plans were afoot for a new building to allow increased enrollment. Unhappily, seven years later, a fire ruined the music conservatory at Sacred Heart. Lost in that conflagration were nine pianos, an organ and an extensive music library with its manuscripts and prints.

The enrollment inched upwards until, by 1991, in the school's sixtieth year, there were 325 day students and ninety residents on campus. The girls hailed from eight counties throughout the state. Boosters asserted that "a school is more than a place of a number of students; it is the spirit and philosophy of the school, the dreams of its youngsters and the achievements of its alumnae."

A Blue Ribbon School of Excellence, the Rose Parade Queen for 2001 was a student at Flintridge Sacred Heart Academy.

IMMACULATE HEART HIGH SCHOOL

Advertised as the "the first private school in Southern California," Immaculate Heart High School, founded in 1906, was nestled on a fifteen-acre parcel of land at the foot of the Hollywood Hills. The schoolhouse was perched at the crown of Western Avenue's northernmost tip, enjoying a pastoral surrounding with an eastern view of a cowpath that became Los Feliz Boulevard.

In the years between 1910 and 1920, with the advent of motor travel, larger numbers of day students were attracted to the school to join the boarders from various communities throughout California.

The course of study included Greek, Latin, physics and chemistry, each more intensively pursued than today when a wider scope of subjects is offered. There was ample time for recreation and the development of school spirit along with the school's excellence in academics.

In the late 1920s, the school facilities and horizons expanded. A swimming pool was added, the boarding quarters were enlarged and more out-of-state girls were attracted to the campus.

Extracurricular activities blossomed in the 1930s. The drama department sponsored a wide variety of productions and there was increasing interest and participation in competitive sports.

During the war years, the school reflected the national patriotism. Students appeared in uniform. A school newspaper, *Viewpoint*, was inaugurated. While fashions changed, traditions held. Graduation ceremonies were held in the Hollywood Bowl and the Church's spirit of renewal was reflected in the expanded religious exercises.

It was time for a physical renewal of the campus in the 1960s. The old chapel facade was to become a memory. The high school struggled to meet the challenges of change and growth.

The girls fared well in outside competition. In 1986, three students among the 550 enrollees were winners in the Annual National Achievement Scholarship program. Several years later, nine members of the speech team won trophies in forensics.

Roger Cardinal Mahony broke ground for a new chapel in 1986. La Capilla de Maria was formally dedicated on December 8, 1987. The small 600 square foot mission style chapel provides a place for daily Mass and quiet prayer. A white marble altar is centered in front of windows that reach from floor to ceiling in the all white structure interior.

As part of the school's 85th anniversary, two new buildings were completed. The 10,200 square foot science facility was built in California mission style along Franklin Avenue. A new office structure adjoined the science building. By that time over 6,000 young women had studied at the high school.

A private Catholic college preparatory school, Immaculate Heart High School being dedicated to the intellectual, spiritual, moral and social development of young women, draws its students from sixty-five parishes.

An alternative to the education offered by the public system and to assure a substantial enrollment for grades 9 through 12, La Reina opened a junior high division in the fall of 1973.

Between 1972 and 1983, Moorpark College used the La Reina facilities as a satellite campus. A major advantage of that association was the opportunity for La Reina's upper class students to enroll in college courses.

Following revision of the school's philosophy to that of College prep, in 1981, the graduation requirements were revised to reflect the standards for admission to the University of California.

Then in 1985, La Reina's softball team won the Tri-Valley prize. A spokesman said, "The whole philosophy here is to produce mature Christian women who can respond to society. We work a lot on attitude, positive thinking and prayer before and after games. We discuss goals and priorities. Playing is a lot more than just hitting and fielding."

Early in 1985, ground was broken for a multi-purpose building. That 43,000 square foot building was to include on the first floor an auditorium-gymnasium with stage and rooms for props, dressing and rehearsals, showers and lockers, recreation rooms, kitchen and cafeteria. The second floor was designed to house classrooms at one end and faculty accommodations at the other.

Outreach was always emphasized at La Reina. In 1986 for example, students and teachers demonstrated their mission spirit by raising $6,000 or an average of $14 for every student. Class competition, teacher enthusiasm and effective publicity accounted for the success of that program.

A full activities agenda complemented the regular curriculum. The Christian service program encouraged student participation in parish and community activities and a chapter of Amnesty International awakened student awareness to human rights and their violations.

LA REINA HIGH SCHOOL

La Reina High School opened on September 8, 1964 under the patronage of Our Lady by the Sisters of Notre Dame who felt that the growing Conejo Valley needed a Catholic secondary school for girls.

A classroom building was finished in 1964, with the administration and library building being completed in April of 1965. To accommodate courses with the proper laboratories, another structure with a chapel was added in 1967. James Francis Cardinal McIntyre dedicated the school on October 15, 1967.

Located in Thousand Oaks, La Reina offered a comprehensive curriculum with classical, scientific, cultural, secretarial and vocational courses. The campus was a fifty-acre parcel of land located near Moorpark Road and the Ventura Freeway.

The attractive buildings, contemporary in design, were among the most functional in the archdiocese. To give students a greater understanding and retention of all phases of the curriculum, a multi-sensory approach was implemented in 1972 and media centers were located around the campus.

LA SALLE HIGH SCHOOL

In its issue for November 11, 1955, *The Tidings*, official Catholic newspaper for the Archdiocese of Los Angeles, announced that "a new Catholic high school for boys, La Salle High School, will be opened by the Christian Brothers in the fall of 1956 "just inside Pasadena's eastern city limits at Sierra Madre and Michelinda Boulevards."

Located on what had been the Hastings Ranch area, the school would accommodate 400 students. The initial building included ten classrooms, two labs, a study hall, drafting room, cafeteria, locker room and offices.

Like other secondary schools erected in that era, the Youth Education Fund that James Francis Cardinal McIntyre established to further the Catholic educational apostolate in Southern California financed La Salle.

The initial academic program encompassed religion, Latin, Spanish, English, algebra, public speaking and life science. Freshmen and sophomores were required to participate in physical education sessions daily. And after sessions, intramural league was sponsored for a large group of interested students. School athletes who fulfilled the designated requirements were awarded the official school "LS" letter and were permitted to wear the official red and blue school sweater. By November of 1956, a track, baseball diamond and football field had been completed as well as a large parking lot.

Two years later, ground was broken for a 16,000 square foot gymnasium which was to double as an auditorium. That structure was of pre-cast concrete construction and included bleachers seating 800 people, a large stage, music room and assembly hall. Large posters announced that the new auditorium would be the "home court" of the La Salle Lancers.

The number of parishes represented at La Salle totaled twenty-four. Soon the Lancers were leading contenders for championships in both basketball and baseball. The newest sport added to the athletic program was a try in "cross country." The school even boasted its own broadcasting station.

In 1959, the first year with a graduating class, the school began offering a special program for parents who wanted to advance their sons' skills in reading, listening, comprehension and independent study enhanced. Literature seminars soon became a staple on the campus. Capacity at La Salle reached 430 in 1960.

Promotional literature told potential students in 1962 that La Salle was composed of "a qualified and dedicated faculty of Christian Brothers and Catho-

lic layman trained in the arts of communication, science and the arts." The school offered a basic curriculum of theology, natural sciences and foreign languages in addition to the traditional subjects. An extra-curricular program included inter-scholastic athletics, journalism, forensics, an artist's guild and intramural clubs.

The Youth Educational Fund added a new wing in 1966. The Parents Association participated in providing part of the cost. The projected library was to have 10,000 books.

When San Gabriel Mission closed its boys' department in September of 1970, the students were welcomed at La Salle. The merger proved to be a great boost and allowed for increased facilities and wider curricular choices.

Officials at La Salle began a formal fund raising program in 1972 to place the institution on a more secure financial footing. That program helped to define to the community the necessity and worth of Catholic schools.

La Salle, coeducational since September of 1991, serves students from Sierra Madre, Arcadia, Monrovia, Altadena and Pasadena.

LOUISVILLE HIGH SCHOOL

The Sisters of Saint Louis announced plans for a new Catholic girls' academy in Woodland Hills in May of 1959. The college preparatory school was to be built on property adjacent to a convent at 22300 Mulholland Drive.

The following September, the school began its first semester with approximately 100 freshmen girls. First buildings on the scenic campus included an administration unit, a classroom wing and a science wing. Other structures were also in the planning stage.

Early in the school's life, arrangements were made for students to travel to Europe. Besides the opportunity of perfecting their French and visiting places of cultural and religious interest, the young travelers were afforded a chance to see their compeers at work and play as they visited other schools operated by the Louisville Sisters in France, Belgium, England and Ireland.

According to an early brochure, the school offered college prep, commercial and general high school courses in an academic program that included religion, English, mathematics, science, Latin, French, Spanish, social studies and business, as well as instruction in music, art, drama and homemaking.

Probably the most outstanding and distinctive feature of the school was a six-foot marble statue of Our Lady as Queen of the Universe that was enshrined above a reflection pool at the school's entrance.

Situated on a gentle curve of a gravel country road in the Santa Monica mountains, Louisville High School provided a picturesque setting amidst giant oak and pepper trees which cast their shadows against Spanish tile roofs.

In 1961, work began on a new classroom building and multi-purpose auditorium with connecting brick and concrete walkways. The auditorium provided seats for upwards of a thousand persons. Intended for student assemblies, concerts, dramas and other related presentations, the contemporary Spanish style buildings formed a "U" around existing shrubs on the twelve-acre hillside campus.

By 1964, eighty-percent of the school's graduates were bound for colleges throughout the nation. Another ten-percent easily found employment in the valley and the remaining ten-percent applied for entry into Louisville Novitiate as postulants. The total enrollment for that year was 470.

Early in the life of the school, an annual "Friendship Brunch" was inaugurated on the campus. Louisville chorus and madrigal singers provided entertainment for the event which became a hallmark of the school.

In 1972, Timothy Cardinal Manning visited Louisville where he offered Holy Mass and shared luncheon with the seniors. He met each of the young ladies and shared with them some of the history of the area and of the Sisters, most of whom came from his native Ireland. He returned eight years later to participate in the school's twentieth anniversary.

A feature story in *The Tidings* for December 3, 1982, noted that there were fifty-two teachers; one priest, nine Sisters and forty-two lay teachers. The writer told how the school was named for Saint Louis IX of France, the patron of the Sisters who started the school. "Louisville stands slightly above the roadway imparting to its students a sharply focused, full-dimensioned vision of life. Louisville is truly a Christian community."

In 1985, the school sponsored a Mock Trial wherein fifteen student barristers advanced to the semi-finals in the countrywide mock trial competition for the second year in a row. Many of the girls went on to formal law schools. In 1996, Louisville High School was designated a National Blue Ribbon School of Excellence.

LOYOLA HIGH SCHOOL

Established in 1911, Loyola High School is the oldest secondary institution for boys in the Archdiocese of Los Angeles. It came about when the Jesuits succeeded the Vincentians as the southland's educators of teenage boys.

With the removal of Loyola College (now University) to Westchester, the Tudor Gothic buildings on Venice Boulevard, erected and blessed in 1917, were devoted to the training of youngsters. It was envisioned as a "feeder" to the university.

The ideal of the school was that of training young men to be Christian gentlemen of character. In a brochure published in 1940, it was stated that "under the Jesuit system the faculty strives to develop a boy in habits of accuracy of mind and strength of will; to train him to think clearly and correctly, and to express his thoughts in accurate and forceful language; to teach him the culture that extends beyond the pleasures of the external senses to those of the mind.

That the school succeeded in its goals is evident from statistics that show that 2,274 alumni served their country during World War II. Over thirty were killed in action, others were missing in action and a number were wounded.

During the 1950 Holy Year, twenty-one students left Los Angeles by train for a pilgrimage to Rome. Loyola High Sodality sponsored the pilgrims. Enroute to the Vatican the group traveled through Portugal and Spain.

In 1952, some new classrooms, together with a physics and microchemistry laboratory were added to the Venice Boulevard campus. Complete renovation of the school's third floor was a feature of the renewal program.

In that same year, a newspaper article reported that the "study of the Catholic faith and military training are compulsory for four years. The classical and scientific curriculum of the school is built around mathematics and the natural sciences and four years of Latin."

Three years later, a new library, complete with 8,000 volumes became available. Including four classrooms, the Crosby Memorial Library was of modern Tudor design blending with the other academic buildings on the Jesuit campus.

Over the years, students excelled in a host of activities. In 1950, seniors won $40,000 in scholarships. Each year they engaged in a "Food for Christmas" campaign for the poor and in one year alone, five seniors were nominated to United States military academies. One year, thirteen graduates entered seminaries.

The football stadium was renovated in 1957 for the 900 enrollees, many of whom took an active part in the "Cubs," the football team. When the school began its forty-eighth year, in 1958, the student roster was advanced another dozen.

Further renovation came in 1961 with three new modern buildings and a main classroom complex renovated to conform to modern ordinances. Replacing an earlier auditorium on 15th Street was a new science and chemistry facility. The old gym was also outfitted with new lockers and shower rooms. A modern two-story dormitory was built for boarders.

A gala golden jubilee for Loyola High School was observed in 1961 at Blessed Sacrament Church in Hollywood. In his homily for the Mass, the Jesuit provincial told how the school was a continuation of the educational work begun in 1865.

In 1964, Xavier Center was blessed. It was a new $500,000 auditorium financed by donations from friends, parents and alumni. A cafeteria was included in the new complex with accommodations for 1,000 at lunch or dinner.

In 1975 Hahn Center was dedicated to house the school's theology and fine arts department, along with space for the campus ministers. It also provided space for student and faculty lounges. There has been extensive building on the campus in recent years.

MARYMOUNT HIGH SCHOOL

In 1923, Bishop John J. Cantwell asked the Religious of the Sacred Heart of Mary of Tarrytown, New York, to establish a school of quality Catholic education for young ladies in the distinguished Marymount tradition. The Sisters purchased the Brockman home on West 28th Street and it was there that Marymount in-the-West opened its doors to five students.

Before long, it became evident that additional space was needed to accommodate the increasing student enrollment. A five-and-a-half-acre parcel of land was acquired across from UCLA in the Bel Air

district and, on February 2, 1932, the bishop dedicated the institution.

Over the years, the present campus was home to Marymount Junior School (which moved to its location in Brentwood in 1947) and to Marymount College, which relocated in Palos Verdes in 1960.

Since 1960, extensive restoration, renovation and construction have provided the high school with the facilities to respond to the educational challenges of a busy era. Cantwell Hall, built in 1936, housed an auditorium and science department and Butler Hall, erected in 1947, originally had quarters for boarders. The latter was transformed into the Leavey Arts Center at a later date, providing photography and language labs, art and ceramic studios and a fashion design center.

In 1982, at the culmination of its first fifty years, the Cultural Heritage Board of Los Angeles announced that Marymount's chapel, high school and auditorium, in their graceful Spanish style, had been named a Historic Monument. The school draws students from Beverly Hills, Bel-Air, Brentwood, Malibu and Pacific Palisades.

A private, independent, all girls' Catholic school, Marymount is a college preparatory institution committed to a quality education that is stimulating and challenging in essence. Its primary goal is that of developing in students a sense of personal worth and dignity; a creative inquisitive mind, a love of scholarship, a global perspective, an appreciation of the aesthetic thus providing competent and caring leaders for the modern age.

Christian service outside the classroom became a hallmark at Marymount. In 1982, upwards of fifty students were performing volunteer work on weekends or after school helping the hospitalized, the handicapped and the aged at a dozen locations. The young ladies learned how to be tolerant, patient and giving to their fellow human beings. Collections of food and clothing were made at both Thanksgiving and Christmas.

The academic program at Marymount kept pace. Girls learned how to use their time well and to probe, evaluate and work hard. Each semester students had to successfully complete a minimum of six courses, including religious studies and four courses from the English, foreign languages, mathematics, science and social studies departments.

There was also a full honors requirement along with several elective courses. Girls were given the opportunity of taking Advanced

Placement courses and the UCLA honors program in the senior year allowed still a further option.

In 1998 Roger Cardinal Mahony celebrated Mass at the school marking its seventy-fifth anniversary. Over a thousand members of the Marymount community, including parents, alumnae, faculty and friends attended that gala event. There were 373 enrollees in that year.

MAYFIELD SENIOR SCHOOL

The secondary phase of Mayfield School for girls was established in 1931 by the Sisters of the Holy Child of Jesus. Situated at 443 South Euclid Avenue in Pasadena, it proved to be conveniently accessible by car, bus and, at the time, the Pacific Electric Railway.

The school was named after its sister-school in Mayfield, Sussex, England. Staffed by the Sisters of the Society of the Holy Child of Jesus, it began with an educational philosophy, traditions and history first enunciated by Cornelia Connelly in 1862.

Her educational programs were progressive and innovative. Believing in education that is available to all classes, she created a system of internal government that stressed individuality for each student. Girls were trained in culture, drama, and all the normal basics, together with poise, self-control and confidence.

Early on, the Sisters identified Pasadena as a place for a school unlike the normal parochial or public school. And there were families there who wanted a program that combined high quality academics with the advantages of Christian training.

A new building for Mayfield was planned in 1950 when the campus was transferred to the former estate of John H. Eagle at 500 Bellfontaine Street. Auxiliary Bishop Joseph T. McGucken blessed the chapel there in November of 1950, dedicated to the memory of Guy Williamson. The next month, James Francis Cardinal McIntyre blessed the school itself.

When the new facilities were occupied, plans were announced for classes in ceramics, home economics and speech in addition to the regular courses previously on the curriculum.

With the inauguration of its twenty-second year, in 1952, there were further alterations at the school, including changes in the library. The French department was enlarged and classes in Spanish were enhanced.

In 1954, Cardinal McIntyre blessed a further addition at Mayfield. That two-story wing consisted of an auditorium, four classrooms and several music rooms. In the south wing was a dining room. The playground was also enlarged. By the time of the school's silver jubilee, the enrollment at Mayfield was 352 students.

Plans for a million dollar expansion program were announced in 1963. The large home on the new 4-1/2 acre site adjoining the present campus was converted to school use. The school then occupied a whole city block on the sunny side of Pasadena. With the acquisition of the former Warner estate, the school had a more sweeping, spacious look.

Students were engaged in community service, some working to care for families of those in prison and others working to help feed the hungry. The girls were also associated with the American Field Service program for exchange students. In 1991, Tannis Ann Turrentine was chosen over 700 fellow contestants as the 1992 Rose Queen. Extensive building has been done on the campus in recent years.

NOTRE DAME ACADEMY

Plans were announced in the summer of 1950 for opening Notre Dame Academy High School for girls in West Los Angeles. A new structure was underway and its doors were opened that fall. Until completion of the new facilities, classes were conducted in the grade school section of the academy on Overland Avenue.

The high school division had begun in September of 1949 when the ninth grade was added to the curriculum. The new three-story building was built of reinforced brick and concrete in the modern colonial architectural theme. There were eight standard classrooms, a library, offices, and cafeteria, art, music, home economics and business rooms. Auxiliary Bishop Timothy Manning blessed Notre Dame Academy on November 30, 1952.

By 1956, there were 430 young ladies enrolled at Notre Dame, representing twenty-nine neighboring parishes. The beautiful chapel, seating 230, dominated the entire school layout and emphasized the religious atmosphere of the school.

Four basic courses were offered: college or nursing preparation, secretarial training, general non-collegiate courses and homemaking. Extra-curricular opportunities included the Sodality of Our Lady, the Legion of Mary, Student Council, Glee Club, Dramatic Club, Forensic League, California Scholarship Federation and the Girls' Athletic Association. Other offerings abounded and included a journalistic program through work on the school paper. The school was accredited with the University of California.

Gearing themselves to meet the renewed emphasis on intellectual excellence, student leaders at Notre Dame planned a program of activities directly related to the needs of the time.

Enrollment continued to grow. In 1963, the numbers advanced dramatically. For the first time, candidates for the school were turned away.

In 1975, educators at Notre Dame inaugurated a pilot program that allowed students to take classes by telephone. The innovation was the result of the Pacific Bell Telephone technology. The company installed a conference telephone at several campuses, which allowed for amplification of the speaker's voice. A microphone allowed talking by the student. The Los Angeles Community College district provided the speaker's voice.

A local newspaper proclaimed in 1983 that Notre Dame Academy was "one of the most creative and influential communities in the nation." Its six-acre campus was walking distance from Century City where many decisions of power and entertainment are determined. Seniors were obliged to devote a minimum of twenty-hours weekly to Christian service.

Over the years, girls won trophies from the Drama Teachers Association of Southern California, the National Achievement Scholarship Program and the United Crusade Art Context. By the time of its golden jubilee, Notre Dame Academy had twice won the national Blue Ribbon School designation. There were 480 girls attending the Academy in 1999.

A chapel/science lab and auditorium were added in 1956. The school also phased out its business, general and home economics tracts in 1969 and became strictly college preparatory. Extensive remodeling of the chapel and auditorium has been done in the last ten years.

NOTRE DAME HIGH SCHOOL

The formal dedication of Notre Dame High School in Sherman Oaks took place in October of 1948. In his inaugural address, Msgr. Bernard Dolan pointed out that Catholic schools are far ahead of public educational institutions. Noting that the first schools in the nation were religious, he deplored the godless type of education so prevalent in the secular sector.

The Holy Cross Brothers were in charge of the school. In the opening class on the twenty-acre campus were 125 boys and the following year that number rose to 280 youngsters from thirty-five parishes in the San Fernando Valley.

The new classroom building accommodated 500 students and consisted of a cafeteria, faculty offices, athletic and storage rooms and fourteen spacious classrooms. Athletic facilities included a football field, cinder track and a baseball diamond.

A new auditorium was added in 1950 with seating capacity for 1,800 persons. It was the third building on the growing Sherman Oaks campus. Its exterior followed the modern Spanish type of architecture.

An arts and drama section were added in 1951 in an overall curriculum that envisioned graduates continuing their education at the college and university level. Provisions were made for those whose formal education would terminate with high school.

With another building added in 1956, the school began anticipating an enrollment of 1,200. New campus sights included a residence wing to the faculty house and an enlarged chapel for the Brothers. A new system of outside lights on the football gridiron and additional handball courts were well received by the students.

By 1957, the roster had grown by 900% to help accommodate San Fernando Valley's growth. Statistics asserted that the Valley was "perhaps America's fastest growing population center." A steady stream of additions and expansions had characterized the school since its inception.

A beautiful statue of Our Lady of Grace was added in 1958. Located in the plaza area, it became the focal center of the school. A large directory with changeable letters was placed in the corridor outside the administration offices.

Students returning in 1959 found that in the math and science curriculum, the latest recommendations of the National Science Foundation had been added. The address at 13645 Riverside Drive had become a measure of pride for students and graduates alike.

The machine age was reflected at Notre Dame. Increased speed and comprehension in reading was the object of the new Craig Reader, a device looking much like a portable television which automatically preserved scientific programmed reading material.

Students at Notre Dame took an active part in outside activities too. For example, in 1971 more than ninety upperclassmen were involved in the school's religious outreach program. Their volunteer work took them to North Hollywood, Valley Presbyterian Hospital, Regis House and other local areas.

Statistics indicated that in 1972, there were more than 4200 alumni of the school distinguishing themselves as community leaders. Students were carrying the ND banner and tradition into all kinds of leadership and service positions.

Among the outstanding youngsters were Jay Whitney who received first place in the annual Future Engineer's competitions, Anthony Riolo who earned first place in the mathematics division of the San Fernando Valley Science Fair and Bernard Kutscher and Ronald Mullin who took first place in the state finals of the American Legion oratorical contest.

In 1998, Roger Cardinal Mahony challenged students at Notre Dame to continue "to nourish and develop young minds and to bring together continually a school community that will care for and nourish minds and souls."

The school, which is now co-educational, is a Blue Ribbon School of Excellence.

PROVIDENCE HIGH SCHOOL

Located in Burbank, Providence High School was founded late in 1955 in a modern building, its design and décor harmonizing perfectly with the surrounding area. A combination of contemporary materials and construction methods was combined with the best features of school planning. Comprised of three wings, the central building was two stories in height overlooking the City of Burbank and the San Fernando Valley. The fireproof structure had air conditioning, forced heat and ventilation and had acoustically treated ceilings with indirect lighting and asphalt floor finishing.

The girls' school opened in 1955 at the corner of Riverside Drive and Buena Vista Street under the direction of the Sisters of Providence. It had accommodations for 500 students in ten classrooms, library, study hall, chemistry laboratory, typing and bookkeeping rooms, and space for art crafts, dramatics and music. There was a meditation chapel, an outside grotto and beautifully landscaped grounds.

The Sisters of Charity of Providence staffed the seventh Catholic high school in the San Fernando Valley. The whole complex was located adjacent to Saint Joseph Hospital.

Once a part of the 4000-acre Rancho Providencia, the high school was dedicated on November 25, 1956 by James Francis Cardinal McIntyre. With all its modern and artistic design, the new school was a very practical and functional plant. The domestic science department was equipped with the latest cooking and sewing machines. The sewing room had a podium with a triple view mirror, six sewing machines, large cutting tables and cabinets.

In its philosophy, Providence High School pledged to provide an education based on Christian principles as expressed in Catholic tradition. The school recognized that the claim to education is the right of each individual and that the students were unique individuals with abilities, insights and needs."

There were an active co-curricular and extra events from the earliest years. Organizations at the school included student council, campus ministry, honor society, drama club, speech and debate, choir, cheerleading, varsity and intramural sports, publications, a literary magazine and student yearbook.

In 1959, there were 500 enrollees at the Burbank campus. In addition to preparatory college courses, were opportunities for further work in commerce, art, home economics and music. Outside activities were geared to the needs of the young ladies of that era.

The school welcomed boys in 1974 and thereafter the athletics program earned them a place in the CIF playoffs. After dominating the Liberty League for years and winning in a goodly percentage of its games, the team earned plaudits in the archdiocesan playoffs. Consistently earning maximum accreditation with the Western Association of Schools and Colleges, Providence graduates won high honors in a host of professional careers.

The enrollment took a dip in the 1980s, but later the prospects improved and the spirit of excellence helped to keep the school on its course of high academic accomplishments. A large part of the credit was due to the spirit of discipline. One teacher explained that "discipline is not something we do to a student, it's something we enforce. Discipline has everything to do with guidance and nothing to do with punishment."

Over the years, youngsters at the Blue Ribbon School excelled in a wide range of activities. In 1966, Penny Moriarty received a medal from Governor Edmund G. Brown as a state finalist in the Veterans of Foreign Wars Voice of Democracy contest and, in 1980, Robert Vega was a Providence medallist for outstanding service to his fellow students and lay employees.

RAMONA SECONDARY SCHOOL

Ramona Secondary School, a resident and day institution for girls, traces its history back to 1889 when it was founded by the Sisters of the Holy Names of Jesus and Mary. It soon became a foremost place among the educational institutions in Southern California. Situated in the historic and picturesque San Gabriel Valley, its extensive campus makes it one of the most beautiful academic centers in all of California.

From the very outset, the purpose of the school was "to cultivate in its students a high regard for scholarship; to awaken in them an appreciation of the cultural richness of their Catholic heritage; to develop individuality and a right attitude towards social obligations in the home and in civic life; to mould characters which will be animated by Christian principles of action and guided by the moral standards which the Catholic Church upholds as the foundation for right living."

One of Ramona's graduates recalled in 1974 that the convent had opened with seven boarders and nine day students. Since that time, 4,000 girls had been graduated and the school's enrollment included 548 day students and seventy residents. The oldest of the institution's graduates, Eugenia Castruccio, left Ramona in 1901. The secondary department of Ramona Convent dates from 1973.

In 1976, the grandson of James deBarth Shorb, the original benefactor, broke ground for two new buildings in Alhambra. He recalled on that occasion that the school had been named for Ramona Shorb.

Even by then Ramona was the oldest school of its kind under continuous operation on the same site in California. Its first day students came in two-wheel donkey carts and horse drawn carriages, little dreaming that their successors would arrive in self-powered automobiles.

The multi-purpose gymnasium and a sixteen-classroom structure dating from 1980 indicate the modernity of the old school whose alumnae rosters read like a history book. By the 1980s, alumnae were in the forefront of Christian service programs and anti-abortion groups.

It was a sad day in 1986 when the historic building, which housed the original, Ramona Convent yielded to the demolishers. Alumnae gathered one last time to view the wonderful old edifice that was so much a part of the southland's land and arts cape. In a moving eulogy, Mildred Harrigan wrote: "Change, change – always change - and so much of it has not been advantageous. It is traumatic but, like the elegant dowagers of yesteryear, we are told that you must fold your silken skirts about you and fade away into history." The new buildings, like fledging grandchildren sprang up on the hill.

In 1988, groundbreaking ceremonies were held for an administration building that would house the chapel, dining area and other needed rooms. The next year, Roger Cardinal Mahony went to Alhambra for the centennial of Ramona.

The personal achievements of past pupils are truly remarkable. Their vigorous efforts for the promotion of civic and intellectual advancement in their local communities are a splendid tribute to the educational work done by their alma mater, a Blue Ribbon School.

SAINT FRANCIS HIGH SCHOOL

Plans were announced in 1946 for the Capuchin friars to open a secondary boarding school for boys in La Canada. Initially, the school was to be primarily a minor seminary. Located in the former Flintridge Country Club building at La Canada-Verdugo Road, the school would be named Saint Francis. The courses offered were geared to college preparation. Boys were also accepted into the high school section who did not wish to pursue a vocation to religious life.

In October 1955, plans were unveiled for a new reinforced concrete eight-classroom building at Saint Francis. Architecturally, the new structure matched the décor of the existing buildings. Because of the new Foothill Freeway, the school's address was changed to La Canada. The enrollment that year numbered 285 youngsters.

Twenty-two parishes were represented in the student body, most of them in the San Gabriel Valley. The chapel was reconfigured with pews to accommodate ninety boys, with another twelve pews in the choir. A local company in Altadena donated beautiful stained glass windows.

The first decade at Saint Francis was quite impressive. Progress was noted in an expanded facility, increased enrollment and, above all, by the quality of the academic curriculum. Added during that period were administration offices, a new lighted football field and an expanded athletic stadium.

In the years that followed, the number of boys grew considerably. To accommodate an envisioned 370 enrollment, an older building was remodeled. In the scholastic field, four students won college scholarships in one year and two received appointments to Annapolis Naval Academy and the Colorado Air Force Academy.

In 1961, word went out "St. Francis sat the Fastest United States Clocking" which meant that the school's basketball team went unbeaten in thirty-three consecutive league meets. Saint Francis won both inside and outside the Parochial League.

The school observed its twentieth anniversary by completing a new three-story structure. The unit contained six classrooms and two science laboratories. The old Flintridge Country Club was demolished to make room for counseling offices. By 1985, students were volunteering at local centers helping the developmentally disabled. It was part of the community outreach of the campus ministry program, with nearly ninety students involved. Others were working with the American Cancer Society and visiting the elderly in rest homes and local hospitals.

SAINT JOHN BOSCO HIGH SCHOOL

Salesians brought to California their motto: "prevention before cure becomes necessary." Their apostolate showered attention on boys mostly of the working class who, because of their conditions and environment, are easiest prey to bad example. The overall philosophy was and is that such boys need only a proper home, good companions, friendly teachers and a fatherly hand that gently guides them through the most dangerous stage of their lives.

Saint John Bosco High School, established in 1940, occupied a forty-five acre campus at 13640 South Bellflower Boulevard, about a mile north of the community of Bellflower.

The autonomous high school unit was ready for occupancy in 1954. A three-story building was dedicated with accommodations for both day and resident students. College preparatory, business and machine shop courses were offered. A chapel was also erected and to its rear were expanded classrooms. The central building had quarters for laboratories as well as facilities for visual aids. In 1954, there were already 225 students, including sixty boarders.

Subsequent expansion provided for shops, typing and driver education followed a year or so later. Generally the school followed the traditional Christian education system modeled on Saint John Bosco himself.

After another five years of consecutive expansion, a new four-classroom building was erected in 1957. A football field and quarter mile track were part of the new features. A watering system allowed for irrigating the six-acre campus. For the first time, Saint John Bosco's team competed in the football section of the Olympic League.

By 1958, the school, located in one of the fastest growing suburbs of Los Angeles, accounted for 500 boys on its roster. The school was described as striving "only for the highest standards." Endeavoring to influence the minds of its students, Saint John Bosco High School formed the minds, trained their will and fostered their Christian life.

School activities and organizations included a well-regulated athletic program, sodalities, choir and band, student council, a mono-gram club, a dramatics and a speech club and such recreational facilities such as swimming and horseback riding.

The new 1,000-seat auditorium-gymnasium was scheduled for completion late in 1961. Over 500 students made use of the newly erected building with its smooth hardwood floor and regulation courts. In 1963, 170 new freshmen were added to the student body, pushing the total enrollment to approximately 600. In that year, students hailed from fifteen states and several nations.

An article in the local Catholic newspaper told how, in 1983, students took to the streets in an attempt to assist the poor in down-town Los Angeles on Skid Row. Each semester from thirty to sixty youngsters could be found working on Wednesday morning in the Catholic Worker Soup Kitchen. The boys took turns chopping onions, dicing mushrooms and spooning out soup in an all-out Christian assault on poverty. By 1990, Saint John Bosco High School was one of the premier Catholic secondary schools in Southern California.

SAINT LUCY'S PRIORY HIGH SCHOOL

The secondary school under the patronage of Saint Lucy is operated by the Benedictine Sisters in Glendora. It offers a liberal curri-culum, intelligent guidance and a thoroughly Catholic philosophy of life. In the words of Pope Pius XI, it will "endeavor to develop the physical and spiritual, mental and moral, domestic and social per-sonality of the young girl."

Situated in the foothills of the San Gabriel Mountains, overlooking Sierra Madre Avenue, between Ben Lomond and Grand Avenues, it's setting is majestic, its classical lines of architecture following the deeply engraved character of Benedictine culture.

The Sisters acquired the Mall Villa in 1952. Later they purchased property from the Silent Ranch Estate for the purpose of building their

high school. The institution opened in 1962 with an initial enrollment of sixty girls. The facilities on the twenty-acre campus began with a tri-level, 6,000 square foot brick schoolhouse.

The concrete and brick structure was trimmed with ceramic tile. Three levels were necessary because of the hillside site. Initially, there was a library, study hall, language booths, physics and chemistry labs, a small theatre and quarters for music, art, ceramics and lunch. Long range plans called for a chapel, auditorium, music hall, gymnasium and guests quarters. The school's stated aim was to mould "the mental, moral, physical, social and especially spiritual" fabric of its students.

James Francis Cardinal McIntyre dedicated the school on February 2, 1964. Clearly the Benedictine spirit was reflected in the architectural design, a combination of classical and contemporary.

From the beginning, Saint Lucy's had one of the largest and best-equipped school libraries in California. It was given to the school by George B. Gillson of San Francisco. The language laboratory was a gift of the Raskob Foundation and Saint Lucy's Guild donated the furnishings.

On the hillside behind the school is a terraced lawn that was envisioned as an assembly area. On the higher level is a locker-shower building and playing fields.

SAINT MARY'S ACADEMY

Originally opened in 1889, at 21st Street and Grand Avenue, Saint Mary's Academy later occupied a ten-acre tract at what is now Slauson Avenue and Crenshaw Boulevard. It was dedicated in 1911 by Bishop Thomas J. Conaty. By 1940, there were five modern buildings equipped with every available facility for the teaching of girls. The ample campus afforded opportunities for swimming, tennis, basketball, volleyball, archery and other sports. Athletic recreation was encouraged as conducive to health, poise and wholesome appearance.

The four-year secondary course was early accredited by the University of California with three courses offered: Latin-Scientific, Literary, and Elective. A pre-secretarial course was also available as an elective.

In 1950, the student body at Saint Mary's was received into the League of the Sacred Heart. Each student pledged herself to recite the daily Morning Offering and to make frequent Communions of reparation to the Sacred Heart.

A new uniform was introduced in 1950. It had the Eton look about it – navy-blue wool suit, white blouse, class tie and blue and white shoes. There was no derby in the outfit but each class wore a different color tie.

The student body was cosmopolitan with young ladies from every part of the United States registering. The enrollment reached 1,150 in 1956, the largest in the school's history. The school was located at 3300 West Slauson Boulevard and the area served was the southwest part of Los Angeles.

The golden jubilee class set all kinds of records: Eighteen girls earned life membership in the California Scholarship Federation. Five graduates boasted "honors at entrance" at Mount Saint Mary's College and others won places in the annual Bank of America's regional awards.

The overall program at Saint Mary's allowed young ladies to take an active part in spiritual, scholastic, social and athletic functions. Languages featured were Latin, French and Spanish. Chemistry and Physics formed part of the science program.

Relocated at Prairie and Grace Avenue, the new campus was closer to Daniel Freeman Hospital, which was also operated by the Sisters of Saint Joseph of Carondelet. It was in 1965 that the school moved to the new campus near Saint John's Chrysosom Church in Inglewood. A two-story building complex was built to accommodate students. Facilities included auditorium-gymnasium, chapel and class-rooms. The old familiar landmark at Slauson and Crenshaw fell to the path of progress, its campus torn down to make way for a shopping center.

Over many years, girls at Saint Mary's were singled out for their excellence, academic and otherwise. In 1948, Doris Bursk won the prize for her poster adopted by the Holy Name Society; the next year, the school itself was given a scholastic award by UCLA based on outstanding academic accomplishments in a given year and, in 1953, seniors Johanna Randall and Donna Dunne won first and third place in the Los Angeles County contest for the Association of American Physicians.

VILLANOVA PREPARATORY SCHOOL

Advertised as "a Catholic resident and day school for boys." Villanova Prep School offers secondary courses in classics and science along with a thorough preparation for college courses. Located on 130 acres in the scenic Ojai Valley a healthful climate and extra-ordinarily natural beauty greatly enhances the institution that opened its doors in 1924.

Already by 1940, the school had grown considerably. A new gym-nasium and swimming pool were added to the original wing. Scholasti-cally the school has always ranked high. One survey showed Villanova Prep well above the average of all schools in the state.

Further construction was announced in 1947 when a dining hall and a modern kitchen were added. Existing buildings were renovated and in keeping with the school's needs, the athletic field was enlarged to six acres and boasted of a track and football field, baseball diamond and lawn tennis courts. The road was extended to the field and other buildings.

When students returned to school in 1949, the roster had grown from the original enrollment of forty boys to 125. Dormitory accommodations were enlarged and new stables, playing field and an outdoor swimming pool became part of the campus. Since its beginning Villanova was accredited by the University of California.

Conducted by the Augustinian Fathers and Brothers, Villanova continued offering fresh opportunities for its students with typing classes and public speaking. A new stage made it possible to present elaborate musical and dramatic works. In 1961, the Fathers Club Hall was opened at ceremonies attended by local community leaders, alumni and friends. The one story structure measured 24 by 60 feet.

A carved marble statue of its patron, Saint Thomas of Villanova, was unveiled at the school in August of 1955. Carved in Italy, the marble statue was placed in the center of the "island" before the entrance to Cantwell Hall.

In 1962, a three year building program was completed with the opening of a pre-fabricated steel building which provided a home for student activities, photography, newspaper and yearbook work. Known as Alumni Hall, the structure provided spacious living quarters for the custodial staff.

Goggin Hall was dedicated on November 6, 1966. Serving as the administration building, it was named to honor Terrence P. Goggin of Glendale, an alumnus of the Ojai School.

Villanova's fiftieth anniversary coincided with its 1000th graduate. Girls were admitted as day students in 1970 and, fifteen years later, the school made provisions for resident female students. Alumni from as far away as South America came to California to help celebrate Villanova's golden jubilee.

A feature story in a local newspaper in 1983 stated students get "benevolent discipline, heavy study load, a full sports program and a very good awareness of their community and the larger world around them."

Graduate William P. Clark, National Security Advisor for the Reagan Administration, attended services commemorating a new gymnasium in 1989. The construction of the 12,500 square foot gym was targeted for completion for the last decade of the twentieth century. The gymnasium had retractable seating for as many as 350 persons. The earlier gym, built in 1929, was reconditioned and used for other purposes.

ARCHDIOCESAN HIGH SCHOOLS

BELLARMINE JEFFERSON HIGH SCHOOL

Monsignor Martin Cody Keating laid the cornerstone for a new parochial high school in Burbank, named Bellarmine Jefferson, in 1945. The original building was parallel to Fifth Avenue. Msgr. Keating named the school after both St. Robert Bellarmine and Thomas Jefferson because of his intense interest in both men and in the ideals that he felt both Bellarmine and Jefferson held in common.

Many years of American history are built into the architectural design of Bellarmine Jefferson High School. The front entrance, foyer and tower, exact replicas of the same found in Philadelphia's Independence Hall, were added in 1950. The bricks used on the exterior walls conform in size and color to those used in the original structure of Independence Hall.

Inside the front door, the rotunda duplicates the foyer, stairway and balcony of Independence Hall. Rising high into the sky is a clock tower that can be seen for many blocks. The side of the clock facing east is permanently set at 8:00 PM to commemorate the signing of the Declaration of Independence on July 4, 1776. The side of the clock facing west is permanently set for 4:00 PM, the hour that the Constitution of the United States was signed on September 17, 1787.

Four years later, Monsignor Keating supervised the construction of the auditorium, modeled after the library of the University of Virginia, which was designed by Thomas Jefferson. Details on one

inside wall of St. Eleanor Hall repeat the floor plan of Independence Hall. There is a ceiling high alcove similar to the spot where Thomas Jefferson sat to sign the Declaration of Independence. The thirteen steps, leading to the auditorium entrance, represent the thirteen original colonies. In March 1980, the auditorium was dedicated as St. Eleanor Hall.

Although the buildings were early American in many architectural details, they were provided with all the modern facilities and educational aids. At the time, the high school was the tallest structure in Burbank.

Courses offered at the school followed the usual format, plus homemaking, sewing, consumer economics, art, general science and trigonometry. At the beginning of the 1950 term, there were students from every part of the San Fernando Valley in attendance.

By the mid-1970s, there were 500 boys and girls enrolled at Bellarmine Jefferson. A newspaper article about the school stated that students were "acutely conscious of their historical heritage from both the Church and the country." Since 1980, the school has been an archdiocesan institution.

BISHOP ALEMANY HIGH SCHOOL

The need for a Catholic secondary school had long been felt in the northern end of the San Fernando Valley. According to an article in *The Tidings* for April 4, 1949, the official newspaper for the Archdiocese of Los Angeles, it was Auxiliary Bishop Joseph McGucken who first recommended a high school "in the west end of the valley."

When the quadrangle area of San Fernando Mission had been restored in the late 1940s educational officials for the archdiocese began planning for a high school in the newly rebuilt facilities. When Saint Ferdinand's High School opened in 1950, it was staffed by the Sisters of Saint Joseph of Carondelet who acquired a residence at 1029 Coronel Street in San Fernando.

In a feature newspaper article about the rebuilt facilities at San Fernando Mission, which appeared on January 24, 1950, a writer noted, "that the mission is now being used as a high school." He went on to note how appropriate it was that the school was located "at the same site where Indian children were taught manual arts, reading and writing by the friars."

In a letter sent for *Recuerdos*, the 1954 student yearbook for the high school, Archbishop J. Francis A. McIntyre said that "the privilege of taking a high school course under the shadow of the Old Mission of San Fernando, has been a highly prized favor and I am confident that many blessings have come to the graduating class from their proximity to this relic of our faith.

As the school's enrollment began expanding, relocation became a paramount goal. The opening of the archdiocesan seminary on adjoining property in 1954 provided a paramount reason why Saint Ferdinand's High School would need a separate campus, one that would also have accommodations for boys. When Cardinal McIntyre announced the opening of the Youth Education Fund in 1956, the relocation of the high school was given top priority among the projected schools.

In *The Tidings* for February 3, 1956, it was announced that Saint Ferdinand's High School, now a girl's school, would "become co-instructional when it moves to a new campus this fall." At the same time, officials at the archdiocesan school system also made it known that the Sisters of Saint Joseph of Carondelet would continue teaching the girls, with the Oblates of Mary Immaculate teaching the boys.

Originally, the new campus located to the north of the seminary across Rinaldi, was to retain its original title. A sign erected at the site proclaimed, "Saint Ferdinand's High School is to be built on this site." However, hoping to appeal to a larger geographical section of the Valley, officials agreed to Cardinal McIntyre's suggestion, made on April 26, 1956, that the co-instructional school would be named after Joseph Sadoc Alemany, the Spanish-born Bishop of Monterey.

By 1959, there were a thousand students at Alemany. A new building erected that year had provision for a science lecture hall, four classrooms and other facilities for the rapidly growing student body. The co-instructional archdiocesan high school had students from twenty-one parishes, most of them in the San Fernando Valley.

As the years moved on, new offerings were made to the curriculum. The field of social sciences was enriched by a course in political and economic geography and homemakers for the future continued to find inspiration in a department that won national acclaim for its accomplishments.

In 1963, the tempo of the jet age was reflected in expanded programs that added Russian to the other foreign languages. An electronic reader accelerated work in remedial, developmental and advanced reading courses.

A new unit was added in 1966 containing additional teaching modules. Smaller classes permitted better teaching techniques. Art, ceramics, drafting, band and choral facilities were added, as well as counseling quarters and storage quarters.

Following the devastating 1994 Northridge earthquake, which destroyed the Rinaldi structures, the high school was relocated onto the spacious ground of nearby Queen of Angels seminary. When the seminary closed, Alemany High School occupied the entire campus, thus allowing it to become the largest Catholic school in the Archdiocese of Los Angeles. A new gymnasium was completed and readied for occupancy in 2001.

Students at the now co-educational high school were Academic Decathlon Regional Champions for 1996, 1997, 1998, 1999, 2000 and 2001.

BISHOP AMAT HIGH SCHOOL

Located in the Bassett-West Covina area, the high school bearing the name of Bishop Thaddeus Amat was begun in 1957 as part of the archdiocesan Youth Education Fund. The first six buildings were separated by an administration wing to close off the quadrangle.

Intended for both boys and girls at the secondary level, Bishop Amat was envisioned to serve a dozen parishes in northeastern San Gabriel Valley. Its acre campus is at Fairgrove and Orange Avenues in present day La Puente.

Originally the school was staffed by the Fathers of the Sacred Hearts of Jesus and Mary, the Sisters of Saint Louis of Monaghan, the Immaculate Heart Sisters and the Benedictine Sisters of Saint Lucy's Priory.

The initial unit included five contemporary-style, frame and stucco buildings grouped around a quad. Fourteen classrooms were available plus homemaking rooms and dean's offices. An attractive chapel adjoined the administration building.

In 1959, the capacity of Amat High School was doubled with another sixteen classrooms and a complete business education department. There were, at that time, 350 freshmen from fourteen parishes. All the new buildings matched the architectural scheme of the earlier structures.

The Lancer football team compiled an enviable record in those first years. At each game, the school band provided musical support at half time. The girls' prize winning drill team also became an important ingredient at sporting events.

James Francis Cardinal McIntyre dedicated the school in 1959, explaining that its patron was the founder of the Catholic educational system in what was then the Archdiocese of Los Angeles. In its third year, there were 800 enrollees at the school.

In 1962, a tilt-up concrete gymnasium-auditorium was ready for the student body which then numbered 1,300. The multi-purpose building would seat over 700 for basketball games and 1,300 for plays, assemblies and retreats.

The schools' multi-track curriculum offered college preparatory business and general courses. By 1962, it was accredited by the University of California and the Western Education Association.

Further expansion came a few years later with the addition of a unit providing a biology laboratory, guidance offices and utility rooms. The science department was equipped with updated features and the library boasted of over 6,000 volumes.

In 1973, Bishop Amat High School moved from a co-institutional to a co-instructional institution in practically all of its classes. The Business Management course was augmented by further studies and communicational arts. Approximately 95% of the school's graduates enrolled in colleges and the class of 1973 was awarded over a quarter million dollars in scholarships.

Bishop Amat High School was among sixty private secondary schools across the United States cited as "exemplary" by the Council for American Private Education in 1984. Schools were judged on their ability to aid students "intellectually, creatively, developmentally and artistically." They also won points for helping students "as growing human beings – their values, their goals, their character, what they believe in, where they are going, and why and how."

Between 1986 and 1990, students from La Puente emerged victorious four times in the Los Angeles County Academic Decathlon. Participants competed in ten categories including economics, fine arts, language and literature, mathematics, science, social science, speech, interview, essay and super quizzes.

BISHOP CONATY
OUR LADY OF LORETTO HIGH SCHOOL

The origin of Bishop Conaty High School can be traced to the early days of this century, when the parochial school of Saint Vibiana's Cathedral was expanded to include secondary classes for girls.

Bishop Thomas J. Conaty, a veteran educator and former Rector of The Catholic University of America, had long wanted to provide such opportunities for the then Diocese of Monterey-Los Angeles and it was he who encouraged the initial steps along those lines.

With the cessation of World War I, Conaty's successor, Bishop John J. Cantwell, approached the Sisters of the Immaculate Heart of Mary with a proposal to purchase the grounds on which their former academy was located as a site for a new diocesan school.

The Sisters had already transferred most of their own educational facilities to Hollywood and the earlier site on Pico Boulevard was thought to be an ideal place for inaugurating a secondary school for girls.

In 1922, Cantwell formally announced plans to adopt a modified form of the "central high school idea" used by Bishop Philip McDevett in Philadelphia. The idea was to accept young ladies from all over the city on a competitive basis.

Cantwell's announcement of plans to erect a new facility in Pico Heights was well received by the local Catholic populace. The old building was razed and in November 1922, the cornerstone was set in place for the new Los Angeles Catholic Girls High School.

In his address for the occasion, Joseph Scott explained the purpose of the establishment and how it was envisioned as the focal point of a whole new educational thrust for the Church in Southern California. Father Peter C. Yorke, the highly respected "labor" priest from San Francisco, then delivered an eloquent panegyric on the necessity of a Catholic education, pointing out that "the first American schools and colleges were religious and we are following the best American traditions when we build schools like this to give fair play to our children…."

The Tudor Gothic structure was hailed by local newspapers as one of the "finest buildings of its kind in all the west." And indeed it became the showpiece of Cantwell's tenure, visited by politicians, celebrities and such churchmen as Patrick Cardinal Hayes and Archbishop Diomede Fumasoni Biondi, the Apostolic delegate to the United States.

It was Cantwell who suggested that the school be named for Bishop Thomas J. Conaty. A beautiful statue of the prelate, carved from a solid piece of white carrara marble, was placed in a niche over the main entrance.

On the first day of classes, September 4, 1923, the school roster numbered upwards of 500 students. On that day, Father Peter Corcoran, the principal, formally inaugurated the first unit of what became the largest and most successful system of private high schools in the nation.

In November of 1942, a new Pre-Flight Aeronautics course was added to the school's curriculum. Its purpose was to prepare girls for subsequent training in war industries. Such a unique course would provide girls with sufficient knowledge for the coming air-age era.

By 1943, ninety parishes were represented at Conaty. There were more than forty members from seven religious orders on the faculty at that time. Examination determined that graduates rated unusually high in civil service examinations.

An archdiocesan Film Library made available educational motion pictures to local Catholic schools in 1948. It was envisioned that the program would eventually provide films of general Catholic interest for use at the parochial level.

A three-classroom addition was announced in 1950 as a means of expanding the school's business education department. The addition would be a second floor to the east wing that had been constructed in 1937. There were 1,100 girls on the roster by mid-1950.

A library wing was added in 1959 through the cooperation of the Youth Education Fund with a seating capacity for sixty and room for 9,000 books. Many of the volumes were purchased with monies given by the Alumnae Association.

Based on figures available at Bishop Conaty, administrators figured that city taxpayers were being saved $359,000 annually by the service of Catholic secondary schools in the Archdiocese of Los Angeles. Each of the students enrolled in the archdiocesan school system was saving Los Angeles $321.79 per year, the cost of educating a pupil in the Los Angeles Unified School System.

James Francis Cardinal McIntyre turned the first sod for Our Lady of Loretto High School for girls on February 21, 1949. Located at 227 North Lake Street, north of Beverly Boulevard, the school served the north central Los Angeles district.

County Supervisor John Anson Ford spoke at the dedication and said the American ideal of a religious school was a place "where God's name is revered and Christ's influence is eloquently felt."

Opened in the fall of 1939, Our Lady of Loretto was one of the first built under the aegis of the "Youth Education Fund." Its curriculum was designed to prepare girls for college, business and Christian living. Required courses included religion, English, history, physical education and family living. Added elective courses allowed for specific avocations in professional and non-professional fields. A cafeteria, bookstore and library were in the original plans. The two story brick structure, with is twenty-one classrooms, was located amidst a fully equipped playground covered with asphalt.

Commercial studies were added in 1950, when the enrollment reached 200. A Christian Family Living Program was designed to prepare young ladies to take their places as Christian women in family and society.

In 1956, a gymnasium was added to the campus. Adjoining the earlier building, it had a seating capacity for approximately 600 persons. The Legion of Mary was always active and visitation of the sick, parochial census work and sewing for the needy were among the many activities occupying their schedule.

A language lab was installed in 1964. Equipped with headsets and boom microphones, students were able to study Spanish according to the audio-lingual method. Textbooks in Spanish and oral conversations were encouraged in a plan that was a pilot program for Los Angeles.

In order to maintain a quality educational program for young women in modern, earthquake-safe facilities, Bishop Conaty and Our Lady of Loretto High Schools were consolidated into a single campus in September of 1988. The need to demolish or repair a major portion of the Conaty building, linked with the changing demographics of the inner city areas were major factors calling for consolidation.

A new schoolhouse, costing upwards of $3 million dollars, was built with a capacity for 500 enrollees. The up-to-date facility, with modern classrooms, a gymnasium, administrative offices and an athletic field, continued the noble tradition as the flagship of Catholic educational system in Southern California

By 1998, over 9000 alumnae claimed Bishop Conaty or Our Lady of Loretto as their alma mater. As one writer put it: "The works of God proceed slowly and in pain, but then, their roots are the sturdier and their flowering the lovelier."

BISHOP GARCIA DIEGO HIGH SCHOOL

Just a mile from the burial spot of the first bishop of Both Californias is the secondary school bearing his name. Bishop Garcia Diego High School was built on a twenty-five acre campus site at San Marcos Pass and La Colina Road in the channel city of Santa Barbara.

Plans were announced for the school in March of 1957. Sixteen classrooms were designed to accommodate its co-educational candidates. In addition to chemistry and physics laboratories, typing and homerooms, study halls and administrative offices were provided. A concrete-masonry gymnasium with permanent bleachers for 800 students and room for another 700 on the basketball court was constructed. The auditorium area also had a permanent stage and dressing rooms.

The school was a continuation, on a new and much larger campus, of the earlier downtown campus of Santa Barbara Catholic High. Like the parent school, the Jesuit Fathers and the Sisters of Charity staffed Bishop Garcia Diego.

The school was opened in September of 1959. Technically, the institution was a co-institutional rather than a co-educational school. Several friars from nearby Santa Barbara Mission were also on the faculty. Boys and girls were separated for most classes, but all shared

the common facilities of chapel, library, science and commerce rooms, gymnasium and lunchrooms.

A newspaper account described the beautifully designed one-story building as a "pleasing geometrical pattern in the foothill valley located against the magnificent backdrop of the nearby Santa Ynes Mountains." James Francis Cardinal McIntyre dedicated Bishop Garcia Diego High School on February 26, 1961.

The Tidings, official Catholic newspaper for the Archdiocese of Los Angeles, said that "the new high school, a product of the Youth Education Fund, was a link between the space age and the era of the old California missions, joining the Christian tradition that brought knowledge of God to the Indians with the modern scientific know-how that has launched the Discoverer satellites."

The early enrollment of 520 students came from nine parishes as far away as Vandenberg Air Force Base. A busload of forty-four students made the 120-mile round trip daily from the missile base and the Lompoc area.

The school offered a three-track curriculum – college preparatory, business and vocational. It was one of two Catholic high schools to receive certificates of merit from the University of California.

Over the years, enrollees at Bishop Garcia Diego won many awards. In 1966, Elizabeth Anne Giannone earned a citation from the Santa Barbara and Ventura counties District Council of the Italian Catholic Federation; in 1967, William Parks placed first in the senior biological division of the California Science Fair and, two years later, the "Cardinals" won their fourth consecutive Tri-Valley League tennis championship.

It was also in 1969 that the school opened its new television and video studio with all the equipment needed to televise a newscast, produce a documentary file or record a live stage performance.

BISHOP MONTGOMERY HIGH SCHOOL

Named for the crusading leader of the Church in Southern California at the turn of the century, Bishop Montgomery High School traces its roots to early 1957, when the co-instructional secondary school was announced for the South Bay area.

Twenty-four acres were acquired for the new institution near the Redondo Beach and Torrance city boundaries. Located only a mile from the Pacific Ocean, the school was to serve Catholic families in Torrance, Redondo Beach, Palos Verdes, Hermosa Beach, Manhattan Beach, Lawndale, Lomita and surrounding communities.

Plans called for erecting five contemporary buildings with a capacity for 600 students. A common use building included facilities for physics, chemistry, art, shorthand, typing and business. There was also a library and bookstore. Covered walkways connected the buildings and central corridors criss-crossed each classroom structure. Most of the interior partitions were movable.

James Francis Cardinal McIntyre dedicated the school on February 23, 1958. The school had opened its doors to 268 ninth graders the previous September. That number represented ten parishes.

Twenty additional classrooms were ready by the fall of 1960. These units allowed the enrollment to reach a thousand students. In addition to the academic offerings, Bishop Montgomery High School fielded several teams that were soon winning football and basketball games throughout the South Bay area.

An essay in a local newspaper in mid-1960 told how the school was "busy building academic traditions." The roster boasted 1,121 boys and girls - 198 seniors, 248 juniors, 305 sophomores and a record setting 370 freshmen.

The school boasted an excellent library, beginning with approximately 4,000 volumes of which 500 were reference works. The periodical section was outstanding, with forty-four magazines for student use and an equal number for the faculty.

Students produced an annual comedy program and there were opportunities for glee clubs, drama productions and an art club for self-expression. Bishop Montgomery also produced a champion baseball team, which took the El Camino League championship. The monthly newspaper, *The Knight Life*, made its appearance with articles by students and faculty.

In 1964, plans were unveiled for a new tilt-up building with a cushioned maple floor and tapered steel beams supporting a wooden roof deck. Bleachers were provided for approximately 1,000 persons.

In 1985, it was announced that Bishop Montgomery High School had forty-eight religion classes, with a campus ministry reaching out to the local communities. A yearly food drive was planned each year for Thanksgiving and the youngsters who personally distributed the food fed several hundred needy people. Students at Bishop Montgomery engaged in outreach with Little Company of Mary Hospital.

BISHOP MORA SALESIAN HIGH

Destined to be a structural landmark in East Los Angeles, Bishop Mora Salesian High School, is clearly visible from the heavily traversed Santa Ana Freeway. Located at 960 South Soto Street, the school offers a comprehensive educational program with complete college preparatory, general secondary, business education and vocational shop courses.

The main building on the three level campus is a concrete and steel structure containing thirty classrooms, laboratories, art and business departments, library, study hall and conference rooms. A modern kitchen and cafeteria was located at one end of the building adjacent to a roofed outside lunch area. The lowest level of the hillside site was developed for athletic fields. The opening of Bishop Mora in September 1958 brought to fifty-two the number of Catholic secondary schools in the Archdiocese of Los Angeles.

Shop areas measuring fifty by sixty feet each were equipped with complete facilities for cabinet making and printing. The printing plant boasted of two large presses of the latest design, one for offset and the other for letterpress.

Functioning in the most densely populated district of the city, the school was blessed by James Francis Cardinal McIntyre on April 26, 1959. When the institution opened, there were 220 freshmen representing forty-five parishes.

Participation in extra-curricular activities has always been an outstanding characteristic of the school. The band, Sodality, Pep and Press Club and other student groups never encountered any difficulty recruiting members.

A reporter noted that Bishop Mora Salesian High was "as bright inside as it was outside. A complete scheme of color dynamics was carried out in the painting. Cheerful pastel hues were chosen to allow for the greatest possible light in the hallways and classrooms."

Father Charles Casassa, the Jesuit President of Loyola University, told a convocation at the school "you see before you a vivid expression of the Church's appreciation of knowledge through history from barbarian times through the Reformation to the present. In a similar address, Cardinal McIntyre described the school "as a civic contribution that would train citizens of noble accomplishment not only for the neighborhood, but for the city as a whole."

In 1959, fifteen additional lots were acquired for expansion of the campus. Twelve thousand cubic yards of soil had to be moved to make the area suitable for recreational use. Entering the second year of its service, Bishop Mora Salesian had 450 students.

The school came of age in 1960 with 800 enrollees. The Boyle Heights campus took its place among the electronic age schools with the introduction of electronics as its fourth vocational shop. A multipurpose auditorium-gymnasium building was erected in 1969 with capabilities for a regulation basketball floor, practice courts, two banks of bleachers and storage spaces.

In 1983, Timothy Cardinal Manning paid a visit to Bishop Mora Salesian where he presided at an historic convergence of past, present and future students. In a moving address, Cardinal Manning recalled his own closeness to the school since its foundation.

CANTWELL-SACRED HEART OF MARY HIGH SCHOOL

The secondary school for boys named for the proto Archbishop of Los Angeles, John J. Cantwell, was opened for registration on September 9, 1946. The first classes assembled on the top floor of Saint Alphonsus elementary school for the early weeks. The high school was officially dedicated on April 13, 1947.

Located on a picturesque seventeen-acre campus in Montebello, the structure contained twenty-one classrooms, science laboratories, administration offices, a cafeteria, typing rooms and a library with six thousand volumes. There was also a gymnasium-auditorium, a field house, track and football stadium, all equipped with lights for evening games.

At the dedication, Bishop Joseph T. McGucken spoke for the archbishop and noted that the school was culmination of an episcopate that began thirty years earlier in what was then the Diocese of Monterey-Los Angeles. Archbishop Cantwell said he would "expect exceptional things" from the students. Saint Philip of Jesus was chosen as patron of the school.

As the flag was raised over the "largest addition to the archdiocesan school system," the legendary Joseph Scott paid tribute to the teaching qualities of the Irish Christian Brothers who constituted the initial faculty. The first unit of Cantwell High School, located at 329 North Garfield Avenue in Montebello, had space for 600 students.

A physics laboratory was added in 1950. That same year, the teams won the Catholic League championship in football and tied for the championship in baseball. Five years later, a new structure was erected with space for assemblies, concerts and dramatic productions, as well as for indoor sports. Cantwell's seventy-voice glee club took part in the dedication ceremonies.

A few years later, it was announced that the "California Institute of Technology and Notre Dame University are but two institutions of high learning training scientists who received their first training in the field at Cantwell."

An intensified guidance program was added in 1959. In cooperation with local agencies, the school was able to offer social and moral guidance, appraisal of personal qualities and interests, information on educational and vocational opportunities, personality and adjustment inventories and self help study aids.

A varied co-curricular activities program afforded students an opportunity to enrich their high school experience. Among those activities are the Sodality, California Scholastic Federation, Glee Club, band, public speaking, art and science clubs.

Another classroom unit was added in 1962, bringing the total enrollment to 650. The new building is an all-steel structure described as portable but not temporary. The campus was further beautified with an irrigation system for the grounds and the planting of trees.

Serving thirty parishes in 1962, mostly in the East Los Angeles area, Cantwell High offers an honors college preparatory curriculum to qualified students as well as college prep, general and terminal programs.

With the closure of nearby Sacred Heart of Mary High School in 1990, the girls attending that institution were incorporated into Cantwell which, thereafter, became co-educational and named Cantwell-Sacred Heart of Mary High School.

DAMIEN HIGH SCHOOL

Pomona Catholic High School, now a girls' secondary institution, was established in 1959 as a co-instructional educational facility. Ten years later, the boys division was moved to La Verne where it occupied the twenty-five acre campus of the former Bonita High School. After extensive renovation to the existing buildings, Damien welcomed its first 120 freshmen on September 14, 1959.

Among the many improvements to the earlier facilities were a new roof, new ceilings in all rooms, complete painting of the edifice, remodeling of the arcades, new chalk boards, fresh flooring, new heating units, extensive plumbing updating and a series of electric fixtures.

Fifteen classrooms and a spacious library were provided. The ample provisions for athletics made possible all the contemporary sporting needs. The gymnasium, baseball field and track and football field proved more than adequate.

The new school served seven parishes, including those in La Verne, San Dimas, Claremont, Glendora, Azusa, Covina and Pomona. Even a few students from the Diocese of San Diego were welcomed.

By 1962, there were 500 students on the schools' roster. Through the instrumentality of the Youth Education Fund, a science-administration building was ready for occupancy that year. Five years later, the title of the boys division became Damien High School in memory of Father Damien De Veuster, the famed apostle of Molokai.

Among the many accomplishments associated with Damien High School has been its debate squad. In 1969, the team of Mike Higelin and Mike Castellini chalked up a record of nineteen wins with only three losses, finishing first in the tournament for that year. The varsity team also excelled that year.

Ground was broken for a new multi-purpose building in 1970. The edifice replaced earlier sporting facilities by offering a gymnasium-auditorium with bleacher seating for 1400.

Interestingly, Damien High School was never officially dedicated. On October 9, 1970, Archbishop Timothy Manning journeyed to La Verne and performed the long overdue ceremony. The seventeen communities served by the school raised $100,000 for the new facilities.

Further additions were made in 1989 when ground was broken for a 15,000 square foot annex to the high school. The two-story combination classroom-office had space for a science and computer laboratory, new classrooms, a chapel, conference rooms and storage space.

DANIEL MURPHY HIGH SCHOOL

(KNOWN EARLIER AS SAINT JOHN VIANNEY HIGH SCHOOL)

With the transfer of Los Angeles College minor seminary for the Archdiocese of Los Angeles to Mission Hills, plans were set afoot to convert the facility at 241 South Detroit Street into a boys' high school. In the fall of 1954, Saint John Vianney opened its portals with more than 200 enlistees.

A full college program was offered in the opening year and business administration courses were added the following year. The campus was enlarged to allow competitive sports programs.

The three-story brick building included a beautiful chapel, theatre-type auditorium seating 300, a gymnasium, cafeteria, library, chemistry and physics laboratories and a dozen classrooms.

Because the old building had become structurally unsound after suffering numerous earthquakes, plans were drafted for a wholly new complex large enough to accommodate 640 students in 1964.

The new three story concrete and steel structure contained sixteen classrooms, a multi-purpose auditorium-gymnasium, study hall, counseling rooms and offices. Contemporary in style, the building had concrete wall panels with horizontal sliding windows. The chapel of the old seminary was detached and remains as one of the loveliest in the southland.

The name of the school was changed in order to honor Dan Murphy, a pioneering developer, businessman, industrialist, civic leader and benefactor of the Church in Southern California. The Dan Murphy Foundation provided funds for the new building. The U-shaped new school wraps around the end of the block at Third Street between Detroit and Cloverdale Streets. James Francis Cardinal McIntyre blessed the new Dan Murphy High School on December 4, 1966.

Over the years, students at the school excelled academically and otherwise. One of the boys accomplished a "first" by capturing four of the awards in a local science fair in 1958; Joseph Bonelli was awarded one of two national scholarships from UNICP national service club in 1960; Peter Galbraith was appointed to the United States Naval Academy in 1961; Louis Siggins won first place among more than 500 parochial schools participating in a contest sponsored by the Los Angeles Herald-Examiner and Foster Montalbano won a place among the nation's leading scientific minds in the Westinghouse Science Talent Search.

JUNIPERO SERRA HIGH SCHOOL

In 1950, a boys' high school was announced for Gardena. It was to be named after the intrepid apostle of California, Fray Junípero Serra. Located on an eighteen-acre campus at Van Ness Avenue and Compton Boulevard on what was then used as a truck garden, the school would be staffed by the Marianists.

The L-shaped campus was erected in stages, with the first unit being ready for occupancy in September. In excess of 200 students joined as freshmen in a plan that would involve expanding one class for four years. The overall structure, bordering the athletic field, had room for 1,500 bleachers with lockers and showers, along with a cafeteria, dining room and snack bar.

The institution offered college preparatory, commercial and industrial courses. Among the latter would be religion, English, history, Latin, Spanish, biology, practical mathematics, algebra, geometry, general science, physics and typing.

Serra High School served an area as large as one of the old missions, nineteen parishes in all, from Inglewood and Southwestern Los Angeles to the Harbor, from the ocean inland to Lynwood and Compton.

The early students caught the pioneering spirit and volunteered to help grade and seed the football field. They were also instrumental in similar projects such as fashioning a baseball diamond and track.

In 1952, Junípero Serra High opened a technical department. Students planning a technical career followed a general arts course during the first two years. A solid basic academic training program was

imparted as a requirement for manual arts. Third year technical students studied religion and other subjects. During the first semester, they were taught the fundamentals of woodwork, metal work, auto machines and electronics.

A stadium was erected in 1954. It was outfitted with lights, new turf and a bleacher capacity of 4,200. On October 26, 1957 Bishop Alden J. Bell blessed a new gymnasium. It was a tilt-up building with basketball courts, a spacious stage and space for student assemblies. In that year there were 610 boys on the school's roster.

Fray Junipero Serra

The amateur radio station at Junípero Serra High acquired a rotary triple beam antenna. A new room was made available for the Poster Club and provisions became available for imparting training in the silk screening process.

An honors program was added in 1958, with special courses for the more gifted students. Those qualifying were trained in special research practices and later in other advanced procedures. Music appreciation was placed in the curriculum and the Serra chapter of the California Scholarship Federation became a member of the National Honor Society.

An announcement in 1959 called attention to the fact that almost 700 young men had been stamped with the Catholic educational tradition. Thirty-two graduates were studying for the priesthood.

Bishop John J. Ward dedicated a new classroom wing in 1967. Included therein were six classrooms and an enlarged library, cafeteria and other office area. This latest project was completed and the educational plant was dedicated to Fray Junípero Serra.

The school became co-educational in the early 1990s.

PARACLETE HIGH SCHOOL

Located amidst the silent Joshuas on the High Desert, Paraclete High School went on the drawing board in 1962 and was on a thirty-acre parcel in Lancaster. The 50,000 square foot complex provided classrooms, administration office, chapel and a shop building.

Architectural balance was achieved throughout by use of a central court separating the two classroom buildings. Concrete block walls with steel framing and metal decking on the roof allowed for maximum use of space. All structures were air conditioned. The school was scheduled to open in 1964 with some 600 Antelope Valley students.

A co-educational institution, the school opened with ninth graders, allowing for the addition of one class annually for the next three years. For the opening term, the school utilized leased quarters in the Administration Building of the Antelope Valley Fairgrounds.

The chapel for Paraclete High School was unique insofar as it had large sliding glass doors that permitted the entire student body to attend Mass from the court area. The school offered a full college preparatory curriculum, plus a second track for students not planning to go to college.

The school grew rapidly, both academically and athletically. It joined the ten member Desert Inyo League and by 1965, the enrollment had risen to 240 students with over half of the boys signing up for varsity and JV football. Plans called for erecting a new unit to Paraclete in 1971. It was to be a multi-purpose gymnasium and, as such, was a milestone for the eight-year old high school.

Paraclete was popular in academic circles. Students traveled great distances, some over fifty miles each day to be a part of the institution. And it was not exclusively Catholic, with fifty of its 350 students professing other religious persuasions.

Cordial relations with the Antelope Valley High School permitted students to take part-time classes not offered at Paraclete. Juniors and seniors were allowed to apply for advance placement courses at Antelope Valley College.

Because the climate in and around Lancaster is freezing much of the winter and blistering hot during the summer months, the heating and cooling systems at the high school were tremendously expensive to operate.

Principals

Parish High Schools

Ms. Rita Dever, Mary Star of the Sea Righ School, San Pedro
Ms. Michelle Purghart, Holy Family High School, Glendale
Mr. Daniel Honi, St. Genevieve High School, Panorama City
Mr. Thom Gasper, St. Monica High School, Santa Monica
Ms. Carolyn Nelson, San Gabriel Mission High School, San Gabriel

Private High Schools

Ms. Ann Gillick, Alverno High School, Sierra Madre
Fr. Tom Elewaut, C.J., Bishop Garcia Diego Righ School, Santa Barbara
Br. John Montgomery, F.S.C., Cathedral Higli School, Los Angeles
Br. Tom Fahy, O.S.F., Chaminade College Prep. West Huis
Fr. Paul Renson, O. Carm., Crespi Carmelite High School, Encino
Fr. Michael Gergen, S.D.B., Don Bosco Technical Rigb School, Rosemead
Sr. Celeste Marie Botello, O.P., Flintridge-Sacred Heart Academy, La Canada
Virginia Hurst, I.R.M., Immaculate Reart Righ School, Los Angeles
Ms. Cecilia Coe, La Reina High School, Thousand Oaks
Mr. Patrick Donacci, La Salle High School, Pasadena
Ms. Kathleen Vercillo, Louisville High School, Woodland Hills
Mr. William Thomason, Loyola High School, Los Angeles
Dr. Mary Ellen Gozdecki, Marymount High School, Los Angeles
Ms. Rita McBride, Mayfield Senior School, Pasadena
Ms. Joan Tyhurst, Notre Dame Academy, Los Angeles

Ms. Stephanie Connelly, Notre Dame High School, Sherman Oaks
Ms. Michelle Schulte, Providence High School, Burbank
Ms. Kathleen Pillon, Ramona Secondary School, Alhambra
Mr. Thomas Moran, St. Francis High School, La Canada Flintridge
Mr. Pat Lee, St. John Bosco High School, Bellflower
Sr. Monica Collins, O.S.B., St. Lucy's Priory, Glendora
Sr. Fay Ragen, C.S.J., St. Mary's Academy, Inglewood
Mr. Anthony Sabatino, Villanova Preparatory, Ojai

Archdiocesan High Schools

Sr. Cheryl Milner, S.N.J.M., Bellarmine Jefferson High School, Burbank
Dr. John Monnig, Bishop Alemany High School, Mission Hills
Mr. Merritt Hemenway, Bishop Amat High School, La Puente
Ms. Sharon Moreno, Bishop Conaty-Our Lady of Loretto High School, Los Angeles
Ms Rosemary Lisbon, Bishop Montgomery High School, Torrance
Mr. Manuel Villarreal, Bishop Mora Salesian High School, Los Angeles
Mr. David Chambers, Cantwell-Sacred Heart High School, Montebello
Fr. Patrick Travers, SS.CC., Damien High School, La Verne
Mr. Denis Munoz, Daniel Murphy High School, Los Angeles
Fr. Sal Pilato, Junipero Serra High School, Gardena
Mr. John Anson, Paraclete High School, Lancaster
Ms. Kimberlee Gazzolo, Pomona Catholic High School, Pomona
Sr. Mary Diane School, O.P., Sacred Heart High School, Los Angeles
Ms. Siobhain O'Reilly, Santa Clara High School, Oxnard
Ms. Lori Barr, St. Anthony High School, Long Beach
Mr. James McClune, St. Bernard High School, Playa del Rey
Br. Paulinus Horkan, O.S.F., St. Bonaventure High School, Ventura
Dr. Teresa Mendoza, St. Joseph High School, Lakewood
Mr. Joseph Myers, St. Joseph High School, Santa Maria
Ms. Margaret Meland, St. Matthias High School, Downey
Mr. Frank Laurenzello, St. Paul High School, Santa Fe Springs
Ms. Susan Abelein, Verbum Dei High School, Los Angeles

SACRED HEART OF JESUS HIGH SCHOOL

The beginnings of Sacred Heart of Jesus High School can be traced back to 1890, the establishment of an academy at Lincoln Heights by the Dominican Sisters of Mission San Jose. Initially it was a boarding and day school for a small group of children in the area. High school classes began in 1907 with eight pupils.

After fifty-nine years of educational service, the academy closed its doors in the summer of 1949. A new Sacred Heart of Jesus High School carried on the academy's traditions at Griffin Avenue and Mozart Street. The capacity of the new institution was envisioned for 500 girls.

Housed in a modern class-A building with Roman brick exterior, floor slabs and a concrete structural frame, the edifice had a composition roof, asphalt tile floors, acoustical tile ceilings and forced air heating.

Administrative offices, a First Aid room, library, study hall, music department and several classrooms were located on the first floor, with art and commercial departments, sewing room and additional classrooms on the second.

College preparatory, commercial and homemaking courses were offered, as well as electives in dramatics, journalism, public speaking and choral training. The school was dedicated on January 15, 1950. On that occasion, Archbishop J. Francis. J. McIntyre announced that $5,000,000 worth of new schools had been built or were in preparation by the archdiocese.

To meet the needs of its students, Sacred Heart provided a three-track program – college preparatory, business and general. The schoolyard was graded and asphalted with new athletic courts for tennis, basketball and volleyball laid out. An auditorium was constructed in 1956.

In 1959, school officials announced that the institution was fully accredited by the University of California. Its 500 enrollment had an integrated curriculum, which allowed for spiritual, moral, intellectual, aesthetic and physical education.

Two years later, the school boasted of having students from forty-four parishes in a program that included Latin, Spanish and French. Academic honors came from a National Latin Society, Loyola University, the American Legion Auxiliary and the Junior Red Cross.

In 1968, at a reunion of graduates, it was announced that fifty of the graduates had entered the sisterhood. And graduates were busily tutoring at local public schools, with special emphasis towards students speaking only Spanish. Sacred Heart of Jesus High School became an archdiocesan school in 1979.

Observing the centennial of its parent institution, seven hundred teachers, students and parents returned to Lincoln Heights in May of 1990. Archbishop Roger Mahony extolled the school and its work over a hundred years, noting that its outreach programs changed the lives of untold peoples in all stratas of society.

POMONA CATHOLIC HIGH SCHOOL

(Known earlier as Saint Joseph)

In April of 1948, a drive was inaugurated to raise funds for opening a co-educational parochial high school that would replace the Academy of the Holy Names in Pomona. Ninth grade classes began in the fall of 1949 and an additional grade was added each year until the new school had a complete secondary curriculum. The school served San Dimas, Chino, Ontario, Baldwin Park, Upland, Azusa, Monrovia and La Verne.

Known as Pomona Catholic High, the institution was the first of its kind in the northeastern part of the Archdiocese of Los Angeles. The Felician Sisters were entrusted with operating the school.

An article in the March 23, 1951 issue of *The Tidings* reported that there were over a thousand freshmen and sophomore boys and girls who considered themselves as "pioneers in a wonderful project" that brought Catholic education to a wholly new area of California's southland.

They watched in the summertime as their parents cleared off seventeen-acres of land, hauling away some 5,000 yards of dirt, leveling the area and starting what became a magnificent athletic field. Figures indicated that the school would save taxpayers some $125,000 per year when it reached full enrollment.

Pomona Catholic offered scientific, academic, general and commerce courses. Subsequently new courses included general science, mechanical arts, geometry and domestic science. Besides a well-developed athletic program consisting of basketball, baseball, volleyball and boxing, the school offered well-integrated musical and dramatic courses. In 1951, classes offered were in chemistry, biology, mechanical drawing, public speaking, business training and fine arts and crafts.

Archbishop J. Francis A. McIntyre dedicated a separate facility for Pomona Catholic, located at 533 West Holt Avenue, on April 27, 1952. The prelate noted in his address for that occasion that the school was in the center of a fifteen-mile radius containing a population of 200,000 persons.

With the new facilities, enrollment began increasing at Pomona Catholic with numbers reaching 400 in the fall of 1952. A physics lab and equipment room were also ready for the opening that year.

Student initiative, civic leadership and experience in Catholic Action were consistently developed through participation in such organized co-curricular activities as the student council, Sodality, dramatics, glee club and athletics. A lighting system was installed for the football field and a beautiful 100 x 50 foot swimming pool was installed.

Over 550 students returning to the school in the mid-1950s found two more classrooms and three new elective courses. Architectural drawing was offered to upper classmen and the business curriculum was enlarged.

By the time the school observed its silver jubilee, there were opportunities for guided independent study in foreign languages and in reading and writing skills. Seniors could obtain credits for job experience in the field of business, beauty, library science and nursery school education.

Since 1962, the school became an archdiocesan high school for girls residing in Pomona, Claremont, Upland, Covina and Montclair.

By 1973, a program known as "Adopt a Grandmother" was in progress. Students began visiting local hospitals where they engaged in assisting the patients in a host of activities. That program also strengthened the collaboration between school and parish.

SAINT BERNARD HIGH SCHOOL

Early in December of 1957, the site for Saint Bernard High School was blessed near Manchester Avenue and Lincoln Boulevard. The first sessions were scheduled to begin in the fall of 1958 at temporary quarters in nearby Saint Anastasia School.

The co-instructional institution, located on twelve acres of land was the latest in the litany of schools financed by the Youth Education Fund. The first unit was a two story, reinforced brick and concrete structure containing seventeen classrooms, nine special service rooms and administrative offices. In the special rooms were science

laboratories, library, study hall, chapel, homemaking, and drafting, as well as typing and business machines. Contemporary in style, the building was fire and earthquake resistant.

Surrounded by a rapidly growing residential neighborhood, the campus was designed to accommodate 1,400 students. College preparatory and general academic programs of study, remedial English classes, public speaking, choral, dramatics and art classes were in the initial curriculum.

When opened, Saint Bernard was advertised as "a school as modern as tomorrow and as ancient as the Christian tradition it represented." Giant jets climbing into the sky from nearby Los Angeles International Airport typified the future for which the students were being prepared.

Saint Bernard was planned to serve the central Santa Monica bay area, as well as populous Westchester. One reporter said, "The buildings are beautiful and permanent. The layout is good. The sea breezes blow continually. It is a perfect place for academics." Less than a mile from the Pacific Ocean, the windswept campus was the gift of the Fritz Burns Foundation. In the small but devotional chapel, unique stained glass windows interpret the seven gifts of the Holy Spirit in relationship to the Beatitudes and sacraments.

There was a ready-made sports arena in a natural bowl on the west side of the campus. A retaining wall in the form of permanent bleachers was erected overlooking the football track. The school had a full athletic program for both boys and girls. The teams were known as the Vikings. Extra-curricular activities included GAA, Lettermen's Club, Spanish, Latin, journalism and speech groups, Sodality and the boys' Radio Club.

In 1960, a large, two story addition was erected containing fourteen classrooms and other facilities. In that year, there were 700 enrollees, with provisions available for a full thousand students.

The first graduates set soaring standards for future classes, with state scholarships going to several students. In 1972, four seniors were among the 1,275 nationwide winners for National Merit scholarships. Regina Anne Aichner won a place at the Los Angeles County Science Fair and Daniel Twomey was the first alumnus admitted to the Air Force Academy in Colorado Springs.

Enrollment inched up to 1,200 in 1962, with spiritual, intellectual, physical and social development forming the school's goal for its students. There was a three-tiered academic program for superior students, college prep and those who needed additional attention. Four years of ethics courses were required covering personal relationships, scripture, Church history, social justice and Christian service.

Another multi-purpose building was completed early in 1965. Lt. Colonel Kevin Chilton came for a visit in 1992. A former student, he was an astronaut and the pilot on the satellite rescue shuttle mission.

SAINT BONAVENTURE HIGH SCHOOL

The first of the schools erected by the Youth Education Fund was dedicated to Saint Bonaventure. A co-instructional institution, the school opened in September of 1963, with a capacity of 600 students. Serving the area of Saticoy, Santa Paula, San Buenaventura, Ojai, Fillmore and other Ventura County communities, the school was located on property adjacent to Assumption parish on Telegraph Road.

Built in a contemporary style featuring vaulted concrete roofs and extensive use of glass, the building's roof vaults rested on concrete columns, while the walls between the columns were of concrete block and glass.

There were a dozen classrooms, three laboratories, a library, home economics department, art room, book store and offices in the edifice. College preparatory, general and business curricula were offered.

The three buildings were connected by arcades with patios between. Starting with the ninth grade, Saint Bonaventure added another grade each year until the full complement of high school classes were in place.

In 1965, a gymnasium-auditorium was put in place, along with space for additional classrooms and offices. Outdoor athletic facilities were added with up-to-date tracks and fields.

When James Francis Cardinal McIntyre dedicated the new school, he noted that the educational apostolate begun by the Franciscan friars 186 years earlier for Indian neophytes was being carried into the 1960s for modern teenagers by Saint Bonaventura High School.

A locker-shower building with facilities for both boys and girls was completed in 1967. By that time, there were 300 students enrolled. High scholastic standards were evident from the outset. Forty-four of the forty-seven pioneer graduates moved on to colleges and professional schools, seven with scholarships.

Over the years, students walked off with many plaudits. Jerry Stone was chosen Player of the Year for 1970 by the All Southern California Board of Baseball; James Posakony was named by President Richard Nixon to attend an international science fair in Sydney; Karen Patterson was named a winner of a coveted scholarship by the Southern California Edison Company and Terry Rooney won first place in the 28th annual Herald-Examiner's Bill of Rights Essay Contest.

As the only Catholic high school for a forty-mile stretch of the California coastline, Saint Bonaventure drew students from a wide expanse of the Archdiocese of Los Angeles. Parents played an active part in the school's activities, participating in such fundraising activities as fiestas and dinner-dances, and supporting the academic and extra-curricular program with volunteer outreaches.

In 1985, the 630 students could sign up for a high school diploma or honors tract. All students took four years of religion and English, two-and-a-half of social studies and two of science and math. Also offered were advanced placement courses in English, United States history and calculus.

SAINT JOSEPH HIGH SCHOOL
(LAKEWOOD)

An archdiocesan high school for girls was established at Lakewood in 1964. Originally unnamed, the school eventually took on the patronage of the Sisters of Saint Joseph of Carondelet who comprised the first faculty.

Only one unit of the new facility was ready for occupancy in the fall, but the rest of the buildings were nearing completion. College preparatory and general curricula were offered. There were four classroom units, an administration-library, home economics, science buildings and a chapel.

James Francis Cardinal McIntyre dedicated the school on March 5, 1967. At that time, there were 395 girls from twenty-one parishes in southeast Los Angeles County. Saint Joseph had close ties with nearby Saint John Bosco High School in Bellflower.

There was a cheery atmosphere in the buildings. All rooms were bright and well lighted. Facilities included well-equipped language, science, food and clothing laboratories, together with art, typing and counseling rooms.

The educational policy at Saint Joseph High School was contained in the following statement taken from an early handbook:

A true education aims at the formation of the human person in the pursuit of his ultimate end and of the good of the societies of which, as a man, he is a member, and in whose obligations, as an adult, he will share. Therefore children and young people must be helped, with the aid of the latest advances in psychology and the arts and science of teaching, to develop harmoniously their physical, moral and intel-lectual endowments so that they may gradually acquire a mature sense of responsibility in striving endlessly to form their own lives properly and in pursuing true freedom as they surmount the vicissitudes of life with courage and constancy.

Along with its educational program, the school urged students to take an active role in their respective parishes. Many of the girls volunteered to work on weekends as Confraternity of Christian Doctrine helpers.

The school sponsored seasonal athletic tournaments for pupils in parish grammar schools in the area. Girls from twenty-six schools participated in one of the early basketball matches.

An incentive program was begun whereby parents agreed to contribute twenty hours of work each month or to pay an additional tuition fee. Most became involved in the program and, after awhile, it became a regular fixture at the school.

An accelerated graduation program was initiated in 1974. That program was designed to prepare students for matriculation at the end of six, seven or eight semesters, depending totally on the needs of the individual students. Those were intellectual, social, financial or whatever else might influence the total development of the person. The program leaned heavily on the well-known fact that students in the Catholic High School traditionally have always completed far more units and courses at any given time than their counterparts in the public system.

SAINT JOSEPH HIGH SCHOOL
(SANTA MARIA)

The northernmost of the secondary schools in the Archdiocese of Los Angeles is located in Orcutt-Santa Maria. Opened in the fall of 1964, the high school was envisioned as serving the whole of the northern Santa Barbara County's Catholic parishes. The eleven unit co-instructional school opened its doors in the fall of 1964 under the aegis of the Josephite Fathers and the Daughters of Mary and Joseph.

The first building on the twenty-acre campus included seventeen classrooms with accommodations for physics, chemistry and biology, together with space for arts, business and homemaking.

In 1967, plans were announced for a new unit to Saint Joseph High School, this one to be a gymnasium-auditorium. It was a concrete frame structure with a wooden gymnasium floor and a roof structure of steel trusses.

The school was dedicated by James Francis Cardinal McIntyre on February 4, 1968. At that time, it was determined that parents of over half of the students were employed at the huge Vandenberg Air Force Base, only ten miles away.

Although still a largely rural farming and grazing country, the area grew quite fast in those years. Students represented seven parishes from Pismo Beach to Lompoc, some traveling over thirty miles each day to school.

Capacity of the school in 1968 was 450 students. Athletic provisions included facilities for basketball, football and baseball. Along with its full academic program, Saint Joseph High School had a galaxy of extra-curricular student activities including the California Scholarship Federation, the National Honors Society, the Junior Statesmen of America, the Forensic League and Our Lady's Sodality.

The Youth ministry among the 600 students at Saint Joseph High was alive and thriving in 1979. Students were involved in a host of reach-out activities including visiting rest homes and working with the handicapped. One class performed in a folk group at liturgies and another met to pray several times each week.

An expansion of the gymnasium was made in 1980, with addition of 2,400 square feet to the existing building. At the time, there were students from Lompoc, Los Alamos and Guadalupe. Even some youngsters were coming from the southern sections of San Luis Obispo country in the Diocese of Monterey. In the new addition to the gym was space for a theatre, stage, ministry office, and kitchen and conference room.

In 1993, Saint Joseph High School was formally honored with the presentation of the United States Department of Education's Blue Ribbon Award. That coveted distinction was given to schools that were exceptionally effective at educating students. Factors determining the award include leadership, teaching, environment, curriculum, parent and community support and organizational vitality.

SAINT MATTHIAS HIGH SCHOOL

With erection of the new elementary school for Saint Matthias parish in Huntington Park in 1960, a girls' secondary school was inaugurated to occupy the earlier building. Beginning with only the ninth grade, the school was to fill out the four-year cycle within that many years.

Remodeled for its new use, Saint Matthias High School provided a science laboratory, home economics department, library and cafeteria. Like the elementary school, the secondary level was staffed by Sisters of Notre Dame. College preparatory, business and general courses were offered. Co-curricular activities included Sodality, Glee Club, Athletic Association, speech, drama and journalism.

With an address at 6003 Stafford Avenue, the school also promised to look into pre-college training in nursing and teaching. The primary school had operated a junior high department for some years prior to 1952.

By 1961, the girls were wearing new uniforms. Their gray plaid skirts with matching gray blazers soon became a popular sight in Huntington Park. The school's curriculum was broadened to include speech and journalism.

A new, two-story concrete masonry building was erected in 1962. The addition was needed to provide for students from twenty-one southwest area parishes. The unit contained a biology-chemistry laboratory, library and administration area, with rooms opening into exterior corridors. A contemporary structure, it covered 5,800 square feet and included provisions for a landscaped patio to the south and the rear of the earlier building.

The first senior class at Saint Matthias coincided with the golden jubilee of the parish. By 1964, there were 350 enrollees. A new feature on the campus in that year was a life-size statue of the school's patron saint.

The 1989 class of seniors made a commitment of their class to Christ. In five clear sentences, their pledge read as follows:

"LORD Jesus Christ, you have been with us, sustaining us from the instant of our conception," the 54 young women recited together.

"We believe you have been especially present to us in the hopes, joys and sorrows of our high school years.

"We thank you for your loving guidance and tender care.

"Give us faith to go out with courage, not knowing where we go, but only that your hand is leading us and your love is supporting us," the young women prayed.

"Grant that in you we may find true peace so that filled with your spirit, we may live for your kingdom."

In March of 1995, *The Tidings* announced that Saint Matthias High School would be merged with Pius X High School on the Downey campus. The school became co-educational for three years until the last of the students from Pius X had graduated, at which time it reverted to its earlier status as a girls' high school.

SAINT PAUL HIGH SCHOOL

In April of 1957, officials for the Archdiocese of Los Angeles announced that a new high school would soon be erected in Santa Fe Springs. The classes actually began in the fall of 1956 in quarters at Saint Mariana de Paredes in Pico-Rivera. Ninety-eight students enrolled for the first semester. The new campus, located on an eighteen-acre campus facing Greenleaf Avenue at Reis Street, included an administration building, chapel and four classrooms with a capacity for 750.

Saint Paul High School served nine parishes in the rapidly developing southeast area of Los Angeles County. Initially called Santa Fe High School, the name was changed when the Unified School District opened a school by that name close by.

The new facility was opened in January of 1958 with 328 students. The contemporary style brick buildings allowed for an atmosphere that was light-hearted and cheery. A parcel of land to the south was leveled to provide more recreational and athletic opportunities.

In 1959, an eight-classroom addition was begun. The new structure provided room for 300 more enrollees. A multi-purpose building was also envisioned which combined auditorium, gymnasium and other facilities.

Dedication ceremonies at Saint Paul High School were conducted on October 25, 1959 by James Francis Cardinal McIntyre. At the event, the cardinal noted that Saint Paul was one of twenty-four high schools opened within a single decade. A co-instructional school, the institution offered college preparatory and general curricula, with complete courses in business education and home economics.

A bright and spacious library, conducive to study and research, provided an up-to-date collection of volumes for student educational projects. The chemistry laboratory had the latest equipment for sciences, as did similar rooms for physics and biology.

The curriculum was revised in 1961 to that of a three-tiered program. At first affecting only the incoming freshmen, it was designed to elicit from each student, the gifted, the average, and the less gifted, the maximum potential. Classes were broken down into A, B and C. Each student was tracked according to results of the school placement test scores, achievement marks in key subjects and the recommendations of elementary school teachers.

Over the years, Saint Paul High School's academic and scholastic achievements have been impressive as attested by the trophies located near the library. Along with the Angeles League trophies won in football and track, are the Model Nations plaque and the APSL Latin award.

In 1985, more than 650 students from Saint Paul High School walked twenty-six miles from East Los Angeles to Santa Monica Beach to raise funds for the Catholic Worker Hospitality Kitchen.

The high mark in enrollment was reached in 1985 when 1,545 students were on the roster. There were sixty-seven teachers and 97% of the students were Catholic.

Student achievers abounded over the years. In 1961, Fred Zahlki and Mike Eberhard won first place in the 7th Model United Nations program; in 1965, Tom Metzler was selected as a participant in the United States Senate Youth program and was given a trip to the District of Columbia and, in 1985, teacher Dan Jiru was awarded the Eleanor Roosevelt Peace Ward.

SANTA CLARA HIGH SCHOOL

Catholic secondary education in Oxnard can be traced to a school opened in 1901 under the title of Saint Joseph Institute. The name was changed in 1930 with establishment of a high school department located on the top floor of the parochial school. Ground was broken in November of 1950 for a new facility that would accommodate 400 students with provisions for future expansion. The completion date was to coincide with the fiftieth anniversary of the first school opened by the Sisters of Saint Joseph of Carondelet.

There were two wings at right angles, comprising the classroom and administration services. Radiating on the diagonal between the two wings was an auditorium-gymnasium.

Included in the institution were chemistry, physics and biology laboratories, together with space for classes in bookkeeping, typing, mechanical drawing and home economics as well as offices, library, chapel, dining facilities and faculty rooms.

The school occupied an eleven-acre parcel of land near the southern limits of Oxnard. Educational provisions had been opened in the city in 1901 when the school auditorium served as a church until the larger one was erected.

The completed concrete and steel plant at Santa Clara was dedicated in April of 1952. Students in the high school included many children of the area's pioneer Catholic families. Opening with

Although functional and economical in design, the buildings at Verbum Dei have a traditional atmosphere. The use of ornamental iron reflects the religious and educational purposes of the school. By the time of its dedication, Verbum Dei had 230 students in grades nine through eleven.

The graceful chapel, facing the entrance, is the pivotal point and the most distinctive structure on campus. A peaked roof and interior arch gives a Gothic atmosphere to the chapel.

Built in a predominantly black area of South Los Angeles, with a financial outlay of $1.5 million, Verbum Dei was described as "the finest of its kind in the west."

An article about the school stated that its "low rate of absenteeism is largely attributable to the fact that the new school inspires pride. The bright colors used in the corridor, the modern lighting facilities, the spic-and-span cleanliness maintained both within the building and on the surrounding campus all combine to command an upbeat response in the students, to demand from them their best."

By 1967, there were 353 students enrolled at the Compton school. They came from backgrounds of varied cultures and social deprivation, from low-income housing involving large families. Without Verbum Dei, students in that area would have had no chance for a Catholic education.

The principal noted in an interview in 1972 that 80% of the graduates would go on to college and 40% would receive scholarships. He noted that "the primary objective of the school is academic and there is a great consolation in seeing the number who go on to positions of leadership."

Over the years, Verbum Dei enjoyed unprecedented success in athletics with three national championships in basketball. Emile Wilson, an alumnus of the school received a Rhodes scholarship. In 1975, he returned to Compton to speak with the students, noting that "I won't be the last" to win such a distinction for the school. In 1983, four students were honored for achieving perfect 4.0 grade averages at the school.

In 1994, there was a $4 million renovation at Compton, part of which was used for a gymnasium and athletic field that was locally advertised as a tribute to the local community who had supported the school from its earliest days. In 2000, the administration of the school was entrusted to the Society of Jesus.

185 enrollees and adding another hundred anticipated for the second year, James Francis Cardinal McIntyre dedicated the institution as part of the 50th anniversary ceremonies for the local parish.

A new wing provided in 1959 allowed for doubling the school's capacity. The co-educational institution offered academic courses, including four years of science, mathematics and foreign languages, as well as courses in commercial arts and home economics. There was also a full athletic program from the very outset.

In addition to an active Sodality whose projects form an important part of student activity, various other groups were active on campus including Latin, Key, CSF and library Clubs and Junior Red Cross.

In 1964, Santa Clara High School expanded into buildings formerly occupied by Saint Anthony's parish elementary school. Projections were then realized for 675 students. The school became archdiocesan in 1967.

By 1978, Santa Clara students had made three trips to Tijuana, Mexico, where they took part in a program to assist in teaching poor youngsters the basics of Catholic education. Some of the students went to orphanages and the others to the local garbage dumps where they sought to feed, clothe and otherwise assist the poorest of the poor.

VERBUM DEI HIGH SCHOOL

It was in May of 1962 that plans were announced for a new secondary school in the Compton area of Los Angeles. Verbum Dei received its name from the Divine Word Fathers who staffed nearby Saint Leo parish.

While construction was being completed on the new institution, classes were begun in the fall with an initial enrollment of sixty-seven boys. Located at 11100 South Central Avenue, all the buildings were designed a contemporary style with reinforced concrete block walls and flat gypsum slab roofs.

Referred to as "one of the most distinctive modern schools in the United States," Verbum Dei High School was dedicated on November 29, 1964 by James Francis Cardinal McIntyre. The building received wide recognition for its architectural beauty and efficiency.

| Los Angeles | Los Angeles | Manhattan Beach | Arcadia |

All Saints

Although the parish of All Saints had been erected in 1926, the school itself did not open until September 13, 1948. That year, four Dominican Sisters of Sinsinawa, Wisconsin, and three lay teachers welcomed 354 students to All Saints School.

Initially All Saints contained only the first six grades; the seventh and eighth were added in 1949 and 1950. During the 1950s, the student population continued to grow compelling the pastor, Father James Nevin, to expand the school plant. In the spring of 1956, the parish completed a six-room, two-story addition. By the end of the decade, the rising enrollment necessitated still more changes. The three rooms on the second floor that had been used as a hall were converted into classrooms and All Saints became a double-grade school.

As Los Angeles moved through the 1960s and 1970s, the city's changing demographics had an impact on All Saint's student population. Consequently, a decision was made to reduce the pupil/teacher ratio. As a result, All Saints gradually became a single-grade school.

By April 1985, a shortage of religious vocations forced the Dominican Sisters to withdraw from All Saints. In order to better serve what had become a predominantly Latino community, a kindergarten program was added in 1991.

At present Ms. Maria Palermo is principal.

All Souls

All Souls, the first parochial elementary school in Alhambra, opened on September 19, 1921 with fifty-three children in grades three through six. The school was staffed by the Sisters of the Holy Names of Jesus and Mary who had been teaching catechism in the parish.

As the school's enrollment increased with the addition of a new grade each year, the original one-story, four-classroom building proved to be inadequate. In 1923, the pastor, Father Henry Gross, added a second story to the original structure in order to provide more classrooms. Just three years after its opening, All Souls was a fully equipped, eight-grade school.

The school continued to use these facilities for the next twenty-five years. Shortly after World War II, the parish acquired additional property adjacent to the school playground. In May 1948, ground was broken for two new buildings. The structures, which contained twelve classrooms as well as a parish hall and kitchen, were ready for occupancy by September 1949, and were dedicated by Archbishop J. Francis A. McIntyre on February 12, 1950. The former school building was renovated for use as a parish recreation center and finally razed in 1962.

Since that time few outward changes have taken place at All Souls. In June 1979, the Sisters of the Holy Names relinquished the school. Within recent years, a kindergarten has been added and the Writing-to-Read program installed.

Today Mr. Anthony Yniquez is principal.

American Martyrs

American Martyrs School opened in September 1947. Staffed by the Sisters of St. Joseph of Carondelet, the school had an initial enrollment of 225 students in grades one through six.

Additional classrooms were added in 1951, again in 1954 and yet again in 1964 until the school plant ultimately consisted of twenty classrooms with 2 1/2 classes for each grade. The school achieved its peak enrollment in 1957 when the student population reached 1,000.

During the late 1960s, however, the Archdiocese of Los Angeles decided to eliminate double grades in the schools. Four of the classrooms were converted to other uses and in 1971 only one first grade was opened. This pattern continued over the next seven years until American Martyrs had a single K-8 configuration.

In the mid 1990s, however, American Martyrs experienced an upsurge in applications. As a result, in 1996, the school began to double its grades again. A second kindergarten was added in 1996 and a second first grade the following year. This pattern of expansion continued until American Martyrs was once again a double-grade school.

The Sisters of St. Joseph of Carondelet had staffed American Martyrs since 1947. In June 1987, however, the community relinquished its administration.

Mr. Kevin Baxter is principal.

Annunciation

Annunciation School in southeast Arcadia actually began at St. Luke's School in Temple City. Although construction of the school had been underway since the previous year, the building was not ready for occupancy by February 4, 1952, the date on which the pastor, Father Dominic Daley, had announced classes would begin. Therefore, the first and second grades initially met at nearby St. Luke's.

The five-classroom building plus a convertible classroom-assembly room were completed in late spring. The following September 1952, 244 children registered for school. Additional classrooms were added to the school plant in 1956, in 1959, and again in 1964. By 1960, the school had sixteen classrooms and a total enrollment of 816. With the waning of the population explosion of the 1950s and 1960s, however, the double grades were gradually phased out. A kindergarten opened in 1987.

Annunciation School was originally staffed by the Sisters of St. Francis of Penance and Christian Charity. Following the withdrawal of this community in July 1989, Sister Marie Therese Gleeson, O.P. became principal. In 1993 Sister was succeeded by Sister Anthony Loos, C.S.S.F.

In 1996, Mr. Christopher Martinez began his tenure as principal.

Los Angeles

Ascension

During the early 1920s, the district around 112th and Figueroa streets was composed primarily of small farms and open fields. In the mid 1920s an imaginative developer subdivided the area and named his potential residential community Athens-on-the-Hill. Shortly after, Bishop John J. Cantwell erected Ascension Parish.

In 1939, ground was broken for a school. Ascension School opened on September 23, 1940 with an initial enrollment of 230 students. In the beginning, classes were held in the four-room classroom building and in the parish hall. In 1954, four new classrooms were added. Shortly afterward, a primary building, containing four additional classrooms, was erected in order to accommodate the student population of nearly 700 pupils. As a result, Ascension became a twelve-room school.

Gradually, however, the school enrollment began to decline as the construction of the Harbor Freeway (Interstate #110) took away the homes of many of Ascension's parishioners. Classrooms were redesigned until, by the mid 1970s, the school itself consisted of only nine grades, kindergarten through eight.

From the beginning, Ascension School had been staffed by the Sisters of St. Joseph of Carondelet. In 1991, the Sisters of Notre Dame of Namur accepted the administration of the school.

Following the Sisters departure in June 1997, Ascension has had a lay principal; at present, Ms. Karen Kallay.

Los Angeles

Assumption

Malabar and Winter streets were quickly replaced by bulldozers and backhoes in the early spring of 1949 when construction began on Assumption School in Los Angeles. The eight-classroom building was ready for occupancy by the following autumn. Regular classes began for 265 children that September. A kindergarten program was added at the beginning of the 1992-1993 school year. A pre-kindergarten opened in September 1994.

The school was initially under the direction of the Sisters of Charity of the Blessed Virgin Mary. Following their withdrawal in June 1979, a lay principal was appointed.

Today Ms. Carolina Gomez is principal.

Pasadena

Assumption of the Blessed Virgin Mary

Assumption of the Blessed Virgin Mary School, Pasadena, opened on September 15, 1952, for 163 children in grades one through four. An additional grade was added each year until the school achieved a grade 1-8 configuration.

Assumption of the Blessed Virgin Mary's plant has been enlarged several times in the school's history; first in 1953 and again in 1958. Eight years later, in 1966, the completion of the new church permitted the pastor to convert the old church into a parish hall. The old hall, in turn, was divided into additional classrooms. A kindergarten was added in 1990.

Assumption of the Blessed Virgin Mary School was originally staffed by the Sisters of the Holy Child Jesus. Due to the reduced number of available personnel, however, the sisters were obliged to withdraw from school at the end of the 1975-1976 school year. Ms. Nancy McKenna was appointed principal for the following year.

A dedicated faculty, with Ms. Mary Jo Wynne as principal, staff the school today.

La Mirada

Beatitudes Of Our Lord

Although Beatitudes of Our Lord Parish was erected in June of 1964, various delays postponed construction of the church and school for nearly two years. It was not until April 17, 1966 that the pastor was able to break ground for the parish plant. Six months later, two eight-classroom units had been completed. Beatitudes of Our Lord School began classes on September 19, 1966. Three hundred seventy-five children enrolled in grades one through six; the first and second grades were double. By the time the first eighth grade graduated in June 1969, the student body numbered over 450 children. The following year, 1969-1970, enrollment peaked at 508 students. That same year, at the request of the archdiocese, Beatitudes School began to phase out its double grades. When Beatitudes School was built in 1966, a six-room area in one of the classroom units served as a temporary parish hall. When the new church was completed in the fall of 1991, the "old church" became the parish hall. As a result, the vacated classroom area was gradually used for other purposes. A kindergarten was begun in September 1992 and a new science lab opened in December of 1993.

The Bernadine Sisters of St. Francis had initially staffed Beatitudes. Lack of personnel compelled this community to withdraw from the school in June 1991. The following September, Sister Bridget Flannery, S.S.L. became principal.

Today Ms. Carolyn Horecsko holds that position.

Hollywood

Blessed Sacrament

Blessed Sacrament School opened on February 1, 1915. Because of the heavy debt incurred in building the original church and renovating the rectory, the parishioners decided to utilize the old hall—a former Protestant church - as a temporary school. Sliding partitions and new desks were installed. Seventeen children, enrolled in grades one through four, made up the first classes. During the following winter, the heavy rains that flooded the property made this building uninhabitable. The pastor managed to erect a small, three-room, screen-sided bungalow into which the students could move. Two more classrooms were added in 1919.

Originally both Blessed Sacrament Church and School were located on three lots on the southeast corner of Prospect Avenue (now Hollywood Boulevard) and Eulalie Street (now Cherokee Avenue). The rapid growth of Hollywood itself, however, as well as the encroachment of the business district soon made this site a less than ideal location. In February 1921, the parish purchased property on Sunset Boulevard. and Cherokee Avenue, and on January 2, 1923 broke ground for a new school. On September 21, 1923, Blessed Sacrament School began classes for 370 students on its present site.

During the first seventy-one years of its existence, Blessed Sacrament School was staffed by the Sisters of the Immaculate Heart of Mary.

In June of 1986, the sisters withdrew. From 1994 to present the principal has been Ms. Ava Haylock.

Los Angeles

Cathedral Chapel

Cathedral Chapel in Los Angeles opened on September 8, 1930 with an enrollment of 510 students in grades one through eight. Tuition was $2.00 a month for the oldest child. In addition, children could purchase hot lunch items in the cafeteria for $.05 each. Since the new school was in the suburbs, transportation was a problem; however, it was resolved in a rather unique way. The students used taxis.

The pastor, Monsignor Bernard J. Dolan, had made arrangements with the local cab companies to transport the children to and from school. The fare was $3.00 a month per child. It soon became a familiar sight to see the cab drivers standing at attention with their passengers during the flag raising each morning.

Originally Cathedral Chapel had been envisioned as having a K-8 configuration. In 1931, however, a ninth grade was opened as part of an experiment by the Diocesan Department of Education. However, the separate junior high division with a departmental curriculum was judged to be detrimental to the lower grades, so the ninth grade was discontinued in June 1933.

In the beginning, Cathedral Chapel was staffed by ten Sisters of the Immaculate Heart of Mary. This community continued to staff Cathedral Chapel until 1968. Since September of that year, the Sisters of St. Louis administered the school. In 1987, this community also withdrew and a lay principal was hired.

Ms. Tina Kipp is principal.

Chatsworth

Chaminade Middle School

The opening of Chaminade Middle School in Chatsworth in 1987 offered the youngsters of the West San Fernando Valley a unique educational experience in the Marianist tradition.

In September 1961, the Brothers of the Society of Mary (Marianists) had moved their four-year high school, then known as Chaminade High School, from West Los Angeles to Canoga Park. The new facility was called Chaminade Preparatory.

Eight years later, in 1969, the Society leased the 18-acre site of St. John's Military Academy in Chatsworth from the Sisters of Mercy. As a result, in September 1969, Chaminade opened a second campus for young men, both resident and day, in grades seven, eight and nine. The instructional program at both sites was expanded further in February 1972 when the schools began to admit young women.

In 1987 the Marianists purchased the Chatsworth property from the Sisters. As a result, grade nine was moved to the Canoga Park campus (now West Hills). The school, now known as Chaminade College Preparatory High School, once again offered a four-year program. At the same time, the addition of the sixth grade at the Chatsworth campus marked the beginning of Chaminade Middle School. Since its inception, Chaminade Middle School has continued to educate young men and women of the San Fernando Valley.

At present, James Adams is president and Ms. Christine Phelps, principal.

Los Angeles

Christ the King

Christ the King School in Los Angeles opened in September 1958. Since the school building itself was still under construction, the 115 children met in a church-owned apartment located on the lower end of the property. Classes were held in half-day sessions as the entire student body could not be accommodated in the small "school building." By the following September 1959, the new building was ready for occupancy.

Christ the King began with grades one through five. A new grade was added each year until the school achieved a 1-8 configuration. A two-story addition containing an auditorium and two additional classrooms was added in 1962. In 1970, however, financial difficulties necessitated the closure of the seventh and eighth grades. The students transferred to Blessed Sacrament. By the mid 1980s, however, support within the school community for the reopening of the junior high division became apparent. As a result, Grade 7 was reinstated in September of 1986, and Grade 8, the following year.

From 1958 to 1970, the Religious of the Sacred Heart of Mary staffed Christ the King School. Personnel problems, however, forced the sisters to withdraw in June of that year. The community was replaced by the Sisters of the Holy Cross, who directed the school for the next twelve years. At the end of the school year 1981-1982, they too withdrew and Sister Sheila Jordan, S. S. L. was appointed principal. Sister Sheila was replaced by a lay principal, Ms. Antoinette Crump, in September 1989.

Dr. Mary Kurban is, at present, principal.

Corpus Christi

Archbishop James Francis A. McIntyre laid the cornerstone for Corpus Christi School in Pacific Palisades on May 27, 1951. The eight-classroom school opened on September 17, 1951. Two hundred ninety children, taught by the Sisters of St. Louis, were enrolled in kindergarten through grade six. Grades seven and eight were added during the next two years so that, by 1953, the school had reached capacity. The facilities soon proved to be inadequate. Consequently construction was begun in 1956 on a ten-classroom addition. By September 1959, the school's total enrollment reached 659 students

The decade of the 1970s brought several significant changes to Corpus Christi. Because two local public schools as well as a private school in the area had excellent kindergarten facilities, the program at Corpus Christi was dropped in 1970. Two years later, the school also began to phase out the double grades. The vacated classrooms were converted to a computer lab and special rooms for art, math, music, reading and science.

At present, Corpus Christi is a K-8 school, staffed by the Sisters of St. Louis, under the leadership of Sister Patricia McGahan, S.S.L.

Divine Savior

Divine Savior Parish in northeast Los Angeles began in 1907 as a mission to serve the Polish-speaking Catholics who worked in the nearby railroad yards. Fifteen years later, when Father F. A. Wekenman, the pastor, petitioned the Superior General of the Sisters of Loretto at the Foot of the Cross, for nuns to staff a parochial school, the population had become predominantly English speaking.

Divine Savior School opened in September 1922. A second wing was added to the existing structure in 1952 in order to provide eight more classrooms. In 1983, a kindergarten program was begun.

The Sisters of Loretto at the Foot of the Cross had staffed Divine Savior School since 1922. Because of declining numbers, however, the Sisters withdrew from the school in June 1978. The following September the first lay principal was appointed.

Today it is Ms. Patricia Van Ness.

Dolores Mission

In 1946, a small community of Belgian sisters, the Missionary Sisters of the Immaculate Heart of Mary, asked Archbishop John J. Cantwell for permission to work in his diocese. He sent them to the small Jesuit parish of Dolores Mission and from this assignment sprang an elementary school.

At first the sisters did social work in the parish. However, they soon added education to their ministry and in September 1950 opened a parochial school. Since ground had not been broken for a permanent structure when classes began, grades one and two met in the back of the church; grades three, four and five, in a wooden structure on the rear of the property. By the following year, 1951, the students were able to move into their three-story, nine-classroom building. As the five original classes moved up, a new grade was added each year until, by September 1953, the school had a K-8 configuration. In 1967 however, the kindergarten was closed in order to make room for the Title I program.

In 1969, the Archdiocese of Los Angeles identified Dolores Mission as one of the potential feeder schools for the new Queen of Angels Middle School near downtown Los Angeles and the seventh and eighth grades were subsequently closed. With the closure of the middle school in 1982, the pastor requested permission to reopen the junior high division. The seventh grade was ultimately reinstated in 1984 and the following year, 1985, the eighth grade was added. The kindergarten was reopened in September 1993.

Mr. Javier Avitia is principal today.

Epiphany

Construction on Epiphany School in South El Monte was completed in March 1959. Classes began for approximately 300 children in grades one through six on September 14th of the same year. In September 1960, a seventh grade was opened, followed by an eighth grade the next year.

The original structure contained eight classrooms. The rapid expansion of the community, however, obliged the pastor, Father Michael Hunt, to enlarge the school facilities. A two-classroom addition was completed in 1963 and a four-classroom unit in 1965 giving Epiphany two classrooms for each of its eight grades. In 1986 salary scale increases and higher tuition rates coupled with the exodus of families to less expensive residential areas of the San Gabriel Valley compelled the school to begin phasing out the double classrooms. A kindergarten program was inaugurated on August 29, 1994 to help stabilize the enrollment.

Today Epiphany School serves a predominantly Latino population. Although the school was originally staffed by the Bernardine Sisters of the Third Order of St. Francis, it now has a lay administration, headed by Ms. Gina Garcia as principal.

Beverly Hills	Pacoima	Arcadia	Ventura

Good Shepherd

Guardian Angel

Holy Angels

Holy Cross

Classes began for 152 children in grades one through eight from Good Shepherd Parish in Beverly Hills on September 8, 1930. Two features set this particular school apart from the other parochial institutions in the archdiocese. The school was not located next to the church as is most often the case. Since the pastor could not persuade the Beverly Hills City Council to change the zoning along Santa Monica Boulevard so that the parish could erect a school, the building was constructed on property south of Wilshire Boulevard on the corner of Linden Drive and Charleville Boulevard. In addition, the school did not bear the name of the patron of the parish. Instead, it was known as "Beverly Hills Catholic School." In 1975, however, the name was officially changed to Good Shepherd School.

During the first forty-five years of its history, the Sisters of the Holy Cross had staffed Good Shepherd School. In 1975, however, the sisters announced their need to withdraw from the school at the end of the academic year. They were replaced by the Sisters of Mary, Mother of the Church, with Sister Mary Leonella Lynch, I.H.M. as principal. After twenty-four years of service, these sisters withdrew in June 1999. Sr. Mary Elena Lopez, C.S.J., was principal from 1999 to 2004. In 2004, Ms. Terry Miller became principal.

When Guardian Angel School, Pacoima, opened in September 1956, its staff consisted of two laywomen who taught grades one and two. The following September, the Congregation of the Religious of Jesus and Mary accepted the administration of Guardian Angel and three sisters joined the faculty. As a result, the school's configuration was expanded to grades one through six. The seventh and eighth grades were added during the next two years so that, by 1959, the student population reached 365 students. In 1988, a kindergarten program was begun through the generosity of the Shea Foundation.

Guardian Angel School is located in the heart of San Fernando Gardens, a low-income federal housing project. Initially, the school served a predominantly African-American population. In recent years, however, the large influx of Latino families into the Pacoima area has impacted the ethnic composition of the school.

Understanding and meeting the needs of these students are a constant challenge for both the staff and administration, headed by Ruben Cortez, principal.

Holy Angels School in Arcadia opened in October 1946. The student population consisted of 187 children in grades one through six. The following year, a seventh grade was added. By the time the first class graduated in June 1949, the school enrollment totaled nearly 400 students.

The post-war housing boom had a dramatic impact on Arcadia. As more and more young families moved into the area and sought to enroll their children in a Catholic school, Holy Angels' plant soon proved inadequate. In 1952, and again in 1956, the pastor had to add an eight-classroom addition plus a junior high library, teachers' lounge and boys' and girls' locker rooms to the school. By 1961, Holy Angels enrolled over 800 students in double grades.

By the end of that decade, however, Southern California's population boom had begun to wane. As Holy Angels began to cut back on its enrollment, the extra classrooms were renovated to meet other curriculum needs. A kindergarten program was inaugurated in 1986, and a computer lab, in 1987. A child care center was opened in 1990, a science room set up in 1994, and a prekindergarten program licensed in 1999.

In the beginning, Holy Angels School was staffed by the Sisters of St. Francis of Penance and Charity. In 1971, these sisters were replaced by the Sisters of St. Felix of Catalice (Felicians). A shortage of personnel as well as the retirement of two of the three sisters on the staff necessitated this community's withdrawal in June 1989.

Today, Mr. Theodore Carroll is principal.

The recent opening of a new three-story Holy Cross School in Ventura represents only the latest chapter in the long history of education in the shadow of San Buenaventura Mission. Although the earliest documented proof of the existence of a school at the Mission is found in a report dated 1829, it was not until 1921, however, that construction of the first Holy Cross School was completed – a single structure consisting of four classrooms and residence for the sisters, members of the Congregation of the Holy Cross who would staff the school. The agreement between the parish and the sisters, however, contained an interesting stipulation; namely that the new school would be named "Holy Cross" in honor of the order.

When classes opened in late September of 1921, the number of students asking to enroll was more than three times the number expected. Consequently the expansion of Holy Cross' original facilities became imperative. In 1925 two additional classrooms and an auditorium were constructed. Four years later, in 1929, another classroom was added at the rear of the building in order to provide a place for the music and dancing lessons that the school offered. Finally in 1955, two more classrooms plus a library, an office and a supply room were constructed.

Holy Cross School as well as the Mission itself had always suffered from a lack of space. In the mid-1990s, the parish launched a building project that resulted in the construction of a multi-purpose building – Junipero Serra Center – as well a new Holy Cross School, which today is headed by Sister Rachel Yourgules, I.H.M., principal.

Glendale

Holy Family

The Sisters of Charity of the Blessed Virgin Mary have been active at Holy Family School since its opening in 1925. In that year the pastor, Monsignor Michael J. Galvin, invited the sisters to staff his newly completed parochial school. Six sisters accepted his invitation thereby making Holy Family School their community's first foundation in Southern California. When the sisters arrived in the summer of 1925, only five of the classrooms were completed. Consequently, Holy Family School began with only seven grades. The eighth grade was slated to open the following year.

By the early 1960s, however, the large enrollment had made Holy Family's original elementary school building inadequate. Therefore, in 1962, the parish broke ground for a new unit that would contain eight classrooms, a multi-purpose room, and a faculty lounge as well as space for library storage. A kindergarten was opened in 1987 and a prekindergarten program established in 1993.

Although the Sisters of Charity have remained active in Holy Family School and parish, in 1990 they relinquished the administration of the school to Mrs. Marion Heintz, a lay woman.

South Pasadena

Holy Family

Although Mass had been celebrated in what was to become South Pasadena as early as 1770, nearly a century and a half passed before the Catholics of the area had a church of their own. In 1906, the diocese acquired title to property at the corner of Fremont Avenue and El Centro Street with the intention of erecting a parish. Three years later, in November 1909, Bishop Thomas J. Conaty formally created Holy Family Parish to serve the people of South Pasadena. Nearly twenty-five years elapsed however, before Father James B. Morris was able to purchase land on which to build a parochial school.

Holy Family School opened on September 7, 1937. Ninety-four students were enrolled in grades one through eight. A preschool was added two years later, and a kindergarten in October 1941.

During the 1940s, the school population continued to grow. As a result, a two-story addition was completed in 1949, which allowed Holy Family to double its enrollment. In June 1998, a special ground breaking ceremony officially launched Holy Family Education Center, a state-of-the art facility that houses both the school and parish religious education program. In the spring of the following year the old school was razed and classes began in the "new" Holy Family School on September 1, 1999.

Initially Holy Family School was staffed by the Sisters of Loretto at the Foot of the Cross. In 1980, however, a shortage of personnel compelled the sisters to withdraw. Since that time the school has continued with an all lay staff.

Ms. Carolyn Strong is principal.

Wilmington

Holy Family

Ground was broken for Holy Family School, Wilmington, on January 8, 1950. Construction of the nine-classroom building was completed in time for the first day of classes on September 11, 1950. At that time, 177 children enrolled in grades one through five. A kindergarten and grade six were opened the following year. Grades seven and eight were added in the next two successive years. By 1953, Holy Family maintained grades kindergarten through eight.

The school plant was expanded in 1957 and again in 1980 when additional property was purchased in order to increase the size of the playground. In 1984 a religious education office and tutoring rooms were added; in 1986, a lunch pavilion, and in 1991, a computer lab and school cafeteria.

In 1996, the Carmelite Sisters of the Most Sacred Heart, who had staffed the school since its foundation, relinquished the administration to Mrs. Cecilia Campos.

The principal at present is Ms. Carolyn Hart.

Long Beach

Holy Innocents

Holy Innocents School in Long Beach was opened in 1958 in response to James Francis Cardinal McIntyre's request that every parish in the Archdiocese of Los Angeles establish a parochial school. Since property near the church was not available, the pastor, Father John J. O'Brien, purchased six lots at 25th Street and Pacific Avenue. Construction was started in March 1958. On September 15, 1958, 176 students in grades one through five began classes. One grade was added each successive year until the first graduation in June 1962.

The school plant has been enlarged three times. In September 1959 the convent was completed. In 1967, a multi-purpose hall that has been used extensively for school activities was added. Lastly, a kindergarten program was begun in 1990 under the auspices of a grant from the Shea Foundation.

The Carmelite Sisters of the Most Sacred Heart have staffed Holy Innocents since 1958. Today Sister Margaret Ann Laechelin, O.C.D. is principal.

Los Angeles	San Dimas	Montrose	Los Angeles

Holy Name of Jesus

A handful of African American Catholics, who gathered in a small wooden building at the intersection of Gramercy Place and Jefferson Boulevard in 1921, was the nucleus of Holy Name of Jesus Parish. Three years latter, in 1924, the second pastor, Father Joseph J. Truxaw, finished construction of a two-story structure on Cimarron and West Jefferson Boulevard that would serve not only as a church-auditorium but as a parochial school as well. The Sisters of Loretto at the Foot of Cross were invited to staff the latter. One hundred fifty students enrolled in grades one through eight when Holy Name of Jesus School opened its doors in September of that year.

Early accounts describe the new school as up-to-date and fully equipped. However, by 1960, the building no longer conformed to the City of Los Angeles' stringent building and safety codes, so construction was begun on a new nine-classroom structure. The new building was completed in April 1961. Shortly after, the old school was razed. The following year, 1962, the pastor, Father Patrick J. Roche, completed the replacement of the original plant by adding an auditorium as well as another classroom. A kindergarten program was begun in 1983.

Holy Name of Jesus has been under the direction of lay principal -- at present Ms. Marva Belisle -- since the Sisters of the Loretto withdrew from the school in June 1978.

Holy Name of Mary

The parish of the Holy Name of Mary, San Dimas, is in reality a consolidation of two former missions, Our Lady of Guadalupe, La Verne, and Our Lady of Mt. Carmel, San Dimas. In 1956, the two chapels were combined into a single parish dedicated to the Holy Name of Mary. On January 4, 1957, the pastor broke ground on a nine-acre site at the corner of Bonita Avenue and San Dimas Canyon Road for a church and school that would serve both communities. Classes began for 156 boys and girls in grades one through four on September 5, 1957. Three Sisters of St. Louis and one lay teacher staffed the school.

During the late 1950s and early 1960s, the population of the east San Gabriel Valley grew rapidly as the citrus groves and small farms gave way to residential subdivisions. The enrollment at Holy Name of Mary kept pace with it. By 1966, the student population had reached 455 and some grades were meeting in double sessions. On February 24, 1966, therefore, ground was broken for an eight-classroom unit as well as a parish hall. By 1968, the school had grown to fourteen rooms.

By the late 1960s, however, the school-age population in the area had begun to decline. Consequently, Holy Name of Mary School gradually phased out the double grade system and converted the extra rooms to other purposes. A kindergarten was added in 1979 and a prekindergarten in 2001

In the spring of 1993, the Sisters of St. Louis announced their intention to withdraw from Holy Name of Mary School at the end of the 1993-1994 school year. Ms. Candice Kuzmickas was named principal for the following year.

Holy Redeemer

When Bishop John J. Cantwell dedicated the newly erected church of the Holy Redeemer he recalled his initial doubts; namely, that this sparsely settled parish lying between the Sierra Madre and the Verdugo Hills could support such an undertaking. Between 1940 and 1950 however the population in the area more than doubled and there was no end in sight. The opening of Holy Redeemer School on September 16, 1946 represented the culmination of Father Patrick Healy's twenty-year dream.

The first months were rather makeshift. Since the classroom building itself was not finished, the teachers met their 158 students in the English Basement of the Community Church. Grades one, three and five attended classes in the morning; grades two, four and six, in the afternoon. On January 27, 1947, however, a new building was completed and the children and their teachers were able to move into their own school. By the beginning of the second year, the student population had nearly doubled. It continued to increase until its peak of 514 students in 1955. A kindergarten program was initiated in 1980.

Holy Redeemer School, like other schools in the archdiocese, was impacted by the State of California's commitment to a free-way system. The construction of the Foothill Freeway (Interstate #210) in the late 1960s took away many homes in the Montrose area. Consequently enrollment declined and the school itself was in danger of closing. This trend, however, reversed itself in the 1990s, and, in 1995, a preschool was begun.

When it opened, Holy Redeemer was staffed by the Sisters of Charity of the Blessed Virgin Mary. In June 1975, the community withdrew. At present the school has a lay faculty and staff, headed by Ms. Susan Fite.

Holy Spirit / St. Mary Magdalen

Holy Spirit / St. Mary Magdalen School was organized in 1970 as the result of the consolidation of two elementary schools – Holy Spirit and St. Mary Magdalen.

Holy Spirit Parish was founded in 1926. Ten years later, in 1936, the school was built and staffed by the Sisters of the Immaculate Heart of Mary. In 1968, the Immaculate Heart Sisters withdrew from the school and were replaced by the Sisters of the Holy Faith.

St. Mary Magdalen Parish was established, in 1930. In 1932, the school was opened and staffed by the Sisters of the Presentation of the Blessed Virgin Mary. When circumstances compelled the community to withdraw from the school in 1970, the decision was made to consolidate the two schools into a single institution under the leadership of Sister Mary Loretto O'Leary, C.H.F. Grades one through four would be located at Holy Spirit while students in grades five through eight would attend classes at St. Mary Magdalen.

In September, 1988, a kindergarten was added to Holy Spirit School.

Los Angeles

Holy Trinity

Although the parish of Holy Trinity in the Atwater Park area of Los Angeles had been erected in 1925, nearly twenty-five years passed before a parochial school was opened. In 1949, the parish hall was partitioned into four classrooms. On September 12, seventy-four students began their education under the direction of the Sisters of the Immaculate Heart of Mary.

By the early 1960s, however, Holy Trinity's original building had become inadequate for the school's growing enrollment. Moreover, the remodeled hall no longer met the City of Los Angeles' building and safety standards. As a result, construction of a new two-story eight-classroom structure was begun in 1964. When it was completed, the original school was demolished to make way for a larger parking area adjacent to the church.

The Sisters of the Immaculate Heart of Mary had been part of Holy Trinity since its opening in 1949. In 1968, however, the sisters relinquished the school to the Sisters of St. Felix of Catalice (Felicians). This community staffed Holy Trinity until June 1991 when a shortage of personnel necessitated their withdrawal. From September 1991 until June 1995, the Sisters of the Immaculate Heart again directed the school. Since 1995, Holy Trinity has had a lay principal and lay staff.

Today Mr. Anthony Grasso is principal.

San Pedro

Holy Trinity

At the end of World War II, the large number of former servicemen and their families who flooded Southern California stretched the limits of the existing schools and churches. In order to alleviate these crowded conditions precipitated by the war, in November 1946, Archbishop John J. Cantwell reactivated Holy Trinity as a separate parish. Four years later the pastor, Monsignor George M. Gallagher, purchased land for a parochial school. Ground was broken on March 5, 1950 and classes scheduled to begin the following September.

As the vacation months came to a close, however, the new building was not finished. Consequently, when school opened on October 4, 1950, the 334 students in grades one through seven met in the three completed classrooms and the auditorium. The school was staffed by the Sisters of the Presentation of the Blessed Virgin Mary. By the time the eighth grade was added the following year, 1951, the new building was ready for occupancy. A kindergarten was added in October 1956.

As the population of San Pedro continued to grow, so did the student population at Holy Trinity. By 1955, the number of children enrolled in the school made it necessary to begin doubling the grades.

Today Holy Trinity in San Pedro is a double-grade school. In June of 1990, the Presentation Sisters gave up the administration of the school. Mrs. Linda Wiley was named principal for the following September.

Los Angeles

Immaculate Conception

Immaculate Conception School has had two different names in its eighty plus year history. Shortly after his arrival in 1903, Bishop Thomas J. Conaty announced his intention to demolish the Cathedral of St. Vibiana and erect a more magnificent structure in the Westlake area. Accordingly he purchased property on the north side of Ninth Street as the future site for the new cathedral. Circumstances forced the bishop to postpone the project so, in 1909, he erected a small chapel dedicated to Our Lady of Guadalupe on the Westlake site in order to serve the Catholics of the area. In 1914, the chapel became the nucleus of a parish in its own right. The pastor's first task was to open a parochial school.

Construction of the first classroom building was completed in 1918. In the fall of that year 225 children began classes under the direction of the Sisters of the Immaculate Heart of Mary.

By the 1920s, however, the Westlake area was deemed unsuitable for a cathedral. Consequently, in 1926, the name of the parish was changed to that of the Immaculate Conception. Plans were make to erect a permanent church and school. The present school building was finished in 1927. A kindergarten was opened in 1989.

In September 1987, Immaculate Conception received nationwide attention when Pope John Paul II met informally with twenty-one seventh and eighth grade students during his visit to Los Angeles. The principal, Ms. Mary Ann Murphy, was also present.

Monrovia

Immaculate Conception

Immaculate Conception School, Monrovia, opened its doors to eighty-three students in September 1922. During the next thirty-seven years, from 1922 to 1959, the continued growth of the student population compelled the parish to expand the original four-classroom plant four times. In 1938 and again in 1951, a two-classroom unit was added. In 1953, three more classrooms were built and six years later, five additional classrooms were completed. By 1959 Immaculate Conception had expanded to sixteen classrooms. Beginning in the late 1960s, however, Immaculate Conception, like many other elementary schools in the archdiocese, began to phase out its double grades. A kindergarten program was begun in 1986.

From 1922 to 1980, the Sisters of Loretto at the Foot of the Cross staffed Immaculate Conception. In September 1980, the administration was turned over to a lay principal, although the Sisters of Loretto continued to teach several grades. In 1986, Sister Ann Carita Corbett S.L. was named co-principal with Sister Mary Agnes O'Connor, a Sister of Charity of the Blessed Virgin Mary. This arrangement lasted until 1988 when the latter religious became the sole administrator. In September 1993, the leadership of Immaculate Conception was again turned over to a layperson, Mr. Norman Mezey.

Ms. Joanne Pellegrino is the current principal.

Los Angeles

Immaculate Heart Middle School

Although Immaculate Heart Middle School opened in 1975, its educational tradition goes back more than a hundred years. In 1903, under the auspices of Bishop Thomas J. Conaty, the Sisters of the Immaculate Heart of Mary purchased, for $10,000, a fifteen-acre plot of land in the Hollywood Hills near what is now Western and Franklin Avenues. At the time, the area was outside the city limits and flanked by olive and orange trees. A wagon road provided the only access to the property. Two years later, on April 24, 1905, ground was broken for Immaculate Heart High School.

In 1975, Immaculate Heart Middle School was established on the same property. Initially the institution consisted of three seventh and three eighth grades and enrollment was limited to 150 students. Sixth graders were added to the student body beginning in 1995.

Today Immaculate Heart Middle School operates as an entity separate from the high school. It provides an excellent academic preparation for students wishing to continue their education in a college preparatory high school.

Ms. Anne Phelps is the Director.

Los Angeles

Immaculate Heart of Mary

Immaculate Heart of Mary, established in August 1910 as a mission chapel of Blessed Sacrament Church, was erected as a parish in its own right on January 5, 1912. The parochial school staffed by the Sisters of the Immaculate Heart of Mary opened on September 8, 1922. In June 1968, this community withdrew from the school. At the invitation of the pastor, Monsignor John O'Donnell, the Religious Sisters of Charity accepted the administration of the school.

Immaculate Heart of Mary Church is located in Hollywood in the shadow of the Griffith Park Observatory, a rapidly growing area of Los Angeles. Consequently, by 1955, the thirty-three year-old school building was no longer adequate for the needs of the parish. Therefore, a new structure was erected on the corner of Alexandria Avenue and Santa Monica Boulevard directly behind the old school. The original building was subsequently razed and the site used for a playground. A kindergarten program was begun in September 1992.

Sister Marsha Moon, R.S.C. is principal.

Glendale

Incarnation

Incarnation School in Glendale opened in September 1937, ten years after the parish itself was established. The 170 students who appeared on opening day, were taught by five Sisters of Charity of the Blessed Virgin Mary, who had accepted the invitation of the pastor, Father Michael Carvill, to staff the school.

The original building at Incarnation consisted of six classrooms and an auditorium. By 1943, however, the enrollment had increased to 300 children. In order to accommodate the growing student population, construction of a new wing was begun in 1948. Another addition consisting of six classrooms was completed in 1962, giving Incarnation sixteen permanent classrooms. Eventually, the enrollment reached its peak of nearly 600 students.

The next two decades brought several significant changes to Incarnation. In the 1970s, in keeping with the policy of the Archdiocese of Los Angeles, the school began to phase out its double grades. A library and media center were opened in the unused rooms. In 1984, the Sisters of the Blessed Virgin Mary withdrew from the school and a lay principal, Mr. Robert Grossi, was hired.

Today Ms. Anne Regan-Smith is principal.

Lompoc

La Purisima Concepcion

In the 1930s and 1940s, Lompoc was a predominantly agricultural area. The advent of the Space Age in the mid-1950s, however, soon changed this, as residential tracts rapidly replaced the small truck farms and cattle ranches. By 1958, the population of the area had expanded from 6,000 to 11,000 individuals and was expected to double again by the end of 1959. To serve the educational needs of the families moving into the area, ground was broken for La Purisima Concepcion School on December 8, 1956. Staffed by the Religious of Nazareth, the school opened on September 10, 1957 for children in grades one through five. By 1959, the presence of approximately 400 students in grades one through eight severely taxed the building's capacity.

The 1970s and 1980s brought several important changes. In August 1969, the Superior General of the Religious of Nazareth announced her intention to recall the sisters to Europe since they were the only members of their order in the United States.

Another significant change took place in 1986 when the government decided to end the Space Shuttle Program at Vandenberg Air Force Base. As a result La Purisima experienced a severe drop in enrollment. This trend, however, gradually reversed itself.

When the sisters withdrew in June 1971, Mrs. Barbara Rowe was appointed principal. The school continued under lay administration until the mid-1980s when Sister Mary Denis Donovan, C.S.J. became principal. Following Sister's retirement, the administration was again in the hands of a layperson.

Ms. Lucy Fahrbach is currently principal.

Gardena

Maria Regina

To Maria Regina School belongs the distinction of being the second parochial school opened in Gardena. The parish itself was erected in May 1956 and dedicated to the Blessed Virgin under her new title of Queen. The pastor, Father Michael J. Casey, broke ground for a parochial school on August 25,1957.

Maria Regina had originally opened with grades one through four. By 1962, the school had achieved a grade 1-8 configuration. The needs of the growing parish were such, however, that construction was begun almost immediately on a second eight-classroom unit. By 1969, Maria Regina had sixteen classrooms in operation. Enrollment peaked at 683 children.

This arrangement lasted for three years. By 1972, changes in the demographics of the area had begun to have an adverse impact on the school's enrollment. As Gardena became more industrialized, many families moved out of the parish. Newcomers to the area, on the other hand, tended to be either non-Catholic or unable to afford the rising cost of a parochial education. As a result, the second first and second grades were closed in September 1972. Grades three, four, five and seven became single classes the following year. By 1975, the school had returned to its original eight grades. A kindergarten program was begun in 1981, which brought Maria Regina to its present K-8 configuration.

Today Ms. Lynnette Felix-Lino is principal.

Pacoima

Mary Immaculate

In the years following World War II, Southern California experienced a building boom. One region in particular was affected by this development: the San Fernando Valley.

Consequently, in April 1956, James Francis Cardinal McIntyre formally erected Mary Immaculate Parish. Two years later, on Easter Sunday 1956, ground was broken for a parochial school. In September 1957, classes began for 314 students in grades one through five.

Although Mary Immaculate was conceived as a sixteen-classroom school, only the first floor of the building was completed. As the enrollment continued to rise, however, the parishioners decided to donate their time and talent on Saturdays to complete the school and renovate the rectory.

Both Mary Immaculate Church and School suffered severe damage during the Northridge Earthquake of January 1994. Thanks to the hospitality of the staff and students at St. Ferdinand School in San Fernando, the children were able to resume their classes in early February. By September portable classrooms had been set up on Mary Immaculate's campus so that students could begin the new academic year on their own site. At the same time, construction was begun on a new school. The building was finished late in 1987 and dedicated by Roger Cardinal Mahony on January 11, 1998.

Today, Ms. Federino Gullano is principal.

San Pedro

Mary Star of the Sea

Father Patrick J. McGrath had a reputation for building schools, churches and convents wherever he was assigned. Mary Star of the Sea Parish, San Pedro, was no exception. In 1914, two years after he was named pastor, he pulled down the shaky steeple on the original church on Centre Street and remodeled the building as a school. Furnished with cast-off desks from the Cathedral of St. Vibiana's basement, Mary Star of the Sea School was ready to open in September 1914. Two hundred students in grades one through six registered on the first day.

In 1921, Father M. H. Benso, Father McGrath's successor, purchased a full city block, bounded by Cabrillo and Meyler Avenues and 7th and 8th Streets, to accommodate the entire parish plant. Construction of a twelve-classroom structure was begun on August 7, 1922 and completed by the following April.

During War II, the construction of three federal housing projects as well as the influx of defense workers doubled the population of San Pedro. Both Mary Star of the Sea School and Church quickly became inadequate for the number of newcomers flooding into the area. Consequently, in 1946-1947, the pastor, Father George M. Scott, undertook a massive fund raising drive in order to replace or expand the existing parish facilities. A new convent was completed in September 1948 and a fourteen-classroom school and auditorium in 1950. A rectory followed in 1952; the high school building in 1953, and finally the church in 1958. A kindergarten program was inaugurated in September 1987. Ms. Noreen Maricich directs the school.

Santa Barbara

Marymount of Santa Barbara

Marymount of Santa Barbara began in 1937 as a high school for girls owned and operated by the Religious of the Sacred Heart of Mary. Originally located in Montecito, Marymount moved to its present location near Mission Santa Barbara in 1941. Major expansion programs during the 1950s and 1960s greatly enlarged the school facilities.

Until 1972, Marymount consisted of two divisions—Marymount High School for girls and Marymount Junior or Elementary School. In addition to day students, the school also accepted boarders for grades seven through twelve. In 1972, however, a decline in the number of available religious personnel coupled with low school enrollment compelled the Religious of the Sacred Heart to close Marymount High School. The junior school, however, continued as a co-ed elementary school, K-9. A lay Board of Trustees conducted the business and policy-making operations of the school.

In 1974, the sisters sold their property in Santa Barbara, including the acreage on which the school was located, to the Battistone Foundation. Three years later, in 1977, Marymount's Board of Trustees purchased the six acres, which made up the elementary campus, from the Battistone Foundation. Mrs. Dolores Pollock was appointed principal.

Mr. Douglas Phelps heads the school.

Mayfield Junior

The Sisters of the Holy Child of Jesus opened Mayfield Junior School in Pasadena in September 1931. The school, named after the community's school at Mayfield, Sussex, England, consisted of a convent and two moveable classrooms and followed the Montessori system of education. Eventually additional buildings were added to the school plant until Mayfield became a fully enrolled institution with grades one through twelve.

Until 1950, both Mayfield Junior and Senior Schools occupied the same site on South Euclid Avenue. In July of that year, Dr. Charles Strub purchased the John H. Eagle estate on Bellefontaine Street from the California Institute of Technology and gave it to the Sisters for the use of the high school. As a result, the sisters on the junior school faculty moved into the residence on Bellefontaine and Mayfield became a school on two campuses.

In 1956, a new eight-classroom elementary building on the South Euclid property was completed in time for the opening of the school in September. In 1963, the sisters purchased additional property and shortly afterward construction of a new two-story junior building was begun.

Further building development continued during the 1980s and 1990s. A multipurpose facility, completed in the late 1990s, is the most recent addition to the school plant.

Ms. Stephanie Griffin is Head of School.

Mekhitarist Armenian

Armenian Sisters' Academy

Mekhitarist Armenian School in Tujunga and the Armenian Sisters' Academy in Montrose are unique among the schools in the archdiocese. Both schools are under the jurisdiction of the Armenian Catholic Exarchate of the United States and Canada rather than that of the Roman Catholic Archdiocese of Los Angeles. Their mission is to evangelize the large number of Armenians who have immigrated to Southern California from various countries of the Middle East.

Father Michael Akian, pastor of Our Lady Queen of Martyrs Parish, Los Angeles, established Mekhitarist Armenian School in 1980. The principal is Rev. Augustin Szekula, C.M. Vind.

The Armenian Sisters' Academy opened in Glendale in 1985 as a Child Center under the direction of the Armenian Sisters of the Immaculate Conception. In the beginning the program was limited to 2 $\frac{1}{2}$ to 5 year-olds. However, a new grade was added each year until it became a complete elementary school.

Sister Lucia Al-Hail, C.I.C. directs the school.

Mother of Sorrows

Construction began in Mother of Sorrows Parish, Los Angeles, for a combination school and convent in the spring of 1948. When the opening day of school, September 13, 1948, arrived, however, workmen were still in the new building so 182 children began classes in the parish hall. This situation was only temporary. By the beginning of 1949, the classrooms were finished; on January 3, 1949, the children and their teachers moved in.

Mother of Sorrows began with grades one through four. The pastor, Father William O'Donnell, however, planned to add a new grade each year until the school had reached capacity. Consequently, in April 1950 he broke ground for a new wing for grades six, seven and eight. The addition was completed by September of the same year. On June 7, 1953, Mother of Sorrows graduated its first eighth grade of forty-seven students. Between 1948 and 1981, Mother of Sorrows School was staffed by the Sisters of Notre Dame de Namur, who had taught religion classes in the parish since August of 1943. In June of 1981, however, the sisters withdrew from the school and the administration was taken over by a lay principal.

In 1999, the Daughters of Charity accepted responsibility for Mother of Sorrows School and Sister Martha Garcia, D.C., was named principal.

Nativity

Nativity School in El Monte opened on September 2, 1947 for children in grades one through eight. At that time the school was staffed by the Missionary Sisters of the Sacred Heart who had agreed to minister in the parish until the pastor, Father Denis Ginty, could find another community of religious women to replace them. In 1949, the Sisters of St. Louis from Monaghan, Ireland accepted Archbishop James Francis A. McIntyre's invitation to teach in the Archdiocese of Los Angeles. They also agreed to staff Nativity School, which became their first foundation in the United States.

Nativity was originally built as a single-grade school. The rapid growth of the student population, however, made the expansion of the plant imperative. In 1953, four additional classrooms were completed. With the addition of four more classrooms in 1964, Nativity became a double-grade school.

In 1970, however, the double grades began to be phased out with the result that, by 1978, Nativity once again had only one grade on each level. A kindergarten was opened in September 1988.

Sister Stacy Reineman, S.S.L. is principal of the school.

South Los Angeles	Torrance	Los Angeles	Santa Barbara

Nativity

Nativity School was established in September 1921 under the direction of the Sisters of St. Joseph of Boston. When this community was recalled to the east coast in 1936, the Sisters of Loretto at the Foot of Cross took their place.

During the first forty-eight years of its history, Nativity was an eight-grade school. In the late 1960s, however, it was identified as a potential feeder school for the new middle school in Holy Cross Parish. Consequently, in June 1969, the junior high division was closed. As a result, for the next twenty-four years Nativity had a grade 1-6 configuration. A kindergarten was added in September 1986.

On January 17, 1994, the Northridge Earthquake shook large areas of Los Angeles. Nativity was among the four parochial elementary schools that were subsequently condemned. At the invitation of the principal of nearby St. John the Evangelist School, the students and staff of Nativity were temporarily relocated to that campus. By September 1994 modular units had been moved onto property adjacent to the original buildings and classes resumed on the Nativity site. At the same time, the pastor, Monsignor Timothy Dyer, campaigned for rebuilding of the school.

In September 1998, a newly renovated Nativity reopened its doors. There was a new grade as well. A seventh grade was added that year and a grade eight the following year.

The Sisters of Loretto were unable to welcome the students to the "new Nativity". A shortage of personnel had compelled the sisters to withdraw from the school in June 1994.

Sister Judith Flahavan, S.N.D. took over as principal in 1997 de N. heads Nativity School today.

Nativity

The discovery of oil in the early 1920s in the southern part of Los Angeles County had a tremendous impact on the area. "Boom towns" sprang up almost overnight. Among these was the "modern industrial city of 2,000 residents" founded by J. S. Torrance. In 1924, Bishop John J. Cantwell canonically erected Nativity Parish to serve the Catholics of this area. A second population explosion – this time as a result of World War II – brought the number of people to 15,000. Consequently, in the fall of 1944, when Archbishop John J. Cantwell sent Father Patrick J. McGuiness to Torrance as the newly appointed pastor of Nativity Parish, it was with the mandate to build a parochial school. In 1946, Father purchased property at Carson Boulevard and Acacia Street.

Construction was completed by the summer of 1948. On September 10, classes began for 303 children in grades one through eight. As the population in the Torrance area continued to expand, the original facilities proved to be inadequate. With the completion of a second eight-classroom unit in 1958, Nativity became a sixteen-room school. This arrangement lasted until 1968 when the double grades were gradually phased out. A kindergarten was opened in 1977 and a prekindergarten program begun in 1990.

In the beginning, Nativity was staffed by the Sisters of St. Joseph of Orange. When their community recalled these sisters in 1970, Sister Bernadette Cahill, I.H.M. became principal. Members of the Immaculate Heart community continued to direct the school until September 1974.

Mr. Michael Falco is currently principal of the school.

Notre Dame Academy

The Sisters of Notre Dame opened Notre Dame Academy Elementary School, Los Angeles, in the early spring of 1946. Construction of the elementary school building had begun on September 7, 1945. Although classes were scheduled to start on February 1, 1946, various delays pushed the opening date back to the first of April. Even then, the building was not finished. Nevertheless, the sisters decided to open as planned. That weekend they cleared out two of the rooms on the second floor of the convent and on the following Monday, April 1, 1946, classes for grades one, two and three began. A week later, two of the rooms were ready so the sisters and their pupils moved into the still unfinished building. When school resumed in the fall, on September 10, 1946, 246 children were enrolled at Notre Dame Academy Elementary School in grades one through six.

With the addition of the seventh grade in the fall of 1947, the elementary building had reached its capacity. Therefore, construction began on a two-story annex, which would provide classroom space for grades seven and eight as well as additional living quarters for the sisters.

When school began in September, a kindergarten was also opened. This program continued until 1956 when it was discontinued in order to accommodate the large elementary school enrollment. The program was reinstated in 1996.

The school currently follows the principal-president governance model with Ms. Katherine Nocella as principal and Sister Mary LaReina Kelly, S.N.D. as president.

Notre Dame

Notre Dame School in Santa Barbara was established in 1974 as the result of the consolidation of two local elementary schools, Dolores School and Our Lady of Guadalupe.

Dolores School was established in 1906 by Father Polydore J. Stockman, pastor of Our Lady of Sorrows Parish, and was staffed by the Sisters of Notre Dame of Namur. The enrollment, however, soon outgrew its original building. The cornerstone of a more permanent building was laid on Sunday, May 3, 1914. This building served the parish's needs until June 29, 1925 when an earthquake destroyed the school as well as the church and the rectory. In September, classes were held in temporary buildings on the southeast corner of Anacapa and Victoria streets until January 3, 1927, when the present building was ready for occupancy.

Our Lady of Guadalupe Parish in the southern section of Santa Barbara was originally a mission of Our Lady of Sorrows Parish. The pastor, Father Villa, S.J., however, felt that education would only be possible for the Latino people of the area if they had their own mission center. Consequently in 1917, he opened Our Lady of Guadalupe School and asked the Sisters of Notre Dame of Namur to staff it.

The two elementary schools operated separately until the early 1970s. At that time, declining enrollment together with increased operating costs at both schools made some type of adjustment necessary. Consequently, in 1974 the two parishes agreed to consolidate their schools into a single institution, which would be located in Our Lady of Sorrows Parish. The new school was named Notre Dame in order to honor both Our Lady and the Sisters of Notre Dame of Namur who had staffed both the schools since their beginning. Ms. Jaqueline Gonzalez is principal.

East Los Angeles	Artesia	Encino	Los Angeles

Our Lady Help of Christians

The parish of Our Lady, Help of Christians in Lincoln Heights in East Los Angeles was established in 1923 in order to minister to the large Italian population in the area. By the time the parochial school was opened in September 1944, however, the neighborhood had become predominantly Latino.

The original school consisted of five small wooden structures. In 1961, however, construction was begun on a more permanent building.

During its sixty-year history, Our Lady, Help of Christians has undergone significant changes both in configuration and staffing. In the beginning the school was comprised of grades kindergarten through eight. In 1969, however, Our Lady, Help of Christians was designated a "feeder school" for the new Queen of Angels Middle School in downtown Los Angeles. Consequently, the junior high division was closed. However, in September 1982, as a result of parental insistence, the seventh grade was reinstated. Grade eight reopened the following year. A kindergarten program, which had been discontinued earlier, was re-started in 1982.

The religious community staffing the school has also changed. In 1953, the Franciscan Sisters from Pennsylvania withdrew. They were followed by the Sisters of St. Louis. In 1962, these sisters were succeeded by the Sisters of the Pious Schools. In September 1975, these sisters were replaced by the Poor Clare Missionary Sisters, who, under the leadership of Sister Esthela Gonzales, M.C., continue to serve in the school.

Our Lady of Fatima

The city of Artesia, which was named for the artesian wells in the area, was once a small farming community inhabited principally by Dutch and Portuguese immigrants. Their spiritual needs were served by a small church on the corner of Corley and 187th Streets dedicated to the Holy Family.

In 1947, however, the pastor, Father Patrick O'Connor, purchased property on Clarkdale Avenue for a parochial school. As a tribute to the efforts of his Portuguese parishioners on behalf of the school, Father decided to dedicate the school to Our Lady under the Portugueses' favorite title, Our Lady of Fatima.

Our Lady of Fatima School opened on September 13, 1948 for grades one through seven and was staffed by the Sisters of the Immaculate Heart of Mary. As the dairy farms gave way to the city of Cerritos and to tract housing, the ethnic make-up of both the school and parish changed. Today, Our Lady of Fatima is composed primarily of families of Filipino, Chinese, Korean and Latino origin.

With the withdrawal of the Sisters of the Immaculate Heart of Mary in 1981, Dr. Larry Thompson became the first lay principal. Currently Ms. Kathleen Meyer is principal.

Our Lady of Grace

The growth of Our Lady of Grace School, Encino, is another example of the phenomenal development of the San Fernando Valley after World War II. When the parish was erected in 1945, Encino was described as a "sleepy town" with a number of nice homes as well as small ones. Ventura Boulevard was a street "without curbs" lined with a few small businesses. The development of housing tracts was just beginning. Classes at Our Lady of Grace School began for 170 students on September 3, 1947 in a single four-room building. This situation, however, would soon change.

In 1950, the parish was compelled to break ground for an additional four-class-room unit. In April of 1955 construction on another eight-classroom building was underway. By the mid 1960s, Our Lady of Grace had an enrollment of over 1000 students. The changing demographics of the Valley, however, coupled with archdiocesan policy, called for the phasing out of double grades in the early 1970s.

The decrease in student population paralleled the increase in lay staff members. In the beginning, Our Lady of Grace was staffed by five sisters of St. Joseph of Cleveland. When their bishop recalled the religious community in 1954, six Sisters of the Immaculate Heart of Mary arrived to staff the school. In 1985, the community turned the administration over to the Sisters of St. Louis. Sister Donna Hansen, S.S.L. was named principal.

Our Lady of Grace School is currently directed by Sister Ann Paul Clare, C.S.J.

Our Lady of Guadalupe

Southern California's close proximity to Mexico has always made it a haven for Latinos exiled from their native land for their political or religious beliefs. In 1922, one such group, who had settled in the Belvedere area of Los Angeles, petitioned Bishop John J. Cantwell to establish a church in honor of Our Lady of Guadalupe. The Bishop agreed and a small clapboard building on Fisher Street became the center of the new parish of Our Lady of Guadalupe.

In 1926, another wave of Mexican Catholics, fleeing the persecutions in their own country, sought refuge in Southern California. Although the people of the tiny parish quickly realized that a Catholic education must be a priority if their children were to preserve both their heritage and their faith, it was not until 1948 that a grant from the Youth Education Fund made it possible for them to open a school.

Since Archbishop McIntyre's school building program had created a shortage of teaching sisters in the archdiocese, the pastor, Father Patrick Kelly, invited the Missionary Sisters of St. Columban to staff his new school. In September 1950, three sisters and two lay teachers from the parish began classes for 250 children in grades one through five. The remaining grades were added in the next three successive years. A kindergarten program was begun in September 1991.

Ms. Beatrice Lopez is principal of the school.

Hermosa Beach

Our Lady of Guadalupe

The church of Our Lady of Guadalupe in Hermosa Beach was originally a mission of St. James Parish in Redondo Beach, erected to serve the needs of the Spanish-speaking people of the South Bay area. In 1923, a group of local residents donated labor and materials in order to erect a small catechetical center. Four years later, in 1927, Father Jose Alva, a refugee from the persecutions in Mexico, began to celebrate the Eucharist in the building. As a result the center was officially designated as a chapel and dedicated to Our Lady of Guadalupe.

In 1958, James Francis Cardinal McIntyre raised Our Lady of Guadalupe to the status of a parish. In 1961, the pastor, Father Samuel Bonikowski O.F.M., opened a parochial school for 200 children. It was staffed by the Carmelite Sisters of St. Therese from Oklahoma City, Oklahoma.

Our Lady of Guadalupe School originally began with the first four grades. A new grade was added each year until it achieved a grade 1-8 configuration. In 1985, a kindergarten program was begun in a small house to the rear of the main school plant. When this property was sold, the class moved into the main building

Six years later, during 1991-1992, extensive renovations and construction provided a new building for the kindergarten as well as a computer lab and a covered lunch area. At the same time, the parish hall was refurbished and the grounds landscaped.

At present Ms. Cheryl Hunt is principal of the school.

Oxnard

Our Lady of Guadalupe

By 1906, the number of Spanish-speaking families in the parish of Santa Clara in Oxnard had grown to such an extent that the pastor, Father John Laubacher, decided that he must do something to provide for the educational needs of their children. As a result, he invited the Sisters of St. Joseph of Carondelet to open a free school for the children of his Latino parishioners in a small building on East 7th Street. Forty-eight children enrolled on the first day.

The Sisters of St. Joseph staffed Our Lady of Guadalupe School for the next twenty years. In 1926, however, a group of Spanish-speaking nuns, fleeing the persecutions in Mexico, sought refuge in Oxnard. As a result, the Sisters of St. Joseph withdrew from Our Lady of Guadalupe and these sisters took over the administration and staffing of the school. Two years later, however, the community was invited to open a school for girls in Los Angeles. Consequently, the sisters gave up Guadalupe and, in 1928, the Sisters of St. Joseph again accepted the direction of the school.

Our Lady of Guadalupe had originally begun as a mission of Santa Clara Parish. In 1958, however, Santa Clara was divided and the mission church and school were incorporated into the newly established parish of Christ the King. Two years later, in 1960, the school, which consisted of a four-classroom unit, was relocated to its present site on north Juanita Avenue and Colonia Road. In 1970, when Archbishop Timothy Manning dedicated the new church, the name of the parish was changed to Our Lady of Guadalupe, the name of the original mission. Three years later, in 1973 construction was begun on four additional classrooms. A kindergarten was added in 1992 under the auspices of the Shea Foundation.

Ms. Siobhain O'Reilly-Hill is principal.

Los Angeles

Our Lady of Guadalupe-Rosehill

The opening of Our Lady of Guadalupe School in the fall of 1957 represented the culmination of a long tradition of Catholic education in the northeast part of Los Angeles. As early as the mid-1920s, a catechetical and social center was located on Mercury Avenue in what was then Sacred Heart Parish. Here the Sisters of Social Service had offered religious instruction to the families of the neighborhood. In 1924, this center became Our Lady of Guadalupe Mission and later the nucleus of Our Lady of Guadalupe Parish.

In 1951, Father Ramon Soriano invited the Missionary Sisters of the Immaculate Heart of Mary to take over the religious education program inaugurated by the Social Service Sisters thirty years earlier. When, in 1956, plans were underway for the construction of a parochial school, it seemed only logical that these sisters would be invited to staff it.

Our Lady of Guadalupe School opened in September 1957 for the children of the neighborhood of kindergarten age, and grades one, two and three. Two years later, in May 1959, construction was begun on four additional classrooms and a social hall. By the time James Francis Cardinal McIntyre dedicated the buildings on January 22, 1961, the school plant was compete.

Since September 1962, Our Lady of Guadalupe has had a K-8 configuration. In 1974, however, financial reasons forced the school to close the kindergarten. The program was reactivated in 1993 through a grant from the Shea Foundation.

Currently, Mr. Juan Carlos Garcia is principal of the school.

Los Angeles

Our Lady of Loretto

Our Lady of Loretto School opened on September 13, 1910. The school building, however, was not finished, so the first students - approximately 100 boys and girls - met their teachers in temporary quarters. Six months later, on March 12, 1911, the classes moved to their new building, one block from the present site. Although a third story was added in the summer of 1914, this building quickly proved to be too small for the school's growing enrollment.

The placing of the cornerstone on July 11, 1928, signaled the completion of the third Our Lady of Loretto School. The plant was enlarged in 1958 when four more classrooms, an office and a music room were added to the original eight-classroom structure.

Since its opening in 1910, Our Lady of Loretto consisted of grades one through eight. This configuration was changed briefly in June of 1974 when the seventh and eighth grades were closed and the students transferred to Our Lady Queen of Angels Middle School. Three years later, in September 1977, at the request of the parents, the seventh grade was reopened. The eighth grade was re-instated the following year. A kindergarten was opened in 1980.

Our Lady of Loretto School was initially staffed by the Sisters of the Immaculate Heart of Mary. In August 1921, this community was replaced by the Sisters of the Presentation of the Blessed Virgin Mary. A shortage of personnel necessitated the withdrawal of these sisters in June of 1974. During the following year, a lay principal, Mrs. Scottie Morrow, headed the school. In August 1975, the Eucharistic Missionary Sisters, who had joined the staff the previous year, accepted the administration of the school.

Today Ms. Fidela Suelto is principal.

Los Angeles

Our Lady of Lourdes

At the turn of the century, Belvedere, a small suburb just east of the Los Angeles city limits, was made up primarily of French, Irish, Slavic, Basque and Mexican families. In 1910, Bishop Thomas J. Conaty erected the parish of Our Lady of Lourdes. Father Gratian Ardans, O.S.B. was named pastor. Four years later, in 1914, Father opened a parochial school. It was staffed first by the Sisters of the Immaculate Heart and, beginning in 1919, by the Sisters of the Presentation of the Blessed Virgin Mary from San Francisco.

No one perhaps could have predicted this area's phenomenal growth. In 1910, the parish was made up of forty families and 200 parishioners. By 1951, the number had risen to 5,000 families and approximately 15,000 parishioners. Since the original four-classroom school was inadequate for the growing student population, Monsignor Patrick J. Dignan, Superintendent of Schools for the Archdiocese of Los Angeles, broke ground for a new twelve-classroom building and auditorium/cafeteria on Mary 26, 1950.

Both students and teachers had hoped to occupy the new building when school began in September 1951. Various construction delays, however, postponed the opening. Since the principal had accepted an unusually large number of new children in anticipation of the availability of the building, there was no choice except to continue to use the original four-classroom structure. Shortly after Christmas, however, the new building was finished and classes could be moved to the larger, more spacious rooms. Our Lady of Lourdes continued as a double-grade school until 1980. A kindergarten was opened in 1984 through the fundraising efforts of the alumni.

Ms. Annette Olivas presently heads the school.

Northridge

Our Lady of Lourdes

The parish of Our Lady of Lourdes in Northridge was erected on September 1, 1958 in order to accommodate the post-war population explosion in the San Fernando Valley. Eight months later, in May 1959, construction of a parochial school was well under way. The following October 12, classes began for 300 children in grades one through four.

By the beginning of the second year, however, 100 new children had registered and all of the eight original classrooms were occupied. It quickly became apparent to the pastor that the school's facilities were inadequate for the growing number of students who wished to enroll. In 1961, eight additional classrooms were opened. The school reached its maximum enrollment in September 1962 with 800 students in grades one through eight.

During the early 1970's, however, in keeping with archdiocesan policy, Our Lady of Lourdes School began to phase out its double grades.

Today, the school has a single grade K-8 configuration. Initially staffed by the Sisters of the Immaculate Heart of Mary, Our Lady of Lourdes currently has a lay administration, faculty and staff with Ms. Patricia Hager as principal.

Tujunga

Our Lady of Lourdes

The history of Catholic education in the Tujunga area begins with a legend. Old timers tell the story that near the turn of the century, a nun, known as Sister Elsie, used to visit the area to teach catechism to the Paiute Indian children who lived in the Verdugo Hills, and to take care of the cattle grazing in the upland area.

Nearly fifty years later, in 1949, during the pastorate of Father Denis J. Falvey, Catholic education assumed a more permanent form when the first two units of Our Lady of Lourdes School were completed. Classes began on September 13, 1949 for 225 children in grades one through six. Three Sisters of Charity of the Blessed Virgin Mary and one lay teacher staffed the school.

Two years later, in 1951, the addition of three more classrooms and an auditorium completed the school plant. These two buildings, however, quickly proved to be inadequate for Our Lady of Lourdes' burgeoning enrollment. In 1969, the erection of an eight-classroom unit across the street from the original buildings completed the sixteen-room structure. Beginning in 1971, however, the double grades were gradually phased out until the school reached its present K-8 configuration. The kindergarten was opened in September 1986.

Ms. Kathleen Jones is principal.

Malibu

Our Lady of Malibu

Of all the schools in the Archdiocese of Los Angeles, Our Lady of Malibu School has perhaps experienced more than its share of natural disasters. Covering a 20-mile long stretch of the Pacific coastline from the Ventura County line to Big Rock Drive, the parish plant has several times been in the path of the various brush fires that swept through the canyons.

Our Lady of Malibu School opened in September 1958, staffed by two Sisters of St. Louis and two lay teachers. The student population was made up of ninety-five children in grades one through six. Grades one and two, as well as grades five and six were combined. Four months later, on December 3, 1958, a giant brush fire erupted in the hills above the parish grounds and threatened both the church and new school. A five-hour fight successfully prevented the flames from destroying parish property although at one point the fire came within fifty feet of the church itself.

Twelve years later, early in September 1970, brush fires swept through the area again. This time, however, Our Lady of Malibu was not so fortunate. Flames severely damaged the church and completely destroyed the newly renovated Reading Resource Center. In November of 1992, a third fire came within fifty feet of the church itself.

Our Lady of Malibu's original school plant consisted of four classrooms, an office, and health and book rooms. Four additional classrooms were ready for use by 1962. Since that time, the school has had a K-8 configuration.

In 2004 Mr. Matthew Weber began his tenure as principal.

Our Lady of Mount Carmel

The parish of Our Lady of Mt. Carmel in Montecito traces its history to the episcopacy of Bishop Thaddeus Amat, C.M.. In 1856, the residents of the area erected a small adobe church on sixteen acres of land donated by Dona Ayala for a parish. A little more than forty years later, a wooden church with a steeple replaced the original chapel. A small white frame cottage served as the rectory. It was in this building that Our Lady of Mt. Carmel School began in 1944. Less than thirty students in combined classes, grades one through six, shared desks and materials when the school opened on September 11, 1944. Grades seven and eight were added in the fall of the next two years.

In the beginning, Our Lady of Mt. Carmel was very much an "old country school." Two students came to school on horseback. During classes the horses grazed peacefully in a sheltered corral in a corner of the meadow—today's athletic field.

The parishioners, however, were eager to have their children in a real school building. On August 17, 1953, ground was broken for a four-classroom, faculty room and office unit. In 1955, an auditorium and kitchen were built and two more classrooms added to the classroom wing; two additional classrooms were added in 1959. The following year, 1960, the original "rectory-school" was razed and two more classrooms were completed. The enrollment reached its maximum at 320 students. A kindergarten was added in 1985-1986 and a computer lab in 1988-1989.

Ms. Karen Regan is the current principal.

Our Lady of Peace

In 1941, the portion of the San Fernando Valley, which today comprises the parish of Our Lady of Peace, was still predominantly rural. By 1944, however, when the Our Lady of Peace was formally erected as a parish, the area then known as Sepulveda could rightfully be described as the "Hub City of the Valley".

In 1951, the pastor, Father James A. Leheny, began construction of a parochial school. Approximately 220 students in grades one through six made up the student body when classes began the following September. The Daughters of Mary and Joseph staffed the school; Sister Mary Catherine, D.M.J. was principal.

In order to keep pace with the San Fernando Valley's rapidly growing population, Father Leheny's successors continued to enlarge the school. By September, 1965, Our Lady of Peace was the largest elementary school in the archdiocese with a total enrollment of 1,150 students, taught by eleven sisters and thirteen lay teachers.

With the beginning of the 1970s, however, this situation began to change. The decision by Lockheed, American Motors and Northrop to relocate their employees compelled many of the families to move out of the area. At the same time, the school was asked to phase out its double grades. When the downsizing was completed, Our Lady of Peace had one grade on each level. A kindergarten program was added in 1985.

In June of 1973 the Daughters of Mary and Joseph discontinued their administration of the school. The following September, Sister Frances Catherine Curran, a Sister of Charity of Levenworth, was named principal. Since 1978 Our Lady of Peace has had a lay administrator. Today it is Ms. Mary Beynon.

Our Lady of Perpetual Help

Our Lady of Perpetual Help School, Santa Clarita, opened in September 1962 with an enrollment of approximately eighty students. Sister Mary Coleman, S.M. of the Sisters of Mercy from Manchester, New Hampshire, and Mrs. Ethel Morris made up the faculty. Mrs. Morris taught combined grades one and two while Sister, in addition to her duties as principal, took grades three and four. The following year a second laywoman, Mrs. Marqua, joined the staff so the school expanded to six grades.

Our Lady of Perpetual Help's original building contained only four classrooms. The opening of two additional grades made the construction of more rooms imperative. Plans for the erection of four more classrooms as well as an auditorium were completed in 1964. By the time the first twenty-three students were ready to graduate in June of 1967, Our Lady of Perpetual Help was a complete eight-grade school. A kindergarten was opened in 1988.

In June 1974, the Sisters of Mercy were recalled to their Motherhouse. In September of the same year, the Franciscan Sisters of the Immaculate Conception began their ministry in the parish. This religious community, under the leadership of Sister Mary Madalene, O.S.F., continues to administer and staff the school today.

Our Lady of Perpetual Help

Downey was another area of Los Angeles County whose population exploded during the post-World War II era. Although Our Lady of Perpetual Help Parish had been erected in 1909, its members had never felt the need for a parochial school. By 1948, however, the number of new families moving into the area had risen dramatically. Consequently, the pastor, Father Patrick J. Carey, decided that the time had come to open a parish school.

Father purchased a large Spanish-style mansion situated amid a three-and-one-half acre park. School was scheduled to begin in the fall of 1948. The cost of property, however, had exceeded the parish's budget; therefore, Father Carey had to postpone construction of the school. Consequently, although the Our Lady of Perpetual Help School formally opened on September 13, 1948, the 124 students in grades one through six had to meet in temporary quarters. This situation, however, only lasted one year. In January 1949, ground was broken for the school. When classes resumed after summer vacation, the new building was ready for occupancy.

The population boom of the 1940s, however, continued into the 1950s. As a result, no sooner had the original building been completed than it was necessary to begin construction of an extension. Three classrooms were added in 1951; four more in 1953. Two years later, 1955, the auditorium was completed and, in 1958, four more classrooms and a library. Beginning in September 1971, the school began to phase out the double grades. A kindergarten program was begun in 1976.

Since opening in 1948, Our Lady of Perpetual Help School had been staffed by the Sisters of Notre Dame. A shortage of personnel compelled the community to withdraw in June 1994.

Ms. Steffani McMains is the current principal.

Long Beach	Ventura	Claremont	Sun Valley

Our Lady of Refuge

In 1945, the Los Altos section of Long Beach was an area of beans, beets and boysenberries. Within three years, however, bulldozers and backhoes had replaced the small truck farms as construction began first on Our Lady of Refuge Church and then, in November 1952, on an eleven-classroom parochial school.

Our Lady of Refuge School opened in September 1953 for 266 children in grades one through five. It was staffed by the Sisters of St. Louis, with Sister Elizabeth Gildea, S.S.L., as principal. Two years later, work began on a two-classroom addition.

During the early 1970s a change in the demographic make-up of the area brought about a significant decrease in enrollment. By the time the Sisters of St. Louis withdrew from the school in 1977, the student population had dropped to 186. This trend, however, began to reverse itself with the opening of the kindergarten program in 1978 and the closing of nearby St. Matthew School in 1982.

Ms. Joan Bravo de Murrillo currently heads the school.

Our Lady of the Assumption

On August 15, 1769, two Spanish friars, Juan Crespi and Francisco Gomez, chaplains in Portola's Expedition, reached a small Indian village on the present day site of the city of Ventura. Since it was the feast of the Assumption of Our Lady, the men named the village "La Asuncion de Nuestra Señora." Nearly two centuries later, in 1952, this name was invoked once again when Archbishop James Francis A. McIntyre erected the parish of Our Lady of the Assumption in Ventura. Four years later, on March 9, 1956, the pastor, Monsignor Daniel Hurley, broke ground for a parochial school. Construction was finished by the summer of 1957.

Although the Sisters of Notre Dame had agreed to staff Our Lady of the Assumption, the community was unable to provide the necessary teachers immediately. As a result, Monsignor Hurley decided to open the school with a lay faculty. Mrs. Margaret Carroll was named principal. One hundred two students in grades one, two and three enrolled on the first day of class.

The following September, 1958, two sisters of Notre Dame joined the staff and Sister Mary Cornelius Ols, S.N.D. became principal. A new grade, the fourth, was also added. This practice continued for the next five years until Our Lady of the Assumption School achieved a K-8 configuration in September 1962. A kindergarten program was added in September 1989.

Following the withdrawal of the sisters in 2004, Ms. Patricia Groff became principal of the school.

Our Lady of the Assumption

Our Lady of the Assumption School in Claremont opened in September of 1955. Two hundred children were enrolled in grades one through six. Two Benedictine Sisters and three lay teachers comprised the original faculty. The following year, 1956, the seventh and eighth grades were added.

Initially Our Lady of the Assumption was planned as an eight-classroom school. By 1965, however, the rapidly expanding enrollment compelled the pastor to add an eight-classroom annex to the parish plant. At that time, 630 children attended the school.

At the beginning of the 1970s, however, Our Lady of the Assumption experienced a sharp drop in enrollment. As a result, in 1972 the newly organized parish Board of Education, in collaboration with the pastor, decided to close three classrooms. The following year, 1973, a fourth class was eliminated. This downward trend, however, gradually reversed itself with the result that the previously closed classes were reinstated. The kindergarten opened in 1987.

In 1965, the Benedictine Sisters, who had initially staffed and administered the school, withdrew and were replaced by the Sisters of St. Felix of Catalice (Felicians). This religious community made up Our Lady of the Assumption's religious faculty until June 1996 when they, too, withdrew.

A lay faculty and administration, headed by Ms. Erica Hamel, currently staff the school.

Our Lady of the Holy Rosary

Our Lady of the Holy Rosary School was opened on September 29, 1950 in order to serve the families of the community of Roscoe, now known as Sun Valley. Students in grades one through four met in the parish hall and in a nearby utility house until the following year, when the first unit of the school was finished. That same year, the parish began constructing a second six-room unit. In 1956, the third unit was completed making Our Lady of the Holy Rosary a double-grade school. A kindergarten was opened in 1981.

From 1950 until 1971, Our Lady of the Holy Rosary was staffed by the Sisters of Charity of Providence. From 1971 to 1983, the school was directed by a lay principal. In 1983, the Sister Servants of the Blessed Sacrament took over the administration of the school.

Today, the community, headed by Sister Remedios Aguilar, S.J.S., continues to staff the school.

Montebello

Our Lady of the Miraculous Medal

Our Lady of the Miraculous Medal School opened its doors on September 3, 1954 under the auspices of the Daughters of Charity. At that time the school was known as "Marian School" since it was the first new school dedicated to Our Lady, opened in the Marian Year. In 1989, however, the name of the school was officially changed to Our Lady of the Miraculous Medal so that it would be the same as that of the parish.

The first student body consisted of 190 children in grades one, two and three. Another grade was added each year with the result that, by 1962, the school had reached its goal of sixteen classrooms - double grades from one through eight. A double kindergarten was built in the summer of 1995. A preschool program was added in 2002 through the generosity of the Daughters of Charity Foundation.

Today, Our Lady of the Miraculous Medal School is a double-grade Pre-K to eighth grade institution. Co-sponsored by the Daughters of Charity, with Ms. Analisa Hernandez as principal, the school continues to maintain the traditions of the religious community that initially staffed it, as well as those of the Vincentians, who originally ministered in the parish.

Los Angeles

Our Lady of the Rosary of Talpa

Love of Our Lady has always been a hallmark of the Latino culture. Over the years it has been strengthened by various appearances of the Blessed Virgin to the people of Mexico. One such apparition took place in the small village of Talpa de Allenda, in Jallisco, in the seventeenth century. During the religious persecutions of 1926-1928, Mexican Catholics brought this devotion with them to Southern California.

One of these immigrant groups settled in East Los Angeles. At first, religious services for these refugees of the faith were held in a private home. Attendance was so large, however, that by 1927, a small chapel was built on East Sixth Street. Spanish-speaking priests from nearby St. Mary Church came each week to celebrate the Liturgy. In 1938, these priests were able to return to Mexico. As a result, the Spanish Vincentians, in the person of Father Jose Cervera, C.M., accepted responsibility for the now burgeoning congregation that remained in the Southland.

Our Lady of the Rosary of Talpa School opened in September 1951, staffed by three sisters of the Daughters of Charity of St. Vincent de Paul, from St. Louis, Missouri, and one lay teacher. The faculty enthusiastically welcomed 250 students on the first day, enrolled in grades one through four. A new class was added each succeeding year until the school achieved its present K-8 configuration.

Mr. Adolfo Mata is principal.

Paramount

Our Lady of the Rosary

Our Lady of the Rosary School in Paramount opened in September 1952 with an enrollment of 400 students in kindergarten through the sixth grade. Mother Mary Loyola of the Daughters of Mary and Joseph was principal; Father Henry J. McHenry, pastor.

By the fall of 1956, the student population reached 595 students. Within the next three years, the kindergarten was discontinued, six additional classrooms were erected, and a sixteen-classroom elementary school was set up. Student enrollment peaked at 720 children, and remained relatively stable during the next decade.

With the arrival of the 1970s, however, changes became necessary. In 1971, Our Lady of the Rosary began to phase out its double grades in order to comply with archdiocesan policy. By 1984, the school had been reduced to its present arrangement as a single grade school. A kindergarten program was reinstated in September 1991.

Sister Anna O'Reilly, D.M.J., is principal today.

Canoga Park

Our Lady of the Valley

Our Lady of the Valley School in Canoga Park opened in 1948 under the auspices of five Sisters of St. Joseph of Carondelet. The first student body consisted of 189 children in grades one through four. The expansion of the plant followed the pattern of other schools in the San Fernando Valley. The original educational construction contained four classrooms, an office and a first aid room. Four more classrooms were added in 1952 and replicated again in 1959. A kindergarten opened in 1974.

Beginning in 1971, however, the school began to phase out its double grades. Over the years, the extra classrooms have been utilized by the school itself as well as by various parish ministries.

Originally staffed by the Sisters of St. Joseph of Carondelet, as of 1989, the school has had a lay administrator.

Ms. Katheleen Delgado currently directs the school.

Compton

Our Lady of Victory

Our Lady of Victory School in Compton opened on September 15,1940, just thirty-six years after the erection of the parish itself. The school, consisting of five class-rooms and an auditorium, was staffed by four Sisters of St. Joseph of Orange and enrolled 188 students the first year.

In 1947, the pastor was able to purchase the Pathfinder Clubhouse on the north side of Palmer Avenue. This acquisition provided additional space for the sixth, seventh and eighth grades. As a result, the following September, Our Lady of Victory's enroll-ment increased by more than 200 students. The construction of a two-story brick building to replace the clubhouse in 1952, together with the addition of three more classrooms in 1961, brought the total number of rooms to sixteen.

The year 1975 brought several significant changes to Our Lady of Victory. In Septem-ber, three Sisters of the Holy Family, from New Orleans, welcomed the students in place of the Sisters of St. Joseph of Orange, who had withdrawn from the school the previous June. In addition, the downward trend in enrollment, which had become apparent in the late 1960s, began to reverse itself. Classrooms were gradually reopened until Our Lady of Victory was once again a double-grade school.

During the late 1980s and early 1990s, however, the demographic make up of the community began to change. As more and more African American families moved out, more and more Latino families moved in. However, the rising cost of Catholic education precluded their attendance at Our Lady of Victory School. As a result, the student population began to decline. Gradually the school went from double grades to combined grades and finally to single grades.

Ms. May Dualan is the currently principal.

Los Angeles

Our Mother of Good Counsel

Vermont was just a long avenue on which vacant lots alternated with homes in 1925 when Father John J. Farrell, O.S.A. was ap-pointed pastor of the newly erected parish of Our Mother of Good Counsel. Four years later, in April 1929, Father launched a fund raising drive in order to build a parochial school. Debts and the Depression, however, delayed the opening for four years.

Finally, Father Farrell's successor, Father Philip L. Colgan, O.S.A., collected enough funds to purchase two small wooden bunga-lows on Ambrose Avenue as the nucleus of the school. On September 11, 1933, classes began for grades one through four. Thirty-seven children were taught by the Sisters of the Immaculate Heart of Mary during the first year. In 1937, the parish purchased an additional cottage on Dracena Drive to use for the seventh and eighth grades. By 1939, Our Mother of Good Counsel School was ready to graduate its first class. In September 1949, these buildings were replaced with the present eight-classroom structure.

Our Mother of Good Counsel School was originally under the direction of the Sisters of the Immaculate Heart. In 1968, these religious withdrew and were replaced by a lay faculty with Sister Joseph Ann, C.S.C., as principal. From 1975 to 1978, the school was administered by Sister Clare Briody, D.M.J.; and from 1978 to 1985, by Sister Margaret Gallavan, I.H.M. In September 1985, Ms. Tina Kipp became the first lay principal. A kinder-garten program was begun on September 5, 1990 for a group of thirty curious five-year olds.

Ms. Andrea Deebs is principal.

Los Angeles

Precious Blood

In the 1930s and 1940s the area sur-rounding Precious Blood Church was composed primarily of vacant lots inter-spersed with large homes. Oil wells dotted Rampart Boulevard. The few children be-longing to the parish were bused to nearby Immaculate Conception School.

Opening a parochial school, however, was a long-standing dream of the pastor of Precious Blood Church, Monsignor Michael O'Halloran. Thus, in 1950, he bought a large home at the corner of Third Street and Occidental Boulevard. Three large rooms downstairs as well as the garage were con-verted into classrooms. The building was ready for occupancy by September 12, 1950. On the first day of classes, an old school bus went around the parish en-couraging the local children to attend. As a result of these initial efforts, 114 children eventually enrolled. In 1952, when the student body reached 200, a new class-room was added.

Initially the Daughters of Mary and Joseph staffed Precious Blood School. In June of 1971 however, these sisters were com-pelled to withdraw. For the next thirteen years, from September 1971 until June 1984, the Sisters of Charity of the Blessed Virgin Mary provided a principal. At the end of the 1983-1984 school year, the school's administration was handed over to a lay-person, Ms. Dawn Cooper.

Precious Blood originally began with grades kindergarten through six. Another grade was added each year until the school achieved a grade 1-8 configuration. How-ever in 1970, Precious Blood School was identified as a "feeder school" for Queen of Angels Middle School. In light of this, the junior high division was closed. Although Queen of Angels Middle School closed in 1982, the junior high program was not reinstated at Precious Blood School until September of 1995, at which time a kinder-garten was also added.

Ms. Dorothy Bessares is principal at pre-sent.

Los Angeles

Resurrection

The establishment of Resurrection School in the southern part of Boyle Heights is a testimony to the determi-nation of the school-age children of the neighborhood, and their desire to have their own parochial school.

Although Bishop John J. Cantwell had erected the Church of the Resurrection on December 12, 1923, there were no plans to open a parochial school on the site. Parents, therefore, had to send their children to nearby St. Mary. Religious education classes either at Resurrection itself, or at Our Lady of Victory, provided the only other opportunity for religious instruction in the neighborhood.

This situation, however, did not satisfy many of the neighborhood youngsters, so they decided to take matters into their own hands. As parishioners were leaving the church after Mass on Sunday, February 24, 1949, they were confronted by a line of children marching up and down the street, carrying picket signs urging them to build a parochial school of their own.

The students' efforts were apparently successful. Shortly afterward, the pastor, Father Henry Alker, purchased property on the corner of Eighth and Lorena. On February 21, 1950, ground was broken for a new school, which would be administered and staffed by the Franciscan Missionary Sisters of Mary Immaculate.

Classes began on September 11, 1950. Two hundred eleven children were enrolled in grades one through four in the school's initial year. In 1953, Father Alker's successor, Father Ramon D. Garcia, added a single story, three-classroom addition to Resurrection. Two years later, in 1955, the school gra-duated its first eighth grade class.

The principal today is Angelica Figueroa.

Covina

Sacred Heart

In the 1930s and 1940s, the community of Covina consisted of approximately fifty families living in an area dominated by citrus groves. The post-war population boom, however, dramatically changed this picture as more and more young families moved into the San Gabriel Valley.

On October 12, 1953 bulldozers began leveling eleven acres of citrus groves along Workman Avenue to make way for Sacred Heart School. The new school opened on October 12, 1953. Four Benedictine Sisters commuted daily from Glendora, in order to teach the 401 students enrolled in grades one through eight.

In the beginning, the school plant consisted of eight classrooms, an auditorium, a health room and a parish kitchen. In 1955, again in 1957, and yet again in 1958, more classrooms were added to accommodate the influx of new parishioners. By 1959, Sacred Heart School was a sixteen-room institution with an enrollment of approximately 820 students.

The 1970s, 1980s and 1990s were decades of change for Sacred Heart. In keeping with archdiocesan policy, the school began to phase out its double grades in 1971. In 1983, the Benedictine Sisters withdrew. For the next three years, the school was under the direction of a lay principal. In August 1986, two members of the Sisters of St. Joseph of Nazareth, from Michigan, joined the staff as co-principals. A kindergarten program was begun in 1983, and then enlarged in 1993. Beginning in 1999, Sacred Heart School was once again in the hands of lay leadership.

Ms. April Luchonok is currently principal.

Lancaster

Sacred Heart

A dream of Father Charles K. Kennedy and the members of Sacred Heart Parish materialized on February 13, 1949, when ground was broken for the new parochial school and convent. The school was completed during the summer of 1949 and opened for classes in September of that year with an enrollment of 112 students in grades 1-8. Sisters of the Immaculate Heart of Mary were the first community to staff the school and continued through June 1968. In September 1968 the Sisters of the Holy Cross took charge of running the school. From the beginning there have been lay teachers on the staff. Since September 1974 there has been a lay principal and since September 1979 the school has been staffed completely by lay personnel. A kindergarten was opened in 1979.

As a parish school, Sacred Heart School has always been under the authority and guidance of the pastor. Since September 1999 co-principals administrate the school. Each teaches one class in the departmentalized junior high. The school which is at maximum capacity currently employs co-principals, two full-time office staff, twelve full-time teachers, four part-time teachers, three full-time aides, one part-time aide, one part-time librarian, and a custodian. The faculty and staff have been at Sacred Heart School for an average of 10 years.

Today Sacred Heart School is a K-8 institution, with Ms. Peggy Horner and Ms. Catherine Schuster serving as co-principals.

Los Angeles

Sacred Heart

The Dominican Sisters of Mission San Jose opened Sacred Heart School on September 1, 1890 with a total enrollment of sixty-two children, ranging in age from five to nineteen, in two classrooms. By mid-October however, the number of children had jumped to 115. In 1894, the first boarders were accepted.

By December of 1893 a kindergarten had been added and plans were underway to enlarge the school building. In 1902, a three-story frame building fronting onto Sichel Avenue was erected, and then connected to the original 1890 school house. In 1913, work began on another addition, at which time the school became known as Sacred Heart Academy, a name it retained until 1923 when the parish financed the construction of a new red brick school building. The new school became known as Sacred Heart Parish School.

The elementary school continued to occupy this building until the present U-shaped, one-story building replaced it in time for the 1961-1962 school term.

The new building at Sacred Heart contained twelve classrooms for grades one through eight, and combination classrooms of one-two, three-four, five-six and seven-eight. Beginning in 1970, the school began to phase out the combination grades and to reduce class size. The vacant rooms provided facilities for a library, a religious education office for the parish, a kindergarten classroom and a computer lab. In 2002, a shaded lunch area was completed.

Sister Maria Elena Gutierrez, O.P. is principal.

Ventura

Sacred Heart

Although the parish of Sacred Heart in Ventura was established in 1973, it was not until 1980 that the pastor, Monsignor Arnold Biederman, finally received permission from Timothy Cardinal Manning to open a parochial school. Two classrooms, which had been used for religious instruction, were quickly refurbished. Three months later, in September 1980, forty students in kindergarten and grade one began lessons under the guidance of two laywomen, Mrs. Kathleen Garcia and Miss Shirley Zimmerman. Six months later, in January 1981, Sister Mary Francelia Klingshirn, S.N.D., was appointed principal.

Almost immediately, the parish began a major building project. The original school unit consisted of four classrooms as well as office facilities for both the school and the religious education program. On March 30, 1983 ground was broken for a new wing containing four more classrooms, offices and a faculty room. In the fall of 1986, a kindergarten, library, science lab and computer room were added.

Ms. Jean M. Alden is principal.

San Antonio de Padua

Los Angeles

The neighborhood served by San Antonio de Padua Parish is one of the oldest and most densely populated in the city of Los Angeles. It is also one of the poorest. Thus it took the parishioners nearly twenty years to liquidate the debt incurred in building the church, so that they could begin saving for a school. By that time only one parcel of vacant land was available in the parish. This property was part of an old family estate. Just about the time, however, that the pastor, Monsignor Fidencio Esparza, felt that the parish had accumulated sufficient funds for a school, the lot came on the market. With assistance from the Youth Education Fund, Monsignor Esparza was able to purchase it.

San Antonio de Padua School opened in September 1950 with students enrolled in grades one through six. The seventh and eighth grades were added in the following two years. The Religious of Jesus and Mary staffed the new school. When these sisters left the parish five years later, they were replaced by the Sisters of the Little Company of Mary.

The plant configuration of San Antonio de Padua has undergone several changes over the years. The school was originally built for eight grades. In 1969, however, San Antonio was identified as a feeder school for Queen of Angels Middle School and the junior high school program was terminated. This arrangement lasted until 1982 when Queen of Angels itself closed. At that time the seventh and eighth grades reopened and a kindergarten was begun.

The kindergarten program lasted until 1984. At that time, the second grade had to move downstairs for reasons of safety to the detriment of the kindergarten. The available space on the property could not allow for the existence of both programs. Happily, in 1990, a two-room module, provided through the generosity of the Shea Foundation, allowed San Antonio to relocate its first grade program to new and improved quarters, and to allow for the re-opening of its kindergarten. Solis Rivas is principal.

San Gabriel Mission

San Gabriel

The year 1912 marked the creation of an elementary school at California's fourth mission, Mission San Gabriel. In that year, construction was begun on a two-story wood and adobe building. At the request of Father Michael Ornate, C.M.F., the Dominican Sisters of Mission San Jose agreed to staff the school. On September 8, 1912, four sisters welcomed the first pupils into the two-room school.

Over the next eleven years San Gabriel Mission School's enrollment grew to nearly four hundred students. Consequently, temporary bungalows were added to the plant in order to accommodate them. In 1931, the completion of a Spanish-style arcade added five classrooms, an auditorium and a cafeteria to the growing institution. The construction of a convent in 1952 allowed the sisters to move out of their original building, although classes continued to be held in the dwelling's downstairs rooms. To keep pace with the expanding enrollment, in 1954, a third building, which became the school's primary wing, was added to the plant. In 1958, a fourth building, housing offices and special classrooms, replaced the original school-house.

Until the mid-1960s, San Gabriel Mission School was a double-grade institution. With the diminishment of the school-age population during the next decade, the double classrooms were gradually phased out.

Today, nine classrooms house an ethnically diverse student population encompassing kindergarten through the eighth grade, under the leadership of Ms. Nancy Nicholas.

San Miguel

Los Angeles

San Miguel School in South Los Angeles opened its doors on September 6, 1966. One hundred ten children made up the first student body. The school was staffed and administered by the Sisters of the Love of God, from Spain, until 1983, at which time Mr. Roy De La Torre became the first lay principal. Although San Miguel began with grades one through four, it soon expanded to a complete eight-year program.

Today the school is staffed by a dedicated faculty and administration headed by Mr. Jesus Vazquez.

Santa Clara

Oxnard

In the late 1800s, as the farming community on the Oxnard Plains grew and prospered, the pastor of Santa Clara Chapel felt that a school for the Catholic families was needed. The school was established as St. Joseph's Institute in 1901 as a parish boarding and day school for primary through high school students. In 1926, the pastor of Santa Clara Parish, Father F. A. Wekenman, announced the inauguration of the fund-raising campaign to replace the old Institute building with a newer, more modern structure. Three years, later, 1929, the new building, which housed grades kindergarten through twelve, was ready for occupancy.

The school enrollment, however, grew to such an extent that by 1951 the building could no longer accommodate two schools. Consequently, the high school classes transferred to their own campus on Saviers Road, a move which allowed the grammar school to utilize the entire building.

The Sisters of St. Joseph of Carondelet administered the school from its beginning until 1990 when Ms. Dorothy Massa became the first lay principal.

Santa Isabel

At the beginning of the last century waves of Mexican immigrants fled to Southern California to escape the revolution and persecutions in their own country. Many of these families sought refuge in the Boyle Heights area of East Los Angeles. In 1914, Bishop Thomas J. Conaty established the mission center of Santa Isabel to serve the needs of the Spanish-speaking families of the area. Thirty-five years later, Archbishop James Francis A. McIntyre invited the School Sisters of Notre Dame to open and staff a parochial school.

Classes began for 380 students in September 1949. The school itself was a one-story L-shaped structure erected along the outer edge of the property along Boyle Avenue and Opal Street. In the mid 1950s the California Department of Transportation embarked upon a massive freeway-building project. First, construction of the Santa Ana Freeway (Interstate #5) split the parish and displaced about 200 families. Then in 1957, the state purchased the entire parish plant in order to make way for the East Los Angeles Interchange. As a result, the church as well as the school moved to Soto Street and Whittier Boulevard.

Despite this disruption to the educational life of the school, the new Santa Isabel School was ready for occupancy in February 1958. The new school year, however, saw significant improvements to the new three-story building. The first floor contained eight classrooms as well as an office, a faculty room, a clinic and lavatories, while the second floor provided living accommodations for the sisters. A multi-purpose room on the lower floor eventually became additional classrooms and a computer lab.

Sister Joanne Marie Otte, S.S.N.D. is the current principal.

Santa Rosa

Santa Rosa opened in February, 1954, with five grades, an enrollment of 151, and a staff of five Franciscan Sisters of the Immaculate Conception. An additional classroom was added each year for the next three years until a total of eight existed.

The school, staffed by Sister Antoinette Clay, O.S.F. and a dedicated faculty, has continued to serve a predominantly Mexican-American student population.

Santa Teresita

Santa Teresita School is located across the street from Ramona Gardens, the oldest Federal Housing Project in Los Angeles. As a result, it has always served low-income families of predominantly Latino descent.

The future parish of Santa Teresita began as a confraternity center for public school children in the neighborhood. In 1922 one of the workers, Mrs. Maude Rice Ibbetson, purchased property and built a hall. This building became the nucleus of Santa Teresita Parish. Twenty-five years later, in 1950, with financial assistance from the Archdiocesan Youth Education Fund, the parish was able to open a parochial school.

Classes began on September 11, 1950. The school, staffed by the Dominican Sisters of Mission San Jose, enrolled 140 children in grades one through four in its inaugural year.

Over its subsequent years, the school plant has undergone major improvements. In 1964, the parish purchased several older houses adjacent to the school. These structures were razed and the property blacktopped in order to provide additional playground space. Seventeen years later, in 1981, a lunch area below the lower yard was built on a small triangle of land which the parish had recently acquired. A kindergarten opened in September of 1987. In 1995, the stage area in the parish hall, as well as the small rooms behind it were converted into a computer lab for a Writing-to-Read program.

Sister Angelica Velez, O.P. is principal.

Saint Agnes

When the parish of St. Agnes was erected in 1903, the pastor, Father Clement Molony, was eager to open a parish school. He was determined, however, that Sisters of the Congregation of the Holy Cross should staff it. Consequently, he was willing to wait nine years until sisters were available to accept the school.

The promised sisters finally arrived on August 3, 1914. On September 8th classes began for 220 students in grades one through eight. The following September, 1915, ninth grade courses were added to the curriculum. By the time the first two seniors graduated in June, 1919, St. Agnes School consisted of grades one through twelve and was the first coeducational high school within the city of Los Angeles.

St. Agnes' school plant has undergone major renovations during its more than eighty-five year history. When the sisters arrived in 1914, their temporary convent was not yet finished so, for the next two months, they were the guests of the pastor's brother, Dr. William Molony. In 1924, the sisters moved into their permanent home. The following year, Father Molony enlarged the school with the addition of classrooms and auditorium wings.

Following World War II, Father Molony's successor, Monsignor Patrick J. Dignan, purchased property south of the school in order to extend the school plant. The construction of four new classrooms relieved some of the overcrowding brought about by the post-war population boom.

In 1959, the City of Los Angeles judged the original three-story building unsafe, so construction was begun on the present structure. St. Agnes opened as an elementary school in its new building in September 1960. A kindergarten was opened in 1990.

In 1998, the Sisters of the Holy Cross withdrew. Mr. Kevin Dempsey is principal.

Los Angeles

Saint Albert the Great Elementary School

Saint Albert the Great Middle School

St. Albert the Great School opened its doors on September 19, 1958. The student body numbered 110 children in the first and second grades. Classes met in temporary quarters on the parish grounds since the school itself was not finished.

By September of the following year, 1959, a four-classroom building had been completed and the third grade was opened. By the time the first eighth grade graduated in June of 1962, St. Albert had sixteen classrooms. In September the enrollment reached 608. The kindergarten was begun in 1965 and a preschool in 1966. By the early 1990s, St. Albert's had nineteen classrooms with double grades from kindergarten through grade eight.

The closure of Queen of Angels High School (formerly Regina Caeli High School) located across the street provided an opportunity for expansion. The seventh and eighth grades were transferred to the former high school campus and the facility rechristened St. Albert Middle School.

When St. Albert opened in 1958, the school was staffed by lay persons since no sisters were available. In September 1962, the Sisters of the Holy Family from New Orleans, Louisiana accepted James Francis Cardinal McIntyre's invitation to staff the school.

Today, Ms. Deborah Parham heads the elementary school and Ms. Tina Johnson, the middle school.

Los Angeles

Saint Alphonsus

In 1923, Bishop John J. Cantwell invited the Benedictine Fathers at Our Lady of Lourdes Church to open a mission in the eastern section of their parish. As a result, the Fathers purchased a lot at Third Street and Ford Boulevard and made arrangements to move the old hall from St. Mary Church onto the property. Within the same year, the chapel was raised to the status of a parish.

By 1935, the old hall proved to be inadequate for the parochial needs of the growing parish. Father Patrick J. O'Dowd, the pastor, elected to purchase property on Hastings Street, and erected a chapel dedicated to St. Alphonsus Ligouri. That same year, the City of Los Angeles not only condemned the church, but also informed Father O'Dowd that they intended to take part of the parish property in order to widen Third Street. Consequently, Father O'Dowd obtained permission to move the entire parish plant to the site of the chapel and to dedicate it to St. Alphonsus. Nearly ten years would pass, however, before the next phase of Father O'Dowd's dream – a parish school – would become a reality.

In 1944, Father O'Dowd was able to break ground for St. Alphonsus School. Despite delays in obtaining building materials, construction was finished in time for the beginning of classes in September 1945. Initially, the school consisted of sixteen classrooms and had a student population of 800 children in grades one through eight. The Religious of the Sacred Heart of Mary who staffed the school, commuted daily from Marymount in Westwood. Eventually the sisters moved to the convent at Sacred Heart of Mary High School in Montebello to be closer to their apostolate.

From the day that it opened, St. Alphonsus School prospered. Within a short time the enrollment reached over one thousand students. In the early 1970s, in keeping with archdiocesan policy, the school began to phase out its double grades. With the eighth grade graduation of June 1980, St. Alphonsus became a single-grade school. It adopted a K-8 configuration in 1985 with the opening of a kindergarten.

A shortage of personnel compelled the Religious of the Sacred Heart of Mary, who had staffed St. Alphonsus since 1945 to withdraw. Ms. Kathleen Hughes is the current principal.

Los Angeles

Saint Aloysius Gonzaga

A one-story frame building on the corner of Crocket Boulevard and Nadeau Street was the original site of St. Aloysius School. Classes began for over 160 students in grades one through eight in the four large classrooms on September 13, 1921. The four Sisters of Mercy who staffed the school commuted from St. John's Military Academy in Anaheim until 1926 when their convent was completed.

The post-war population boom, however, taxed St. Aloysius' capacity to serve its population, with the result that many children had to be turned away due to lack of room. Consequently, on May 14, 1950, the pastor, Father William O'Regan, broke ground for a new church-school. By the following September 1951, a nine-classroom building was ready for occupancy. During the following decade, the enrollment peaked at over 400 students.

Initially St. Aloysius School had a predominantly Irish, German and Italian student population. The Sisters of Mercy, who had withdrawn from the school in June 1976, returned in September 1989 with the appointment of Sister Anna Marie Law, R.S.M. as principal.

Today St. Aloysius Gonzaga has a lay administration with Ms. Lilia Covarrubias as principal.

Los Angeles

Saint Anastasia

The Westchester-Playa del Rey area was among the many sections of Los Angeles impacted by the population explosion after World War II. As a result, late in 1952, James Francis Cardinal McIntyre established the parish of St. Anastasia. The parishioners, however, could not wait for a school to be built so in September 1953, St. Anastasia's initial first graders began class in a bungalow on the grounds of the neighboring parish, St. Mark in Venice.

By March 1955 construction of St. Anastasia's eight-room school building was underway and grades one through four were able to begin classes on the property in September of that year. The faculty members were two Sisters of the Holy Names of Jesus and Mary, and two lay teachers.

Attendance at St. Anastasia grew rapidly. Each year from 1956 to 1959 an additional class was added. In 1960, construction on a third unit of the school site began. From 1959 to 1963 a second class was added to each grade. By the 1963 - 1964 school year, St. Anastasia had sixteen classes of students.

The gradual expansion of the Los Angeles International Airport caused a corresponding reduction in the size of the parish as well as in the number of children attending the school. By 1978-1979, St. Anastasia consisted of eight grades and eight classrooms. A kindergarten was added in 1984.

In June 1981, the Sisters of the Holy Names of Jesus and Mary withdrew, and the following year the school was under a lay administrator. In September 1982, Sister Lillian Thomas, C.S.J. assumed administrative duties.

Ms. Rosemary Connolly is principal.

Pasadena

Saint Andrew

St Andrew School began in October 1897 as the Academy of the Holy Names in a rented house on Fair Oaks Avenue in Pasadena and was staffed by four Sisters of the Holy Names of Jesus and Mary. The Register of Pupils lists seventy-seven pupils in grades one through ten for the initial school year.

The enrollment increased steadily. Consequently by the 1913-1914 academic year, the Academy of the Holy Names had become a full twelve-grade school. In 1918, St. Andrew's parishioners purchased the Academy from the sisters and it became a parochial elementary and high school. In 1923, the elementary division was renamed St. Andrew School and occupied a building on Chestnut Street. In 1949 this structure was demolished and the current school building erected.

By the late 1960s, however, the enrollment in both the elementary and high school began to decline as construction of Interstate #110 (the Arroyo Seco Freeway) and housing redevelopment forced several hundred families in the immediate area to relocate. Over time, as the resident population continued its decline, the high school program was discontinued in June of 1980.

The closing of the high school gave the elementary school additional instructional space. A kindergarten as well as computer labs and a multi-purpose room now provide students with a variety of new learning experiences.

Today Sister Daleen Larkin, S.N.J.M. is principal.

Santa Monica

Saint Anne

On September 7, 1908, forty-seven students gathered for the first time in a small mission chapel that was part of St. Monica Parish. This 24-by-40-foot frame building was situated amid the chicken coops and barren fields, which dominated that part of Santa Monica. The faculty was composed of two Sisters of the Holy Names of Jesus and Mary from St. Monica's convent, who drove to St. Anne each morning in a "surrey with a fringe on top." By the time the first three students graduated eight years later, in 1916, the school's enrollment had risen to 87 students. During the next sixty-five years several important changes took place at St. Anne Mission. In 1923, the students moved into a new six-classroom building. On June 12, 1951, Archbishop James Francis McIntyre erected St. Anne as a separate parish and appointed Father Cyril J. Woods its first pastor. During the next three years, Father Woods acquired additional property and erected two additional classrooms as well as a new church. By 1954, the student population had reached 270 children in grades one through eight. A kindergarten was opened in 1989 through the generosity of the Shea Foundation.

The years 1994 and 1995 were traumatic ones for St. Anne School. The Northridge Earthquake, which took place on January 17, 1994, severely damaged the main building. At first the classes were relocated into overcrowded rooms around the parish grounds. In April, however, the children were able to move into temporary modules, which had been erected on the playground-parking lot. This arrangement lasted until September 1995, at which time repairs to the original structure were completed, and students were able to move back into the original building.

As part of these renovations at St. Anne's, the parish decided to convert the sisters' convent into a pastoral center.

Mr. Michael Browning is the principal.

El Segundo

Saint Anthony

The adage "From small beginnings big things grow" can easily apply to St. Anthony School in El Segundo. Like most new schools, St. Anthony's began, in 1956, in a small way – three grades in a single building taught by the Daughters of Mary and Joseph. The fourth grade was added the following year. By 1958 a second building had been completed which allowed the school to grow into an eight-grade, single-classroom school.

This configuration continued until the mid 1970s when a decline in enrollment necessitated combining classes. By 1979, St. Anthony's student body included grades one through eight in four classrooms. In the mid 1980s however, this enrollment trend reversed. Beginning in 1986, grades were separated so that by the fall of 1989, St. Anthony was once again an eight-grade single classroom school.

This growth continued. An after school child care program was initiated in the spring of 1987 and a kindergarten opened the following September. In 1988-1989 plans were underway for the construction of an additional classroom as well as the expansion of the office and faculty room. Lastly in 2002, work was completed on a new gymnasium/parish hall to provide space for student and parent gatherings and a venue in which the school athletic teams can practice and play.

Currently, Ms. Joanne Svarda is principal.

Long Beach

Saint Anthony

St. Anthony School in Long Beach opened twice. The first "opening" took place shortly after the arrival of Father James A. Reardon as pastor. At that time, the school, located on 7th Street near Alameda, consisted of s single un-plastered room in a rented house. The enrollment was made up of seventy-seven students spread over nine grades. Father Reardon had envisioned St. Anthony's as a "free school" and relied on pledges from the parishioners to support it. However, within two years, the school was in serious financial difficulties and was forced to close.

Father Reardon, despite this set-back, was unwilling to relinquish his dream. In 1919 he secured the services of four Sisters of the Immaculate Heart of Mary. With this foundation, St. Anthony's reopened that September in a building adjacent to the rectory. The student body numbered 125 boys and girls in grades kindergarten through eight.

Despite the fact that the parish had added a second story to the school building in 1920, the facilities at St. Anthony quickly proved inadequate. Consequently in the early 1920s, Father Reardon's successor initiated a massive building program. The result was a three and one/half story building which served in subsequent years as both St. Anthony Elementary and High Schools.

By 1941, another building drive was underway. Its outcome was the addition of another story to the elementary school. Fifteen years later, in 1954, construction of the present two-story, twelve-classroom elementary school began. In 1981, an all-day kindergarten program was added and a licensed preschool initiated in 1996.

The Sisters of the Immaculate Heart of Mary had staffed St. Anthony School since 1916. In 1967, the community withdrew and the Sisters of the Third Franciscan Order of Syracuse, New York, replaced them. Today the school is administered by Mr. Robert Lines and Ms. Deborah Cherry as co-principals.

Oxnard	San Gabriel	Gardena	Long Beach

Saint Anthony

St. Anthony began on September 11, 1956. The school, which was located at Laurel Street and Saviers Road adjacent to Santa Clara High School, was planned to serve the needs of the young families settling in the rapidly growing South Side district of the city. Sister Mary Edward McLaughlin, C.S.J., the principal, together with two sisters of St. Joseph and two lay teachers welcomed 300 students, enrolled in grades kindergarten through four, on the first day.

In June 1959, St. Anthony became a parish in its own right with Father Michael J. Condon as pastor. Almost immediately, Father undertook a building project. By 1964 a new sixteen-room school on South "C" Street had been completed. The classrooms at the Laurel Street facility became part of Santa Clara High School.

St. Anthony's enrollment peaked the following year, 1965, at 869 students. In 1973, the school began to phase out the double grades in keeping with archdiocesan policy. With the graduation of the last double-grade class in 1979, St. Anthony became a single-grade school.

During the following years, however, St. Anthony School did not remain static. In June 1989, the Sisters of St. Joseph withdrew. The Sisters of Mercy accepted the administration of the school. The following year, 1990, the kindergarten program, which had been terminated in 1960, was reinstated.

Ms. Barbara Dettlaff is principal.

Saint Anthony

Since its inception in 1948, growth has been a hallmark of St. Anthony School. The school opened on September 12, 1948 with 308 children enrolled in classes from kindergarten through grade eight. In 1956, the parish purchased two acres of land in order to add four additional classrooms. But the expansion of the plant had just begun.

By 1962, the school had grown to sixteen classrooms. In 1967, another construction program was undertaken in order to erect a school library, faculty wing, and multi-purpose building. In 1988 a mobile unit was renovated as a computer lab and, in the summer of 1990, the library was remodeled to add a kindergarten classroom. The fall of 1998 saw the educational ministry of St. Anthony's expanded to include three and four-year-olds with the opening of the new preschool. In a few short months, "Pooh's House" and "Tigger's House" had become an integral part of the St. Anthony's family.

Mr. Raymond Saborio is presently principal of St. Anthony School.

Saint Anthony of Padua

St. Anthony of Padua School opened on September 16, 1940. Eighty-two students were enrolled in grades one through eight. A ninth grade was added the following year. The 1940s and 1950s were decades of phenomenal growth. By 1953, the school's enrollment had reached 670. Attendance peaked in 1963 at 1,036 making St. Anthony of Padua one of the largest elementary schools in the archdiocese.

The expansion of the school plant kept pace with this increase. When it opened in 1940, St. Anthony consisted of a four-class room building on 163rd Street. Shortly afterward, the influx of students compelled the pastor to convert the parish hall into classrooms and to add a two-classroom unit. In 1953-1954, he began construction on a new eight-classroom structure and auditorium on the north side of 163rd Street. In the meantime, four large tents were erected in the playground area in order to accommodate the burgeoning student population. A new wing, consisting of eight additional classrooms, was completed in 1958. Four years later, two more classrooms were opened in temporary structures north of the school. By 1963, St. Anthony of Padua School had eighteen classrooms with two and sometimes three sections of a grade on each level.

The 1970s, however, saw a drop in school enrollment due to the rising cost of Catholic education and the changing demographics of the Gardena area. As a result, St. Anthony of Padua gradually cut back the number of classrooms. Space previously used for instructional purposes was converted into music and art rooms, a library and faculty lounge. A grant from the Target Corporation in 1999 provided funds with which to create an area where science could be taught in a more hands-on way.

The current principal is Sister Ann Stephen Stouffer, S.P.

Saint Athanasius

Located in north Long Beach, St. Athanaius School opened on September 13, 1948 with an enrollment of 336 students in grades one through six. Members of the religious community of the Franciscan Sisters of Mary Immaculate of Amarillo, Texas comprised the staff. In September of 1996, a kindergarten and after-school program were established to serve more children and to help stabilize the enrollment.

St. Athanasius School provides a variety of educational experiences. In September of 1996, a kindergarten was added.

Sister Rita Campos O.S.F. is principal.

Culver City

Saint Augustine

On August 28, 1926, the Feast of Saint Augustine, a pioneer group of religious women - three Irish, three English, and one Dutch – members of the Daughters of Mary and Joseph, arrived in Culver City to open a new parochial school. Classes officially began on September 7, 1926, with an enrollment of 123 children in four classrooms located in the newly renovated parish hall.

Because of the population growth of Culver City and the surrounding neighborhoods, additional bungalows were provided in 1938 to accommodate the growing enrollment. The present building was completed in 1947. By the latter part of the 1960s, St. Augustine was a double-grade, K-8 school.

During the 1970s the double grades were phased out. Today, St. Augustine School, staffed by a commited faculty headed by Mr. Norman Mezey, principal, continues to exert a positive influence in the community by offering a strong spiritual and academic program to a diverse student population.

Long Beach

Saint Barnabas

September 1994 was a memorable month for the members of St. Barnabas Parish since it marked the arrival of seven Sisters of the Holy Cross who had come to Long Beach, at the invitation of the pastor, Reverend Thomas J. Foley, to staff

the new parochial school. Classes began on October 3, 1946 for 290 pupils enrolled in grades one to eight.

As the population of Long Beach continued to expand in the post-war years, St. Barnabas began to double grades. This configuration continued until 1969, when the enrollment began to decline and the double grades were phased out. In 1977, a kindergarten was opened and, in 1988, Spanish and a computer lab were added to the curriculum. Because of time constraints, Spanish was dropped from the curriculum in 1993. With the withdrawal of the Sisters of the Holy Cross at the conclusion of the 1993-1994 school year, St. Barnabas came under lay administration.

The addition of a child-care center in the former convent has enabled the faculty, headed by the principal, Catherine Urbigkeit, and staff to continue to meet the needs of Catholic families in Long Beach.

La Cañada / Flintridge

Saint Bede the Venerable

St. Bede the Venerable School actually began at Flintridge Sacred Heart Academy. When the six Sisters of St. Louis arrived in the parish in September of 1952, the school building was not ready for occupancy. Therefore, they began classes in borrowed classrooms on the nearby high school campus. By January 5, 1953, work had been completed and the sisters and their 500 students were able to move into their own building.

St. Bede's student population continued to expand and eventually seven more classrooms were added in order to accommodate the increasing enrollment. In 1970, however, in keeping with archdiocesan policy, the school began to phase down to a single class per grade level. To better serve the community and to help ensure enrollment, a kindergarten program was opened in the fall of 1977.

Lastly a massive capital campaign, launched in the late 1990s, resulted in the construction of a new Education Center, which was blessed by Roger Cardinal Mahony on October 12, 2003.

The Sisters of St. Louis withdrew from St. Bede in 1987 due to a need to consolidate personnel. Since that time, a lay administration, today headed by Mr. Ralph Valente, and faculty have staffed the school.

Montebello

Saint Benedict

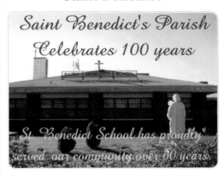

St. Benedict Parish was erected on September 30, 1906 in the area once known as Lugo Ranch, under the leadership of Father Leo Garriador, O.S.B., from Sacred Heart Abbey in Oklahoma. The parish grew slowly but steadily over the next thirty years. In 1941, plans were made to open a parochial school.

St. Benedict School, staffed by the Sisters of the Presentation of the Blessed Virgin Mary, opened its doors for the first time on Wednesday, September 22, 1941. Two hundred sixty children were enrolled.

By 1951, however, the original six classrooms could no longer accommodate the growing student population, and a new wing was added. Double grades continued from grades one though eight. During the summer of 1958, a school library and an additional classroom were added in the main building. In order to help children develop the skills necessary to begin a reading program upon entering grade one, the school added a kindergarten program in September of 1980.

Today Saint Benedict is under the direction of a lay principal, Mr. Frank Loya.

| Los Angeles | Bellflower | Los Angeles | Woodland Hills |

Saint Bernadette

The first Mass was offered in St. Bernadette Parish on August 24, 1947 in what was the clubhouse of the former Sunset Field Golf Course. Eight years later, on September 12, 1955, the Sisters of St. Joseph of Cardondelet opened St. Bernadette School with kindergarten through grade six. The first faculty was composed of four sisters, with Sister Eva Francis, C.S.J. as principal, and three lay teachers. Although painters and plumbers were still underfoot and there were not enough desks for everyone, the children were delighted to be there.

The Sisters of St. Joseph left St. Bernadette School in June 1974. For the next four years the administration and the faculty were composed entirely of lay teachers. At the request of the pastor, the Reverend Aidan Day, the Sisters of the Presentation of the Blessed Virgin Mary came to the school in September 1978. In the fall of 1991, when the Presentation Sisters were unable to provide a principal for the school, Sister Joan Mary O'Dwyer, C.S.J. was appointed principal of St. Bernadette School.

The present principal is Ms. Barbara Davis.

Saint Bernard

St. Bernard School in Bellflower opened October 7, 1946 as a four-room parish school staffed by the Sisters of St. Joseph of Orange and with an initial enrollment of 178 students. Despite several adjustments in the parish's boundaries, the school population continued to expand. Consequently in 1950 and again in 1952, a two-room unit was added to the complete the eight-room school. In 1965, this building was replaced with a new two-story structure, erected on property adjacent to the original site. A five-room complex which included a kindergarten, computer lab, music room, library and Science/Art rooms, was added in 1991.

In June 1986, the Sisters of St. Joseph of Orange withdrew from the school and the first lay principal was hired. Today St. Bernard's school population is enriched by the rich cultural diversity – Latino, Filipino, multi-racial, Caucasian, African American and Asian – which it serves.

The principal is Ms. Melissa Oswald.

Saint Bernard

St. Bernard School opened in September of 1941, seventeen years after Bishop John J. Cantwell established St. Bernard Parish in the area known as Glassell Park. Four Sisters of Charity of the Blessed Virgin Mary from Dubuque, Iowa, with Sister Mary Gilbert, B.V.M. as principal, staffed the school—a simple one-story, four-room building. One hundred twenty six pupils registered for eight classes. During the summer of 1945, four additional classrooms were added to the second floor of the original building. In September of that year, four additional Sisters of Charity joined the faculty.

Today St. Bernard School, under the leadership of Ms. Laurin Boadt, offers instruction to grades kindergarten through eight and provides child care as well. The school population, once of a predominantly Italian background, is racially and ethnically mixed.

Saint Bernardine of Siena

On March 1, 1964 ground was broken for the new parish of St. Bernardine of Siena that was destined to serve the families of the Woodland Hills area of the San Fernando Valley. By the following September, the school building was completed and staffed by four Sisters of the Immaculate Heart of Mary and four lay teachers in grades one through four. In the spring of 1968, the Sisters of the Immaculate Heart of Mary withdrew and four Sisters of Notre Dame, with the assistance of thirteen lay faculty members, staffed the school. By the fall of 1968, the school had increased to double grades, one through eight. However, beginning with the 1971-1972 academic year, St. Bernardine of Siena School began phasing out the double grades beginning with grade one. In the fall of 1982, a kindergarten was inaugurated.

Because of a shortage of personnel, the Sisters of Notre Dame withdrew from the school in June 1990. A preschool with 150 students was established in September of 1997.

Ms. Theresa Valenzuela is principal.

| Los Angeles | Van Nuys | Whittier | Los Angeles |

Saint Brendan

St. Brendan School, located in the mid-Wilshire district of Los Angeles, has the distinction of being among the oldest parochial schools in the archdiocese. The original school, located on Western Avenue north of Third Street opened in 1912, staffed by the Sisters of the Immaculate Heart. At first, the sisters lived in Immaculate Conception Parish until the pastor, Father William Ford, could rent a house in the neighborhood for them.

Teaching in a building that faced Western Avenue demanded resiliency from both teachers and students. It was not unusual for classroom instruction to come to halt whenever one of the yellow streetcars passed or a fire engine or two from the nearby station careered by with sirens, horns and bells blaring.

In 1927, the Immaculate Heart Sisters withdrew and the Sisters of Charity of the Blessed Virgin Mary took over the administration of the school. As the population of Los Angeles burgeoned, so did the student body at St. Brendan until the building could no longer accommodate the children safely. In 1960, the school was relocated on the opposite end of the schoolyard on Manhattan Place.

Sister Maureen O'Connor, C.S.J. is the current principal.

Saint Bridget of Sweden

St. Bridget of Sweden School opened on September 10, 1957, three years after the parish was erected. In the beginning, the pastor, Father Patrick Goldrick, had intended to erect a sixteen-classroom school. With the establishment of the new parishes in the surrounding area, each with its own school, the plan was altered to the present single-grade structure.

The school was initially staffed by the Irish Sisters of Charity, who remained until 1982. A lay administrator -- Mr. Robert Pawlek -- has continued to direct the school since that time.

Saint Bruno

St. Bruno School opened in 1956 with an enrollment of 293 students in grades one through four. By the fall of 1963, the school offered a full double-grade program for grades one through eight. As enrollment declined the classes went first to one and one-half rooms per grade and then to a single room for each grade. The last double class graduated in June 1982. A kindergarten was opened in September of 1986 with two half-day sessions. In 1990 it expanded to a full day and the following year the class was split into two kindergartens, each with its own classroom. At this same time an extended day care program was opened for all students. In the winter of 1997, the Father Cooley Parish Center was completed which provided additional space for educational use.

The Sisters of Mercy staffed the school until June 1983. The following year a principal from the Sisters of St. Joseph of Orange was appointed and served the school for two years, together with an entire lay faculty. In the summer of 1985 a lay principal was appointed.

Ms. Peggy Vice is currently principal.

Saint Casimir

St. Casimir School was initially established to serve the educational needs of the Lithuanian families in the Archdiocese of Los Angeles. It began on September 15, 1955 with eighteen kindergarten students in a small classroom in the parish rectory. The faculty consisted of two Sisters of Saint Casimir, a Lithuanian community.

The changing demographics of the city, however, gradually attracted more and more families, not necessarily of Lithuanian descent, to the neighborhood. In order to meet the growing needs of the parish, a three-room school was built in 1959. Three years later, the academic program was expanded to include eight grades. In June 1965, four students made up the first graduating class.

The Sisters of St. Casimir remained in the school until June 1977. When classes resumed in the fall of that year, St. Casimir had a lay principal and staff. Although the school itself remains firmly rooted in its Lithuanian heritage, a significant number of students are either of Filipino or Latino descent.

Mr. Eric Von Brockdorff is principal.

Torrance

Saint Catherine Laboure

St. Catherine Laboure School in Torrance was established in January 1952. The Sisters of St. Joseph of Cluny opened the school and continued to staff it for forty years. Because of declining numbers in their order, they withdrew from the school at the close of school year 1990-1991. Since that time, lay personnel have staffed the school.

Ms. Kathleen Gorze is the current principal.

Reseda

Saint Catherine of Siena

St. Catherine of Siena Parish in Reseda was canonically established in May 1949 and construction of the first unit of the parish school begun in 1951. By September 1952 classes were ready to begin.

Because of the rapid growth in the area, a second unit was added to the school in 1953 and in 1956 another addition was made. In 1971, however, in compliance with an archdiocesan mandate, St. Catherine began phasing out the double classrooms—one each year—until, by 1978, it had become an eight-classroom school. A kindergarten was opened in 1981

The Sisters of St. Joseph of Carondelet served St. Catherine of Siena for twenty-three years. They were followed by a lay principal for one year. Beginning in August 1975, an Adrian Dominican Sister assumed the administrative responsibility. This community remained at St. Catherine until June of 1983 at which time Mrs. Marion Falchi was appointed principal.

Today Ms. Theresa Glenn holds that position.

Los Angeles

Saint Cecilia

St. Cecilia School was opened on September 11, 1916, with two hundred pupils and Sister Mary Paul, C.S.J. and a faculty of Sisters of St. Joseph of Carondelet in charge. The original building was a three-story brick structure, which served the parish until 1959 when it was replaced with the present edifice.

Originally, St. Cecilia was organized as an eight-grade school. When the archdiocese opened Holy Cross Middle School in 1969, grades seven and eight transferred to that campus. With the closure of Holy Cross in June of 1999, the junior high program was reinstated at St. Cecilia.

Ms. Michelle Flippen is the current principal.

North Hollywood

Saint Charles Borromeo

St. Charles Borromeo School opened on September 5, 1939. Five Sisters of Charity of the Blessed Virgin Mary taught 200 students in portable bungalows. The permanent school opened September 1947 with fourteen classrooms, a cafeteria, library, and auditorium. Later two classrooms were housed in a small building across Moorpark Street.

As the number of Sisters of Charity in residence decreased, archdiocesan officials recommended that enrollment gradually be reduced to one class per grade. The last double-class graduated in 1976, and St. Charles Borromeo became an eight-classroom school.

The Sisters of Charity of the Blessed Virgin Mary continued to provide a principal until 1982, at which time the community withdrew from St. Charles. The following two years, lay principals were appointed. In 1984, the pastor, Monsignor Thomas Kiefer, secured two Benedictine Sisters from Saint Lucy's Priory: one to serve as principal and one to serve as the school's Religion Coordinator. That same year a kindergarten was established.

In August 2000, Ms. Jayne Quinn began her tenure as principal.

West Covina

Saint Christopher

St. Christopher Parish was established in March of 1954 and ground broken for the school in August of that same year. On February 1, 1955, the school was opened to the first four grades with an enrollment of 270 students.

The Benedictine Sisters of Saint Lucy's Priory in Glendora originally staffed the school. In 1979, however, the ever-growing demands on the resources of religious communities compelled the sisters to withdraw from the school. That summer, the Franciscan Sisters of Christian Charity of Manitowoc, Wisconsin moved into the convent. In addition to serving at Bishop Amat High School, the sisters provided both a principal and teachers for the school. Due to shortages in the Franciscan Order, the sisters had to withdraw from St. Christopher School in 1997. In May 1997, the first lay principal, Ms. Gail Fernandez, was hired.

Today Ms. Adela Solis serves as principal.

Los Angeles

Saint Columbkille

The story of St. Columbkille School in South Los Angeles offers a good example of the dramatic changes that can occur in a community's demographics. Opened in 1923, under the direction of the Sisters of Notre Dame de Namur, the school primarily catered to working-class European-American families. By the middle part of the twentieth century, however, the student population had become predominantly African-American. At present, the school serves a predominantly Latino community.

Throughout its history, St. Columbkille has also experienced several changes in its configuration. Originally, the school provided an educational program for children in the first through the eighth grade. In 1969, the junior high classes were transferred to Holy Cross Middle School and St. Columbkille became a grade one-six school. With the closure of Holy Cross in 1999, the seventh and eighth grades classes were reinstated and St. Columbkille returned to its original eight-grade configuration.

The reopening of the junior high challenged both the faculty and administration. Until December 2001, the seventh and eighth graders lacked formal classroom space. Thanks to the efforts of the school's Development Board construction of two additional classrooms and a learning center was completed and the students were able to move into a space of their own in January 2002. The learning center was dedicated to St. Julie Billiart, foundress of the Sisters of Notre Dame de Namur, who had staffed the school.

Ms. Karla Briceno is now principal.

Long Beach

Saint Cornelius

In September 1953, St. Cornelius School opened its doors to 240 students for grades one through three. The faculty consisted of four Sisters of Charity, newly arrived from Ireland, who taught two first grades, one second grade and one third grade, with the principal teaching full time.

As the sisters continued to arrive from Ireland, two grades were added each year. Lay teachers were employed as the need arose. With the gradual growth and development of two new neighboring parishes as well as changes in St Cornelius' boundaries, there was the gradual merging of classes at the same grade level. This continued each year until September of 1971, when St Cornelius became an eight-classroom school. In 1979 a kindergarten was opened with twenty-eight students.

St. Cornelius School is presently staffed by a lay faculty, headed by Mr. Leonard Payette, and includes nine grades, kindergarten through eight.

Long Beach

Saint Cyprian

St. Cyprian School is a K-8 school established by the Sisters of St. Louis in 1950 with a student population of 307 children in grades one through six. The school reached its peak enrollment in 1963 with 731 students in sixteen classrooms in grades one through eight.

Beginning in 1968 a gradual decrease in registrations necessitated a reduction in the number of classrooms. By 1971 there were eight grades of one class each. In 1988 a single kindergarten class was opened. An extended child care program was opened in 1988 to assist families needing before and after school care for their children.

The Sisters of St. Louis administered St. Cyprian School from 1950 to 1997 with a faculty composed of religious and lay teachers. In 1997 there was a change in administration, and since that time there has been a lay principal -- Ms. Dawn Still at present.

Encino	Sylmar	Los Angeles	Bellflower

Saint Cyril of Jerusalem

St Cyril of Jerusalem School was opened in 1950 to serve the Catholic families of Encino. The school was staffed by three Sisters of St. Joseph of Carondelet. The first permanent building was completed in 1952. By the time St. Cyril School graduated its first eighth grade in June of 1958, the school had eight classrooms. It had expanded to include sixteen classrooms by 1960.

In 1970, at the recommendation of the Archdiocese of Los Angeles and the Sisters of St. Joseph of Carondelet, the elimination of one classroom each year began.

At the present time, St. Cyril School, with Ms. Lelana Moran as principal, has nine classrooms, kindergarten through the eighth grade.

Saint Didacus

St. Didacus School, located in the northeast section of the San Fernando Valley, opened on September 15, 1958. Four laywomen taught the students in grades one through three. The following year, three Sisters of St. Joseph of Peace joined the staff, and the student body expanded to include six grades. By 1961, the school had the necessary facilities to accommodate all eight grades, and an enrollment of 493 children. A prekindergarten opened in the fall of 2002.

Religious sisters continued to minister in the school until 1982-1983. In September of 1983, the administration of St. Didacus School was turned over to Mr. Frank Cantu. Ms. Kathryn Sweeney is the current principal.

The preschool was established in 2004 located in the new parish center which was open in 2003.

Saint Dominic

St. Dominic School was established in 1925 when the Dominican Friars who ministered in the parish invited the Dominican Sisters of San Rafael to staff the school. The first classes shared space in the church, a building on the northeast corner of Maywood and Merton Avenues.

The student body numbered 110 children. When the new church was built in 1941, the section of the building that had been used for worship was converted to classrooms. By September of 1964 St. Dominic's enrollment had reached 720 students in sixteen classrooms.

Over the years the parish acquired additional properties along Merton and Chickasaw Avenues. DePorres Hall (the original wood frame church) was renovated for an extended child-care program. In 1991 a kindergarten program was established and, in 1993, moved to a converted residence on the southwest corner of the church property. In the fall of 1997 the new Library/Computer Center and the Science/Art Lab were dedicated and made available for student use.

In 1998 no Dominican sisters were available to administer the school so the first lay principal was hired. In September 2005, Ms. Elida Lujan began her tenure as principal of the school.

Saint Dominic Savio

In August of 1956, three Salesian Sisters of St. John Bosco from New Jersey arrived in Bellflower to assume the administration and partial staffing of the newly built elementary school in St. Dominic Savio Parish. The school opened its doors on September 11, 1956, with grades one through five. By 1959, all eight grades were in place, and by 1962 the enrollment had so mushroomed as to warrant double grades and the construction of two more wings.

Towards the end of the 1960s, however, the forced sale of a massive number of homes in the area for the projected Interstate #105 freeway, and the relocation of the aerospace industry from the Downey-Bellflower area brought about a drastic and relatively sudden reduction in the parish's population and in the school's enrollment. Consequently, the double grades were rapidly phased out with the result that by 1970 St. Dominic Savio was once again an eight-classroom school.

In 1977 one of the wings was remodeled to house a kindergarten classroom and a spacious school library and storage area. In 1987, further remodeling was done to accommodate a computer lab. In 1994 a prekindergarten was opened to serve the needs of the growing number of working mothers and to respond to changing educational trends.

Sister Barbara Campbell, F.M.A. is now principal of the school.

Glendora

Saint Dorothy

St. Dorothy School opened its doors under the direction of the Sisters of St. Benedict in 1960. The original school building contained five classrooms, grades three through seven. An eighth grade was added in 1962; the second grade in 1965 and the first grade in 1973 with the result that St. Dorothy became an eight-grade elementary school. Two new classrooms were built in 1987 and a kindergarten and after school child-care program were opened in September of 1988. Morning child-care was added in September of 1991.

After twelve years of service, the Benedictine Sisters withdrew from the school in June of 1972 due to a lack of personnel. Between 1972 and 1984 the school was under lay leadership. In September of 1984, however, the administration of the school again was under the auspices of the Benedictine Sisters. In September of 1987 St. Dorothy again returned to lay leadership.
Ms. Carol Burke is now principal.

Van Nuys

Saint Elisabeth of Hungary

The first day of classes at St. Elisabeth of Hungary School found the children gathered in a rented storefront on Van Nuys Boulevard. The staff was composed of four Sisters of Providence of St. Mary of the Woods. The date was September 11, 1928.

Expansion has been the key word at St. Elisabeth ever since. As soon as the workmen left, the faculty and students moved into the two-story facility on Tobias Avenue. The structure consisted of four classrooms on the first floor and an auditorium on the second. The latter, however, was soon converted into classrooms. By 1950 the pastor, Father Patrick O'Dwyer, had broken ground for a second building. In 1954, he added a third building, bringing the total number of classrooms to sixteen.

By 1987 St. Elisabeth had returned to a single classroom per grade. One of the extra rooms was renovated as a kindergarten. Ten years later, in 1997, a preschool was added and later enlarged to include a prekindergarten program as well. In 2001, the old library of the original school building was converted into a Computer Lab and Multi-Media Center.

St. Elisabeth of Hungary School is headed by Ms. Barbara Barreda, the current principal.

Altadena

Saint Elizabeth

St. Elizabeth School opened on September 22, 1919 with an enrollment of thirty-nine students in grades one to five. Until November classes were held in the home of Dr. Margaret Holt, directly across the street. Once construction on the school building itself was competed, faculty and students moved into their quarters.

The original school buildings, located on the west side of Lake, were destroyed by fire. The north school building was built in 1955. By 1964 the west and south wings were completed. School enrollment reached a peak in 1967 with 729 students in sixteen classrooms. Decreased enrollment during the early 1970s and the subsequent phasing out of classes brought St. Elizabeth to its present configuration of a single grade K-8 school.

Two Sisters of the Holy Names of Jesus and Mary, Sister Clara and Sister Gertrudis, were part of the first faculty. These sisters lived with their community in St. Andrew Parish in Pasadena until 1927 when their own convent was completed. The community withdrew from the school in 1981, and, in 1990, the former convent was converted into a parish center.

Among the noteworthy events in St. Elizabeth's history is the visit of Cardinal Eugenio Pacelli, who made an informal visit to the school and parish in 1936, three years before he became Pope Pius XII.

Ms. Jeannette Cardamone is principal.

Lynwood

Saint Emydius

St. Emydius School was established in 1949 under the auspices of the Sisters of St. Joseph of Orange. Initially, the school had a student population of 270 children enrolled in grades one through six. Additional grades were added in subsequent years. Because of the rapid population growth in the Lynwood area, in September 1956, St. Emydius added a new building. This structure, detached from the main school building, contained four spacious classrooms. This year also saw the beginning of a double-grade school.

As with the history of all small cities, the population of Lynwood has grown and diminished; therefore, in the mid 1970s, in compliance with archdiocesan directives, classrooms were gradually closed. In 1979, however, the first grade was doubled again. By 1986, St. Emydius School had eight double grades, with a student enrollment of 635. A double session kindergarten began in September 1987, bringing the student population to 666. A second kindergarten opened in 1990. However, 1996 saw the closure of one kindergarten room.

The Congregation of the Sisters of the Holy Faith, headed by Sister Merlyn Galway, C.H.F., who have served the school community since 1971, currently staff the school.

Los Angeles

Saint Eugene

On September 21, 1948, St. Eugene opened with an enrollment of 300 students in grades one through six. The Sisters of St. Joseph of Carondelet were given charge of the educational program.

Between 1953 and 1956, eight additional classrooms were added to the school plant. During the 1970s and 1980s the educational facilities were improved through the addition of a conference room, library, computer center, and art center. In 1998 the art center was converted into a second computer lab for the intermediate and junior high students.

In 1987, the Sisters of St. Joseph withdrew from St. Eugene. The congregation's educational traditions, however, were carried on by Ms. Lillian E. Morse, a St. Joseph of Carondelet Associate, who became the school's first lay principal.

Mr. John Quarry is principal now.

Granada Hills

Saint Euphrasia

St. Euphrasia, the second parochial school in Granada Hills, began in 1964 in a renovated building on the grounds of St. John Baptist de la Salle Parish. By 1966, however, construction of an eight-classroom school on property at the northwest corner of the intersection of Shoshone and Mayerling Streets was completed. In September of that year 250 students, enrolled in grades one through five, were able to move in. An additional grade was added each consecutive September until all eight grades were in attendance with approximately 432 students.

A kindergarten was established in September 1987, and class was held in the school library. A permanent building for the kindergarten as well as for a library was added in the spring of 1990. The latter was dedicated to Mrs. Leonora T. Mahoney upon her retirement after twenty-five years of service as teacher and principal at St Euphrasia School.

The Sisters of Our Lady of Mount Camel of New Orleans staffed St. Euphrasia until 1972, at which time they were recalled to their motherhouse in order to staff their schools in Louisiana. During the next three years, the school administration was in the hands of three Sisters of Providence of St. Mary of the Woods, Indiana. In 1975, this community also withdrew from St. Euphrasia. The following September a lay principal was employed. During the following year, the school moved to an all-lay faculty, today headed by Ms. Mary Blair as principal.

San Fernando

Saint Ferdinand

St. Ferdinand School opened in 1929 in a simple two-story building in the city of San Fernando. Eight classrooms were located on the main floor while church services were held on the second. The school was staffed by the Sisters of Divine Providence.

The expanding population of the San Fernando Valley after World War II necessitated the expansion of the existing facilities. Consequently, in 1952, the second unit, consisting of eight classrooms, was constructed on the property between Pico and Coronel Streets. It was at this time that the Sisters of Divine Providence withdrew from the school and the Sisters of St. Joseph of Carondelet took over the administration of St. Ferdinand.

Since the original school was near the business district, the city bought the property in 1960. Construction of a modem, air-conditioned, well-equipped eight classroom building began immediately and was completed in 1961.

The Northridge Earthquake that shook the San Fernando Valley in 1994 inflicted only minor damage on St. Ferdinand's parish plant. Mary Immaculate School in nearby Pacoima was not so fortunate, so St. Ferdinand School offered hospitality to both Mary Immaculate's faculty and students until May of 1994 when classes could once more be held on the Pacoima campus.

Sister Eleanor Marie Ortega, C.S.J. is principal today.

Burbank

Saint Finbar

Although Archbishop John J. Cantwell had erected St. Finbar Parish in 1938, the United States' entry into World War II precluded any thought of erecting a school. By 1944, however, the war was drawing to a close. Consequently in November of that year, St. Finbar's parishioners began a fund raising campaign for a parochial school.

Although ground had been broken in May 1945 and students had registered for the fall term, the shortage of building materials made it impossible to have the school building ready by September. Consequently, for the first two months the Sisters of Charity of Providence, who staffed the school, held classes in tents, in the church sacristy and even outside on the playground. On October 22, the first students were able to move into their new school building.

Ten additional classrooms were added to the school in 1955, making a total of sixteen permanent rooms and a music department. By 1956, the school enrollment had more than doubled from the original 350 students.

The Sisters of Charity of Providence served St. Finbar School from the opening of the school until 1984. At that time the school administration passed from religious to lay administration, currently headed by Mr. Michael Marasco.

Saint Frances of Rome

St. Frances of Rome School opened in September 1952, beginning with five grades, and was staffed by the Sisters of St. Benedict. In 1953, the sixth grade was added; followed by the seventh grade in 1954 and the eighth in 1955. Beginning in 1956, pre-fabricated class-rooms were added as needed with the result that by 1963 the school plant consisted of fourteen classrooms. In 1971, following a proposal by the arch-diocese, St. Frances of Rome School began phasing out double grades until there remained single rooms for grades one through eight. In 1985, the kinder-garten was added

At present, St. Frances of Rome is a single-grade school offering a strong educational program to children in grades kindergarten though eight. The staff, under the leadership of Ms. Linda Cassidy, is commited to carrying on the tradition of the Benedictine Sisters who pioneered an educational institution of which the parish and the city of Azusa can be proud.

Saint Frances Xavier Cabrini

A few miles east of the Los Angeles International Airport is St. Frances X. Cabrini School. Since the school building was still under construction, the school annals record the events of that opening day, September 14, 1951 as: "Saint Frances X. Cabrini School opened its 'school' doors in the parish hall at 9 o'clock this morning… The enrollment was 139 children"

Construction was completed within the following month and on October 1, 1951, the children of grades one through four and their teachers, the Dominican Sisters of Mission San Jose, moved into their permanent building.

St. Frances X. Cabrini School began with the first four grades. Another grade was added in each succeeding year. By September 1961, enrollment had reached 791 and there were double grades for all classes. Eventually this configuration was eliminated and the last double eighth graders graduated in June 1986.

Initially the majority of the families in the school were of Irish and German descent. In the summer of 1965, the Watts area of Los Angeles became the scene of racial rioting which spread to other areas of South Los Angeles. As a result, the ethnic composition of the school began to change and the number of African-Americans in the school popu-lation began to rise.

Saint Frances X. Cabrini School currently serves the African-American and Latino communities of the area under the leadership of Sister Carol Ward, O.P. and the Dominican Sisters

Saint Francis of Assisi

St. Francis of Assisi School opened its doors to the parish community of the same name on September 6, 1938. Staffed by the Sisters of Notre Dame, it began with an enrollment of ninety-two students in eight grades. The first building was a two-story structure that had been renovated to serve as both a school and convent. This arrangement lasted until 1951 when this building was replaced by both a new school and separate convent.

At present St. Francis of Assisi School has a K-8 configuration; a kindergarten was added in September of 1983. The Sisters of Notre Dame withdrew from the school in June of 2004. Mr. Frank Cavallo began his tenure as principal the fol-lowing September.

Saint Francis de Sales

St. Francis de Sales School, with Reverend James O'Mahoney as pastor and under the direction of the Religious of the Sacred Heart of Mary, was established in September 1949. Initially the school enrolled 300 students in grades one through eight. In 1960, the pastor, Monsignor Patrick Dignan, received permission to build an eight-room school addition. With its com-pletion in September 1961, St. Francis de Sales School enrolled 700 students, accommodating two classes of each grade.

Between 1970 and 1990, a significant rise in property values as well as an increasing number of apartment com-plexes discouraged families with school age children from moving into the Sherman Oaks area. As a result, student enrollment declined. Today St. Francis de Sales School is a single-grade school, enrolling children in nine grades, kinder-garten through eight.

Sister Ellen Marie McGovern, R.S.H.M. is principal.

Burbank	Panorama City	Los Angeles	Bell Gardens

Saint Francis Xavier

St. Francis Xavier Parish in Burbank, established on July 16, 1954, has a special link to St. Frances Xavier Cabrini, America's first citizen saint. Mother Cabrini herself had donated the plot of land on which it stands to the Diocese of Monterey-Los Angeles shortly before her death in 1917.

On September 17, 1956, St. Francis Xavier Elementary School opened its doors to approximately 300 students. The school was equipped with eight classrooms, a social hall and a kitchen. At that time, the Missionary Sisters of the Sacred Heart, the order founded by Mother Cabrini herself, operated the school. In 1966, a second eight-classroom structure was completed on the upper level of the property along with a larger parish hall and kitchen.

In 1970, the Missionary Sisters of the Sacred Heart withdrew from Southern California altogether. Consequently, St. Francis Xavier became among the first parochial schools in the archdiocese with an all lay faculty

Today, Dr. Paul Sullivan is principal.

Saint Genevieve

St. Genevieve School, located in the hub of the San Fernando Valley, opened on September 17, 1951, a little more than a year after the parish itself had been erected. The school consisted of the first four grades. An additional grade was added each year.

As a result of the tremendous growth of the San Fernando Valley in the post-war years, St. Genevieve's original facilities soon proved to be inadequate. In January of 1955 construction on eight more classrooms was completed with the result that the school quickly became a double-grade institution. The single half-day kindergarten program, introduced in the fall of 1991, was expanded into two full-day classes in the fall of 1998.

When St. Genevieve opened in the fall of 1951, the pastor, Father Michael Ryan, was fortunate to secure the services of the Sisters of St. Joseph of Newark. In June 1970, the community was no longer able to staff the school so for the next five years, 1970-1974, the Sisters of the Holy Names of Jesus and Mary provided a principal. In 1974, the Salesian Sisters of St. John Bosco took charge of the school. This community ministered at St. Genevieve until 1998 at which time the Sister Servants of the Blessed Sacrament took over the school.

Today, Sister Teresa Lynch, C.S.J. is principal.

Saint Gerard Majella

St. Gerard Majella School dates from September 1953, when it opened in temporary quarters at St. Mark Parish. The student body consisted of 234 children in grades one through three who were taught by the Sisters of the Holy Names of Jesus and Mary. Construction on an eight-classroom school was begun in November of the same year and the students moved into the new building in May 1954. As the enrollment increased, additional classrooms were added to accommodate the increased student population, eventually bringing the total number of classrooms to sixteen.

Changing economics and demographics in the area within recent years have had an impact on St. Gerard. As the double grades were gradually eliminated, the space was utilized for various parish and school activities including a kindergarten, which opened in 1981. Four of the classrooms have been converted to a parish hall and kitchen.

In July 1995, the Holy Name Sisters left St. Gerard Majella, and the first lay principal was hired in August. With the exception of a brief period during which a Sister of the Holy Faith served as principal, a lay person-- today Ms. Camille Fau-- has headed the school.

Saint Gertrude

Twelve years after the formal erection of St. Gertrude Parish in Bell Gardens, Archbishop James Francis McIntyre dedicated St. Gertrude School. Classes began the following day, September 11, 1952, with 110 students. During the early 1980s, St. Gertrude experienced tremendous growth with the addition of three new classrooms. In 1987, a modular classroom was added for the eighth grade and a library. Three years later, in 1990, two more modular buildings were incorporated into the plant, one to serve as a kindergarten classroom, and the other as a computer lab.

Initially, St. Gertrude School was staffed by the Sisters of the Immaculate Heart of Mary with Sister Mary Giovanni, I.H.M. as principal. In 1968, the administration of the school was given over to the Salesian Sisters of St. John Bosco, with Sister Mary Helen Tafoya, F.M.A. as administrator. Mr. Juan Carlos Martinez is principal now.

| Los Angeles | Whittier | South Gate | Pico Rivera |

Saint Gregory Nazianzen

St. Gregory Nazianzen School opened in a temporary residence in September 1925 with forty-eight children enrolled in the first four grades. Two Sisters of the Holy Names of Jesus and Mary, who traveled each day from Santa Monica, staffed the school. The fifth through eighth grades were added in successive years. By the time the first graduation took place in June of 1929, the school enrollment had reached 136 students.

Until 1959, at least two of the grades shared a room. In that year, because the enrollment had reached over 300, an additional classroom was built enabling each grade to have a separate room.

St. Gregory School has experienced several transitions since its beginning. From September 1925 to September 1975, the Sisters of the Holy Names of Jesus and Mary staffed the school. In September 1975, the Poor Clare Missionaries assumed its administration, but withdrew in June of 1980. During the next five years, 1980-1985, the Sisters of the Holy Names again administered and staffed the school. In June of 1985 this community found it necessary to withdraw because of a shortage of sisters. Presently, the school is staffed by a lay faculty and administrative staff with Ms. Zulay Chavez as principal.

Saint Gregory the Great

St. Gregory the Great School opened on September 20, 1954 with an enrollment of 450 students in the first four grades (double grades). It was staffed by four Dominican Sisters of Houston, and four lay teachers.

Enrollment grew rapidly until the school reached its peak of 929 students in grades one through eight in 1958 and 1959. With the advent of Vatican Council II, changes were being experienced in different areas of church life and many sisters chose to work in ministries other than education. As a result, the Dominican Sisters decided to withdraw from positions of administration at St. Gregory the Great School and Mrs. Vernie Meagher became the first lay principal. Beginning that same year, the school began to phase out one grade per year until it reached a single grade configuration.

In 1976, four Sisters of the Presentation of the Blessed Virgin Mary moved into the convent, two of which joined the teaching staff. In 1984 Sister Sheila Keen, P.B.B.M. became principal. In 1997, Mrs. Dominik succeeded Sister Sheila and two years later, in June of 1999, the Sisters of the Presentation of the Blessed Virgin Mary withdrew from St. Gregory the Great altogether.

Today, Ms. Pauline Ortega heads the school as principal.

Saint Helen

St. Helen School was established in September 1941, during the pastorate of Reverend Terrence O'Donnell. Since the building was not finished in time for the opening of school, the students were taught by the pioneer faculty of eight Sisters of Notre Dame in the original St. Helen Church located at the corner of Firestone Boulevard and Madison Avenue. It was not until December 9, 1941, that the eight-classroom school was ready for occupancy. The following year, 1942, the parishioners requested the addition of a ninth grade, which continued to be a part of the school until 1950.

In 1990, St. Helen was a recipient of a Kindergarten/Computer Lab Grant from the Riordan and Shea Foundations. The first kindergarten class began in October of that year. A year later, in 1991, the kitchen and storage building was built on the southwest corner of the property. Finally, in January of 1998, plans were submitted for a computer lab to be constructed on the northeast corner of the property. The new lab was upgraded to include Internet access for the students. The existing computer lab was remodeled and readied for a pre-kindergarten classroom that opened in the fall of 1998.

Sister Mary Francis Wahl, S.N.D. is at present principal of the school.

Saint Hilary

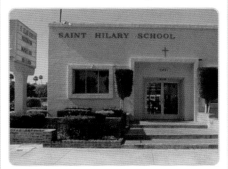

On June 29, 1952, the first Mass was celebrated at St. Hilary Church in Pico Rivera. Three months later, St. Hilary School opened with grades one through four staffed by the School Sisters of Notre Dame. Another grade was added each year thereafter until 1956 when the school achieved an eight-grade configuration.

Enrollment continued to escalate during the 1950s, reaching a peak of 677 in 1961. Eventually the double classrooms were phased out in order to adjust to changing demographics and to reduce class size.

In 1966 a wing for the primary grades was added to the main building. A computer lab was installed in 1987 and renovated in 1999-2000. Between 1997 and 2001, the entire school plant was enclosed for added security.

Sister Richardine Rempe, S.S.N.D. is principal.

Los Angeles

Saint Ignatius of Loyola

The educational tradition of the Dominican Sisters of Mission San Jose has been apparent at St. Ignatius of Loyola School from the first. Beginning with Sister Frances Dunne, O.P. the first principal, down to the present administration of Sister Georgette Coulombe, O.P., Dominican Sisters of Mission San Jose have continued to provide the students of the Highland Park area with a quality Catholic education.

St. Ignatius of Loyola School opened on September 5, 1922. The initial enrollment was 127 pupils, but within the first two years that number had nearly doubled. By 1944 it had grown by more than 300%. As result, the decision was made to add an additional eight classrooms to the school plant. Shortly before construction was completed, the archdiocese issued a directive requesting parochial schools to decrease enrollment. Consequently, St. Ignatius ultimately remained a single grade school. A kindergarten opened in 1977 with two half-day sessions and expanded to a full day in 1987.

In the summer of 1995, the Dominican Sisters of Mission San Jose agreed to provide additional support to their Dominican Schools in the inner city by establishing regional development offices through the Vision of Hope Program. The following year, the East Los Angeles Development Office was inaugurated at St. Ignatius. Since that time, the school's development efforts in conjunction with the Vision of Hope Program have brought in a significant number of grants and continue to gather support from alumni, foundations and local businesses.

Torrance

Saint James

In 1918 ground was broken by Bishop John J. Cantwell for St. James School, Redondo Beach. Three sisters of St. Joseph of Carondelet came at the invitation of the bishop to teach seventy children. In 1954 four classrooms were added at the Redondo site. By 1958 a third building was necessary. This made a total of twelve classrooms.

By 1967 the enrollment had reached its peak of 1,060 and the physical plant had grown from four classrooms to twenty-four. St. James was among the largest schools in the archdiocese.

As the population in the South Bay area continued to grow, an eight-classroom school building was erected in Torrance and called St. James Annex. This enabled the children to attend whichever school was geographically closest to them. In 1971 the decision was made to utilize the Annex as a primary/intermediate school and the Redondo Beach plant for a junior high.

By 1989, the school population had greatly decreased and it became financially and logistically necessary to combine the two schools into one site. The move was completed by September 1990. St. James School, under the leadership of Sister Mary Margaret Kreuper, C.S.J., is currently single-grade school located in Torrance.

La Crescenta

Saint James the Less

The Reverend Christopher Barry established St. James the Less Parish in 1955 in La Crescenta as an outcome of the population explosion of the post-World War II years. The following year, September 11, 1956, St. James the Less School opened its doors to 240 pupils. A kindergarten was begun in September 1985.

St. James the Less was staffed by the Daughters of Mary and Joseph. When they arrived in the parish, however, they had no place to live. The parish was able to purchase a small bungalow next to the school, which was renovated as a convent. In 1961, this building was replaced by a more commodious structure. The sisters continued to staff St. James the Less School until the retirement of Sister Mary Aquinas, D.M.J., at which time the administration was turned over to Ms. Barbara Gallian, the first lay principal.

Mr. David Burroughs is principal at the present time.

North Hollywood

Saint Jane Frances de Chantal

Although the parish of St. Jane Frances de Chantal was erected in 1948, a lack of funds and insufficient students delayed the opening of a parochial school until 1951. On September 17th of that year, classes began for grades one through four under the direction of the Sisters of St. Joseph of Carondelet. Since the permanent building was still under construction, the children met in makeshift quarters – three grades in St. Jane's Hall and one grade in the garage. By November of 1951, the classrooms were ready for occupancy. Initially the cost to attend was minimal. There was no tuition; only a $6.00 book fee. Gradually a charge of $4.00 a month per family was levied,

The school population continued to expand throughout 1952 and 1953. More classrooms were added and tuition was raised to $5.00 per month. By 1968 it was decided to reduce the size of the school to one class per grade level. A kindergarten was added in 1971, and a Pre-K program in 1986. The Sisters of St. Joseph, who had served the school since 1951, withdrew in 1977-1978.

A lay principal -- currently Mr. Joseph Brown -- and lay faculty have staffed St. Jane Frances since that time.

Los Angeles	Los Angeles	Inglewood	Chatsworth

Saint Jerome

St. Jerome School opened in 1952 with eight classrooms, serving students in grades one through eight. By 1961, St. Jerome had grown to sixteen classrooms, with two classrooms for each grade.

Beginning in 1971, and responding to archdiocesan directives, one section of each grade was eliminated annually. A kindergarten was added in 1973 in one of the unused classrooms. The remaining rooms, vacant since 1971, were gradually converted into computer labs, a library, office, mailroom/parent workroom, an activity/meeting room and an area for an extended child care program. Beginning in 1987, this last service was provided on campus by Catholic Charities and later by the parish itself.

At the present time, St. Jerome School serves students in kindergarten through grade eight. The Sisters of Saint Joseph of Carondelet have served St. Jerome School from its beginning until the present.

Sister Donna Anne Bachman, C.S.J., is principal today.

Saint Joan of Arc

St. Joan of Arc School opened on September 15, 1947 with an enrollment of 239 students in grades one through eight. The school was originally built with four classrooms; additional classrooms were added in 1954 and 1955.

The Sisters of Notre Dame administered St. Joan of Arc School until 1992 when a lay principal became the administrator. The Sisters of St. Joseph of Carondelet accepted the administration in 1993 until 1998. Since that time St. Joan of Arc has had a lay faculty and principal.

At present Mrs. Diane Conrad is principal.

Saint John Chrysostom

St. John Chrysostom School began in 1923 in a combination church and school building on the corner of Locust and Manchester. Staffed by the Sisters of St. Joseph of Carondelet with Sister Mary Dolores Murphy, C.S.J. as principal, it welcomed 120 students when the doors opened that year.

When World War II broke out in 1941 and a continuous stream of defense workers poured into the area, the need to erect a new parish plant became apparent. With the generous assistance of Mrs. Grace Freeman Howland, daughter of Daniel Freeman, the parish purchased the present site on Florence Avenue and began construction of a new church and school.

The present school was completed in 1953. A kindergarten was established in 1982. The faculty, headed by Sister Antoinette Czuleger, C.S.J., continues to offer a quality Catholic education to the families of the Inglewood area.

Saint John Eudes

In 2006, St. John Eudes School will celebrate forty years of providing a Catholic education to children of the northwest corner of the San Fernando Valley. When the school opened in 1966, the parishioners of St. John Eudes were still attending Mass at Rancho San Antonio. Nevertheless, the pastor, Father Philip Grill, was determined to have a parochial school. Therefore, he obtained the services of four Sisters of the Pious Schools and in September 1966 began classes for 170 students in grades one through four.

It was Father's intention to open an additional grade each year as needed. However, when the first fourth graders completed the seventh grade in 1970, the newly organized Parish Council was reluctant to add an eighth grade. The faculty and students intervened and the following year, the school achieved an eight-grade configuration.

Since that time, St. John Eudes has continued to implement innovations to both its plant and curriculum. In the summer of 1992 a Writing-to-Read lab was installed through the efforts of the Parent-Teacher Support Organization and the Riordan Foundation. In 1997 a former garage and office space were remodeled, and play ground equipment assembled for a kindergarten.

Ms. Barbara Scanlon Danowitz is principal today.

Palos Verdes

Saint John Fisher

St. John Fisher School was founded in 1961 by Monsignor Thomas J. McCarthy. The permanent school building was completed in 1962 and staffed by the Daughters of Mary and Joseph. By 1965, the school had reached its peak enrollment of 654 students with two classes of each grade, from first through eighth. A kindergarten opened in 1994 and in the 1990s the classrooms were enlarged to include computer stations and research centers.

In 1969, the process of changing to single classes for each grade was begun. In 1970, due to a shortage of personnel, the Daughters of Mary and Joseph withdrew, and the Sisters of the Immaculate Heart of Mary accepted administration of the school.

The principal today is Ms. Anne Marie Hudani.

Norwalk

Saint John of God

Ground was broken for St. John of God School on March 22, 1953 under the parish's first pastor, Father Louis Buechner. The Sisters of the Holy Faith had agreed to staff the school but difficulties with immigration delayed their arrival until mid-October. As a result, when classes began on September 6, 1953, eight women from the parish made up the temporary staff.

During the years from 1953 to 1958, St. John of God made use of temporary one-classroom units as well as the parish hall in order to handle the expanding enrollment. In 1964, the new eight-room structure, built to accommodate grades five through eight, was completed, eliminating the need for the temporary classrooms and the use of the hall.

In 1971, because of substantial parish debt and in conformity with a directive of the Archdiocese of Los Angeles, the school intentionally decreased enrollment with the ultimate goal of one class per grade. This phase-out was completed in June 1978. A kindergarten was opened in September 1983 and, in 1993, a prekindergarten program added.

Currently the principal is Ms. Mary Pekarcik.

Baldwin Park

Saint John the Baptist

St. John the Baptist School opened its doors in 1952 under the direction of the Reverend John G. Flack and the Benedictine Sisters. The student body numbered of 280 in grades one through five. In September 1953, a sixth and seventh grade were added. By 1955, however, the enrollment had increased to 498 students. Due to over crowded classrooms, the first three grades were forced into half-day sessions, and an eighth grade was added to the school. These conditions prompted new construction. In September 1959, St. John the Baptist School doubled the number of classrooms. The new St. Elizabeth Building housed grades five through eight and the St. John Building housed grades one through four.

In 1978, the school administration felt the need to seriously consider reducing some of the classes. The first, second, and third grades were reduced over a three-year period to a single class per grade level. In September 1982, two of these vacated classrooms were converted into a library and a study hall. In September 1987, however, double classes for the first eight grades were reinstated.

The Sisters of St. Benedict staffed the school until 1972. At that time, they felt the need to withdraw due to the decrease in the number of sisters available to adequately staff the school. In September 1972, the Sisters of the Love of God took their place, thus providing for a smooth transition in the administration of the school.

Sister Invencion Canas, R.A.D. is the principal.

Granada Hills

Saint John Baptist de la Salle

The area today known as Granada Hills, was once part of the extensive holdings of Mission San Fernando. Even in the early 1950s citrus groves and onion fields still dominated the landscape. By the mid-point of the decade, however, this picture had changed significantly. The community boasted a flourishing new parish, St. John Baptist de la Salle. Its members had recently completed construction of a church, which would seat 700 persons, and were looking forward to the opening of a parochial school.

De la Salle School opened in September of 1955. Two hundred thirty students were enrolled in grades one through four. Initially classes were held in bungalows, which had been built in 1943 and had served as the original church for Visitation Parish in West Los Angeles. Remodeled into classrooms and moved to Granada Hills, these structures served the needs of the teachers and students until the permanent eight-classroom structure was completed the following year, 1956.

This building, however, quickly became inadequate. In 1958, eight more classrooms as well as a faculty room and library were added to the parish plant in order to accommodate the rapidly increasing enrollment. By September 1965, the student population peaked at 960 children.

Three Sisters of St. Joseph of Carondelet and a lay teacher staffed de la Salle when the school opened in 1955. In 1974 this religious community was replaced by the Sisters of Charity of the Blessed Virgin Mary. These sisters ministered in the parish until June 1984. The following September Mrs. Patty Baldwin was named principal.

Today Ms. Patricia Melch is principal.

| Los Angeles | Hawthorne | La Puente | Long Beach |

Saint John the Evangelist

St. John the Evangelist School began in September 1926 in a region of Los Angeles then known as Hyde Park, a rural area considered "way out in the country." Initially classes began in the parish hall.

As the number of families increased, the plans were made for a new school building. On February 27, 1927, the Right Reverend John J, Cantwell dedicated the structure. In spite of the depression years, the enrollment continued to grow. Four new classrooms were added in 1950 to the area west of the present church. At this time, the enrollment reached almost 1,000 students. With the establishment of new parishes to the north and west, the enrollment leveled off to 780 students by 1962.

At the recommendation of the Safety and Building Commission, the original school building was razed and, in 1962, the pastor, Monsignor McNicholas announced plans to erect a new two-story building with twelve classrooms. Two classrooms were also to be added to the previously built primary building. The first kindergarten at St. John was opened in September of 1973. That same year the decision was made to close one classroom each year until the school consisted of nine classrooms including the kindergarten.

The Sisters of St. Joseph of Carondelet ministered at St. John the Evangelist Parish and School until June of 1996.

The principal is Ms. Beulah Flowers.

Saint Joseph

Construction of St. Joseph School, Hawthorne, began in the spring of 1928. On September 10, 1928, five religious, Sisters of Providence from St. Mary of the Woods, Indiana, welcomed 165 children who enrolled in four classrooms representing grades one through eight.

St. Joseph's original school building consisted of two stories with four classrooms on the first floor and an additional classroom as well as an auditorium and kitchen on the second. In order to keep pace with the rising enrollment resulting from the increase in the number of aircraft plants in the area, the second floor was remodeled to provide more classrooms. Additional classrooms were added in 1951 and again in 1957 with the construction of the north and west wings. A kindergarten as well as a pre-K program was eventually added.

Ms. Christine Whelan is principal.

Saint Joseph

St. Joseph Parish, erected by Bishop Thomas J. Conaty in 1908 to serve the Mexican and Basque families of the area, has the distinction of being among the oldest parishes in the San Gabriel Valley. It was not until 1950, however, that it had a parochial school of its own.

Ground was broken for the school in April of 1950. By the following September, classes were underway for children in grades one through six. During the 1950s, the total enrollment peaked over the 800 mark, forcing double sessions for the twelve classes (grades one-eight and four classrooms with double grades). As parishes and schools were established in the surrounding areas, the need for double grades lessened. As a result, St. Joseph gradually returned to a single grade configuration.

Initially, three Sisters of the Immaculate Heart of Mary staffed the school. In 1968, this community withdrew. At the request of James Francis Cardinal McIntyre and Reverend Edward V. Callahan, the pastor, the Carmelite Sisters of the Most Sacred Heart of Los Angeles assumed responsibility for St. Joseph School.

Sister Madeleine Keeps O.C.D. is principal today.

Saint Joseph

St. Joseph Parish in Long Beach is an example of how quickly a new parish could grow in the 1950s. Erected in April of 1955, the first Mass was celebrated the following June. Ten months later, April 1956, the congregation had moved into the almost completed hall and in October, the first eight classrooms in a parish school were ready for occupancy and approximately 415 children had enrolled for grades one through five.

In early 1957, it was evident that more classrooms were needed; therefore work began on a four-classroom structure. By the spring of 1959, the builders were on the scene again breaking ground for the final block of rooms. Unfortunately, this block was not completed until January 1960, and that necessitated double sessions for four classes during the first semester.

By 1961, St Joseph had double grades from one through eight with an enrollment reaching a peak of 850 in the mid-1960s. In the early 1970s, the school gradually phased into a single grade school, one though eight. The need for a kindergarten was met with the inauguration of the program in 1976.

With the completion of the 1990-1991 school year, the Sisters of St. Louis could no longer provide a principal for the school. In July 1991, Ms. Brigid Considine, the first lay administrator, began her tenure as principal of St. Joseph School.

Pomona	Canoga Park	Westlake Village	Compton

Saint Joseph

Shortly after being named the first pastor of St. Joseph Church in 1886, Reverend P. J. Fisher took a survey of his parish, which revealed that many Catholic families were educating their children in boarding schools outside of the area. Consequently, he invited the Sisters of the Holy Names of Jesus and Mary to open a school in the parish. On September 11, 1889, classes began for students in grades one through ten at the Academy of the Holy Names in Pomona. In 1926, the parish itself built a small six-room elementary school on the northeast corner of Huntington Boulevard and William Street to accommodate the primary and intermediate grades while the junior high students continued to attend the nearby academy.

Nineteen forty-eight brought a number of significant changes for both schools. First Monsignor Thomas English, the pastor at St. Joseph, purchased an eighteen acre tract on west Holt Avenue for a new parish plant. Then, in May of 1952, he dismantled the elementary school on Huntington and William and transported half of it to its new location. Reconstructed and enlarged, it opened in mid-September 1952, with twelve classes in session. A kindergarten was opened in 1989, and a science/computer lab in 1990.
The Sisters of the Holy Names administered both the Academy of the Holy Names and St. Joseph School until 1948, when the Sisters of St. Felix took over the administration.

Today St. Joseph School is a fourteen room school under the leadership of Ms. Gail Fernandez.

Saint Joseph the Worker

St. Joseph the Worker School opened its doors in February of 1958 with an enrollment of 360 students in grades one, two and three. The teaching staff consisted of two Sisters of St. Joseph of Carondelet and four lay teachers. The original building consisted of eight classrooms, and in 1960 eight more classrooms were added to complete the sixteen-classroom structure.

The school continued as a sixteen-classroom school until 1971 when the archdiocesan office requested that the parish close one grade each year until it became an eight-classroom school. As the classes were eliminated, the vacant classrooms were accessible for various needs—a Religious Education Office, library, conference room, and computer labs.

With the addition of the kindergarten program in September 1982, St. Joseph the Worker adopted a K-8 configuration. In October of 1986, an extended child-care program was opened to serve the growing needs of the one-parent families and two-parent wage earners. In 1998, a Pre-K was added.

Sister Barbara Joseph Wilson, C.S.J. is principal.

Saint Jude the Apostle

St. Jude the Apostle Parish was founded in 1970 by Monsignor Thomas O'Connell. Twelve years later, on September 7, 1982, the doors of the school opened for the first time. Ninety-three students in kindergarten through second grade, under the administration of the Sisters of Notre Dame, occupied the transformed rooms of the existing Religious Education Center and the parish hall. Ground was broken for a permanent building in May 1984. Classes began in September 1985 in the new building with 209 students in grades kindergarten through five. Each year a class was added until the full student body of 300 occupied the school in September of 1988.

In June 1990, the Sisters of Notre Dame ended their administration of St. Jude. In September 1990, Ms. Mary Lou McGee was appointed the first lay principal. A departmentalized program for grades six, seven and eight was established during the 1990-1991 school year. Next the Writing-to-Read program, sponsored by a Riordon Foundation grant, was implemented for grades kindergarten and one. At the same time, improvements continued to be made to the school plant. A new two-story building was constructed which had a multi-purpose room on the first floor and housed the fourth grade classroom and a computer lab on the second.

These additions plus other changes in the curriculum have enabled St. Jude, under the leadership of Ms. Patricia Chaimowitz, to demonstrate an on-going commitment to Catholic education to the people of Ventura County.

Saint Lawrence Brindisi

The first school building in St. Lawrence Brindisi Parish was a Spanish-style stucco structure on the corner of Compton Avenue and East 101st Street. When classes began in September 1924, the student population consisted of 220 pupils, primarily the children of migrant workers, in grades one through eight in four furnished classrooms. It was staffed by the Sisters of Notre Dame.

In March of 1959, the original building was declared unsafe. The present red brick structure was subsequently erected on the property. The students and faculty moved in April 1961. The kindergarten program was added in 1993.

Growth at St. Lawrence was slow. Between 1924 and 1940 it remained stable at 200. By 1950, however, enrollment had increased to 300 students. In 1960 the school population had reached the point where it was necessary to employ eight full-time teachers and eight classrooms were opened.

This trend reversed itself in the mid-1960s when, as a result of the Watts Riot and the subsequent Watts Redevelopment Project, many African American families moved out of the area. At the same time, the number of families from Mexico and Central America increased. The parish is 80% Latino at least and 20% African American. The school is the same and is now full.

In September 2005, Ms. Lillian Paetzold began her tenure as principal at St. Lawrence.

Saint Lawrence Martyr

Before World War II, Redondo Beach was a small community surrounded by gently rolling hills. By the mid-1950s, however, it was well on its way to becoming the flourishing area it is today. From its beginning, St. Lawrence Martyr School has been an indicator of this growth.

St. Lawrence Martyr Parish was erected in 1955 and by early 1956 construction of a temporary church, rectory and twelve classrooms of a projected sixteen-room school was underway. Classes began on September 20, 1956 for grades one through six. Four Sisters of St. Joseph of Carondelet and two lay teachers taught 360 students; that is an average of sixty students per class. By 1957, the enrollment had doubled and four classrooms were added. The peak enrollment came in 1961 with 960 students in sixteen rooms.

Today St Lawrence Martyr has nine grades, K-8, and continues to have a strong religious and academic program under the leadership of a capable lay administration, headed by Ms. Shannon Gomez, faculty and staff.

Saint Linus

September 10, 1963 was a "red-letter" day for the Catholic families of the Norwalk area since it marked the opening of St. Linus School. The Sisters of the Holy Faith welcomed the first 287 students in grades one through six. Thereafter, additional classrooms were added annually until sixteen classrooms were utilized. Beginning in 1987, however, St. Linus School began to decrease the number of classrooms and by 1990 had become a nine-classroom school (K-8). In 2000, a preschool program was added.

Since the mid-1970s St. Linus School has experienced several notable demographic changes as well. First, in addition to the Norwalk area, the parish now includes a portion of the City of Cerritos. Second, the student population has moved from a mainly Latino and Anglo enrollment to a primarily Latino and Filipino enrollment.

Ms. Theresa Valenzuela is principal.

Saint Louis de Montefort

St. Louis de Montefort School was opened in September 1964 in order to serve the needs of the families in the agricultural community of Orcutt. On September 14, 112 children in grades one through three met their teachers for the first time.

St. Louis' building was designed for eight classrooms. Three rooms were ready for use when school began in September. The remaining five-classroom area was left un-partitioned in order to serve as a temporary church/hall. When the fifth grade opened in 1966, a wall was added to the open space. In each successive year, place was made for the new grade by adding a partition to the hall. By September 1969, St. Louis de Montfort was an eight-grade school. A kindergarten was begun in 1982. In 1992, this class moved into a modular unit next to the main school.

Currently Ms. Mary Kathleen Crow is principal.

Saint Louis of France

St. Louis of France School, staffed by the Sisters of St. Louis, opened on September 17, 1956 with eight grades. During subsequent years a significant increase in enrollment made the construction of additional classrooms a necessity. By 1960, four new classrooms were ready for occupancy. In 1963 four additional classrooms and an auditorium were completed, bringing the school to its full capacity. In 1969, however, St. Louis of France School began phasing out one grade each year until 1977 when the school was once more reduced to eight grades.

In October 1986, in order to meet the needs of working parents, an after-school program was established. The following year, September 1987, the school itself was expanded to include a kindergarten program.

Since its beginning the Sisters of St. Louis have ministered in both the school and parish. In June of 1996, after forty years of service, the community withdrew.

Beginning in September the school had a lay administration, which is today headed by Ms. Patricia Jackson.

| Covina | Long Beach | Temple City | Pomona |

Saint Louise de Marillac

St. Louise de Marillac Parish was officially established in 1963; Father James
Walsh was the first pastor. The following
year, 1964, he began construction of an
eight-classroom school and parish hall,
the latter to serve as a temporary church.
St. Louise School opened its doors on
September 20, 1965 with an enrollment
of 200 students in the first four grades.
The school was staffed by four Sisters of
Notre Dame de Namur. Grades five and
six were added in 1966; grades seven
and eight, in 1967 and 1968.

In 1988, St. Louise's parishioners embarked on an ambitious building program. The result was the erection of a
new parish hall, a school library and a
kindergarten classroom, as well as the
expansion of the computer lab. In
September, 1990, the kindergarten welcomed its first class of thirty-six students.
A Campaign Development Plan, launched in 1998, enabled the parish to add a
new multi-purpose building with a large
kitchen, meeting room, bathrooms, a new
lunch area, new playground, new basketball courts and added storage areas to
the plant

Ms. Elizabeth La Dou is principal.

Saint Lucy

The first four grades of St. Lucy School
opened in September of 1950. A new
grade was added in each successive
year until the 1954-1955 school year
which saw the first eighth grade graduation. The peak enrollment was reached in 1958 when 503 children attended
the eight-classroom school.

The original building, however, could not
keep up with the growth and needs of
St. Lucy's student body. Consequently,
the school moved into other areas of the
parish plant. A library was established in
the old rectory building in 1990. In 1991-
1992 a kindergarten and a computer lab
for the Writing-to-Read program were
added through the generosity of the
Shea and Riordan Foundations. The
transfer of the library in 1999 to another
location created space for new administrative offices. The former offices in turn
became a faculty resource room and a
combination health room/athletics office.

During its fifty-five year history, St. Lucy
School has been administered by three
religious communities. Initially, the Sisters
of the Mother of God staffed the school.
In 1954, they were replaced by the
Missionary Sisters of the Immaculate
Heart of Mary. In 1973 to 1976 the Domi-
nican Sisters took over the school.

Today the faculty and staff, with Ms.
Diane Pedroni as principal, are lay.

Saint Luke

St. Luke Parish opened its school in
September 1947, a year after Archbishop
J. Francis A. McIntyre had established
the parish. Because the parish itself was
heavily in debt, construction of a permanent building was out of the question.
Therefore the first six classrooms were
temporary frame buildings. By 1956, however, construction of a new wing had been
completed and fourteen classrooms were
in operation. Within two years, sixteen
classrooms were being used to educate
more than 800 students.

From 1970-1978 the school was reduced to a single class per grade school
and the student enrollment decreased to
approximately 300 students. The additional space was utilized for a computer lab
for the Writing-to-Read program (1988),
and a kindergarten (1991). Also in 1991,
the school underwent major renovations
and a science lab, art and music rooms,
new lighting, storage space as well as
air-conditioning were added.

When St. Luke opened in 1847, the
Sisters of the Immaculate Heart of Mary
had charge of the school. In June 1969,
the sisters, under the direction of Sister
Anita Caspary, withdrew. The sisters
under Sister Eileen MacDonald, however,
agreed to continue to administer the
school. This community remained at
St. Luke until June 1990 at which time a
lay principal was appointed.

Mr. David Zuber is principal.

Saint Madeleine

As with many of the schools in the
archdiocese, classes at St. Madeleine
School began under somewhat unusual
conditions. Shortly after the formal inauguration of the parish of St. Madeleine in
May 1963, the pastor, Father Robert
Gara, had leased a store on Holt Avenue
to serve as a temporary chapel. At the
same time, he promptly began construction of permanent buildings for both the
church and a school. The church, however, was not completed when the lease
on the store expired so the parish moved
into the school building which was ready
for occupancy. As a result, the first
students at St. Madeleine had to share
their rooms with both the parish church
as well as the hall. As soon as the church
was completed, however, these rooms
were available for instructional purposes.
As St. Madeleine grew from five grades
to eight, they were converted into classrooms.

Ms. Lucia Saborio at present directs the
school.

Los Angeles

Saint Malachy

The story of St. Malachy School is a good example of the changing demographics of Los Angeles itself. St. Malachy School opened in the fall of 1948 with 303 students in grades one through seven under the direction of the Ursuline Sisters of the Roman Union. The eighth grade was added the following year. At that time, the ethnic make up of the school as well as of the people of the surrounding community was primarily of Irish and Italian descent.

By the mid 1950s the neighborhood experienced an influx of African Americans and Latino immigrants. By 1965 the school population was predominantly African American with a small percentage of Latino. During the 1980s, however, the Latino population gradually increased so that by 1990, the student body was equally made up of Latino and African American children. By the time a kindergarten was established in 2000, the population had become predominantly Latino but there are a small number of children of African American and Filipino descent.

Today St. Malachy is a K-8 school, headed by Mr. Daniel Garcia.

Lomita

Saint Margaret Mary Alacoque

St. Margaret Mary Alacoque School was established in September of 1953 in the Los Angeles suburb of Lomita. From 1953 to 1986, the school was staffed mainly by the Salesian Sisters of St. John Bosco. During the late 1970s and early to mid 1980s the Sisters of Charity of Rolling Hills were also part of the faculty. Since 1986, however, the faculty, staff, and administration have been made up entirely of lay persons.

Presently, St. Margaret Mary School is a K-8 institution, headed by Mr. Joseph Des Barres, serving families from the areas of Lomita, Torrance, Wilmington, San Pedro, Harbor City, Palos Verdes, Carson, and Gardena.

Long Beach

Saint Maria Goretti

St. Maria Goretti School was founded in 1957 at the request of James Francis Cardinal McIntyre, Archbishop of Los Angeles. The school opened on February 4, 1957, staffed by five lay teachers with an enrollment of 276 in grades one to four. The following year, three Sisters of St. Joseph of Carondelet joined the staff as full-time teachers and as administrator. An additional grade was added each year so that by 1960 there were eight grades with fourteen classrooms and a teaching staff of six sisters and eight lay teachers. The enrollment increased proportionally and in 1964 reached 801.

In September 1981, the school began a phasing-out program in order to reduce the number of classrooms to one class per grade.

Changes have been inevitable over the course of the years. When the St. Joseph Sisters found it necessary to withdraw from staffing the school in 1974, the parish was fortunate to obtain Sisters from the Dominican Order of St. Catherine of Siena. The Dominican Sisters continued to work in the parish until 1987. Illness, retirement and the Vocation shortage eventually made it impossible for the order to continue to staff the school. In 1987, Miss Sandra Brosnahan and an all lay faculty began a new era for the parish school, but the tradition of quality Catholic education has continued!! In September 1988, a kindergarten class and a fully equipped Writing-to-Read lab were added. A child care program was opened in 1997.

Mrs. Mary Ann Fitzpatrick is the current principal.

Pico Rivera

Saint Marianne de Paredes

According to the School Chronicle of the Sisters of Notre Dame de Namur, the proposed site of St. Marianne de Paredes School was "part orange grove and part junkyard" when the sisters arrived in Pico Rivera in August 1953 to staff the school. The first unit consisted of seven classrooms and office areas. Nine more classrooms were completed in September of 1955 parallel to the original structure and joined to it by a covered walk

Warmth and generosity have always been hallmarks of St. Marianne de Paredes Parish and School since the first day of classes on September 15, 1953. In 1955, the new parish of St. Pius X in Santa Fe Springs used part of St. Marianne's facilities to begin their parochial school. In September of 1956 a section of their plant provided space for the charter class of St. Paul High School.

St. Marianne de Paredes School has been staffed by School Sisters of Notre Dame since its establishment in 1953. The school presently has a lay administration, headed by Karen Lloyd as principal, and staff.

Venice

Saint Mark

Although St. Mark Parish was established in 1923, parents wishing to have the benefits of a Catholic education for their children had to enroll them in either St. Augustine or St. Clement schools. In 1949, however, the pastor purchased three bungalows and moved them onto the parish site. Classes met for the first time at St. Mark School on September 12, 1949, with 150 children enrolled in the first three grades. More bungalows were added annually until construction began on the Coeur d'Alene Avenue property in 1952. The new school opened in October of 1953 with a total enrollment of 658 pupils in eleven classrooms.

St. Mark School reached its peak enrollment in 1957 and became a sixteen classroom school the following year. As the years progressed, various factors contributed to a steady decrease in school population, and, in 1972, a plan for gradually phasing down to eight classrooms was devised. A kindergarten was opened in September of 1981 and expanded to a full time program in 1993. At the same time, a Pre-K enrichment program was also offered.

The Sisters of the Holy Names of Jesus and Mary had begun their educational ministry in St. Mark in 1927. Therefore when the parish opened its parochial school in 1949, it was only natural that this community accept charge of the school. In September of 1988, a shortage of personnel caused the sisters to withdraw and the school administration was turned over to the laity.

Mrs. Mary Jo Aiken is principal.

Valinda

Saint Martha

St. Martha School opened in September 1960 under the direction of the Sisters of the Love of God. Initially the school consisted of 160 students in grades one through four. An additional grade was added each year until, by September 1964, the school had a grade 1-8 configuration.

The Sisters of the Love of God, under the leadership of Sister Azucena del Rio, R.A.D., continue to staff the school.

Christian education also includes over 1000 elementary children in Religious Education led by Sara Monte, DRE and seventy-five volunteers.

The high school youth ministry and confirmation program is coordinated with the young adult ministry with over 250 teens and seventy-five young adults. Lawrence Dacanay is the Coordinator of Life Teen Youth and Young Adult Ministry.

Los Angeles

Saint Martin of Tours

St. Martin of Tours School was opened on September 13, 1954 to serve Catholic families in the Brentwood area of West Los Angeles. Until 1979, the school was administered and staffed by the Sisters of St. Joseph of Carondelet. Since 1979, it has had both a lay administration and faculty.

Throughout its more than fifty-year history, St. Martin of Tours School has sought to educate its students by means of a challenging academic curriculum infused with Gospel values Early additions to the school plant included a resource room, computer lab and kindergarten. In September 1997 a religious resource area, counseling offices, fine arts room, library, art room, and science lab were added, all of which contribute to St. Martin of Tours' long tradition of community spirit, academic excellence and strong art and athletic programs.

Ms. Cecilia Oswald is principal.

Los Angeles

Saint Mary

St. Mary School, erected in 1905 on the corner of Fourth and Breed Streets, was the third parochial school established in Los Angeles. Because of difficulties in securing a religious community to staff it, the building remained unoccupied for two years. In 1907 the Sisters of the Holy Names of Jesus and Mary took charge of St. Mary and classes for 171 students met for the first time on September 17th.

St. Mary began as an eight-grade school. In 1912, a two-year business program for girls was added and eventually expanded to a three-year program. In 1940, the commercial course was replaced by a ninth grade for boys and girls. This class was discontinued in 1943.

The prosperity experienced by Southern California after World War II as well as the support of the Youth Education Fund enabled the pastor to purchase two lots facing St. Louis Avenue and to bring the school and convent next to the church and rectory.

In June of 1992, due to the declining number of teaching sisters, the Sisters of the Holy Names withdrew from the parish. The Salesian Sisters of St. John Bosco took over the administration of St. Mary School.

Sister Joseph Ochoa, F.M.A. is principal.

| Palmdale | Camarillo | Santa Maria | Whittier |

Saint Mary

In the fall of 1960, St. Mary, an eight-room parochial school in Palmdale, opened its doors to seventy-two first and second graders. The following year, the addition of the third, fourth and fifth grades caused the enrollment to almost double.

During its initial year, St. Mary was staffed by three parishioners, including Mrs. Rae Henry who served as the first principal. At the invitation of the pastor, Father Martin Hiss, three Sisters of the Immaculate Heart of Mary took over the school. These sisters continued this ministry until June of 1968, when their community withdrew from the parish. The following September, the Salesian Sisters of St. John Bosco assumed the administration and partial staffing of the school.

Today St. Mary, under the direction of Ms. Carolyn Gries, offers a K-8 program to the families of the Palmdale, Acton, Littlerock and Lake Los Angeles areas, one of the fastest growing regions in Los Angeles County.

Saint Mary Magdalen

The history of St. Mary Magdalen School in Camarillo is closely linked with the story of the Camarillo family itself. In 1914, two brothers, Juan E. and Adolfo Camarillo, decided to replace the small overcrowded family chapel with a more permanent structure as a memorial to their parents. Ground was broken on July 1, 1913, and a year later, on July 4, 1914, the new chapel was formally dedicated and named after the brothers' eldest sister, Magdalena.

The Church of St. Mary Magdalen continued to serve as the Camarillo family chapel until 1940. In that year the family deeded the building as well as additional acreage for a school to the Archdiocese of Los Angeles for use as a parish church. The school, however, did not become a reality for another fifteen years. Finally on March 19, 1954 Adolfo Camarillo turned the first shovel of dirt in order to break ground for a four-classroom building.

Classes began on September 14, 1954 for eighty-nine students in grades one through three. The pastor, Father John Moclair, planned to open a new grade each year. In 1956, a second four-room unit was added. By September of 1958, the school had a total of eight grades. The kindergarten was added in 1999.

The Sisters of the Immaculate Heart staffed St. Mary Magdalen School from 1954 until 1968. In September of that year, the school was turned over to the Sisters of Notre Dame. This community administered St. Mary Magdalen until 1997 at which time Mr. Don Huntley became the first lay principal.

Saint Mary of the Assumption

Santa Maria was a small agricultural community with a population of 8,000 when excavations began for St. Mary of the Assumption School on June 17, 1938. Construction was completed in record time and regular classes began on September 14. Fifty-nine students were enrolled in grades one through eight under the guidance of the Franciscan Sisters of Penance and Christian Charity. On June 16, 1939, six eighth graders – three boys and three girls – became St. Mary of the Assumption's charter class.

The original building at St. Mary consisted of a four-room unit; two grades shared a single classroom. This arrangement lasted until 1948 when construction of a second four-classroom unit was begun. At the same time, the parish also purchased the property across Cypress Street from the church, which was subsequently fenced in for the main playground. In 1960-1961 and again in 1963-1964 two more four-room units were added. By September 1964 St. Mary of the Assumption was a double grade school.

Growth at St. Mary of the Assumption during the ensuing years was steady but slow. By 1971, however, the presence of another parochial school in Santa Maria coupled with archdiocesan policy dictated the gradual elimination of double grades. The "phase-out" was completed by 1975-1976. A kindergarten was opened in 1985.

Today Ms. Carmen Vadillo is principal.

Saint Mary of the Assumption

St. Mary of the Assumption, located in Whittier, opened in 1923 with an enrollment of 107 pupils in grades one through six and staffed by the Dominican Sisters of Houston, Texas. An eight-room school building was added to the campus in 1961. The school year 1984-1985 brought the addition of a kindergarten, and participation in the Title I program.

On October 1, 1987, the city of Whittier experienced an earthquake, which caused major damage to the original school building on Pickering Avenue. As a result, that portion of the school plant was condemned and demolished. Construction of a new building was begun almost immediately on the site.

The new building was ready for the students in December 1990. In addition to classrooms, the structure contained computer labs and a library as well as ample office space. At this time, a covered lunch area, grass area, gardens and kindergarten playground were added. In 1998, the computer labs were updated and Bishop Joseph Sartoris was able to bless them in time for St. Mary of the Assumption's 75th Anniversary Celebrations.

Ms. Gloria Napoli is principal.

Huntington Park

Saint Matthias

The first school in St. Matthias Parish was located at the corner of Belgrave and Stafford in Huntington Park. When it opened its doors in 1924, it consisted of just four classrooms. The grades were combined and four Sisters of Notre Dame taught 215 children. This arrangement lasted until 1932 when the school was enlarged to include five additional classrooms, a library, a music room, offices, and an auditorium. The ninth classroom provided space for a ninth grade.

In 1933-1934, however, two major earthquakes shook the area seriously damaging the parish plant. Only the persistence of Sister Mary Bernard, S.N.D. and the intervention of Bishop John J. Cantwell convinced the pastor to rebuild the school. By September, 1937, the renovated school was ready for occupancy. A kindergarten and tenth grade were added in 1943 which boosted enrollment to nearly 600 children.

By 1960, plans were underway to convert the elementary school building into a four year high school for girls. A new building adjacent to the church on the corner of Florence Avenue and Mission Place was planned for the elementary school.

Since 1960 St. Matthias has continued to grow. In 1989, St. Matthias opened a kindergarten and initiated the Writing-to-Read Program. In September of 1998, St. Matthias School opened a pre-kindergarten. Following the withdrawal of the Sisters of Notre Dame, the school was in the hands of a lay administrator who today is Ms. Lorraine Selva-Speights.

Woodland Hills

Saint Mel

St. Mel School in Woodland Hills was established in February 1957 with an opening enrollment of 368 students. Three sisters of the Immaculate Heart of Mary and four lay teachers taught grades one through five in double sessions. The following year, the Sisters of St. Louis assumed the administration and grades six and seven, also in double sessions, were opened. The eighth grade was added the following year.

During the ensuing years St. Mel has continued to expand. In 1962 twelve more classrooms and offices were added to the school plant. Another new building, erected in 1984, provided facilities for a computer lab, reading lab, and faculty lounge.

The previous year, 1983, the school had opened a half-day kindergarten. In 1993, the expansion of this program to a full day necessitated the addition of two portable classrooms. Since that time, a child care program as well as a prekindergarten have been initiated.

The current principal is Ms. Marilyn Kadzielski.

Los Angeles

Saint Michael

In September 1903, two Dominican Sisters of Mission San Jose made the first trip from their convent in St. Joseph Parish to the newly built school of St. Michael. In reality, St. Michael School was a small, two-room building located at the corner of Manchester Boulevard and Vermont Avenue. Classes began on September 9, 1903 for forty-three students in grades one through eight.

Throughout its more than one hundred year history, St. Michael School has continued to grow. In 1926, the main building of the present school was erected. In 1953, an annex was added in order to accommodate the growing enrollment. The opening of a Writing-to-Read Computer Lab in 1986, through a grant from the Riordan Foundation, expanded the Language Arts curriculum.

The ethnic makeup of St. Michael's students provides an example of Los Angeles' changing demographics. Following the Watts Riot of 1965, the school served predominantly African-American families - Catholics from Louisiana as well as Baptists. Since the 1980s, families from Mexico and Central America together with a large number of Black Catholics from Belize have joined the school community. At the same time, the parish itself continued to reflect an increasing enrollment of economically disadvantaged Latino families. As a result, St. Michael School today, under Dominican Sister Carol Ward's leadership, boasts of an educational environment rich in both cultural diversity and in religious background.

Santa Monica

Saint Monica

On September 4, 1889, just thirteen years after the founding of St. Monica Parish, the Sisters of the Holy Names of Jesus and Mary opened Holy Names Academy in a small frame building on the corner of Fourth Street and Arizona. The school served as the elementary school for St. Monica Parish until 1930 when Monsignor Nicholas Conneally, the pastor, was able to erect his own building next to the parish church, which became known as St. Monica School. The elementary division of Holy Names Academy was transferred to the new site and the sisters agreed to staff the parochial school. In 1974, the sisters withdrew from the school altogether. Beginning with the new school year, 1975-1976, St. Monica has operated with an all-lay staff.

Earthquakes have frequently impacted Southern California schools and St. Monica was not an exception. On January 17, 1994, the school building was badly damaged by the Northridge quake. After a series of inspections, classes were able to resume on January 31.

Since that time, St. Monica School has benefited from a number of parish construction projects. In 1995, the Special Projects Committee of the parish remodeled the lower level of the school building. At the same time, the Trepp Library was erected at the north end of the campus.

Ms. Joan Morris is principal.

Los Angeles	Lakewood	Thousand Oaks	North Hollywood
## Saint Odillia	## Saint Pancratius	## Saint Paschal Baylon	## Saint Patrick

Although St. Odilia Parish, the Mother Church of the African American community in Los Angeles, was established in 1926, plans for a parochial school did not materialize until 1948. Finally, through the efforts of the pastor, Father Patrick Shine, S.M.A, who went door-to-door in the neighborhood soliciting funds, and the support of the Youth Education Fund, St. Odilia School became a reality.

Classes began in September, 1950 taught by the Sisters of St. Joseph of Carondelet. One hundred thirty-one students in grades one through four made up the charter classes. Grades five, six, seven and eight were added during the next four years. In 1969, however, St. Odilia was identified as a "feeder school" for Holy Cross Middle School. Consequently, the junior high grades were transferred to that campus.

The 1990s were book ended by significant growth for St. Odilia. A kindergarten was opened in 1990. With the closure of Holy Cross Middle School in 1999, the school administration began planning for the reinstatement of the seventh and eighth grades. Additional property was purchased and a building erected. With the dedication of the new unit St. Odilia once again became a K-8 school.

Ms. Sharon Oliver is currently principal.

St. Pancratius School opened September 1955 with an all-lay faculty of four teachers, a teacher/principal and an enrollment of 270 students in grades one through four. The following year, four more classes were added, attendance rose to 500 children and six Sisters of Charity of Seton Hill joined the faculty. By 1956, there were two classes for every grade. A kindergarten was added in 1981 and a child care program in 1989. Eventually, in accordance with the archdiocesan plan, St. Pancratius School began to phase out its double grades.

Although a member of the Sisters of Charity continued to serve at St. Pancratius until 2001, the community withdrew from the administration of the school in 1979 at which time a lay principal was appointed.

Today, St. Pancratius School has a single grade K-8 configuration under the leadership of Ms. Carol Kulesza.

Class began on September 10, 1963 at St. Paschal Baylon School. In 1966 a second four-classroom unit was added and a double first grade was begun. St. Paschal Baylon continued to "double" its grades for the next four years. In the fall of 1970, however, a single first grade was reinstated in compliance with archdiocesan policy. As classes were eliminated, the vacant rooms were utilized for other purposes including a kindergarten and a state-of-the art science lab.

Changes in staffing took place as well. In June 1997 the Sisters of Notre Dame withdrew from St. Paschal Baylon. Mrs. Suzanne Duffy began her tenure as principal the following September.

St. Patrick School was established in 1952, just four years after the parish itself had been erected. The beginning of classes was delayed until September 27th since construction workers were still in the building. The faculty consisted of seven sisters, Religious of the Sacred Heart of Mary, and one lay woman who taught children in grades one through six. Within two years the school had expanded to eight grades with a total enrollment of 280 students.

Over the years, changes occurred in order to accommodate the population shifts which impacted the area. In 1960 and again in 1963 additional classrooms were added with the result that St. Patrick became a double-grade school. When the second classes were phased out during the 1970s, the space became available for program development.

The Religious of the Sacred Heart of Mary withdrew from St. Patrick in 1987.

The school at present has both a lay administration headed by Ms. Rosselle Azar, and staff.

Los Angeles	La Mirada	Los Angeles	Lynwood

Saint Paul

From the very beginning, Monsignor Thomas Blackwell realized that a parochial school was an important means of strengthening the educational system of St. Paul Parish. Therefore, in 1922, he began construction of a one-story building and asked the Sisters of the Holy Cross to take over the academic program. Within a few short years, however, the enrollment had increased to the point where a larger building was needed. As a result, a second story was added. In 1962, this structure was replaced with the present building.

In September of 1973, the Holy Cross community relinquished St. Paul. Their place was taken by Brother Charles Philpot, bsfc and the members of the Brothers of St. Francis of the Cross. In June of 1987, this community disbanded and the archdiocese appointed Mrs. Iris Trouillier as principal. In 1999 to provide a better religious education in the school, Sisters Servants of Blessed Sacrament were invited to help the school. Ms. Jennifer Grenardo is principal.

Saint Paul of the Cross

St. Paul of the Cross School was established in September 1957 during the pastorate of Monsignor Owen P. Jinks with an enrollment of 379 students in grades one through six. Three Bernardine Sisters of the Third Order of St. Francis and four lay teachers staffed the school.

As enrollment increased and additional rooms opened, a second building was added to the school plant. By 1959, St. Paul had two classrooms per grade on each level, one through eight. The process of phasing out one class at each grade level was begun in 1970, and by 1977, the school had achieved a single grade 1-8 configuration. The kindergarten program was added in September 1988.

Ms. Lorraine Mendiaz is principal.

Saint Paul the Apostle

St. Paul the Apostle School was established in 1935 under the guidance of the Daughters of Mary and Joseph and the supervision of Reverend Francis Quinan, a member of the Paulist Community. The school originated with six classrooms and over the next six decades expanded to a double grade, K-8 school. Today the principal Sister Stella Enright, D.M.J. and her committed faculty and staff continue to provide a wide variety of learning experiences to the children of the parish.

Saint Philip Neri

Saint Philip Neri School opened as a four-classroom school staffed by the Sisters of the Holy Cross. In 1954, four more classrooms were added to complete the eight-grade configuration. A kindergarten program was begun in 1993.

Although the Sisters of the Holy Cross continued to serve at St. Philip Neri until 1984, they relinquished administration of the school in 1974. At this time, the first lay principal was appointed.

Like many of the schools in the archdiocese, St. Philip Neri is a reflection of Los Angeles' shifting demography. Initially both the school and parish served an essentially middle class Caucasian community. Beginning in the early 1970s, this pattern began to change. Today, the majority of St. Philip Neri's population is Latino. There are also a significant number of African Americans in the parish and school community.

Ms. Mary Greggins is principal.

| Pasadena | Carson | Santa Fe Springs | Los Angeles |

Saint Philip the Apostle

St. Philip the Apostle School opened in September 1927, and was originally staffed by the Sisters of Charity of the Blessed Virgin Mary. Sister Mary Dominic Burke B.V.M. was the first principal. Fifty students were housed in what was described as "a fortress-built structure" known as the "South School". In 1958 the growing school population necessitated the construction of a second building north of the parish church, known as the "North School".

The Sisters of Charity continued to direct and staff the school until 1974 when a lack of personnel necessitated their withdrawal. In that year, Sister Benedict Joseph Doherty, a sister of the Holy Names of Jesus and Mary, assumed the administration of the school. In September 1977, Mrs. Celeste Justice was appointed the first lay principal.

At present St. Philip the Apostle Parish has undertaken a building program in order to expand the school and accommodate its growing enrollment. When completed, St. Philip the Apostle School will be a double-grade facility, with grades kindergarten through eight.

Today Ms. Jennifer Ramirez directs the school.

Saint Philomena

St. Philomena School opened on September 15th 1958 with 172 children in grades one through four. An additional grade was added each year until the school achieved a K-8 configuration. By 1969, the enrollment had reached 698 children and sixteen classrooms were in use. In 1972, at the request of the archdiocese, the double grades were gradually phased out. In September of 1997, St. Philomena began a special program especially designed to help children who will turn five years old on or before December 31st, prepare for kindergarten.

Since its opening, the Carmelite Sisters of the Most Sacred Heart of Los Angeles have administered St. Philomena. Today, the school is a single grade K-8 institution serving a rich diversity of families - - Filipino, Hispanic, Samoan, Black, Korean, Vietnamese, and Anglo -- in the Carson area.

Sister Martin Marie King, O.C.D. is presently principal.

Saint Pius X

As often happens with a new school, construction was still in progress when it came time for classes to begin. This was true at St. Pius X in Santa Fe Springs. As a result, in September of 1955, the initial first graders, 100 boys and girls, gathered in two classrooms leased from St. Marianne School in Pico Rivera. By the time the Sisters of Mercy arrived the following year to staff the school, the first unit of the plant had been completed.

The original plans for the parish plant had included an eight-classroom elementary school and a convent. The large enrollment, however, necessitated expanding the school to sixteen classrooms. The period of double grades lasted for twelve years, 1960-1972. The adjustment of parish boundaries that took place in 1970 meant that approximately 250 families were incorporated into the adjacent parishes. Consequently, beginning in 1972, St. Pius X started the transition to a single grade school. In the fall of 1983, the first kindergarten class began.

In the fall of 1988, the Sisters of Mercy were no longer able to staff St. Pius X School.

Today, Ms. Margaret Alvarez is principal.

Saint Raphael

Located in South Los Angeles, St. Raphael School has been a vital part of the community since it was established in 1947. Construction of the school actually began in 1946 and was completed in time for the opening day of classes on September 2, 1947. Within the next two years, a kindergarten as well as a seventh and eighth grade were added and the playground expanded. In 1980, a Montessori School was opened under the direction of the pastor, Reverend Matthew Sprouffske, O. Carm.. This program was discontinued in 1986 when Father was transferred.

St. Raphael School was originally staffed by the Adrian Dominican Sisters. Since the withdrawal of the community in 1984, the school has had a lay administration, presently headed by Ms. Barbara Curtis, and faculty.

| Goleta | Downey | Sierra Madre | Burbank |

Saint Raphael

The story of St. Raphael School in Santa Barbara began with the prayers of a nun, Sister Alix Mitchell, D.C.. In 1931, Sister had been assigned to St. Vincent Orphanage in Santa Barbara. Besides caring for the children, she also taught religious education classes in the small parish of St. Raphael. It was Sister Alix's hope, however, that a parochial school would someday be built in the Goleta Valley. To this end, in 1935, she buried some medals at the parish site on Mandarin Avenue.

Nearly thirty years later Sister Alix's dream became a reality. In 1961, Father William R. Harvey moved the parish to a seven-acre site on Hollister Avenue. Two years later, he started construction of a parochial school. Classes began on September 10, 1963 for 189 students in grades one through four. A new wing containing four classrooms as well as an equipment room and lavatories was completed in 1966.

The Sisters of the Immaculate Heart staffed St. Raphael until 1968. In that year, the sisters withdrew. The Sisters of the Holy Names of Jesus and Mary assumed the administration of the school. Seven years later, in 1975, this religious community turned the school over to a lay principal, who at present is Ms. Ellen Manning, and staff.

In addition to a complete instructional program for grades kindergarten through eight, the school offers KinderKlasse, which opened in 1977. A full-day program for young fives opened in 1992, and a preschool began in 1993.

Saint Raymond

St. Raymond School opened on September 19, 1957 under the supervision of Reverend Patrick L. Cleary as pastor, and the guidance of the Sisters of the Holy Faith. The student body consisted of 250 children in grades one through four. Four additional classrooms were added in 1959 and another four in 1961.

In 1971, because of decreasing enrollment and to comply with archdiocesan directives, only one first grade was enrolled. By 1979, the school was operating with eight grades. In 1988, a kindergarten as well as a child care program were added. A computer lab opened in 1990.

The principal is Sister Margaret Dullaghan, C.H.F.

Saint Rita

St. Rita School was founded in 1922, fourteen years after the parish itself was erected. The original plant consisted of a four-room structure on Baldwin Avenue. By 1942, the school enrollment had reached 114 children in eight classrooms.

In 1952, the parish began construction on a two-story building on East Alegria Avenue. Ten years later, in 1962, another eight-room building was erected on the west side of Baldwin Avenue. By 1967, St. Rita's enrollment had reached 610 children in sixteen classrooms for grades one through eight, with an east and west campus.

During the 1970s, the school began to implement the archdiocese's plan to phase out double grades. By September 1979, all eight grades had been reduced to one room per class. At the same time, a kindergarten was opened. The east campus housed the primary grades, kindergarten through third; the west campus, the intermediate and junior high grades, four through eight.

Throughout its history, St. Rita School has been staffed by various religious communities: the Sisters of Loretto at the Foot of the Cross (1923-1924), the Sisters of St. Joseph from Brighton, Massachusetts (1924-1936), Sisters of the Presentation of the Blessed Virgin Mary (1936-1942) and the Sisters of St. Francis of Penance and Christian Charity (1942-1979).

At present the school has a lay administration headed by Ms. Patrice Cantrell, and faculty.

Saint Robert Bellarmine

The parish of St. Robert Bellarmine began on December 12, 1907. At the time, the church was located in the Odd Fellows Hall on San Fernando Road and Olive Avenue and its name was "Holy Trinity". By 1909, however, the parishioners had moved into a building of their own. In 1936 construction of a new church was completed and the old building then became the parish elemen-

tary school. St. Robert Bellarmine School (still known as Holy Trinity) opened in September with grades one through four and an enrollment of eighty-eight pupils. By 1938 the number of students had risen to 185 pupils in eight grades. In November of that year Archbishop John J. Cantwell blessed the school and renamed it St. Robert Bellarmine. The school continued to grow until, in 1955, it reached a maximum of 645 pupils occupying twelve classrooms. In September 1969, due to a decline in enrollment, four classrooms were converted to other functions.

From its beginning, St. Robert Bellarmine School was staffed by the Sisters of Charity of the Blessed Virgin Mary from Dubuque, Iowa. In June of 1988, after fifty-one years of service, the community withdrew. The following September, St. Robert Bellarmine was administered by a lay principal -- currently Dr. June Rosena.

| Maywood | Simi Valley | Los Angeles | Santa Paula |

Saint Rose of Lima

St. Rose of Lima School is located in the heart of the city of Maywood, an area known as "Little Mexico" due to its high concentration of Latinos. Opened on September 28, 1930 with an enrollment of 185 children, the school was staffed by the Sisters of the Notre Dame with Sister Mary Balbina, S.N.D. as principal. As the student population grew, so did the school. Two additional classrooms were added in 1936 and again in 1941. St. Rose reached its peak enrollment at 420. A kindergarten as well as a Writing-to-Read lab were opened in 1990 and 1991 through grants from the Riordan and Shea Foundations.

The Sisters of Notre Dame staffed St. Rose of Lima School until the close of the 2001-2002 school year. The following September, Mr. Mathias Vairez, Jr. was appointed principal.

Saint Rose of Lima

The tremendous growth that took place in Southern California as a result of World War II continued unabated throughout the 1950s. By the early 1960s, the population of the San Fernando Valley had begun to spill through the Santa Susanna Pass into the Simi Valley. In 1960, the region had a population of 7,440. By 1963-1964, this figure had jumped to nearly 30,000 as the orange and walnut groves gave way to new homes and shopping centers. The number of families moving into the community created the need for a parish school. Consequently, on January 5, 1964, Father Patrick McDonagh broke ground for St. Rose of Lima School.

Classes began on September 14, 1964 for 213 children enrolled in grades one through four. They were taught by three Sisters of Notre Dame and a laywoman. A new grade was added in each successive year. By 1969, the school had a student population of 356 in grades one through eight.

The Sisters of Notre Dame withdrew from St. Rose of Lima in June of 1993. The following September Mrs. Patricia Pryor was appointed principal. Ms. Katherine Barrantes is principal today.

Saint Sebastian

St. Sebastian School opened In September 1950 staffed by the Daughters of Mary and Joseph. The sisters commuted from their convent in St. Augustine Parish, Culver City, until a convent was built on the site of the old parish hall. A shortage of personnel compelled the community to withdraw from St. Sebastian in 1972. The following September, the Sisters Servants of the Blessed Sacrament from Guadalajara, Mexico took over the administration of the school.

When these sisters left the school, the first lay principal was hired. In 2005, the school came under the governance of the Department of Catholic Schools. A school council assists Cort Peters, the present principal, in the administration of the school.

Saint Sebastian

St. Sebastian School in Santa Paula can be known as the school with "two lives." The school initially opened in 1952 and was staffed by the Sisters of the Humility of Mary from Ottumwa, Iowa. In 1969 a decline in enrollment compelled the sisters to withdraw from the school. As a result, the pastor decided to close it.

In 1987, Father James Rothe was appointed pastor. With the encouragement of the parishioners, he decided to reopen St. Sebastian as a middle school. In September 1988, classes began for eighty-nine students in grades six, seven and eight.

Two years later, in 1990, the school expanded to kindergarten through grade eight. Because of the limited number of rooms available, classes were combined. Two years later, in 1992, a preschool program was inaugurated to accommodate working parents and to prepare children for kindergarten. With the addition of four portable classrooms to the plant, each of the elementary grades became self-contained.

Today St. Sebastian with Kathleen Garcia as principal enrolls students in kindergarten through grade eight. The elementary curriculum together with the preschool program provides families of the Santa Paula and Fillmore areas with an opportunity for a quality Catholic education.

Monterey Park

Saint Stephen Martyr

St. Stephen Martyr School began on September 11, 1926 in four classrooms to accommodate 130 students in six grades. The seventh and eighth grades were added in successive years. The present "L" shaped structure was completed in 1964 and a Title I instruction mobile unit added in 1976. In 1981 the parish added the hall and adjoining rooms and the enclosed playground on the rear campus.

The diversity of the community of Monterey Park is evident in the high Asian population in the school. In addition, the Ming Yuan Institute utilizes a number of classrooms for an after school Chinese Catholic children's education program.

St. Stephen School was originally staffed by the Sisters of Holy Names of Jesus and Mary. In 1993, the community withdrew from the school and a lay administrator was appointed.

The principal today is Ms. Josefina Solomonson.

Los Angeles

Saint Teresa of Avila

St. Teresa of Avila School opened for 150 students on September 19, 1949 under the direction of the Sisters of Providence of St. Mary of the Woods, Indiana. For the first two months, classes were taught in the parish hall. Grades one, three and five attended the morning session; grades two, four and six, the afternoon. On November 2, 1949, the building was completed and the classrooms were ready for use. The seventh and eighth grades were added in the next two years.

In the spring of 1969, St. Teresa of Avila was identified as a "feeder" school for Queen of Angels Middle School near downtown Los Angeles. As a result, the seventh and eighth grades transferred to that campus.

When Our Lady Queen of the Angels Middle School closed in 1982, the parish initiated plans to reinstate the junior high division. A seventh grade class began in September 1987; an eighth, the following year. During the 1988-1989 school year, plans were developed for a kindergarten and a Writing-to-Read lab, both of which opened in September 1989.

In 1983 the Sisters of Providence turned the administration of the school over to the current principal, Ms. Christina Fernandez-Caso, although the community has continued to be actively involved in the parish.

Alhambra

Saint Therese

St. Therese School is located in a residential section of Alhambra adjacent to the San Marino area. A combination church-school building was dedicated on November 7, 1926. The first graduating class consisted of five boys and one girl.

As the parish grew so did the school. In 1950 the parish completed construction of a new church with the result that the old church was converted into a parish hall. The former parish hall, in turn, was converted into two classrooms and a small meeting room. In the early 1960s, the increased student enrollment necessitated another extension of the school. In 1963, the new school building was completed. A kindergarten was added in 1988.

St. Therese School was originally operated by the Dominican Sisters of Mission San Jose. In 1930, the Sisters of Providence took over and served the school until 1994 when the administration was handed over to a lay principal and staff.

Today Mr. Christopher Haygood is in charge of the school.

Monterey Park

Saint Thomas Aquinas

St. Thomas Aquinas School opened its doors in September of 1963, with an enrollment of 200 pupils. Only four classrooms had been built to accommodate the first four grades. Each successive year, an additional grade was added. The first kindergarten class was opened in 1977. The Sisters of St. Joseph of Peace staffed the school from 1963 until 1982. At present, the faculty consists of a lay principal and lay teachers supported by classroom aides and office personnel.

Like its neighboring school, St. Stephen Martyr, St. Thomas Aquinas has opened its facilities to the Asian community in the area. In the fall of 1992, the Shu Guang Chinese School began an after school education program in four classrooms on the campus. Within recent years, this school has expanded to include a Chinese cultural education program on Saturdays.

Ms. Anne Bouvet is principal of St. Thomas Aquinas School.

Saint Thomas More

St. Thomas More School opened its doors for the first time on September 15, 1952, with a faculty of five Dominican Sisters of Sinsinawa, Wisconsin. At that time, there were 108 students enrolled in grades one through four. Classes were temporarily held in the parish hall while construction of a permanent school building was in progress. By January 1953, the students were able to move into the present building. By opening an additional grade each year, St. Thomas More was able to serve pupils in grades one through eight by 1956.

Five additional classrooms were added by the beginning of the 1963 school year with the result that the school reached its peak enrollment of 511 students in thirteen classrooms. As the student population decreased, however, and space became available, the extra classrooms were converted to a computer lab, a music room, and religious education office. A kindergarten was opened in 1987. In 1991, a portable building was used to house a library.

In 1985, the first lay administrator of the school was appointed. Since that time, with the exception of a brief period in the 1990s, St. Thomas More has had a lay principal, faculty and staff.

Today Ms. Judith Jones and Ms. Jennifer Schmidt serve as co-principals of the school.

Saint Thomas the Apostle

According to early parish records, St. Thomas the Apostle School was originally located on the present site of Bishop Conaty - Our Lady of Loretto High School on Pico Boulevard. During the mid 1920s, the elementary school first moved into a building adjacent to the church and finally, in 1929, into the building which it now occupies.

Initially St. Thomas served children of several old California families. The neighborhoods from which the school drew its students were predominantly German and Irish. During the 1940s the school population shifted as families with a Spanish-speaking background moved into the area.

When St. Thomas opened, the faculty was composed of Sisters of the Immaculate Heart of Mary. This community continued to minister in the school until 1968 when the Sisters of Mercy assumed responsibility. In September of 1988, the administration of the school was turned over to the Sisters of the Holy Names. In 1990, St. Thomas School employed a lay principal and lay faculty for the first time. Today it is Karen Velasquez.

In May 1993, St. Thomas the Apostle School received The National Blue Ribbon Award from President Bill Clinton at a special ceremony in the White House Rose Garden.

Saint Timothy

St. Timothy Parish was erected in 1943; however, due to a shortage of building materials during World War II, parishioners worshipped in a storefront on Pico Blvd., a few blocks west of Beverly Glen. Once construction of the permanent church was completed in 1949, the pastor, Father William O'Shea, turned his attention to opening a parish school. It was not until 1958, however, that he was able to acquire the land adjacent to the hall and break ground.

St. Timothy School opened in 1958 with 100 children in grades one through four. In 1959, grade five and a kindergarten were added. Another grade was added each year until, in 1963; the enrollment reached 400 students in kindergarten through eighth grade. In 1978 the kindergarten was closed and did not reopen until 1991.

The Sisters of Notre Dame staffed St. Timothy School until 1989 when Dr. Rita G. Lapple was appointed the first lay principal.

At present Ms. Iselda Richmond is principal of the school.

Saint Turibius

Although Bishop John J. Cantwell had established St. Turibius Mission in 1927, the dream of its first pastor, Father Francis Redman, O.F.M., and his successors to open a parochial school did not materialize until the late 1940s. On February 27, 1949, through the generosity of the Youth Education Fund, Bishop Timothy Manning blessed the foundation of St. Turibius School. Classes began for 265 children the following September.

Today St. Turibius has a K-8 configuration; however, this was not always the case. When it opened in 1949, the school consisted of six grades. As the original sixth grade moved up, a new grade was added each year so that by 1952 St. Turibius was an eight grade school. In 1969, however, St. Turibius became a participant in the Archdiocese of Los Angeles' Middle School Project. As a result, the junior high division was closed and the seventh and eighth-grade students attended either Queen of Angels or Holy Cross Middle Schools. When Holy Cross Middle School closed in June 1999, St. Turibius reinstated grades seven (1998) and eight (1999). A kindergarten had been added in 1993.

Today St. Turibius is a nine-grade school – kindergarten through grade eight. Staffed first by the Franciscan Missionary Sisters of the Immaculate Conception and then by the Sisters of St. Francis of Penance and Christian Charity, the school today is directed by Ms. Claudia Moreno as principal.

Los Angeles

Saint Vincent

The history of St. Vincent School began in 1911 when the Vincentian Fathers discontinued St. Vincent College, located at Washington Boulevard and Grand Avenue. At the suggestion of Father Aloysius Meyer, C.M., the Sisters of St. Joseph of Carondelet agreed to take over the buildings for a parochial school. In 1923 a new school with nine classrooms, an office, and an auditorium was built at Adams Boulevard and Flower Street, one block east of the present church.

In 1953 St. Vincent relocated once again, this time due to the construction of the Harbor Freeway. The new structure, at its current location at Adams and Figueroa Street, was built in a record time of four and a half months. Occupied since the spring of 1954, the present school consists of nine classrooms, a library/computer lab, administrative offices, a kitchen/cafeteria area, and an auditorium. In the spring of 1987, a Writing-to-Read Lab opened. St. Vincent Center provides office space for Esperanza Housing Project as well as for a Headstart and child care Program.

The Sisters of St. Joseph of Carondelet staffed St. Vincent School until 1987 at which time the school came under lay leadership. In 1997, the school administration was transferred to the Daughters of Charity who co-sponsor the school today.

Sister Cabrini Thomas, D.C. is the principal.

San Marino

Saints Felicitas & Perpetua

Saints Felicitas and Perpetua School, located on a three-acre site in San Marino, was established in 1950. Four Sisters of the Holy Names of Jesus and Mary, who commuted from Ramona Convent, and two lay teachers, staffed the school. Classes began on September 11, 1950 with 240 children enrolled.

In 1981, the Carmelite Sisters of the Most Sacred Heart of Los Angeles assumed the administration of Saints Felicitas and Perpetua School. Today, students at Saints Felicitas and Perpetua are provided with a Catholic education in a living Christian environment through the efforts of a dedicated faculty and principal, Mr. Lawrence Fitzgibbons, as well as a concerned parent and parish community.

Wilmington

Saints Peter & Paul

Saints Peter and Paul School has provided the opportunity for a Catholic education to the community of Wilmington for more than sixty years. The first school, founded in 1945, was staffed by the Franciscan Sisters of Penance and Christian Charity. When the current plant was built in 1951, the Franciscan community was unable to provide additional sisters, so the pastor, Reverend John Dunne, invited the Sisters of St. Joseph of Cluny to staff the school.

At first the student body was small, since the original school had two grades to a room. With the new facility, however, the enrollment steadily increased. In 1988-1989, a kindergarten was added and after school day care was organized under the auspices of Catholic Charities. In 1993, the empty lot north of the school yard was landscaped. While providing additional play area for the students it also enhanced the community of Wilmington.

Currently Mr. Kevin Sherman is principal.

Los Angeles

Transfiguration

When Transfiguration School opened in 1937, the population of Los Angles was less than one million. One hundred fifty-five children made up its student population. By 1959, the city had risen to 2.3 million and Transfiguration's enrollment had reached 759 students in sixteen classrooms. In the mid-1970s, efforts were made to reduce class size. Although this plan had resulted in a decrease in enrollment, it also made space available for a library, administrative center, faculty room and additional support facilities.

In September 1985, Transfiguration instituted an extended child care program. A "Writing-to-Read" lab was created in 1986 for the primary grades. A preschool for three and four year old children was started in 1996 and has added another dimension to Transfiguration School whose mascot is the eagle.

The Monsignor Havard Computer Lab was established at the turn of the century and allowed the school to offer technology classes to the wider community.

The Sisters of St. Joseph of Carondelet served the school from 1937 to 1993. Mr. Oscar Pratt left a legacy of thirteen years with the eagles, and Mrs. Terry Dicks became pincipal in 2006.

Los Angeles

Visitation

Until the late 1920s the community, familiarly known as Westchester, could still be described as "rural". In 1930, however, Mines Field became Los Angeles Municipal Airport and aircraft companies began moving into the area. With the advent of World War II, the growth of the airport due to the movement of military aircraft and cargo through Westchester coupled with the tremendous influx of people needed in the aircraft plants led Archbishop John J. Cantwell to establish Visitation Parish in 1943.

Visitation School opened in the fall of 1947 with all eight grades under the direction of the Sisters of Charity of Leavenworth, Kansas. Although the building was completed, furnishings were sparse. The second graders, for example, did not have desks so they sat on folding chairs at card tables. As a result, their books, crayons, pencils, etc. were always sliding to the floor.

Eventually Visitation expanded to a double grade school. By the early, 1970s, however, airport expansion had claimed approximately 35% of the homes in the parish. As a result, the school gradually phased out the second classrooms.

The Sisters of Charity continued to staff Visitation School until 1972 when they withdrew in order to meet more urgent commitments. Between 1972 and 1980, the school was directed by Sister Joan Patrice Clement, B.V.M. In 1980, the administration was assumed by Dr. Carol Ann Crede.

CATHOLIC
EDUCATION
FOUNDATION
Invest in Children™

The Catholic Education Foundation

The Catholic Education Foundation for the Archdiocese of Los Angeles was established by Roger Cardinal Mahony in 1987 as an independent charitable trust committed primarily to providing tuition assistance to the most financially deserving students attending Catholic elementary and high schools that serve an economically disadvantaged population. The Foundation is committed to providing a quality, value-orientated education in the safe and nurturing environment of a Catholic school, especially for poor and disadvantaged children living in inner-city area.

As a result of the generosity of donors, during its twenty-year history the Catholic Education Foundation has made over 86,600 tuition awards with an aggregate value of over $77 million through its two core tuition assistance programs – TAP, the basic Tuition Awards Program, and SOS, "Save Our Students". These awards have made a significant impact on the educational choices, skills development and achievements of the recipients, as well as having a tremendous positive impact on the schools and their surrounding communities.

The Foundation also supports leadership development education for qualified teachers and administrators within the archdiocese. It has also developed a long term strategy to raise significant gifts through a Planned Giving Program.

These Catholic Education Foundation's programs are funded through donations made by individuals, corporations and foundations for program expenditures and for investment in the Foundation's core endowment. The Board of Trustees meets quarterly to review overall performance, the allocation of funding and to oversee development activities.

CATHOLIC HEALTH CARE

BACKGROUND

healing of both physical and spiritual illnesses has been an integral part of the Catholic Church's ministry since Jesus dispatched His disciples "to teach and to heal". Saint Matthew's Gospel tells about the Savior healing a variety of illnesses along with His commissioning the twelve "to heal every disease and every infirmity."

The early Church Fathers spoke about the care of the sick and poor as a mark of authentic Christianity. The Council of Nicea identified the need for distinct facilities for the sick and poor and the Emperor Constantine called for the erection of hospices and hospitals. Such care developed in monastic communities as they began to grow and, as early as 800, monasteries were providing hospitality and services for the sick and pilgrims.

With the emergence of active communities of religious women, groups like the Daughters of Charity began providing nursing services in public hospitals, prisons and clinics.

In the New World, a Catholic hospital was started at Mexico City in the 17th century and, in the United States, the story of Catholic health care begins in the nineteenth century. Mother Frances Cabrini opened hospitals in New York, Chicago and the Northwest. In Maryland, Mother Elizabeth Seton's followers served in public facilities as early as 1823, before beginning their hospitals. Women religious provided major health care during the Civil War and the Spanish-American War.

In 1915, the Catholic Hospital Association was established with the goal of providing education for Sisters involved in hospital work through educational programs. In the 1980s, the Catholic Hospital Association of the United States changed its name to Catholic Health Care Association in order to more adequately reflect its membership and the growing emphasis on wellness.

The Catholic Church in the United States is unique within the universal Church for its maintenance of Church-related systems of health services. Statistics indicate that Catholic institutions and agencies now represent about one-sixth of the overall health services provided in the United States.

While the documents of Vatican Council II remained silent on health care, the hierarchy in the United States became increasingly vocal on health issues. Both Popes John XXIII and Paul VI championed the individual's right to medical care and to healthful social conditions. Under the leadership of Pope John Paul II, the first International Congress on Catholic Health Issues took place during which the Holy See's Pontifical Council for Pastoral Assistance to Health Care Workers was formed.

In 1948, the National Catholic Welfare Conference formed a Bureau of Health and Hospitals in its Social Action Department and, in 1971, issued its "Ethical and Religious Directives for Catholic Health Care Facilities." A decade later, the bishops of the United States released a collective pastoral letter "Health Care" which outlines principles for a national health policy.

This discussion attempts to sketch the story of Catholic health care in what is now the Archdiocese of Los Angeles. Our concentration here is on the historical establishment and subsequent evolvement throughout the ensuing years. Little attention has been paid to the recent challenges brought on by the ever-growing burden of financial costs.

Inasmuch as the titles and mission statements of the various health care systems have changed over the years, they are herein enumerated and categorized as they appear in the latest edition of the Catholic Directory for the Archdiocese of Los Angeles.

Production of this treatise was something of a challenge for a host of reasons. Even where there was a traceable paper trail, there were almost insurmountable factual challenges. One of the hospitals never opened, the names of several others were changed and ownership of others remains unclear.

CATHOLIC HEALTH CARE

Catholic health care is a ministry whose roots reach back to the healing works of Jesus and to the compassionate care of religious men, women and lay persons around the world over many centuries. The medical history of the area now comprising the Archdiocese of Los Angeles can be traced to the cradle of the new Spanish province where the sword, the cross and the scalpel proceeded hand-in-hand.

There were all kinds of medical challenges in missionary California. Battle casualties and accidental wounds coupled with the natural scourges of pneumonia, scurvy, consumption, typhoid, small pox and cholera presented serious obstacles to the work of the friars. Despite it all, the spirit of Francis of Assisi was evident in those hectic days! "If anyone of the brethren should fall ill, the others shall serve him as he would wish to be served himself."

Treatment was frequently crude and primitive. On one occasion Fray Junípero Serra ordered the same poultice applied to his lame leg as was used on mules - with astonishing results! Medical care progressed so rapidly, however, that on his deathbed, Serra had the services of a naval surgeon, Juan Garcia. The Indians had their healers and, surprisingly enough, many of the native remedies were successful. The Indians exhibited a remarkable facility with such difficult problems as the setting of bones.

The friars did what they could for the sick and infirm. Among the 1,760 books constituting the large collection of provincial volumes on display at San Fernando Rey de España Mission, are sixty-four titles in the general category of *Medicine* that were brought to Alta California during mission times. Among those tomes were Broun, *Medicina Domestica*; Tissot, *Medicina Domestica*; Buchan, *Medicina Domestica* and Stanciffer, *Florilegio, Medicinal* (Medical Anthology).

As was the case in all the California missions, the hospital erected by the friars at San Gabriel in 1814 contained bedrooms and corresponding *salas* or reception rooms for the convenience of the sick. There was a chapel for the administration of the sacraments to the sick, as well as rooms for the nurses and a storage facility for medicine and other requisites of the hospital. Furthermore, documents attest to the existence of a wall separating the patio of the hospital from the various shops of the mission. The wing was built of adobe and roofing tiles. In 1810, the friars reported that their hospital was crowded with from 300 to 400 habitually infirm patients. The total number of neophytes at San Gabriel was 1,199.

The likelihood is that in time the neophytes would have built up an immunity to white man's diseases. Certainly they were not all destroyed by those scourges. The considerable number of Indian neophytes and their offspring residing in the vicinity of the various missions as late even as 1890 and on into the twentieth century attest to this fact. Their descendants, many of mixed blood, are still living in numerous parts of the state.

While medical practices in California were highly undeveloped, it must be remembered that the entire profession was only then coming into its own. One author reminds readers that at the time of the founding of the missions, the science of surgery had only recently been separated from the trade of barber. Probably the "first original contri-

bution ever offered by a resident of California in the field of medicine" was a paper written by Fray Vicente Francisco de Sarria in 1830, on the morals and method of caesarian section.

Another friar reported in 1813 that "we missionary Fathers are careful, as far as possible, that the mission lacks nothing in the way of medicine." Fray Luis Martinez noted in 1814 that "I have a little book of medicines, and am guided by it in order to apply some kind of remedy, as there is such a dearth of drugs in the country..." The missionaries were not as adept physicians of the body as they were of the soul but, in times of urgent need and in default of a physician, they did a tolerably good job of improvising in a field totally foreign to their education.

The friars utilized many of the herbs and remedies used for centuries by the native Californians. Father Andrew Garriga (1843-1915) compiled a manuscript on that subject which he based on his own research, and that done earlier by Father Doroteo Ambris. There were fifty-eight entries in the Garriga manuscript which eventually found their way into print. Garriga had served at San Luis Obispo Mission and, at the time of his death, was eulogized by Bishop Thomas Conaty as "a man beloved by all who knew him because of his devotion to the priestly office and the people confided to his care."

That history is generally reflected in persons is nowhere more obvious than in California where the activity of a trilogy of physicians stretches from the earliest times to almost the contemporary scene.

Though there may well have been physicians with Juan Rodriguez Cabrillo in 1542, and Sebastian Vizcaino in 1602, Pedro Prat was the first doctor actually to practice the profession in California. While his family name was a common one in Catalonia, the best evidence available about this dynamic man who held the rank of Captain in the Royal Spanish Army, is that he was either of French birth or extraction. To all intents and purposes, however, he was probably as much a Spaniard as were the people with whom he cast his lot when he arrived in San Diego.

Prat came with Gaspar de Portola and Fray Junípero Serra in 1769 and, almost immediately after his arrival, was hard at work treating victims of the scurvy then decimating the tiny community. As could be expected of a graduate from the University of Barcelona, Dr. Prat was also a skilled botanist. When his scant supply of medicines was depleted, he gathered quantities of green mustard leaves, wild horseradish and watercress, and from these crude elements, he concocted effective remedies for his patients. Even though he himself fell victim to the dread scurvy, brought on by lack of fresh vegetables and fruit and an extensive diet of salt meats, the indefatigable physician continued treating the afflicted in his tent hospital at the *Punta de los Muertos*.

After laboring unceasingly at San Diego for nearly a year, Prat accompanied Junípero Serra to Monterey, where he spent additional months caring for the sick. According to Fray Francisco Palou, "the surgeon performed his office with the highest extremes of benevolence. Indeed, according to reports of all who composed the expedition, he had no equal."

The tremendous physical strain of his many medical activities soon had their effect on California's first surgeon general. In mid-1771, "his mind had been so harassed by the harrowing experiences that he became demented." In June, authorities deemed it wise to send the stricken doctor to Guadalajara for hospitalization. Soon after his arrival there on the ship *El Principe*, the "skilled surgeon of the royal armies of His Majesty" quietly gave up his noble soul.

His charity and efficiency in California were "officially reported to Madrid" where even today the name of Pedro Prat is held in high repute in medical circles. California's pioneers were deeply indebted to this generous man, for had it not been for Pedro Prat, it is probable that the projected province would have miscarried and never withstood the travail of its birth.

On the local scene, the name of Richard Somerset Den (1821-1895) is deeply engraved in the annals. Having received his medical degree in Dublin, in 1842, Den came shortly thereafter to Los Angeles where he began performing "some difficult surgical operations." By 1845, he had established a quasi-hospital where he cared for victims of smallpox. Den was able to influence state legislation whereby two percent of the fines and the sales of confiscated smuggled goods were applied to his free hospital. So revered did Den become in the medical profession that many said: *"despues de Dios, Doctor Don Ricardo"* (After God, comes Dr. Richard)

Den attended Holy Mass daily at the Plaza Church of Our Lady of the Angels. He would then go immediately to the Convent of the Daughters of Charity to examine and treat any infirm nuns or orphaned children. Afterwards he would make himself available to the general public. One contemporary commentator ventured the remark, "old Dr. Den will be remembered not only with esteem, but with affection. He was seldom seen except on horseback, in which fashion he visited his patients and was, all in all, somewhat a man of mystery. He rode a magnificent coal-black charger, and was himself always dressed in black. He wore, too, a black felt hat and beneath the hat clustered a mass of wavy hair as white as snow. In addition to all this, his standing collar was so high that he was compelled to hold his head erect and, as if to offset the immaculate linen he tied around the collar a large black scarf. Thus attired and seated on his richly caparisoned horse, Dr. Den appeared always dignified and even imposing."

At the time of his funeral in Saint Vibiana's Cathedral, the local press noted "Dr. Den was always a practical Catholic. He was deeply interested in the progress of the Church as well as various educational institutions connected with it, and a liberal patron of charitable institutions. Richard Somerset Den, the first foreign physician to establish a medical practice in California, was buried at the very hill-top from which, a half century earlier, he had first looked down upon the infant *Pueblo de Nuestra Señora de Los Angeles.*

Shortly after the turn of the century, a young graduate of the Medical Department of the University of California attached his name to a small office on the second floor of a rooming house at Fifth and Broadway. He lived on to treat great grandchildren of those patients and, by the time of his demise, was the oldest practicing physician in Los Angeles.

William R. Molony (1879-1976) was the son of Richard Molony and Catherine Fermessy. He was baptized in the old Plaza Church of Our Lady of the Angels. He was in the first class of the parochial school opened by the Sisters of the Immaculate Heart of Mary at the cathedral in 1886. He vividly recalled the many times he served Holy Mass for Bishop Francis Mora during his years at Saint Vibiana's.

Young Molony subsequently studied at the University of Denver. It was there that he met Leona Egerer. They were married in Denver's Cathedral of the Immaculate Conception on July 3, 1897. The five youngsters born from that bond grew to eleven grandchildren and twenty-two great grandchildren. After finishing his studies at the College of Medicine of the University of Southern California, Molony took his internship at the California Hospital. In 1901, he became resident physician at Idyllwild Sanitarium.

Of all his charitable contacts through the years, the doctor cherished most his long-time association with the Little Sisters of the Poor. The venerable physician spent his Wednesdays at 2700 East First Street, dispensing medical advice to the "oldsters" cared for in Saint Anne's Home for the Aged.

Later he returned to the College of Dentistry of the University of Southern California as Professor of Anatomy and Associate Clinical Professor of Medicine in charge of forensic jurisprudence. Despite his manifold duties, the doctor had been engaged in private practice without interruption since 1901. Prior to 1905, when he purchased a Saint Louis one cylinder automobile, he made his house calls by streetcar (during the daytime) and by bicycle (after midnight when the railway closed down). In later years, when his office was in the Mason Building, the doctor was frequently visited by Mother Frances Cabrini whom he remembered as "a woman of saintly appearance, very humble, with a pleasant face and appealing eyes."

Though he never sought nor held political office, Dr. Molony was an active supporter of his party over the years. He was known personally by every governor since 1913, when Hiram Johnson appointed him to the California Board of Medical Examiners, a post he held for twenty-seven years, many of them as president. Molony was one of those rapidly vanishing "general practitioners." When he first began medicine, there was not a single "specialist" in the city and every doctor, by necessity, was surgeon, family physician and specialist simultaneously.

Dr. Molony served as president of the County Medical Association and for twelve years as a member of the American Medical Association's House of Delegates. He took an active part in the battle against subsidized medicine in the early New Deal days and later when similar proposals were suggested by Governor Earl Warren for California. In 1942, Molony became president of the Catholic Medical Association.

Although later sharing office space with his physician son, Dr. Molony never had an assistant. Among the 3,300 babies he delivered were the three Cremins brothers, all of whom became priests in the Archdiocese of Los Angeles. Molony was a familiar figure in Catholic organizations. He joined the Newman Club in 1905, and later served a term as its president.

The story of "premier" hospital in California's southland dates back to a January day in 1856 when a heavy stage coach rolled into the *Pueblo de Nuestra Señora de los Angeles* to the boom of the town's cannon heralding the arrival of the Daughters of Charity. The history of the Daughters has been a history of firsts. They were the first community of women to live and work outside cloistered walls; the first to take annual vows; the first to consecrate their lives to the service of God's poor and the first to found a Catholic hospital in the United States, the old Mulanphy Hospital in Saint Louis, Missouri.

It was only on May 29, 1858 that the city witnessed the opening of its first medical dispensary in the home of Don Cristobal Aguilar, a small adobe building at Bath and Alameda streets near the Plaza. The Sisters subsequently purchased property from Don Luis Arenas on Chavez Lane in the early 1860s and moved into a two-story building. There was no water in the four room house and all linen had to be carried to the river bank to be washed.

On May 30, 1858, the Sisters were ready to receive patients at their new hospital at the Cristobal Aquilar home, just north of the Plaza Church. On May 29, 1858, the following paid advertisement appeared in the Los Angeles *Star*:

> The County Hospital is now ready to receive patients. It is situated in a quiet and airy part of the city in the house belonging to Cristobal Aquilar, north of the church. The sick will be attended by the Sisters of Charity, under the direction of the best medical advice in the city. In addition to the Charity Ward, there is a Ward for patients who can pay.

In December 1858, the Los Angeles *Star* published a human interest story about the hospital and the Sisters, giving the following statistics:

> Since the establishment of the hospital, there have been fifty-two charity patients and eleven private patients admitted. During that time, only ten have died. It is intended to increase the accommodation of the hospital so as to have three private rooms. For private patients wishing to avail themselves of the careful nursing of the establishment, the charge is $2.50 per day. For private patients in a ward, $1.50 per day. Dr. Griffin is the visiting physician of the hospital, assisted by Dr. Welsh. Patients who desire it, may have the attendance of other medical gentlemen.

From that moment onward, the story of "Saint Vincent Hospital" paralleled that of the *pueblo* it has served so long and so diligently. An example would be the host of new "miracle" drugs that have changed the whole concept of medical care.

More than 2,300 years ago, Hippocrates, the Greek "Father of Medicine," prescribed willow leaves to treat women at childbirth. Those leaves contained salicin, a natural compound related to aspirin. In 1826, two Italian researchers isolated the magic ingredient and, twenty-seven years later, a French chemist produced acetylsalicylic acid in his laboratory. Chemists employed by the Bayer Company in Germany continued experiments with aspirin in the 1890s. They discovered its value as a pain reliever and fever reducer. Aspirin was first marketed by the Bayer Company in 1899 and the new medication was hailed as a wonder drug in medical circles. It has been relieving aches, pains, swelling and fever ever since.

The first of the little white pills were brought to Los Angeles from the Paris motherhouse of the Daughters of Charity in 1901. Since that time, aspirin has become a household curative throughout the United States. Over twenty billion aspirins are sold every year in this nation alone and that averages out roughly to ninety-one pills for every man, woman and child.

It is not only the world's safest drug, but the most widely used. Marketed worldwide under scores of labels, aspirin is also still sold under the label of its originator, the Bayer Company. In more recent times, researchers have discovered that aspirin also has anti-blood clotting properties that can be used to treat cardiovascular diseases. After all these centuries, medical science continues to be puzzled by this deceptively simple drug. Its anti-fever effect is a mystery for it lowers body temperature only when there is a fever. To their eternal credit, the Daughters of Charity can be thanked for introducing this "curative medicine" to the western part of the United States over a century ago.

In 1924, physicians and others attached to Saint Vincent Hospital played an important role in an outbreak of bubonic plague which began on a hot summer day in a bustling Hispanic neighborhood east of the downtown area. Jesus Lajun was recounting a humorous tale of how he had come across a dead rat beneath his house.

Less than a month later, the gossip around the area had stopped. Lajun began to nurse a bloody cough and a painfully swollen gland. He was mourning the death of a daughter who had been declared a victim of "double pneumonia" by the coroner. A neighbor, Lucena Samarano, had also died recently. By the end of October, Lajun was dead too. So were three other boarders in his house. Within days, there had been a dozen unexpected deaths in the immediate neighborhood.

Once properly diagnosed as the plague, according to medical records, the community between Alameda Street and the Los Angeles River and from Macy Street to Alhambra Avenue was placed under strict quarantine. Rope barricades were set up and armed guards were brought in. Food was rationed, a temporary medical facility established and undertakers throughout the city were instructed not to embalm any bodies until health inspectors had been called in.

Priests were cautioned by Bishop John J. Cantwell about the outbreak and told to report any unexpected deaths or extraordinary illnesses. Funerals of known victims were to be conducted privately, with only family members in attendance.

Due mostly to the careful enforcement of strict health measures, the Los Angeles epidemic was quickly over, although before its end forty people were known to have been infected, and all but three of them died. Medical historians now believe that the plague that infected Los Angeles came from San Francisco, apparently aboard a ship that had entered San Francisco Bay from the Orient.

In all the areas where Saint Vincent Hospital was a pioneer, none was more important than its work in training nurses. Over the years, a number of Catholic hospitals in the archdiocese had apprentice programs for training nurses, some of them quite advanced. The two "formal" schools with greatest influence in health care in California's southland operated in fairly close proximity.

Of the ten young ladies who began their two years of training at Saint Vincent's College of Nursing in 1890, only three actually completed their courses, donned their white uniforms and received their diplomas from Bishop George Montgomery on November 27, 1901. A few years later, the program was lengthened to three years.

In 1915, Saint Vincent Hospital Alumnae Association was established. During World War I, nursing graduates of the school played an important role in the armed forces both at home and abroad. A unit of graduates journeyed to Italy to care for the wounded soldiers. The school was officially recognized with the Los Angeles City Health

Department in 1924 and during the following years, many progressive initiatives were implemented. The first school annual appeared in 1925.

Following a fire in 1927, the School of Nursing moved to new headquarters at Third Street and Figueroa, and the school was afforded additional space for teaching and clinical experience. In that era, the School of Nursing was affiliated with Mount Saint Mary's College. At that time, the nurses were encouraged to further their education in other areas of learning. The traditional blue and white striped uniform was changed to all white in 1932. Three years later, the school was accredited with the Los Angeles County General Hospital in Communicable Diseases, Pediatrics and Neuro-Medical diseases. The staff nurses at the hospital organized in September of 1938 and this enabled the graduates to unite more closely.

In 1941, after the beginning of World War II, Saint Vincent School of Nursing proved itself equal to the challenge of war demands, with many members responding to the call for active service. A close relationship with the United States Cadet Nurse Corps was forged. In 1950, Saint Vincent unveiled its new, expanded School of Nursing.

Records of one of the west coast's earliest nursing schools are available at the hospital's Historical Conservancy. The files date from 1899 and include administrative documents, curricula and personal papers of graduates. A large collection of over 2,000 photographs forms a major portion of this collection and provides a glimpse into nursing care and how it has changed and progressed through the years.

The "Training School" at nearby Queen of Angels Hospital began in the fall of 1926 with an opening class of twelve young women. First student enrolled was Hilda Shepard. Classes were initially conducted in a five-room cottage that was known as Queen of Angels Training School.

Paramount in the curriculum was the Franciscan philosophy of nursing which portrays the world as being "full of God". The student nurse strove to achieve a development of inner sight, seeing the image of God in each patient, each fellow worker and each neighbor. By 1945, there were thirty-seven "cadets" at the School of Nursing. Many of them served in World War II.

Students attended Belmont High School for their basic and preparatory class instructions, which included nutrition, chemistry and English. A contemporary report declared the school as remarkable for its phenomenal growth and rapid formulation of curriculum. The diploma program stretched over twenty-eight months.

In 1945, the school's affiliation with Immaculate Heart College was broadened to provide a wider basis of interest and a larger field of cultural and mental development. In August of 1953, the school's name was changed to Queen of Angels School of Nursing.

In a manuscript written by Eva Stockonis, a nursing graduate in 1954, the following criteria were enumerated as the backbone of the education provided to students:

Nursing service is the provision for and the administration of safe, adequate, economical, and Christ-like nursing care of the sick admitted to the hospital.
We believe that in this artful service, the needs of the supernatural as well as the natural order of mankind are to be considered.
Therefore, the primary objective of the Queen of Angels Nursing Service is the provision of such administration to the sick that it will include in its scope of care the optimum welfare of the patient's spiritual, mental and physical well-being.

Plans for a half-million-dollar addition to the college were announced in 1951. The contemplated six-story addition was designed to increase the capacity of students from 165 to 220. A new library was envisioned in the reinforced concrete edifice. By that time, the school was among the oldest of its kind in the southwest. In keeping with trends in nursing education, the Board of Directors of Queen of Angels Hospital had authorized the incorporation of Queen of Angels College of Nursing on April 7, 1938.

The college grew dramatically over the years. In 1952, there were fifty-three graduates who received their diplomas from James Francis Cardinal McIntyre. Several religious women were among the graduates that year. Those proudly exhibiting the college diploma had grown to 1,000 by 1963.

Two years later, "mature" or older women were invited to join the college. The ideal candidate was considered to be a housewife between forty and fifty-six years of age and free of day-long family obligations. Refresher courses were also offered to former students, a program designed to update the professional skills of those who had been professionally inactive.

After forty-seven years of service to the southland, Queen of Angels School of Nursing was closed down in June of 1973. By then, over 1,400 nurses had been trained at the facility. The hospital itself was leased to a proprietary firm two years earlier.

Finally there was and is the program for nurses training begun and continuing at Mount Saint Mary's College since early 1950s.

This was the first baccalaureate program offered in an era when almost all existing nursing programs provided only a three-year diploma.

The Sisters of Saint Joseph inaugurated this wholly new approach with unwavering determination, futuristic vision and extensive nursing know-how. Accredited by the Board of Nurse Examiners for the State of California, the four-year program offered a bachelor of science degree in nursing along with a public health certificate. Students spent the first two years and intervening summers doing clinical work at Saint Francis, Saint Vincent, Queen of Angels, Brentwood Veteran or Children's Hospital.

From bedside nurse to head pediatric coordinator, students faced challenges that confronted their personal and professional lives. The overall program earned high marks for its ability to adapt and prepare students to perform beyond expectations. The figures indicate that 98% of the graduates taking the State Board passed with commendation.

A new ADN program, begun in 1992, allowed students to take classes on weekends and evenings at Mount Saint Mary's downtown campus. It was one of only three such programs in California. Lastly, a new thirty-seven-unit program was started in 2002 that offered courses in advanced nursing theory and practice, a program that allowed students to become fully aware of the latest changes taking place in the health care world.

Believing as he did that "the work of Catholic charity in any diocese takes first place among our responsibilities," Bishop John J. Cantwell totally reorganized and coordinated diocesan activities along those lines by establishing, in 1919, the Associated Catholic Charities.

Under the supervision of Father William E. Corr, existing facilities were brought under the jurisdiction of a central office. Included among the earliest of the far-flung operations of the association were seven orphanages, two settlement houses, a preventorium, an infant home, two clinics, two homes for the aged and a day nursery. New departments were subsequently inaugurated for child and family welfare, correctional service and immigrant needs

Bishop Cantwell succinctly outlined his concept of the Associated Catholic Charities as that of coordinating the work of all Catholic charitable organizations and institutions, modernizing and increasing the efficiency of existing facilities, promoting needed additional works, guiding and encouraging benefactions, establishing a liaison with other public agencies and gathering sociological information useful for rendering even more efficient the operation of Catholic activities.

By 1923, thirty-seven professionally-trained persons were employed to direct and supervise twenty-eight institutions throughout the diocese, including several boarding schools for dependent children, a correctional school for wayward girls, a maternity hospital, two homes for unemployed ladies and one for men, two salvage shops, three community hospitals and two branch offices, all in addition to those agencies already functioning under the Bureau's aegis.

Cantwell's uncanny ability for utilizing the talents of his priests was nowhere more evident than in the field of charitable work. The naming of Father Robert Emmet Lucey as diocesan Director of Charities in 1921, for example, brought to that office a young priest intensely attuned to the work of promoting such causes as those favoring labor and racial equality. During his tenure, Lucey became a brilliant and respected exponent of the principles of social justice.

With the appointment of Lucey to the Bishopric of Amarillo, Texas, in 1934, his long-time assistant, Father Thomas O'Dwyer, succeeded to the directorship. This unassuming, Irish-born priest became, over the ensuing decades, something of a legend for his tireless dedication to the social needs of the area's Catholic populace. The structural realignment of the Associated Catholic Charities, in 1921, as the Bureau of Catholic Charities and again, in 1926, when it became the Catholic Welfare Bureau, is additional evidence of concern for the needy.

The loosely-knit umbrella of Catholic hospitals in the Diocese of Monterey-Los Angeles, the Diocese of Los Angeles-San Diego and the Archdiocese of Los Angeles fell under the direction of the Catholic Welfare Bureau in the early years of the twentieth century.

In the 1931 report of the *Catholic Social Services in Southern California* for the Catholic Welfare Bureau, the following excerpt for Health Service gives an overview of one phase of Catholic outreach:

Types of Health Service

Medical, surgical, nursing or hospital care was given to 14,370 persons in the diocese during the year through the Catholic Welfare Bureau, its affiliated health units and branch offices, and the Catholic hospitals. The service included several thousand clinical examinations and subsequent treatments, the filling of medical prescriptions, the applying of surgical dressings, medical appliances, artificial arms and legs, dental work, and eye glasses for individuals and families in need.

Out-Patient Department of Hospitals

With a growing number of persons scarcely able to pay for physicians' service, free dispensaries and medical social service are being developed in Catholic hospitals as out-patient departments.

Such out-patient departments exist in this diocese in connection with St. Francis Hospital, Santa Barbara; and with the Queen of Angels and St. Vincent's Hospitals in Los Angeles.
The out-patient department of St. Francis Hospital reports a total attendance of 5,428 during 1931.

A decade later, the director of the Catholic Welfare Bureau told the Catholics of the Archdiocese of Los Angeles that Catholic Hospitals had been affiliated with the Catholic Hospital Association, with the approval of the American College of Surgeons and the recognition of the American Medical Association. He also noted that there were 185 Sisters working and caring for the sick. That encompassed eight Religious Orders: The Daughters of Charity, the Franciscan Sisters of the Sacred Heart, the Sisters of Charity of the Incarnate Word, the Sisters of Saint Joseph of Orange, the Sisters of Mercy, the Sisters of Saint Francis of Penance and Christian Charity, the Carmelite Sisters and the Maryknoll Sisters.

After carefully pointing out that only 84% of the patients were able to pay all or part of their bill, the report said the "tremendous cost of the hospital operation" could only have been met "because of the large number of Sisters who devote their lives without pay to the service of the sick." The report concluded with these words:

The hospital today is an integral part of the community it serves and carries on a function that is vital to the well-being of all. The Catholic hospitals of the archdiocese participate in the activities of the various hospital associations, national, state and local. Carrying active membership in health and hospital agencies and associations has enabled our Sister superintendents and administrators to keep abreast of what is going on in the hospital field, and to equip themselves to employ new developments and techniques for the improvement of their services to the sick. Through these public relationships, the Sisters also have an opportunity for reflecting the Church in action through its services to the sick.

It was shortly after his installation in Los Angeles that Archbishop J. Francis A. McIntyre asked Msgr. Thomas J. O'Dwyer to put aside his duties as Director of the Catholic Welfare Bureau in order to devote full time to the newly established and autonomous Department of Catholic Hospitals.

The overall statistics for Catholic hospitals in the archdiocese and the country as a whole continue to be impressive. There were 637 Catholic hospitals in the United States (or 17% of all such institutions) along with 122 home health care agencies.

HEROINES OF CATHOLIC HEALING CENTERS

Throughout California's history, the Catholic Church has been at the forefront of health care. This is particularly evident in the accomplishments of the women religious who followed often-hazardous routes from faraway places to the Pacific Slope.

The simple and unselfish zeal with which the Catholic Heroines of Health Care braved the horrors of pestilence and disease to care for the sick, nurse the injured and comfort the dying unquestionably has asserted a memorable civilizing and moralizing influence on contemporary society. Their concern from the earliest days of California is clearly among the most impressive factors in the story of the Golden State. The contribution of Sisterhoods to the physical and moral stature of our commonwealth is reflected in their wholesome regard for God's gifts of life and health to the millions they have and continue to serve.

Interestingly, very little has been written about the nursing Sisterhoods and their hospitals in California, possibly because their selfless spirit defies description in mundane terms. Years ago, Father Bernard C. Cronin said, "certain manifestations of the inner life of the Sisterhoods and their works may be discernible in physical and tangible events. A spirit of love is clearly reflected in the sacrifices that the Sisters have made of home and homeland to come and care for sick strangers on the shore of a strange and foreign land. In the establishment of hospitals on California soil that would shelter and save the sick and wounded, one perceives a unique embodiment of devotion and sacrifice."

Those who want to enjoy the fullest impact of the California story will need to know something, even if it be sketchy, of those noble heroines who brought the gift of healing to that segment of the Lord's vineyard now served by the Archdiocese of Los Angeles.

DAUGHTERS OF CHARITY

It was Bishop Thaddeus Amat, the Vincentian Bishop of Monterey-Los Angeles, who invited members of the largest religious community in the Church to establish a foundation in Southern California. There was little angelic about the City of Our Lady of Angels when the "Angels of the Battlefield" began their apostolate of teaching, running orphanages and conducting hospitals.

Founded in 1633 by Saints Vincent de Paul and Louise de Marillac, the Daughters of Charity began in Paris where the Order represented the organization of Christian charity as a permanent heritage of the poor and downtrodden.

That great antagonist of the Catholic Church in France, Voltaire, had a special love for the Daughters of Charity. He once said "perhaps there is nothing grander on earth than the sacrifice which the delicate sex makes of beauty, youth and high birth, to relieve in hospitals that mass of human miseries the sight of which is so humiliating to our pride and so revolting to our delicacy." Throughout France, these wonderful women were known as the *soeur grises* by reason of the bluish gray hue of the habits.

Having established their first motherhouse in the United States at Emmetsburg in 1809, the Daughters came to California in 1855. Later, they began their hospital work in the home of Christobal Aguilar, the *Alcalde* for the city of *Nuestra Señora de los Angeles*. There, they were soon treating smallpox victims felled by an especially dry winter.

THE CONGREGATION OF THE LITTLE SISTERS OF THE POOR

This congregation began in 1839 at Saint-Servan in Brittany when a humble servant, Jeanne Jugan, received into her poor dwelling some elderly women. Being unable to provide for them, she went out to beg for her charges. From the very first, Marie Jamet and Virginie Tredaniel joined to help in her charitable enterprise. Then, blessed by God, the work prospered.

The principal object of the congregation is the sanctification of its members, both the Sisters and the aged poor. The Religious strive after holiness by the practice of the vows of poverty, chastity, obedience and hospitality, and the elderly by the Christian life they lead in the homes. The latter are free to walk about and no pressure is brought to bear upon them.

The immediate object is the succor of the aged poor, regardless of creed. To be admitted, potential residents must be sixty years of age. All that is required is that they conform to the simple family rules of the house.

The work depends entirely on Divine Providence. Daily, the Little Sisters go out begging and the necessaries have never been lacking. Very often Providence intervenes in a marvelous manner on behalf of the poor.

Legacies are accepted, but not annuities. In Los Angeles, the Little Sisters of the Poor opened Saint Ann Home for the Aged in 1906.

FRANCISCAN SISTERS OF THE SACRED HEART

Three of the Catholic hospitals in Southern California were founded by the Franciscan Sisters of the Sacred Heart, a community tracing its origins to 1886 in a small town in the German province of Baden. Its four founders had joined together to dedicate their lives to the care of the ill and aged, as well as those injured on the battlefields of the Franco Prussian War.

Civic appreciation, however, proved short-lived. A few years after the war, Chancellor Bismark confronted the Sisters with the alternatives of suppression of their Order or exile. There was really no choice but to leave Germany. There was no choice but to go to America, the land of the free.

The Sisters came to the United States in 1876 where they served in Indiana and Illinois. During the early years of his ministry, Patrick W. Riordan had worked with the sisters and, after he became Archbishop of San Francisco, he invited them to the City of Saint Francis, the town that grew up around the mission founded on the shores of the bay bearing the seraphic imprint. In California's southland, the Franciscan Sisters established Saint Francis (Santa Barbara), Queen of Angels and Saint Anne Maternity (both of Los Angeles).

SISTERS OF MERCY

By the time of California's admission to the Union, San Francisco had been established as the primary metropolis along the Pacific Slope. Described as a "seaport town in a land of fortune," San Francisco served as the gateway to the gold fields of the north. Life in the frontier town was rough, brusk and often cruel, and there was little time to look after the sick and infirm. When Joseph Sadoc Alemany arrived as archbishop in 1853, he saw the need for serving the sick and sinful. He sent Father Hugh Gallagher to Ireland with an invitation for the sisters of Mercy to come to California.

The community had been founded in Dublin in 1831 by Mother Mary Catherine McAuley. She launched a worldwide apostolate for the ill, especially the victims of cholera. By the time of her death, more than 400 women had joined her apostolate. It was to these Sisters that Florence Nightingale came for advice and training.

On December 8,1854, a contingency of eight Mercy Sisters arrived to begin working in San Francisco's hospitals under the direction of Sister Mary Baptist Russell. From those brave beginnings, the Sisters spread their mission of mercy throughout the west.

In 1912, a small band of the Sisters of Mercy settled in Oxnard to provide hospital service for its people. The local pastor, Father John Laubacher, took the initiative, with John Borchard donating a tract of land as a site. In May of 1912, a temporary facility was ready for occupancy. A forty-five-bed hospital was dedicated three years later.

SISTERS SERVANTS OF MARY

Founded by St. Maria Soledad in Madrid in 1851 for the specific purpose of caring for the sick and elderly, the Sisters Servants of Mary came to the United States from Mexico in 1914. They opened a convent in Los Angeles at 2400 South Gramercy Place, which Bishop John J. Cantwell dedicated in 1928.

SISTERS OF CHARITY
OF THE INCARNATE WORD

This Congregation of Sisters was given its present form and purpose in September, 1866, by Bishop Claude Dubuis, second bishop of Galveston, when he visited his native France for the purpose of securing Religious for hospital work in his mission field. He obtained three Sisters from the Hospital of Antiquaille, Lyons. On September 23, 1866, the three young women who had volunteered for the noble purpose of caring for the sick in the New World were invested in a new religious habit that was patterned after that of the Order of the Incarnate Word and Blessed Sacrament but better adapted to hospital service.

The Sisters arrived in Galveston on October 23,1866. In April of the following year, their first hospital, the first private hospital in Texas, was completed and ready for patients. It is known today as St. Mary's Infirmary. Its establishment marks the foundation of the Congregation of the Sisters of Charity of the Incarnate Word. These Sisters are now engaged principally in the care of the sick, the aged and orphans in the West and Southwest sections of the United States. It was in 1923 that the Sisters opened Saint Mary's Hospital in Long Beach at the invitation of the Right Reverend John J. Cantwell.

SISTERS OF
SAINT JOSEPH OF CARONDOLET

The Sisters of Saint Joseph began in France in 1650 as a union of two ideals, the contemplative life and the active apostolate. Their clothing reflected that worn by widows of the period. They were disbanded during the French Revolution, but later continued their ministry under a modified rule. They were among the first band of Sisters to leave France for the New World. Coming to the west in 1870, they opened a hospital in Tucson and, in 1954, dedicated Daniel Freeman Hospital in Inglewood. In 1994, Santa Marta Hospital, a long-time institution among the poor of the southland, joined what was then the Carondelet Health System.

FOREIGN MISSIONARY
SISTERS OF SAINT DOMINIC

This congregation of American women, known far and wide as the Maryknoll Sisters, are dedicated to the service of the Church in Catholic foreign missions. Founded in 1912 by Mother Mary Joseph of Jamaica Plain, they work closely with the Maryknoll Fathers. They came to California's southland in 1920 and, a decade later, they took charge of the Maryknoll Sanatorium at Monrovia.

CARMELITE SISTERS

In the late 1920s, a contingent of the Discalced Carmelite Sisters of the Third Order was forced to leave their native Mexico during the religious persecution that was taking place there. Bishop John J. Cantwell welcomed the Sisters to the Diocese of Los Angeles-San Diego and invited them to inaugurate a sanatorium for victims of tuberculosis in Duarte.

SISTERS OF SAINT JOSEPH OF ORANGE

This community was founded in 1912 to continue the traditions of charity and humility associated with the others gathered under the banner of Saint Joseph. They were active in nursing those affected by the 1918 flu epidemic. They opened a hospital in Eureka, California and, in 1933, they established Saint Luke Hospital in Pasadena.

SISTERS OF NAZARETH

The origin of the Nazareth Sisters is in the Archdiocese of Westminster in London where they answered the call of Nicholas Cardinal Wiseman. The foundress was Victoire Larmenier, known in religion as Mother Saint Basil. The order grew rapidly in the British Isles and soon took root in Australia, New Zealand and the United

States. It was in 1924 that Bishop John J. Cantwell asked the order to staff the Catholic Children's Home in San Diego. A decade later, they came to Los Angeles to staff Nazareth House.

SISTERS OF SAINT FRANCIS OF PENANCE AND CHRISTIAN CHARITY

This community was founded in 1835 at Liege by Catherine Daemen, a penniless Dutch woman then in middle-life who belonged to the Third Order of Saint Francis. Becoming Mother Magdalen, she and a group of like-minded women went about nursing the sick. Before she died in 1858, her congregation had already spread to Germany.

Soon after her death, the Sisters expanded their work to the Dutch West Indies, to South America and then, in 1874, to the United States. From their original establishment at Stella Niagara, New York, two other foundations were made, one in Denver and the other in Monrovia, California.

The Sisters, in addition to operating hospitals, conducted retreat houses for women, homes for business girls, elementary, high and normal schools, orphanages, day nurseries, kindergartens and Indian Missions. They came to Santa Maria where they opened Our Lady of Perpetual Help Hospital (now Marian Medical Center) in 1940 and Saint Francis in Lynwood in 1945.

SISTERS OF CHARITY OF LEAVENWORTH

This is a community whose background, history and institutions are thoroughly and exclusively American. Originating in Kentucky, many of the original members were daughters of frontier people. During the troublesome days of the American Civil War, they carried the blessings of a Christian heritage to the illiterate, the sick and the orphaned throughout the Indian territories. The Sisters of Charity of Leavenworth answered the call of Bishop John J. Cantwell in 1942 to establish Saint John Hospital in Santa Monica.

SISTERS OF CHARITY OF PROVIDENCE

The Community of Sisters of Charity of Providence was founded in Montreal in March of 1843. A widow at the age of twenty-seven, the wealthy Madame Mary Emily Travernier Gamelin became a servant of the poor.

At first, the love of this woman for her fellowmen found expression in visits to the homes of poor and sick outcasts of society. Gradually, she founded a number of shelters for poor, homeless women whose pitiable conditions required immediate and long-term care.

In time, word of Madame Gamelin's work reached the local bishop who was impressed by the woman's zeal and organizational ability. Eventually he entrusted the program of charity within the Diocese of Montreal to her and her helpers, and arranged for their canonical establishment as a Congregation of Religious in 1843.

Just a century after the community's establishment, the Sisters opened a hospital in Burbank, the entertainment capital of the world.

SISTER SERVANTS OF MARY

The Sister Servants of Mary is an order of trained nurses who visit the sick in their homes. Originating in Madrid, the Sisters came to Los Angeles in 1928 where they worked at the bedside of both the wealthy and the poor, asking only donations for the upkeep of their convent. In 1960, the Sisters opened Mary, Health of the Sick, Convalescent and Nursing Hospital in Newbury Park.

LITTLE COMPANY OF MARY SISTERS

The genesis of this community can be traced back to London where Mary Potter was born in 1847. This young lady of humble origins gathered a few like-minded ladies around her to begin a new work of service under the banner of the Little Company of Mary. She met and befriended Pope Leo XIII who encouraged her to establish a hospital in the Eternal City for English speaking residents. Her followers subsequently spread their work in many directions. In 1960, they established the Little Company of Mary Hospital in Torrance.

SISTERS OF THE HOLY CROSS

Founded at Le Mans, France in 1841, by Abbe Basil Anthony Moreau, the silver heart bearing the emblem of our Lady of the Seven Dolors, which the Sisters wear on their habits, dates back to the time when their community was known as the Congregation of the Seven Dolors.

It was in 1843 that four Sisters of the Holy Cross came to the United States to work in the great missionary field of the mid-west. A little, rose covered blacksmith shop in Bertrand, Michigan, served as the Sisters' first convent. There they trained American candidates for the religious life. It was from that institution that the Sisters went out into the vast stretches of land west of the Mississippi on missions of charity to Native Americans.

During the Civil War, seventy-one Sisters of the Holy Cross, at the request of General Lew Wallace, cared for the wounded and dying in military and naval hospitals and aboard the hospital ship, *Red Rover*. Following the war, the Sisters opened their first private hospital in Cairo, Illinois. At the time of the Spanish-American War, one of the Sisters of the Holy Cross from their hospital in Columbus, Ohio, was placed in charge of two hospital trains that were put in service in Puerto Rico. It was in 1961 that the Sisters of the Holy Cross opened their hospital in Mission Hills.

The Sisters of the Holy Cross were officially recognized as the forerunners of the Naval Nurse Corps as they were the first women to receive salaries from the United States government.

IMMACULATE HEART SISTERS

Founded at Olot, in the Spanish Province of Catalonia, the Immaculate Heart Sisters were brought to California in 1871. Their early years were given to teaching in Gilroy, San Luis Obispo and San Bernardino. In 1886, they opened a convent in Los Angeles at Saint

Vibiana Cathedral. Later, they began Immaculate Heart Academy, which evolved into Bishop Conaty - Our Lady of Loretto High School.

In 1962, the Sisters established Queen of the Valley in West Covina. Presently that institution is known as the Citrus Valley Medical Center.

• • • • • •

These are the Sisters' hospitals high on the hills, deep in the valleys and out on the shores of California. More lasting than bronze and marble shafts, they recall perilous voyages from shores across the seas, weary days on the hot, dusty trail, years of work and service. Raised by self sacrifice, with fortitude Christian and heroic perseverance, they stand today as monuments to the weak and afflicted who found treasures of health, life and love in California.

Through the years, the Sisters have traveled over the hills and through the valleys along the shore of the land by the western sea on a mission that men hesitate to undertake, accomplishing tasks that only hardy pioneer women dared attempt. They established hospitals wherein doctors could practice their healing arts and the Sisters could nurse their patients in the name of the Divine Physician.

In a long essay written in 1936, Msgr. Thomas J. O'Dwyer, Archdiocesan Director of Hospitals, wrote an about the "Hospitals of the Archdiocese." Among other things he said: "The history of the hospital development is intimately connected with the history of Christian charity. From the Catholic viewpoint, hospital care is concerned with both the physical and spiritual. The basic motive of our hospital efforts is charity, love of man because of love of God. We are solicitous for the body, shattered by disease and sickness, because we want to help also the immortal soul which resides therein."

The individual hospitals, medical centers and skilled health centers which have evolved over the years since 1858 will now be delineated.

SAINT VINCENT HOSPITAL
LOS ANGELES

Among all the hospitals in California's southland, the primacy of honor goes to Saint Vincent, the first established in the *Pueblo de Nuestra Señora de los Angeles* in 1858. In five locations, the facility, operated by the Daughters of Charity, has been providing health care uninterruptedly for 148 years.

The proto medical dispensary was opened in the Aguilar adobe on Eternity Street or what is now North Broadway as the Sisters' Hospital. It was advertised as the "County Hospital" in the May 29, 1858 issue of the Los Angeles *Star* which located it "in a quiet and airy part of the city, north of the Plaza Church." There the sick were "attended by the Daughters of Charity under the direction of the best medical advice."

It wasn't long before larger quarters were needed and the hospital was moved to a two-story brick building on Ann Street, between Main and San Fernando Road, near the railroad yards. Sheepherders, stagecoach drivers, miners, livery stable keepers and sea captains were among the patients listed on the admitting register. In 1869, the hospital was incorporated as the Los Angeles Infirmary.

In 1884, a third structure was erected on a six-and-a-half-acre site at the corner of Sunset Boulevard and Beaudry Avenue and there the victims of the smallpox epidemic were treated. This was the first hospital in Los Angeles to be standardized by the American College of Surgeons. That handsome building, known as Saint Vincent Hospital since 1918, was destroyed by fire.

The fourth hospital was opened at the corner of Third and Alvarado Streets in 1927. An eight-story structure, built in Italian Renaissance style, was described as being "in keeping with the dignity and material progress of the city." When it opened in 1927, a journalist said: "Crowning a hill that rises above Sunset Boulevard, there stands an institution which carries us back through seventy years of growth and progress of the city." The first open heart surgery on the West Coast was performed there in 1957.

The latest location for the hospital, known as Saint Vincent Medical Center since 1974, is a nine-story, 385-bed facility with a 132–bed skilled nursing unit, an alcohol treatment section, an education and training center and an adjacent eleven-story medical office building.

One entire floor is occupied by a special care facility geared to achieving the ultimate in twenty-four hour observation and care of the critically ill. That sixty-bed unit includes separate pavilions for coronary care, cardiac surgery, medical/surgical intensive care and a six-station hemodialysis unit for patients with kidney disease.

Located on the fourth floor is a special care facility where cardiac patients are looked after immediately following their operations. All patient rooms are private with glass doors providing visibility and soundproofing. Every patient has physiological monitoring and closed circuit television.

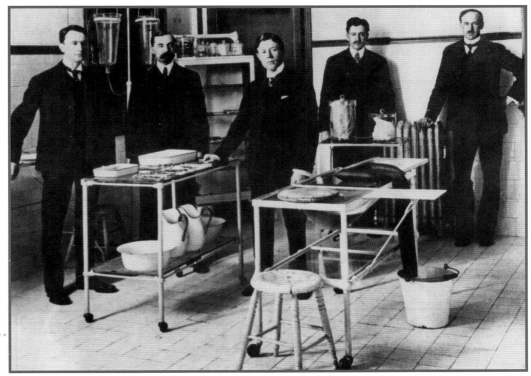

Operating Room at Saint Vincent's Hospital, 1908

Each of the other floors specializes in the latest medical offerings. The overall design of the area is intended so that no room is more than thirty-five feet from a monitoring station. There is even a satellite pharmacy.

Always alert to the need for recording its history, the Daughters of Charity provided an area for an Historical Conservancy in 1995, wherein the story of the oldest medical institution in Los Angeles houses its archives in a 3,000 square foot facility with 100,000 documents and artifacts open to the public.

Saint Vincent Medical Center

SAINT JOHN MEDICAL CENTER
OXNARD

Responding to an appeal from Bishop Thomas J. Conaty, the Sisters of Mercy came to Oxnard in 1912 to begin their apostolic work. An eight acre property for the proposed hospital was donated by John Borchard who, with the support of other local Catholics, responded generously to a drive for funds. The population of Oxnard was then only three thousand people. Bishop Conaty blessed the new foundation on May 19th. Civic leaders and prominent citizens of all creeds were present.

The initial building was a six-room structure, constructed mostly by community volunteers. Two years later, the first permanent hospital was completed with twenty-five beds. Early on, the institution was approved by the American College of Surgeons and the American Medical Society.

During its early years, Saint John Hospital occupied an important place in the life of the county. It was especially praised for its services during the influenza epidemic. Near the end of World War II, expansion plans were announced. A successful campaign was launched to permit

groundbreaking, in 1951, for a new seventy-bed hospital. Completed near the end of the next year, the authorities then tore down the earlier facility.

Three years after its completion, the hospital once again reached its peak operation. By 1957, the hallways were being used for emergencies and admissions doubled in a six year period. Sometime later, a thirty-bed nursing home was finished adjacent to the acute hospital. Twenty more beds were added to this unit in 1963.

Expansion continued. By 1964, work was started on the four-story north annex. This building program added 152 beds, new radiology, laboratory and physical therapy departments, a cysto-fracture room for surgery, a nineteen-bed recovery room, two delivery rooms and additional quarters for delivery.

In 1968, the emergency room was expanded and a data processing program was begun for hospital records. A cardiac care unit was opened with four beds and later it was expanded. A pulmonary medicine department was inaugurated in 1967, with inhalation therapy added to the home health program. A neuro-medical laboratory was added in 1969 to allow for more accurate and rapid diagnoses. A school for radiology technicians was opened in 1969 and, a year later, its first students were graduated and the school was officially certified.

The dietary program dates from 1970. A cardio vascular laboratory opened in 1970 and subsequently the first open-heart surgery was performed at Saint John. The next year, a chemo-dialysis center began providing services for kidney patients. A modern, sophisticated facility for the treatment of acute cases began in 1972, together with a facility for burn patients. During 1983, the hospital's physical therapy department was approved.

In mid-1986, just a year prior to its seventy-fifth anniversary, hospital authorities announced that a 260-bed hospital would replace Saint John Regional Medical Center. Groundbreaking took place at the southeast corner of Rose Avenue and Gonzales Road. The not-for-profit hospital was by then a division of Catholic Health Care West, the largest religious sponsored healthcare system in California.

Roger Cardinal Mahony was on hand to dedicate the new Medical Center on August 29,1992. The "health park", on a forty-eight acre site, was the culmination of a dream by the Sisters of Mercy. The facility represented a radical departure from traditional hospital construction insofar as it provided a full range of services including acute care, ambulatory center, medical office building, rehabilitation center and a retail mall. The diagnostic and treatment services were the most advanced of anything previously built in the State of California

SAINT MARY MEDICAL CENTER
LONG BEACH

It was in 1923, in response to a letter from the pastor of Saint Anthony Parish in Long Beach, that the Sisters of Charity of the Incarnate Word responded to an invitation to launch a hospital in Long Beach. There the Sisters acquired the yellow brick Long Beach Sanitarium that Dr. Truman O. Boyd was anxious to sell. Renamed Saint Mary Hospital, the institution was solemnly dedicated by Bishop John J. Cantwell on August 26,1923.

The growth of the original sleepy resort city into a thriving modern metropolis demanded that the Sisters respond in kind. Oil had been discovered on Signal Hill and, in the ensuing years, the hospital shared the community's fortunes and misfortunes. The area was under-hospitalized and a growing demand motivated several fund raising drives for added facilities.

The depression, followed by the earthquake that rocked Long Beach in 1933, slow progress. In fact, that catastrophe left the Sisters without a hospital, a chapel and a convent.

The Sisters sent out a plea for support that told the 160,000 people then living in Long Beach about the vital necessity of having a fully staffed and professional hospital in their city. They promised to build a modern, fireproof, standardized, completely equipped hospital for the care of anyone needing it, irrespective of creed, station, race or condition.

In 1936, ground was broken for a new structure, a 100-bed, four-story building that became the south wing of the later building. The north wing was opened in 1949 and, in 1962, a $4.5 million east wing brought the bed capacity to 341 patients.

For the hospital's golden anniversary year, there was even a more dramatic expansion, thus placing the institution on the threshold of becoming one of Southern California's major medical centers.

Bauer Professional Building, a huge edifice erected adjacent to the existing hospital, opened in the fall of 1973. With that addition, there were 555 beds at Saint Mary's. Among the benefactors, none surpassed Evelyn and Modestus Bauer who contributed $4 million dollars for the facility. He told the press that Saint Mary would "provide the maximum patient care, outstanding medical education and stimulating research, all of which will be of great help to the people of today and the generations to come."

On the occasion of the fiftieth anniversary, hospital officials unveiled their "master plan" calling for a "comprehensive and flexible development plan, which emphasized dynamic and dramatic expansion of patient services."

It was early in 1974 that the name of the hospital was changed to Bauer Hospital-Saint Mary Medical Center. The name change paved the way for a new medical thrust into the local community. Patient care services were updated along with Out-Patient Care departments, in keeping with the latest practices in the ever developing medical profession.

At the dedication of the new Bauer Hospital at Saint Mary Medical Center, in mid-1974, Timothy Cardinal Manning came to Long Beach where he declared that the real Queen Mary was not in the nearby water, but in this huge curative complex where God's people are served with compassion and love. Surely that was true in the new ten-story hospital which newspapers called a "bastion of helping." The cardinal added his own aside for the ceremony, hoping that the hospital "could soon find the cure for sinus problems."

The Superior General of the Sisters looked ahead and predicted that "the coming years will see sweeping changes in the method of health care delivery. Regardless of the system or systems that may be adopted, one thing that will remain unchanged is the dedicated care provided by the Sisters."

SANTA MARTA HOSPITAL
LOS ANGELES

This institution can be traced back to 1924 when it was founded by Dr. Francis Anton. It struggled during its early years and was closed in 1932 for about eight months. During part of that time, the hospital was served by the Sisters of the Precious Blood from Mexico. In 1924, the Sisters were reassigned to other duties and a board of directors took charge of Santa Marta Hospital and clinic. In 1948, the ownership and direction of the hospital passed into the loving care of the Sisters of Misericorde. From its inception, there were twelve beds for maternity patients plus an outpatient clinic for the scores of people who knocked at the doors for medical assistance.

Located at 328 North Humphreys Avenue, the hospital was housed in a stucco building, with the adjoining clapboard, spic and span, squeaky-clean clinic. Its spotless linoleum floors, plasterboard walls and a new green paint job were typical of the care given by the Sisters.

During 1958, the hospital served 1,563 low-income families, while the clinic that same year treated 54,705 patients. The Sisters were praying for a new facility that they hoped would accommodate 100 beds.

Plans were announced in 1961 for a "second spring" for the old hospital. James Francis Cardinal McIntyre wanted to rejuvenate and expand the institution. The cardinal noted that over the years, the hospital had "experienced a depression, change in ownership and survived even a closing. Yet it has survived as a poignant symbol of Christ's admonition that the poor you have always with you."

When the Sisters of Misericorde returned to Canada in 1961, the Spanish speaking Daughters of Saint Joseph took over administration of the hospital. At that time, people representing all races, creeds, colors and ability to pay were coming from a wide area, including Pomona, Norwalk, and Pico Rivera.

In May of 1968, Cardinal McIntyre announced that the archdiocese was planning to construct a fifty-bed general hospital in the heart of the city's eastside Hispanic community. It would replace Santa Marta Hospital and Clinic whose facilities were limited and outdated. Cost of the new hospital, including a dental clinic, would be $2.5 million.

President-elect Richard M. Nixon agreed to speak at the Cardinal's Community Dinner to raise funds for the new Santa Marta, which the newspapers at the time described as the "best charity in town." Speaking to 1,400 persons at the Century Plaza Hotel, Mr. Nixon told about his earlier visit that day to the hospital. There, he saw firsthand what challenges were being faced by the Sisters and how important the new facility was. He said that support of the Sisters should be made "regardless of our religious background. Christians call it charity. My Quakers call it concern for fellow men and women. In Hebrew, it is expressed by the word *tzedakah*." It was at that dinner that Sir Daniel Donohue pledged a million dollars for the new hospital.

Groundbreaking for the new facility took place on December 5, 1969. The three-story edifice was to be ready for occupancy by mid-1971. In the meanwhile, the 500th baby was born at the old hospital in July of 1970.

By early 1972, the hospital was in full operation with 110 beds. It was furnished with laboratories, pharmacy, radiology, dental, intensive and coronary care departments. Located at North Humphreys and New York Avenues, the new facility was the pride of East Los Angeles.

The Santa Marta Hospital was dedicated by James Francis Cardinal McIntyre and Archbishop Timothy Manning on February 19, 1972. The eastside's only non-profit hospital, Santa Marta was built totally without any state or national funds. Within a few years, newspapers were calling the institution "one of the leading health care facilities in Los Angeles."

In 1977, a new pediatrics department was opened on the third floor with sixteen beds. A Special Care Nursery provided care for babies struggling with special medical problems.

It was announced that, by the end of 1979, 32,680 babies had been born at Santa Marta over the preceding fifty years. A new emergency room was dedicated and blessed in 1989.

In 1994, Santa Marta Hospital joined the Carondelet Health System. The transfer of sponsorship afforded the hospital access to medical, administrative and fiduciary resources previously unavailable.

The hospital bade farewell to the Daughters of Saint Joseph early in 1988 and thereafter, the institution was staffed solely by the Sisters of Saint Joseph of Carondolet.

Santa Marta Hospital observed its seventy-fifth anniversary in 1999. Unhappily at the time, the hospital was operating at an annual loss of several million dollars due mostly to cutbacks in Medicare reimbursement.

SANTA TERESITA HOSPITAL DUARTE

It was in 1930 that a group of Carmelite Nuns from Guadalajara purchased acreage in the foothills of the San Gabriel Mountains for a tubercular sanatorium. Located on a small parcel of land in Duarte, an old farmhouse, a garage and two small buildings were readapted for hospital use.

On March 17,1935, Bishop John J. Cantwell blessed a new chapel at the site, giving eloquent testimony of the progress made during the early years as the Sisters took care of young girls stricken with tuberculosis. Within a short time, the institution was recognized as a thoroughly equipped center for treating its patients. Members of nearby Olive View Sanatorium supervised the medical treatment and the county board of education provided grammar and high school teachers for the girls.

Groundbreaking ceremonies were held in 1949 for a new addition to the Santa Teresita Sanatorium, one that would provide living facilities for the Sisters who staffed the institution. At that time, there were 115 beds for tubercular girls of all races. Included also were facilities for major surgery, a dental clinic and an ear, nose and throat unit. This new addition was named Villa Cantwell in memory of the late Archbishop of Los Angeles.

In May of 1959, Santa Teresita opened its doors as a complete general hospital for the people of the San Gabriel Valley. Now in a greatly enlarged facility with forty-six beds for all types of patients, the hospital had an X-ray department, pharmacy, laboratories and two surgical units. An additional sixteen beds were set aside for ambulatory ladies and five for men.

Villa Cantwell was described by one account as a modern reinforced brick building with air conditioning. There were eighty-five doctors on staff, along with forty-three Carmelite Sisters serving the patients.

By the time of its silver anniversary, Santa Teresita was serving 2,000 Spanish-speaking girls afflicted with tuberculosis. There were nineteen buildings on the campus - fifteen of them stucco, one framed and three brick. The entire facility stretched over eight acres of land. The hospital, located on Royal Oaks Drive, was being operated completely independent of the sanatorium.

Within eight months of its establishment as a general hospital, Santa Teresita was fully accredited by the Joint Commission on Accreditation of Hospitals. But growth continued and plans were set afoot for a new administration building and other additions to house outpatient and maternity departments. Mount Carmel, a second edifice for elderly women, was also opened. The hospital, then the smallest in the Archdiocese of Los Angeles, was located in two cities, with nine acres in Duarte and two-and-a-half acres in Monrovia.

In 1959, there were 155 beds at Santa Teresita. A new chapel, long a dream of the sisters, neared completion. It was blessed by James Francis Cardinal McIntyre on October 3rd. At that time, with medical advancement made in the treatment of tubercular patients, the unit at Santa Teresita was transferred to Maryknoll Sanatorium in Monrovia.

Another wing was dedicated in 1963, this one with an intensive care unit, a medical library, inhalation therapy room, an audio-visual call system, built-in-oxygen and television systems.

Two more units were inaugurated in 1966, including a pediatrics facility. That new hall was a two-level brick structure with a 60 x 60 foot auditorium, classrooms and office. The seventeen-bed building was fabricated of brick and concrete, designed to meet the highest standards of the Crippled Children's Program.

Then came a new surgical wing in 1984. Outfitted with the latest in the art of operating rooms, it also housed a recovery unit and other facilities. By now, Santa Teresita had 283 beds for acute care and skilled nursing.

MARIAN MEDICAL CENTER SANTA MARIA

Located on a six-acre site on Airport Avenue in Santa Maria, Our Lady of Perpetual Help Hospital was dedicated by Archbishop John J. Cantwell on June 23, 1940. Operated by the Sisters of Saint Francis of Penance and Christian Charity, the hospital was the fifth erected by the Sisters in the United States.

Opening with thirty-five beds, it was a general hospital and represented the highest type of development in modern equipment and therapy. Civic business, industrial and medical leaders of Santa Barbara County had long urged the erection of a Catholic hospital in Santa

Maria. Our Lady of Perpetual Help was a two-story building of modified Italian architecture, equipped with surgery, delivery room, nurseries, laboratory and X-ray facilities.

Statistics in 1948 indicated that 2,063 patients were treated at the facility, with 720 infants born within its walls, a sharp contrast from the initial year when the number was only 312. Additionally 5,770 out-patients were served during that year.

In 1953, Captain G. Allan Hancock came forward with an offer to complete the hospital's second wing of 1,700 square feet area, which had formerly served as a sun deck. Already the facility was crowded and expansion was of the utmost necessity. The new addition brought the bed count up considerably.

An essay in a local paper in 1955 noted "speeding motorists had discovered the hospital." Travelers from all sections of the country were being served at the hospital. Injured persons brought in from accidents were treated with the same gentle care long associated with the Franciscan Sisters.

The northernmost city in the Archdiocese of Los Angeles, Santa Maria had growth pains as did the other urban areas in the southland. In 1956, further expansion plans were announced and the following May, Bishop Alden Bell dedicated a new wing that accounted for an almost fifty percent increase in the number of beds.

Next came a new X-ray wing at the northernmost section of the hospital. That facility was of concrete construction, with a red tile roof matching the earlier edifice. It accommodated a waiting room, reception office, two radiographic fluoroscopic rooms separated by a dark room and several dressing rooms. Space for future expansion was also included. Installed in the new unit was the latest machinery, including a 500 milliampere unit with a ceiling-mounted tubular stand.

An unprecedented population jump, due to the expansion of the Vandenberg Air Force Base, came in 1961. Located only thirty miles from the hospital, the missile base provided work for thousands of workers, many of whom moved into the housing tracts in and around Santa Maria. In a three-year period, the local population doubled. The space program put new demands on Our Lady of Perpetual Help Hospital where 1,279 babies were born in one year.

Responding to its growing needs, the hospital made plans once again to increase its bed capacity. A drive was launched and local business leaders appealed for funds for a totally new hospital. By that time, the existing institution was serving an area with a population of 127,000.

An 80,000 square foot five-level building would replace the original structure and would accommodate 250 patients. Captain Hancock donated ten acres of prime land for the hospital on Main Street east of the 101 Freeway. The finished structure, now known as Marian Hospital, was dedicated by James Francis Cardinal McIntyre on April 22, 1967.

The five-level hospital featured a double-corridor, central-core plan for most efficient patient care. Basement facilities included the kitchen, dining rooms, X-ray and physical therapy rooms and storage. The first floor was devoted chiefly to business offices, outpatient and emergency room, X-ray, laboratory and pharmacy.

On the second floor were surgery and surgical patients' rooms. Surgical facilities included four operating rooms, a cystoscopic surgery room, a recovery room and an intensive care unit.

The third floor had facilities for obstetrics and gynecology patients, labor, delivery and recovery rooms, together with three nurseries. On the fourth floor were twenty-two bedrooms for medical patients and the pediatrics department. Between the hospital and the Sisters' convent, was the distinctive chapel.

On the opening day, forty-seven patients were moved into the new hospital. Seven ambulances, loaned by the nearby Air Base, were used to effect the transfer. By this time, Captain Hancock had died but his memory lives on in the hospital he made possible.

New units were added in 1983 that included a building and several renovation projects, together with quarters for the Cardio Vascular Laboratory that allowed the medical center to detect potential stroke victims and to diagnose thrombophlebitis and other circulatory difficulties. Such treatment was mostly non-invasive and did not require overnight stays.

SAINT JOHN HEALTH CENTER
SANTA MONICA

A proposal was made to the Sisters of Leavenworth in 1920 that they consider establishing a hospital in Santa Monica. Pledges were sought from people in Beverly Hills, Westwood, Venice, Culver City, Inglewood, and West Hollywood for the purchase of property. A five-acre parcel of land was finally acquired in Santa Monica at Arizona and Twenty-Second Streets. Groundbreaking took place on May 14,1941 for the new facility that commanded a panoramic view of the mountains to the east and the broad expanse of the Pacific to the west. The six-floor building was fireproof and earthquake resistant. The second floor Maternity Department had the first nursery of its kind in Southern California. There were eighty-nine beds and thirty-five bassinets in the completed building. Archbishop John J. Cantwell dedicated the new hospital on October 25,1942.

In the 1940s, the hospital was described in these words:
"Constructed of reinforced concrete floors, exterior walls, columns, beams, etc., and designed especially to withstand earthquake stresses, the hospital's exterior walls were furred on the inside with metal lath and plaster. The outside was stuccoed, interior partitions were hollow terra cotta tile laid up with cement mortar. The finished floors generally were of terazzo for the private rooms and wards, with tile floor and wainscoting in the kitchen, toilets, baths, etc., and with rubber tile flooring in the corridors. All roof surfaces were covered with a twenty-year guaranteed built-up roofing. The plumbing fixtures and piping, as well as the heating and high-pressure steam systems, were of the best material obtainable and were designed especially to withstand hospital use. The specifications and drawings would cover the installation of everything that will be built into the hospital."

The first twenty-five years of the hospital's service in Santa Monica was highlighted in 1967 by an ambitious and fascinating book on Saint John's and Its People. Therein, Sister Julia Gilmore tells her story with colorful descriptions and anecdotes.

In 1960, a new form of service to the community was inaugurated at Saint John's. An outpatient psychiatric clinic to benefit marginal income families was inaugurated. Space for a new Intensive Care Unit was also provided, as well as an eleven-bed care unit for critically or seriously ill patients. Later that year, the addition was named Xavier Clinic and was formally blessed by Bishop Alden J. Bell.

The next year, hospital officials turned their attention to heart maladies that, by then, were the leading cause of death in the United States. New diagnostic concepts and procedures were being advanced. Work was also begun for the Kennedy Child Study Center.

By 1963, plans were afoot to double the size of Saint John Hospital. The previous year, officials had to turn away 2,500 patients for lack of space. A nun gave her "recipe" for the new hospital:

Clear an area nearly one-half of a city block.

Dig a hole at this site some sixty feet deep.

Into this hole, mix the following ingredients in proper order:

Eight million dollars.
15,000 cubic yards of cement;
1,100 tons of steel reinforcing bars;
400 kegs of nails;
600,000 bricks;
290,000 board feet of lumber.

Approximately three years will be needed to have these portions form the new south wing at Saint John's.

The new seven-story wing was planned to include four medical and surgical units in addition to extensive expansion of X-ray, surgery, research, laboratory, intensive care and ancillary services to keep pace with the advances of medicine. Dedication of the new wing took place on February 19, 1967 when James Francis Cardinal McIntyre blessed the 475-bed facility.

Another 147 beds were added in 1973 with the purchase of a four-story building across the street from the existing hospital. The new Kennedy Regional Center for the Developmentally Disabled was established in 1974. An expanded Ambulatory Care Unit was added in 1978. Now known as Saint John Hospital and Health Center, a new nursery was opened in 1984. And the following year, a magnetic resonance imaging facility was installed.

Extensive earthquake damage in 1994 motivated a wholly new hospital at Santa Monica. After a brief closure for repairs, the hospital was re-opened later that year. In 1998, plans were unveiled for a new complex on the old site in order to best serve the local community in the 21st century.

• • • • • •

In 1959, the Joseph P. Kennedy, Jr. Memorial Foundation provided a grant to Saint John Hospital for the erection of a Child Care Center. That institution was to be available to children of all faiths and nationalities. The center was to be located on land acquired for that purpose adjoining the hospital at 20th Street and Santa Monica Boulevard.

The center was devoted to the diagnosis, treatment and schooling of emotionally disturbed, brain damaged and mentally retarded children. It was also to serve as a training center for personnel engaged in that type of work.

Formally activated in September of 1961, the Kennedy Child Care Center already had 134 youngsters receiving treatment by the following January. Financial support for the new center was derived largely, in the early years, from the Archbishop's Fund for Charity.

James Francis Cardinal McIntyre dedicated the new Child Care Center on March 18, 1962, as a memorial to Lieutenant Joseph Kennedy, a young navy pilot killed during World War II. At that time, there were twelve similar institutions in other parts of the country.

The center's reinforced concrete building, containing forty-two rooms, included six classrooms for special education, an observation nursery, library, examination, counseling, interview and therapy rooms and offices.

Among the center's ancillary services are those encompassing medical, psychiatric, psychological evaluations, speech, hearing, occupational and physical therapies and family counseling. From the outset, the Sisters of Charity of Leavenworth had to assume most of the responsibility for operating the center.

PROVIDENCE SAINT JOSEPH MEDICAL CENTER BURBANK

It was Archbishop John J. Cantwell who asked the Sisters of Providence to open a hospital in the east San Fernando Valley. The new building, a rambling one-story edifice fashioned from wood and brick was erected on a ten-acre site in Burbank donated by the Lockheed Aircraft Corporation. Saint Joseph Hospital was dedicated in November of 1943 and opened for patients the following February. On that occasion, the archbishop said "a hospital is a more civilizing influence in a community than schools."

Beginning with a hundred beds, hospital administrators soon developed plans for a first addition of another fifty beds, located adjacent to the earlier building at the corner of Alameda and Buena Vista Streets.

So successful was the institution that a new 175-bed unit was soon in the planning stages. This was to be placed on acreage acquired from

SAINT FRANCIS MEDICAL CENTER LYNWOOD

Shortly after the inauguration of plans for a new hospital in Lynwood in mid-1944, a group of public-minded sponsors issued a statement in which they promised that theirs would be "one of the finest hospitals in the west."

To be operated by the Sisters of Saint Francis, the hospital was located on a fourteen-acre site at Century and Imperial Boulevards. The large, modern, five-story reinforced concrete building was designed to have an initial capacity of 100 beds. The surgical, obstetrical and other facilities were planned for a facility with double the original plans. The hospital would serve Lynwood, Huntington Park, South Gate, Maywood, Compton, Bell, Downey and Vernon. Archbishop John J. Cantwell journeyed to the site and blessed the new Saint Francis Hospital on April 29,1945.

The building was arranged so that clinical equipment, including X-ray, laboratory, pharmacy, physiotherapy, together with specialty examination and treatment rooms would be readily available as an out-patient department. This department was located on the first floor with an entrance from the parking area so that outpatients could have the benefit of these facilities.

In another wing on the first floor, there was the administrative unit, the general lobby, waiting rooms, a suite of quarters for the doctors, an emergency operating suite near the ambulance entrance and a large staff room.

A third wing on the first floor contained the mechanical services such as the boiler room, laundry, electrical service rooms, the main

the city of Burbank, a steel and concrete structure which embodied the latest developments of design. Medical, surgical and pediatrics were to be located in the new eight-story edifice.

Not long after the latest unit was added, statisticians determined that "the San Fernando Valley had grown far beyond any expectation." Experts estimated that another 300,000 persons would settle in the valley in the following decades.

Formal dedication of another unit took place on August 30, 1953. James Francis Cardinal McIntyre was present for the ceremony and mentioned that hospital care was at the top of Catholic priorities in the Archdiocese of Los Angeles.

One of the nation's first "Intensive Treatment Centers" was located at the Burbank hospital in 1959. The center coordinated external use of artificial organs with physiological monitoring equipment to maintain a constant check on the condition of the patients.

Traditionally a "reach-out facility," Saint Joseph Hospital opened a Children's Clinic in 1965 which was available two mornings a week for youngsters of limited income families. The clinic was partly financed by the Burbank chapter of the National Charity League. Another unit opened the following year that was involved with rehabilitating heart patients wishing to return to work.

Figures published in 1966 indicated that Saint Joseph Hospital had served 18,554 patients the previous year. Noting that "the Patient's Welfare Was Always Our Principal Concern," the statistics listed a Clinical Laboratory, a Department of Radiology, a Surgery Department and an Obstetrics and Intensive Nursing Unit. Plans were also announced for Coronary Care and Work Evaluation Units.

Construction of a fourth building was begun in March of 1971. With that facility, the institution's capacity reached 514 beds. Additional parking lots were added on what was left of the twenty-acre hospital grounds. April 28,1973 was the target date for opening a new era in the medical center's devoted operations. By 1973, there were 1,200,000 Californians living in the San Fernando Valley. The completed hospital consistently operated with a census between ninety and a hundred percent.

kitchen and the various dining rooms and coffee shop for the use of the staff, employees, and the public.

On the second floor there was a wing for two major surgeries and two minor surgeries, a fracture room, a cystoscopic room and necessary facilities. Another wing on the second floor included a nursing unit for surgical patients.

On the third floor was a wing with two delivery rooms, three labor rooms, two nurseries and other facilities. A nursing unit included twenty-five beds for maternity patients. The fourth floor included a nursing unit with twenty-five beds for medical cases. On the fifth floor there was another nursing unit with twenty-five beds for medical cases.

Among the pro-active outreaches at Saint Francis Hospital was a series of bi-monthly "reports" which discussed the daily functions of the hospital. The issue for November 1956, for example, told about plans to expand the Department of Physical Medicine and the Saint Francis Hospital-Compton College vocational nursing school.

Other issues featured interesting aspects of hospital life that often go unnoticed by observers. An example was the coverage given the laundry services and their importance to the overall well being of the institution. At the time, there were some eighty different departments responsible for specialty care. The laundry was located in an off-wing of the hospital. Tons of laundry were cleaned daily to keep the facility supplied with linen. The complicated logistics of changing 400 beds daily, moving the soiled laundry to the proper stations, the actual cleansing process and then the return of it to the rooms was carefully explained.

A statistical glance at a single year is most revealing. In 1974, for example, the hospital treated a total of 134,171 patients, admitted 17,380, brought 1,893 new lives into the world, while 578 died. The average stay at the facility per patient was 7.8 days. There were 7,925 surgeries performed and an additional 82,268 persons were examined or treated as outpatients in the following departments: Radiation therapy and nuclear medicine - 1,428, Electrocardiography - 2,889, Cardio-pulmonary Laboratory - 211, Electroencephalography - 1,370, Physical Medicine and Rehabilitation - 2.360 and Emergency - 74,010.

Despite the fact that the hospital ranked tenth of all medical facilities in the United States in terms of quality of patient care and though it was a statewide leader among non-profit hospitals, providing medical care for children, Saint Francis was close to bankruptcy by the end of the 1970s. In 1981, the Daughters of Charity assumed sponsorship and began to reverse the cash flow.

A Child Abuse Program was inaugurated, as well as a Lung Cancer Laser Center. In the latter department, new procedures allowed for the latest advancement in the detection and treatment of lung ailments.

Construction was begun in November of 1989 for a new Health Services Pavilion at Imperial Highway and Martin Luther King, Jr. Boulevard. The four-story, 160,000 square foot structure was dedicated by Roger Cardinal Mahony on December 13, 1991. Statistics for that year indicated that the Medical Center was admitting 14,000 patients per year and delivering 400 babies every month. It had the busiest private emergency department in Los Angeles County, serving some 60,000 patients annually. As part of the Daughters of Charity National Health System, Saint Francis was the largest not-for-profit care system in the nation.

LITTLE COMPANY OF MARY HOSPITAL TORRANCE

At a press conference in July of 1956, the Little Company of Mary, a community of Sisters specializing in the care of the sick, announced plans for a hospital on a ten-acre site in Torrance. The multiple story edifice was envisioned to serve the 500,000 residents of Redondo Beach, Hermosa Beach, Manhattan Beach, San Pedro, Wilmington, Palos Verdes and Rolling Hills.

A survey by the state showed that at least 600 hospital beds were urgently needed to accommodate the growth of industry and population in the area. The new institution would join the forty-three other hospitals operated by the Sisters around the world.

Groundbreaking ceremonies took place on December 19,1957. The hospital was to rest on 400 columns extending thirty-five feet into the sandy soil. James Francis Cardinal McIntyre dedicated the hospital on December 12,1959. The five-story reinforced concrete building was engineered to accommodate three additional stories in future years. In addition to the emergency unit, there were medical and surgical units, four operating rooms with recovery wards, labor and delivery rooms with obstetrical recovery and a pediatric department. Total cost of the hospital was disclosed at $3,500,000.

During the inaugural month of the hospital's service, a total of 309 adult patients were given surgical and medical care at the modern 150-bed facility. The staff consisted of eleven Sisters, 350 registered nurses, lab technicians, interns, clerical workers, aides and a staff of over 200 doctors.

An auxiliary guild was formed in May of 1959 and within a year its membership advanced to 550. When the hospital doors opened on January 3,1960, the guild members began performing corporal works of mercy and serving as nurses' aids. With the passage of only a few years, Little Company of Mary Hospital was serving 8,764 patients annually. Its pediatric department operated at an 84% capacity.

Medical research is part of the story for all hospitals. At Little Company of Mary, funds were acquired for research in comparative cardiovascular pathology. The project was carried out in conjunction with Marineland of the Pacific and investigated arteriosclerosis in sea mammals.

In 1962, officials at the hospital reported the birth of the 5,000[th] baby, Megan Mass. The infant, born on the hospital's third anniversary, belonged to members of American Martyrs parish in Redondo Beach.

A story in the local press compared Little Company of Mary Hospital with a church where dedicated men and women were sensitive to the sacredness of life. They reflected the high goal of God's hand in every patient. Nearly 600 families were involved in some form of voluntary service to the hospital and its patients. The avenues for that work were a junior auxiliary that numbered about 150 teenage girls and a 400 member women's auxiliary. The adult group gave the hospital some 50,000 hours of service in tasks within their competence.

In keeping with the space age, a heliport was installed at the Torrance hospital in 1965. There, the Los Angeles County Sheriff's Department and the United States Coast Guard brought in patients from areas usually inaccessible to ambulances, including the coastal islands and ships at sea.

One of the first coronary units was established at Little Company of Mary in 1966. The idea was new then and heart disease was the nation's single greatest health problem. The unit was located in a quiet area at the end of the hospital where the latest in electronic devices were located.

A nuclear medical unit was added a short while later. Included in the new equipment was a scanner with a five inch detector crystal which permitted radioactive scanning of various organs in addition to the thyroid, including the brain, lungs, liver, spleen, pancreas, kidneys and bones.

Typical of other hospitals in those days, there was always the need to enlarge. In its short lifetime, there was a continual increase of admissions and newborns. Radiology examinations increased from 6,645 to 31,756. Yet, Little Company of Mary Hospital met those challenges, with a Physical and Rehabilitation Therapy unit, a Nuclear Diagnostic department and a Pulmonary and Inhalation Therapy department. Because of the tremendous population growth in the area, those treated by the hospital increased by 88%.

In 1975, a new five-story unit was built on a 95,000 square foot expansion, extending in front of the existing hospital. New facilities were provided for radiology, physical medicine, maternity and coronary care. The unit was blessed by Timothy Cardinal Manning on January 27,1979. Twenty years later, Little Company of Mary joined with Providence Health System in order to better deal with Congressional cuts for patients in and out of Medicare.

PROVIDENCE HOLY CROSS
MEDICAL CENTER
MISSION HILLS

In what was then America's fastest growing community, the sprawling San Fernando Valley, plans were announced in mid-1957 for a new Catholic general hospital to provide for the area's health needs. A twelve-acre site near Alemany High School was selected for the institution to be staffed by the Holy Cross Sisters, a community whose nursing tradition dates back to the Civil War.

Concrete foundations were laid in May of 1959 for the 240-bed hospital. The completely integrated medical center was to serve the Valley's vast northwestern area with a quarter million population. At the time, only 28% of the minimum beds were in place for the fast-growing population. There were to be six surgical rooms, an emergency department, three delivery rooms for obstetrics, dental facilities for surgery and modern laboratories for pathological and radiological work. Built on a site close to the proposed Golden State Freeway, the hospital was to have 140 two-bed rooms and sixty private rooms.

James Francis Cardinal McIntyre dedicated the new facility on June 3, 1961. Local newspapers reported that the hospital incorporated many revolutionary concepts in hospital design along with an ingenious use of automation. A series of guilds were established to further public recognition, perform ancillary functions and operate various volunteer programs.

Within the first year it became necessary to expand. A separate convalescent and chronic disease unit was added across Indian Hills Road from the main facility. There were rooms there for forty-nine long-term patients. The one-story, 16,200 square foot unit was built in

the shape of a Greek cross with a main nursing station at its center. On duty at both units was a staff numbering 272 doctors, thirteen Sisters and 340 lay employees.

A Cardio-Pulmonary Lab was installed in 1964 for those suffering from severe respiratory disabilities. A timing unit enabled regulation of heartbeats until that vital organ could resume its normal operation. The following year, a new photo scanner was added for work in the Division of Nuclear Medicine.

An earthquake registering 6.5 on the Richter scale hit the Mission Hills area of the San Fernando Valley on February 5, 1971. All patients were evacuated from the main building. The extent of structural damage was devastating. Walls and floors were cracked, the bond beam was cracked and most of the windows broken. According to a previously arranged procedure, the forty most-enfeebled patients were taken to other hospitals in the city. Mobile Units were brought in for emergency service. Still deeply in debt after ten years of operation, Holy Cross Hospital had to be abandoned.

The hospital re-opened with thirty beds early in 1972 for those not requiring surgery. The beds were located in the one-story convalescent wing. Several mobile units housed the administrative quarters. Meanwhile work was underway on the first floor in the hospital's north wing for surgery and intensive care. That wing was opened in April of 1972.

In 1974, plans were approved for a new 209-bed facility. The new structure would include expanded units of physical medicine, pulmonary function and emergency service. On April 16, 1977, Timothy Cardinal Manning dedicated the new Holy Cross Hospital on the very locale where the previous structure had been destroyed. Its four-story, 2,000 ton structured steel frame was supported by reinforced concrete piles thirty feet deep. It was destined to be among the most advanced medical centers in the Los Angeles area. A new cancer center opened in November of 1993. That 11,000 square foot center expanded the existing services by providing for oncological surgery.

Because of the changing nature of health care, traditional modes of hospital administration gradually gave way to new priorities. The need for inpatient acute care, for example, declined sharply. Also, increased financial pressures, changes in reimbursement and other issues affecting operational costs made it imperative that Holy Cross become part of a larger system. Hence, it was announced on December 29, 1995, that the two San Fernando Valley Catholic Hospitals would join forces within the same corporation. Providence Health System purchased Holy Cross Medical Center which, thereafter, became known as Providence Holy Cross.

Queen of the Valley, 1962, later Citrus Valley Medical Center

CITRUS VALLEY
MEDICAL CENTER WEST COVINA

Plans for a 125-bed hospital for the Covina area were announced in March of 1958. To be staffed by the Immaculate Heart Sisters, the hospital would serve the entire East San Gabriel Valley from El Monte to Pomona and from the San Gabriel mountains to the Whittier highlands.

Queen of the Valley would help to fill the need for an additional 500 beds lacking in such communities as Azusa, Baldwin Park, Charter Oaks, Glendora, City of Industry, La Puente, San Dimas and Covina. Departments in the new facility would include surgery, obstetrics, pediatrics, emergency services, geriatrics and a clinic for the emotionally disturbed.

When the contract was let for the hospital, arrangements were made whereby the building would be finished in 732 working days. The four-story edifice was to be located on a thirty-two acre parcel of land, formerly owned by William Berger at Sunset and Merced Avenues.

Maximum use of automation and efficiency techniques was used to allow the nurses more time for direct patient care. The ground floor of the new hospital included a pharmacy, laundry, storage, personnel office and areas for sterilization, electrical and telephone equipment. The maternity department would be on the second floor, with the third floor devoted to fifteen pediatric beds and thirty-nine medical-surgery beds. On the fourth floor were forty-six beds and an eight-patient intensive care unit.

The hospital was dedicated on October 6, 1962 by James Francis Cardinal McIntyre. A local community newspaper noted "the beautiful new Queen here is like a flower facing the bloom of its first summer." It "sits bright and radiant in the middle of the East San Gabriel Valley where there is a young new life and everything is growing."

There were 150 doctors on staff at the inauguration. Three medical buildings were erected within a half-block of the hospital. A convent provided housing for the Sisters of the Immaculate Heart of Mary.

Electronics provided instrumentation for cardiac monitoring and resuscitation. Nuclear medicine was represented by a magnescope, and a radiological device whose previous licensing was reserved to the Atomic Energy Commission.

A commentator writing in *The Tidings* for May 21,1965 said "the future is the cornerstone of Queen of the Valley Hospital. The four-story concrete and glass building stands tall like a jewel of mercy and succor a few blocks from the San Bernardino Freeway." Since its opening, the facility had operated at between 85% and 90% of capacity and, in addition to the normal functions of general hospital work, was caring for more than 10,000 emergency cases each year.

A new Home Care Program was inaugurated in mid-1966. This called for the visitation to persons in their homes by hospital staff to administer health benefits that did not require hospitalization.

Expansion plans were announced shortly thereafter. Capacity would be enlarged to allow for 272 beds by adding two floors and extending the building forty-feet on the south and west sides.

A trauma center was opened in 1984. Victims of serious accidents could be moved into surgery within minutes of arrival at the emergency department. In subsequent years, well in excess of 1,000 trauma victims from throughout the eastern Valley were brought into the hospital. A cardiac surgery suite was begun the next year and, in 1987, an intercommunity chest-pain unit was in operation.

In 1994, after years of caring for people in the valley, Inter-Community Medical Center, its hospice and Queen of the Valley Hospital joined together in order to provide even better services. Two years later, Inter-Community Medical Center and Queen of the Valley merged to form one medical center with two campuses.

In more recent times, Citrus Valley Medical Center has served as a non-denominational or community hospital. Its administrators recognize the need for preserving human dignity, as well as the spiritual and emotional well being of its patients and their families. It still serves as the compassionate, loving heart of the community.

SAINT JOHN
PLEASANT VALLEY HOSPITAL
CAMARILLO

The city of Camarillo, situated in a fertile agricultural plain and incorporated since 1964, has a population of 65,000 people. Residents boast of having the best climate anywhere. Mild Pacific breezes help maintain temperatures that are generally in the low to mid-70s. The City enjoys more than 300 days of sunshine annually. Rainfall occurs most often in January and February, with an average of thirteen inches each year. Located just seven miles from the ocean, Camarillo is accented by rolling hills, colorful agricultural fields and avocado and citrus orchards.

Camarillo's mild climate and clean, healthful air add greatly to the quality of life. City leaders are committed to attracting industry and business that will not affect the year-round smog-free skies. The Federal threshold for ozone (the primary ingredient of smog) has never been exceeded in the city. Camarillo's remarkable record for clean air can be credited to the city's location, adherence to its General Plan and comprehensive land use and transportation planning in the community development process.

The Pleasant Valley Hospital was opened on July 29, 1974 as a health care facility for the burgeoning rural community of Camarillo

and its environs. It was founded by two physicians on the staff of Saint John Hospital in Oxnard, a facility operated for many decades by the Mercy Sisters.

Later, the hospital was sold and for a time served as a "district" hospital, subsequently becoming a non-profit institution. On February 19, 1993, the hospital merged with Saint John Medical Center as a satellite of the Oxnard establishment - one hospital - one corporation and one medical staff on two sites. In January of 1994, both hospitals became a mini-system with Catholic Healthcare West.

SAN PEDRO PENINSULA
HOSPITAL
SAN PEDRO

San Pedro Peninsula Hospital began as a community hospital and then became affiliated with the Sisters of the Little Company of Mary in 1992. It has 256 beds in addition to a Pavilion which provides facilities for another 328 less acute patients.

SAINT ANN HOME FOR THE AGED
JEANNE JUGAN RESIDENCE

The mail delivery of September 16, 1904, brought an offer to Bishop Thomas J. Conaty, as casual as it was monumental. After outlining the charitable work already accomplished by the Little Sisters of the Poor in San Francisco, Edward J. LeBreton asked the Southern California prelate if he would be "disposed to invite this religious community to start a house in Los Angeles." If so, LeBreton offered to purchase a seven or eight acre site and build quarters thereon where the nuns could accommodate 200 elderly patients.

Bishop Conaty did not know LeBreton personally. Had he inquired in the Bay Area, however, he would have found that Edward J. LeBreton was recognized among his contemporaries as "a man of irreproachable character and saintly life" and "a man of God who loved his religion and faithfully followed its precepts."

Edward Joseph LeBreton was born of French parentage in Folsom, California, in 1852. He had been educated in France and Germany and, by the time he was advanced to the presidency of the French Savings Bank in San Francisco, he had reached "the honorable distinction of being a successful man of affairs and by his industry and integrity he accumulated a fortune."

LeBreton had been associated with the apostolic endeavors of the Little Sisters of the Poor since their arrival at San Francisco, in 1901. One of the nuns reported that at their initial meeting LeBreton said: "You will find in me a friend and a protector as often as you will choose to have recourse to my assistance or my advice in your needs." In addition to financial assistance, LeBreton visited the Home for the Aged Poor every Wednesday and Saturday, where he performed the most menial tasks. Frequently he would send elderly patients on a day's outing in his private carriage. Such activities were a natural outgrowth of his philosophy that "to give one's money is little, but to give oneself is better."

The prospect of introducing the Sisters in the Diocese of Monterey-Los Angeles was most appealing to Bishop Conaty, and he arranged to meet with Mr. LeBreton in San Francisco, in October of 1904. After making some preliminary arrangements, the Little Sisters of the Poor arrived early in 1905, and immediately took up their apostolate among the elderly citizens of all races and creeds. LeBreton acquired property on East First Street and construction was soon underway for permanent quarters. A four-story red-brick building was ready in mid-1907, and Bishop Conaty dedicated the handsome American colonial structure on March 25, 1908. LeBreton absorbed the total cost of the institution which amounted to over $400,000.

In the following years, the generous San Francisco benefactor frequently visited the Sisters. A newspaper account recalled "how edifying it was to see this man of affairs, this successful businessman moving among the old people in the homes which he had built for them, sharing their simple meal, always delighted to wait on them at table." When asked by the nuns if they could display his portrait in the foyer, LeBreton replied that some sort of religious picture would more properly express their gratitude for his assistance.

For over seventy years, Saint Ann Home for the Aged served the poor, elderly and infirm of Los Angeles. When the brick structure would no longer pass the strict building codes, the Archdiocese of Los Angeles gave the Sisters the campus of Fermin Lasuen High School in San Pedro where today the Jeanne Jugan Residence continues the apostolate of the Little Sisters of the Poor.

NAZARETH HOUSE
LOS ANGELES

Begun in 1934, on Kenmore Avenue in Los Angeles, Nazareth House was moved to Clarington Avenue where the Poor Sisters of Nazareth provided sanctuary for elderly, homeless women. In their beautiful five-acre site, the Sisters were able to accommodate fifteen women at a time by late 1949.

The next year, plans were afoot for a larger building to care for the ever-growing number of patients wishing to avail themselves of the facility. In those early years, the Nazareth House Auxiliary was greatly influential in raising funds for the operation of the institution.

Archbishop J. Francis A. McIntyre presided at groundbreaking ceremonies for a new unit in Cheviot Hills on November 25, 1950. Built to accommodate sixty guests, the new two-story reinforced brick unit was outfitted with a tile roof. It faced Manning Avenue across from the California Golf Club. The structure had a non-institutional and home-like atmosphere. Single and double rooms were grouped in small wings with sun parlors and sitting rooms in each. There was also an up-to-date infirmary and a large dining room. The new facility was ready for occupancy in mid-1952.

Six years later, a new wing was constructed which boosted the capacity of Nazareth House to a hundred residents. It was announced that the new wing, with ten more double rooms with private baths, would also provide accommodations for men.

Oldsters living at Nazareth House never grew old from worry. Rather, they aged securely content in the knowledge that the Sisters would provide for their every need. Guests were free to come and go as they pleased. And friends were always welcome.

Midway through 1963, another appeal was made to further expand Nazareth House. The Sisters wanted to construct an auditorium to increase recreational facilities for their guests. Space was available for movies, playing cards, sewing circles and other social events. Late in 1974, ground was broken for another twelve-bed infirmary.

Timothy Cardinal Manning journeyed to the west side in 1978 for the anniversary of Nazareth House. He spoke glowingly of the works

provided by the sisters in their sixty-eight houses located throughout America, Australia, Great Britain, Ireland, New Zealand and South Africa.

SAINT JOHN OF GOD RETIREMENT AND CARE CENTER LOS ANGELES

It was in 1941 that the Hospitaller Order, the Brothers of Saint John of God, came to Los Angeles. They opened a hospital in the San Fernando Valley, conducted Rancho San Antonio Boys' Home and began a hotel for transient men in downtown Los Angeles. In 1943, the Brothers relinquished their work and moved into a dwelling at Adams Boulevard and Western Avenue. There they opened a "hospital-sanitarium" that Archbishop John J. Cantwell dedicated on July 11th.

The thirty-three-bed facility was quickly filled to capacity and soon they were planning a larger structure where they could also accommodate the elderly. It was an inviolable part of their program that only 40% of their patients pay in full. The rest were cared for from funds raised by the Brothers. On May 3,1952, Archbishop J. Francis A. McIntyre blessed and laid the cornerstone for a new Saint John of God Sanitarium. The first wing of the new building was ready early the next January. The three-story, forty-six bed facility enabled the Brothers to double the number of their patients.

Geriatrics, the care of the aged and chronically ill, continued to be the prime work of the Brothers in Los Angeles. With the increased life expectancy among the general population, ever more demands were made upon the Brothers.

By 1957, the hospital already had exceeded its capacity and the need for additional expansion was urgent. The Brothers wanted to erect a new wing that would bring total capacity to 180 beds. The proposed expansion would include physical, hydro and occupational therapy facilities, a laboratory, an X-ray department, a surgery suite and an administrative suite. Over the years, the average stay of patients was 179.5 days for long-term male patients.

Bowing to pressures of society, the Brothers decided in 1968 to admit women patients. Improvements and enlargement of the hospital's facilities made it possible to admit women patients, most of whom, at least in the early years, came from larger hospitals for periods of convalescence.

During 1971, Saint John of God adopted the theme of "We Care" in its dealings with patients. Extra services such as maintenance physical therapy, dental care, films, birthday observances, occupational and recreational therapy and family picnics were among the activities provided for patients.

When the new three-story edifice at 2035 West Adams Boulevard was completed in July of 1973, the earlier building was converted for occupational therapy and administration. Adjacent to the new structure was a chapel. The Brothers were happy to announce that the hospital was built without any Federal or State funds. Timothy Cardinal Manning dedicated the new Saint John of God on September 29,1973.

The beautiful, new, fully fireproof steel and reinforced concrete building with its adobe-colored stone finish, became a landmark in one of the oldest sections of Los Angeles. The Brothers were especially pleased with the kitchen area and the fully equipped laundry rooms.

In 1989, the Brothers announced plans for an Apartment Complex for active, older adults. There the Brothers tried to provide an environment that "directs their lives towards freedom and wholeness of Christ." A descriptive account of the new facility stated that it was "literally an oasis in the heart of the city." The entire campus was built in the attractive southwestern style of architecture with thick walls, view windows, balconies and courtyards.

A decade later, an improved residential care facility was opened at Saint John. That included apartments for independent seniors, residential independent living and residential assisted living. This latest addition accommodated ninety new units. The upgraded center also provided a variety of recreational facilities and services such as gardening, pet companionship, an indoor pool, a fitness center and an art gallery.

MARYCREST MANOR CULVER CITY

The Irish Sisters of Charity came to Los Angeles in 1953 where they engaged in a teaching apostolate in Long Beach. In 1962, they took charge of Marycrest Manor as a ministry for the spiritual and temporal needs of the elderly, the sick and the infirm.

Their residence, located on a wooded hilltop overlooking Santa Monica Bay, was at 10664 Saint James Drive in Culver City. The institution provided comfortable private and semi-private accommodations for twenty-one guests. Most of the spacious rooms had adjoining private patios. The modern facilities included a large living or common room, a solarium, library, swimming pool and a chapel. The two-story structure was constructed of fireproof masonry and finished in an attractive Mediterranean design.

A new wing was added to Marycrest Manor in September of 1968 with facilities for another twenty-nine residents, plus a dining room, treatment center and physiotherapy rooms. It is now operated by the Carmelites.

MARY, HEALTH OF THE SICK
NEWBURY PARK

It was in April of 1960 that the Sisters Servants of Mary began planning for a convalescent home in Newbury Park. It had long been the practice of this community to go to their patients by bus, streetcar and other vehicles during the daytime. Whether they cared by day or night at the bedside of the sick, the Sisters served without remuneration.

The Sisters wanted to erect a convalescent home and novitiate in Newbury Park. Patients frequently needed a period of convalescence after leaving a hospital. Often, elderly people had no family left to care for them. The new facility would occupy thirteen acres and provide twenty-five beds that would increase as the years rolled by.

Named Mary, Health of the Sick, work on the initial building began in late 1962. Bishop Timothy Manning was present for the groundbreaking on September 15th. The non-profit, non-sectarian facility was designed to provide care for medical, post-operative and geriatric cases.

The apostolate of the Sisters was reported by a journalist from Los Angeles: "A small band of humble, charming, black-robed Spanish nuns have traveled the streets and highways of Los Angeles ministering day and night to the sick and infirm in their homes, regardless of creed or social status."

Before opening their facility, the Sisters made an agreement whereby patients at their convalescent hospital needing surgical or other treatment could be admitted to Saint John Hospital in Oxnard. The new Mary, Health of the Sick Convalescent Hospital was dedicated on June 20, 1964 by James Francis Cardinal McIntyre. There were thirty-nine beds in the one-story facility including eleven single rooms. The hospital was erected on twelve beautifully landscaped acres.

One of the hospital's distinguishing features is that it catered only to women. Its residents came not only from the local community but from throughout the state. Others took up residence in the Conejo Valley just to be near the institution.

With an eye toward a homelike atmosphere, the hospital's chief attraction was the high visibility of the Sisters. Their personal involvement with residents, their availability to laugh and cry provided support for both days of happiness and moments of sorrow.

In 1986, a program for much needed expansion was begun. The physical therapy department as well as the outpatient unit needed attention. At that time, there were sixty-one residents, half of whom were Medi-Cal patients. The Sisters made up whatever financial deficit emerged.

SAINT JOSEPH HEALTH
AND RETIREMENT CENTER
OJAI

Saint Joseph Health and Retirement Center, operated by the Hospitaller Brothers of Saint John of God, is located on a thirty-acre tract of land in Ojai, California. Purchased in 1955, the original estate included the main house and several guest houses. The single family main structure was built in 1928 in English Tudor style.

When the Brothers moved to Ojai in 1956, these facilities were utilized as the first nursing home with six male residents. Today, this building serves as the main dining room, Brothers' living quarters and guests rooms. In the subsequent years, the ministry opened a small skilled nursing facility to complement the novitiate building and a large chapel. The entire property still retains the charm of its original English setting in the midst of acres of orange groves.

In June of 1958, Bishop Timothy Manning presided at groundbreaking services for "Saint Joseph Health and Retirement Center". Then, on December 8, 1959, James Francis Cardinal McIntyre dedicated the new facility. The twenty-two-bed nursing home and adjoining novitiate was located on the former Lombardy Ranch, just two miles east of Ojai. The rambling, one-story concrete structure provided treatment facilities for long term patients, with emphasis on physiotherapy and occupational therapy.

Saint Joseph Health and Retirement Center is a twenty-nine-bed skilled nursing facility. The Christian Community Center, in the renovated novitiate, accommodates twenty-five active seniors.

LITTLE COMPANY OF MARY
ACUTE CARE CENTER
TORRANCE

This 200-bed facility, begun in 1957 as the Bay Harbor Hospital West, was purchased by the Sisters of the Little Company of Mary in 1998 and now operates as the Little Company of Mary Acute Care Center in Torrance. It is an intermediary care center established to look after patients who no longer require or qualify for full hospitalization and yet are unable to return to their homes.

PROVIDENCE SAINT ELIZABETH
CARE CENTER
TOLUCA LAKE

Saint Elizabeth Care Center was originally part of the American Hungarian Social Service Board. From July of 1963 to June of 1973, Sister Magdolna Margit Heczke, a member of the Sisters of Social Service, served as a fulltime worker at the facility. In 1973 she became executive director of what was then known as Saint Elizabeth Toluca Lake Convalescent Hospital, a position she occupied until late 1982.

Providence Saint Elizabeth Care Center, 1953

On January 16, 1984, Saint Elizabeth became a subsidiary of Holy Cross Hospital in Mission Hills. It was then a fifty-two-bed facility licensed for both male and female patients. An article in *The Tidings* later reported that Saint Elizabeth was more than just a facility offering convalescent health care. It was also a community of senior citizens living and working together in a compassionate Christian atmosphere of good care, nutrition, kindness and love.

The facility offered a warm and caring religious environment coordinated by the Holy Cross Sisters who oversaw the many formal Christian activities in addition to assuring that all patients were treated with warmth, respect and dignity.

Saint Elizabeth was one of the very few convalescent health care centers directly supervised and operated by a major acute-care hospital. As such, its medical services, resources and professional oversight are unique in the San Fernando Valley. Since April 16,1996, Saint Elizabeth has been owned and operated by Providence Health Care of Burbank.

TOGETHER IN MISSION

Since 1993 the Catholics of the Archdiocese of Los Angeles have participated in an annual appeal for funds called " Together in Mission ". Priests, religious and laity join forces at the parochial level to demonstrate the oneness of their faith commitment.

This united appeal endeavors to keep open the doors of thirty-two parishes and forty-six schools for those who cannot do so alone. This is done in recognition that Catholics in the Archdiocese of Los Angeles are a single family working out their salvation under the Good Sheperd.

Generally Catholics are more attentive to far-away areas of the world where bringing the Good News, the Word of God, is restricted by a host of challenges. But in "Together in Mission", Catholics are addressing the needs of their own locale where many people are unable to share in the basic blessings of their own society.

Scripture proclaims that "charity begins at home" and for that reason, Roger Cardinal Mahony appeals on behalf of those who are unable to share in the basic needs of Church and school.

Catholics have traditionally been quick to assist the less fortunate, to heal the sick, feed the hungry, defend the oppressed who walk in our streets, inhabit our own city and worship the one true God.

Some feel that the government or some other agency should be looking after those needs and that may be true in some respect. But in the worship of God and the instruction of the faith, others are called upon to provide for those wbo bear or want the same imprint of Baptism that marks their neighbors.

The annual goal is roughly 8% of a parish's annual income. The overall campaign is audited by an outside firm to guarantee that all monies raised are properly accounted for.

Each year 284 parishes meet and exceed their goal in the Archdiocese of Los Angeles. In 2005, 118,510 Catholics donated $18,651.460 to those living in financially disadvantaged neighborhoods in the three county archdiocese. Almost three million dollars was rebated to parishes exceeding their goals.

The Catechism of the Catholic Church says that: "God blesses those who come to the aid of the poor and rebukes those who turn away frorn them. It is by what they have done for the poor that Jesus Christ will recognize His chosen ones."

CEMETERIES AND CATHOLIC MORTUARIES

CATHOLIC MORTUARIES

According to an article in the Los Angeles *Times*, archdiocesan officials said that Catholic mortuaries would draw the faithful back into the Church's final embrace, reversing a twenty year trend in which parishioners increasingly have chosen not to be buried in Catholic Cemeteries. The proportion of Catholic burials in archdiocesan cemeteries declined alarmingly from 85% to 35% between 1965 and 1985. The concern was far more than financial because the connection of the Church to its people does not end with death.

The Vicar General for the archdiocese of Los Angeles said "we are committed to providing Catholic families throughout the Archdiocese of Los Angeles with the very finest and most convenient services and facilities during their time of bereavement."

Each facility, designed to make families feel welcome and peaceful, includes a beautiful courtyard with flowing fountains and lush greenery.

Catholic Mortuary Services, a group within Stewart Enterprises headquartered in Santa Fe Springs, announced its value statement as follows:

• To ensure that every family will receive accurate information regarding the choices available to them;

• To provide all services in a manner that fully respects Catholic tradition and practice;

• To promote an atmosphere of caring service to all families;

• To build good relationships with local parish communities;

• To provide accessibility to both the funeral home and the cemetery at one convenient location, thus simplifying the arrangement process;

• To provide every family an opportunity to select from a wide range of affordably priced funeral options;

• To ensure that no one will ever be turned away for lack of funds.

HISTORICAL BACKGROUND

The change from mission to diocesan status for the Church in California involved a radically different jurisdictional concept. After the 1840s, Catholics along the Pacific Slope were divided geographically into units known as dioceses that were broken down further into parishes. Today, the area originally served by twenty-one missions comprises two archdioceses, nine dioceses and 1,067 parishes with a total population of 10,110,452 or about 30% of the population. Things have changed! And so have cemeteries. The burial practices at the California missions were based on the European notion where a cemetery was presumed for every parish (Canon 1208). Hence, there were cemeteries at all the missions, generally located outside the Gospel side of the Church. With the passing of the mission era, the notion of area cemeteries for Catholics gradually emerged, but where there were no "exclusively Catholic" cemeteries, it became common to inter Catholics in public cemeteries, with a priest blessing the ground for each interment.

Prior to the opening of New Calvary Cemetery in 1896, the bishops of Southern California had little to say and less to do about Catholic burial places. Most members of the faith were interred in the "Catholic section" of a public cemetery.

Bishop Francis Mora, who pioneered New Calvary Cemetery, provided wisely and well for the Diocese of Monterey-Los Angeles, establishing Catholic cemeteries at Castroville (1875), Salinas (1875), San Luis Obispo (1879), Fresno (1885) and Santa Barbara (1896).

As will be noted in a later section of this book, Calvary Cemetery was the first diocesan cemetery. The following observations about Calvary were prepared by Mora and later incorporated into the 1898 Diocesan Catholic Directory:

Calvary is a most appropriate title for a Catholic graveyard, because the name of Calvary is indissolubly associated with our Lord's death; it designated the spot where Christ died that we might live, where by His death He overcame death. The life of a Christian is the following of Christ, and Calvary is the end of his earthly journey. "If any one come after Me, let him take up his cross and follow Me." St. Paul says that in life he was nailed with Christ to the Cross. The Cross on which Christ paid the price of our redemption was buried on the spot of the crucifixion, and was discovered by the mother of Constantine. The Pagans, to obliterate all memory of the death of Jesus Christ, built a temple to Venus on the spot where He had died; but tradition kept watch and ward over the hallowed ground, and the Christians of the fourth century, then living in Jerusalem, could point out to the Empress the exact place where the true Cross had stood. Removing the temple and digging down into the ground, three crosses were exhumed. To test the true one, they were all applied to a sick man; the two first not availing his cure, the third was applied, when he rose from his bed whole. A Christian Church was then built over the place, which remains to this day. Pilgrims visiting the Holy Land find the very way marked out which our Lord traveled carrying His Cross, and the fourteen stations of the Way of the Cross are given with the unerring accuracy of love's imperishable memory.

Where on earth a better place for man to be buried than where God died for men? The roads of our "Calvary" bear names taken from the history of the Passion, the *Via Dolorosa* leading to the "Great Cross," and the other ways called after those who accompanied Jesus on that sorrowful journey.

Mora's greatest contribution to the Church in Southern California was the opening of Calvary Cemetery in 1896. The first interment there was made on October 28th of that year. The grounds contained about one hundred and fifty acres, one-fourth of which was surveyed and fenced in. The general design of the cemetery is that of a park. Rising gently from the main entrance, its long avenues winding round and round, shaded by a variety of trees, and away from the noise and bustle of the city, nature and art have made it the tranquil dwelling place of the city's dead.

With his grammatical facility, Bishop George Montgomery left little to the imagination of his people. In the case of deaths and funerals, he issued a statement in 1898, outlining his thoughts relating to Catholic Cemeteries:

THE CHRISTIAN CEMETERY

The word "cemetery" means a dormitory, or place of sleep. The early Christians always called death a sleep. When their friends died they closed their eyes and mouth, not only to take away the hideous stare and expression of death, but to symbolize the sleep into which the dead had gently fallen. Above the unknown graves of thousands is written the simple legend, *"in peace."* The dead sleep awaiting the resurrection. The grave, the ceremonies of burial, the laying out of the body, all symbolize the Christian faith in the resurrection of the dead. At the head of the grave is placed the sign of life's victory over death. The body in the coffin is clothed in the white robes which typify the winding sheet in which our Lord's limbs were wrapped during the three days He remained in the tomb.

In the early days, the Christians celebrated the holy sacrifice of the Mass on the graves of the martyrs, with their little raised mounds for altar stones. When peace was given to the Church she erected churches over those graves, and that custom is preserved in our day, little sepulchres being cut into the altar stones for the reception of relics of the saints. Moved by an impulse of the communion of saints, the Christians, after the dawn of peace, sought the neighborhood of the churches to lay them down in death. Hence the name long borne by cemeteries, "churchyards," and "God's acre." When it became inconvenient to bury the dead in or around the churches, place was found for them along the roads leading to the cities. The graves were placed near the highways, that the dead might be refreshed by the prayers of the living, who were thus constantly reminded of their own mortality, and of the duty they owed to the departed.

The Church loves to linger, like Magdalene, near the tombs of her children, for whose eternal repose she prays a hundred times a day: *"Fidelium animae per misericordiam Dei requiescant in pace.* If there is a sermon in stones, the tombs of our cemeteries preach of immortality. It is the one doctrine of all time and of all men; it will not die, and is found nowhere so vital and strong as among the graves and monuments of the dead.

CHRISTIAN SEPULTURE

A Christian cemetery is a place set apart, consecrated by a bishop, and devoted to the sepulture of saints. Those who do not die in the grace and friendship of God, die not in the state of sanctification, are not saints, and are out of place in a Christian cemetery. In all times, the Church has claimed the right to deny Christian sepulture to those whom she deems unworthy to rest in consecrated ground. She made many concessions to the civil power, especially in the last century, but this right she would never surrender. A consecrated cemetery is polluted by the notorious burial of one not entitled to a grave in it.

Those excluded from consecrated ground are those who are not baptized, those who do not belong to the Church, and public sinners who have died in impenitence. In other words, those not entitled to the sacraments while living are not deserving of a Christian grave in death.

Besides the consecrated ground of a Christian cemetery, there is often found land set apart for the burial of non-Catholics, and other persons not admitted to the cemetery. While non-Catholics and bad Catholics cannot be buried in consecrated ground, good Catholics may be buried in unconsecrated ground. In cases of mixed marriage, where the non-Catholic party has died outside the Church, the Church does not wish to separate in death those who were united in life, and she buries them all in unconsecrated ground, blessing the graves of her children one by one as they die, and saying over them the prayer of her burial service.

The Church is slow to condemn, and inclines ever to mercy; so in every case of doubt as to the right to Christian burial the Bishop of the Diocese must be consulted; and his judgment is final. Christian burial is not merely the few prayers said at the grave; the service begins properly at the house, is continued in the Church, where a Mass of Requiem is said and ends with the service at the grave. Hence the custom of almost universal observance in Catholic countries, and among Catholics everywhere, of having funerals in the forenoon. Afternoon funerals and funerals on Sunday, when a requiem mass cannot be celebrated, can scarcely be called Christian sepulture.

THE CROSS

As a symbol of triumph, the Cross has always held the first rank. It is the sign of the Son of Man that will appear in the Heavens on the day of final resurrection, and it is the banner of the Risen Lord, who blotted out "the handwriting of the decree that stood against us, nailing it to the Cross." The Church declares the Cross our only hope: *"Ave, Spes Unica."* The instrument of Christ's death is the instrument of our resurrection. According to St. Paul, those who are buried with Christ will be raised from the dead with Christ. The Cross is a monument to the victory of Christ over death and it proclaims in triumphant accents, "O Death, where is thy sting? O Grave, where is thy victory?"

Since the days of Constantine the Great, who quartered it on his banner, the Cross has been everywhere accepted as the one aggressive symbol of heroic Christianity. Other symbols, expressive of the Christian's hope, would be appropriate in a Catholic cemetery, but they should be associated with Calvary, and recall the bloody tragedy of Good Friday. Statues of the Mater Dolorosa, the cock, the Angel of the Resurrection, the anchor, and the Instruments of the Passion, are all appropriate; but the urn, the broken shaft, and the inverted torch are symbols of Paganism, and are out of place in a Catholic cemetery. But the Cross is a silent and sleepless sentinel over the graves of the Church's heroes. The Fathers represented Christ as asleep on the Cross. As Eve was formed out of the rib from the side of the sleeping Adam, so was the church formed out of the pierced side of the second Adam, asleep on the Cross. The Christian who has borne his cross faithfully through life goes asleep under it, and awaits the trumpet call of the resurrection to take his place once more in the ranks, not to battle again, but to receive the unfading laurels of deathless victory. The Cross is our strength in life, our hope in death, and our glory in eternity. "God forbid that we should glory in aught save the Cross of Christ, by which the world is crucified to us, and we to the world."

CREMATION

The custom of burning the bodies of the dead is of comparatively recent date. The Jews always buried their dead. The people of China, and the Goths and Huns, practiced inhumation from the earliest times. The statement that cremation was practiced among the Germanic people before they embraced Christianity is disproved by the regulations of Charlemagne, who compelled the Saxons to adopt Christian sepulture, they having formerly observed a great variety of forms of burial according to the standing of the deceased.

The Greeks were the first of European nations to adopt cremation, but it was a dire expedient of unsuccessful war. To the Greek the most terrible of misfortunes was to lie unburied, as it prevented the passage of the spirits into the happy beyond. To kill a man was not as great an injury as to leave his body unburied. To insure entrance into the future state of happiness, it was necessary that one's body should be buried, and that the deceased have the price of ferryage across the River Styx. The pious Greek always placed a piece of money in the mouth of his dead relative for that purpose. After their wars with the Persians, we find cremation introduced. They had met with many disastrous defeats in their conflicts with the nation to the west of them, and many times they were compelled to leave their dead in the hands of the enemy. The bare possibility of their not being buried forced them to the grim alternative of burning the bodies of their fallen companions on the battlefield.

The custom passed over to Rome, but that it was not originally the practice of the Romans to burn their dead is evidenced from one of the laws of the Twelve Tables, which forbade the burying of the dead within the city.

The people of India adopted cremation, no doubt, for the same reason as the Greeks. People always at war with each other, and strongly imbued with the belief in a future state of happiness, and the necessity of burial to attain it, were forced to adopt a mode of sepulture in keeping with their roving and adventurous social habits. But their methods of disposing of their dead, whether by inhumation or incineration, evinced their belief in the immortality of the soul, and the existence of a future state.

The revival of the practice of cremation dates from the French Revolution. The infidel philosophers of the last century found that the graveyard was, even more than the Church, a nursery of Christianity, and they invaded both, overturning monuments, breaking off crosses, and destroying all symbols of religion they found there. Since their day, crematories have been established in a few places in Germany, Italy and elsewhere; but we have more in the United States than in all the Christian world beside, owing to the presence of large bodies of German infidels, and their undying hatred of the Christian religion.

Men who write for encyclopedias are apt to follow received opinions without inquiring into their truth. From them we learn that cremation was universally practiced in India and northern Norway in early times. A visit to those countries will teach the contrary. Those ancient lands are filled with mausoleums, tombs, tumuli, and sepulchral mounds many dating back to ages beyond any historic record. Cremation was first a religious necessity. It then became a conceit of art, and in our day an infidel fad. The best physicians of the world have lately pronounced upon the hygienic reasons of cremation, and declared them childish. It is grand to behold a sacred ruin crumbling to decay, but only a vandal would profane it, either by artificial destruction or vulgar restoration. Dust we are, and unto dust we shall return, but let us leave the time and method to the Author of life and death.

THE RESURRECTION OF THE BODY

In the Apostles' Creed, which was the catechism or compendium of Christian doctrine in the days of the Apostles, we declare our faith in "the resurrection of the body." Man is made of soul and body and without either he would not be man. As men we live, and labor, and suffer, and merit; and as men shall we be rewarded in Heaven. The body's final home is not the graveyard, but Paradise. The body will be rewarded as well as the soul, and the delights of Heaven will be for both.

Hence our bodies are called, by St. Paul, temples of the Holy Ghost, and we purify them in baptism, and keep them clean, that they may be fit dwelling places of the Blessed Trinity. "If any one love Me," says our Lord, "My Father will love him, and We will come and take up Our abode with him."

The beauty of the material temples of the Church is but a faint type of the beauty of the souls of the saints. The body of a holy man or woman partakes of such holiness, and it should receive the respect that belongs to all holy things. The material view, that our bodies belong to the earth, and should be returned to their mother after death, as a clod of the valley, is based on the assumption that a man is all spirit, which would make the mystery of death not only a mystery, but a meaningless enigma. God will restore our bodies, those wondrous mechanisms which are almost spiritual in their subtlety, and will make us in Heaven all we were on earth, plus the attributes of the glorified body. To those chemists who would tell us that the resurrection is an absurdity and unintelligible to science, we can say that we know much more about the resurrection of the body than they do about chemistry, and can explain the identity of the risen body much better than they can the diversity of the parts of which it was composed.

MOURNING

We put on black for the adult dead, and white when children die. When the former are buried and bells are tolled; when the latter are brought to the church they ring out a merry peal. In the church, black is permitted at funerals everywhere, except on the altar. The mourning color of royalty is violet, and when services are held for the adult dead, the tabernacle of the King of Kings is decked in that color. On the coffins of children, the Church, in her ritual, commands that flowers be laid, to symbolize that the innocent dead are like flowers plucked from the garden of the Church, and made to bloom in Paradise. No flowers should be laid on the coffin of the adult; nothing but a cross, as rich as may be desired, but a cross, plain and prominent. Flowers on the graves of both young and old are not to be condemned, as they are quite consonant with Christian thought and feeling.

• • • • • •

The Diocese of Monterey-Los Angeles was considered by Rome to be a missionary area well into the 20th century. Little attention was given to funerals and cemeteries by bishops, especially those in the west, whose time and efforts were occupied almost entirely by looking after the living.

Though he probably would have preferred a uniform policy on cemeteries, Bishop Thomas J. Conaty was satisfied to utilize his predecessor's guidelines. Only once did he refer to the notion and that was in a letter written to the clergy in 1905, wherein he said that, in accordance with the teachings of the Baltimore Councils, "no funerals were to be held in houses, or in English, and funeral orations were discountenanced." He frowned on burying in consecrated ground

anyone who, by his life and the neglect of the sacraments, cut himself off from the body of the Church." Interestingly though, his own funeral "orations" were classic, easily the most eloquent of any of his contemporaries.

When Bishop John J. Cantwell came to California's southland, as Bishop of Monterey-Los Angeles in 1917, there were a few options for burials in Catholic cemeteries. With one exception, all the Church's burial plots were parochial. Only Calvary Cemetery in Los Angeles served the far-flung diocese. He pointed out that "the cemeteries in Chicago were further away from the vast majority of the Catholic people than Calvary cemetery is from the people of that city." He even urged that where priests do not have ready access to a Catholic cemetery, "they should make arrangements for the establishment of a cemetery in the immediate vicinity of their parish church." There is no evidence that any took his suggestions to heart.

In any event, on December 24, 1931, the bishop informed the clergy that the Church, ever concerned for the welfare of her children, "does not restrain her tender solicitude even when they have passed upon the tideless sea of eternity." Cantwell stressed that the Church "extends itself to the care of the body" as well as the soul. And he noted "it has ever been the mind and practice of the Church that those who belonged to her communion upon earth, who lived fortified by the graces of the sacraments, who prayed at her altars, should in the hour of death rest side by side in holy and consecrated places."

Cantwell explained that in conformance to the wishes of the Plenary Councils of Baltimore and the pioneer priests of the United States, bishops, even "in the days of extreme stress," should make provisions for the Christian interment of the faithful departed.

Observing that "we have in this diocese a number of parochial cemeteries" he went on to commend "the foresight of my lamented predecessors" that there was a cemetery worthy of this diocese.

He was speaking, of course, of historic Calvary Cemetery. He said "it behooves the pastors to see to it that the Catholic people are instructed in the traditions of their Church in the matter of Christian burial and that they be made to realize how much it means to have their bodies rest in a place visited by those who believe as they believed."

The bishop told his priests "it is an unheard thing in a Catholic community that a priest should assist at obsequies in a non-Catholic cemetery." He went on "to solemnly forbid any priest enjoying the faculties of the Diocese of Monterey-Los Angeles to officiate at a funeral in a non-Catholic cemetery." Though he remained open to special circumstances, he reserved permission to act otherwise to himself.

The bishop's regulations were incorporated in the statutes of the diocese that were released in December of 1927. He wanted crosses on all markers and all other non-Catholic insignias omitted. Repeated were Cantwell's earlier prohibitions, a ruling that was later included in the archdiocesan synod of 1942.

Actually, the mandate of using only Catholic cemeteries and not officiating at ceremonies in non-Catholic cemeteries was honored in the breach. If the bishop ever compared the number of reported deaths to the quantity of interments at Calvary and the few parochial cemeteries, he would have seen the inconsistency. One old-timer claimed "Cantwell was too clever to push us on that issue."

The annals record that only one priest, Father Alexander Bucci (1875-1959), openly defied Cantwell's prohibition about officiating in non-Catholic cemeteries. Bucci had been suspended for violating the Volsted Act and, in the mid-1930s, he began performing funerals and witnessing weddings at Forest Lawn Cemetery.

In May of 1935, Father Bucci gained national notoriety by offering Holy Mass in the "Wee Kirk o' the Heather" chapel at Forest Lawn for Trent Durkin, a popular teenage film star who had been killed in an auto crash. The Los Angeles *Examiner* featured a photograph of "Father A. Bucci, retired Catholic priest of Burbank" leading a procession of mourners to the grave.

Then, two months later, Bucci once again hit the headlines when the Los Angeles *Times* reported that he officiated at Forest Lawn for the funeral of Leland Deveraigne, known in Chicago's underworld as "Two Gun Louis" Alterie. "Two Gun" was killed when enemies fired twelve shotgun slugs into his body after he allegedly turned government informant on a bond case. Another story in the *Examiner* said that "Bucci, now resigned from an active pastorate, was a friend of Alterie." Bucci continued his unorthodox ministry until his own health began to fail. In his later years, he lived quietly in Burbank with a younger sister. He remained on close terms with Msgr. Martin Cody Keating and was reconciled to the Church prior to his death. He was the first priest interred in the "new" San Fernando Mission Cemetery in 1959.

Shortly thereafter, the bishop announced that daily Mass would be offered at All Souls' Chapel in Calvary Cemetery every Saturday morning for the eternal rest of those interred there. Four years later, he began the annual Memorial Day Mass at Calvary.

Upon his arrival in California's southland, Archbishop J. Francis A. McIntyre found that the Catholic cemeteries operated much differently than those in his native state. In addition to the legal differences growing out of California's "Corporation Sole" legislation, there was a tradition, dating from the Synod of 1927, which stipulated that "the remains of Catholics may not be interred in secular cemeteries." McIntyre always felt that rule was more restrictive than the *Code of Canon Law* that simply stated that "the bodies of the faithful must be buried in a cemetery… which has been blessed." An earlier canon stated that ecclesial burial consisted of being "interred in a place legitimately designated for the burial of the faithful departed." Though he realized the rationale behind the regulations, McIntyre was never comfortable with that stipulation though he was convinced by his advisors to leave it on the books. On more than one occasion, he said that "back in New York," a phrase which greatly irritated his priests, the practice was to bless the grave at the moment of interment, which allowed for being buried in non-Catholic cemeteries. Interestingly, McIntyre rarely wrote or spoke about cemeteries and when it became necessary to remind the clergy and others about archdiocesan regulations, he generally delegated that chore to the director of cemeteries.

Beyond personally re-drafting existing burial regulations and bookkeeping procedures at the various sites, McIntyre eventually centralized the whole operation by bringing the ledgers and day-to-day operation under the umbrella of the Chancery Office. Within the first year, the financial figures increased dramatically, much to the dismay of local administrators.

Included in the annual exhortation about burying Catholics in consecrated ground, McIntyre insisted that daily Mass be offered for the repose of those interred in Catholic cemeteries. Where possible, this was to be a public Mass to which the faithful were invited. Emphasis was always made that non-Catholic spouses were also welcomed in Catholic cemeteries. Annual Masses were scheduled on All Souls and Decoration Day, generally at an outside altar where greater crowds could gather. The following exhortation, written by McIntyre, was included with every letter on the subject:

Let us also surround the funeral of our beloved dead with the truly Catholic atmosphere of reality, of reverent prayer. How consoling it is to have the rosary recited together, with the body of our beloved present, before the altar of the parish church, the solemn ritual of the High Requiem Mass, all uniting to speed the departed soul to "the place of refreshment, light and peace" to live with God forever. Let us offer to the surviving family the comfort and strength of our religion by having Masses offered for the repose of the soul of the departed. Thus will our faith and our love follow after the soul who has gone to join its Creator, and will guard in the bosom of the Church, in "God's Acre", the mortal remains which await the Resurrection of the Last Day.

An interesting thing happened in mid-1956 when the Archdiocese of Los Angeles announced plans for a cemetery in La Puente. There were objections to the site by neighbors who argued that the cemetery would create traffic problems, create a danger of water pollution, create an eyesore to a nearby school, depreciate land values and injure the sale of better homes. Finally, after almost a year of controversy, the local supervisors agreed to the notion of a cemetery.

Partly due to that problem and others caused in adjoining areas, the Western Regional Conference of the American Society of Appraisers did a study and ultimately issued the following results on February 17, 1957:

Values are not adversely affected by the establishment of memorial parks, but on the contrary, they have been enhanced on the same ratio as have parcels of land removed from the cemetery zone of influence," reported Appraiser Herbert N. Bair. His report is based on a survey of 13 Los Angeles area memorial parks and property near them.

Mortgage bankers "do not consider cemeteries, churches, schools, airports and neighborhood shopping centers, *per se*, as detrimental factors, mortgage-risk wise," he reported.

McIntyre could never be accused of being a "canonist," a term which he abhorred. He was once heard to tell a friend that "the Vatican Council would never have been necessary had not canonists gotten us so embroiled in nitpicking." When, in mid-1961, the director of cemeteries took it upon himself to issue a new legalistic version of the directives for Catholic burial, the cardinal was not pleased. In those rules, it was said that the "honor of being buried in sacred ground may not be rejected at will without forfeiting all other rites and ceremonies provided by the solicitude of the Church for the repose of the deceased and the comfort of the family." Then, to make matters worse, it was stated "where permission is obtained for burial in a non-Catholic cemetery, neither the place of burial nor the Church where the funeral ceremonies are to be held may be published or announced."

Later that year, McIntyre attempted to clear the air by issuing one of his rare messages about Catholic burial to the priests, one which stressed the "pastoral" aspect of the matter. Vintage McIntyre, it bears repeating *in toto*.

We are all aware of the continuing efforts needed to provide the services of the Church to the ever-increasing number of the faithful of the archdiocese. Because of the mobility of population, it is difficult to establish long-time relationships with many parishioners who, nevertheless, need and are entitled to, counseling on the benefits available to them.

A particular problem in this regard has come to our attention. We note an increasing number of families who, at the time of a death, are confused because of lack of information and misinformation as to the suitableness and availability of interment under the aegis of the Church. Among other reasons, this is caused by our desire to limit our sphere to the Christian care of the dead and not to enter the business activity of advertising and home salesmanship. At the same time, we desire to offer every possible consideration to a bereaved family. Advantage is sometimes taken of these decisions and families ultimately suffer.

We would hope that if, from time to time, you could remind your families of the nature of cemeteries under the care of the Church and of their availability, some families might avoid mistakes through ignorance.

Cemeteries are located in several strategic areas in the archdiocese. They are the common resting place of those who in life openly professed their common faith. They are set aside by the Church with a special blessing for the care of the dead. Mass is offered each day for all interred therein. When they are finally closed to interments they will be cared for by the Church and not by an impersonal and inadequate business fund. Only in such sacred ground can the ritual of the Church be fully exercised.

The cardinal wanted Catholics to understand the true nature of a cemetery and why it was considered a holy place. He envisioned funerals as prayerful occurrences, surrounded with the beauties and comforts of the Church's liturgy. He was especially anxious that there by a rosary recited, preferably the night before and in the parochial church if that was feasible. He encouraged a friendly but business-like rapport with local morticians and urged periodic meetings with them to discuss the nature of Catholic burials.

As part of his annual report made during the clergy retreats at Saint John's Seminary, Camarillo, McIntyre kept the priests abreast of activities impacting the cemeteries. On one occasion, he pointed out that "with the increased population of Los Angeles, our cemeteries are responding accordingly." He reflected on problems that developed from time-to-time and urged priests "to consult the Cemetery Office when any unusual circumstance arises."

On July 18, 1962, the cardinal had an occasion to address the archdiocesan cemetery board. He reported that a recent audit reflected satisfactorily on operation, but pointed out that there were several features that did not meet "the increased requirements of our times and the efficient conduct of what has become a large business." In particular, he wanted accounting procedures tightened, monthly meetings held of the cemetery board, along with periodic reports for members. As was always the case when he became personally involved, McIntyre commended workers for their performance, but emphasized those areas where improvement was expected.

The cemeteries were one of the few financially lucrative operations of the archdiocese and their efficient management helped to make possible the growth of the school system, their major beneficiary. A typical operational report, dated April 1963, indicated some fascinating statistics.

In 1941, when Bishop Joseph T. McGucken became auxiliary, the then Father Timothy Manning was given care of Catholic cemeteries. In addition to parochial cemeteries in such places as Santa Barbara, Oxnard and San Gabriel, there were two archdiocesan cemeteries, Calvary and Holy Cross. Resident directors residing at both locations directed daily operations. Even after becoming auxiliary bishop, Manning retained his position as "director" of cemeteries until 1952. He enjoyed celebrating the liturgy in the beautiful and artistic Mausoleum chapel at Calvary that was designed by the same architect who worked on the chapel at Saint John's Seminary in Camarillo.

In the summer of 1970, Archbishop Manning wrote that:

Every church has a facility known as the *"sacrarium."* It is a disposal place into which is put the residue of holy things that have served their function. Sacred oils, the ashes of sacred objects that have been burned as required by ritual, the washings of sacred linens. The disposal empties directly into the earth and not into the common sewer. Such is the respect the Church has for material things that, when they have fulfilled their sacred purpose, they may not be profanely discarded, but reverently enfolded in the earth.

If this be the measure of respect for material objects, we can have some concept of the regard which the Church has for the human body when it becomes a corpse. In life, it was the envelope of the soul, anointed in baptism, a housing for the Eucharist, made sacred again in the oils of Confirmation, hallowed in suffering and pain. It lays down life in the hope of rising again in the same, but glorified flesh. For all these reasons the Church will not allow a profane discarding of human remains. She reverently incenses them, sprinkles them with holy water, blesses the earth in which they will lie and stands watch over their holy ashes, until doomsday and the resurrection from the dead.

A few months later, Manning observed that "the liturgy speaks of a place of light, happiness and peace, which we wish for those who have gone before us marked with the sign of faith. Our Catholic cemeteries are in a way sacramental signs of that eternal blessedness. There is an abiding quality of repose and peace which descends over these holy acres. It is a wholesome thing for us to visit them, and there, in a communion of Saints to pray for those from whom we are separated for a while." Then Manning suggested that the Catholic cemetery "offers us graphic evidence that the ultimate goal of our earthly lives is to prepare ourselves to go home to God." It is "a reliquary of the saints, just as surely as the catacombs were in the earliest centuries of the Church. Already in the next world, those buried there have left us something of themselves aside from their memory, love and prayers." He concluded by saying that a Catholic cemetery is "first and last and always a blessed sanctuary wherein rest the faithful, awaiting the fullness of Christ's redemptive action, on the day of our resurrection unto life eternal."

The question of allowing cremation for Catholics finally was addressed in 1972. Manning remained personally opposed to the practice, but he did notify his priests that exceptions to the general practice would now be permitted. In issuing this directive, he said that "it is not recommended that this be given any general publication, but merely be available for pastoral counseling individual cases."

1. The practice of burying the bodies of the faithful is by all means to be kept; hence Ordinaries should, by appropriate instructions and exhortations, see to it that Catholics do not practice cremation and that, except in cases of necessity, they do not abandon the practice of burial, which the Church has always kept and which she consecrates with solemn rites.

2. However, lest difficulties arising from present circumstances be unduly increased, and lest the necessity of dispensing from existing laws in this matter become more frequent, it has been wisely determined to mitigate somewhat the prescriptions of canon law concerning cremation, so that the provisions of canon 1203 2 - (prohibiting cremation) and those of canon 1240 1, 5 - (denying ecclesiastical burial to persons who ordered that their bodies be cremated) be henceforth binding, not universally, but only when it is certain that cremation was chosen because of the denial of Christian dogmas, or because of a sectarian spirit, or through hatred of the Catholic religion and the Church.

3. It follows that persons who chose to have their bodies cremated are not for that reason to be denied the sacraments or public suffrages, unless it is certain that they made that choice for the above-mentioned reasons inimical to the Christian way of life.

In 1983, Manning once again wrote the priests, reminding them that the archdiocese "maintains cemeteries with a great deal of pride, effort and expense, so that there may be places of faith, hope and love for both the living and the dead." He worried that "many of our Catholic people do not seem to be fully aware of the importance of the Catholic cemetery in their life of faith."

November, the month dedicated to the Holy Souls, gives us a perfect opportunity to remind our people that the blessed end of the earthly life of the faithful Christian resides within the Catholic Cemeteries. May we ask your support through preaching, announcements and education on the value and the necessity of burial in our Catholic Cemeteries?

The cardinal emphasized that "for many of us, as well as our people, these thoughts carry us to our own cemeteries where our dead have found their final resting place. These holy places give hope and inspiration for us pilgrims on our journey to be with our Heavenly Father."

In 1975, Cardinal Manning issued new guidelines for burials that reflected advances made in the field of ecumenism:

Non-Catholics in Catholic Cemeteries:
The Catholic cemeteries in the Archdiocese of Los Angeles are available for burial to those not of the Roman Catholic religion, such as parties to a mixed marriage and close relatives. In such cases, clergymen of other religions may conduct graveside services.

Catholics in Other than Catholic Cemeteries:
The most recent synodal decrees for the Archdiocese of Los Angeles direct that "the bodies of the faithful must not be buried in secular cemeteries." Only for compelling circumstances, and with specific permission of the archbishop or his delegate, are priests allowed to perform graveside services in other than Catholic cemeteries. Exceptions are made for veterans wishing to be interred in a National Cemetery or converts utilizing property acquired before the profession of the Catholic Faith.

Burial Services in Other Christian Traditions:
When requested by the family, priests may officiate at the funeral services of other traditions in funeral homes and at the graveside. By the same token, they may, if invited, participate in the funeral services conducted by the decedent's minister. Whenever a priest officiates at or takes part in such a funeral, he should use prayers and Bible readings suitable for the occasion. Priests may not officiate at church funerals of other communions but, when asked by the family and the resident pastor, they may be present in the sanctuary or chancel to offer prayers and expressions of sympathy.

In recent years, there has been some criticism about a policy inaugurated during the later days of the Manning regime whereby parcels of undeveloped archdiocesan cemetery properties were sold, apparently in disregard of future needs.

The evolution of that policy can be traced to the early 1960s when the whole notion of burial plots was being reviewed. The argument was that much of the area in the earlier forecasts would be wasted in walks, copings and fencing.

In addition to the traditional mausoleums, there came about garden crypts that were erected without the expense of constructing enclosed chapels, decorative art and inner hallways and vistas.

Then came a novel method of interment known as "multiple depth" which was widely considered a better and more effective use of land. With new mechanical digging devices, it became possible and legal to install lawn vaults up to six deep for what effectively results in an underground mausoleum.

With these new advances, prognosticators opined that the need for future expansion of cemeteries would not be necessary. Whether that was a wise decision or not is open to question, but it was developed on a reasonable premise.

The question of cremation came up in 1963 and Church officials continued to "prefer" burial over cremation. At that time, cremains were not allowed to be present during the funeral Mass. In 1997, the Vatican gave the bishops of the United States permission to allow the celebration of the obsequies with the cremains present. The Church continued to encourage that the actual cremation take place after the full funeral liturgy. Prohibition of scattering the ashes remained in place.

With the exception of Good Shepherd Cemetery in Lancaster and the Mausoleum in the new Cathedral of Our Lady of the Angels, no other burial facilities have been inaugurated during the tenure of Roger Cardinal Mahony. Each of the existing facilities was expanded and during the early years of the 21st century, their overall *raison d'etre* was revised and updated as follows:

MISSION STATEMENT

We provide well cared for sacred places for Christian burial, with all attendant rites of the Church, to Catholics and members of their families.

VALUE STATEMENT

We proclaim through our ministry:

- the virtue of hope through a belief in the resurrection of the dead
- the sacredness of the human body and
- our dedication to strengthening faith in the Church as family

Near the end of the century, the National Catholic Cemetery Conference issued a publication entitled *The Catholic Cemetery. A Vision for the Millennium.* Among the many suggestions was one encouraging Catholic cemeteries to "consider operating their own funeral homes" as had been done successfully in the Archdiocese of Denver.

The Catholic Cemeteries in the Archdiocese of Los Angeles and Stewart Enterprises, one of the nation's leading providers of mortuary services, then began finalizing plans for Stewart to construct and operate mortuaries on land leased from the various cemeteries in the archdiocese. The first one to open was All Souls' Mortuary in Long Beach that began as a fully licensed, for-profit facility governed by the applicable laws of the State of California.

Msgr. Terrance Fleming, Vicar General for the archdiocese, said that "Catholic cemeteries embarked on this project to expand and enhance the Church's ministry to bereaved Catholic families." He said that "offering mortuary services that fully comply with Catholic traditions would enable them to more fully serve the Catholic community."

Initially, plans were announced to locate Catholic mortuaries at Holy Cross Cemetery in Culver City, Calvary Cemetery in Los Angeles, Queen of Heaven Cemetery in Rowland Heights and San Fernando Mission Cemetery in Mission Hills.

Again, it was noted that "this program marks the beginning of a new era in providing Catholic families throughout the Archdiocese of Los Angeles with the very best and most convenient services and facilities during their time of bereavement."

As the new program was launched, Roger Cardinal Mahony issued a statement which read as follows:

Our Catholic Cemeteries are an extension of our church community. They are a unique and sacred testament to our belief in the resurrection of the body. They are holy places where we give witness to the communion of Saints and draw strength from our faith during times of great need. By making important decisions beforehand, you can greatly ease the burden you and your family must endure at the time of death of a loved one.

I urge you to consider preparing in advance of such need by sharing in the information and services available through our Catholic Cemeteries and the Catholic Mortuaries.

1885 ONWARD

SANTA CLARA CEMETERY OXNARD

El Rio was a settlement near the center of the Ventura Valley. Located at a fording place on the east side of the Santa Clara River, the town was initially looked after spiritually by priests attached to San Buenaventura Mission. About once a month, Mass would be offered, confessions heard and the other sacraments administered.

Father Cyprian Rubio was a frequent visitor to El Rio, which was renamed New Jerusalem about 1876, reportedly by one of the local merchants, Simon Cohn. Rubio, a colorful man, was the last of the Castilian pioneers in Southern California and one known for his "active

interest in progressive measures" that affected his people. Rubio remained at the Old Mission until poor health brought about his retirement in 1895.

One of Rubio's predecessors, Father Juan Comapla, had overseen the erection of a church in 1877. Rubio was assiduous in outfitting the small edifice and it was he who asked Bishop Francis Mora to appoint a canonical pastor in the person of Father Juan Pujol. In 1885, Bishop Mora entered into an agreement with Max Geisler for a thirty-acre parcel of land from the old *Rancho El Rio de Santa Clara* which he designated as a burial ground for local Catholics. The deed was signed on April 20th.

The initial interment at the El Rio Cemetery, as it was originally known, was that of Kate Donlon, the first wife of Irish-born John Donlon, who farmed 400 acres of choice land just outside the town of El Rio. That interment took place on January 17, 1885.

From the outset, the cemetery was parochial and when the seat of the parish was moved to Oxnard in 1901, El Rio Cemetery retained its adherence to Santa Clara parish which was advertised as being in the "Biggest Little City on the Coast."

During the last years of Father John Laubacher's pastorate at Santa Clara Parish in Oxnard, a mausoleum was erected on the cemetery grounds at El Rio. When the subscribers defaulted in covering the cost of that edifice, Father Laubacher agreed that the parish would purchase half of the vaults. The mausoleum was dedicated on June 6, 1919, by Archbishop Edward J. Hanna of San Francisco. Ironically, the first interment in the mausoleum was that of Father Laubacher who had died from the flu epidemic the previous November 5th.

In his homily, the archbishop reminded those present that burial in such places as the newly blessed mausoleum accorded with the practice of Christians from the earliest times whose reverence for the bodies of their dead was but a natural consequence of their belief in the high dignity conferred upon the body in life and its sublime destiny after the resurrection. The prelate said also that "such an occasion recalled the consoling Christian teaching that the dead will one day rise" and it "is still in our power to assist those gone before us by our prayer." After Mass, a procession of the clergy made its way to the temporary vault where Father Laubacher's remains had rested since his death. His body was borne to a crypt in the new mausoleum where the archbishop gave the absolution.

The mausoleum, standing at the north end of the cemetery, contains 360 crypts. It was erected at a cost of $85,000. Ultimately the mausoleum debt was liquidated by James T. O'Connor.

In his end-of-the-year Annual Report for 1920 to parishioners, Father John J. Clifford had this to say:

> The mausoleum in the cemetery at El Rio is now completed. My beloved predecessor purchased one-half of the crypts at the cost of $30,000, with the expectation of selling them to members of the parish. Father Laubacher had planned to dispose of the crypts at an increased price, and to use the funds that remained over and above the amount that he paid to the builders, for the care of the cemetery and mausoleum. I intend, as far as it lies in my power, to carry out his plans. It will not be possible even to attempt at carrying out these plans unless the crypts are purchased. The present indebtedness resting on the cemetery makes the actual

carrying out of the present plans impossible. This indebtedness now amounts to $29,552.00.

> The plan, aimed at keeping El Rio cemetery a decent place for interment of our beloved dead, consists chiefly of placing the entire cemetery under *perpetual care*. To do this, there is need of installing a *water plant*; there is also need of keeping a man constantly employed in caring for the plots and graves. As you are aware, these aims require funds and the only means of securing the necessary funds is by selling the crypts. It is to the best interests of those who have already bought crypts to approach people over whom they have any influence and succeed in having them purchase one or more crypts. I would suggest to those who own crypts, that they appoint themselves a committee of one to secure another purchaser and, in this way, it will be easily possible to get the necessary funds for the complete care of the cemetery.

In 1963, it was announced that a new mausoleum unit would be built at what has become Santa Clara Cemetery. Erected in a classic style of reinforced concrete trimmed in emerald pearl granite, it contained another 360 crypts. The edifice was blessed the following year by James Francis Cardinal McIntyre. During the early months of 1964, the parochial cemetery became archdiocesan thus allowing families in the rest of Ventura County to utilize its facilities.

(NEW) CALVARY CEMETERY
LOS ANGELES

Bishop Francis Mora's selection of a new site for the Catholic cemetery in Los Angeles was hailed "as one of the last of the many monuments which attest his untiring zeal in a long and laborious episcopate." Fortunately, after the land boom of the 1880s, the bishop had purchased a fifty-two acre tract of land on the eastern edge of Los Angeles. In September of 1895, Mora went before the City Council to announce that "realizing the growth of the city, taking into account general sanitary conditions and desiring to meet the necessities of a

large congregation" he had determined "to close as early as possible the old cemetery grounds situated on Buenavista Street." And he told the council members that the Church was anxious to see its already acquired property authorized for burial purposes.

The Boyle Heights site was approved by the Board of Health but because of the pressures from the powerful American Protective Association, Bishop Mora soon announced that the diocese had exchanged the Colgrove property for acreage further out of town and would "establish New Calvary Cemetery beyond the city limits" on Stephenson Avenue "only a half mile beyond the Odd Fellows' Cemetery, on a direct line to Whittier."

Considerable planning was involved in the new site and many of the remains from the old graveyard were transferred. Minute regulations were issued for the first of Los Angeles' planned memorial parks. Among other requirements, there was to be "no woodwork of any kind around the graves, such as fences, cribs or other contrivances of the kind ... excepting a temporary small cross of wood marking the head and foot of each grave." Those charged with laying out the new area noted that "nothing in the way of general ornamentation of a cemetery excels the lawn or grass plot."

In his address at the dedication of Calvary Cemetery, Bishop Francis Mora said that "the bodies of our deceased must not be treated lightly or disregarded, particularly the bodies of the faithful or of virtuous people; for these bodies were used by their souls in a holy manner as instruments and agents for the performance of all their good works."

One of Mora's earliest decisions was to locate a memorial to those moved from Old Calvary at the North end of the new burial grounds. An appropriate plaque there attests to that factor.

Containing 136 acres of gently rolling land, with more than five miles of paved roads, Calvary Cemetery became what was then among the first of the southland's beautifully landscaped parks. An early descriptive account said:

> The gentle slopes of Calvary are dotted with the monuments of the first families of Los Angeles. Here are to be seen memorials to the names that live in the record of achievement and on the roll of honor of our community. Calvary is the resting place of those pioneers who succeeded the Mission friars in laying the foundation of a great metropolis. Reading the names inscribed here, the Catholic heart swells with pride in the realization that to our forebears in the Faith belongs the aristocracy of honor. A certain consolation comes with the thought that one day we will be laid side by side with those whose memory is in veneration and to whom we are united in one Catholic family by the Communion of Saints.

Anxious to avoid the criticism associated with Old Calvary, the bishop was one of the first to call for a "perpetual care" arrangement that would insure the beauty of the new cemetery. Here is how it was described by an early commentator:

The care which is now evidenced in the well-kept condition of Calvary was guaranteed in perpetuity. Perpetual care at Calvary is not to be measured by a mere fund of money. Its guarantee is backed by a really perpetual organization—the Catholic Church. The Roman Catholic Bishop of Los Angeles, a Corporation Sole recognized by the State of California, is responsible for the Perpetual Care of Calvary. The Church is the oldest organization in the State of California. It will be when all other existing organizations have ceased to be, for it is built upon the Rock of Peter. Our more than adequate perpetual Care fund is therefore in the custody of an organization of unquestionable integrity and endurance. Calvary is not operated for the profit of stockholders or any other individuals whatsoever. The Church is the sole recipient and custodian of the funds it produces.

In December of 1962, Bishop Mora's remains were returned from Spain to Los Angeles where they reposed in the Episcopal Vault of Calvary Mausoleum until the summer of 2002 when they were removed to the crypt of the Cathedral of Our Lady of the Angels.

1930 ONWARD

CALVARY MAUSOLEUM LOS ANGELES

There were many devotional and picturesque additions made to the cemetery over the years since its inception, the first of which was All Souls Chapel erected in 1906. Later, the outside Stations of the Cross, a replica of the Pieta and numerous shrines were added and, finally, in the late 1920s, plans were announced for a magnificent mausoleum.

It was decided that the architectural plan would follow closely the Catholic tradition and be designed in a Christian style of architecture, rather than the classical tradition to which most of the diocesan mausoleums in the United States adhered. The mausoleum of Theodoric, the Ravenna Baptistry, the mausoleum of Galla Placidia, and the Roman tomb of Santa Constanza, offered the inspiration for the architectural conception of the Calvary Mausoleum.

The first building, of fireproof and earthquake-proof reinforced concrete, marble, and bronze, was completed in 1930, and dedicated by Archbishop John J. Cantwell on Memorial Day of that year. It contained 1,262 crypts, seventeen family sections and eighteen private rooms. It embodied every modern appointment, and is so built as to assure a waterproof and lasting final resting place. Located on the highest hill in Calvary Cemetery, the mausoleum is 240 feet long, 56 feet wide and three stories high. In 1934 and 1935, a second unit of one thousand crypts was added to the mausoleum. Two hundred and fifty crypts were intended for children and seven hundred and fifty for adults. On May 30, 1936, the archbishop dedicated a new chapel in the Mausoleum.

The altar is authentic in its liturgical arrangement and appointments, thereby conforming to the contemporary ceremonials required by the Church. A Calvary group with the Blessed Mother on one side of Our Crucified Saviour, and the beloved disciple St. John on the other, forms the culminating feature of the reredos.

In the niches on the left side of the reredos, are statues representing St. Matthew and St. Mark, and on the right side, St. Luke and St. John.

The symbols of the Evangelists are incised in stone over their respective niches, adding to the ornamental embellishment of the *reredos* as a whole.

Within the chapel is a crypt, intended for the deceased prelates of the diocese. The first bishop interred in the Episcopal vault was the Right Reverend Thomas J. Conaty on July 18, 1936. His remains had been in a receiving vault since 1915. The beautiful room, on the Gospel side of the main chapel, is a simple yet lovely marble altar where Masses are offered periodically for deceased bishops. A gorgeous art glass window, imported from Munich, depicting Christ the King, fills the area with its painted light.

A contemporary brochure referred to the mausoleum in these words:

> Calvary Mausoleum is an everlasting shrine surrounded by well-kept lawns and parks. Calvary combines three things - the Catholic faith, art and science. The Faithful departed lie so sacredly close to the Catholic heart that for them we seek the help of religion, the beauty of art and the safety of modern science. This noble edifice is as enduring as any work of man can be, constructed as it is of the most permanent of materials - steel, bronze, marble and reinforced concrete.
>
> Recently erected, it is lovely to look upon, yet a century from now, when its walls shall be covered by ancient vines and it shall be shaded by giant trees, time will have but enhanced its charm. Its walls are massive beyond the strictest requirements of earthquake engineering, and are solidly braced by the honeycomb of reinforced crypts. Like the pyramids, it has been constructed to remain as a monument to the ages. Our children's children shall

see in it the respect we have for those "whom we have loved and lost awhile." It shall inspire them as we have been inspired by the monuments of antiquity. Science and engineering have made it more strongly built than the tombs of the ancients that have endured through the centuries.

The mausoleum is a dry, permanent and respectful method of entombment. The interior is as sweet and wholesome as any home for the living. Within its consecrated walls our loved ones may await the general resurrection. Not only is mausoleum entombment an ideal modern method of laying the dead to rest, it is traditional for Catholics. Christ Himself was entombed in the stone sepulchre of Joseph of Arimathea. The catacombs, which were the first Catholic cemeteries, were mausoleums. The mausoleum in some form has been adopted by all peoples at the period of their highest development.

A new mausoleum unit was added after World War II to what was already hailed as "one of the most beautiful buildings of its type in the country."The new edifice made an additional 2,187 crypts available. Decorative scheme of the new building followed that of the Roman Catacombs used in the original. Another wing came in 1957, with a further 3,300 crypts.

Over subsequent years, a Guadalupe Mosaic was installed on the cemetery grounds and, in 1988, a new office building on Whittier Boulevard replaced the one destroyed earlier by earthquake. In 1994, a bronze plaque honoring Pope John Paul II's visit in 1987 was dedicated. The large cross at the northwest corner of the cemetery was originally used at the Dodger's Stadium for the visit of Pope John Paul II in 1987.

1896 ONWARD

CALVARY CEMETERY
SANTA BARBARA

The *Santa Barbara Weekly Herald* told its readers on July 31,1896 that "a new Roman Catholic Cemetery was being laid out near the Hope schoolhouse." Located on a ten-acre plot of ground and consisting of beautifully wooded land and enclosed behind an attractive stone wall, it was to succeed the burial plot near Hollister and Modoc roads that had belonged to the Thomas Hope Estate. First interment at Calvary Cemetery was John Charles Kays who was buried on September 3,1896 by the legendary Father Polydore Stockman, pastor at Our Lady of Sorrows parish.

Interestingly another newspaper report, this one on Memorial Day of 1897, explained the dedication of the twelve-foot monument to the soldiers buried at the cemetery. Readers were told that "the ceremonies were impressive, the music was excellent, the cannon worked like a marvel and was heard at the Montecito cemetery." There was a procession from the old cemetery to the new one.

Calvary Cemetery was described at length by a journalist in February of 1900:

> The Catholic Cemetery, situated three miles from the Courthouse, near Hollister Avenue, is, although far from completed, worth a careful visit...

It is beautifully laid out, with broad avenues that sweep in graceful curves around and through the grounds. Italian cypress in their slender but tall form, point out to the visitor the main and longest avenue; a species of eucalyptus graces the border of another, and *casuarinas* outline the last avenue, which, semicircular in form, rests upon Cypress Avenue as a base, and points out in bold relief the culminating point of landscape, the block on which stands the imposing chapel.

Calla lilies and white roses in great abundance and of endless variety line the different avenues on either side, and form with the fore-mentioned trees and the undulating surface of the ground a panorama most pleasing to behold.

When one enters the cemetery, a mere glance will suffice to impress the visitor with the religious character of the plan for this city of the dead… He is struck with the imposing life-sized angel standing on a pedestal of stone dominating the highest ground nearby… Saint Gabriel pointing with one finger to heaven…

He spies to the left and evacuation… The section will tell the visitor that here is to be constructed the house of Nazareth. He may show, if he is asked, the group of statues that will be placed in the house representing the death of St. Joseph.

To the right on another eminence, a dainty Gothic chapel looms up from among the shrubbery, not unlike a dais, with a canopy supported by four equal columns that shelters from the rain and storms a huge crucifix.

We have come now to the place where the main avenue branches off nearly at right angles. We follow the avenue leading to the left and we come immediately in front of a group of figures in high relief… We come to the first station of the 14 stations of the Cross placed at regular intervals around the main drive…

Our attention is naturally attracted to the open chapel not far from the last station. It is a graceful building of a severe Grecian style, with massive columns and a stone altar, well carved, surmounted by what is known as a calvary of three statues, a crucifix, the Virgin and St. John.

Back of the chapel, a semicircle of bamboo and silver cypresses form a pleasing background to the chapel when viewed in front…

From the chapel, we descend by the right to the tomb of Our Lord …The whole is built of rocks, with a concrete roof. We come to the iron door by a short, narrow lane, closed in by two walls of stone… The visitor enters the Angel's Chapel, the walls of which serve as vaults, and can accommodate 16 bodies.

Directly in front, a low entrance with a huge rolling stone, not unlike a millstone, brings us onto the main tomb…

A mausoleum was erected in the western portion of the cemetery with four tiers of niches containing twenty-five vaults to accommodate the remains of 200 people. Today, there are still places available in the garden type facilities for those wishing to be buried above the ground.

In 1912, most of those interred in the old cemetery on Modoc Road were transferred to Calvary Cemetery. Promotional literature proclaims that even today "Calvary is park-like in its setting. Inside the trumpet-vine lined fence screening Hope Avenue, there's a tranquil serenity, with mountains capped by 3,900 foot La Cumbre Peak rise above."

When the centennial of Calvary was observed in 1996, the local regional bishop noted that the "cemetery will continue to be a place of devotion and of reverence. Its presence in our midst will be a constant reminder of our belief in the resurrection of the dead."

1904 ONWARD

HOLY CROSS CEMETERY
POMONA

In 1904, Father Joseph Nunan, pastor at Saint Joseph parish, acting upon the advice of his city officials, decided that the old Palomares Cemetery was inadequate for a town that even then was experiencing growing pains. He gave the option that anyone buried in the earlier cemetery could be moved to what he christened as Holy Cross Cemetery which became available for people living as far away as Claremont, La Verne, Azusa, La Puente, Covina, Ontario, Upland and Cucamonga. Along those moved was Dolores Garrion who had been buried at Palomares in April of 1886.

A number of significant changes were made after World War II. The careful planting of trees and shrubs added a note of beauty to the area. Acquisition of modern machinery further facilitated the efficient operation of the cemetery. New macadam roads were installed throughout and the widening of the road to a circle at the center of the property lent itself to the erection of an impressive Calvary Memorial to the Catholic war dead. It was dedicated on Memorial Day in 1946.

The rock work, done by a noted stone mason, embodies multi-colored stones from nearby San Antonio Canyon. At the base of the crucifix is a regular-sized altar where Holy Mass is offered occasionally. Additional property was acquired over the years to accommodate the ever-growing population of the area.

HOLY CROSS CEMETERY
CULVER CITY

Shortly after the elevation of Los Angeles to the ecclesial status of a Metropolitan District, Msgr. Joseph T. McGucken urged that consideration be given for a new cemetery for the southland's Catholics on the western side of the city. A choice parcel of property was acquired to the north of Slauson Avenue, about a mile and a half west of La Brea Avenue, across the street from what was then the Fox Hills Country Club.

The original forty acres were laid out in roads and landscaping as one of the first of the nation's memorial parks. In this configuration, there were to be no standing memorials, only flat markers. The acreage developed was part of a 180-acre tract of a beautifully rolling plain. The contour of the grounds proved ideal for a cemetery. The site was equipped with an excellent drainage system and abundant well water. According to an early brochure, "The landscaping is carried out in

accordance with the most modern trends in memorial park developments."

Archbishop John J. Cantwell dedicated Holy Cross Cemetery in colorful ceremonies on the afternoon of Memorial Day, 1939. The main speaker for the occasion opined that "today's services mark one of the highlights of a long and eventful archiepiscopate." He also foresaw that a massive mausoleum would eventually be erected at the site.

Over the subsequent years, several areas of the cemetery were further developed with statues to Saint Joseph and other popular saints, many of them ethnic. The most noteworthy and attractive feature was the Lourdes Grotto, installed after World War II, by Ryozo Fuso Kado. So majestic was that shrine, on a barren hill overlooking the cemetery, that it was described by the *Saturday Evening Post*, as "an eye-filling spread of gardens surrounded by a massive 400-foot rock wall out of which arises a thirty-foot-high grotto."

HOLY CROSS MAUSOLEUM
CULVER CITY

Surely the most ambitious innovations at Holy Cross was the new mausoleum which one newspaper called a "majestic edifice" and another described as "truly imposing." Constructed of reinforced concrete and dominating a hilltop overlooking the Pacific Ocean, the facility provided, in its initial unit, 6,500 crypts. The mausoleum was the dream of Msgr. Edward Wade, who served for many years as director of Catholic cemeteries. Following the dedicatory ceremonies on April 8, 1961, James Francis Cardinal McIntyre presided at a Solemn High Mass in what was known as "The Sanctuary of the Risen Savior." Bishop

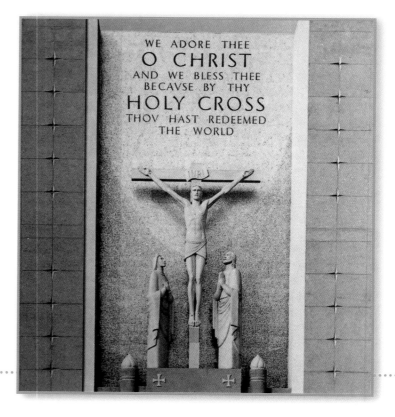

WE ADORE THEE
O CHRIST
AND WE BLESS THEE
BECAVSE BY THY
HOLY CROSS
THOV HAST REDEEMED
THE WORLD

Timothy Manning preached a homily in which he proclaimed "this new building stands here in massive assertion of our holy and consoling faith." Rooted in the Christian tradition of the catacombs, "the existence of this mausoleum will be proof of the pledge and the promise" of what the Church is all about.

Among the many features of the blue and white mausoleum was providing a place for daily Mass. In addition to a scheduled liturgy, the ornate chapel also provided a place for the funerals of those wishing to utilize that service.

In 1988, the artist Isabel Piczek, was engaged to paint a huge mural of the Resurrection on a 1,300 square foot wall immediately behind the altar. The sketches, original-size drawings and actual painting process were a gigantic task that occupied her time for over twenty-eight months. Roger Cardinal Mahony observed that the artist had captured "in these splendid mural paintings the totality of our belief and understanding of the Resurrection of Jesus Christ." He hoped that those who viewed the mural would "find new hope and joy for their lives in a world which is too often cynical and unbelieving."

On February 27,1994, Cardinal Mahony dedicated a second chapel, this one named for the Holy Redeemer and an adjoining garden mausoleum. In his homily, the cardinal noted "the chapels here, the wonderful statuary and the beautiful paintings are all reminders to us of the vision of Christ who suffered, was crucified and then rose from the dead." The new chapel had its own treasury of lovely artifacts, including a carrera marble statue of Saint Anthony and the Blessed Mother with Child. Probably the most ornate item was the chapel's main glass entrance consisting of twelve panels, thirty-two feet high, constructed of leaded hand-blown antique glass, depicting a crowned cross and heralding angels.

1950 ONWARD

ALL SOULS' CEMETERY
LONG BEACH

In a letter to the priests of the Archdiocese of Los Angeles, dated October 2,1950, Archbishop J. Francis A. McIntyre said that two years earlier he had acquired property, a tract of land on Cherry Avenue, in Long Beach that was being developed to serve as All Souls' Cemetery. He pointed out that the new cemetery would serve the areas of Long Beach, San Pedro, Wilmington, Artesia, Compton, Lynwood, Paramount and Huntington Beach.

An ad placed in the local newspapers described the new cemetery property as "one of the most modern developments in America." It was located on twenty-five acres of a 150-acre parcel that would provide ample future expansion.

Opened in June of 1950, All Souls' Cemetery was dedicated on October 15th by Archbishop McIntyre and numerous other civic and ecclesial dignitaries. Msgr. Bernard Dolan, the homilist, said "Our bodies are laid to rest in blessed ground, not with the harsh finality of pagan disbelief, but with the shining hope of a glorious resurrection." The first unit of the new garden mausoleum complex was made of reinforced concrete and had a height equal to that of five crypts. The

overall structure was a perimeter type and had the advantage of compactness of arrangement combined with ample room for access and for artistic adornment. An article in *The Tidings* said "the new property will signify the eternal solicitude of the Holy Mother Church for her departed children."

In his address for the occasion, the archbishop reminded listeners that "next to the Church, the tabernacle of the living God, is the Catholic cemetery." He went on to say:

The Catholic Cemetery, the last resting place of our beloved departed, is sacred and holy ground. Our loved ones are not forever lost to us. In tender memories, with faith and love, they are enshrined in our hearts. Dear to our hearts is their tomb, blessed and dedicated by Mother Church, where they await the promised joys of Resurrection.

From the moment of our birth until God calls us to our eternal reward, the Church, like a loving mother, watches over us, strengthening our faith and our devotion, leading us to God, the while invoking the intercession of our Blessed Mother and the saints.

To the Church, our bodies are sacred things. At Baptism and Confirmation, they are anointed with holy chrism. In Holy Communion our hearts are the repositories of the Holy Eucharist, "the compendium of all miracles." At Confirmation, the Divine Paraclete comes to us, and our bodies become the temples of the Holy Ghost. In Matrimony, God's church endows the union of man and woman with the dignity and indissolubility of a sacrament. The efficacy of Extreme Unction prepares the soul for its entrance to glory and frequently eases the pain-racked body. Thus the Divinely instituted ministrations of Mother Church attend us from birth to death.

Would it not be strange if the Church ceased to be solicitous when the soul departs and the body returns to the dust from whence it came? The Body of our Redeemer was tenderly anointed after death and placed in a tomb. Ever since the Church has been unfailing in her practice giving due respect for her deceased members. Protected by the sacred canons and by secular legislation, the Catholic Cemetery bespeaks in its very name and in the very fact of its being, the beauty and strength of the Faith by which we live and in which we hope. Even our memorials in stone and metal are prayerful reminders that the Church Militant on earth, the Church Suffering in purgatory and the Church Triumphant in heaven are one and indissoluble in the Communion of Saints.

In holy faith and good works, in the daily memento of the Mass, in the traditional devotion of our Church, in the prayers and indulgences that rise like incense from the blessed graveside, we can truly say *"non omnis moriar"*—I shall not wholly die. Our bodies are laid to rest in blessed ground—in God's Acre, not with the harsh finality of pagan disbelief, but with the shining hope of a glorious Resurrection.

A year later, a reporter told the people of Long Beach that All Souls' was "fast becoming one of the most beautiful and modern cemeteries" in the southland. Two years later, a statue of Our Lady of Peace was dedicated in memory of America's war dead. Members of all the armed services attended the opening ceremony of dedication. Among the other shrines erected over the subsequent years is one honoring the Holy Family.

Bishop Carl Fisher blessed a 30-foot high marble outdoor altar at All Souls' cemetery on Memorial Day of 1990 and then offered Holy Mass at the newly developed ten acre site at the cemetery's north-end section. Bishop Fisher said that "our gathering here this morning is a sign of our belief in the words of Jesus Christ that new life for our loved ones has sprung forth." He went on to affirm "it is our belief in the resurrection from the dead that compels us to gather and pray to God." He concluded by saying "this cemetery, so alive and so green, serves as a fitting testimony that our loved ones are alive and living in eternity."

1952 ONWARD

RESURRECTION CEMETERY
MONTEBELLO

In 1949, plans were formulated to open a new cemetery, named for the Resurrection of the Lord, which would be located at the corner of Arroyo and Potrero Grande Drive in the Potrero Heights district, on property formerly owned by Henry H. Wheeler. The declaration of intent was recorded at the Los Angeles County Recorder's Office on September 16, 1949.

Three years later, Archbishop J. Francis A. McIntyre announced that "the needs of the San Gabriel Valley and surrounding communities for a cemetery has long been felt." Designed to serve the areas of Pasadena, Arcadia, Monrovia, San Gabriel, Whittier and South Gate, the archbishop invited interested Catholics to attend the official blessing which took place on Sunday, the 30th of November, 1952.

Following the dedicatory Mass, the raising of the flag, appropriate addresses and Benediction of the Blessed Sacrament, the new Resurrection Cemetery was formally opened. Over the ensuing years, various embellishments were added. On September 30, 1999, a massive new mausoleum was blessed for the Montebello cemetery.

1961 ONWARD

QUEEN OF HEAVEN CEMETERY
ROWLAND HEIGHTS

A memorandum in the archdiocesan archives attests that on July 5, 1956, James Cardinal McIntyre approved the title Queen of Heaven for the proposed cemetery to be located on property in La Puente. As was often the case, there was some initial opposition from local residents for the envisioned 280-acre site at the southwest intersection of Fullerton Road and Fifth Avenue. The County Board of Supervisors ultimately approved the proposal and gave authorization to begin landscaping. Dedication of the new cemetery, destined to serve twenty eastern San Gabriel Valley parishes, was scheduled for Memorial Day, 1961.

During the Dedicatory Mass, the then Auxiliary Bishop Timothy Manning preached a magnificent homily, parts of which are herein reproduced:

At one time or another, especially on the occasion of a funeral, each of us has been exposed to the narrative of the resurrection of Lazarus. We do not need to recount the details. We would propose to reflect on three aspects of it that excite our wonder and dispose us to hope and adoration.

First of all, we draw attention to the successive stages of the illness of Lazarus. The message sent to Jesus, in hiding across the Jordan, was as crisp as a telegram—"He whom thou lovest is sick." After some delay, on His way to Bethany, He tells His disciples, "Lazarus, our friend, sleeps;" then, later, "Lazarus is dead." When they arrive at the village of Martha and Mary, they find that their brother is already buried "four days in the tomb." When they reach the place of burial, Jesus asks that the tomb be opened, but Martha protests, "By this time, he is already decayed." Sickness, sleep, death, burial, and decay.

Is there not in this sequence a mirroring of the sad story of humanity itself? There is the initial sickness caused by the first sin and a progression of calamity until we reach the fetid decadence of a culture from which Christ is absent. Could it not be also the story of own individual sinfulness, "the slippery way in the dark," prostrating us in helplessness and without His redemptive visitation, destined for decay?

The second suggestion for our attention is the emotion of Jesus when He meets the two sisters and when He stands before the tomb. When he saw Mary weeping and her friends also weeping, "He groaned in spirit and was troubled ... and Jesus wept." The Jews said, "See how he loved him."

Jesus wept. An emotion of deep origins from within His sacred humanity surfaced to His countenance. Tears welled up in His eyes and flowed down His cheeks. He wiped them away, in manly gesture, with the fingers of His hand. We stand aghast at this revelation of the tenderness of the human heart of Christ. In His tears, all our tears are sanctified. The grief for those whom "we have loved long since and lost awhile" is now incorporated into the sorrow of our Saviour and we bear it in unison with Him. Just as He sanctified the waters of the world when He stepped into the Jordan for His baptism, so He sanctified all our sorrows when He stepped into the river of our bitter tears. See how He loved Lazarus! See how He loved us!

After the incident of tears, Jesus "again groaning in Himself, came to the tomb." Some Scripture scholars interpret this emotion of groaning as one of anger. The scope of His view allowed Him to see sickness and death as the result of the primal sin of Adam and as the banners of Satan's triumph over humankind. Jesus was now going to begin His final assault on this fortress of the Evil One, the tomb. The resurrection and the Life is going to be locked in combat with death and the grave.

Standing thus before the tomb calls to mind the young shepherd, David, standing in confrontation before the giant Goliath. David was naked of any of the battle instruments and armors of the day. He had only that which he carried over his shoulder, the sling and the five pebbles taken from the brook. So, it would be that Christ would go out against Satan with only that which He carried over His shoulder, the cross and the five components of His five wounds. With these He would enter into the valley of death, invade the ranks of the buried dead and duel to the victory that would bring Him forth in Resurrection and Life.

(NEW) SAN FERNANDO MISSION CEMETERY MISSION HILLS

It was in October of 1951, that the Archdiocese of Los Angeles announced plans for developing a new cemetery, located north and west of the mission-era burial grounds, on a seventy-eight parcel of land that formerly served as a mission orchard.

When a local newspaper reported that the new cemetery would be located on acreage "adjoining San Fernando Mission," a lawyer for the Church assured local inhabitants that there would be no headstones above the surface of the ground, and that the area would be tastefully landscaped.

The spacious and beautiful grounds on Stranwood Avenue were opened for interments on December 15, 1952. The initial interment occurred when Sinferosa Real Ruiz was buried from Santa Rosa Church in San Fernando. She had been raised on the *Camulos rancho*, made famous by the Ramona pageant. In his message for the dedication, which took place the following November 1st, James Francis Cardinal McIntyre pointed out that the "Body of our Redeemer was tenderly anointed after death and placed in a tomb." Ever since, the cardinal observed, "the Church has been unfailing in her practice of giving due respect for her deceased members."

The area, now known as San Fernando Mission Cemetery, was developed as a massive "memorial park" in keeping with contemporary practices. Artistically landscaped, the cemetery is maintained by a "perpetual care fund" which guarantees its long-term service to the community.

Wide, paved roads meander in leisurely curves between attractively arranged graves. An impressive wrought iron gateway marks the former entrance that exits onto a buffer street for Sepulveda Boulevard. Inside the grounds and near the gates stand modern office facilities, and parking sections. Visitors are awed by a striking outdoor altar beneath four graceful pillars supporting a baldachin canopy. Several additional pieces of property acquired in subsequent years have tripled the capacity of the cemetery, as have several large lawn-crypt mausoleums. Among the many statues adorning the cemetery is a carrera marble depiction of Fray Junipero Serra, the founder and *proto Presidente* of the California missions.

ASSUMPTION CEMETERY
SIMI VALLEY

The only cemetery opened during the tenure of Timothy Cardinal Manning as Archbishop of Los Angeles was dedicated to Our Lady's Assumption on November 7, 1970. Property for the new burial grounds, 160 acres, had been purchased in 1962. Only part of the area was dedicated to burial purposes while the other acres were set aside for future expansion.

Assumption Cemetery was envisioned to serve Catholic families in the Simi Valley and surrounding areas of Ventura County. The artistic centerpiece of the cemetery is a marble statue of Our Lady of the Assumption that towers over those interred there.

In his homily at the dedication of the cemetery, the cardinal responded to a request for the secret of holiness:

Man was made to serve God, his Creator, and so save his soul. Everything else in creation was made to help him toward that end. "Even before the world was made, God had already chosen us to be His through our union with Christ, so that we would be holy and without fault before him."—To know this, and to do it is holiness. Jesus called it love.

Chapter five of the Dogmatic Constitution of the Church, *Lumen Gentium*, enacted by the Fathers of the Second Vatican Council on November 21, 1964, gives us the best treatise on holiness in our modern day. Unfortunately, it is a Cinderella chapter outshone by the other more honored and quoted chapters that make up the Constitution. It deserves prayerful reading and study.

Holiness is not a garment we wear like a Sunday suit, nor is it a posture as of one given to ostentatious piety. Christ had scorn for such attitudes. It is intrinsic to our state of life with its source in word and sacrament, inseparable from the humdrum thoroughfares of our daily journeys.

Housewives, office personnel, journeymen workers, students in a class-room; tinker, tailor, soldier, sailor—bishop and priest—all are called to become holy in the exercise of the duties of their state in life. The invalid and those who only stand and wait are equally called to holiness.

Holiness is patience. It is kind. It is not jealous, it does not put on airs, it is not snobbish. It is never rude, it is not self-seeking, it is not prone to anger, neither does it brood over injuries. It does not rejoice in what is wrong, but rejoices with the truth.

What is important then in life is not to be immortalized with a bronze star set into the concrete sidewalk of Hollywood Boulevard, nor to make a sensational catch at a disputed ball game, nor to be canonized in the *Guinness Book of Records*, nor to be a center-spread in adolescent pornography, nor any of those feats which, for a moment, illuminate the marquee, the scoreboard or the front page.

The familiar prayer, the Our Father, contains within it the formula of holiness. We are alerted to the constant presence of God in our lives. Whether we eat or drink, the Apostle says, or whatever else we do, we should do it for His glory. It matters not what we are doing, we can try to do so in His presence. This is holiness.

Then His all-holy name and the desire to spread His glory have a priority in our lives. Daily bread and daily forgiveness are needs basic to our tranquility. The pursuit of sustenance, security and shelter are a common cause of all our occupations. God is the source of all our being. Not a sparrow falls to the ground unnoticed in His infinite care; and we are worth more than many sparrows. And forgiveness is a bridge across which we clasp God's hand and walk in peace with our fellow-pilgrim. That is holiness.

And always, there is the recurring premonition of our end, no matter how much we turn the other way. To remember it is holiness. To ask God to strengthen us for that final encounter is holiness. To know Him and love Him, to live in His presence each day is genuine holiness, for the kingdom and the power and the glory are His, now and forever.

GOOD SHEPHERD CEMETERY
LANCASTER

In February of 1988, the Los Angeles County Board of Supervisors granted a Use Permit to the Archdiocese of Los Angeles for a cemetery in the Quartz Hill section of the city of Lancaster. Located at 43124 - 70th Street West, Good Shepherd Cemetery was envisioned as providing Catholic burial plots for the growing Antelope Valley. The total parcel of land amounted to sixty acres.

The initial dozen or so acres would include administration and service buildings, several lawn sections and an atrium shaped area with a Shrine of the Good Shepherd. The area would be enclosed by forty-eight two-high crypts and forty-eight niches along with space suitable for the offering of Holy Mass. With sensitivity to the needs of the desert, the landscaping was designed to be water economical and drought resistant while also practical and pleasing to the eye.

Construction began the last week of April of 1990, with the opening scheduled by the end of the year. Counselors were dispatched to move among the Catholic families of the area to acquaint them with the cemetery's location and the availability of its property The first burial took place in 1990, when a member of the Riani family was laid to rest in a temporary lawn crypt.

2002 ONWARD

CATHEDRAL MAUSOLEUM
LOS ANGELES

A centuries-old tradition allows for bishops and certain distinguished Catholics to be interred in cathedrals and certain other churches and shrines. Though generally reserved to members of the hierarchy, the privilege of occupying such places of prominence has been extended to laity for the first time in the United States at the Cathedral of Our Lady of the Angels in Los Angeles.

The crypt of the magnificent new Cathedral contains 1,275 casket spaces and 5,000 columbarium niches for cremains. The entire crypt area has been outfitted with the colorful stained glass windows formerly in the old Saint Vibiana Cathedral.

On June 22, 2002, the remains of James Francis Cardinal McIntyre and Bishops Thaddeus Amat, Francis Mora, Thomas J. Conaty and Carl Fisher were moved into the central area of the crypt immediately below the cathedral's main altar.

CATHOLIC ACTION

Early in 1934, the Bishop of Los Angeles-San Diego began preparations for "Catholic Action Week" which was to be held between April 29th and May 3rd. For that occasion, Bishop John J. Cantwell issued a thirty-six page *Catechism, on Catholic Action: Its Theory and Practice* whose purpose was that of giving "our Catholic people a clearer understanding of the meaning of Catholic Action." In retrospect, it is clear that the Church in Southern California was considerably out in front of its sister ecclesial jurisdictions in the field.

In his foreword to the *Catechism*, the bishop noted that—

Many lay organizations have already been established in this diocese to further the participation of the laity in the apostolic work of bishops and priests. A campaign of education is necessary that all our people should come to understand that the profession of religion means much more than the personal observance of a code of belief and conduct. It means that the graces received be constantly stirred up and called unto fruitfulness. Numbers of very good living people have forgotten the injunction of our Blessed Lord that our "light should shine before men." Instead of an ardent, burning faith, many there are who turn the lamp as low as they possibly can without extinguishing it.

The old distinction between the Church Learning and the Church Teaching should not be so emphasized as to permit the laity to think that they have fulfilled all obligations when they attend Church, pay their dues and receive the sacraments. The laity must know what the priest's life is. They must participate in his apostolic work and be like the early Christians, of one heart and one mind.

Reprinted in the *Catechism* were excerpts from an address by Archbishop Amleto Giovanni Cicognani in which the Apostolic Delegate to the United States explained the relevance of "Catholic Action" to the world of the 1930s.

The Holy Father, charged with the government of the Universal Church, realizing the prevalence of evils that threaten the destruction of human society, conscious of the needs of the whole human family, issued as early as 1932 a call to Catholics throughout the world to enlist in the apostolate of Catholic Action. This was in reality not a new call. It was rather the call of the Vicar of Christ, re-echoing throughout the Christian centuries, urging all to obey the precept of old: "God gave to every one of them a commandment concerning his neighbor." This call reminded the Christian world of the fulfillment of its duties in a holy militia to which all Catholics belong by virtue of their membership in an ecclesiastical society - the Church - which membership imposes upon the individual definite obligations to society.

He who strives to be good individually does well. But this is not sufficient. He cannot ignore the divine command concerning his neighbor but must keep ever in mind the new law of Christ: "Thou shalt love thy neighbor as thyself." He must enter, therefore, into the soul of the social body. This has been done since the dawn of the Christian ages by the disciples, the deacons and the holy women who, as St. Paul says, "labored with me in the gospel." This labor has varied with the changing conditions of the centuries, fitting itself to the needs of each age.

In our day the Holy Father, the vigilant sentinel of the world, viewing from his sacred watch-tower the conditions of all peoples and knowing their spiritual needs as no one else knows them, has deemed it necessary to unite through Catholic Action the activities of the faithful and to bring them into closer association with the labors of the hierarchy.

Pope Pius XI has in a few words defined Catholic Action with marvelous clearness: "It is the participation of the laity in the

apostolate of the hierarchy." This is a world-embracing program, excluding nothing that pertains to the divine mission of the Church of God. Catholic activity that is not *de facto* and officially made participant in the mission of the bishop of the diocese is not Catholic Action.

Catholics of America must show their zeal for every good work, for every holy crusade, sanctifying others by their example. In his individual life and in the life of the family, by his observance of the sanctity of the marriage state, by his zeal for the education of youth and by his generous cooperation in every movement to which he is called by his spiritual leaders, the true Catholic will respond to the invitation of Pope Pius XI and thus render an inestimable contribution to the Church and to the nation. He will answer whole-heartedly the call of Catholic Action!

While no extant minutes of the Catholic Action Week have yet surfaced, a speech given by J. Wiseman Macdonald found its way into the pages of *The Tidings*. It is vitally important because it gives the perspective of a prominent member of the laity.

The term "Catholic Action" as a name-unit, is of very recent origin —that is to say, it is only within the past few years that the words "Catholic" and "Action" have been fixed together in juxtaposition so as to form a special name or appellative.

The very day that our California was founded was *the* day that Catholic Action commenced here — and, mark this well — *it was Catholic Action itself that founded the State* — nothing more, and nothing less.

In the year 1769, the saintly Fray Junípero Serra and some of his brother Franciscan monks, left the College of San Fernando in Mexico City, and, in two parties, passed overland, going by way of the most northerly of the missions of Lower California, bent on their work of evangelizing Upper California.

From the Missions of Lower California, the good friars brought with them, for immediate use and future sustenance, and to aid in founding the new territory, hundreds of heads of horned cattle, horses, hogs, sheep and domestic animals of other kinds. They carried provisions, medicines, clothing and abundant necessaries of life.They brought farm and agricultural implements, and experienced craftsmen to use them thereby to cajole into productiveness the faces of Mother Earth.

In their *carretas*, or old-fashioned, springless wooden carts, they carried building and industrial implements of many kinds to aid in developing the new territory. Grape vines, slips of olive and other fruit trees, and quantities of grain seed, were in their train, and, later, all were planted and grew profusely in the fecund soil of our own California.

It is well for us to know that *every single grape and olive*, and every blade of barley and grain, originally grown in this great state, *was here produced directly through Catholic Action*, for Catholic money paid for all of them, and Catholic hands planted everything.

Every animal which the good friars brought to California in 1769, and later, for food and for labor, and every industrial and agricultural instrument, every plow and harrow which they

Interior - Our Lady of Angels Cathedral

Archbishop Amleto Cicognani, Apostolic Delegate to the Church in the United States

carried with them, distinctly represented Catholic Action. *Catholic money paid for it all, and Catholic hands did the work.* Every penny that was spent by the good Missionary friars on animals, implements, fruits and grains, was money obtained from *"El Fondo Piadoso de las Californias"* — The Pious Fund of the Californias — a great charitable trust fund between a million and a million and a half dollars, *contributed by Catholics in Spain and Mexico*, and assembled by the Jesuit Fathers in those countries in the first half of the Eighteenth Century for the specific purpose of evangelizing both Californias —Upper and Lower — then, of course, Spanish colonies. A notable reflection in this connection is that *even the wages of the few soldiers who accompanied the friars for protection against Indians, came from Catholic Action. Those wages were paid from the same Pious Fund.*

Catholic Action indeed began very early in California. Seventy years before 1769, it had incepted in Lower California, when the Jesuits commenced the foundation of their thirteen missions in that territory.

Great, spreading arrays those pioneers of our State and their animals presented, as they marched slowly and resolutely to commence the building of California — to open up its great destiny; and I say, and declare to you that, *when the first of those* historic marchers stepped across the imaginary line then stretching between Lower and Upper California, and placed his evangelizing foot on the soil of Upper California, our own California of today — at that very instant Catholic Action commenced in this State, and, ever since that moment, it has continued efficiently, progressively, gloriously and with every-widening range, until the present moment.

The twenty-one great Mission buildings in this state subsequently erected by the friars, running from San Diego, northerly, six hundred miles to the Mission of San Francisco Solano, forty miles north of San Francisco, were built through Catholic Action, and those buildings, today the pride and joy of all Californians; irrespective of creed—some of them in the disintegration of sad but beautiful and romantic ruins; others restored to stately strength and grandeur and still performing their sacred functions—all remain as glorious monuments attesting the zeal, the fervor, and the charity of a bygone and unforgettable century, and they stand as wonderful tributes to Catholic Action, dating back to the very first day of the state's existence.

We have selected some examples of Catholic Action inaugurated along the Western Slope of the United States since 1865. There were many more, of course, but these randomly chosen "reach-outs" are quite enough to demonstrate how Catholics in the Golden State were heroic pioneers by their involvement in the apostolic work of the Church.

ANCIENT ORDER OF HIBERNIANS

Historians trace the origin of the Ancient Order of Hibernians to the Emerald Isle's County of Kildare in the Province of Leinster. There in 1565, Rory O'Moore and his "Defenders" rallied the Irish people to a defense of their religion and country against the English invaders.

During the stormy penal days, members accompanied the priests in their midnight missions of mercy. They were entrusted as sentinels to guard the heights and defend the priest and his flock from surprise attack. The annals relate how, sometimes, in spite of their vigilance, "they were surrounded, the kneeling congregation was slaughtered, and the venerable white-haired priest at the rude altar was slain and his lifeblood flowed near the Adorable Body and Blood of the Redeemer he was offering up for the living and the dead."

Through the following centuries the A.O.H. has continued to be the great defender of its native land and the chosen rulers of the Irish people. In the stirring days of the "Land League" the mighty moral and financial support of the society was largely responsible for the nation's eventual emancipation.

The Ancient Order of Hibernians was formally established in the United States in May of 1836, when that bigotry and prejudice which assailed Irish Catholics in their homeland was transplanted with added virulence to the New World. In the constitution adopted by the A.O.H.

in 1908, the intent and purpose of the fraternal society was geared to promoting friendship, unity, and Christian charity.

Loyalty to Catholic principles has been a trademark of the Ancient Order of Hibernians. Each county chaplain was instructed by the constitution to see that nothing is done or countenanced within his jurisdiction which is contrary to the laws of the Catholic Church, the decrees of the Plenary Councils of Baltimore and the Synodal Constitutions of the Diocese.

To this oldest Catholic fraternal society in existence "belongs the honor and distinction of being the first American society to raise $50,000 for the support of The Catholic University at Washington, as an endowment of a chair for the preservation of the language, literature, history and antiquities of Ireland." The initial division of the A.O.H. in Los Angeles was instituted on September 17, 1875, and "for a good many years the shock troops of Catholic Action in the diocese were the members of that order which insists upon the qualification of Irish birth or descent through either parent."

By the turn of the century, the Ancient Order of Hibernians had the largest membership and the strongest financial standing of any Catholic organization in Southern California. When disaster struck the Golden State in 1906, earthquake and fire victims of San Francisco received substantial assistance from the A.O.H., which promptly raised $40,000 for the Bay City's homeless refugees. The Ancient Order of Hibernians in California has faithfully carried on the good work intended by its founders. Its activities have extended to all the corporal and spiritual works of mercy. Whether it was caring for the needy, visiting the sick, burying the dead, comforting the sorrowful or praying for the living, the A.O.H. has set an enviable record of Christian accomplishment

ARCHCONFRATERNITY OF BLESSED JUNÍPERO SERRA

The origins of the Archconfraternity of Blessed Junípero Serra can be traced to July of 1988, when Archbishop Roger M. Mahony authorized the inauguration of such a pious association "to coincide with the friar's beatification" which was scheduled to take place in Rome on September 25th of that year. The motivating objective was to launch "a prayer crusade" that would eventually culminate in Serra's canonization.

On July 26,1988, the archbishop enthusiastically endorsed the proposal. After agreeing to become the canonical "protector" of the new archconfraternity, he directed that the program proceed.

The formal establishment of the archconfraternity took place on October 1st, at a con-celebrated Mass in the chapel of the Convento de San Bernardino, just a few steps from the house where Junípero Serra was raised in the tiny village of Petra de Mallorca in the Baleric Isles.

Assisting this writer at that Liturgy were Fathers Salustiano Vicedo, Vice Postulator for the Serra Cause in Spain and Father Thom

Form 3547 Requested

THE CALIFORNIA HIBERNIAN

FRIENDSHIP · UNITY · TRUE CHRISTIAN CHARITY · A·O·H·—U.S.A.

THE OFFICIAL STATE
QUARTERLY NEWS BULLETIN
OF THE

ANCIENT ORDER OF HIBERNIANS IN AMERICA

Blessed Fray Junípero Serra, The Apostle of California

Davis, a priest attached to the Archdiocese of Los Angeles. Among the forty charter members enrolled at Petra were two non-Catholics: Marla Daily of Santa Barbara and Mervin Eide of Granada Hills, California.

Canonically the archconfraternity is an ecclesial association having the three-fold purpose of advancing the canonization for Fray Junípero Serra, promoting vocations to the priesthood, religious life and lay ministry and intensifying the spiritual lives of members. By virtue of its authority of aggregating to itself confraternities erected for the same objectives in other localities, the association was referred to as an "archconfraternity." Members in the Archconfraternity of Blessed Junípero Serra, along with other confraternities established elsewhere, share in all the spiritual blessings, indulgences and works of virtue performed by associates throughout the world.

In addition to several newspaper accounts of its establishment, the first official recognition of the archconfraternity occurred in the 1989 issue of the *Los Angeles Catholic Directory* where it was described as a "nonprofit organization dedicated to the canonization of Fray Junípero Serra."

In notices circulated to prospective members, it was stated that the names of enrolled and/or affiliated members would be recorded in the central headquarters. Membership is perpetual and requires only a daily prayer incorporating the objectives of the archconfraternity.

On November 9, 1988, this writer suggested to Bishop Thaddeus Shubsda that he consider establishing a branch of the association in the Diocese of Monterey. The bishop was initially hesitant only because he didn't have a priest available to direct the project. When it was explained that sacerdotal leadership was not necessary, the bishop reconsidered and, in mid 1989, he asked the late Martin Morgado to begin the Confraternity of Blessed Junípero Serra in the Diocese of Monterey.

The origins of the archconfraternity's newsletter, later issued under the title *Siempre Adelante*, go back to 1983 and the first issue of the *Serra Bicentennial Commission Newsletter*. The eleven newsletters published between April of 1983 and September of 1985 were devoted to outlining the proceedings of the ten meetings held by the Serra Bicentennial Commission in various parts of the State.

There were several subsequent editions issued under the watchful eyes of Miriam Downie and Elizabeth Hilleary. In January of 1990, the newsletter became the official organ for the Monterey branch of the Confraternity of Blessed Junípero Serra. Its title was changed to *Siempre Adelante* by its new editor, Martin Morgado.

CATHOLIC BIG BROTHERS AND SISTERS

The stated objective of the Catholic Big Brothers was to assist problem boys in adjusting themselves to the community by becoming practical Catholics and better citizens.

Catholic Big Brothers was organized in 1926 at the direction of Bishop John J. Cantwell. The organization was incorporated three years later with departments governed by a Board of Directors consisting of nine members. By 1934, the enrollment had grown to 419 laymen from many parishes in the diocese. Potential members could apply with the recommendation of their pastor and an already certified member.

Archbishop J. Francis A. McIntyre greets E. L. Morneau of the Big Brothers in January of 1952

Duties were divided according to individual ability and interests. Physicians rendered medical service, dentists provided dental care and attorneys gave legal advice. Big Brothers became counselors and friends to individual boys and leaders of club groups. Many also served on boards and committees seeking community support. Over the years, members received many Apostolic blessings.

Closely aligned were the Catholic Big Sisters. They functioned in the field of Catholic social services, looking after girls from the age of fifteen to twenty-one who were in need of friendly supervision and assistance. The girls under their care were called "Little Sisters."

Like its counterpart, Catholic Big Sisters was governed by a constitution and by-laws under the supervision of the Catholic Welfare Bureau. The organization held monthly meetings for the purpose of spiritual inspiration and continued training.

The duties of these organizations encompassed religious supervision, moral, physical and mental development of youngsters by providing the example of Catholic grown-ups carrying forth the gospel of Christ to those less fortunate.

CATHOLIC BOY AND GIRL SCOUTS

The Boy Scouts of America organization was founded in the Diocese of Los Angeles-San Diego in the 1920s under the supervision of Father Vincent Shepherd. Earliest specific reference to the Boy Scouts appeared in *The Tidings* for June 12, 1925 when Troop 87 was celebrating its first anniversary.

At that time, the Deputy Commissioner for scouting reported that there were already twenty Catholic Troops organized in the diocese. A contingency of Boy Scouts from Los Angeles journeyed to Rome in

June of 1926 for a giant assemblage presided over by Pope Pius XI. During their visit to Saint Peter Basilica, they were accorded the rare privilege of being blessed by the veil of Saint Veronica.

In 1934, Bishop John J. Cantwell sent a letter to all the faithful in the diocese urging that each parish become interested in the Catholic Boy Scout Program. In his letter the bishop characterized the Boy Scout Movement as successful in directing the life of boys into wholesome and constructive channels. Under Catholic auspices, he said, it promotes spiritual welfare and develops the natural virtues.

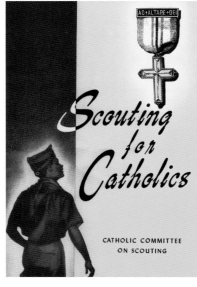

appointed by the Most Reverend Bishop to assist the Diocesan Director of Scouting. The Committee includes representatives from each of the seven Scout Councils within the diocese. Policies are formulated by an Executive Committee and assistance is given to local Scout officials in the promotion of a healthy program. The service rendered by organized troops in the various parishes has merited the commendation of pastors. At the present time, there are seventy troops under Catholic auspices.

The internal workings for scouting was spelled out in a catechism issued during the mid-1930s:

The organization cooperates with the regional and local councils of the Boy Scouts of America within the diocese, and promotes scouting under Catholic leadership. It correlates the scout program with the entire parish program in order that the religious life of the Catholic boy in scouting shall receive adequate attention, and that scouting activities may become an integral part of the youth program of the Catholic Church. The organization arranges special events, under Catholic auspices, and suitable retreats for boys and adult members of the organization. It provides special facilities and supplementary study in Catholic doctrine and principles to Catholic men trained in leadership for Catholic boys in scouting.

In 1936, Father James E. Dolan was named chaplain and, at that time, the Catholic Boy Scouts became an official division of the Catholic Youth Organization. Statistics in 1940 indicate over a hundred troops, with 2,200 registered scouts under the supervision of 507 adult leaders. By 1970, the Los Angeles Area Council of the Catholic Boy Scouts of America had reached a high of 57,614 scouts, including cub, Boy and Explorer scouts.

This movement, the letter concluded, has already been established in many of the dioceses of America, including our own. However, in the past there has been great difficulty experienced in securing a sufficient number of qualified and interested men to act as leaders. Yet the development of a boy's character and the preservation of this faith is one of most practical and constructive forms of Catholic action a good laymen may follow. In a report for Catholic Welfare Bureau in 1935 was this entry for "Boy Scout Troops:" Satisfactory progress was made in the diocese during the past year in the development of the youth programs of the Boy Scouts of America. Many new troops were organized, and special events for Catholic troops were successfully promoted. New leaders were recruited and trained. A committee of Catholic laymen was

Though never as extensive as their male counterparts, there were twenty-three Catholic Girl Scout Troops in the various parishes of the archdiocese in 1940.

Throughout subsequent years, the archbishops of Los Angeles have played a vital part in the Scouting Program. The manual for scouting became the second all-time best seller after the Bible, with 32,565,000 copies printed between 1910 and 1988.

Msgr. James Dolan and Bishop Alden J. Bell present Ad Altare Dei *Merit Badge to Bobbie Labonge.*

CARDINAL MCINTYRE
FUND FOR CHARITY

As all social workers can testify, needy people often slip through the cracks, even in charitable programs operated by the Catholic Church. Cardinal McIntyre was aware of that and called together a group of businessmen and other prominent leaders to whom he proposed the idea of establishing a program for just such persons. One of those attending that meeting was John B. Rauen who gave McIntyre a check for $1,000, along with the suggestion that the new support group be called the "Archbishop's Fund for Charity."

McIntyre defined the purpose of the new fund as "the collection and maintenance of monies which can be used to support otherwise unprovided for charitable and corporal works." It was incorporated on November 15, 1951. The fund itself was to operate no charitable programs.

Through its Board of Directors, comprised of fifty members of the clergy and laity of the archdiocese, it was to collect and receive memberships and contributions, which it would then distribute to needy and worthwhile programs, agencies and institutions not supported by Community Chest or other sources.

In his first appeal to the faithful of the archdiocese, McIntyre told how the fund had been inaugurated "for the purpose of rendering aid and assistance to the poor and needy, particularly in instances where required relief and service is not available from established sources." He explained that membership in the fund would consist of a two dollar offering each year. Saying that the fund "will bring a much desired and necessary assistance to our charitable programs, he encouraged everyone to take part. He concluded by saying that "our efforts on behalf of the needy will be doing for Christ because they will be for His least brethren."

In its coverage of the new program, *The Tidings* noted that there were already twenty-six programs operating under the umbrella of the archdiocese, many of which had needs not covered by existing sources. "The present sources of revenue are by no means adequate."

Those wishing to take part in the Archbishop's Fund could specify that his or her gift, be it large or small, could be used for any specific field of charity, child welfare, the mentally or physically handicapped, family assistance, health care or any other. Gifts could be designated for use in any geographical area of the archdiocese. Gifts were encouraged from corporations and from individuals while living or under their wills. Holy Mass would be offered every day of the year for enrollees.

The first drive was immensely successful. A total of $93,542 was raised from parochial memberships, a most respectable sum for those days. Blessed Sacrament Parish in Hollywood recorded the most memberships, raising $2,217.

In the first three years of its operation, the Archbishop's Fund for Charity allocated $255,994 to charitable programs in every part of the four county archdiocese, with forty-two charitable agencies and institutions participating in the fund. A total of $69,179 was used for direct relief and assistance to needy families, $84,180 for the needs of dependent and neglected children, $32,800 for youth services, $47,944 for health care and the rest for the aged and miscellaneous charitable activities.

The Archbishop's Fund for Charity remained among McIntyre's favorite works and he reserved the active administration of that work to himself personally. Only rarely did he miss a meeting of the Board and he was extremely solicitous that every penny be disbursed in accord with the wishes of donors. In 1955, he reported that the fund had been instrumental "in providing assistance to many thousands of families and children whose needs would otherwise have not been met."

He repeated every year that "this fund for charity gives to each person an opportunity of participating directly or vicariously in some of our most real and needy works of charity." A year later, he noted that "the Archbishop's Fund for Charity had recently inaugurated a Child Guidance Center" to provide care for emotionally disturbed children. He was fond of recalling that works supported by the fund "are most worthy, and in many instances urgent. They constitute charity in the true sense of relief and service to needy children and persons for whom no other provision is made."

Of all his apostolic works in Los Angeles, Cardinal McIntyre was happiest with the establishment and success of the Archbishop's Fund for Charity. At the annual meeting of the Board of Directors in May of 1971, his name was given to the program, which thereafter was and is known as the Cardinal McIntyre Fund for Charity.

CATHOLIC YOUTH ORGANIZATION

The Catholic Youth Organization was founded in 1931 by Auxiliary Bishop Bernard J. Sheil of Chicago. Its aims were to contribute to the development of young people, especially those phases of their environment that did not fall within the ambit of home or school.

Bishop John J. Cantwell established the C.Y.O. in Los Angeles in 1936 to serve as a coordinating center for archdiocesan activities of young people. Its purpose was to unite and encourage youths to provide for their needs under parochial leadership. Programs were instituted for recreational, social, cultural and religious nature according to age groups. The initial director was Father James E. Dolan.

The athletic program begun in 1932 was placed under the sponsorship of the C.Y.O. In its first year, nearly 8,500 youth participated in the various inter-school and inter-parish games.

Over subsequent years, the C.Y.O. and allied programs reached out to every Catholic youngster in the archdiocese. Such groups as the Catholic Youth Federation and a host of similar organizations insured a Catholic presence among young peoples throughout Southern California. James

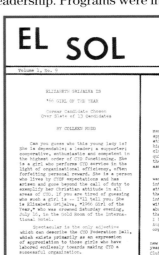

Francis Cardinal McIntyre echoed the common view that C.Y.O was "the most influential and important institution in the lives of Mexican Americans."

In April of 1947, 1,200 members of the Catholic Youth Foundation, comprised of fifty-two young peoples clubs, held their annual communion breakfast at Blessed Sacrament Church in Hollywood. They then marched five blocks down Sunset Boulevard to Vine Street with banners proclaiming their various parochial components. Five years later, a C.Y.O. Federation of Young Peoples Clubs rallied at Immaculate Heart High School, where they were addressed by Father John Sheridan on the moral obligations affecting Catholic youth in modern society.

Bishop Alden J. Bell spoke at the annual meeting of the C.Y.O. in February of 1957. A total of 4,516 boys and girls representing 141 archdiocesan parochial schools on 211 teams heard the bishop speak about the challenges facing young people at the time.

Statistics in 1968 revealed that 464 laymen were serving C.Y.O area boards, not including athletic coaches and other volunteers. Major General J. S. Blaymeier spoke at the annual gathering.

In 1970 Jose Vargas, administrative director of the C.Y.O., told how the organization operated to narrow the distance between the poor and these willing to assist them at the parochial level. He noted that from the earliest days, C.Y.O. had a presence in the barrios, in the neighborhoods and with the poor. Over many years the C.Y.O had received much of the best professional and volunteer help from the very people it helps. He envisioned the C.Y.O. as being in the top echelon of groups keeping in touch with the challenges then confronting young Catholics.

"Service to the total person" was the proclaimed goal of the C.Y.O. program in 1971. The parent agency, Catholic Community Services, funneled a wide variety of programs through five centers, which sponsored picnics, sea trips, summer sports and cooking classes. American Martyrs parish served as the prototype for the program in other parishes.

Two years later, the C.Y.O. began comprehensive outreach aimed at lessening and even preventing delinquency. Young people were openly encouraged to take full advantage of the educational and cultural opportunities. The C.Y.O. worked closely with federal and city agencies in assisting gang work with experts especially trained for that

type of ministry. Along with its direct work with individual youth groups, the C.Y.O. labored closely with local families, schools and public agencies.

In 1975 the Catholic Youth Organization's lunch program served about 100,000 meals during July and August at thirty-six churches, schools and mostly in the poorer sections of Los Angeles County. United Way dollars were greatly helpful to the C.Y.O. In that same year, for example, United Way allocated almost $394,000 to the C.Y.O. from the 18 million public dollars distributed to 250 human-care agencies. Those funds helped to conduct neighborhood day camps, community centers and other programs for which there were no Church funds.

In 1981 young people in the archdiocese were invited to "celebrate summer" with a five part program of fellowship and learning sponsored by the C.Y.O. That outreach was expanded in subsequently years when more attention was concentrated on South Central and East Los Angeles areas.

By 1996, a thirty-two member volunteer board was overseeing the activities of the C.Y.O. Among other activities, C.Y.O. established a gang deterrent agency with the idea of keeping youngsters too busy in good works to think about other pursuits. Though the structure, financing and oversight evolved over the years, the C.Y.O. has continued to serve youth in a unique fashion.

CONFRATERNITY OF CHRISTIAN DOCTRINE

The practicality of founding a branch of the Confraternity of Christian Doctrine in the Diocese of Monterey-Los Angeles was initially broached by Verona Spellmire, a public school teacher long active in catechetical work among the ever-growing community of Mexican-Americans. Father Robert Emmet Lucey, Director of Catholic Charities, was responsive to the idea and arranged for a series of exploratory discussions during which the need for a local unit of the Confraternity was thoroughly studied.

Episcopal endorsement came on March 11, 1922, with Bishop John J. Cantwell's call for an organizational meeting at which he gave his unqualified approval of the CCD. Father William J. Mullane was named director of the new unit, which closely followed the pattern of the Pittsburgh Missionary Confraternity in its activities among the immigrants scattered through the rural districts of southwestern Pennsylvania.

While the work of the CCD in Los Angeles was not restricted to Hispanic immigrants, it was among that segment of the Catholic population that its earliest and most far-reaching accomplishments were realized. The first foundation, on the parochial level, was made at Saint Mary's Church in East Los Angeles. On April 16, 1923, a formal constitution was approved, and, shortly thereafter, the initial catechetical center was opened under the patronage of Santa Maria at Belvedere Park.

James Francis Cardinal McIntyre with the board of the Confraternity of Christian Doctrine in 1956.

The apostolate was warmly supported by Bishop Cantwell who expressed grave concern for the "thousands of children in and around our city, especially among our immigrants, who are in danger of being lost to the faith" through lack of proper catechetical instruction. Of those heeding the prelate's invitation for personal involvement in the CCD objectives, more than 300 completed the training course and qualified for assignment in one or another of the twelve centers in key locations of the diocese.

Further expansion came, on March 5, 1924, when the bishop lent his support to the parish unit system of organization, which he endorsed for adoption in all of Southern California. With the establishment of a Diocesan Union of Confraternities, minutely structured programs were inaugurated for teacher-training, home visitation, transportation of students and relief to the poor and needy. What began as a missionary movement on behalf of children living in the immigrant districts had blossomed into a well-knit bond of parochial confraternities.

A new phase of involvement came in the years after 1926, with the appointment of Father Leroy Callahan to the directorship. Among the first of his innovations was the affiliation of the Los Angeles branch with the Archconfraternity of Christian Doctrine in Rome. Father Callahan, a recognized scholar, initiated a series of model catechetical lessons, which were widely utilized as a pioneer handbook for CCD teachers. Within a few years, some thirty-five comparable publications were circulating around the country bearing the Los Angeles imprint.

In 1928, the CCD ambit was further enlarged to encompass courses for religious vacation schools. *The Handbook of Suggestions for the Daily Vacation School*, the first compilation of its kind ever produced, was subsequently adopted by over fifty centers in the eastern and southern parts of the United States.

The planning, vitality and spirit of CCD activities in the Diocese of Los Angeles-San Diego prompted similar undertakings in other areas. Father Callahan's hope of seeing the Confraternity established nationally was championed, in the early 1930s, by Father Edwin V.

O'Hara of the Catholic Rural Life Conference, who recognized the program's merits and its relevance to the Church on the national scene.

To O'Hara, the Los Angeles plan provided a partial answer to the perplexing challenge posed by the tremendous numbers of children unable to participate directly in the already functioning Catholic school system.

Timothy Cardinal Manning greets Cursillistas in June of 1972.

There were other epoch-making proposals emanating from California's southland such as the formation, within the CCD framework, of teacher institutes and study groups to better equip members for their particular apostolate. By 1936, the Confraternity of Christian Doctrine in Los Angeles was a vital organization with an effective catechetical program reaching the largest number of public school children in the country.

The manifold accomplishments of the Confraternity of Christian Doctrine in its earliest years helped to create interest, encourage programs and upgrade instruction in CCD activities in practically every area of the nation. Eventually, a goodly portion of the country's affiliated branches had adopted the basic guidelines used so effectively in Southern California.

By 1937, the CCD program was so widespread that it required a full-time director. Msgr. John Clarke became director, a post he held until 1970. Within his thirty-three years, the CCD registration of participants grew from 30,000 to more than 200,000 in 1969.

CURSILLO

The contribution of the Isle of Mallorca to Provincial California was outstanding, varied and continuous. Sixteen of the early missionaries invested 341 man-years in spreading the Christian message to the Indians along the Pacific Slope.

Father Maynard Geiger, the Franciscan historian, has stated that "the state of California owes much to persevering and determined men from a small island in the Mediterranean. Mallorca, especially in the beginning, provided many of California's early conquering heroes. For this reason, the isle of calm and beauty was and remains California's spiritual god-mother."

Nor did that contribution stop in 1856, with the death of Fray Juan Cabot, the last of the Mallorcan friars. Indeed, there is much of that same missionary enthusiasm evident almost two centuries after the passing of those early pioneers. In 1944, Eduardo Bonnin, a convert from Judaism, invited about thirty priests and laymen to join him in counteracting the personal immorality and religious indifference then creeping into Spanish society. His aim was to transform the small group into militant Catholics whose lifestyles would revolve about the sacra-

ments. Shortly thereafter, Bonnin approached the Right Reverend Juan Hervas y Benet, and asked the Bishop of Mallorca for guidance and approval of the movement. Bishop Hervas heartily endorsed the proposals and personally assumed direction of what would later be known as the *Cursillos de Christianidad*. From the very outset, the prelate insisted that the retreat-like movement be carefully structured.

The *Cursillo*, as envisioned by Hervas, was to be "a short, intensive course, in which priest and lay leaders, in close collaboration, develop a particular method, the aim of which is the Christian renewal of the *Cursillistas* and their apostolic projection into society, so that they will extend the Kingdom of Christ." The prelate's apostolic zeal is further revealed in an article written for *The Americas*, in January of 1950, in which he called for a re-kindling, in a new generation, of "that same peace and good-will of the Gospel which Fray Junípero (Serra) succeeded in planting in the New World."

After completing a carefully prepared course of instruction, a squad of teachers conducted the first *Cursillo* on January 7, 1949, in Palma's Convento de San Honorato, under the personal supervision of the bishop. Teams were subsequently sent to Barcelona and from there to the other major population centers of Spain. Within a few years, the "spiritual revolution" had spread through much of Latin America as well.

In May 1957, two flyers from the Spanish airforce, Agustin Palomino and Bernardo Vadell, while on a training program in Waco, Texas, joined with Father Gabriel Fernandez, to launch the *Cursillo* program in the United States.

The initial *Cursillo* was held in Los Angeles under the direction of the Claretian Fathers, in 1962. James Francis Cardinal McIntyre welcomed the movement and, within four years, thirty-three *Cursillos* had been conducted in the archdiocese.

Bishop Hervas, later the Prefect Apostolic of Ciudad Real, described the *Cursillo* as "an instrument of Christian renewal in which the most modern pedagogic, religious, social and psychological methods are brought into harmonious fusion with the traditional

doctrine of the Church." Today, the intensive apostolic collaboration of priest / laymen teams are busily bringing to modern generations of believers what Fray Junípero Serra and his companions brought to the pagans of earlier times: "faith, tenacity and self-sacrifice." And Mallorca once again lights a candle in the New World!

FAMILY THEATRE OF THE AIR

The apostolate of Father Patrick Peyton on behalf of family prayer has no parallel in United States Catholic annals. Since January 1942, the tireless Holy Cross priest devoted himself to strengthening the family unit through daily corporate prayer, especially the Rosary. A vital part of Peyton's campaign involved utilization of radio as a means for furthering the notion that "the family that prays together stays together."

After meeting with the leaders of network radio in Hollywood, Father Peyton decided on a format for the "Family Theatre of the Air" patterned after that used by professional shows: a "drama" to gain audience, followed by a "commercial" to sell the product. The drama would be presented in a family setting, so as to prepare the listeners for the message of daily corporate prayer, which Peyton termed the "lost notion of our age."

The first office of the Family Theatre in Hollywood was a room at the old Immaculate Heart Convent. That and "sundry telephone booths" served as headquarters until permanent facilities were acquired at 7201 Sunset Boulevard. The initial program was aired over the Mutual network on February 13,1947. It was a play entitled "Flight from Home" and starred Loretta Young, James Stewart and Don Ameche.

The reaction of the general public was overwhelmingly favorable. Eventually 700 stations throughout the United States subscribed to the program. The Armed Forces Radio network beamed them to troops overseas and independent stations in other countries also picked up the series. Even certain areas behind the Iron Curtain heard the program by short-wave.

The tremendous impact of the program in favor of family prayer was sustained. Four hundred and eighty-two separate presentations were carried by the Mutual Broadcasting System every Thursday evening at 7 o'clock, for almost ten years.

The "Family Theatre of the Air" was also well received in professional circles. It won the Thomas Edison Award, as well as the American Legion award. *Time* magazine called the series "outstanding" and *Radio Daily* selected it as the Mutual network's best of the year.

The program continued into the mid 1950s, until the radio media began losing much of its audience to television. Even a decade later, however, reruns of earlier shows were reaching 150 stations, as well as millions of listeners in Latin America, Spain, Australia and the Philippines.

Though Father Peyton's radio productions were only one of his many-faceted endeavors on behalf of daily family prayer, they were perhaps his most important. His identification with those programs provided an exposure, which eventually enabled Father Peyton to project his Rosary and prayer crusades to diocesan, national and international audiences.

Father Peyton's pioneering radio apostolate anticipated by fifteen years Vatican Council II's decree advocating "Catholic broadcasting" as an ideal means for bringing listeners "into communication with the life of the Church."

HOLY NAME SOCIETY

The inauguration of the Holy Name Society as an organized effort to promote that reverence enjoined by the Second Commandment can be traced to the thirteenth century and the violent attacks then being made on the Divinity of Christ and His supernatural character. The society itself, founded in 1274, was an outgrowth of attempts by the Council of Lyons to foster special devotions in reparation for the excesses of the Albigenses and other blasphemers.

In succeeding centuries, crusades honoring the Holy Name were led by the illustrious personages of the time. When the ravages of a violent plague ceased in Portugal during the 1430s, a series of lectures advocating devotion to the Holy Name was credited as divine approval of the devotion. A grateful nation responded with a gigantic public procession.

The movement received its societal orientation at Burgos, Spain, in 1450. The objective of the society as then stated "was the suppression of blasphemy, perjury and the profanation of the Sacred Name in conversation." On April 13, 1564, Pope Pius IV elevated the society to the status of an ecclesiastical confraternity. At that time the primary purpose was stated as "the honor and glory of God and the personal sanctification of its members by acts of love and devotion to the Holy Name." In addition, affiliates were exhorted "to suppress blasphemy, perjury, oaths of any character that are forbidden, profanity, unlawful swearing, improper language and, as far as possible, to prevent those vices in others."

On the second Sunday of Lent, in 1809, Father Charles Nerincks established the first Holy Name Society in America at Saint Charles Church, Hardin's Creek, Marion County, Kentucky. To Bishop Thomas J. Conaty must be given credit for initiating the Holy Name Society in Southern California. In 1910, his campaign to check profanity and indecent language resulted in the foundation, by Father Thomas F. Fahey, of a branch of the society in Holy Cross Parish under the presidency of M. H. Kearney. A new impetus was given to the movement, in November of 1920, when Bishop John J. Cantwell named Father Frederick A. Wekenman as diocesan director. The Illinois-born priest inaugurated a campaign for increased membership in the course of which he "proved the adaptability of the Holy Name Union as a vehicle for organizing lay effort."

On January 15, 1922, the scattered units of the Holy Name Society, the only lay confraternity then existing in the Church with a purely spiritual objective, were organized into a diocesan union. The growth of the Holy Name movement has continued into present times. Later membership of the 230 parochial units in the Archdiocese of Los Angeles exceeded 100,000 affiliates.

During the post-conciliar years, the Holy Name Society, in addition to fulfilling its original historical purpose of spreading and increasing love for the Sacred Name of Jesus through word and example, exhorted its members to "witness Christ" in all their personal and social actions through a carefully planned program of information, which covers relationships in the family, the parish, the Church, the world of work, the community and society at large.

ITALIAN CATHOLIC FEDERATION

California is the story of a heritage fulfilled, resources developed and beauty cultivated. Catholicism in the Golden State is likewise the narrative of saint-named cities and mission-marked heroism brought to the twenty-first and promise.

The influence of Italians in the mosaic of California Christian life can be traced to the dawn of another century when the Florentine navigator, Alesandro Malaspina first anchored in the warm waters along the Pacific Slope. Since that time, Italians have participated in agriculture, fishing, mining, constructing, manufacturing, wholesaling, retailing, farming, law, politics and almost every other field of human endeavor.

Luigi Providenza was co-founder of the Italian Catholic Federation with Father Albert Bandini

In the early 1920s, a survey indicated that a vast majority of the Italians and Italo-Americans in California had become alienated from the traditions of their Catholic religion. Mainly responsible for that sad condition were such factors as anti-clericalism, lack of Italian-speaking priests, poor education and, above all, the mentality that economic and social betterment would be accelerated by breaking all ties with their background, foremost of which was the Catholic faith.

In an attempt to reverse that trend, Father Albert Bandini and Mr. Luigi Providenza decided to establish an organization whose primary and ultimate aim would be the reactivation of the spiritual seed, which was dormant in so many Italian hearts and souls. The first meeting of the Italian Catholic Federation took place on June 15, 1924, in San Francisco's Church of the Immaculate Conception. Archbishop Edward J. Hanna approved the structure and statutes and, on December 7, the initial branch of the I.C.F. was inaugurated with 300 members.

It was the founders' intention that the I.C.F. should be the instrument for anchoring Italian descendants to a family apostolate, uniting husband, wife, children and relatives in sacred enthusiasm. That ideal was further implemented through establishment of the *Bollettino*, which has been published monthly since 1925.

From the very outset, the Italian Catholic Federation sponsored missions, retreats and radio programs by Jesuits, Salesians, Josephites, Franciscans and Dominicans to awaken "a more intense Christian life among the Italian population of California." The I.C.F. was introduced to California's southland in 1931, with foundation of the San Rocco branch at Santa Barbara, on November 22. Presently, the Archdiocese of Los Angeles is the largest field of work for the I.C.F., with fifty-eight branches in the three county area.

Though envisioned as primarily a parochial society upon which the local pastor could rely for his work, the I.C.F. was destined by God's grace to encompass a spirit and vitality that has grown to 225 active branches and 25,000 persons. The Italian Catholic Federation observed the golden jubilee of its establishment in 1974, with publication of a 112 page book on *The First Fifty Years*. Therein, the "reason" for the I.C.F. was nobly stated by Msgr. Robert Brennan: "to bring back people to the Body of Christ."

The long-time archdiocesan director of the I.C.F. for Los Angeles went on to describe the organization as "an ideological, beautiful expression of Catholic Action."

KNIGHTS OF COLUMBUS

In mid 1904, Joseph Scott was asked to write an article for *The Monitor* outlining the rationale for the Knights of Columbus. He was ideally suited for that task, inasmuch as he was then serving as State Deputy.

The Knights of Columbus were founded by Father Michael McGivney, a priest serving in New Haven, Connecticut. He was a far-sighted man with a keen knowledge of human nature. New Haven, the home of Yale University, was for years honeycombed by influences diametrically opposed to the welfare of the Catholic Church and this in spite of the educational enlightenment of Yale's educational center. The bigotry and prejudice to all things Catholic was phenomenal.

Father McGivney felt that his little band of devoted Catholic men needed the strength of organization to keep them together for mutual protection and support. Accordingly, he assembled a few of the leading spirits among his congregation and established in a very quiet, unpretentious way, the society of the Knights of Columbus.

Originally, the Knights were envisioned as simply a fraternal insurance organization, with the usual beneficial advantages that accompany such associations. Gradually the unselfish and devoted efforts of Father McGivney and his followers attracted attention throughout Connecticut and the Order spread until its ramifications were in every quarter of the "Nutmeg State."

It was hardly anticipated by its most sanguine members that the Order would ever branch outside of its native jurisdiction. Yet it crossed into Rhode Island with some trepidation and, in 1893, it landed in Boston. Its total membership at the time was 3,500. From its entry into Massachusetts until 1904, the development of the Order was most rapid and wonderful. In fact, at times, the growth alarmed its more conservative element. Shortly after the turn of the century, there were 125,000 members in almost every state of the Union.

Mr. Scott assigned several reasons to the rapid growth. At the outset, a solid Catholic faith was impregnated into its very vitals by the respected Father McGivney. And those lessons continued to impress younger people. Further, those elected to national office were men of unquestioned integrity. Their obviously sincere faith and devotion to the Catholic Church was unyielding.

The various state jurisdictions have generally been well operated. In the west, though the membership was initially smaller, men of sound judgment and unspoiled character were called to leadership. There never was any class distinction in the Knights, socially, financially, racially or politically. Candidates need only be men of sterling Catholic character and reasonable intelligence.

Mr. Scott then outlined the various charitable activities engaged in by the Knights, noting that they had just recently endowed a Chair in History at The Catholic University of America, in Washington, D.C. The work resulting from the endowment of that Chair would demonstrate that the Catholic Church had converted thousands of Indians into devout adherents "long before the Pilgrim Fathers landed on Plymouth Rock."

He concluded by noting that the work of the Knights will be carried on "with charity to all and with fear of none and with the firm hope and belief that there is enough disposition of fairness in the average American to do adequate, if tardy, justice to the facts of Catholic history."

KNIGHTS AND DAMES
OF THE HOLY SEPULCHRE

The Equestrian Order of the Holy Sepulchre of Jerusalem has the distinction of being the oldest and certainly the most celebrated of the Pontifical Military Orders in the long history of the Catholic Church. The Order traces its lineage back to 1099, when it was established by Sir Godfrey de Bouillon, the Duke of Brabant. Godfrey bestowed his own insignia, the red cross of the Five Wounds of Christ, on the Order.

Today the insignia (consisting of a large central cross surrounded by four smaller ones) can be seen at all the sacred shrines cared for by the Franciscans in the Holy Land. This "Crusader's Cross" is also mounted atop each of the stations along the *Via Dolorosa*.

Following the crusades, the Knights of the Holy Sepulchre returned to their countries of origin. During the ensuing centuries, the Order maintained its identity in most areas of Europe. In the 13th century, the Order was placed under the leadership of the Franciscan Custos of the Holy Land and members were entrusted with the maintenance of churches, abbeys, convents, shrines, hospitals and schools within Palestine.

In 1847, when the Holy See restored the Latin Patriarchate in Jerusalem, Pope Pius IX placed the Order under the jurisdiction of the new patriarch. Forty years later, Pope Leo XIII approved formation of the Ladies of the

Sir George Zorn, our Lieutenant for the past seven years received a standing ovation from the assembled Knights and Ladies as he turned over the leadership reins to our new Lieutenant, Sir James F. McGlone at the Sunday morning business meeting.

Sir James F. McGlone is Our New Lieutenant

Holy Sepulchre and thereafter women were admitted to full membership, in all degrees of rank.

The present apostolate of the Knights and Ladies of the Holy Sepulchre remains essentially that enunciated by Pope Pius IX, namely the support of the living Church, the poor Christian community attached to the Patriarchate of Jerusalem. Though the Order had been formally constituted in the United States for only fifty years, there are already four Lieutenancies and one Magistral Delegation. The Western Lieutenancy, which includes California, was created in 1973.

According to the 1977 statutes, the Knights and Ladies of the Holy Sepulchre are chosen "from among persons of a deep and practical Catholic Faith and of unblemished moral reputation who have acquired particular merits on behalf of the Works and the Catholic Institutions of the Holy Land and the Order." While membership in the Order is considered a great honor, it carries with it the serious responsibilities in keeping with its original character, requiring its members to serve the Church with their prayers, alms and activities.

Since its inception, the Western Lieutenancy has held annual meetings in San Diego, San Francisco, Tucson, Anchorage, Los Angeles and Honolulu. In 1975, members had the opportunity of visiting Jerusalem, where they received the Pilgrim Shell, the ancient badge of pilgrims, from Patriarch James. J. Beltritti.

Ancient as it is, the Order still represents something alive, functional and excellent in the modern Church. Their well-defined charitable objectives and duties confirm the Knights and Ladies of the Holy Sepulchre as a valid and vibrant force in a troubled world.

Father Patrick Peyton preaches a Rosary Crusade in New Zealand in 1954. Over 152,000 persons participated.

KNIGHTS OF MALTA

The Hospitallers of Saint John of Jerusalem were founded in the middle of the 11th century. Their earliest work was that of financing and staffing a hospital in the Holy City for pilgrims. During the Crusades, the hospital was enlarged and the Knights endowed it with their properties.

With the advent of the Moslems, the Knights retired to Acre and later to Cyprus. They participated in the conquest of the Isle of Rhodes, which they fortified as a Mediterranean military stronghold.

The Order enjoyed sovereign rights and, following the victory at Rhodes, became an autonomous state, with its own laws, army and naval forces. Knights fortified its rocky coast and established a fleet to patrol the Mediterranean and cleanse it of Turkish pirates. The Order of Malta ultimately became one of the foremost naval powers in Europe.

The "Knights of Malta" occupied the island for almost three centuries, until Napoleon forced their surrender in 1798. Four years later Admiral Horatio Nelson captured the island. With their departure from Malta, the Knights ceased to be a military or political body. They wandered from place to place until Pope Leo XIII invited them to locate their headquarters at Rome.

In all their peregrinations, the Knights made establishment of hospitals for the poor and needy their first priority. That apostolate was subsequently enlarged to include all the works of charity.

So well recognized has been its charitable and hospital work that under the Geneva Convention the Cross of Malta became entitled to the same recognition by belligerents in war as is accorded the Red Cross.

Although long deprived of its territorial autonomy, the Order retains its sovereign character. It issues its own passports and entertains diplomatic missions and legations in several countries. In 1927, the American Chapter of the Knights of Malta was established by Pope Pius XI at the special request of Alfred E. Smith. There are about a thousand members currently in the states.

In California's southland, the Knights of Malta have an enviable tradition of charitable works. They maintain a free clinic in Los Angeles, provide transportation for the elderly and occasionally arrange for terminally ill patients to visit Lourdes.

The Maltese Cross, with its four equal arms expanding outwardly in width, is the badge of the Order. The four arms of the cross represent the virtues of temperance, prudence, justice and fortitude. The white in the arms of the cross symbolizes the purity of deeds, and the eight points of the cross are in honor of the eight beatitudes as proclaimed by Christ in His Sermon on the Mount.

The Grand Master, elected for life, enjoys the rank of prince. He is referred to as the "Custodian of Christ's Poor." The Grand Prior is generally a member of the Sacred College of Cardinals. The constitution and by-laws of the Association of Master Knights of the Sovereign Military Order of Malta in the United States were promulgated on November 7th, 1932 and amended on April 30, 1977.

Establishment of the Knights of Malta along the Pacific Slope links the Catholic life of California with the history, traditions and glories of the Church's medieval peoples.

KNIGHTS OF PETER CLAVER

In november of 1909, four Josephite priests and three black Catholic laymen joined forces to establish the Knights of Peter Claver at Mobile, Alabama. The purpose of the fraternal order was "to give financial help to the members and their beneficiaries, solace to the sick and disabled and to provide social and intellectual fellowship for members".

Another objective envisioned by the founders was that of encouraging members in their practice and propagation of the Catholic faith. Bishop Edward Allen of Mobile suggested the name "Knights of Peter Claver" be given to the nascent order.

The patronage of Saint Peter Claver (1602-1654) had special significance. That famed Jesuit missionary spent his whole life ministering to the spiritual and material needs of the sick and wretched at Cartagena. During the forty years Claver spent as a "Slave of the Negroes," he baptized more than 300,000 persons. The Catalan priest was a familiar figure at the chief slave market of the West Indies.

From the very outset, membership in the knights was intended to embrace the whole family. Thus the Junior Knights (1917), the Women's Auxiliary (1922) and the Junior Daughters (1930) were inaugurated in succeeding decades. The first council of the Knights of Peter Claver established in California was Queen of Angels-87. Chartered on April 20, 1941, this proto council was headquartered in Los Angeles. It was the first branch west of San Antonio, Texas.

One of the largest and oldest of the Catholic fraternal orders, the Knights of Peter Claver are mostly Black, though membership is open to Catholics of all races and colors. James Francis Cardinal McIntyre once remarked that the Knights were "always a source of comfort, consolation and edification." He had work-

James Francis Cardinal McIntyre distributes Holy Communion at a gathering of the Knights of Peter Claver

ed closely with them while serving in the Archdiocese of New York. After his transfer to Los Angeles, McIntyre became even more outspoken in his regard for the Knights.

Timothy Cardinal Manning was no less supportive of the Knights of Peter Claver, whom he once described as the "stand-ins for Christ." In 1977, he became personally involved in a drive to recruit members and, at that time, he difined the aims and goals of the order as that of supporting the local clergy, participating in parochial and archdiocesan activities, promoting civic improvement, creating brtoherhood and furthering a love of Church and community.

KNIGHTS OF SAINT GREGORY

Peoples of the Pacific Slope have long held the memory of Pope Gregory XVI in high esteem. He was the pontiff who created the Diocese of Both Californias, on April 30, 1840, and appointed the first bishop in the person of Fray Francisco Garcia Diego y Moreno.

Gregory XVI (1765-1846) was the first of the "modern" popes. Formerly a Camaldolese monk, he had occupied many positions in the curia prior to his election to the Chair of Peter, including that of Prefect for the Sacred Congregation of Propaganda Fide. His fifteen year pontificate marked an important milestone in the effective exercise of papal authority.

The great revival of missionary activity, for example, dates from Gregory XVI who created seventy dioceses and vicariates apostolic, including ten in the United States. The former Bartolomeo Cappellari was both an accomplished theologian and a skillful diplomat.

Among the Holy Father's many innovations was the establishment of the Order of Saint Gregory the Great in 1831, as a way of honoring people of unblemished character who had "promoted the interests of society, the Church and the Holy See." Because of his great admiration for Saint Gregory the Great (540-604), the pontiff named the new order for his illustrious predecessor and namesake.

There were no knights appointed for the United States in those earliest years after 1831, mostly because of the commonly held belief that it was improper (and possibly unconstitutional) for Catholics in this country to receive titles from the head of a sovereign government. Recall that prior to the suppression of the Papal States, the popes were also temporal kings. (That, by the way, explains why there were no cardinals in the United States until 1875.)

Shortly after re-organizing the Order and making it more responsive to the needs of contemporary society, Pope Pius X issued a decree on February 7, 1905, extending to local bishops the prerogative of nominating candidates for the papal knighthood.

It was in 1919 that Bishop John J. Cantwell first responded to the Holy Father's invitation by proposing Joseph Scott as a Knight Commander of the Order of Saint Gregory. Cantwell bestowed the honor at a pontifical Mass offered at Saint Vibiana's Cathedral on Pentecost Sunday, May 15,1921. The Bishop of Monterey-Los Angeles praised the recipient for "having interested himself during his entire career in all questions affecting the welfare of the people."

Three years later, the Order was again conferred on an outstanding Catholic layman, Isidore B. Dockweiler. At that investiture ceremony, on June 5,1924, a writer for *The Tidings* said Dockweiler's "talents have ever been at the command of the Church."

Others cited in subsequent years were W. T. Moore (1935), P. H. O'Neil (1937) and Harry E. Johansing (1944). Though the record keeping has been less than perfect, it would appear over a hundred have been invested into the Order of Saint Gregory the Great since 1921.

KOLPING SOCIETY

In the view of Father Adolph Kolping (1813-1865), "active charity heals all wounds." Well over a century ago, this German-born "Apostle of the Workingman" noted that if the life of the people is again to become more according to the spirit of the Church, then the Church must again become popular.

Even before the first of the Vatican Councils, Father Kolping recognized that the priest "must concern himself with the social, the civil, the community life of the people; that he ought to stoop down to the ground to lift up any one or every one who stretches forth his hand imploring help." Imbued with the motivation that working people should recognize God better and love Him more deeply, Father Kolping organized the Catholic Journeymen Society at Cologne, on May 6, 1849. Interestingly enough, just two blocks away, on that very night, Karl Marx was urging workers of the world to unite against God and country.

Envisioned as a spiritual family to substitute or supplement a young person's home conditions, the society was to encourage Catholic men, young and old, to be good Christians in the Kingdom of God, industrious workers in their respective trades and professions, solicitous fathers in their families and loyal citizens in the community of their people. Fittingly, the work of the society was placed under the patronage of Saint Joseph. In an effort "to bring back the active charity of Christ among the people as a healing power for the social evils of the time," Kolping asked teachers, master-craftsmen and artists to give

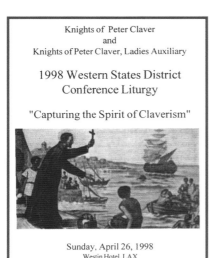

Knights of Peter Claver
and
Knights of Peter Claver, Ladies Auxiliary

1998 Western States District
Conference Liturgy

"Capturing the Spirit of Claverism"

Sunday, April 26, 1998
Westin Hotel, LAX
5400 Century Boulevard
Los Angeles, California
8:30 a.m.

Pope Saint Gregory the Great
BISHOP OF ROME (590-604)
HEAVENLY PATRON OF THE ORDER

Dedication

KOLPING HOUSE

LOS ANGELES

NOVEMBER 18th, 1945

lectures on the means of rising above the educational level of ordinary workers.

Father Kolping's basic formula to help young workingmen is shown in his writings: "Give these men a moral background, extend a helping hand, let them have a decent meeting place, sound instruction, social entertainment, corporal religious practices and so forth, and such means will give the journeymen joy in God and cheer in labor."

The Catholic Kolping Society, as it later became known, was brought to the United States in 1863. In order to provide opportunities for social life in suitable Catholic surroundings, a branch was inaugurated by Anton B. Voss, in Los Angeles, around a group of German immigrants who gathered in Saint Joseph's parish hall on February 23, 1928. Four years later, plans were formulated for a Kolping House on South New Hampshire Street. Although the scope of the society was broadened to meet the needs and customs of the Los Angeles area, its character, aims and traditions were retained intact.

On November 18, 1945, Archbishop John J. Cantwell officiated at the dedication of the refurbished Gillett Mansion, 1101 South West-moreland Avenue, as the 323rd residence of its kind in the world. Subsequently another site was begun on South Union Avenue.

Aside from regular monthly payments made by members to cover room and board, the society depends mostly on its social activities for support and maintenance. The Kolping Society's claim as "the first union of a genuine social character in the entire world" is one of which its members are justly proud. Surely the wide success of the movement is due to its founder's realization that happiness has its foundations in personal achievements, in religious and civil virtues; the future of the people rests in a well-skilled youth.

KOLPING MONUMENT IN COLOGNE

THE TOMB OF FATHER KOLPING
COLOGNE, GERMANY

LAY MISSION HELPERS

The Lay Mission-Helpers Association was born into a world in which one-third of humanity had never heard the name of God. Founded by Monsignor Anthony J. Brouwers to help correct this universal tragedy, the organization was canonically erected as a Pious Association under the patronage of His Eminence, James Francis Cardinal McIntyre, Archbishop of Los Angeles.

A constitution was drafted outlining the specific duties and obligations of the Mission-Helpers. Members receive no salary, but are given a monthly allowance for food and clothing, enabling them to have the same standard of housing, board and medical care as do the local clergy. Their transportation is paid, but it is understood they will remain at their posts for a minimum of three years.

A contract is signed with the local bishop stipulating the particular functions of each Mission-Helper. Men and women between twenty-five and thirty-five years of age are eligible and, beyond normal health, applicants are required to take the Minnesota Multiphasic Personality Inventory. Once accepted, they take no Religious vows and wear no distinctive garb.

By September of 1956 there were eight workers in Africa, where it was soon discovered that lay missionaries are frequently able to enter into the life of a community more completely than priests or nuns. So quickly did the organization develop that within a year after its establishment, a similar group was set up by Bishop James A. McNulty of Paterson, under the title of the Association for International Development.

A carefully trained staff conducts an intensive training program lasting an entire year including such courses as ascetics, theology, Scripture, first aid and history of the area of assignment. Reports from members already in the field are carefully examined and scrutinized in seminar sessions.

While college-trained applicants are preferable, others have been accepted. Teachers, doctors, mechanics, carpenters, electrical and metal workers, pressmen, journalists, social workers, pilots, radiomen and farmers are but a few of the skills and trades represented over the past years. The training period emphasizes the spirit of personal mortification. Prospective members are acquainted with the climatic discomforts, transportation inconveniences, strange foods and pesty insects they may encounter.

The Lay Mission Helpers and its sister organization, the Mission Doctors Association, are geared to provide skilled lay men and women to assume tasks that will advance the cause of Christianity on the mission frontiers. Members undertake no regular form of community life but they follow a well-organized plan of spiritual practices. Daily Mass, regular prayers, reading of Scripture, obedience to authority, monthly reports and annual retreats are their chief spiritual weapons.

Monsignor Brouwers' Lay Mission-Helpers antedated the papal volunteer program by several years and served as a "pilot system" for that world-wide organization set up by the late Pope John XXIII. Another proof of its effectiveness is seen by the fact that by 1960 there were seven separate diocesan groups on the national level paralleling the Los Angeles foundation and functioning in Brooklyn, Evanston, Paterson, Chicago, Washington, D.C., and Weston, Massachusetts.

As could be expected of any agency in the jurisdiction of James Francis Cardinal McIntyre, the Lay Mission-Helpers was and is an economically healthy organization. Compared to the cost for a three-year period in the Peace Corps, a Mission-Helper can be transported to and from his post and maintained for his tour of duty for approximately of what it costs the Peace Corps.

Embedded in the minds of these dedicated soldiers of Christ was Pope Benedict XVs reminder that "missionary work surpasses all other works of charity."

LEGION OF DECENCY

The first organization of Catholics in the movie industry was launched by Bishop John J. Cantwell in June of 1923, under the title of Catholic Motion Picture Actor's Guild of America. While the Guild served a useful purpose, it was never recognized as anything more then a social agency and was unable to wield any lasting influence in bettering motion pictures.

Bishop Cantwell's concern for the blatantly irreverent attitude exhibited in certain of Hollywood's productions convinced him that some sort of officially sponsored organization was needed to inform Catholics about the dangers inherent in such entertainment.

At the 1933 annual assembly of the American hierarchy in Washington, the Bishop of Los Angeles-San Diego read a detailed status-report on Hollywood's productions in which he confirmed what many of the prelates had long suspected about the movies and their producers. Cantwell noted that, in many cases, the films had taken "to preaching a philosophy of life" and were overly concerned with such delicate social problems as "morals, divorce, free love, race suicide, and unborn children" with no obvious restraint.

At the first meeting of the newly established Episcopal Committee on Motion Pictures, in June of 1934, the prelates established the Legion of Decency to act as a clearing house for their subsequent activities. Sole purpose of the Legion was "to arouse millions of Americans to a consciousness of the dangers of salacious and immoral pictures and to

take action against them." Catholics throughout the nation were urged to enroll in the Legion of Decency and subscribe to its pledge of avoiding "indecent and immoral motion pictures" and those that "glorify crime and criminals."

In the Diocese of Los Angeles-San Diego, Bishop Cantwell's campaign was tremendously successful. Talks were given throughout the southland to various Catholic and non-Catholic groups, and much of the Legion's support came from sources outside the Church.

Results of the nationwide campaign were soon obvious. By the end of 1934 the Committee announced that many theatres were reporting a curtailment of patronage directly traceable to Catholic boycotting of objectionable films. The columnist, Raymond Moley, was to say two decades later that "the Catholic Church has had a vital part in the 35 years' revolution which transformed a rowdy and tasteless film world into an orderly, self-regulated industry."

Bishop Cantwell, as a prime mover behind the Legion of Decency, had no illusions about the problems still facing the group, realizing as he did that "the task before the Church in striving to improve the productions of Hollywood is a difficult one." But with all the obstacles connected with such an undertaking, the Bishop of Los Angeles-San Diego never faltered in his determination to elevate the moral tone of the movies. His contribution to this first national attempt by the Church to discipline, according to Catholic morals, an industry dealing with all Americans, an industry at once the richest, most influential and most tightly coordinated of all pressure groups in the United States, was a major factor in the ultimate effectiveness of the Legion of Decency.

NEWMAN CLUB

The Newman Club was established, on May 25, 1899, by John Filmore Francis and several other Catholic laymen of California's southland with the avowed purpose of promoting religious toleration in accordance with the Constitution of the United States, and considering and discussing subjects germane to Catholic thought and history and giving expression, on proper occasions, to the sentiments of members about matters of Catholic concern.

According to John Alton, "the idea of such a club had its inception in the mind of that American Churchman whose memory we all revere and cherish, the late Most Reverend George Montgomery," during his years as Bishop of Monterey-Los Angeles. An early journalist noted that "the formation of the Newman Club came at a most opportune time, and its object was mainly to have a body of laymen whose tact and firmness would be a great assistance to the Catholic people in general." Such an observation is understandable when one considers that the Newman Club was launched in an era when many citizens believed that a Catholic American was not a fit person to be a citizen.

Meeting of the Newman Club with Francis Montgomery and Dr. Richard Molony, 1971

Though it was essentially a literary organization, one of the Club's principal purposes was the defense of those few Catholics in public positions whose religious convictions subjected them to injustice or oppression. That the Newman Club achieved its purpose is obvious from remarks recorded just a few years after its establishment: "Whilst maintaining the strictest Catholicity, the club has done a noble work ... in giving to the Church in this community a standing among the non-Catholic body that it never had before." It has done "a generous service in breaking down unhappy prejudices that have too long made enemies of those who should be friends."

These outstanding effects on the educational life of Los Angeles were recognized by Bishop Montgomery, who reckoned that the Newman Club was "one of the promising features of Catholic life in the city and for the diocese."

Men of prominence in the professional and business life of the community have always considered membership in the Newman Club a distinct privilege. Even in 1903, it was noted that the organization "is made up of some of our best men in almost every walk and profession of life. They are men who enjoy the respect and confidence of their fellow citizens, irrespective of party or denomination."

At the same time, social status has never been a criterion for membership. The Newman Club is open to Catholics in all walks of life, provided only that they have "a liberal education and sufficiently culti-vated literary taste ... to appreciate and discuss the activities, which under the purview of the constitution, may be brought up in the papers which each in turn will be required to present."

The passage of time has not altered the Club's original format. Since May of 1899, when Madame Modjeska read her paper before the group on "Christianity and the Stage," members have met monthly to hear and discuss the major problems encountered by the Church in an ever-growing community. Over sixty years ago, the Newman Club was referred to as "probably the only society of its kind in the United States," a distinction that would very likely go unchallenged even today.

It would be hard indeed to improve on the observations of the poet, publicist and author, James R. Randall, who wrote, in 1905, that "The Newman Club, of Los Angeles, is a splendid representative body of Catholic men. It is an admirable combination of religious and literary motives and purposes."

NOCTURNAL PERPETUAL ADORATION SOCIETY

In the first sermon preached by a Roman Catholic since the Reformation, in Oxford's Church of Saint Mary the Virgin, Gordon Wheeler said:

> The call to holiness is specially underlined by Vatican II. And it would be a terrible impoverishment of the Church's life if mere activism took its place.... What we are and what we do interact on one another. Personal renewal is the key to the right kind of reform. And this postulates prayer.

Surely it is appropriate, while experi-menting with new methods of popularizing Catholic devotional life, that perpetual adoration of the Blessed Sacrament would continue as a climactic part of that intricate pattern of prayer woven around the Mass and the Church's other liturgical and paraliturgical practices.

For over thirty years, the members of the Nocturnal Perpetual Adoration Society have spent 5,110 man-hours annually kneeling "in the subdued light of an alcove chapel, where most of the radiance comes from flickering tapers guarding a sacra-mental presence. "The old Plaza Church of *Nuestra Señora de los Angeles* has been the scene of special eucharistic devotion since April 1,1921, when a group of ladies organized the *Vela Perpetua*, to keep a guard of honor before the tabernacle through the daylight hours.

The *noche feliz*, or noctural adoration, inaugurated on the third Saturday of each month, was subsequently launched by a dedicated corps of Mexican American parishioners in the downtown area. On May 13,1932<, the Pious Sodality was recognized as an autonomous affiliate of Rome's Convent of the Perpetual Adoration. On October

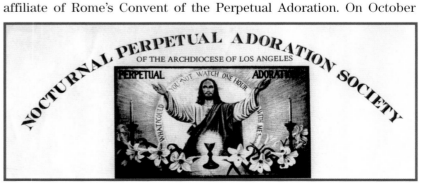

27,1938, Joseph Scott gathered a group of men at the Plaza Church to discuss the possibility of extending the practice of daytime adoration around the clock. Preparations were made for appointment of thirty-one captains, each responsible one evening each month for seeing that every hour is supplied with a sufficient number of adorers.

The inauguration of nocturnal adoration took place in 1939, following a colorful procession through the streets of Los Angeles. Saint Basil's Holy Name Society had the privilege of keeping the first night watches, with two men on duty hourly from 10 o'clock until 5 in the morning. Timidly begun by a few simple but faithful people, the practice prospered under the spiritual tutelage of Father Victor Marin, C.M.F. The adoration has continued, uninterrupted, in succeeding years. Even during the period of church reconstruction, the watch was maintained at temporary quarters, 755 North Hill Street.

Joseph Scott, the founder and first president of the Nocturnal Adoration Society, considered that work "one of the most consoling of my humble activities," noting how edifying it was to see the variety of ages, races, occupations and social strata united faithfully in devoting an hour each month in adoring Our Blessed Lord. Indeed, the membership represents a cross section of the southland's manhood. Doctors, lawyers, merchants, mechanics, laborers and priests bring to the little chapel every sort of local community, each "united in one objective, to stimulate devotion to our Eucharistic Lord in the Sacrament of His love."

Members of the Nocturnal Adoration Society still gather at the historic *Iglesia de Nuestra Señora de los Angeles*, one of California's truly cherished religious shrines, to recite the appointed prayers with uplifted voices. There, secluded before the Blessed Sacrament, they perpetuate a public cult that stretches back to the 13th century. That spiritual work, performed during the dark and lonely hours of the night, is a Catholic "first" along the Pacific Slope. Perpetual Adoration, the first and highest privilege of the angelic choirs, certainly carries with it a special assurance of heavenly favor in Los Angeles, where it thrives under the patronage of Our Lady of the Angels.

PROPAGATION OF THE FAITH

The early bishops of California are uniformly on record with crediting a woman for underwriting most of the missionary work in their areas from the 1850s onwards. The woman in question was not a wealthy duchess, a royal patron or an influential religious personality. She was a penniless French maiden who lived a most unpretentious life. Her name was Pauline Jaricot.

Born on July 22, 1799, young Pauline took a perpetual vow of virginity on Christmas Day of 1816. The next year she founded the Union of Prayers in Reparation of the Sacred Heart, an organization for servant girls. From that group, she first solicited contributions to the foreign missions. In 1820, she formed an association to aid the Society of Foreign Missions of Paris. Each member was asked to recite a decade of the rosary daily, to circulate good books and distribute articles of piety. Later she established a home for working girls, promoted the Association of the Holy Childhood and engaged in other apostolic works for women of all classes.

Pauline's main concern and preoccupation, however, was to help the foreign missions through the alms and prayers of the faithful. In 1822, she joined her efforts to those of Angelo Inglesi, Vicar General of New Orleans, under the title of the Society for the Propagation of the Faith, then known as the Saint Francis Xavier Society.

Pauline Jaricot is the acknowledged "founder" of the Society for the Propagation of the Faith (1822) which began funding missionary activity all over the world, especially in the western part of the United States.

Pauline's fund raising techniques were unique at the time. It was a simple system whereby a promoter found ten persons to contribute a penny a week. Those funds were turned over to another person in charge of ten promoters and so on. In 1822, the Society collected $4,000 in this fashion. It is known that Pauline was very much influenced and motivated in her work as almoner of the missions by the parish priest of Ars, Pere Jean-Marie Baptiste Vianney. For reasons known only to God, Pauline Jaricot never entered religious life, but remained at her humble work until January 9, 1862, when she returned her magnificent soul to the Lord.

In 1930, her cause for beatification was introduced by the Archdiocese of Lyons and, on February 25, 1963, the Sacred Congregation of Rites declared that she had practiced virtue to a heroic degree. She now bears the title "venerable."

The archives for the Archdiocese of Los Angeles are crammed with requests and responses from the Society for the Propagation of the Faith. Letters attached to those petitions tell much about the needs and goals of the Church in California during the 1850s, 1860s and 1870s. And it all began with Pauline Jaricot-a venerable lady indeed!

In 1884, the Third Plenary Council of Baltimore endorsed a suggestion made by James Cardinal Gibbons for a national organization of the Society of the Propagation of the Faith. It became a reality in 1897 with the appointment of a national director.

The Society for the Propagation of the Faith was established in the Diocese of Los Angeles-San Diego in 1925, by Bishop John J. Cantwell. Its first director was Father John J. Devlin.

SAINT VINCENT DE PAUL SOCIETY

The story of the Saint Vincent de Paul Society in the United States can be traced to November 20, 1845, when it was launched in Saint Louis, Missouri, by Bryan Mullanphy. Just a dozen years earlier, a young Frenchman, Frederic Ozanam, with a group of seven or eight men, inaugurated the society in the offices of a Catholic newspaper in Paris.

Ozanam, an apologist, writer, historian, lawyer and professor had in mind an organization that would counteract attacks against the Catholic Church by the unbelievers, deists, and rationalists of his time. After the very first meeting, Ozanam carried a supply of wood to a poor family and those symbolic logs ignited a tremendous conflagration of charity that spread throughout the world.

The first parochial conference of the Saint Vincent de Paul Society was established at Los Angeles in 1904 in Saint Vibiana's Cathedral parish. From there it rapidly spread to scores of parishes reaching a high of ninety parochial conferences with more than 750 active members.

When Bishop John J. Cantwell founded the Bureau of Catholic Charities in the Diocese of Monterey-Los Angeles, in 1919, the Saint Vincent de Paul Society was made part of the Family Welfare section. Five years later, with the establishment of the Catholic Welfare Bureau, the Saint Vincent de Paul Society was restored to its original autonomy. At that time, the field of the society's work was defined as including all parochial welfare and relief cases, supplemental relief to families, society welfare problems for the homeless and spiritual and temporal works of mercy.

By 1945, in the words of Archbishop Cantwell, the society organized when "we were yet a little more than an outpost of the Catholic world," was "strong and healthy with that vigor which emanates from the charity of Christ." By then it was made up of a network of parochial conferences that served the entire Catholic population in the four county archdiocese. All of the funds from poor boxes in the parish churches were turned over to the Society to enable it to carry on its work among the needy. Thousands of worthy recipients received assistance each year.

The objective of the conferences was to sustain its adherents "by mutual example, in the practice of a Christian life." Members visited the

poor, brought them needed assistance and afforded them religious consolation. Arrangements were also made for Catholic instruction for the imprisoned, through the distribution of moral and religious books. No work of charity was considered foreign to members of the Society.

In 1945, the central headquarters for the Society in Los Angeles was located downtown at 254 South Broadway, Room 228. That office was headed by the secretary and three assistants who were on duty eight hours daily. Legal and medical aid were provided by members of the Lawyers and Doctors Guild which had been established in 1927.

Beyond the poor boxes, one of the chief sources of support for the Society was the salvage operation begun in 1917. By 1945, there were four stores and a central warehouse with trucks traveling the streets of the city and county.

Archbishop Cantwell believed that "of all organizations of the laity," the Saint Vincent de Paul Society came "closest to the heart of Christ for His heart was love personified. It sees Christ in the person of every human individual, but especially in those who are needy, for with them Christ has specifically identified Himself."

Founded in the days when charity still resided in the churches and other local organizations, the Saint Vincent de Paul Society was the forerunner of today's social welfare programs. Especially was that true in Los Angeles.

Cardinal Mahony joins politicians in prayer
Photo credit: VICTOR ALEMAN / 2MUN-DOS.COM

Photo credit: VICTOR ALEMAN / 2MUN-DOS.COM

A SAMPLING OF OTHER INSTITUTIONS

ARCHDIOCESAN CATHOLIC CENTER

Originally designed by Pereira & Luckman in 1957, the building at 3424 Wilshire Blvd. was erected for IBM with construction well in excess of existing standards and codes. In 1984 Olivier Vidal of La Sopha Group was the architect for re-designing and enlarging all public areas, with a new lobby and a security station manned by round-the-clock guards. The mezzanine level cafeteria was expanded with outdoor patio dining. Newly designed elevator cabs were installed as well as upgraded restroom facilities.

Pei Shang Yu & Partners, in association with William Heffner, further refined the architectural features of the building in 1991. Some of these elements include terrazzo steps and lobby flooring. In addition, Maguire Thomas Partners undertook a complete retrofit of the fire protection and life safety systems of the building and provided a state-of-the-art CCTV security system installed within new consoles in both the Ground Floor and Mezzanine lobbies. Other elements enhanced the computer areas which include a salon and pre-action fire suppression system, in conjunction with the development of the Mezzanine level conference facilities.

Constructed of cast-in-place reinforced concrete slabs, steel beams and columns and concrete sheer walls, the 186,221 square foot building, with its five story, 580 car garage, became one of the showplaces in the mid Wilshire District.

Located on the southeast corner of Wilshire Boulevard and Mariposa, adjacent to the former Ambassador Hotel and across from Equitable Plaza, the twelve story building embodied all the modern features of the building trade.

The Catholic population of the archdiocese had advanced to 3.6 million since the previous chancery had opened at 1531 West Ninth Street. In 1995, approximately 400 employees worked for the archdiocese in its central office and four satellites.

In receiving the donation of the 18 million dollar edifice, Roger Cardinal Mahony said:

"In accepting this gift, I ask the Catholic community, as well as all of our other brothers and sisters in the Southland to recommit ourselves to building God's kingdom by sharing food and drink with the hungry and thirsty; by clothing and housing the naked and the homeless; by educating and providing opportunity to the ignorant and unemployed; by offering care and comfort to the sick and the suffering, and by welcoming and embracing the strangers and the marginalized in our midst."

HISTORICAL SKETCH - ARCHIVAL CENTER

The dedication of the new Archival Center for the Archdiocese of Los Angeles in 1981 was the latest phase of a program inaugurated over two decades earlier by the late James Francis Cardinal McIntyre.

Though an archivist had been named for the old Diocese of Los Angeles-San Diego, as early as 1927, Msgr. Peter Hanrahan never functioned in any other but a titular role. He later described the collection of those early days as "a mass of unarranged materials in a walk-in vault with a combination lock at the old cathedral rectory."

Charles C. Conroy served the ecclesial community of Southern California for many years as unofficial historiographer. A retired University professor, Dr. Conroy utilized the archives for his monumental treatise on *The Centennial 1840-1940*, but he never made any headway at organizing the holdings.

In the final months of 1962, Cardinal McIntyre had a new wing added to the northeastern end of the Chancery Office which was located at 1531 West Ninth Street in Los Angeles. An archivist was formally appointed and, on the following July 8th the Chancery Archives were formally blessed and designated as an archdiocesan department.

A reporter was present for that ceremony and he later ventured the opinion in the Los Angeles *Times* that the Chancery Archives would "eventually constitute the largest collection of ecclesiastical documents in the Western United States." Indeed there was a prophetic ring to those words.

During the next nineteen years, efforts were made to augment and catalogue the widely diversified assortment of documents, brochures, books and other historical mementos associated with the development of the Catholic Church in California's southland. The initial holdings were quadrupled within the first decade and it became increasingly clear that the quarters on Ninth Street would not be able to adequately serve the ever-growing needs of the archdiocese.

On a number of occasions, the necessity for larger quarters was discussed with Timothy Cardinal Manning and Msgr. Benjamin G. Hawkes. Several possible solutions were presented, all of which were carefully studied by His Eminence and the Vicar General.

Early in 1980, Msgr. Hawkes, a member of the Board of Directors for the Dan Murphy Foundation, presented a letter from the cardinal requesting a grant with which to build a wholly separate structure for the archives on property adjacent to San Fernando Mission. With the endorsement and encouragement of Sir Daniel Donohue, the foundation generously agreed to erect a building which would serve as the major participation by the Catholic Church in the bicentennial celebrations for *El Pueblo de Nuestra Señora de los Angeles*.

Ground was broken on the Feast of Saint Pius V, April 30th. On the following February 5th, the first of twenty-three truckloads of historical materials arrived from the Chancery Office, thus launching the Archival Center on its tenure of service. It was especially fitting that this first independent archival facility erected under diocesan auspices in the United States be located within the shadow of a California mission for it was among those venerable foundations that it all began for Christ along *El Camino Real*.

The Chancery Archives exists to preserve and make available documents and other pertinent historical materials essential to the effective administration of the Archdiocese of Los Angeles. As the final repository for the permanent records of the Church in Southern California, the collection is a treasure-trove for historians, economists, political scientists and many others.

OUR·LADY·of·the·ARCHIVES

CARDINAL MANNING HOUSE OF PRAYER

When ground was broken for the new Cardinal Manning House of Prayer for the clergy of the Archdiocese of Los Angeles, the memory of Earle C. Anthony cast a long and memorable shadow over the proceedings.

The property on which the new facility is located, more recently known as the Villa San Giuseppe, was developed by one of California's most innovative and fascinating characters. Earle C. Anthony was a radio executive (KFI), a composer ("What Hawaii Means to Me"), a bridge-builder (San Francisco Bay Bridge) and a television pioneer—all in one lifetime!

But above all those accomplishments, Earle C. Anthony is credited, as early as 1927, with making Los Angeles "a completely motorized civilization." Anthony sold Packard automobiles to Los Angeles as a total way-of-life.

Kevin Starr tells how he did it: When a person purchased a Packard from Anthony, he bought into a club as well as a franchised service system. Anthony established a chain of gasoline stations, which he lighted with neon lights (a concept he imported from Europe), so that his clients might gas up or have their Packards serviced in uniformly identifiable surroundings.

"Like Helena Rubenstein or Ralph Lauren in the years to come, Anthony understood that in conditions of emergent taste, a brand, a label, a neighborhood, a specific make of car anchored identity. Nowhere was this anchoring more necessary than in Los Angeles of the 1920s and nothing could do it more dramatically than an automobile, especially a shiny new black Packard."

Anyway, in 1923, Anthony acquired eight and a half acres in the Los Feliz area overlooking Los Angeles, Hollywood, Burbank and Glendale. There he decided to build his dream home. Earle dreamed big. He and his wife traveled throughout Europe gathering thousands of photographs of castles and other historic buildings. He entrusted the plan for the building to renowned architect, Bernard Maybeck, who had earlier designed such landmarks as San Francisco's Court of Honor.

Maybeck, a proponent of mixing styles, eventually settled on a medieval, Gothic-styled mansion unlike any other ever erected in the west. Stone was imported from France, tile from Spain and wood from Italy. The completed specifications called for a classical Mediterranean estate, patterned after the early Renaissance.

Beginning in 1927, the building of the mansion stretched over three years. When completed, it covered over 23,000 square feet and became the largest house under one roof on the west coast, with twenty-eight rooms and sixteen bathrooms.

The Earle C. Anthony estate was purchased in the 1950s by Sir Daniel and Countess Bernardine Donohue. It was then christened Villa San Guiseppe in honor of Saint Joseph. The Donohues landscaped the gardens and added European art treasures throughout the mansion. The property was entrusted to the Sisters of the Immaculate Heart of Mary in 1971 and has since become the community's motherhouse. Donohue Manor, now used as a convent, was added in 1983.

Earle C. Anthony's wife died within the embrace of the Catholic Church. Surely she and her husband would rejoice at seeing how their estate at 3431 Waverly Drive is being used seventy-seven years after its birth in the Los Feliz Hills.

THE CATHEDRAL OF OUR LADY OF THE ANGELS

From 1876 until 1996, the Cathedral of Saint Vibiana served as the Mother Church for the Diocese of Monterey-Los Angeles, Diocese of Los Angeles-San Diego and the Archdiocese of Los Angeles.

Shortly after the turn of the century, it became obvious that Saint Vibiana Cathedral, dedicated in 1876 and constructed of brick and mortar, was starting to deteriorate badly. In addition, the size of the cathedral no longer suited the growing Catholic population of Southern California.

On January 27, 1904, Bishop Thomas Conaty petitioned the Congregation de Propaganda Fide for permission to "move the cathedral and demolish the present one." Pope Pius X granted the permission on June 28, 1904.

However, the financial depression of 1907 caused a significant delay in the project. In addition, Bishop Conaty's gradually declining health resulted in further delays and with his death in 1915, the notion of a new cathedral was put on hold.

When Bishop John J. Cantwell came to Los Angeles in 1917, his thoughts also turned to the possibility of a new cathedral. But other economic factors placed the project in abeyance. Between 1921 and 1922, Bishop Cantwell had a vestibule, choir loft and sacristy added to the old structure in order to meet immediate needs until such time that the plans to build a new cathedral could materialize.

A second economic depression began in 1929, delaying the plans yet again. Undaunted, in the early 1940s, Archbishop John Cantwell again set his sights on building the new cathedral. At that time, however, World War II had begun and he was forced to put the plans on hold once more.

Toward the end of the war Archbishop Cantwell acquired property on the corner of Wilshire and Rimpau and began plans once again for a new cathedral. He made the formal announcement for what was to be called the Cathedral of Our Lady of the Angels, in the August 31, 1945 issue of *The Tidings*, the Golden Jubilee edition of the Archdiocesan Catholic newspaper. The archbishop's death in 1947 halted any further work on the proposed Wilshire Boulevard Cathedral.

Installed at Los Angeles in 1948, Archbishop J. Francis A. McIntyre faced the tremendous post-war growth throughout Southern California. He devoted his energies and resources to opening and building new parishes and schools throughout the four county archdiocese.

In 1970, Archbishop, later Timothy Cardinal Manning, assumed the leadership of the archdiocese and continued the pastoral works of his predecessor.Cardinal Manning refurbished the existing cathedral in preparation for the nation's bicentennial in 1976. In addition to interior cosmetic changes, the bells were removed because of the weakened tower's inability to support them.

When Archbishop Mahony arrived in 1985, he faced many urgent pastoral priorities, including the increasing numbers of newly arrived Catholics from Mexico and Central America. Efforts to assist the inner city parishes and schools became paramount, as well as other outreach programs to provide for the spiritual needs of four million Catholics.

Plans were underway to renovate Saint Vibiana Cathedral when the Northridge Earthquake of 1994 virtually destroyed the building. Three options emerged for the future: rebuild the 1876 structure; replace it with an expanded building or relocate and build a wholly new cathedral at a different location. Eventually the decision was made to sell the 1876 structure and relocate on an expansive site above the Hollywood Freeway.

Following substantial pledges from Daniel Donohue and the Dan Murphy Foundation, Kathleen McCarthy and the Thomas and Dorothy Leavey Foundation and the Rupert Murdoch Family Foundations, a massive drive for financial support was launched. Orchestrated by Bill Close, a team of dedicated fund raisers began a campaign for the 193 million dollars needed for what would be the largest church along the Pacific Slope.

Property was acquired at Temple Street and Grand Boulevard, and Jose Rafael Moneo, an internationally known and renowned architect was selected for the project. Roger Cardinal Mahony broke ground for the new cathedral on September 21, 1997 and several months later the site was officially blessed and permanently designated for the Cathedral of Our Lady of the Angels.

Among the features of the new Cathedral are the 200 base isolators which will allow the massive structure to move up to two feet and three inches during a severe earthquake. Another unique element included the use of alabaster windows which flood the interior spaces with a milky "spiritual" light, another were tapestries portraying a panoply of Saints and Blesseds flanking the walls.

The 5.3 acre site of the cathedral is considerably more extensive than the worship area itself. The outdoor plaza, parking area, conference facilities and clerical residence are just a few of the spaces attached and akin to the cathedral.

Of all the ancillary spaces, none is more traditional, beautiful and conducive to prayer than the mausoleum with its 1,200 crypts and 5,000 cremation niches which will serve as the final resting place for many of the southland's Catholic clergy and laity. Visitors are impressed with the stained glass windows from the earlier cathedral which are electronically back-lighted for greater visibility.

The Cathedral of Our Lady of Los Angeles, reportedly "the third largest in the world" was formally dedicated September 2, 2002 by Roger Cardinal Mahony. Speaking to hundreds of cardinals, archbishops, priests and laity he said:

"Millions of people travel the 101 Freeway each year. I expect that many will have their lives brushed by God - some profoundly changed - as they gaze at the great cross on the east side, or the grand campanile on the west side. The road which leads to this spot becomes a different kind of *camino real*, closer to the route the friars first imagined, a road to Christ our King. Many motorists may exit the freeway allured by this towering icon of God's dwelling with us. Within every human heart stirs some, often unnamed, thirst for its creator. No substitute can ever quench that deep-seated thirst. In the shadow of his outpost cathedral, the Bishop of Hippo, St. Augustine, wrote: "You have made us for yourself, Lord, and our hearts are restless until they rest in you."

SAINT VINCENT'S CARDINAL MANNING CENTER (FORMERLY MISERERE HOUSE)

Among Cardinal McIntyre's priorities when he came to Los Angeles was his desire to provide a place "out of the free-eating and free-lodging house category" for needy men. He knew from his experiences in New York that the need existed.

A 15,000 square foot, two-story building was acquired at 231 Winston Street, in the heart of the city's skidrow district, in 1954. It was remodelled at a cost of $100,000 and opened on February 21,1955 as Miserere House.

Maintained and operated by the Saint Vincent de Paul Society, the steel and concrete building included a chapel with a seating capacity for 200 people, counseling offices, reading quarters, letter writing and smoking rooms, space for showers, television and games. It was unlike any other similar facility in the area.

A survey among the early clients of Miserere House revealed that most of them were seasonal workers, living in neighborhood hotels or halfway houses. Others saw Miserere House as a wholesome environment for transients between jobs and residents of the poorer neighborhoods, many of whom were living on small pensions or holding odd jobs.

In the beautiful and peaceful second floor chapel Mass was celebrated daily at 12:07 p.m. by one of the priest counselors who was also available for confessions and other types of spiritual services. Assisting the priests in their work were several professionally-trained workers who rendered advice or provided social rehabilitation to clients and users of the facility.

Miserere House was open from eight in the morning until eight at night. An estimated seventy-five men used the shower facilities every day and 150 the shaving provisions. On opening day alone, more than 600 men dropped in and within two weeks that number reached 10,000. The first year, 350,000 names were listed on the rolls. The house was not only a haven for migratory workers, but "a visible sign of an earnest effort to restore temporarily disadvantaged men to their rightful place of human dignity."

Miserere House was advertised as "something clean and fresh in a drab area." Its programs gave a promise of hope and a pledge of the "good life" to many who had fallen on bad times. Supported wholly by donations and through proceeds from the Saint Vincent de Paul Society, Miserere House provided a base of operation for men in the course of their rehabilitation. In addition, it gave users a healthy place to pass their leisure time.

There were all kinds of services available. For example, through employment services provided by Matt Campion, the House was able to find employment for 3,260 men during the first ten months of its existence. In an early mission statement for Miserere House, it was recorded that its main purpose was to provide "for the mental and spiritual upbuilding of homeless and transient men" in whatever way possible.

Miserere House was Cardinal McIntyre's own special project for needy men. A local newspaper article about the facility stated that McIntyre "saw the clients of Miserere House not as bums, but as souls in need of salvation."

CATHOLIC NEWSPAPERS

THE TIDINGS

Pope Saint Pius X once said, "In vain you win churches, give missions, found schools—all your work, all your efforts will be destroyed if you are not able to wield the defensive and offensive weapon of a loyal and sincere Catholic press."

Establishment of a Catholic newspaper in Southern California was occasioned by the religious bigotry of the American Protective Association. Fearful of losing its advertisers and readers, the Southland's secular press of the 1890s maintained a policy of strict silence in face of the A.P.A.'s campaign to exclude Catholics from equal opportunities in the business world.

In 1890, the Right Reverend Francis Mora, Bishop of Monterey-Los Angeles, asked Joseph Mesmer to establish a diocesan paper and with assurances from local merchants, the *Cause* began publication on October 4th. Shortly thereafter, the name was changed to the *Voice* but before long that enterprise also failed and Southern California was still without a journal sympathetic to Catholic principles.

Four years later, the Junípero Serra Club of San Diego took steps to counteract the malicious public statements being made against the Church. Three of its members, Patrick W. Croake, James Connolly, and Kate Murphy went to Los Angeles and there, on June 29, 1895, launched the *Catholic Tidings* from an office on the second floor of a building on New High Street. Founded on a capital of $400, the first issue had a circulation of fewer than 1,000 copies. The eight-page, four-column weekly was the product of "Irish working girls and working men who had nothing to lose and who gave willingly of their meager salaries to rally public support for the struggling journal."

In the initial editorial, the proprietors announced their purpose: "The field which the *Catholic Tidings* will humbly aim to occupy is a wide fertile one. In territory, it includes the whole of Southern California, and in population more than sixty thousand Catholics… In all matters pertaining to the best interests of the nation, state and city, the *Catholic Tidings* will be abreast of the most progressive."

Psychologically, the advent of the journal was well timed and "it was but a brief time before conditions commenced to improve" in the Church's relations with non-Catholics. There continued to be opposition to the journal, however. Several lay committees urged the editor to abandon the publication, claiming that "it caused the A.P.A. leaders to be more antagonistic than before." As a gesture to those outside the Church, the editor did agree to drop the word "Catholic" from the masthead on April 17, 1897. Though he had no financial investment in the paper, Bishop George T. Montgomery "did all in his power to help it along." Together with Croake, the prelate organized a branch of the Catholic Truth Society for the southland. The lecture program of the new organization received unlimited publicity from *The Tidings* over the early years and by the time of William McKinley's election, "the small and ridiculous figure it [the A.P.A.] cut in the campaign was an eye opener even to the most stupid politicians."

Soon after the arrival in California of the Right Reverend Thomas J. Conaty the new Bishop of Monterey-Los Angeles called a meeting of prominent Catholic businessmen at Cathedral Hall to consider a plan to acquire the paper as the official diocesan organ. *The Tidings* Publishing Company was subsequently formed and on October 7, 1904, *The Tidings* was purchased by the Church.

Subsequent decades have been no less challenging and while *The Tidings* has had its problems, it enjoys an enviable record in measuring up to John Steven McGroarty's ideal for the Catholic press which, he felt, must be "dignified, pure, and true, kindly and sweet, but above all, charitable."

VIDA NUEVA

There is a long and rich historical precedent for *Vida Nueva*, the Spanish language newspaper inaugurated on April 10, 1991 by *The Tidings* Corporation for the Archdiocese of Los Angeles. Catholic journalistic influences stretch back to August of 1846, when the *Californian*, the first newspaper published in the state, was printed on a press "found in the cloisters of one of the missions."

Since that time, the Catholic press has consistently been an active force in California life. As early as 1850 the *New York Freeman's Journal and Catholic Register* carried a regular column from a Sacramento correspondent signed only as "Philos," probably the pen name for Dr. Gregory Phelan.

The first Catholic weekly newspaper published on the Pacific Coast originated at San Francisco under the auspices of Father Hugh Gallagher. The *Catholic Standard*, launched on May 6, 1854, advertised itself as "an organ of the Catholic Church."

Apart from the long list of English-speaking newspapers sponsored by the Church or issued "under Catholic auspices," *La Cronica* has the distinction of being the first published in California for the Hispanic community. Edited by E. F. Teodoli, *La Cronica* was described by a writer in the Los Angeles *Star* as "a substantial paper, published semi-weekly."

La Cronica appeared fairly consistently between 1872 and 1892 when the newspaper got into financial straits and ceased publication. It was succeeded by another Hispanic weekly known as *Las dos Republicas*.

A Portuguese newspaper was distributed in the Bay area under the masthead of *O Vox Portuguesa* between 1884 and 1888 by Antonio Vicente. A second paper, begun in 1884 under the title *O Progresso Californiense*, limped along for five years and was then made over to *A Unaio Portuguesa* by Manuel Trigueiro.

Der Californischen Volksfreund was a Catholic paper printed in the German language in San Francisco. Begun in 1885 by Carl Doeing and Frank Diepenbrock, the publication lasted until 1906. *O Amigos*

dos Catolicos originated at Irvington in 1888. The Portuguese publication was inaugurated by Fathers Manuel Francisco Fernandez and Jose Francisco Tavares. After a year the paper passed to lay control and moved to Pleasanton.

From 1892 to 1896 it was printed at Hayward. The name was changed to *O Arauto* in 1896 and until 1917 it was published at Irvington under the editorship of Messrs. Lemos and Quaresma. In the latter year, Pedro L. C. Silveira purchased the paper and merged it with his *Jornal de Noticias*.

L'Imparziale was first published from San Francisco in 1891 by Joseph Morgana. The paper was inactive for some years but was revived between 1897 and 1909 as the *Impartial Californian* under the direction of P. S. Bergerot. In 1901 the Saint Louis *Review* called it "the only Italian Catholic paper in the United States."

Luigi Muzio edited a newspaper known as *La Verita* at San Francisco between 1893 and 1894. The venture started and finished as an Italian Catholic publication.

"Devoted to the instruction in Catholic truth and doctrine" of the Spanish speaking people in Southern California was *La Actualidad*, printed from 1895 at San Bernardino under the direction of Father Juan Caballeria. The eight page weekly ceased publication about 1902. In 1897, Constantino Soares originated *O Reporter* at Oakland. From 1910 to 1914 the weekly was owned and issued by the Reverend Jose Silva.

CATHOLIC DIRECTORIES

A Catholic census of the City of Los Angeles was taken in 1899 in preparation for a directory. A total of 18,857 Catholics are represented (those fifteen years of age or older), plus another 418 "inmates" of Religious Houses. Another ninety-three living outside the city limits were added for various reasons. Each person listed in the directory was identified with his or her parish. The Catholics residing in Los Angeles, in September, 1899, were divided into the six parishes of Saint Vibiana, Our Lady of the Angels, Saint Vincent, Saint Joseph, Sacred Heart and Saint Mary. Of the parishes then canonically functioning, only Saint Joseph lacked specific boundaries. It was established for the accommodation of the German-speaking Catholics of the whole city.

According to the directory, there were ninety priests serving in the 75,984 square mile diocese. There were twenty-three seminarians (eight studying for the diocese and fifteen for religious orders), forty-six churches with resident priests, forty-two mission churches, twenty-nine station churches and two chapels. Educationally, there were 2,497 enrollees in twenty-two academies and twenty-four parochial schools. Eight orphanages cared for 1,198 orphans, as well as 400 children in three Indian schools.

At that time, the jurisdiction was bounded by Arizona, the Pacific Ocean, Peninsular California and the 37th degree, 5th minute northern latitude. It embraced the portions of Merced, Santa Clara and Santa Cruz counties lying south of that line.

Unfortunately, like many literary compendia, the directory was not financially successful, nor was the labor involved in its production properly acknowledged. But the book was, nonetheless, a monumental accomplishment, perhaps most appreciated by those of us living in a later era. California's southland would not see another such compilation of ecclesial statistics for forty-five years!

The first of the Catholic directories issued in California's southland is now a rare and prized collector's item. It was conceived and produced by one of the area's great literary forebears, Frederick L. Reardon (1879-1906). Born in Peoria, Illinois, he was the son of a well-known officer in the Union Army. His parents brought their family of five youngsters to Los Angeles "when Fred was a little lad in knickerbockers".

Throughout his relatively short life, Reardon was a dominant personality in his many endeavors. A friend recalled that even as a student at Saint Vibiana School, Fred "led us all, and on the tree-shaded playground, as well as in our holiday rambles over the hills, he was our leader. We realized his ability and accorded him recognition, looking up to him and following in his footsteps".

Reardon's intellectual acumen was equally outstanding. He achieved a splendid record at Saint Vincent's College, winning practically every medal or other scholastic honor offered to students. While there he organized a monthly paper and launched it upon the seas of college journalism, reason enough for the Vincentian faculty to regard him "as one of the brightest young men ever enrolled in the college".

After obtaining a master's degree at The Catholic University of America in Washington, D.C. Reardon returned to California, proudly displaying his most treasured possession, a volume of Maurice Francis Egan's poems inscribed on the fly leaf with the writer's prediction that his young friend would become the laureate of the Pacific.

By that time, Reardon had determined to issue a Catholic directory to serve the far-flung Diocese of Monterey-Los Angeles, an ambitious project for which the energetic and talented writer was well trained. Reardon's principal motivation for the directory was that of "making Catholics known to each other and so foster the many good things that would necessarily result from a more perfect union between our co-religionists". A contemporary revealed that Reardon "labored hard and persistently, traversing the length and breadth of the vast district gathering the necessary names, information and statistics".

The 377 page volume, handsomely bound and profusely illustrated, was issued in September of 1899. Printed by L. R. Jones, whose firm was then located at 235 West First Street, Los Angeles, the book contained several hundred advertisements, mostly from the various religious institutions then serving the area.

Since 1947, *The Tidings*, official Catholic newspaper for the Archdiocese of Los Angeles, has published an annual *Catholic Directory* for the Church in Southern California. The issue for 2006 was Volume 60 and released under the editorship of Hermine Lees.

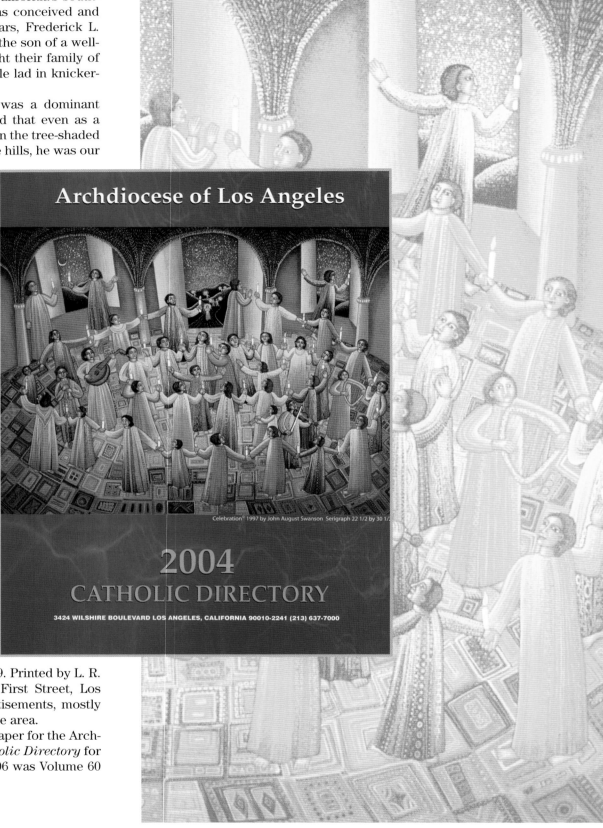

Archdiocese of Los Angeles

Celebration© 1997 by John August Swanson Serigraph 22 1/2 by 30 1/2

2004
CATHOLIC DIRECTORY

3424 WILSHIRE BOULEVARD LOS ANGELES, CALIFORNIA 90010-2241 (213) 637-7000

THE CALIFORNIA CARDINALATE

A faint thread of purple moire or watered-silk in California's Catholic heritage can be traced to September 17, 1875. In a letter to his cousin, Luigi Cardinal Amat, the Right Reverend Thaddeus Amat, Bishop of Monterey-Los Angeles, expressed his happiness about Pius IX's elevation of New York's Archbishop John McCloskey to the cardinalate, noting that "someday, possibly within a century, that honor will come to Los Angeles." The Vincentian prelate went on to say that "when I asked the Holy Father to move [my] episcopal *sedes*, it was from a contention that Los Angeles would one day rank among the great cities of the republic and even the world." Bishop Amat concluded by observing that he was planning "a cathedral fit for an eminent Cardinal!"

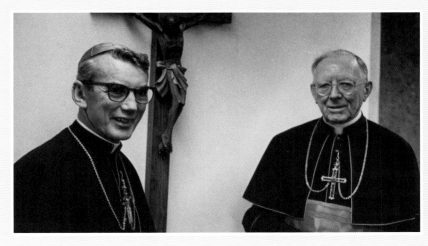

The Golden State was honored, in the latter part of 1887, with a visit by James Cardinal Gibbons, the ranking dignitary of the Catholic Church in the United States. After a brief stop in San Francisco, the prelate proceeded to the southland. The first cardinalatial visitation to the City of Our Lady of the Angels began with a liturgical ceremony at Saint Vibiana's Cathedral and an official greeting by the Right Reverend Francis Mora, Bishop of Monterey-Los Angeles.

In responding, His Eminence of Baltimore observed that the growth and progress of the Pacific Coast far exceeded his "wildest expectations." The prelate went on to say that "the glory of your State after all lies not so much in your climate and soil, but your prosperity consists in your manhood, intelligence and the zeal and earnestness which the American people bring to every enterprise they undertake." The cardinal's biographer later wrote that the presence of Gibbons in the far west "aroused a great deal of interest and enthusiasm among the Catholic people of those regions. It was their first glimpse of a prince of the Church, and their pride in playing host to a member of the College of Cardinals was heightened when they observed the generally friendly manner in which their non-Catholic friends and neighbors greeted the visitor."

The cardinalatial dignity ultimately came to the Golden State in 1953, with Pope Pius XII's bestowal of the red hat on J. Francis A. McIntyre, Archbishop of Los Angeles. The nation's twelfth cardinal was welcomed by the Catholic populace of the Southland, in Amat's "cathedral fit for an eminent Cardinal," on January 21, 1953.

The distinction was renewed two Popes and twenty years later by Pope Paul VI's elevation of Archbishop Timothy Manning, as America's twenty-eighth member of the Sacred College.

Los Angeles, one of the nine cities in the continental United States honored with the cardinalate over a span of ninety-eight years, enjoyed the further distinction of being one of the five ecclesial jurisdications in all the world possessing two living cardinals at one time.

Pope John Paul II's appointment of Archbishop Roger M. Mahony to the cardinalate on May 29, 1991, confirmed a precedent and renewed a commitment to the spiritual well-being of the faithful in Southern California.

Cardinals are commonly referred to as "brothers of the Pope," a terminology especially apt for the Shepherd of God's People in Southern California. There is much that binds the City of *Nuestra Señora de los Angeles* to the See of Peter.

CALIFORNIA — FIRST MASS

In the closing months of 1931, a bronze plaque attached to a three ton boulder near the present site of the Fort Guijarros Monument was solemnly dedicated by the Very Reverend John Hegarty who represented Bishop John J. Cantwell. On the plaque were these words: 'This boulder erected November 1, 1931 by Court San Diego De Alcalá, No. 1099 of the Catholic Daughters of America, to commemorate the first Holy Mass celebrated in California, November 11, 1602 upon the arrival on this site of Sebastian Vizcaino who named the port San Diego in honor of the feast of Señor San Diego de Alcalá and who was accompanied by three Carmelite friars Fray Andrés de la Asumpción, Fray Antonio de la Ascención and Fray Tomás de Aquino."

The story of the three priests with the Vizcaino expedition can be traced to November 24, 1601, when the Viceroy of New Spain asked Carmelite officials to appoint chaplains for the contemplated voyage up the California coast. They were to have two major tasks - administering the sacraments to those aboard the expeditionary ships and instructing and converting "all heathen Indians" in the area.

The trinity of ships left Acapulco on May 5, 1602. The voyage up the coast of peninsular California proved to be extremely treacherous. After a journey of more than six months, the ships finally arrived off the Southern California coast.

On November 10, Vizcaino had his ships anchor in a bay off what later became known as Ballast Point. Two days later, on the Feast of San Diego de Alcalá, Vizcaino, his officers and chaplains went ashore.

According to the captain's diary, once on shore "a hut was built and Mass was said in celebration of the feast of San Diego." Since there were three priests, one can presume that it was a Solemn High Mass. Con-celebration was not then allowed, so it is unclear which of the friars was the actual celebrant of the Mass on that historic day in California's history.

It was another three hundred years before there was any commemoration of that important event. It came about in July of 1911 in conjunction with the groundbreaking of the Panama-California

Explorer of California 1542
29 USA
Juan Rodríguez CABRILLO

THE FIRST MASS IN CALIFORNIA

by
Msgr. Francis J. Weber

MM
Old Monterey Book Company

Exposition buildings. The military sponsored a Mass on the shores of San Diego Bay at the exact location of the 1602 celebration. Bishop Thomas J. Conaty came to represent the Diocese of Los Angeles-San Diego.

It wasn't until 1932 that plans were finalized for dedicating a plaque to commemorate the first Mass in California. Speaker for that event was Father Martin Cody Keating who paid tribute to the adventurous Spaniards who carried the cross of Christianity and the banner of their king to what was then the rim of Christendom.

Unfortunately, because of military restrictions, the area in which the marker was placed proved to be almost totally inaccessible to the general public. In 1963, the United States Navy moved the plaque to its present location in front of the submarine base chapel.

CARDINAL'S AWARD DINNER

The Cardinal's Award Dinner began in 1990 as a means of recognizing men and women who had provided significant leadership in improving the lives of people in Southern California.

Since then the Award has been bestowed annually "to extend appreciation and gratitude to persons who have given extraordinarily of their time or treasure in ways that benefit the quality of life in the local community.

In 1989, an advisory committee was formed to plan for the annual event. The Award itself was a statue of the Blessed Virgin Mary. There were five honorees the first year at the event which was staged at the Regent Beverly Wilshire Hotel on February 1, 1990.

The design of the award was changed slightly two years later when Archbishop Roger M. Mahony became a member of the Sacred College of Cardinals.

Since 1996 the annual proceeds of the Awards Dinner have been assigned to benefiting the poorer parishes of the archdiocese. The cardinal himself decides on the parishes to be assisted.

During subsequent years_____ people have been honored as recipients of the Cardinal's Awards. In 1998, because of increased attendance at the Dinner, it was necessary to move the event to a larger ballroom at the Beverly Hilton Hotel.

Every effort has been made over the years to select honorees who represent the geographic and ethnic diversity of the three county archdiocese. The Development Committee works diligently to have the event underwritten by companies and individuals.

Cardinal's Awards Dinner

1990 - 2005
Sixteen Year Report

THE C.C.D. CONGRESS

In 1970 the annual Confraternity of Catholic Doctrine Congress was moved to the Anaheim Convention Center where it hosted over 10,000 Catholics in the opening year. From that time onwards, the Congress has become an annual staple in the religious life of the whole western part of the nation.

The first Youth Rally was held in 1971 for students. It became a model for the present Youth Day which attracts youngsters from all around the southland to the opening day of the Congress.

At the Congress in 1972, Timothy Cardinal Manning presided at a Liturgy commemorating the fiftieth anniversary of the beginnings of a formal religious education in the Diocese of Monterey-Los Angeles by Bishop John J. Cantwell.

The term "Religious Education Congress" was adopted in 1973 and scores of workshops in Spanish were offered for the first time that year. Each year the number of workshops escalate as do the crowds swarming to hear the speakers and engage in the various outreaches.

Today the Congress supports the diverse needs of parish leaders by offering workshops in evangelization, liturgy, theology, Scripture, spirituality, morality, parish leadership, detention ministry, peace and justice, as well as adult elementary and early childhood catechesis and youth ministry.

GREAT SEAL OF LOS ANGELES

The City of Our Lady of the Angels has always taken cognizance of its Catholic beginnings. One obvious example of that historical awareness is the official seal prominently displayed at all civic functions.

According to one explanation, the seven-decade rosary surrounding the sixty year old seal "suggests the part played by the Mission friars in founding the City." At the time of the seal's adoption, there was considerable anti-Catholic feeling in Los Angeles, most of it spawned by the American Protective Association. It was through the efforts of the Native Sons of the Golden West, who insisted that the missionaries be remembered, that the rosary was included. The original seal, formally adopted on March 27, 1905, contained ten decades. In the interest of correct heraldry, some slight modifications were made in 1949, and now the traditional seven decade Franciscan crown rosary encompasses the four-part pictorial emblem.

Herbert L. Goudge, one-time deputy city attorney and designer of the seal, felt that the crown rosary was the most characteristic reminder of the gray-robed pioneers of California, both because of its traditional association with the friars and because of the actual name bestowed on the area in 1781.

The rosary itself has an interesting history. It was introduced in the early 1400's by a young Franciscan novice to commemorate the Seven Joys of the Blessed Mother. It later became customary to add two additional beads to coincide with the seventy-two years Mary was thought to have lived on earth. Sprays of olive, orange and grape just outside the field suggests the fertile location of Los Angeles in a semi-tropical land of picturesque scenery. The shield within the circlet of beads contains four significant emblems. The lion of Leon and Castile recalls Spanish dominance over the tiny *pueblo* from 1781 to 1822. An eagle holding a snake in its mouth represents the Republic of Mexico whose sovereignty over the City of Our Lady of the Angels lasted from 1822 to 1846.

The era prior to the Golden State's entry into the union is represented by the old Bear Flag of the California Republic. The emblem of the stars and stripes shows that Los Angeles has been under democratic forms of government, both Federal and State, from its incorporation in 1850 to the present time. Certainly it is fitting that the nation's largest city dedicated to the Blessed Mother should publicly recognize that fact in its official seal.

~Meaning of City Seal~

The lion of Leon and the castle of Castile are from the Arms of Spain and represent Los Angeles under Spanish control 1542—1821.

The eagle holding a serpent is from the Arms of Mexico and represents the period of Mexican sovereignty 1822—1846

The Bear Flag typifies the California Republic of 1846.

The Stars and Stripes indicate the present status of this City in an American State.

The sprays of Olive Grape and Orange suggest the location of Los Angeles as a City set in a garden. ~~~ The beaded circle surrounding the shield represents a Rosary suggesting the part played by the Mission Padres in founding the City.

Compliments of the Board of Public Works.

OUR LADY OF CALIFORNIA

California's early friars were clients of Mary and were responsible for introducing her devotion to the area, so much so that the Vice Postulator of Junípero Serra's cause has said that "If Mother Church should raise the Apostle of California to the honor of the altars, we know whose hand will weave for him the garland of sainthood."

Nuestra Señora de Belen, christened *La Conquistadora* by Galvez, had been shipped to Monterey and was used in taking possession of the land there for Spain. The statue was later returned to Mexico, but found its way back to Mission San Carlos in subsequent years. Special veneration to Mary during the colonial period is attributed to that statue and today it is considered California's oldest and most historic replica of the Mother of God.

Two missions in Alta California, *La Purisima Concepcion* and *Nuestra Señora de la Soledad* were dedicated to Our Lady as were seven of the twenty-five establishments in Baja or peninsular California.

The first Bishop of Both Californias, Francisco Garcia Diego y Moreno, was consecrated in the magnificient Marian Shrine of Our Lady of Guadalupe near Mexico City where the Virgin is venerated as the "Empress of the Americas" and, on January 4, 1843, Bishop Garcia Diego declared Our Lady, Refuge of Sinners, the Patroness of the Californias. This patronage has never been revoked and the feast has recently been restored to the state's liturgical calendar.

Old Saint Mary's Cathedral in San Francisco was dedicated to Our Lady in 1854, under her title "Saint Mary, Ever Virgin and Conceived Without Sin." This century-old edifice was the first cathedral in the entire world named in honor of the Immaculate Conception after that doctrine was defined.

A second cathedral in the Bay City was also a Marian Shrine. Dedicated in 1891 to Mary's Assumption, it was in constant use until the fall of 1962, when it was reduced to ashes by a ravaging fire. Stockton's Saint Mary of the Ascension Cathedral also claims the protection of the Blessed Virgin.

California's largest city was named in honor of *Nuestra Señora de los Angeles del Rio de Porciuncula*, where Portola's expedition camped enroute to Monterey in 1769. The virgin's name was given to numerous other towns and villages.

The seminary, erected by Bishop Garcia Diego at Mission Santa Ines in 1844, was dedicated to Our Lady of Guadalupe and served the diocese for several decades, first as a training center for prospective priests and later as a boarding school. Among seminaries bearing Mary's name are Immaculate Heart Novitiate at Kentfield and Our Lady of New Clairvaux at Vina. Two diocesan institutions, that of Immaculate Heart in San Diego and Queen of Angels at San Fernando were also given a Marian orientation.

Personal devotion to the Mother of God has always characterized California's Catholic heritage. For example, on May 7, 1873, Father Joachim Adam wrote from Santa Cruz, "The image of Our Lady has been venerated in this place for more than fifty years, first in the Old Mission Church, now in ruins, and since July 4, 1858, in the new frame church, on the main altar. In 1870 I built a nice side-chapel in one of the towers of the Church, and the image was taken in solemn procession from the main altar to the new chapel, March 25, 1870, where it has been venerated since, with great devotion by people of every condition in life."

California's devotion to Mary forms a chapter all its own and we have space here only to mention in briefest outline the more prominent manifestations of this allegiance. But, from these few words, it can be seen that the Mother of God deserves a lion's share of the credit for California's spiritual and material attainments.

MEMOIR OF A PAPAL VISIT - 1987

If ever my diary or even parts of it are published, I suspect the most intriguing entry will be that made for September 16, 1987, the day Pope John Paul II dropped by for lunch.

At the outset, it should be pointed out that the Holy Father's presence at what *Time* magazine called "the lovely San Fernando Mission," was anything but a casual visit. A goodly portion of the preceding year was spent getting ready for what proved to be the most singular event in the almost two hundred year history of California's seventeenth missionary outpost.

And though one might fantasize that the Roman Pontiff came just to see "the best of the California missions," or "the finest of the nation's Catholic archives," the real reason was to meet with members of the National Conference of Catholic Bishops during Pope John Paul's second pastoral visit to the United States.

There were weekly and then daily briefings with members from the Papal Visit Office, the Secret Service, police and fire officials, traffic controllers, caterers, representatives from the United States Catholic Conference, media pools and other concerned agencies and individuals. San Fernando Mission became an integral part of the most elaborate and intensive preparations ever made for the visit of a foreign dignitary to the United States.

The already scheduled maintenance programs for the Old Mission were revised, updated and advanced in order to have the building and grounds in top shape for the papal visit. *Las Damas Archivistas* inaugurated plans for commemorating the event with appropriate splender by commissioning the renowed artist, Isabel Piczek, to design and fabricate a giant tile portrayal of the Holy Father being welcomed to the Old Mission by Fray Junípero Serra. The ladies began raising the necessary funds sponsoring bake sales, boutiques and other service-related projects. Theirs became the most visible and surely the most colorful of all the preparations and involved the largest number of people.

There were others involved in looking after the needs of the papal visit, including Frederick's of Santa Maria (food services), Martinez and Murphey (altar and sanctuary furnishings) and David Jones of Hollywood (floral arrangements).

On the eve of the Holy Father's arrival, a gigantic "spit and shine" party was staged on the grounds. Forty-five volunteers brought brooms, rakes, dusters, clippers and bags to complete the final preparatory phase. Thousands of fallen leaves and flower buds were picked up, bagged and removed. By mid-afternoon, the five acres comprising San Fernando Mission resembled a giant Hollywood movie set, except that ours was real. We prayed long and hard for good weather, and the Lord answered our supplications favorably.

A veritable army of Secret Service agents, police and fire personnel, Air Force bomb specialists, journalists, television crew and ecclesial officials began arriving at 2:00 AM. on the targeted day of September 16th.

The entire area was "swept" by electronic sensors and then "snuffed out" by three specially-trained canines. That the security net worked is confirmed by the fact that an "intruder" was indeed detected, discovered and placed in custody. The only mishap of the day occurred when an overly-zealous policeman accidentally set fire to a dry area of the adjoining property. Happily, the local incendiary squad reacted promptly and successfully.

A contingency of *Las Damas Archivistas* was processed through the command post at 6:30 A.M. and they quickly set about to complete preparations for feeding the bishops. About an hour later, the first episcopal contingency arrived from the New Otani Hotel.

The seven other buses bringing the cardinals, archbishops and bishops from the LAX Hilton rolled in on schedule at 7:45 A.M. Each of the prelates was greeted and then escorted to a staging area, where a continental breakfast was served by the colorfully costumed ladies.

At 8:45, the 305 members of the hierarchy were ushered to the mission church. The simple house-of-worship decorated tastefully but simply by yellow and white gladiolas and tuberose lilies, symbolized the roots of the Church along the Pacific Slope. Towering over the assembled prelates was the stately figure of San Fernando Rey de España, the same statue that presided over the establishment of the mission in 1797.

"Marine #1," the helicopter bringing the Holy Father from Saint Vibiana's Cathedral, arrived precisely at 9:05 A.M., landing on the field of Queen of Angels Seminary. Three additional khaki-colored helicopters transported the rest of the papal party.

After his Holiness had been officially welcomed to "Mission Hills International," he entered a limousine with Archbishop Roger Mahony for a short motorcade around the western perimeter of the seminary to the gate leading into the mission cemetery. During his short walk towards the Church, the Holy Father blessed the graves of the almost 1,200 Indians interred there between 1797 and 1840.

As he approached the church, the Holy Father glanced upward at the magnificent tile portrayal commemorating his visit. The smile that came across his face was likely inspired by the depiction of the little Sheltie doggie, smallPAXweber, which sits ever-so-quietly at the feet of Fray Junípero Serra.

At the entrance to the church, the Holy Father was presented with an artistically embroidered stole. He blessed himself and his party with holy water and then entered the church where he was greeted by applause from the assemblage.

Lauds or Morning Prayer was sung and recited by the Pontiff and the American hierarchy. In his homily, Pope John Paul II exhorted the bishops to "be examples to the flock," saying that "we shall be precisely that to the extent that our lives are centered on the person of Jesus Christ."

At the completion of Lauds, Archbishop Mahony acting on behalf of the local Catholic community, presented the Holy Father with a beautiful oil painting of the Old Mission together with the historical concordance entrusted to Fray Junípero Serra by his Mallorcan confreres in 1749.

Afterwards, the Pontiff was led through the mission gardens to the seminary dining hall where he was officially welcomed by the cardinals, archbishops and bishops of the United States. In what *Time* magazine described as "an exceptionally cordial encounter," Pope John Paul II listened intently to several interventions by representatives of the episcopacy and then engaged in a dialogue that lasted well beyond the allotted time. Details of that meeting were divulged through official channels.

Following a short pause in the Old Mission's rectory, the Holy Father returned for a buffet luncheon in the garden area. About an hour later he rose, thanked the episcopal conference, and went back to the rectory for a brief rest. It was exactly 2:30 when "Marine # 1," lifted majestically into the sky.

As requested, the Holy Father left behind his signature in our guest book, on an autograph card and on a white zucchetto. In addition he presented a chasuble and stole with a papal crest to the Historical Museum, together with a small box of rosaries and medals "for your dear friends."

It took several days for those of us at San Fernando Mission to digest the happenings of those five and a half hours - to fully appreciate that Pope John Paul II had prayed in our church, lunched in our garden and rested in our quarters. Hereafter and forever, San Fernando will be the "papal mission," the first of those great frontier establishments along the Pacific Slope, visited by the Vicar of Christ.

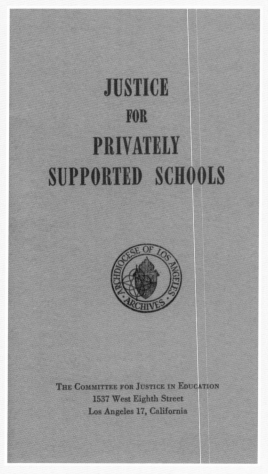

JUSTICE FOR PRIVATELY SUPPORTED SCHOOLS

THE COMMITTEE FOR JUSTICE IN EDUCATION
1537 West Eighth Street
Los Angeles 17, California

TAXATION OF CHURCHES IN CALIFORNIA

Traditionally, church property has been exempted from taxation for the same reasons that apply to governmental property, namely, that churches perform a public service in lieu of and in advance of taxation. The moral and cultural values afforded by religious influence have always been recognized as beneficial to the public, necessary to the advancement of civilization and conducive to the promotion of society's overall welfare.

Inasmuch as religious societies are deemed to be public benefactors, the practice of exempting church property from taxation is one which has become deeply imbedded in the fabric of this nation. Such an attitude rests on the immemorial custom which developed when the parish was as much a municipal corporation as towns, villages and cities are today. It continued after the reason for it had disappeared, and was then bolstered by statutory enactments, constitutional provisions, or by a combination of the two.

California's constitution of 1850 however, absolutely prohibited the legislature from exempting any but public property from taxation: 'Taxation shall be equal and uniform throughout the State. All property in this State shall be taxed in proportion to its value, to be ascertained as directed by law." The constitution further provided that assessments and collections should be made by local officers elected for that purpose in the districts, counties or towns where the property was situated. The fact that on the local level no real attempt was made to pressure the churches into paying taxes only confirms the generally held view about the crudities in the revenue system adopted.

The state's earliest lawmakers regarded "all property" as "all taxable property" and, in the Revenue Act of 1853, passed legislation whereby "churches, chapels and other public buildings used for religious worship, and lots of ground appurtenant thereto and used therewith, shall be exempt from taxation." The constitutionality of that action was sustained in 1854, when Chief Justice Hugh C. Murray ruled that "the power of the Legislature to exempt (from taxation) the property of religious and eleemosynary corporations has not been doubted." When the Revenue Act was amended in 1857, the clause exempting church property was continued. When that legislation was challenged six years later, Chief Justice Edward Norton agreed with the earlier interpretation and ruled that the failure to tax a portion of the land in the state did not thereby render the Revenue Act of 1857 void.

A complete reversal came in 1868, when Chief Justice Augustus L. Rhodes over-ruled the former decisions and directed that a tax be levied on all property, except that owned by the state or federal government. The jurist apparently acted with reluctance, however, noting that his decision would bring California's churches and charities under a burden not contemplated by the framers of the constitution. Between 1868 and 1879, the minimum of valuation was accessed against church property because of the general understanding that the churches had fallen victim to an unintentional injustice.

When the constitution for California was adopted in 1880, a considerable number of petitions were received asking that churches and schools be given explicit exemption. Unfortunately, however, the same spirit that called the convention controlled and adopted the new constitution and churches, along with colleges, asylums, charities, libraries, museums and even cemeteries failed to win exemption.

In 1885, Dr. C. C. Stratton, then President of the University of the Pacific, tried unsuccessfully to induce the legislature to submit an amendment for the relief of churches and schools from the tax rolls. Nine years later, however, an amendment did carry exempting free libraries and free museums from the tax rolls.

Early in 1896, the Reverend F. D. Bovard wrote an important article in the *Overland Monthly* in which he said that "the State by this unjust taxation has scoffingly demanded tribute of its benefactor." He called for removing the taxation of church property, arguing that (1) church property is unproductive, (2) that taxation is an unfair drain on the liberality of church membership, (3) that churches provide useful and important moral dimensions to society, (4) that churches are assisting the state by conducting orphanages, private schools and the like, (5) that church goers are effectively taxed an additional 4 to 6% for the privilege of worshipping God and (6) that taxation of churches is entirely foreign to the traditional spirit of California. He also contended that taxation had literally impoverished many church organizations, much to the detriment of the commonweal.

Bovard concluded his forceful appeal by suggesting that the State of California should acknowledge "in a delicate but substantial manner its obligation to (the Christian) religion by exempting from taxation the property dedicated to the worship of God."

The legislators paid attention to Bovard's pleas, as did many others among the general electorate. A further attempt to extend the 1894 provision was made three years later, but owing to the large number of amendments proposed and the lateness of the legislative session, no effectual, action was taken at the time.

In 1898, the Presbyterian Synod of California took the initiative and organized a committee to work for tax relief of church property. Their work was rewarded on February 14, 1899, when both houses of the state legislature passed the following measure:

> All buildings and so much of the real property on which they are situated as may be required for the convenient use and occupation of said buildings, when the same are used solely and exclusively for religious worship, shall be free from taxation.

That legislation was approved by the voters of California on November 6, 1900.

PATRONAGE

On June 8, 2006, The Vatican Prefect of the Congregation for Divine Worship and Discipline of the Sacraments, Francis Cardinal Aririze, notified Catholics in the California's southland that Our Lady of the Angels has been named principal patroness of the Archdiocese of Los Angeles, a decision approved by Pope Benedict XVI.

The earliest ecclesiastical patronage in California dates from January 4, 1843, when the first bishop, Francisco Garcia Diego y Moreno, placed his jurisdiction under the spiritual protection of Our Lady, Reflige of Sinners. When the diocese was divided in 1853, the Archbishop of San Francisco adopted another heavenly intercessor while the southland retained its earlier allegiance. On September 1, 1856, Pope Pius IX gave the Diocese of Monterey as its patroness Vibiana, a saint unearthed in the Roman catacombs a few years earlier.

The term "Los Angeles" had been a part of the episcopal title since 1859, but that appellation, a shortened form of *Nuestra Señora de Los Angeles*, never figured in the original religious patronage of Southern California.

It was suggested that a transfer of patronage to Our Lady of the Angels would be highly appropriate for the Archdiocese of Los Angeles. Possibly the late Archbishop John J. Cantwell had that in mind when plans were drafted for a proposed cathedral by that name in the 1940s. That the title of the archdiocese had no connection with its patronage, however, is not without precedent in the United States where only four of the twenty-eight archdioceses identify title and patron.

Fray Juan Crespi recorded in his diary that late in the afternoon of July 31, 1769, the expeditionary force of Gaspar de Portola crossed an *arroyo* of muddy water and stopped a little further on in a wide clearing. He stated that the following day was set aside to celebrate the jubilee of Our Lady of the Angels de Porciuncula. The next morning on the vigil of the feast, the party continued its journey and came through a pass between two hills into a broad valley abounding in poplar and alden trees. A beautiful brook crossed the valley and later turned around a hill to the south. After traveling another twenty miles, the Spaniards camped along a river which they fittingly named in honor of *Nuestra Señora de Los Angeles* de Porciuncula, a title derived from the day's liturgical calendar.

According to canonical procedures, the patron of a place is the saint honored as the special protector of that locale. In the case of Los Angeles, this distinction was accorded to Our Lady of the Angels when the name given to the Rio Porciuncula was extended in its alternate from to the *pueblo* founded in the fall of 1781.

Since the feast of Our Lady of the Angels of the Porciuncula was not observed in the universal liturgical schema, the patronage of Mary under that title could not applied to the *pueblo* as a formal ecclesiastical patron except by privilege and even then only after consultation with the clergy and laity of the place. In this, as in other similar cases it has been the practice of the Holy See to bestow as the titular feastday, that of Mary's Assumption into heaven. Hence as early as 1814, Fray Luis Gil of San Gabriel spoke of laying the cornerstone of the church at Los Angeles on the 15th of August on which it, the *pueblo*, celebrates its titular feast.

Although canonical legislation pertaining to patrons of places applies less strictly to churches (the patron or title of a church is the person or mystery to which the edifice has been dedicated), it is also an established custom that churches dedicated to the Blessed Virgin Mary, without the addition of one of her liturgical tities should celebrate their patronal feast on the 15th of August. Thus it is that the city's oldest church, located on the plaza, also observes Assumption Day, not August 2nd, as its annual feast day.

To rephrase it more succinctly, until now religious patronage in the Archdiocese of Los Angeles had no connection with that of the City of Our Lady of the Angels, which proudly saluted its patroness each year on the 15th of August under her original title, *Nuestra Señora de Los Angeles.*

The feastday for Our Lady of the Angels, which some years ago was moved to coincide with the anniversary of the city's establishment, will continue to be observed on September 4th.

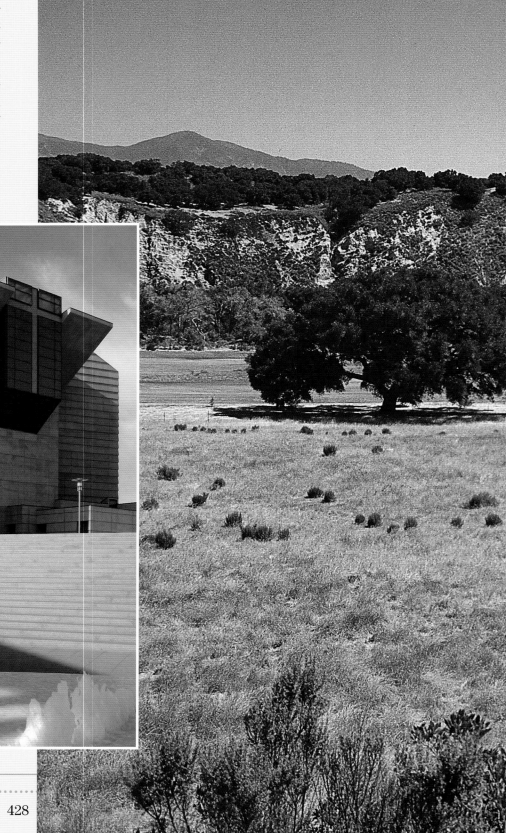

Archdiocese of Los Angeles
Significant Occurences
(1936-2006)

Metropolitan Archbishopric of Los Angeles, 1936

International Marian Celebration, 1937

Saint John's Seminary, 1940

Centennial of California Hierarchy, 1940

Pilgrimage to Mexico City, 1941

First Auxiliary Bishop, 1941

Biblical Campaign, 1941

Synod, 1942

Catholic Press Council, 1948

Mary's Hour, 1948

Catholic Information Center, 1948

Archbishop's Christmas Party, 1949

Department of Hospitals & Health, 1950

Archbishop's Fund for Charity, 1951

Annual Motion Picture Breakfast, 1952

Vocation Department, 1952

Cardinalate to Los Angeles, 1953

Queen of Angels Seminary, 1954

Lay Mission Helpers, 1955

Mission Doctors Association, 1959

Synod, 1960

Chancery Archives, 1962

Department of Radio & Television, 1962

Cursillo Apostolate, 1962

Liturgical Commission (reorganized), 1963

Ecumenical Commission, 1967

Instructional Television Department, 1967

Department of Special Services, 1967

Music Commission, 1968

Right to Life League, 1969

Finance Council, 1970

Priest Senate, 1970

Diaconate Program, 1972

Clerical Placement Board, 1972

Family Life Bureau, 1972

Retirement Plan for Priests, 1972

Episcopal Vicars, 1973

Team Ministry, 1973

Continuing Education for Clergy, 1973

Encuentro Hispano de Pastoral, 1973

Commission on Aging, 1974

Communications Commission, 1974

Charismatic Renewal, 1974

Marriage Encounter, 1974

House of Prayer, 1975

Conciliation and Arbitration Board, 1977

Pastoral Councils, 1977

Retirement Plan for Chancery Employees, 1977

Multilingual Apostolate, 1978

Peace and Justice Commission, 1983

Ad Hoc Womens Task Force, 1985

Archdiocesan Pastoral Regions, 1986

Tercero Encuentro Hispano, 1986

Proposal Immigration Initiatives, 1986

Education Foundation, 1987

Papal Visit, 1987

Cardinals Awards, 1990

Vida Nueva, 1991

Together in Mission, 1993

Clergy Misconduct Oversight Board, 1994

Archdiocesan Catholic Center, 1996

Catholic Mortuaries, 2001

Our Lady of Angels Cathedral, 2002

Synod, 2003

RELIGIOUS INSTITUTES OF MEN-BROTHERS

- Augustinian Recollect Brothers
- Benedictine Brothers
- Brothers of the Christian Schools
- Brothers of Holy Cross
- Brothers of Our Lady, Mother of Mercy
- Brothers of St. Patrick
- Claretian Missionaries
- Divine Word Missionaries
- Franciscan Brothers
- Franciscan Capuchins
- Friars of the Sick Poor of Los Angeles
- Hospitalier Brothers of St. John of God
- Jesuit Brothers
- Little Brothers of Good Sheperd
- Marianist Brothers
- Missionaries of Charity Brothers
- Missionaries of St. Charles
- Passionist Brothers
- Salesian Brothers
- Vincentian Brothers

RELIGIOUS INSTITUTES OF MEN-PRIESTS

- Atonement Friars
- Augustinian Community
- Augustinian Recollects
- Benedictine Monks
- Canons Regular of the Immaculate Conception
- Capuchin Franciscans
- Carmelite Friars (Calced)
- Carmelite (Discalced) Fathers
- Claretian Missionaries
- Columban Fathers
- Comboni Missionaries
- Congregation of St. John the Baptist
- Congregation of St. Joseph
- Divine Word Missionaries
- Dominican Friars
- Franciscan Friars
- Guadalupe Missioners
- Jesuit Fathers
- Josephite Fathers
- Legionaries of Christ
- Marianists
- Maryknoll Missioners
- Mekhitarist Fathers
- Minim Fathers
- Misioneros Del Sagrado Corazon y Santa Maria de Guadalupe
- Misioneros Vicentinos
- Missionaries of the Holy Spirit
- Missionaries of Jesus
- Missionaries of St. Charles Scalabrinians

- Missionary Servants of the Most Holy Trinity
- Norbertine Fathers
- Oblates of Mary Immaculate
- Oblates of St. Joseph
- Oblates of Virgin Mary
- Operarios Del Reino de Cristo
- Passinist Community of Mater Dolorosa
- Paulist Fathers
- Piarist Fathers
- Precious Blood
- Redemptorist Fathers
- Redemptorist Fathers, Vietnamese
- Rogationist Fathers
- Sacred Hearts of Jesus and Mary, Congregation of
- St. Joseph's Society of the Sacred Heart
- Salesians of St. John Bosco
- Society of Christ
- Society of St. Paul
- Trinitarian Fathers
- Vincentian Fathers

RELIGIOUS INSTITUTES OF WOMEN

- Adrian Dominican Sisters
- Armenian Sisters of the Immaculate Conception
- Augustinian Recollect Sisters
- Benedictine Sisters
- Bernardine Sisters of the Third Order of St. Francis
- Bethany, Sisters
- Blessed Sacrament Sisters of Charity
- Caritas Sisters of Miyazaki
- Carmelitas de San Jose
- Carmelite Sisters of the Most Sacred Heart of Los Angeles
- Charity of the Blessed Virgin Mary, Sisters of
- Charity of the Incarnate Word, Sisters of
- Charity Sisters of Leavenworth, Kansas
- Charity Sisters of Seton Hill
- Chinese Dominican Sisters
- Columban Sisters
- Company of Mary Our Lady
- Congregation of Kkottongnae
- Daughters of Charity of St. Vincent de Paul
- Daughters of Mary
- Daughters of Mary Help of Christians
- Daughters of Mary and Joseph
- Daughters of St. Paul
- Dominican Sisters of Christian Doctrine
- Dominican Sisters of Houston Texas
- Dominican Sisters of Mission San Jose
- Dominican Sisters of Sinsinawa
- Eucharistic Franciscan Missionary Sisters

- Evangelizadoras Eucaristicas de Los Pobres
- Felician Sisters of the Southwest
- Franciscan Missionary Sisters of the Immaculate Conception
- Franciscan Sisters of Little Falls
- Franciscan Sisters of Mary Immaculate
- Franciscan Sisters of Perpetual Adoration
- Franciscan Sisters of the Sacred Heart
- Good Sheperd Sisters
- Guadalupan Missionaries of the Holy Spirit
- Guardian Angel Sisters
- Hermanas Misioneras Servidoras de la Palabra
- Hermanitas de la Annunciacion
- Holy Child Jesus, Society of the
- Holy Cross, Congregation of the Sisters of
- Holy Faith, Congregation of Holy Family, Sisters of
- Holy Names of Jesus and Mary, Sisters of the
- Humility of Mary, Congregation of
- Immaculate Heart Sisters
- Korean Martyrs, Sisters of
- Little Company of Mary Sisters
- Little Handmaids of the Most Holy Trinity
- Little Sisters of the Poor
- Loretto Sisters at the Foot of the Cross
- Love of God, Sisters of
- Lovers of the Holy Cross Sisters
- Maryknoll Sisters
- Medical Sisters of St. Joseph
- Mercy, Sisters of Missionaries of Charity
- Missionaries of Jesus Crucified
- Missionary Benedictine Sisters
- Missionary Sisters of the Immaculate Heart of Mary
- Missionary Sisters of Christ the King
- Misioneras Eucaristicas de Maria Inmaculada
- Nazareth, Sisters of
- Notre Dame Sisters
- Notre Dame de Namur Sisters
- Olivetan Benedictine Sisters of Pusan
- Our Lady of Victory Missionary Sisters
- Poor Clare Missionary Sisters
- Providence Sisters
- Providence, Sisters of
- St. Mary of the Woods
- Religious of Jesus and Mary
- Religious Missionaries of St. Dominic
- Religious Sisters of Charity
- Sacred Heart of Mary, Religious of
- St. Francis Mission Community
- St. Francis Sisters of Joliet
- St. Joseph Sisters of Carondelet
- St. Joseph Sisters of Cluny
- St. Joseph Sisters of Nazareth
- St. Joseph Sisters of Orange
- St. Joseph Sisters of Peace
- St. Louis, Sisters of School

- Sisters of Notre Dame
- Servants of the Blessed Sacrament
- Servants of the Immaculate Child Mary
- Servants of Mary
- Sister Disciples of the Divine Master
- Sisters for Christian Community
- Sisters of the Immaculate Heart of Mary of Mirinae
- Sisters of Little Jesus
- Sisters of the Immaculate Heart of Mary, Mother of the Church
- Sisters of the Pious Schools
- Sisters of the Presentation
- Sisters of the Sacred Heart of Mary
- Sisters of St. Francis of Assisi
- Sisters of St. Francis, Millvale
- Sisters of St. Francis, Oldenburg
- Sisters of St. Francis of Penance and Christian Charity
- Sisters of St. Joseph Congregation
- Sisters of St. Joseph of Lyon
- Sisters of St. Joseph, Third Order of St. Francis
- Sisters Servants of Mary
- Sisters of the Third Franciscan Order
- Social Service, Sisters of
- Society Devoted to the Sacred Heart
- Theresian Sisters
- Union of Sisters of the Presentation of the Blessed Virgin Mary
- Ursuline Sisters of the Roman Union
- Verbum Dei Missionary Fraternity
- Visitation Congregation

CLOISTERED COMMUNITIES

- Discalced Carmelites
- Dominican Nuns of the Order of Preachers
- Franciscan Poor Clare Nuns

SECULAR INSTITUTES

- Fr. Kolbe Missionaries of the Immaculata
- Institute of the Heart of Jesus Cor Unum
- Institute of Our Lady of the Annunciation
- Society of Our Lady of the Way

ASSOCIATIONS OF THE FAITHFUL

- Community of the Holy Spirit
- Charity of Rolling Hills, Sisters S.C.R.H.
- Daughters of St. Mary
- Oblates of the Heart of Jesus
- Puso NG Carmelo Community
- Sacred Heart
- Sisters of the Sick Poor of Los Angeles
- Trinitas

Published by
Éditions du Signe
B.P. 94 – 67038 Strasbourg – Cedex 2 – France
Tel (+33) 388 789 191
Fax (+33) 388 789 199
info@editionsdusigne.fr

Publishing Director
Christian Riehl

Director of Publication
Joëlle Bernhard

Publishing Assistant
Marc de Jong

Design and Layout
Sylvie Tusinski

Photoengraving
Atelier du Signe - 107039

Photos
Frantisek Zvardon

Courtesy of the Cathedral of Our Lady of the
Angels Archives, Archdiocese of Los Angeles

Copyright Text
Archdiocese of Los Angeles

© Éditions du Signe 2006
ISBN 10: 2-7468-1291-6
ISBN 13: 978-2-7468-1291-8